U*nder the Editorship of*

M. F. N<small>IMKOFF</small>, *The Florida State University*

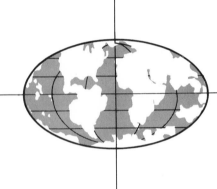

Race and

HOUGHTON MIFFLIN COMPANY
BOSTON

Ethnic Relations

THIRD EDITION

Brewton Berry

OHIO STATE UNIVERSITY

Picture Credits

Preface TO THE THIRD EDITION

History is being made at a rapid pace in the area of race relations. In the United States the walls of segregation are crumbling, and elsewhere in the world racial and ethnic minorities are pressing their demands for equality. These developments are gratifying to all who wish to see justice prevail, including of course the authors of textbooks in the field of race relations, who are, at the same time, faced with the continuing task of revising their work.

When the first edition of this book was written, around 1950, no one would have predicted that within the short span of 15 years changes so revolutionary could have occurred. The second edition, too, which appeared in 1958, soon stood in need of revision. The new census and the admission of Alaska and Hawaii to statehood necessitated up-dating the demographic data on American minorities. Statistics also became available on the ethnic groups in the Soviet Union, South Africa, Israel, and other foreign countries. Available also were new data on the progress of school integration, the economic and political status of the Negro, and various other minorities in our society. The 1960's witnessed the acceleration of the Negro protest, the recrudescence of racism, historic decisions by the courts, and the passage of far-reaching Civil Rights legislation. In other parts of the world the conflicts between racial and ethnic groups mounted to frightening proportions. All the while American sociologists were conducting important research and developing significant new theories.

This third edition of *Race and Ethnic Relations* incorporates all these factors without, however, compromising the author's basic conviction that the primary function of a textbook is not to record current events, but to suggest a way of looking at the world around us. A textbook should provide understanding and perspective, rather than up-to-the-minute factual information. The latter can be more readily obtained from almanacs and year books. Race problems are by no means a new phenomenon in the world. One who gains historical perspective will realize that prejudice is as old as mankind and that the struggle for status has always been with us.

In this volume the author attempts to describe and analyze the phenomena which arise when groups of people who differ racially and culturally come into contact with one another. His interest is in *relations*, which include much more than prejudice and discrimination. He challenges the assumption, all too common, that the race problem is essentially one of Negro-white relations, or that it is peculiar to the United States, or more acute here than elsewhere. To be sure, much of the discussion in these pages pertains to the United States, and the Negro comes in for extended treatment. This is due partly to the fact that we have more information about race problems in this country than in other regions, and partly to the fact that the book is addressed primarily to American college students, who are more concerned with issues near at hand. Even so, we can best appreciate our own problems by avoiding the provincial point of view which has been a fault of more than one area of American sociology, and by adopting instead the comparative point of view which has proved so valuable in helping us gain an understanding of various other social phenomena.

In addition to the inclusion of a world-wide view, as contrasted with a national or sectional view, this book seeks to add other new dimensions to our understanding of racial problems. One of them involves the consideration of other than strictly racial groups. Properly speaking, races are zoological categories, and we do not have social relations between zoological categories. We do indeed have relations between people distinguished by marks of racial descent; but race relations are not so much the relations that exist between members of different races as between people conscious of those differences, thereby affecting the individual's conception of himself and his status in society. Our analysis includes the relations between people who differ culturally as well as racially. Sociologists have long called attention to the fact that the problems confronting the immigrant from Europe, or even the rural migrant to the city, are not fundamentally different from those of the Negro, the Jew, the Indian, or the Mexican. Cultural differences are augmented and sustained by differences in physical traits, and the physical traits themselves would be less significant if they were not symbols of differences in culture.

Still another dimension is that of time. The treatment of race problems suffers when it is focused too heavily on the contemporary. While a sociologist does not ordinarily approach his problem historically, he does recognize the fact that social situations have historical roots, and that current situations, in turn, function as roots for the problems of the future. This book reflects the author's conviction that a knowledge of the past is essential to an understanding of the complexities of the present.

Race and Ethnic Relations has been written for college students, most of whom will have had at least one course in sociology. Accordingly, free use has been made of certain sociological concepts without subjecting them to thorough analysis and definition. At the same time the technical terminology has been kept to a minimum, for the author has happily discovered that the book reaches many others besides sociology students.

Some will be disappointed at the book's failure to espouse a program of action or to offer solutions for racial problems. The author believes it is important in the matter of race relations that we demonstrate and encourage honest and objective thinking, and the habit of gathering and weighing evidence prior to forming conclusions. His hope is that the book will neither foster cynicism, despair, or indifference on the one hand, nor, on the other, encourage a romantic zeal for quick and easy remedies.

The author's indebtedness to others is very great, and he hesitates to select any for special mention. He owes much to his teachers of sociology and anthropology at Wofford College, Yale, and Edinburgh, and to his colleagues at The Ohio State University. Among his former students are many whose comments, research, and criticisms have contributed to such merit as the book may have.

BREWTON BERRY
COLUMBUS, OHIO

Contents

Race and

Ethnic Relations

1

The Point
of View

The sociologist is concerned with
understanding society.

PETER L. BERGER
Invitation to Sociology

S amuel Taylor Coleridge, who was a critic and philosopher as well as a poet, used to say that in order to understand any book one had to know the answers to only three questions: (1) What is the author trying to do? (2) How well has he done it? and (3) Was it worth doing?

We shall begin this book, accordingly, with an account of what we are trying to do, and of the point of view from which we approach the problem. The answer to the second question must rest with the reader, and will be delayed, we hope, until he has finished the book.

As for the third question, none can doubt the seriousness of racial conflict in the world today, and the necessity for all of us to be informed as to its nature and scope. Daily we read and hear of the conflict between Jews and Arabs in the Near East, between the white man and the brown in Asia, between Europeans and natives in Africa, and between Indians and *mestizos* in Latin America. From the Republic of South Africa come disturbing reports of the white man's desperate efforts to maintain his dominance over the more numerous Negroes, Indians, and the mixed bloods known as Cape Coloureds. Here in the United States we are continually reminded of boycotts and riots, of demonstrations and "sit-ins," of discrimination based on creed or color, of the plight of the American Indian, of the Puerto Rican invasion, of refugees and wetbacks, of Jim Crow and Judge Lynch, of civil rights, poll taxes, anti-Semitism, N.A.A.C.P., K.K.K., CORE, and White Citizens' Councils. These, moreover, are only the more glaring of the problems of intergroup relations. For each of these instances which are considered newsworthy, there are innumerable others which pass unnoticed in the press. For example, race prejudice leads to humiliating experiences which leave their scars upon the personality. No reporter takes note of these, but the Negro poet Countee Cullen has captured them in these haunting lines:

> Once riding in old Baltimore,
> Heart filled, head filled with glee,
> I saw a Baltimorean
> Looking straight at me.
>
> Now I was 8 and very small,
> And he was no whit bigger,
> And so I smiled, but he poked out
> His tongue and called me "Nigger."
>
> I saw the whole of Baltimore,
> From May until December,
> Of all the things that happened then
> That's all that I remember.[1]

[1] "Incident," from *Color*, by Countee Cullen (Harper & Brothers, 1925), p. 15. Copyright, 1953, by Ida M. Cullen. Copyright, 1925, by Harper & Brothers.

Small wonder that many thoughtful people regard the relations between racial groups as "our greatest domestic problem," and there are many who give it high priority on the international scene. As a matter of fact, the distinguished historian (or is he philosopher, theologian, or poet?) Arnold J. Toynbee thinks that such contacts are far and away the most significant events of our times. Says he:

> What will be singled out as the salient event of our time by future historians, centuries hence, looking back on the first half of the twentieth century and trying to see its activities and experiments in the just proportion which the time-perspective sometimes reveals? Not, I fancy, any of those sensational or tragic or catastrophic political and economic events which occupy the headlines of our newspapers and the foregrounds of our minds; not wars, revolutions, massacres, deportations, famines, gluts, slumps, or booms, but something of which we are only half conscious, and out of which it would be difficult to make a headline. . . .
>
> Future historians will say, I think, that the great event of the twentieth century was the impact of the Western Civilization upon all the other societies of the world of that day. They will say of this impact that it was so powerful and so pervasive that it turned the lives of all its victims upside down and inside out — affecting the behavior, outlook, feelings, and beliefs of individual men, women, and children in an intimate way, touching chords in human souls that are not touched by mere external material forces — however ponderous and terrifying. This will be said, I feel sure, by historians looking back on our times even from as short a time hence as A.D. 2047.[2]

Russia has long played the role of the champion of underprivileged peoples in their struggle for freedom and equality. Through her propaganda and diplomatic activities she has encouraged and exploited the resentment of Africans, Asians, and Latin Americans against their real or fancied oppressors.

However, for all her sneers at the democracies and her pious professions of tolerance, Russia has anything but a clean record for her own treatment of minorities. Reports continue to come from behind the iron curtain that numerous ethnic and racial groups within the Soviet Union are none too happy over their condition and prospects. Their loyalty to the Soviet system is highly dubious. Many of them, as a matter of fact, welcomed the Germans in World War II as liberators and cooperated with them, until Hitler spurned their help, committing thereby what some have regarded as his most disastrous blunder. Many informed persons today insist that Russia's greatest weakness lies in her failure to win the loyalty and support of her many ethnic minorities.[3]

The problems that arise from the contacts of peoples who differ from each other either racially or culturally, and which are commonly referred to as "race relations," are of more than contemporary and historical interest. They may

[2] "Encounters between Civilizations," *Harper's Magazine*, April 1947, pp. 289–290. From *Civilization on Trial*, by Arnold J. Toynbee. Copyright 1948 by Oxford University Press, Inc.
[3] Cf. F. Lorimer, *The Population of the Soviet Union: History and Prospects*, especially Ch. 5; *Tensions within the Soviet Union*, Senate Document No. 69, 83rd Congress, 1st Session. Also, see Chapter 10, pp. 229–232.

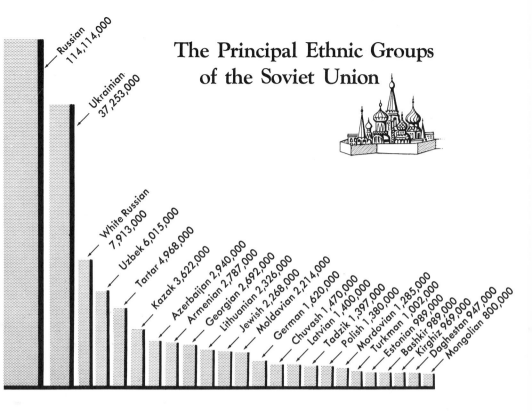

The Principal Ethnic Groups of the Soviet Union

Russian 114,114,000
Ukrainian 37,253,000
White Russian 7,913,000
Uzbek 6,015,000
Tartar 4,968,000
Kazak 3,622,000
Azerbaijan 2,940,000
Armenian 2,787,000
Georgian 2,692,000
Lithuanian 2,326,000
Jewish 2,268,000
Moldavian 2,214,000
German 1,620,000
Chuvash 1,470,000
Latvian 1,400,000
Tadzik 1,397,000
Polish 1,380,000
Mordovian 1,285,000
Turkman 1,002,000
Estonian 989,000
Bashkir 989,000
Kirghiz 969,000
Daghestan 947,000
Mongolian 800,000

well prove to be of even greater significance in the future. For all their current import, race problems as a world issue may not seem today to be as acute as either communism or nationalism; but communism diligently exploits racial feeling, and nationalism frequently fuses with it. Most Westerners still think of the race problem as one of maintaining white supremacy in the face of the demands of the colored people of the world for full equality of status. This conception of the problem, however, is already outdated. It is no longer a question of whether or not the red, brown, black, and yellow people will achieve equality. The question is, Will the whites lose it altogether, or will mankind move safely toward a system of equality, tolerance, respect, and cooperation? There is no certainty here. The whites are outnumbered, and the disproportion is steadily increasing. A world organized on the basis of anti-white hatred is by no means inconceivable.

Variety of Viewpoints

Sociologists, from the earliest days of their science, have been aware of the problem of race, and have given it much thought and study; but the subject, certainly, is not their monopoly. Historians, journalists, clergymen, anthropologists, novelists, biologists, psychologists, poets, politicians, and a host of others have written about it. Race, moreover, presents not a single, clear-cut problem, but a multitude of problems. Consequently, there are many facets to be observed, many areas to be explored, and many angles from which the questions of race and race relations can be approached. How does the sociologist differ from others who venture to write about these things? Before we attempt to answer that question, let us look at some non-sociological points of view as reflected in the recent literature.

The Apologist

There are those who have approached the problem from the standpoint of defending, justifying, or rationalizing the status quo. A well-known exemplar of this point of view was the late Senator Bilbo. Shortly before his death he published a book[4] in which he expounded those opinions which he had so often voiced on the floor of the United States Senate and in the press. His thesis was this: When two races are brought together, and attempt to live side by side, only two outcomes are possible — mongrelization or segregation. The evil consequences of mongrelization, he argued, are numerous, familiar, and disastrous. The other alternative is segregation, which is the wiser choice, and the one the South has followed. Bilbo not only defended the racial system of his section as the lesser of two evils, but espoused it as a positive good.

Following the historic decision of the United States Supreme Court in 1954 declaring "segregated schools inherently unequal" there have been numerous attempts on the part of Southern leaders and intellectuals to justify the existence of separate school systems for whites and Negroes. In a volume entitled *The Case for the South*, the author, W. D. Workman, Jr., maintains that the Supreme Court in 1896 laid down the principle of "separate but equal" which is as sound today as it was then. He espouses "state sovereignty, constitutional government, and racial integrity," and holds that no amount of pressure can force a people to accept a pattern of race relations contrary to its will. He rejects the doctrine that the races are inherently equal in intelligence, and asserts that Negroes are by nature amiable, obedient, sociable, dilatory, and contented. So different are the races in their capacities, temperaments, values and codes of conduct, he says, that integrated schools are unwise, impractical, and catastrophic.

Take another example from the other side of the world. Nowhere are problems of race relations more acute than in the Republic of South Africa. This nation, with a population of 15,841,128 in 1960, is dominated economically and politically by people of European descent who constitute only about 20 per cent of the population. There are, in the nation, approximately 10,000,000 Negro "natives," nearly half a million Asiatics, and 1,488,267 "Coloured," a mixed group formed mainly by interbreeding between early white settlers, the aboriginal Bushmen and Hottentots, and peoples from Madagascar, the East Indies, the eastern coast of Africa, and elsewhere. To deal with the situation the government has embarked upon a policy known as *apartheid* (an Afrikaans word,

---

[4] T. G. Bilbo, *Take Your Choice: Separation or Mongrelization.*

pronounced ə-pärt'hĭt, and meaning "apartness"). This policy of *apartheid* calls for the biological, territorial, social, educational, economic, and political separation of the various racial groups which compose the Republic of South Africa.

The Republic's ambassador to the United States, Dr. John E. Holloway, formerly of the University of South Africa, has written in defense of his government's policy.[5] The racial groups in South Africa, he maintains, are so vastly different in civilization, culture, ways of thinking, and standards of living that *apartheid* is the only humane, feasible, and reasonable way to resolve the difficulties. The alternative to *apartheid* is integration; but, he says, "Except in very small fringes the desire for social integration is completely nonexistent." He maintains that integration of peoples of European and Negro stock in large numbers and on a community basis has nowhere been successfully achieved. He points to the northern states of the United States and insists that even there one finds no "completely integrated white-black community in which people of both races are normally seen living together, eating together, playing together, and intermarrying." And yet, he says, in those northern states the conditions are far more favorable for integration than they are in South Africa, where the Negroes are lacking in education, skills, knowledge, and attitudes essential for participation in the European civilization which has been transplanted to South Africa, and upon which the whole population, black and white, is dependent for its survival. Too hasty integration, he maintains, would create more problems than it would solve. *Apartheid*, on the other hand, would enable each race to develop in its own way, and at a rate suitable to its wishes and capacities.

Many others have taken a similar approach to the problems of race relations, defending white domination of preliterate peoples (the white man's burden), the confining of Indians to reservations, evacuation of the Japanese from California, exclusion of Orientals, or the institution of slavery. For that matter, even the members of minority groups themselves not infrequently come to the defense of the social system of which they are the victims. For example, the distinguished Negro educator, Joseph Winthrop Holley, has published a book in which he attempts to justify the discriminations to which the members of his own race have been subjected. Says he:

> I, a Negro of some education, favor segregation in the Southern States for the time being. . . . I do not turn from non-segregation as an ideal; but in impatient and intolerant pursuit of it, I can see only trouble and even tragedy. . . . Ideally there should be brotherhood among human beings. . . . Ideally all the Christian churches should be one. . . . Ideally there should be a workable federation of nations. . . . Most of us agree that all these are goals to aim for; even if we cannot find accord as to method or speed or faith in ultimate complete success. There is exhilaration in playing leap frog with the stars in our thoughts; but programs and progress have to be anchored to solid earth and mass psychology.

[5] "Apartheid," in *The Annals of the American Academy of Political and Social Science*, Vol. 306, July 1956, pp. 26ff. See also Hilgard Muller, "The Official Case for Apartheid," *The New York Times Magazine*, June 7, 1964.

ractically we are limited to the world of things as they are, and not as we would
ave them. In the Southern States there are special conditions of comparative
umbers of Negroes and whites and inbred psychological attitudes and customs
that constitute as deep-seated a problem as the tangled situations in Ireland,
Palestine, and India. Tact and time are necessary parts of the cure.

You cannot legislate tolerance. . . . Laws to enforce non-segregation will react disastrously if they arouse resentment against the Negro and if they result
in friction. . . .

I favor segregation just as long as those conditions exist which warrant it.[6]

The Critic

Others who have written on the subject of race have assumed that the present
situation is undesirable or intolerable, and that something ought, must, or inevitably will be done about it. Change is the dominant note in such books.
Many examples of this type of approach might be found in the literature, but
none illustrates it more forcibly than a volume by Congressman Powell.[7] His
is no calm, dispassionate analysis of the race problem, but a highly emotional
one. "I am a radical and a fighter," the author says, and his book bears him out.
He criticizes the "rotten, decaying political life of America," and sneers at her
"pseudo-democracy." He castigates the "hypocrisy of the Christian church"
(although he himself is a Baptist minister) and denounces the American Federation of Labor as a "disgrace to the working class movement." The South he
bitterly dismisses as "hopeless," and thinks that Negroes must migrate to the
northern and western cities. He does not deplore race riots, and insists that
some good has followed each of them; but he looks rather to the picket line,
the boycott, and the ballot as the weapons that will bring about the desired
change.

Let us take another example of a book written from the standpoint of criticism
of the racial situation. In 1953 a group of educators, clergymen, and civic
leaders became aroused over the prevalence of racial and religious prejudice
and discrimination within American college fraternities and sororities. They
formed themselves into a committee to assemble the facts and, if possible, to
correct the abuses. Two years later the committee's report,[8] written by the
chairman, was published. It offers abundant evidence to prove that fraternities
and sororities are guilty of discriminating against students on the basis of race,
ethnic origin, and religion. The author maintains that the fault lies, not so
much with the undergraduate, but with the alumni and alumnae who exercise
control over the policies and practices of these organizations. It is the committee's belief that social fraternities can provide social experiences for young men
and women on college campuses, and can make useful contributions to the edu-

[6] *You Can't Build a Chimney from the Top*, pp. 210–212.

[7] A. C. Powell, Jr., *Marching Blacks*.

[8] A. M. Lee, *Fraternities without Brotherhood: A Study of Prejudice on the American
Campus*.

TABLE 1.1

The Racial Structure of the Population of the Republic of South Africa*

| Year | European | | Non-European | | | | | |
| | Number | Per cent of total population | Native | | Coloured | | Asiatic | |
			Number	Per cent of total population	Number	Per cent of total population	Number	Per cent of total population
1904	1,116,806	21.6	3,491,056	67.4	445,228	8.6	122,734	2.4
1911	1,276,242	21.4	4,019,006	67.3	525,943	8.8	152,203	2.5
1921	1,519,488	21.9	4,697,813	67.8	545,548	7.9	165,731	2.4
1936	2,003,857	20.9	6,596,689	68.8	769,661	8.0	219,691	2.3
1946	2,335,460	20.7	7,735,809	68.7	905,050	8.0	282,539	2.6
1956	2,907,000	20.9	9,306,000	66.9	1,281,000	9.2	421,000	3.0
1960	3,067,638	19.4	10,807,809	68.2	1,488,267	9.4	477,414	3.0

* Based on Ellen Hellman (Ed.), *Handbook of Race Relations in South Africa*, Ch. 2, and on data furnished by Republic of South Africa Government Information Office, New York.

cational process, but that, because of their discriminatory policies, they are "schools of prejudice" and "a threat to democracy." The book cites numerous instances where steps have been taken to make fraternities more democratic.

The Strategist

Still other writers have been primarily concerned with the question, how? — How can the changes be brought about; or, for that matter, How can the status quo be preserved? An illustration of this type of approach is to be found in a volume by James Weldon Johnson.[9] He, no less than many others, believes that the racial situation must be changed; but his primary concern is with the most effective means for making progress toward that goal. He rejects riots, insurrection, and bloodshed (not, however, for ethical reasons, but simply because he regards them as futile); he examines the role of the Negro church, the press, and various other organizations and institutions. He says: "I do not offer . . . a program. I do not believe that any one man or set of men can formulate a complete and practicable program. The most that can be done is to lay down certain lines along which a program may be worked out. . . . Nor shall I devote any part of this book to cataloguing the wrongs and humiliations that are put upon us. I do not rehearse them for the simple reason that we all know them by heart. The thing we seek to know is: what to do about them."[10] He then proceeds to analyze and assess the resources the Negroes possess and the techniques by which he thinks it possible to achieve the end of integration with American society. He discusses education (including the education of the whites), the use of the ballot, organization, interracial contacts, leadership, and the blasting of stereotypes.

The question of strategy remains a major concern with Negro leaders. The Urban League continues its patient program of uplift and persuasion, while the N.A.A.C.P. relies upon the use of political power and winning court decisions. The Southern Christian Leadership Conference, inspired by the Rev. Martin Luther King, Jr., pins its hope upon non-violence, and resorts to demonstrations and boycotts. Negro students, disillusioned by the slow, legalistic approach of their elders, decided upon "direct action," and staged the first "sit-in" in Greensboro, N.C. Their technique won immediate support from other young Negroes, who promptly organized the Student Nonviolent Coordinating Committee ("SNICK" for short) and proceeded to register their protest far and wide. The first Freedom Ride was organized by the Congress of Racial Equality (CORE), which inclines toward more sensational and dramatic demonstrations, and which some Negro leaders have described as "a bunch of loonybirds and crackpots."[11] And so, Negro leaders, as well as the rank and file, continually debate on their goals, and the effectiveness of methods of achieving them.

[9] *Negro Americans, What Now?*
[10] *Ibid*, p. vi.
[11] *Time*, Jan. 12, 1962, p. 15.

The Theologian

Religious thinkers and writers have also been aware of the differences and conflicts between racial and ethnic groups, and have regarded these problems from their own particular viewpoints. One may even say that the Old Testament itself is such a book, for running through it is the theory that God had a purpose in creating the world, and that He selected one ethnic group for the execution of that purpose which, by the way, involves all the others. Other religions, or sects, would have quite different opinions with regard to the out-group, depending upon their doctrines and the degree of their exclusiveness. Therefore no one volume could be representative of the theological viewpoint toward race relations; but a book by a professor at Union Theological Seminary illustrates a point of view and shows the contrast with other possible ones.[12] The author assumes that God, through the vital forces of the universe, is working toward worldwide human brotherhood. Evidence for such a purpose he finds not only in Christian thought and history but also in the course of secular history and prehistory. Obstructing the realization of this divine plan, however, are racial differences, cultural diversity, tribal ethics, and nationalism. The problem, therefore, if man is to cooperate in the achievement of this divine plan for a world community, is to substitute the Christian ethic for the primitive, provincial, tribal ethics; to minimize racial differences; to "deepen our respect for unlikeness," and to "transcend our differences."

Since so many people are disposed to look at racial problems from a religious point of view, let us cite a recent book by Father Trevor Huddleston, a member of a religious order of the Anglican Church, and for many years a resident in South Africa.[13] Father Huddleston was an outspoken critic of the Republic's racial policies, a courageous fighter for the rights of the Negro, and, quite understandably, became *persona non grata* with the government. He left Africa eventually, under somewhat mysterious circumstances, and shortly thereafter published a book in which he recounts his experiences and expounds his philosophy. He says, quite frankly, "What I shall try to avoid is that most common and persistent error — the attempt to be impartial . . . I shall write this book as a partisan." His starting point, in considering problems of race relations, is thoroughly Christian. "I believe that because God became Man, therefore human nature itself has a dignity and a value which is infinite. . . . Any doctrine based on racial or colour prejudice and enforced by the state is therefore an affront to human dignity and *ipso facto* an insult to God Himself. It is for this reason that I feel bound to oppose not only the policy of the present government of the Union of South Africa but the legislation which flows from this policy."[14]

[12] D. J. Fleming, *Bringing Our World Together.*
[13] *Naught for Your Comfort.*
[14] From: *Naught for Your Comfort* by Trevor Huddleston. Copyright 1956 by Trevor Huddleston, reprinted by permission of Doubleday & Co., Inc., and of Wm. Collins Sons & Co. Ltd., pp. 17ff.

Father Huddleston rejects the *apartheid* policy as vicious and futile, and presents his own:

> I *know* the solution. I know it from experience: an experience which 99.9 per cent of my fellow South Africans have never had and would not care to have. It lies in the simple recognition that *all* men are made "in the image and likeness of God;" that in consequence each *person* is of infinite and eternal value; that the state exists to protect the person but is itself always of inferior value to the person.
>
> And all these truths white South Africa implicitly or explicitly denies. Therefore, no social order *can* emerge in which the problems of South Africa have a chance of solution.
>
> Only we, who in our ordinary daily life accept and at least try to act upon these truths, know how easy is the answer.[15]

The Assimilationist

The view is widely held that racial and cultural differences are undesirable, that homogeneity is preferable to heterogeneity, that conflict is inevitable as long as unlike peoples try to live together. The only solution for the problem of racial and ethnic groups, therefore (if, indeed, it is not inevitable) lies in the mixing, blending, and combining of the diverse elements. Our own philosophy of the "melting pot" and our program of "Americanization" are reflections of this attitude. The assimilationist viewpoint is manifested in books dealing with various minority groups; and, in the case of Brazil, this is the dominant policy of the nation, with regard to the various groups that make up its population. An example, however, of a book written from this point of view deals with the American Indian.[16] The point of view adopted is that we must "get away from the sentimental and romantic and think in terms of the realistic." It is unwise to attempt to revive and perpetuate the traditional Indian cultures, to "keep the Indian Indian," to set him apart, to give him special privileges and treatment. The Indian must be "a full participant in our common life," and our policies should be directed to that end. The author quotes the remarks of a young Navajo to illustrate his viewpoint:

> Everywhere we Indians go you white boys ask us where our feather headdress, our moccasins, and our "real Indian" costumes are. . . . Don't you know that those are the ways our great-grandparents dressed a very long time ago? All those things belong back in the past. Let them stay there. . . . The problems we are facing will never be solved by feathers.[17]

The assimilationist point of view is reflected in a series of books which have come from the State of Israel. Small wonder, for this young, small nation is

[15] *Ibid*, pp. 249ff.
[16] G. E. E. Lindquist, *The Indian in American Life.*
[17] *Ibid*, p. vi.

confronted with the urgent task of unifying a multitude of people of various backgrounds. No sooner had Israel become an independent nation in 1948 than she declared that her gates were open to Jewish immigrants from the four corners of the globe. In the years that followed a tidal wave of immigrants poured in, coming from almost every country under the sun. Absorbing so many people, at so rapid a rate, was a formidable task. It could not be shirked, however, for one of the basic reasons for the establishment of Israel was to give every Jew the right to find a home there. This right was embodied in the Declaration of Independence, and was made one of the fundamental laws of the state — "The Law of the Return."

Israel, having been established by pioneers of European background, possessed a culture of the Western type; but more than half of all immigrants who came after the establishment of the state hailed from culturally backward areas of Asia or Africa (Yemen, Iraq, Iran, Kurdistan, North Africa) and brought with them an Oriental type of culture. The task of integration, assimilation, and absorption consequently captured the interest of teachers, social workers, government officials, and social scientists. They have reported their activities in a recent volume which begins with these words:

> The vital problem confronting the State of Israel in all spheres of its economic, social and spiritual existence is how to assimilate, within a definable culture, the masses of new immigrants coming from different environments and to create a unified and homogeneous nation. For other countries the problem of "absorbing" newcomers means interpreting to them the social and ethical standards of the dominant majority and of making them accept those standards by way of active education and guidance. The task is different in Israel, where a social norm has not yet had time to take root and to crystallize.[18]

The book proceeds to describe how, through the schools, youth groups, foster-placement schemes, and numerous other devices the process of assimilation has been accelerated.

The Pluralist

On the other hand, there are those who regard cultural diversity as highly desirable, as a source of strength to a nation, as a stimulus to cultural growth, as giving color and interest to a society. They dislike seeing a group lose its identity and uniqueness, discard its traditions, and permit its values, its folk dances and arts, to perish from want of nourishment. They refer to "the melting pot mistake" and the "failure of the Americanization program." They denounce the efforts of our government to force our culture on the Indian and to destroy his faith in his own religion, his age-old culture, and his tribal leaders. They espouse "cultural democracy," and they resist the trend that would "reduce us all to a dead level of uniformity," Louis Adamic writes from this point of view.[19] He would correct the prevalent view that the United States is, or ever was, an "Anglo-Saxon country, with a white-Anglo-Saxon-Protestant civilization struggling to preserve itself against other civilizations brought here by foreigners and Negroes." Diversity itself is the American pattern, according to Adamic, and this is one of the most important sources of our strength. The ideal of freedom of worship, insists the pluralist, should be extended to other phases of culture — to the language of one's choice, to habits of food and dress, to arts, and folkways, to ideals and values.

The pluralist viewpoint is manifested in a recent provocative book about the five largest ethnic groups of New York City.[20] Nathan Glazer, son of Jewish immigrants, and Daniel Patrick Moynihan, grandson of Irish immigrants, maintain in their book that the melting pot has done very little melting. The Irish, Italians, Jews, Puerto Ricans, and Negroes of New York have indeed changed

---

[18] C. Frankenstein (Ed.), *Between Past and Future*, p. 13.
[19] *A Nation of Nations.*
[20] N. Glazer and D. P. Moynihan, *Beyond the Melting Pot.*

over the years, but they have retained their identity and differ as much as they ever did. Nor do the authors deplore this fact. On the contrary they insist that it adds to the richness and charm of our national life.

The Realist

Here we include those whose approach to the problem of race relations is this: What must be done in this particular situation to reduce the conflict or to preserve the peace? This is the point of view of "the practical man." He is not primarily concerned with the justice or injustice of the situation, with the ethical issues, or with the problem of whether the groups change their cultures or retain their individuality. Nor is he interested in broad, universal principles of race relations, and most assuredly not in determining what the divine plan is for the world.

Many books and articles dealing with problems of race relations have been written from this point of view. Their authors have included colonial administrators responsible for keeping the peace, superintendents and principals of schools located in mixed neighborhoods, and statesmen whose constituents include persons of diverse races and cultures. Let us cite, as an example of a book representing this category, a volume prepared for the instruction and guidance of police.[21]

Many American cities, fearful of racial tensions and eruptions, have undertaken to train their police officers to deal effectively with such disorders. Many excellent publications have appeared for use in these training programs. Among the first was one from Chicago, where serious problems of race relations had developed as a result of the tremendous influx of Negroes from the South, to say nothing of immigrants from the corners of the globe, representing every conceivable race and nationality. This book is concerned with the problems of achieving an "orderly social life" in a community where "men of different color, religion, and language must work together," and is focused upon the role of the police in that task. The volume describes the heterogeneous character of Chicago's population, the situations in which tensions between groups arise and fester, the facts about race and nationality which modern science has discovered, the nature of crowd and mob behavior, the influence of rumor, the content of the laws which affect race relations, and the most effective measures to be employed when racial disorders arise.

Others

There are many other points of view writers on problems of race have adopted. There are those who "view with alarm" the course of events but whose writings throw little light on the causes of the trends, and offer slight hope of correcting them; and there are those who adopt an "ain't-it-awful" approach,

[21] J. D. Lohman, *The Police and Minority Groups.*

deploring the situation and documenting beyond peradventure of doubt the sad state of affairs. On the more serious side we find that historians, biologists, physical anthropologists, and psychologists have all manifested an interest in one phase or another of the problem of race, asking the type of questions with which their science is concerned and seeking answers by using the techniques which they have found efficacious. Psychologists, for example, have long been interested in the intellectual, mental, and temperamental differences and characteristics of the various races, and the physical anthropologists have been interested in the racial criteria and classification of mankind.

This does not exhaust all of the possible approaches, nor is it presented as a logical classification. Most books, as a matter of fact, combine several of them. Anyone who speaks or writes about problems of race makes certain assumptions, holds to certain values, and adopts some point of view, whether or not he explicitly states it or is even aware of it.

No attempt is made here to evaluate these various approaches, to discard any of them as invalid, to insist that one is better than another, or that one is most fruitful or illuminating. We shall not even defend the sociological point of view as the best, and certainly not as the only legitimate one. A question so complex and so vital as that of race permits, even demands a variety of attacks. Sociologists are convinced their approach is valuable, able to shed light upon the interesting and crucial phenomena of intergroup relations.

The Sociological Point of View

Race has always been one of the major concerns of sociologists. The first two sociological books published in the United States, a century ago, dealt with the problem.[22] Both writers sought to justify the prevailing institution of slavery. Fitzhugh undertook to prove that morality and discipline could be maintained only in a society founded upon slavery and Christianity; while Hughes ingeniously denied that slavery existed in the South! Slaves, he said, were people who had no rights at all; but in the South, he insisted, the so-called slaves did possess rights. Therefore, American society was not built upon a system of slavery, as everyone supposed, but instead was a "warranty commonwealth," a type of social organization having numerous advantages over other types.

This interest in problems of race is reflected in the writings of American sociologists of the latter decades of the nineteenth century (Ward, Sumner, Cooley, Small, Ross, and Giddings) — the men who were primarily instrumental in establishing sociology as an academic discipline.[23] Those who followed them (especially Thomas, Reuter, Ellwood, Odum, Park) cultivated this field of study, with the result that nowadays race relations constitutes one of the major interests of sociologists, both in research and in teaching.

[22] H. Hughes, *Treatise on Sociology, Theoretical and Practical;* G. Fitzhugh, *Sociology for the South: or the Failure of Free Society.*

[23] E. F. Frazier, "Sociological Theory and Race Relations," *The American Sociological Review,* Vol. 12, No. 3, June 1947, pp. 265ff.

Sociologists, however, have not been in perfect agreement as to the nature and scope of their study of race, nor as to their conclusions, and it is not entirely correct to speak of *the* sociological point of view.[24] From the pens of professional sociologists have come books written from the viewpoint of the apologist, the critic, the realist, the assimilationist, and the pluralist, many of them excellent, scholarly, and important books.

Moreover, the point of view from which sociologists have approached the study of race has changed over the years. E. B. Reuter, who himself played no small part in developing the field, thinks that there have been three stages through which sociologists have moved.[25] The first period was marked by an emphasis upon biological problems. Sociologists were fascinated by the task of classifying mankind, of studying the physical and mental characteristics of races, and of measuring these differences. They spent their efforts in the futile attempt to explain social phenomena in biological terms. The second period witnessed a shift to a cultural frame of reference. The realization dawned that the significant differences between people were not their hereditary, physical features, but language, customs, beliefs, technologies, and institutions. It is these differences, all of which are learned, rather than the hereditary differences, which arouse prejudice and lead to conflict. The belief prevailed, therefore, that the key to understanding racial problems lay in the study of social heritages. The third period is marked by an emphasis upon relationships between the races, rather than upon either their physical or their cultural characteristics. The contact and interaction between groups came to be the focus of interest. In this book, accordingly, we shall attempt to reach an understanding of the phenomena which arise when so-called racial groups enter into relations with one another. Our point of view has six important features which require some further explanation.

Understanding

It is our purpose to understand race relations rather than to espouse causes or to propose solutions. Most assuredly do we insist that we have no panacea for racial problems. We even doubt that one exists. The problems are too complex to admit of easy, simple, and universal solutions. Take, for instance, the American Indian. The situation on one reservation is quite different from that on another, and programs which would be quite feasible on the one would be disastrous elsewhere. So with the Jews. To some of them, the homeland in Palestine is of greatest importance, while to others Zionism is anathema; some regard assimilation as the proper course; but others hold tenaciously to the ancient tra-

[24] B. Berry, "The Concept of Race in Sociology Textbooks," *Social Forces*, Vol. 18, No. 3, March 1940, pp. 411–417. For a continuation of this study, see C. L. Hunt, "The Treatment of 'Race' in Beginning Sociology Textbooks," *Sociology and Social Research*, Vol. 35, March–April 1951, pp. 277–284.

[25] "Racial Theory," *American Journal of Sociology*, Vol. 50, No. 6, May 1945, pp. 452–461.

A group of school girls near Honolulu show a variety of ethnic backgrounds

ditions and values and would deplore their loss. To speak, therefore, of the answer to the race problem betrays either quackery or naïveté.

There are those, to be sure, who will have little sympathy for such a point of view, insisting that what is needed nowadays is action, not investigation. Some will maintain that "everybody knows the answer; it is only a question of applying it." Others will say that "while you fiddle about leisurely," studying the problem, "the whole thing may blow up in your face." We fully appreciate the seriousness and urgency of the situation, but we believe that knowledge and understanding are prerequisites for wise and effective action. We are sympathetic, for instance, with the medical research scientists who work away in their laboratories while an epidemic rages in the community. Why, some will say, do they not do something immediately useful? Why not put into practical use such knowledge and skill as they have, imperfect though it be? Why waste their efforts on research when the times demand action? It is our opinion that, in the long run, the research scientists will relieve more suffering by their investigations than by abandoning their study and devoting themselves to therapy.

Objectivity

The sociologist, unlike the reformer, the apologist, or the moralist, tries to examine the relationships between the so-called racial groups as objectively as possible. We shall endeavor, therefore, to take a neutral position, to refrain from making judgments as to the justice or injustice, the right or wrong, the good or bad in a situation. We shall avoid placing blame and bestowing praise. We shall try to look upon the relations of races as objectively as the zoologist looks upon kangaroos or the palaeontologist upon a fossil.

Now there are those who insist that social scientists cannot adopt a position of neutrality on matters in which they are so vitally involved, and that the only alternative is for them to state their biases frankly.[26] The point is well taken. The mere fact that we choose to investigate race relations is indicative of our interest and concern; and our decision to study relationships rather than biological traits betrays our belief that the former are "more significant" than the latter. The writer, like most persons reared in the American culture, has had inculcated in him the values of the American Creed (democracy, human dignity, good sportsmanship, humanitarianism, and the like), and would find it extremely difficult to look with complete impartiality upon a contest between democracy and authoritarianism, or between freedom of speech and its suppression, or between science and superstition. On the other hand, one sometimes feels that objectivity is regarded in some quarters as the supreme virtue, an end in itself. We look upon it, instead, as a means to an end, as an indispensable part of the equipment of the scientist and the scholar. And even though we may agree that a completely disinterested social science is impossible of achievement, we maintain that the sociologist must discipline himself to develop an open mind and to look as objectively as possible upon the problem he investigates.

Relations

Sociologists are primarily concerned with the phenomena which arise when people and groups enter into relationships with one another. The contacts between racial groups frequently result in conflict, and sociologists have sought to understand the riots, insurrections, strikes, boycotts, and the other forms which such conflict has assumed. The interactions of racial groups, however, are not limited to antagonism; groups learn to cooperate, they adjust their differences, one group dominates the other, members intermarry, they adopt each other's ideas and customs, they develop myths and creeds regarding themselves and those with whom they come into contact, they become prejudiced, and they organize movements either to defend or to change the social patterns. It is these phenomena, more than the physical and cultural traits of racial groups, which primarily interest the sociologist. This is not to say that racial features (skin color, types of hair, and so on) are ignored, or that the history and the social heritage of a group are of no concern. Physical characteristics and cultural heritages of groups are studied by anthropologists, historians, and human geographers; but sociologists are not greatly interested in such matters per se. When groups come in contact these traits take on meaning and assume importance.

---

[26] G. Myrdal, *An American Dilemma*, Vol. 2, Appendix 2, pp. 1035ff. See also C. Bowman, "Must the Social Sciences Foster Moral Skepticism?" *American Sociological Review*, Vol. 10, No. 6, December 1945, pp. 709–715.

Groups

Sociology is concerned only incidentally with races; its main concern is with the interrelations between groups of people who are different. The term "race" most properly applies to those large biological divisions of mankind, to the categories developed by biologists and physical anthropologists for classifying the people of the earth on the basis of their hereditary physical features. Sociology is interested only incidentally in these classifications, but it is vitally interested in groups of people who are conscious of the physical features which distinguish them from others, and who allow that consciousness to influence their behavior. We are interested in the relationships between American and Mexican, between white man and Negro, between Gentile and Jew, between European and Asiatic, between Boer and Hottentot. These are groups, but not races in the strict sense. The subject matter of sociology, on this big problem, might better be described as the interactions between racial and ethnic groups, rather than the interactions between races. These terms will be defined at a later point.

Perspective

"The race problem" is synonymous in the minds of most Americans with "the Negro," and even more specifically with the Negro in the United States. College courses in sociology bearing such titles as "Race Relations" have often so restricted the field, and popular textbooks have reflected this common tendency. To some it is a problem peculiar to the South; to others it is uniquely American. The fact is, however, that racial and ethnic groups have come into contact the world over and for untold centuries, and the phenomena we seek to understand are worldwide in their scope. Sociology is concerned with the interactions of people wherever and whenever they occur, and we shall, accordingly, not limit ourselves to the American scene. Unfortunately, our data on race relations in other lands are sketchy. We are in great need of comparative studies of intergroup relations in the various biracial and multiracial areas of the world. Only when such materials are available will it be possible to develop a science of race relations. Meantime we must enlarge our perspective with the best available information from other lands and generalize with caution and reservation.

Dynamics

Human society is undergoing a continuous process of change, and race relations are no exception to this rule. What we are attempting to understand, therefore, is not some fixed and static phenomenon, but a dynamic, ever-changing pattern of relationships. Consider, for example, the story of the contacts between the Indian and the white man in the area of the present United States. For a long time each racial group was bent upon the extermination of the other, and the attitudes and policies of our government were based upon the assumption that the Indian was a "vanishing race." Later on there was a shift to a policy of isolation and segregation, and the Indians were confined to reservations and subjected to a paternalistic relationship. Somewhat later the emphasis changed from segregation to forced assimilation, and steps were taken to "civilize" the Indian and to integrate him into American society. More recently there have arisen doubts concerning the justice, desirability, and practicability of a policy of rapid and compulsory assimilation, with the result that there has emerged a philosophy of fostering and perpetuating many of the features of Indian society. The fact is that, from the moment the Europeans arrived in the New World, the nature, forms, and patterns of the interactions and adjustments between the white man and the red have undergone tremendous changes, and they continue.

The same is true for the Negro. The American white man has always been convinced that the Negro has a "place" in our society, but that "place" is continually changing. For two and a half centuries slavery was that "place," but slavery itself was never a permanent, unchanging relationship. Instead, throughout American history before the Civil War, slave status never ceased undergoing a process of redefinition in both the laws and the folkways. Consequently, the slavery of 1850 was quite a different thing from the slavery of 1650. Since the abolition of slavery the pattern of Negro-white relationships has continued to change, and they have never changed more rapidly than at the present time. One does not have to be reminded that the system of segregated schools is being undermined, that Negroes are entering occupations from which they were excluded a short time ago, that they have made great strides in achieving the franchise and in using it with effectiveness, that one state after another has adopted fair employment legislation, that recreational facilities such as golf courses and swimming pools are letting down their racial hurdles, and that cracks are beginning to appear in the rigid pattern of residential barriers. In short, the caste-like segregation system which characterized Negro-white relationships in the early decades of the twentieth century are giving way to democratic pressures, testifying to the fact that the Negro's "place" is continually changing and that race relations are highly dynamic.

Race relations, then, are a worldwide problem, not peculiar to the South or even to the United States. So serious is the problem that thoughtful people in all walks of life have directed their attention to it, each in his own way and from his own point of view proposing some solution, espousing some cause, or contributing something to our understanding of it. The sociologist, without claiming he alone holds the complete answer, does insist his discipline has something worthwhile to say about the matter. He believes that by adopting an objective point of view, not an emotional one, we may hope to gain an understanding of the dynamic phenomena which emerge when groups of people who differ racially and culturally enter into relationships. In later chapters we present and analyze what the sociologists have thus far learned.

2

The Concept
of Race

The term "race" is one of the most
frequently misused and misunderstood
words in the American vernacular.

PETER I. ROSE
They and We

Strictly speaking this book is not concerned with problems of race. Only incidentally does it raise such questions as: What is a race? How many races are there? How are races classified, and by what criteria? Are some races more intelligent, more artistic, or more warlike than others? Psychologists and anthropologists may address themselves to such questions, but they are not the focus of this book. We are concerned, rather, with the problems that arise when groups of people who are different are brought together in face-to-face contact and are confronted with the task of having to live together — groups such as Jews and Arabs, Indians and Englishmen, Mexicans and Texans, Negroes and whites, Japanese and Irish, Puerto Ricans and Yankees. These are groups, loosely held together, but they are not races. However, they often *think* of themselves as races, and they are often so regarded by others. The problems that arise from their association are usually called race problems, the attitudes engendered are called race prejudice, and the interactions that take place are called race relations. We might choose not to designate such groups as races, but it is important that we come to some understanding of this term which we reject.

Race is an explosive term. Our language no doubt has its full quota of "loaded" words (*communist, tory, scab,* plus many others which we modestly refrain from enumerating); but when it comes to arousing people's prejudices, loyalties, animosities, and fears, none is the equal of race, and of the innumerable synonyms, slurs, and epithets related thereto. Race is a subject few can discuss dispassionately. "Would you want your daughter to marry a Negro?" is still regarded by many white people as the trump card which can win any argument.

Race an Ambiguous Term

Race is also a vague and ambiguous term. All sorts of groups are referred to as races, and various and sundry criteria are used to assign people to their proper categories. Consider, for example, the following letter written to the "advice-to-the-lovelorn" column of the St. Louis *Post-Dispatch.*

> Dear Miss X:
>
> My work makes it necessary for me to call at a certain city department every day to consult their records and files, and during the past several years I have made many friends there. Last spring I became friendly with one of the girls. I wanted to ask her for a date but one of the other fellows did, and she told him she was going steady. I have since learned that she only told him this because she wanted to turn him down without hurting his feelings. She lost her job several months ago and I have not seen her since, but am anxious to, as I can't get her out of my mind. Would it be all right for me to call her? Our acquaintance was confined to the office, except once, when I drove her home. Also, *she is of a different race. Will this matter?*
>
> Anxious.

What does he mean by "different race?" Is he referring to the color of her skin, her religion, her nationality, her eyes, her hair, her language, or her

*Market scene in Quetta,
West Pakistan*

ancestry? The answer given by the columnist does not throw any light upon the problem:

Dear Anxious:

You seem to know a good deal about this girl, and I see no reason why you should not try to date her if you like. As to race, some people are prejudiced in this regard and others not.

Miss X.

Scholars themselves do not have a clear record when it comes to precise use of the word race. Historians, psychologists, musicologists, philologists, and others are guilty of using the term very loosely. Even the sociologists, who might be expected to define a word they have employed so commonly for decades, have failed to agree.

Who Is an Indian?

This ambiguity so characteristic of the general term "race" is also true for the definitions of the specific groups which are commonly called races. Consider, for example, the American Indian. Who is an Indian? There comes to mind the image of an individual with black, coarse hair, yellow-brown or red-brown skin, wide cheek bones, and a high-bridged, convex nose. Many Indians, however,

24 *The Concept of Race*

would not fit this description; and, as a matter of fact, there are Indians (the writer has seen them on the Cherokee Reservation in North Carolina) who have blue eyes, fair skin, and blond hair. The United States Census Bureau has had to make its own definition of an Indian, as follows:

> In addition to fullblooded American Indians, persons of mixed white and Indian blood are included in this category if they are enrolled on an Indian tribal or agency roll or if they are regarded as Indians in the community.[1]

Mr. J. Nixon Hadley, a statistician of the Office of Indian Affairs, proposed that an individual in the United States, to be classified as an Indian, should satisfy *at least three* of the following conditions:

1. Enrollment with an organized tribal group or on a reservation census roll. This would imply acceptance by the tribal group.
2. General recognition by members of his local community as an Indian. Such recognition would include certain individuals not enrolled with any tribal group.
3. Ability to speak an Indian language.
4. The following of such typical pursuits as the manufacture of Indian arts and crafts or the use of special Indian techniques of agriculture and hunting. This and the immediately preceding criterion is strong indication of a considerable retention of Indian culture.
5. Ownership of restricted property.
6. Residence on an Indian reservation.[2]

Thus, even in the United States, there is considerable doubt as to just who constitute the group we call Indian, and what the criteria are for inclusion in that group. When we look to the Latin American countries the difficulty increases. Throughout most of South and Central America the definition of an Indian is entirely cultural rather than biological. An individual who dresses, lives, and speaks like an Indian is regarded as one; but should he put away those habits and adopt the Spanish or Portuguese language, European dress, and the ways of Caucasians, he would be regarded as a *mestizo* (literally, "mixed" or half-breed) regardless of his hereditary, physical features. In view of this wide diversity in definition, it is impossible to say just what the size of the Indian population of the Americas is. The estimates of competent scholars range all the way from eight million to eighty million.[3] While census data for

[1] *U.S. Census of Populations 1960. United States Summary, General Population Characteristics*, p. xi.
[2] M. Gamio, "Some Considerations of Indianist Policy," in R. Linton (Ed.), *The Science of Man in the World Crisis*, p. 414.
[3] Cf. J. H. Steward, "The Changing American Indian," in R. Linton (Ed.), *The Science of Man in the World Crisis*, pp. 282ff.; D. D. Brand, "The Present Indian Population of the Americas," *New Mexico Anthropologist*, Vols. 6–7, No. 4, 1943, pp. 161ff.; J. N. Hadley, "Demography of the American Indians," *The Annals of the American Academy of Political and Social Science*, Vol. 311, May 1957, pp. 23ff.

the various nations are admittedly inadequate, most of the difficulty lies in our inability to agree on just what we mean by the term Indian, and what criteria we should use in assigning a person to the category.

Who Is a Negro?

The same sort of uncertainty prevails in the definition of a Negro. Most people carry in their minds a picture of the typical Negro — an individual having a dark skin color, woolly hair, broad nose, thick lips, and various other delimiting physical features. The biologist, intent upon classifying mankind, would use a combination of such hereditary characteristics in formulating his definition. Thus Hooton[4] enumerates the criteria of the Negro race: hair form, woolly or frizzly; facial prognathism, pronounced; skin color, black or dark brown; bridge of the nose, low and broad; lip form, thick, puffy and everted; head form, prevailingly dolichocephalic; eye color, dark brown or black; hair color, black; hair texture, coarse and wiry; stature, above medium or tall.

There is a *legal* definition, however, which differs from the foregoing. The fact is there are *many* legal definitions, for the various states which have defined the term either in court decisions or by statute are not in agreement. Missouri, for instance, makes "one-eighth or more Negro blood" the criterion, while Georgia and a number of other states classify as colored all persons with "any ascertainable trace of Negro blood in their veins." Virginia does likewise but makes an exception for individuals having one-fourth or more Indian blood and less than one-sixteenth Negro blood. These Virginia regards as Indians so long as they remain on a reservation. Should they move, however, they are to be regarded as colored. As for the legal definition of the Negro, the situation in the United States has been summarized as follows:

> There is no definite or uniform holding upon the question of who is a Negro, and, in the states where the question has been raised, the courts have been far from unanimous as to the proportion of African blood necessary to classify an individual as a Negro. Some states have defined the term by a general statute, while others have defined it only with respect to particular subjects treated by their laws, such as marriage or education. In a few states, the definition of the term varies according to the subject under consideration.[5]

There is, finally, a *social* definition which takes precedence over both the biological and the legal criteria. According to this definition, which holds throughout the United States, anyone is a Negro who has any *known* trace of Negro ancestry, regardless of how far back one must go to find it. "One drop of Negro blood makes one a Negro" is the popular way of expressing the idea. The Bureau of the Census instructs its enumerators to report as a Negro any person who has a mixture of Negro and white blood, no matter how small the percentage of Negro blood. The agency adds, by way of explanation:

[4] E. A. Hooton, *Up from the Ape*, p. 619.
[5] C. S. Mangum, *The Legal Status of the Negro*, p. 1.

The concept of race, as used by the Bureau of the Census, is derived from that which is commonly accepted by the general public. It does not, therefore, reflect clear-cut definitions of biological stock. . . .

NEGRO. In addition to persons of Negro and of mixed Negro and white descent, this classification includes persons of mixed American Indian and Negro descent, unless the Indian ancestry very definitely predominates or unless the individual is regarded as an Indian in the community.[6]

This social definition, which is the decisive one in most life situations, pays little heed to the hereditary physical features of the individual or to whether the percentage of Negro blood is one-fourth, one-eighth, or one-sixteenth. The American criterion of a Negro has been a popular theme in literature and on the stage, and was used by Sinclair Lewis as the basis for a novel, *Kingsblood Royal*. That it is not a mere fiction, however, is proved by the following news item:

Davis Knight had lived in Mississippi all of his twenty-three years, except for three years in the Navy. He married blonde, blue-eyed Junie Lee Spradley and farmed a poor piece of land. One night the county police arrested him. Knight was a Negro, they said; Junie Lee was white. In Mississippi that kind of marrying was against the law.

Knight said they were wrong. But a relative, irked by an old family feud, had dug up Davis Knight's genealogy. His great-grandfather had been Cap'n Newt Knight, who deserted the Confederate Army and set up "The Free State of Jones" in Jones County. Cap'n Newt had children by Rachel, a Negro slave girl. Rachel was Davis Knight's great-grandmother.

Through succeeding generations the Knights had married white men or women. Davis Knights' own parents had not known of the Negro strain in their ancestry. The story the relative dug up would affect a number of other families in the neighborhood, all sprung from the loins of Cap'n Newt and Rachel. Last week a court in Ellisville convicted Cap'n Newt's great-grandson of miscegenation, sentenced him to five years in jail.[7]

This social definition — the prevalent one in the United States — is not followed elsewhere. In the Latin American countries one may possess many negroid racial features, and may even have known Negro ancestors, and still be regarded as white. Regarding the practice in Brazil, Pierson writes:

Whereas in the United States one drop of Negro blood, if it be known, makes a man a Negro, in Bahia many individuals are listed in the census as white (and, one might add, are so considered by their friends and associates) whose grandmothers were Negroes of pure African descent. . . . It is clear that many individuals are considered white at Bahia who not only have Negro ancestors but whose physical characteristics definitely attest this fact.[8]

[6] *Op. cit.*, pp. x–xi.
[7] Courtesy of *Time*, Copyright Time Inc., December 27, 1948.
[8] D. Pierson, *Negroes in Brazil*, pp. 127–128.

It is much the same in Puerto Rico. Rogler describes the situation as follows:

> Any mulatto who is not in physical features, pigmentation, and hair texture too close to the negroid type may be classed as a mulatto or a white person. He is one of these two, but not a Negro. . . . The light mulatto is regarded as a white person.[9]

In the Republic of South Africa a sharp distinction is drawn between the "natives" and the Cape Coloured, who are Negro-white hybrids. The latter, at least until recently, were accorded privileges denied to the Negroes, and they enjoyed a social position intermediate between that of the dominant whites and the subordinate blacks.

Thus we see that definition of the Negro is subject to considerable variation from country to country, and from time to time.

Who is a Jew?

There are approximately thirteen million Jews in the world, five million of whom reside in the United States. We have to say "approximately," for it is no easy matter to determine just who is a Jew or to know exactly what kind of group the Jewish group is. There is the popular belief, of course, that there are certain physical features which characterize this group; and one frequently hears the expression "the Jewish race." Of one thing we may be certain, however; there is no Jewish race, if we restrict the word race to its biological meaning. There are many Jewish people who do not have the type of nose, for instance, which, in the popular imagination, is a criterion of the group, and there are many non-Jews who do have that particular nasal form. As a matter of fact, in the Jewish group one will find all kinds of noses, all shapes of heads, a wide range of pigmentation, various sorts of stature, blond and brunet, a diversity of hair types, and blue eyes and brown. There are even synagogues of Negro Jews.

If they are not a race then, are the Jews a religious group? Are they not a group such as Methodists, Christian Scientists, or Hindus? Not entirely; for there are among the Jews atheists and agnostics as well as converts to Roman Catholicism and to the various Protestant denominations. Religion has without doubt been the bond which has held the Jewish group together through the centuries, and it is not without its cohesive force today; but the group which is generally regarded as Jewish is not identical with the group which adheres to that particular faith.

Nor is it correct to regard the Jews as a nation. They were a nation at one time in their past; and more recently there has been established the State of Israel, as a homeland for Jews. This new nation, however, includes Arabs, Moslems, and Christians, and does not include the millions in other lands who regard themselves as Jews.

[9] C. C. Rogler, *Comerio: A Study of a Puerto Rican Town*, pp. 37–38.

It is difficult, therefore, to define the Jew, or to determine exactly what the essential criteria are for inclusion in that group. Perhaps it is *the consciousness of being a Jew* that is crucial; and, however unsatisfactory it may be as a definition, it approaches the reality of the situation to say that a Jew is a person who thinks of himself as a Jew and is treated by others as a Jew, regardless of the physical features which he bears, the language he speaks or the nation of which he is a citizen.

Even in Israel the question is a perennial one. The traditional view is that a Jew is one whose mother is Jewish. Members of the Cabinet have repeatedly disputed this definition, and onetime Prime Minister Moshe Sharett has even suggested that "being a Jew is so difficult that anyone professing to be one should be believed."

The matter came to a head in 1958, when a certain Oswald Rufeisen, who had been born and bred a Jew in Europe, but who had joined the Roman Catholic Church and become a Carmelite monk, sought to enter Israel as an immigrant. Brother Daniel, as he had come to be known, was extended the privilege of seeking naturalization, but he rejected that offer on the grounds that he was a Jew, and that the law states: "Every Jew has the right to immigrate to Israel." The case was taken to the Supreme Court, where it was debated at great length, and a decision was finally reached on December 6, 1962. The majority of the justices rejected Brother Daniel's claim, declaring in substance that one cannot be both Jew and Christian at the same time. The Court upheld a decision of the Cabinet to the effect that "A person who in good faith declares himself to be a

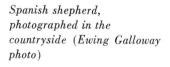

Spanish shepherd, photographed in the countryside (Ewing Galloway photo)

TABLE 2.1

Estimated Jewish Population By Countries, 1962*

Country	Jewish Population
United States	5,586,500
Soviet Union	2,385,000
Israel	2,035,000
France	500,000
England	450,000
Argentina	450,000
Canada	254,000
Rumania	180,000
Morocco	130,000
Brazil	125,000
Republic of South Africa	110,000
Hungary	90,000
Iran	80,000
Australia	66,000
All other countries	558,500
Total	13,000,000

* Source: *The American Jewish Year Book*, Vol. 64, 1963.

Jew and does not belong to another religion shall be registered as a Jew." One of the justices, however, offered a dissenting opinion, maintaining that the clause, "does not belong to another religion," was not supported by proper authority. It appears, then, that if Oswald Rufeisen had repudiated all religion he would have encountered no obstacle in entering the country and becoming a citizen.[10]

Current Uses of the Term "Race"

A speaker once amused his audience by making the facetious observation that "women are a peculiar race." The term "race," however, is rarely used to designate the male and female divisions of mankind. Nor are Methodists, Republicans, blonds, carpenters, or Elks referred to as races. We speak of such groups as sects, denominations, parties, occupations, or fraternities — but not as races. However, an almost equally wide variety of human groups are commonly designated races. Among these are English, French, Arabs, Jews, Gypsies, Scotch, Welsh, Basques, Indians, Eskimos, Aryans, Negroes, Hindus, Latins, Nordics, and Celts. Obviously these are not comparable or similar groups, and yet they are all frequently spoken of as races.

[10] *The Israel Digest*, Vol. 5, No. 26, December 21, 1962, pp. 4–5.

In current use, then, the term "race" is applied to the following kinds of groups and categories:

1. The citizens or subjects of a particular nation, state, or country. Thus, the British and the Japanese are often designated "races." "Nation" or "state" would doubtless be more appropriate terms.
2. Those who speak a certain language or type of language. Latin, Aryan, and English are examples of this use of the word "race."
3. A religious group. Hindu, Sikh, and, to some extent, Jew, are illustrations of this use, or misuse, of the term.
4. A caste. One often hears the expression "the Gypsy race." The Gypsies are, admittedly, a strange group, neither a nation nor a religion, and certainly not a race. The term "caste" would better describe them.
5. A local population, which has, by reason of its isolation, become fairly uniform. Thus, the Cornish people or the Basques.
6. A hypothetical "pure" type which is assumed to have existed in the distant past, such as the Nordic or the Germanic.
7. A recognizable type, such as the Arab, the American Indian, or the Eskimo. The Arabs, for example, are not a nation, for there are several Arab nations. Nor are they a religion, for even though most of them are Moslem, there are also Christian Arabs, and there are Moslems who are not Arabs. (Webster's Dictionary defines an Arab as "one of a swarthy race occupying Arabia, and numerous in Syria, Northern Africa, etc.")
8. One of the major biological divisions of mankind, such as the Mongoloid, the Caucasoid, or the Negroid.
9. A race-conscious group or what Dr. Robert Redfield has aptly called "the socially supposed races." Examples are the American Negro, the Mexican, and the Japanese-American. Such groups do possess certain visible, physical marks, which set them apart, and which tend to enhance their feeling of group solidarity and uniqueness.
10. A group having a common culture and traditions. Some of these groups have, in the past, been nations, such as the Scottish; others aspire to become nations.

This list does not by any means exhaust all the current uses of the word "race." It is apparent, however, that race is a vague, ambiguous term. All kinds of groups and categories of people are designated races, whether the bond that holds them together be biological or cultural, hereditary or acquired.

Such vagueness offends the sensibilities of scholars and scientists, who try to give definite and precise meanings to the words they use. Accordingly, many of them have proposed that we discontinue altogether the use of the word "race." Thus, Barzun regards it as "a modern superstition," and says, "The notion of race is a myth which all intelligent people should discard." [11] Huxley and

11 J. Barzun, *Race: A Study in Modern Superstition*, p. 8.

Haddon are in substantial agreement with Barzun, and "in order to avoid the unfortunate connotations of the word race," they prefer to talk about *minor sub-species, major sub-species,* and *ethnic groups.*[12] Many sociologists, feeling that the word "race" is too vague and misleading, have chosen to employ such terms as "minorities," "nationalities," "ethnic groups," and the like.

Race and Culture

Some of the difficulty with the term "race" arises from the fact that people do not make the proper distinction between that which is biological and heredi-tary, on the one hand, and that which is learned and acquired, on the other. No one denies that we come into the world devoid of political convictions, religious affiliations, recreational interests, and literary tastes. We *learn* all these, and we learn them from those with whom we associate. If it be the American society into which we are born, the probability is that we shall acquire an interest in football rather than bull fighting, baseball rather than cricket, bridge and poker rather than mah jong. It is a safe bet, too, that we shall learn to speak English rather than Romansch, that we shall affiliate with a Christian church rather than a Buddhist, Shinto, or Hindu temple, and that our political activities will follow those of the American pattern rather than those of Brazil, Bulgaria, or Thailand. In short, we are born, ignorant and helpless, into a group which possesses a great body of knowledge, beliefs, attitudes, laws, customs, traditions, and skills. We proceed immediately to imitate and acquire these "group habits" of thought, feeling, and behavior; and the members of the group, at the same time, set about to indocrinate us with those behavior patterns which they regard as right, proper, and natural. The term "culture" is used by social scientists to designate the complex of learned behavior patterns which are characteristic of the members of a group.

Much of what a person becomes is a result of the culture into which he hap-pens to be born. The individual, however, is not simply a carbon copy of his culture, for if that were true then all the members of a society would be identical. The fact is that a culture is a rich and complex phenomenon, and no individual acquires all of his group's culture. Even the simplest societies known to anthro-pologists possess an amazingly complicated pattern of behavior. Ours, of course, is far beyond the powers of any single person to encompass. A culture, then, can be carried and perpetuated only by a group of people, and some members of the group are privileged to carry more of it than others.

Certain parts of a culture are acquired and followed by nearly all members of a society. We have our prohibitions against incest, our dislike for cannibalism, our habit of driving on the right, using the English language, and wearing cloth-ing. Folkways and mores of this type, which apply to all members of a society, Linton has called *universals.*[13] There are other customs, however, which afford

---

[12] J. S. Huxley and A. C. Haddon, *We Europeans: A Survey of "Racial" Problems,* pp. 107ff.

[13] R. Linton, *The Study of Man,* pp. 272–275.

A Ghanian student does graduate work in economics in the United States

us some range of choice. These are known as *alternatives*. None of us eats meat raw; but we may broil, roast, or bake it, and prefer it rare, medium, or well done, and still remain within the bounds of convention. Finally, there are the *specialties*, or those patterns of behavior which are restricted to certain persons in the society. Thus, the Boy Scouts acquire knowledge, skills, and customs which others do not bother to learn; Masons and Elks have traditions known only to themselves; and lawyers, doctors, and soldiers have their own peculiar vocabulary, ethics, and techniques, which are strange and incomprehensible to engineers and priests — and sometimes to each other. Here, then, is another reason why the members of a society are not "a mob of unnecessary duplicates," as Herman Melville once cynically remarked.

Finally, we come into the world with certain characteristics which we have inherited, and which we do not have to learn. We have a certain type of blood, about which we have no choice whatever. We do not have to be taught to sneeze, to blink our eyes, or to make our hearts beat. Nor does one have very much control over the amount of pigment in his skin, the type of hair on his head, the width of his nose, or the color of his eyes. These are all the products of the genes one inherits from his parents. The genetic make-up of an individual, then, is fixed at the time of conception; and, while this make-up is somewhat variable, depending upon the internal and external environment experienced by the individual, the degree and extent of this variability are definitely limited. Hence a person retains throughout his life those features which he acquires through heredity.

It is not so with his cultural characteristics. These may be changed a number of times during a lifetime. It is no easy matter for one to change the culture he has acquired, but it can be done. Thus one may learn a new language and forget the language of his childhood; one may forsake his religion and become converted to another; and one may change his nationality any number of times.

One's personality, therefore, is a product of several interacting factors — the physical environment in which he develops, the biological characteristics he brings into the world with him, the culture into which he is born and in which he lives, and the unique experiences to which he is subjected. These factors make it possible for an infinite variety of personalities to be developed, with the result that no two individuals are identical.

We may recognize the fact, then, that each individual has his own unique personality, and we may insist that it is unwise and unfair to lump people together, and to "think of them in bunches." Despite their differences, however, people do form themselves into groups on the basis of a wide range of interests. Also, we make classifications or categories of people, since it is obviously impossible always to think of the three billion human inhabitants of this earth as unique individuals.

The variety and aptness of these classifications which we persist in making has been well described by Hoebel:

> Classification is nothing more than a grouping of phenomena in accordance with certain of their qualities. There are as many possible and valid classifications of a group of things as it possesses qualities or traits. Any classification is valid, providing the basis or criterion for classification is a true attribute of the thing being classified and providing the criterion is held constant throughout that particular classification. When the requirements of validity of criterion and consistency of application have been met, one classification is as *true* as another.
>
> Classifications have greater or lesser significance and usefulness, however, depending upon the interests of the investigator and the problems he is attempting to solve.
>
> Take a barrel of mixed apples. What possibilities for classification are there in it? Color, size, shape, flavor, juiciness, number of seeds, and toughness of skin are obvious attributes. You may properly and scientifically classify your apples by using any one of these attributes as a criterion for grouping. But if you are going to select the best apples for cider making, then the only classification of significance will be one based upon flavor and juice content. Color and shape are irrelevant. On the other hand, if you want to select apples to be sold in *bon voyage* baskets, color and size will be the criteria of greatest significance.[14]

Human beings possess so many qualities and traits that there is no limit to the possible classifications to which they are susceptible. We may group them according to their religious affiliations, their political beliefs, their economic status, the language they speak, or the occupations they follow. We may classify

---

[14] E. A. Hoebel, *Man in the Primitive World*, p. 437. Copyright 1949. Courtesy of McGraw-Hill Book Co.

them, too, as freshmen, sophomores, or juniors, depending upon the academic credit they have accumulated, by fair means or foul. A university will use certain criteria for classifying the people with whom it deals, the army still other criteria, while psychiatrists, merchants, physicians, and politicians will select those traits, and make those classifications, which suit their respective purposes.

The general feeling among scientists is that, for all its ambiguity, the word "race" — like sex — is here to stay; and the solution of the problem lies, not in discarding the word as Barzun and others propose, but in divorcing it entirely from all associations with cultural, political, linguistic, and religious characteristics, and rigidly restricting it to a biological meaning. To that end numerous definitions of the word "race" have been made, one of the best being the following, formulated by Krogman:

> A race is a sub-group of peoples possessing a definite combination of physical characters, of genetic origin; this combination serves, in varying degree, to distinguish the sub-group from other sub-groups of mankind, and the combination is transmitted in descent, providing all conditions which originally gave rise to the definite combination remain relatively unaltered; as a rule the sub-group inhabits, or did inhabit, a more or less restricted geographical region.[15]

The Biological Concept

Making the word "race" a strictly biological concept is easier said than done. To be sure, people have always shown a disposition to classify themselves and others. The most primitive tribes recognize the difference between "we" and "they"; and lower animals, including insects, make a distinction between those who belong and those who do not. The earliest people of whom we have records seem to have classified mankind into such categories as infidels and faithful, lost souls and saved, bond and free, civilized and savage, Greeks and barbarians.

The idea of classifying mankind on the basis of skin color, hair form, and other biological features which we call "racial" seems, however, to be a rather modern practice. The origin of the word race is not known. Many authorities suspect that it is of Semitic origin, coming from a word which some translations of the Bible render "race," as in the "race of Abraham," but which the Authorized Version translates "seed" or "generation." Other scholars trace it to the Czech word *raz*, meaning artery or blood; others to the Latin *generatio*, or the Old French *generace*, or the Basque *arraca* or *arraze*, referring to a male stud animal. Some trace it to the Spanish *ras*, itself of Arabic derivation, meaning head or origin. In all these possible sources the word has a biological significance, implying descent, blood, or relationship.

Whatever its origin, we do know that it entered the European languages at a relatively recent date. *Razza* makes its appearance in Italian literature in the

---

15 W. M. Krogman, "The Concept of Race," in R. Linton (Ed.), *The Science of Man in World Crisis*, p. 49.

*Swiss woman knits as she carries
her baby with her*

fourteenth century. It occurs first in the French in 1684, where there is a
reference to "especs ou races d'homme," meaning stem or family. In 1696
Leibnitz used the word for the first time in the German language. Its first
appearance in English dates from 1570, where we find "the race of Abraham"
mentioned in Fox's *Book of Martyrs.* In 1667 Milton refers to the "race
of Satan" in his *Paradise Lost.*

Why did Europeans begin to become so race-conscious in the sixteenth and
seventeenth centuries? Why did they begin then to pay so much more attention
to hair and skin color, and to attach so much more significance to them, than
they had ever done before? Why did the racial features of individuals take on
so much importance that a new word was needed in the European languages?
Huxley and Haddon have the ingenious theory that the introduction of the word
race, and the thought-content it conveys, is bound up with the rise of nationalism.[16] When people began to think of themselves as belonging to groups known
as nations, something other than a mere political bond was necessary to hold
them together. It has always been one of the main preoccupations of statecraft
to establish, develop, and regulate group-sentiment among the multitudes composing the nation-state. Now the blood relationship bond is one of the oldest
in human history. Huxley and Haddon believe, therefore, that the concept of
race served to transfer to the new aggregate of the nation some of the age-old
sentiment and loyalty which had hitherto been devoted to family, clan, and other
blood groups. Not only nations, but various human associations, such as religious bodies and fraternities, also attempt to appropriate some of this age-old

[16] *Op. cit.,* pp. 1–3.

family sentiment and solidarity-feeling by employing such terms as brother, father, mother, and sister. Others think that the concept of race helped the white Europeans justify to their own satisfaction their exploitation of strange peoples whom they encountered when Europe began to expand into all the corners of the earth.

But whatever the reason for the popularity of the race idea, the fact is that Europeans began to give thought to the subject, and began to classify the peoples of the earth on a racial basis. Perhaps the first to do so systematically was the French traveler, Bernier (1625–1688). Mankind, he decided, fell into the following categories:

1. Inhabitants of Europe, North Africa, and parts of Asia. (Bernier noted that Egyptians and Indians were somewhat dark, but he attributed this fact to the climate.)
2. Africans: "thick lips, flat nose, black skin, scanty beard, woolly hair."
3. Asiatics: "broad shoulders, flat face, small squab nose, little pig's eyes deep set, and three hairs of beard."
4. Lapps: "little stunted creatures, with thick legs, large shoulders, short neck, face elongated immensely, very ugly, and partaking very much of the bear."

He was undecided about American Indians and South Africans.

Next to try his hand at classifying mankind was the Swedish naturalist, Linnaeus, who proposed the following around 1738:

1. Europaeus albus: "lively, light, inventive, and ruled by rites."
2. Americanus rubesceus: "tenacious, contented, free, and ruled by custom."
3. Asiaticus luridus: "stern, haughty, stingy, ruled by opinion."
4. Afer niger: "cunning, slow, negligent, and ruled by caprice."

Somewhat later the German physiologist Blumenbach classified the human species into five varieties: Caucasian, Mongolian, Ethiopian, American, and Malayan. He used hair, skin color, bodily structure, and especially the form of the skull as his principal criteria. Blumenbach's scheme became very popular, and has survived to this day, inasmuch as one occasionally hears of the five races — white, black, brown, yellow, and red.

Innumerable others have followed these pioneers. There was the French scientist, Cuvier, who derived mankind from the three sons of Noah, Japhet being regarded as the progenitor of the Caucasian, Shem of the Mongolian, and Ham of the African. The divergence of these types is not explained, except that Ham's blackness was attributed to Noah's curse. Then there was Bory de St. Vincent, who, in 1827, chose the type of hair as the chief criterion, and produced a twofold division of mankind, (1) Leiotrichi, or straight-haired, and (2) Ulotrichi, or woolly-haired.

These, and the host of others who tackled the same problem, seem to have arrived at no satisfactory answer, but two principles of classification have emerged from their efforts. First, certain human differences have proved to be of no value in making biological classifications of mankind. Among these are temperament, habits, beliefs, customs, and attitudes. Other differences, such as pigmentation, hair, nose form, eyes, lips, and stature have assumed greater importance. Second, any valid classification must rest upon a combination of traits rather than upon a single characteristic.

The Criteria of Race

No two people are exactly alike. There are differences of height, weight, and girth; differences in intelligence, musical ability, and athletic prowess; in political, religious, and artistic preferences; in occupations, skills, education, sex, marital status, age, and so on *ad infinitum*. Now the fact that people are so different makes it possible, and even imperative, that we place them together into groups and categories. The merchant, for example, will construct categories based upon his customers' bill-paying habits; the telephone company will classify its patrons according to the initial letter of the surname; government statisticians are continually classifying all of us on the basis of our annual income, our age, or whether we are employed, unemployed, or unemployable. Thus the classifiers are continually putting each of us into this pigeon-hole or that, we being unaware most of the time that we are being so handled.

None of these categories is absolute and eternal. The validity of any classification depends upon the purpose of him who does the sorting. There is no "right" way, for example, to classify the millions of books in the world. Some libraries use one system and some another; and each of us, in his own private library, uses his own special system. Or consider the various ways of classifying animals. The writers of the Bible used a threefold system — birds of the air, beasts of the field, and the fishes of the sea. This was entirely adequate for the needs of the time. Modern biologists, however, have quite a different purpose in mind. They want to classify animals on the basis of genetic relationship; and, accordingly, they group together bats, whales, people, and cattle, which they designate the "Class of Mammals."

So it is with the scientist who attempts to classify mankind into races. He, too, seeks a scheme which will show genetic relationship. Therefore he disregards all human differences which are cultural, acquired, learned. He rejects as criteria the differences of political and religious beliefs, of attitudes and customs, of capacity and temperament. He chooses, instead, as useful criteria those differences which are biological and hereditary. He has found especially useful the following: skin color, hair color, hair form, eye color, nasal form, head form, and stature. There are numerous other hereditary features which are also used.

The selection of these criteria, however, does not solve the problem, for they are all extremely difficult to handle. For one thing, they represent differences which are *continuous*, rather than *discrete*. Blood differences are of the latter sort. One's blood is either *O*, *A*, *B*, or *AB*. Consequently, the classification of people according to blood type is relatively simple. Not so with racial criteria, however. There are no sharp distinctions with respect to head form, but a gradual and continuous variation from narrow to round. So it is with skin color, hair form, nasal index, and the others. This means that dividing *Homo sapiens* into racial categories is a somewhat arbitrary affair. Some scientists will make a twofold division, some a threefold, some a fivefold, or more. The problem is more complicated than that of the teacher who, at the end of the year, is required to divide his students into categories designated *A, B, C, D,* and *F,* the arbitrary nature of such divisions being obvious to every teacher and to most students. The customs of the institution determine for the teacher how many categories he will have, but this is not the case with the scientist constructing racial categories.

Another difficulty arises from the fact that the various racial criteria are independent of one another. That is, any form of hair may occur with any skin color; a narrow nose gives no clue to the amount of pigment or the texture of the hair of the individual. Thus the Australian aborigines have dark skins, and broad noses, but an abundance of curly to wavy hair; and the Asiatic Indians have much pigment in their skins, but have narrow noses and straight hair. This gives no end of trouble to the classifier; for if he assorts people on the basis of color, he will have all kinds of noses, hair, and head forms in his category; and if he chooses head form as the major criterion, he ends up with an equally diverse, but different, aggregation of physical types in his pigeon-hole.

It must also be pointed out that the racial traits scientists use are not biologically important, but are secondary and incidental human characteristics. A narrow head is not one whit inferior to a round head; a Mongoloid eyefold does not make for a less efficient eye; woolly hair is no handicap in the biological struggle for existence. As a matter of fact, human beings, along with several other mammals, have lost most of their hairy covering, and it would not be fatal, or even serious, if they were to lose the rest of it.

There are still other difficulties in handling the racial criteria upon which the classification of mankind is based. There is the disturbing fact that these physical features, while hereditary, are not immutable, but are plastic and changing; and they are not immune to environmental influences and human manipulation.[17]

Modern Classifications

It is no wonder, then, that present-day scientists are far from agreement on a racial division of mankind. Thus Kroeber chooses a threefold classification of Caucasoid, Mongoloid, and Negroid, but has a fourth category of doubtful people, which includes Australians, Veddoid, Ainu, and Polynesians.[18] Goldenweiser divides mankind into five races: Negro, Australian, Mongolian, American Indian, and White.[19] Lowie inclines toward a fourfold division: Australoid, Negroid, Mongoloid, and Caucasoid; but this leaves out the Polynesians, whom he regards as "unclassifiable."[20] Stibbe believes there are six races: Mediter-

[17] For a discusion of these criteria, see A. L. Kroeber, *Anthropology,* pp. 126ff.
[18] *Op. cit.,* pp. 131–141.
[19] A. Goldenweiser, *Anthropology,* pp. 20–24.
[20] R. H. Lowie, *An Introduction to Cultural Anthropology,* pp. 4–6.

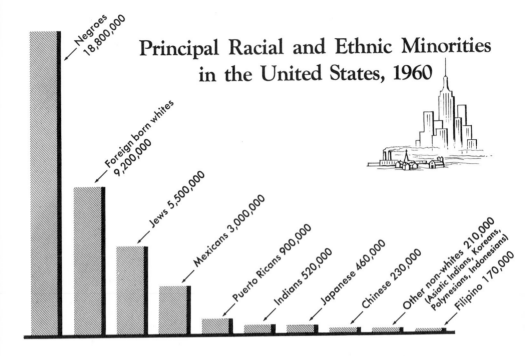

Principal Racial and Ethnic Minorities in the United States, 1960

Negroes 18,800,000

Foreign born whites 9,200,000

Jews 5,500,000

Mexicans 3,000,000

Puerto Ricans 900,000

Indians 520,000

Japanese 460,000

Chinese 230,000

Other non-whites 210,000 (Asiatic Indians, Koreans, Polynesians, Indonesians)

Filipino 170,000

ranean, or "Brown," Alpine, Nordic, Mongoloid, Negroid, and Australoid.[21] Hooton prefers the threefold division of Caucasoid, Negroid, and Mongoloid, but makes a fourth "composite" group, into which he places Australians, Dravidians, Indonesians, Malaysians, Eskimos, Polynesians, and American Indians.[22] Linton's classification results in about seventeen races. These he groups into three basic "stocks" — Caucasoid, Negroid, and Mongoloid — but he is left with the Bushman-Hottentot, Australian, Polynesian, and Ainu races, which, he says, "defy classification."[23] More recently, Boyd, who defines a race as "a population which differs significantly from other human populations in regard to the frequency of one or more of the genes it possesses,"[24] has come up with a classification as follows: (1) Early European, (2) European, (3) African, (4) Asiatic, (5) American Indian, and (6) Australoid.

Garn and Coon deplore this failure of the scientists to agree upon how mankind ought to be classified, and undertake to resolve the problem.[25] They note that "there is considerable disagreement as to how many races there are. Different taxonomies have listed as few as two races and as many as two hundred.

21 E. P. Stibbe, *An Introduction to Physical Anthropology*, pp. 149–160.
22 Hooton, *op. cit.*, pp. 423–661.
23 Linton, *op cit.*, pp. 22–45.
24 W. C. Boyd, *Genetics and the Races of Man*, p. 207.
25 S. M. Garn and C. S. Coon, "On the Number of Races of Mankind," *American Anthropologist*, Vol. 57, No. 5, October 1955, pp. 996ff.

Of two books that appeared in 1950, one distinguishes six races . . . while another described thirty races." They maintain that the problem would be solved if we were to recognize the difference between *geographical races* and *local races.* They define a geographical race as "a collection of populations having features in common, such as a high gene frequency for blood group B, and extending over a geographically definable area." On this basis, they say, we might agree upon six or seven races: (1) Caucasian, (2) Northern and Eastern Asiatic, (3) African, (4) Indian, (5) Micronesian and Melanesian, (6) Polynesian, and (7) Aboriginal American. By *local race* they mean "a breeding or Mendelian population," a unit that can be subjected to study. Such local races, they say, "can be identified, not so much by average differences, as by their nearly complete isolation." They think that the number of local races is "upwards of thirty," and cite as examples the Pitcairn Islanders and the inhabitants of Tristan da Cunha. Classification of mankind into the large geographical races, they say, is to a large extent a matter of convenience, useful more for pedagogical purposes than as units for empirical investigation. Local races, however, "not only are susceptible to direct study but also afford insight into the evolutionary mechanisms still at work in shaping man."

Estel believes that the term "race" ought to be used *only* for such local breeding groups. Says he: "Man is an extremely mobile animal but occasionally a breeding group becomes isolated long enough to develop a complex of genetically inherited characteristics that distinguishes this group from other human populations. . . . The term race should be reserved for these isolated breeding groups."[26] Estel makes no attempt to determine how many races there are but he insists that most human beings would fall into a mixed or indeterminate category.

So confused is the problem of racial classification that the President of the American Anthropological Association, Dr. S. L. Washburn, was moved to discuss it in his presidential address at the annual meeting of the Association in 1962. Said he:

> There are no three primary races, no three major groups. The idea of three primary races stems from nineteenth-century typology. . . . If we look to real history we will always find more than three races. . . . If we attempt to preserve the notion of three races, we make pseudo-typological problems. . . . The majority of anthropological textbooks need substantial revision along these lines.
>
> Since races are open systems which are intergrading, the number of races will depend on the purpose of the classification. . . . If we are classifying races in order to understand human history, there aren't many human races, and there is very substantial agreement as to what they are. There are from six to nine races, and this difference in number is very largely a matter of definition. . . . If one has no purpose for classification, the number of races can be multiplied almost indefinitely.[27]

[26] L. Estel, "Race as an Evolutionary Concept," *American Journal of Physical Anthropology,* Vol. 14 (New Series), No. 2, June 1956, p. 378.

[27] S. L. Washburn, "The Study of Race," *American Anthropologist,* Vol. 65, No. 3, Part 1, June 1963, pp. 523–524.

Conclusions

Let us summarize this discussion of the biological concept of race by venturing the following propositions:

1. The term "race," as used by most biological scientists, refers to a set of categories rather than to discrete, invariable entities. Races are not so much real things which man has discovered as they are pigeon-holes which man has constructed. These categories, to be sure, are based upon clusters of hereditary, physical characteristics.
2. No classification yet proposed has won universal acceptance by scientists. Whatever the system of classification, there are many groups which do not fit into the proposed categories.
3. The criteria upon which racial classification is based are non-adaptive, physical, secondary, and have little survival value. Certain societies, however, have come to attach great social significance to these biological trivia.
4. Most of these racial criteria are phenotypically continuous rather than discrete; they overlap; they are dynamic, not static; and most of them can be transmitted independently of one another. These facts make racial classification an appalling and difficult task, if not an impossible one.

The Social Concept

Most of us, when we use the word "race," are not thinking of the biological categories constructed by the anthropologists, though it would perhaps help matters considerably if we would all fall into that habit. Instead, however, we prob-

Deep-water fisherman of Thailand embarks with his net

ably have in mind one or more of the other kinds of groups mentioned earlier in this chapter. We are thinking of British or Japanese, or Jews, Gypsies, or Arabs. To refer to some of these groups as races is unpardonable. No informed person would designate as a race a group which more properly should be called a state, a religion, or a linguistic family. Only the unenlightened, for example, will believe that there is an Aryan or a Latin race. There is no justification for our speaking of the Russians or the British as a race. Whatever they are, Jews, Gypsies, and Chinese are certainly *not* races. But what about the American Negro, the Indian, the Mexican, and the Japanese-American? Are not these races, and are not their problems racial problems? Certainly they are not identical with the categories devised by the biological scientists. They have occasionally been described as the "so-called races" or the "socially supposed races."

Some sociologists, in order to avoid the confusion, have proposed that the word "race" be restricted to the biological concept discussed above, and that other terms be used for the "so-called" races. Some will enclose the word "race" in quotation marks when they are forced to use it, thereby somehow absolving themselves of the guilt of using so ambiguous an expression. The literature abounds in new concepts and phrases, adopted in the hope that thereby the phenomena with which the sociologist is concerned will be set apart from those of the biological fields. Let us examine a few of these terms.

Intergroup Relations

In some quarters the expression "intergroup relations" has supplanted the older and more familiar "race relations." It *is* important that we distinguish between a category and a group. *Category* simply denotes that several objects are *thought of* together, are classified together because of some point of similarity. There need be no contact or even proximity between the objects themselves. Thus, *fiction* is a category under which we think of a great variety of books; but books may be organized into an infinite number of categories — according to size, color, language, content, and so on. People, too, are continually being thought of in categories, based upon health, age, sex, marital status, income, size of family, and cause of death. *Group*, on the other hand, denotes interactivity, interstimulation, interaction. It consists of any number of people who are bound together by the fact that they hold in common at least one *interest*. The members composing a group need not be in close contact; their relations may be indirect and at a long range. Gypsies, Arabs, Hindus, Jews, American Negroes, then, are indeed groups. So are the Scottish people, the British, the Canadians, and the Portuguese; and so, too, are the Elks, Floridians, Californians, Bostonians, and the American Medical Association. These all think of themselves as "we," and speak of outsiders as "they." They regard themselves as a group, however tight or tenuous the bonds may be, and they are considered a group by those on the outside.

The colorless term "group," therefore, avoids some of the pitfalls inherent in the word "race." The difficulty, however, is that it is *too* broad a term. Sociologists who study so-called race relations are not concerned with the relations of *all* kinds of groups. They are not investigating the relations between nations (though these are groups), nor the relations between college football teams, between Catholics and Protestants, or between the Smiths and the Joneses. It is only the relations between *certain kinds* of groups which concern us here.

Minority

Another term which sociologists have adopted, in preference to race, is *minority*. Donald Young, in one of the first systematic analyses of the problem of race relations, employed the concept extensively. Said he:

> Race, in the strict meaning of the term, is not the subject of this study. We are primarily concerned with social behavior; and the people whose behavior is under consideration neither know nor care whether the Jew, the Italian, the Scandinavian, the American Negro, or the Mexican is a representative of a particular race in the strict biological sense. With superb disdain for the findings of the scientists, popular belief lumps biological, language, cultural, political, and other groups under the one heading of "race," and behaves accordingly. Our use of the term race, then, must conform to that of the ordinary citizen, for it is his behavior, not that of the scientists, that we are studying.
>
> There is, unfortunately, no word in the English language which can with philological propriety be applied to all these groups, that is, which includes groups which are distinguished by biological features, alien national cultural traits, or a combination of both. For this reason, the phrases, "minorities of racial or national origin," "American minorities," or "minority peoples" are here used as synonymous with the popular usage of the word race.[28]

Literally, of course, minority means simply "the smaller number." Accordingly, there is an infinite number of minority groups (the Prohibition Party, chess players, and the admirers of Picasso's art), and all of us belong to many minorities. Sociologists, however, have restricted the term to certain kinds of groups, have divested it of all statistical meaning, and have looked upon discrimination and exclusion from full social participation as the essential characteristics. Thus, Wirth defines a minority as "a group of people who, because of physical or cultural characteristics, are singled out from the others in the society in which they live for differential and unequal treatment, and who therefore regard themselves as objects of collective discrimination."[29]

Nationality

Others have sought to use the term *nationality* to refer to those groups, often called races, which are united by ties of cultural homogeneity, sympathy, we-

---

[28] D. Young, *American Minority Peoples*, p. xiii.
[29] L. Wirth, "The Problem of Minority Groups," in R. Linton (Ed.), *The Science of Man in the World Crisis*, p. 347.

*Indian boy of the
Hopi, a southwestern
United States tribe*

feeling, and a desire to share a common life. They would distinguish between a nation and a nationality, insisting that when a nationality achieves a political structure and territorial establishment it becomes a nation. The individuals who compose a nationality may be scattered among various states (e.g., the Germans), and a particular political unit may be composed of several nationalities (Switzerland, Great Britain, or Czechoslovakia). Hankins attempted to establish this usage in sociology, declaring:

> A full-fledged *nation* has three characteristics, namely, a relatively homogeneous culture, a consciousness of common origin and destiny, and independent possession of and loyalty to a definite territory. A *nationality* falls short of a nation either because, like the Jews, it is not identified with a definite territory, or because, like the Poles before World War I, it lacks political independence.[30]

More recently Fairchild employed the term "nationality" as the designation for groups which are held together by the possession of common culture, sentiments, traditions, institutions, values, folkways, mores, and standards.[31]

This distinction between nation and nationality, however, is not generally accepted. Professor E. K. Francis has pointed out[32] that scholars of the British

[30] F. H. Hankins, *An Introduction to the Study of Society*, p. 758.
[31] H. P. Fairchild, *Race and Nationality*, pp. 36ff.
[32] "The Nature of the Ethnic Group," *American Journal of Sociology*, Vol. 52, No. 5, March 1947, p. 393.

school have tended to emphasize the political aspect, offering as one of the characteristics of a nation "the idea of a common government whether as a reality in the present or past, or an aspiration of the future." Those of the Continental school, on the other hand, have tended to minimize the political aspect, and have emphasized as characteristics of a nation those very qualities which Fairchild and Hankins have selected as the criteria of a nationality. Most sociologists do not make this distinction between nation and nationality, but use the words interchangeably. MacIver, for example, does so, making the "desire for a common government" an essential element of a nationality, and declaring, "We distinguish here *nation* from *people,* meaning by *people* any large group possessing some degree of cohesion but without implying a political or other specific bond of union."[33] The term *ethnic group,* however, is coming into general use in sociological literature to designate the type of group Fairchild and Hankins refer to as a nationality, and which in popular usage is often called a race.

The Ethnic Group

The ethnic group is a human group bound together by ties of cultural homogeneity. Complete uniformity, of course, is not essential; but there does prevail in an ethnic group a high degree of loyalty and adherence to certain basic institutions, such as family patterns, religion, and language. The ethnic group often possesses distinctive folkways and mores, customs of dress, art and ornamentation, moral codes and value systems, and patterns of recreation. There is usually some sort of object to which the group manifests allegiance, such as a monarch, a religion, a language, or a territory. Above all, there is a consciousness of kind, a we-feeling. The ethnic group may even regard itself as a race, a people with a common ancestry; but the fact of such common descent is of much less significance than the *assumption* that there is a blood relationship, and the *myths* which the group develops to substantiate such an assumption. Ethnic groups, of course, are not all alike, and none would embody all the features enumerated above. Some will emphasize certain of these characteristics to the exclusion of others. Religion may serve as an important object of allegiance to one and be of little import to another. Furthermore, ethnic groups are dynamic; the folkways may change, the institutions become radically altered, and the object of allegiance shift from one trait to another, but the sentiment of loyalty to the group and the consciousness of belonging remain as long as the group exists. The ethnic group may or may not have its own political unit, it may have had one in the past, it may aspire to have one in the future, or its members may be scattered through existing states. Political unification is not an essential feature of the group. The term, accordingly, would include such groups as Arabs, French Canadians, British Canadians, Welsh, English, Flemish, Walloons, Scots, Jews, and Pennsylvania Dutch. The Soviet Union itself is com-

33 R. M. MacIver, *Society,* p. 155.

posed of more than a hundred ethnic groups, including, for example, Polish, Kazak, German, Armenian, Georgian, Tartar, and Ukrainian.

The Racial Group

There are other groups, however, with which we are concerned, but which have few of the characteristics of ethnic groups. The American Negro is an outstanding example. The "Jamaica whites," of the island of Jamaica, the Cape Coloured of South Africa, and the Anglo-Indians of India are other examples.[34] These are, indeed, groups; they are tied together by a common interest; they speak of themselves as "we," and are regarded as "they" by those on the outside. However, they lack most of the usual characteristics of ethnic groups. They have no unique culture of their own. In language, religion, value systems, and customs they are similar to other groups around them. They are bound together, however, by the fact that they have in common certain hereditary physical features (color, hair, eyes, and so on) on the basis of which they are ascribed a status in their society and are excluded from full participation in the life of that society. Sociologists refer to such as racial groups, or race-conscious groups. Williams defines the racial group as "one whose members through biological descent share distinctive common hereditary physical characteristics."[35] There are those, such as the Japanese-Americans, which might be classified as both racial and ethnic groups; others, like the French Canadians, which are only ethnic groups; and still others — Eurasians, for example — which are clearly racial groups.

We cannot hope, in one chapter, to rescue the word "race" from the slough of confusion into which it has fallen with centuries of misuse. Nor do we feel that the word can be discarded, for the literature of sociology, anthropology, psychology, to say nothing of the language of the layman, abounds in an infinite number of such expressions as "race differences," "race relations," "race problems," "race riot," and "race prejudice." To substitute another term appears to be impossible and unnecessary. We can, however, bear in mind that race has both a biological and a social meaning, and it is the latter which takes precedence in the affairs and thinking of most of us. When the sociologist speaks of race relations, he has reference, not to the biological categories of the anthropologist, but to those human groups which may perhaps be more accurately designated as racial and ethnic *groups*. When he does use the word "race" (as we must in the following chapter) he would prefer to insert "so-called" before it, if that were not so clumsy a device.

---

[34] See E. V. Stonequist, *The Marginal Man*, pp. 12–24, for descriptions of these groups.
[35] R. M. Williams, Jr., *The Reduction of Intergroup Tensions*, p. 42.

3

Race
Differences

. . . the problem is beset by so many contingencies and pitfalls that exact proof can be brought only rarely, . . .

A. L. KROEBER
Anthropology

The fertile imagination of Al Capp brought forth, a few years ago, a remarkable region known as Lower Slobbovia, the likes of which has never been equalled. By no means the least of its unusual features was the fact that the inhabitants had no use for the place whatsoever. They could not understand why anybody would voluntarily come there, why he would remain once he had seen it, or why any native would hesitate to leave if he had the opportunity.

This is all quite contrary to what sociologists have discovered about real societies. A rare case has been reported from the island of Tristan da Cunha, far away in the South Atlantic — a tiny, bleak spot inhabited by the descendants of British soldiers who were garrisoned there in the early years of the nineteenth century.[1] The Tristan islanders, we are told, suffer from a genuine inferiority complex and have no illusions about their being better than folks elsewhere in the world. "We's only low and poor people," they continually tell the occasional visitors to their land. They address any foreigner with a humble "Sir," whether he be an admiral or a coal trimmer; and they never drop the "Sir" even in free and playful speech. The islanders are thoroughly conscious of the fact that they live a very primitive life compared with the outside world, and they know full well that they are supported in many ways through the charity of Europeans. But such instances of group modesty are hard to find.[2]

Instead, sociologists and anthropologists have found that people everywhere seem to feel that the groups to which they belong are the best, their ways the right ways, their morals superior, their religion the true one. Years ago a pioneer sociologist, William Graham Sumner, observing this well-nigh universal characteristic, coined a term for the phenomenon. He called it *ethnocentrism*, and defined it as the emotional attitude that "one's own group is the center of everything, and all others are scaled with reference to it. . . ."[3] Sumner insisted that each group nourishes its own pride and vanity, regards itself as superior, and looks with contempt upon outsiders. This attitude applies not only to the nation or tribe of which one is a member, but to one's other groups as well — church, political party, race, fraternity, college, social class, and community. Sumner found that even primitive, "backward" peoples, who would seem to have no basis whatsoever for such conceit, were no less immune than the rich and powerful. The simple Lapps, for instance, call themselves (as distinct from outside groups) "human beings," the Kiowa Indians' name for their tribe is "real or principal people," the Tungus refer to themselves as "men," and so on around the world. Outsiders are dubbed in various unflattering ways — infidels, bar-

---

[1] A volcanic eruption in 1961 forced the removal of the Tristan islanders to Great Britain, where they lived for two years. For an account of this experience and its effect upon the people, see L. Griggs, "Violent End for Lonely Island," *Life*, Vol. 51, No. 19, Nov. 10, 1961, pp. 21ff.; C. Mydans, "Far-off Exiles of Tristan," *Life*, Vol. 55, No. 2, July 12, 1963, pp. 72ff.; M. Wall, "They Reject the Twentieth Century," *The New York Times Magazine*, May 6, 1962, pp. 74ff.

[2] P. A. Munch, "Cultural Contacts in an Isolated Community," *American Journal of Sociology*, Vol. 53, No. 1, July 1947, p. 6.

[3] W. G. Sumner, *Folkways*, p. 13.

barians, idolaters, pig-eaters, the uncircumcised, or "the great unwashed." When it comes to racial and ethnic groups, we in the United States are guilty of displaying our ethnocentrism by the use of many labels, which are never appreciated by the people to whom we apply them: bohunk, chink, dago, frog, limey, greaser, nigger, sheeny, and wop are only a few of them.[4]

Ethnocentrism serves a useful purpose, and this fact accounts for its widespread occurrence. It promotes the loyalty and esprit-de-corps without which no group would long endure. It performs the functions of discipline and social control essential to all group life. At the same time, it can be very irritating and disruptive; and when it gets out of hand may be dangerous and even fatal. Sociologists believe that their science is especially well suited to temper and counteract the spirit of ethnocentrism — which is a good reason for the inclusion of sociology among the academic disciplines.

Now it is all very well to say that human beings are the same everywhere, that we are "brothers under the skin," that we are members alike of one species, that "there is only one race, the human race." These statements, moreover, are basically true, and not mere sentiment and wishful thinking. Our likenesses *are* infinitely more numerous than our differences; hence a medical student may learn his anatomy from a Negro corpse, and then go out to practice on Caucasians, Mongolians, or "come what may."

There is no denying, however, that racial and ethnic groups are different. Some peoples are very tall, some short, and some are pygmies. Some are famed for their production and appreciation of music, while others are barely interested in it. Some are warlike and show great esteem for martial achievement, while others are unfamiliar with warfare altogether and take pride in their peaceful pursuits. With some, religion and other spiritual values are paramount, while with others they are of little consequence. Crime rates are by no means identical for all groups, and in the United States the Japanese, Chinese, and Jews can boast of their good records. Negroes and Indians are rarely driven to suicide, while high rates prevail for Jews, Chinese, and Japanese. Cancer strikes heavily among whites, diabetes among Jews, and tuberculosis among Negroes. Certain groups have earned a reputation for the sensitivity and acuity of their visual and auditory powers, others for their musical or athletic prowess, and still others for their scientific and intellectual achievements. It is commonly believed, not without reason, that some groups are lazy and improvident, some aggressive and ambitious, some emotional and impulsive, some reserved and stoical. Races are generally thought to have their distinctive odors, to differ in their moral laxity or rectitude, and to be far apart temperamentally, physically, and intellectually.

The crucial problem, however, is this: To what extent are these differences the result of hereditary, biological factors, and to what extent are they learned, acquired, and cultural? Popular opinion has always insisted that such common characteristics are "in the blood," that Jews are inherently aggressive and mer-

---

[4] For other such derogatory terms, see A. A. Roback, *A Dictionary of International Slurs.*

cenary, Indians naturally stoical and furtive, Negroes cheerful and improvident, British humorless, and Italians volatile. Others, without denying that groups are different, have maintained that "blood" and "heredity" do not provide the proper key to understanding those differences. John Stuart Mill said, "Of all vulgar modes of escaping from the consideration of the effect of social and moral influences on the human mind, the most vulgar is that of attributing the diversities of conduct and character to inherent natural differences."[5] The distinguished sociologist, E. A. Ross, put it this way: " 'Race' is the cheap explanation tyros offer for any collective trait that they are too stupid or too lazy to trace to its origin in the physical environment, the social environment, or historical conditions."[6]

The differences between racial and ethnic groups have always fascinated people, and their causes have long been the subject of debate and speculation. Herodotus, the "Father of History," wrote about the problem in the fifth century B.C., no doubt to the great delight of his fellow Greeks. The following is taken from one of his books:

> Concerning Egypt . . . the people, in most of their manners and customs, exactly reverse the common practice of mankind. The women attend the markets and trade, while the men sit at home at the loom. . . . The women likewise carry burdens upon their shoulders, while the men carry them upon their heads. They eat their food out of doors in the street, but retire for private purposes to their houses. . . . In other countries the priests have long hair; in Egypt their heads are shaven. . . . All other men pass their lives separate from animals; the Egyptians have animals always living with them. . . . Dough they mix with their feet; but they mix mud, and even take up dirt, with their hands. . . .
>
> They are religious to excess, far beyond any other race of men. . . .
>
> On the field where a battle was fought I saw a very wonderful thing which the natives pointed out to me. The bones of the slain lie scattered upon the field. . . . If you strike the Persian skulls, even with a pebble, they are so weak that you break a hole in them; but the Egyptian skulls are so strong, that you may smite them with a stone and you will scarcely break them in. They gave me the following reason for this difference, which seemed to me likely enough: The Egyptians from early childhood have the head shaven, and so by the action of the sun the skull becomes thick and hard. The same cause prevents baldness in Egypt, where you see fewer bald men than in any other lands. . . . The Persians, on the other hand, have feeble skulls, because they keep themselves shaded from the first, wearing turbans upon their heads.[7]

Aristotle, a century later than Herodotus, was convinced that some men are born to be masters, and other slaves; and he reasoned that it was entirely proper and natural that the superior Greeks should govern the barbarians. The subject has never ceased to fascinate. Tacitus extolled the virtues of the tall, blond Ger-

[5] *Principles of Political Economy*, Vol. 1, p. 390.
[6] *Social Psychology*, p. 3.
[7] Quoted in A. L. Kroeber and T. T. Waterman, *Source Book in Anthropology*, pp. 3–7.

mans, whom he declared to be brave, tough, adventurous, virtuous, freedom-loving, and jealous of their racial purity. Within the past century a host of students have carried on the tradition of speculating about the differences between peoples and their possible explanations. Prominent in this line of inquiry have been Arthur de Gobineau, H. S. Chamberlain, Ludwig Woltmann, Otto Ammon, Vacher de Lapouge, Madison Grant, Lothrop Stoddard, and, of course, Adolf Hitler.[8] They all emphasize one point: the races are very, very different.

Science and Race Differences

It has only been somewhat more recently that scientists have turned their attention to this perennial problem of race differences. And the task has proved to be a most difficult one, far more complicated than the philosophers, militarists, and "men-in-the-street" ever supposed it to be. The obstacles that the scientist has to overcome, if he is to answer the question, are numerous and baffling. First of all, he needs to know what a race is; and that, as we saw in the preceding chapter, is itself a problem of no small proportions. How can we generalize about the Negro race until we decide who belongs to the race? Should the Australian aborigines be included, as some insist? Or do they belong with the Caucasians, as others maintain? Or do they constitute a separate race of their own? Again, it is manifestly wrong to draw conclusions about the Negro race on the basis of studies made of the American Negro — a group which includes people as light as the late Walter White, and millions of others with varying admixtures of Indian and European blood.

Yet that problem, so far insurmountable in itself, is only one of many. Suppose we could agree on our races, and suppose we could establish the high prevalence of some particular characteristic in one of those races, would that prove a causal relationship? The Negro suffers from tuberculosis more than the white man does; but the authorities know that social conditions are primarily responsible for these high rates, though they are not prepared to rule out the racial factor entirely. Syphilis, too, has not the same frequency for all races, but here again genetic differences may be of no significance whatsoever. On the other hand, sickle-cell anemia is virtually confined to Negroes, a fact which can hardly be explained by environmental conditions.[9] The American Indian's susceptibility to trachoma, and the Negro's high resistance to it, may well be partly due to their racial affiliations. Cancer is far more serious for whites in all parts of the world than it is for Negroes, Chinese, Indians, and others. It is known, however, that mortality from cancer is related to occupation, climate, the proportion of aged people in the population, and so on. This is not to say, however,

---

[8] For an account of the development of this line of thought, see O. Klineberg, *Race Differences*, Ch. 1; Ruth Benedict, *Race: Science and Politics*, Ch. 7; J. Barzun, *Race: A Study in Modern Superstition*; P. A. Sorokin, *Contemporary Sociological Theories*, Ch. 5.

[9] Cf. A. L. Kroeber, *Anthropology*, p. 187; Lois W. Mednick and M. Orans, "The Sickle-Cell Gene: Migration Versus Selection," *American Anthropologist*, Vol. 58, No. 2, April 1956, pp. 293ff.

that race is *not* a factor, but that the extent of its influence is difficult to define and has not yet been reliably determined. Kroeber summarizes the status of our knowledge of racial pathology in these terms:

> While it is as good as certain that races differ genetically in their pathology, as in other traits, the problem is beset by so many contingencies and pitfalls that exact proof can be brought only rarely, and in general we are lucky if reasonable probabilities can be determined.[10]

It is much the same with the other supposed physiological and psychological differences between the races. Many people believe, of course, that certain groups are naturally venturesome while others are cautious, some more capable of bearing pain, some shrewd and others simple; and every reader of James Fenimore Cooper has been amazed at the remarkable auditory and visual powers of the American Indian. Periodically we read such pronouncements as the following, which future research may or may not prove to be true:

> Negroes can see at night far better than white men. This startling find has been reported by two scientists at Fort Bragg, N.C.
>
> In the past month, Drs. Harry Reginald DeSilva of Yale and Walter Richard Miles of the National Research Council have tested over 4,000 men for Army truck-driving jobs. After noticing that the Negroes seemed to have keener night vision, Dr. Miles picked at random seven white and eight Negro soldiers, lined them up in a field on a dark night. Then he walked to a point 100 feet away, held up a stick with a square white cardboard on each end. The soldiers were asked whether the stick was horizontal or vertical.
>
> Every Negro could tell; but nary one of the whites — most of them had to get within 50 feet of the stick before they could make it out. Said Dr. DeSilva: "We never even suspected this phenomenon before. . . . This may lead us to conclusions never before dreamed of.[11]

And this:

CHINESE AND WHITE DIFFER CHEMICALLY

ANN ARBOR, MICH. — Discovery of a "highly significant" difference in body chemistry between Chinese and Caucasians is announced by H. Eldon Sutton and Philip J. Clark, University of Michigan biologists.

The difference is that Chinese excrete significantly greater quantities of amino acids than Caucasians. Diet is not a principal factor in this difference.

Amino acids are sometimes called building stones of protein. Eating and environment both play substantial roles in the production of amino acids, the Michigan scientists point out. However, they believe the difference they discovered is basically hereditary and racial.

The Chinese studied had been living under Western conditions for at least two years. Two of them were native Americans. Yet, urinary samples, after a series of delicate laboratory tests, fell into distinct racial categories.

[10] *Op. cit.*, pp. 189ff.
[11] Courtesy of *Time*, Copyright Time Inc., June 30, 1941.

*Members of the Royal Order of
Ethiopian Hebrews in their
synagogue, Harlem*

"It was found that the amino acids most influenced by the change to a uniform diet were the ones which show considerable individuality in excretion patterns, and the individuality did not decrease significantly when the subject consumed identical foods," the scientists state.

In essence, they maintain that the world is divided into huge racial chemical factories whose products may resemble one another but which, after careful analysis, are found to be truly distinctive.[12]

A great deal of evidence has been collected, though not enough, on group differences with respect to blood pressure, pulse, basal metabolism, reaction time, glandular functioning, odors, smell, hearing, vision, and the like.[13] The results invariably show that the groups tested are not identical, but the interpretation of the results is no simple matter. Blood pressure, for instance, reflects wide variation, on the average, from Europeans and Americans at one extreme, to Hindus, Filipinos, Japanese, and Chinese at the other. Some have supposed, therefore, that race is a factor in systolic blood pressure. It is known, however, that there are other influences, including diet, climate, exercise, and emotional disturbances. There is abundant evidence, too, that the total pattern of the culture, and its tempo, are significant. Studies have shown that Americans who have moved to the Orient, and have lived there long enough to acquire some of

[12] *The New York Times*, August 21, 1955.
[13] For a summary of the evidence, see Klineberg, *op. cit., passim.*

its spirit, have experienced a lowering of blood pressure. So with sense perception, visual and auditory sensitivity, the sense of smell, and other matters. The differences, such as they are, are more likely the result of cultural conditioning and training. Klineberg says, "The available material suggests, though it does not prove, that group differences in physiological activity can be adequately explained without recourse to the racial hypothesis."[14]

The Question of Racial Superiority

The problem of the physiological and pathological differences between racial groups has been greatly overshadowed by the debate on the question of superiority and inferiority. This has been a perennial problem, at least since the time of Aristotle. Each group, if it thinks about the matter at all, invariably reaches the conclusion that it is superior, and finds evidence of a sort to support its claim. Some writers have attributed the superiority of their people to favorable geographical influences, but others incline to a biological explanation. The Roman, Vitruvius, maintained that those who live in southern climates have the keener intelligence, due to the rarity of the atmosphere, whereas "northern nations, being enveloped in a dense atmosphere, and chilled by moisture from the obstructing air, have but a sluggish intelligence." A certain Ibn Khaldun argued that the Arabians were the superior people, because their country, although in a warm zone, was surrounded by water, which exerted a cooling effect. Bodin, in the sixteenth century, found an astrological explanation for ethnic group differences. The planets, he thought, exerted their combined and best influence upon that section of the globe occupied by France, and the French, accordingly, were destined by nature to be the masters of the world. Needless to say, Ibn Khaldun was an Arab, and Bodin a Frenchman. The Italian, Sergi, regarded the Mediterranean peoples as the true bearers of civilization and insisted that Germans and Asiatics only destroy what the Mediterraneans create. In like manner, the superiority of Nordics, Alpines, Teutons, Aryans, and others has been asserted by those who were members of each of these groups, or thought they were.

This question of racial superiority and inferiority is by no means a dead issue. Powdermaker, for instance, found that whites in the Mississippi community which she studied held "almost unanimously" to the belief that "Negroes are innately inferior to white people, mentally and morally."[15] Nor are such articles of faith limited to Southerners. In 1939 *Fortune* conducted a survey for the Carnegie Corporation Study of the Negro in America, and in all sections of the country the majority of those interviewed expressed a belief in the Negro's inferiority, the percentages varying from 60 in some sections to 76.9 in others. A public opinion survey conducted for *Newsweek* in 1963 indicates that there has been a slight shift, but very slight, in this respect. When asked, "Do you

[14] *Op. cit.*, p. 131.
[15] Hortense Powdermaker, *After Freedom*, pp. 23, 381ff.

believe that Negroes have less native intelligence than whites?" an answer of "Yes" was given by 50 per cent of the whites in the nationwide sample and by 73 per cent in the South.[16]

It is the same beyond the borders of the United States. The fantastic racial doctrines of the Nazi were not universally condemned, and were actually approved by many who rejected the other aspects of their totalitarian philosophy. The belief in white supremacy is nowhere more firmly planted than in the Republic of South Africa, and one finds it in some degree in almost every biracial and multiracial area.

Even the scholars, who presumably have weighed the evidence, have not discarded the doctrine of the inequality of races. Hooton, the anthropologist, says:

> Science can make no valid assertion that this or that race is either superior or inferior to another. For that matter, it is equally unable to put forward the claim that all races are equal biologically or in cultural capacity. We know that in every race there exists a range of mentality from idiots to geniuses, with many more of the former than the latter and a regrettable piling up of the frequency curve in the area of low intelligence. These ranges of mentality in the different races overlap to such an extent that, if we really put an accurate and comparable test into effect whereby to determine them, we might find them to be wholly coincident. On the other hand, there might be some greater or smaller racial differences.[17]

Many other scientists and scholars might be cited to show that the belief in the inequality of races is not limited to demagogues and ignoramuses, but one further reference must suffice. The sociologist, Sorokin, has this to say on the subject:

> That there are mental differences among races seems to be definitely established. . . . No partisan of a belief in the uniformity of all races can disregard the differences in the historical role and in the cultural achievements of the different races. . . . The difference in the cultural contributions and in the historical roles played by different races is excellently corroborated by, and is in perfect agreement with, the experimental studies of race mentality and psychology. . . . So far as I know, all studies of the comparative intelligence of the contemporary Negro and white races . . . have unanimously shown that the I.Q. of the blacks, or even the Indians, is lower than that of the white or yellow. . . .
> The only conclusion which it seems possible to make from the above and similar studies is that the mentality of various races . . . is different.[18]

The question of the native endowment of the races (or racial and ethnic groups) has been approached from many angles, but principally the anatomical, the historical, and the psychological.

[16] *Newsweek*, October 21, 1963, p. 50.
[17] E. A. Hooton, *Up from the Ape*, p. 660. Used with the permission of The Macmillan Company. Copyright 1946.
[18] Sorokin, *op. cit.*, pp. 291–301.

It has been argued that the various races are not equally advanced in the evolutionary scale, some being much closer to the brute ancestors of mankind than others. The whites, they say, are the most human, while the Negroes are most simian. Proponents of this theory will point to the receding forehead of the Negro, his prognathous jaw, his broad, flat nose, to prove his close relationship to the ape. They overlook, however, those physical traits which reverse this order of kinship. Take the texture of the hair. The Negro, with his woolly or frizzly hair, is farthest removed from the apes, who have straight, coarse hair. So with the quantity of the hair; the Negro's relative hairlessness makes him most unlike the other primates, and places hairy Caucasoids closest of all. The Negro's thick, outrolled lips, too, are in sharp contrast to the thin, grayish, mobile lips of the apes. As to the shape of the head, the apes are inclined to be brachycephalic, the Negro dolichocephalic. It is obviously impossible, then, to arrange the races in any evolutionary order, for none proves, on close examination, to be consistently more simian than the others. (See Table 3.1)

TABLE 3.1

Comparison of the Primary Races*

	Most simianlike	*Less simianlike*	*Least simianlike*
Cephalic index	Mongolian	Caucasian	Negro
Cranial capacity	Negro	. . . .	Mongolian, Caucasian
Eye color	Negro, Mongolian	. . . .	Caucasian
Nasal index	Negro	Mongolian	Caucasian
Hair form	Mongolian	Caucasian	Negro
Hair length	Caucasian, Mongolian	. . . .	Negro
Body hair	Caucasian	. . . .	Negro, Mongolian
Lip form	Mongolian	Caucasian	Negro
Lip color	Mongolian	Caucasian	Negro
Facial prognathism	Negro	Caucasian	Mongolian
Eye form	Caucasian, Negro	. . . .	Mongolian

* From E. A. Hoebel, *Man in the Primitive World*, p. 86. Courtesy of McGraw-Hill Book Co. Copyright 1949.

The size of the brain, too, has been offered as evidence of the superiority of certain races. It is true that many measurements of cranial capacity have been taken, and some racial or ethnic groups average higher than others.[19] The

[19] For a summary of the results of these studies, see Klineberg, *op. cit.*, pp. 84, 86.

Scotch, for instance, average 1478 cc., the Dutch 1530, the Swiss 1546, and the Parisians 1559, while the primitive Hottentots average only 1317 cc., the Australian aborigines 1347, and the Tasmanians 1406. Caucasians generally are found to have larger brains than Negroes, a fact the racialists have seized upon and taken to indicate that whites have superior intellectual powers.

There are many objections, however, to drawing such a conclusion. For one thing, the averages noted above fail to reveal the wide range which prevails in each of the groups measured. The Scotch, for example, range from 1230 to 1855, the Swiss from 1250 to 1930, and the Hottentots from 1183 to 1620. Moreover, the preliterate Eskimos have an average of 1535, and a range of 1418 to 1624; and other peoples of simple culture, such as the Polynesians, Chukchee, Kaffirs, and Javanese can boast of large cranial capacity. If we followed the reasoning of the racialists, we should have to acknowledge the Eskimos as our intellectual superiors, and even the extinct and primitive Neanderthal man would rate as our equal, perhaps even our superior. In short, the mere size of the brain appears to give no indication of the capacities or achievements of ethnic groups, any more than it does for individuals within any particular group.[20]

The Historical Approach

A common-sense, pragmatic, practical approach to the problem of racial quality would seem to lie in a consideration of the achievements of the various races. Certainly not all of them have produced great civilizations, developed vast empires, made important contributions to the world's culture, given birth to geniuses, artists, inventors, explorers, and conquerors. "Look at the record," says the racialist, and it will be obvious that not all groups are equally gifted. "By their fruits ye shall know them," he repeats with pride and satisfaction. The Australian aboriginal, hugging a campfire trying to keep warm, ignorant of agriculture, architecture, metals, domesticated animals, writing, and arithmetic, is hardly the equal of those races which have produced skyscrapers, machinery, television, jet planes, symphonies, and penicillin.

John W. Vandercook, who has traveled widely among the "backward" people of the earth, defends them as follows:

> Most people have a very clear picture of what a primitive man is. He wears no clothes. His small, enfeebled mind is filled with terror and superstition. He is sullen, bloodthirsty, dangerous. . . . He is, of course, stupid; he is incurably "inferior" — and his women do all the work.
> That picture, word for word, is wrong. . . .
> Uncivilized man tends to be friendly because, quite often, he has rather a good

[20] For one of the most thorough studies of the relation between brain size and intelligence, see K. Pearson, "On Our Present Knowledge of the Relationship of Mind and Body," *Annals of Eugenics*, Vol. 1, 1925–1926, pp. 382–406. Pearson concludes: "When we come to associate mental and bodily characteristics, we find no correlation whatever of prognostic value. . . . To predict the intelligence of an individual you must test it directly, or measure it in the immediate ancestors of the individual."

mind. That individuals in a crude and never-changing forest commonwealth can be intelligent seems impossible. It is hard, when squatting on a dirt or bamboo floor with all joints cracking, to comprehend that one's host, who has never even invented chairs, may have an alert and adult mind, deep curiosity and the ability to learn. But it is true.

The assumption that all "natives," whatever their color or their country, are more or less half-witted is based on an odd method of comparison. We compare our best to their worst; and we judge bushmen by their behavior, not in their own world, but in ours. Your middle-class tropical planter will point contemptuously to a black boy asleep under a palm tree in the back yard. "Can you imagine that brute," he demands, "or his descendants ever producing a Shakespeare?" Being polite, you do not answer, "No, nor yours either."[21]

This habit of reasoning from performance to potentiality betrays an ignorance of the history of culture, a lack of perspective, and a misunderstanding of the dynamics of civilization. In the first place we have no good standard to measure achievement. We insist, of course, that all people be judged by those things in which *we* excel. We are proud of our machines, our science, and our power, but we fail to see that not all peoples envy us, nor would they agree to use these as criteria of excellence. We would not come out so well, in proving our superiority, if our opponents insisted upon using as criteria, not science and machines, but ability at sand painting, physical endurance, complexity of grammar, multiplicity of taboos, respect for the aged, ability in hunting, closeness to nature, fear of the deity, reverence for the soil, freedom from authority, disregard for material goods, the absence of neuroses, or peace of mind. The fact is that no racial or ethnic group excels in all things, but each has its own interests and values, goals toward which it strives, and channels into which its efforts are directed.

In the second place, the very civilization in which we take pride, and to which we point as proof of our superiority, is not entirely the product of our genius. Most of it, in fact, we have taken over from others. We are not alone, to be sure, in our readiness to appropriate the inventions and discoveries of others, for every culture is largely a medley of borrowed elements. The students of the history of culture have dealt a blow to our ethnocentrism by proving a foreign origin for many of our most cherished possessions. Thus Cressey has shown how much we Americans owe to the Chinese, from whom we have learned about silk, paper, porcelain, tea, lacquerware, kites, umbrellas, screens, fans, goldfish, azaleas, chrysanthemums, camellias, papier mâché, grapefruit, soybeans, ephedrine, and many other articles which have become integral parts of our civilization.[22] The classic statement on the subject, however, comes from Ralph Linton, who has expressed in succinct and convincing fashion the extent of our indebtedness to strange and distant races and peoples. As he puts it:

[21] "The Misunderstood Savage," *Harper's Magazine*, Vol. 170, No. 1030, March 1935, pp. 446–452.
[22] P. F. Cressey, "Chinese Traits in European Civilization: A Study of Diffusion," *American Sociological Review*, Vol. 10, No. 5, October 1945, pp. 595–604.

Our solid American citizen awakens in a bed built on a pattern which originated in the Near East but which was modified in Northern Europe before it was transmitted to America. He throws back covers made from cotton, domesticated in India, or linen, domesticated in the Near East, or wool from sheep, also domesticated in the Near East, or silk, the use of which was discovered in China. All of these materials have been spun or woven by processes invented in the Near East. He slips into his moccasins, invented by the Indians of the Eastern woodlands, and goes to the bathroom, whose fixtures are a mixture of European and American inventions, both of recent date. He takes off his pajamas, a garment invented in India, and washes with soap invented by the ancient Gauls. He then shaves, a masochistic rite which seems to have derived from either Sumer or ancient Egypt.

Returning to the bedroom, he removes his clothes from a chair of southern European type and proceeds to dress. He puts on garments whose form originally derived from the skin clothing of the nomads of the Asiatic steppes, puts on shoes made from skins tanned by a process invented in ancient Egypt and cut to a pattern derived from the classical civilizations of the Mediterranean, and ties around his neck a strip of bright-colored cloth which is a vestigial survival of the shoulder shawls worn by the seventeenth-century Croatians. Before going out for breakfast he glances through the window, made of glass invented in Egypt, and if it is raining puts on overshoes made of rubber discovered by the Central American Indians and takes an umbrella, invented in southeastern Asia. Upon his head he puts a hat made of felt, a material invented in the Asiatic steppes.

On his way to breakfast he stops to buy a paper, paying for it with coins, an ancient Lydian invention. At the restaurant a whole new series of borrowed elements confronts him. His plate is made of a form of pottery invented in China. His knife is of steel, an alloy first made in southern India, his fork a medieval Italian invention, and his spoon a derivative of a Roman original. He begins breakfast with an orange, from the eastern Mediterranean, a cantaloupe from Persia, or perhaps a piece of African watermelon. With this he has coffee, an Abyssinian plant, with cream and sugar. Both the domestication of cows and the idea of milking them originated in the Near East, while sugar was first made in India. After his fruit and first coffee he goes on to waffles, cakes made by a Scandinavian technique from wheat domesticated in Asia Minor. Over these he pours maple syrup, invented by the Indians of the Eastern woodlands. As a side dish he may have the egg of a species of bird domesticated in Indo-China, or thin strips of the flesh of an animal domesticated in Eastern Asia which have been salted and smoked by a process developed in northern Europe.

When our friend has finished eating he settles back to smoke, an American Indian habit, consuming a plant domesticated in Brazil in either a pipe, derived from the Indians of Virginia, or a cigarette, derived from Mexico. If he is hardy enough he may even attempt a cigar, transmitted to us from the Antilles by way of Spain. While smoking he reads the news of the day, imprinted in characters invented by the ancient Semites upon a material invented in China by a process invented in Germany. As he absorbs the accounts of foreign troubles he will, if he is a good conservative citizen, thank a Hebrew deity in an Indo-European language that he is 100 per cent American.[23]

[23]R. Linton, *The Study of Man*, pp. 326–327. Copyright 1936.

Pueblo Indian children who live in Santa Ana, one of the ancient native villages in New Mexico

Thirdly, a reasonable regard for the perspective of time will deflate the claims of the racialists. The Sumerians might well, at one time, have pointed to their civilization as proof of their superior blood, and asked why the peoples of Europe had never risen above their barbarism. Three millenia ago the Egyptians might have used the same argument to prove their superiority to the primitive Greeks; and the Romans, a thousand years later, might have invoked precisely the same argument to prove their superiority to the northern Europeans. As a matter of fact, they did exactly that, for in a letter to Atticus, Cicero said; "Do not obtain your slaves from Britain because they are so stupid and so utterly incapable of being taught that they are not fit to form a part of the household of Athens."

The civilization of a people, accordingly, is hardly a trustworthy clue to their intellectual quality. It is a product of many factors — historical, environmental, accidental — and the sheer size and density of the population would have something to do with it. Race, however, on close inspection appears to be of little or no consequence.

The Psychological Approach

Half a century ago psychologists set about testing the intellectual powers of people; and the intelligence test became immediately popular with those interested in the problem of race differences. Here at last, they thought, was an instrument that would enable them to settle this problem of superiority once and for all in an objective, scientific manner. Accordingly, tests have been administered to various and sundry groups, and wide differences have been found. In comparison with white American norms, certain groups like the English, Scotch, Jews, and Germans come very close to the norm. Negroes in general do poorly, and American Indians score lowest of all. Mexicans do slightly better than the Indians; and Italians, Poles, and Portuguese fall somewhere between the Mexicans and the Negroes. Chinese and Japanese, on the other hand, have made high scores, showing relatively little inferiority in this respect to the whites. Ethnic groups from northwestern Europe, such as the British, Dutch, Germans, and Scandinavians, have proved themselves superior on the tests.

Klineberg presents in tabular form the results of a great number of these intelligence tests:

TABLE 3.2

Summary Table of Ethnic Differences in I.Q. *

Ethnic Group	Number of Studies	I.Q. Range	Median I.Q.
American control groups	18	85–108	102
Jews	7	95–106	103
Germans	6	93–105	100.5
English and Scotch	5	93–105	99
Japanese	9	81–114	99
Chinese	11	87–107	98
American Negroes	27	58–105	86
Italians	16	79– 96	85
Portuguese	6	83– 96	84
Mexicans	9	78–101	83.5
American Indians	11	65–100	80.5

* Otto Klineberg, *Characteristics of the American Negro*, p. 35.

The results of the intelligence tests, so flattering to some ethnic groups and so disparaging to others, have not gone unchallenged. For example, it is pointed out that not all the groups tested have the same facility with the language of tests. Some people are bilingual; and while the ability to speak two languages equally well is certainly a valuable accomplishment, it is definitely a handicap when one is taking an intelligence test.[24] Moreover, American Negroes speak English, and some of them flawlessly, but many of them speak it poorly. On one occasion it was found that Negro children were unable to give the "opposite"

[24] For the evidence that bilingualism affects intelligence test performances, see Klineberg, *op. cit.*, pp. 167–168.

of certain familiar words, until the discovery was made that they did not know the meaning of the word "opposite." In various other ways subtle and unsuspected differences in the cultural background of those tested affected the scores made. Among some peoples speed is highly valued and time is regarded as a precious commodity; but there are groups which place a negative value upon speed and are hardly time-conscious at all. Indian children, it was found, who did miserably at drawing a picture of a man, did much better at drawing a horse; and while they proved themselves inferior on many of the tasks assigned to them, they excelled when it came to tests involving bead work, or when they were asked to match photographs of feet. In short, cultural differences, values, and experiences have a definite effect upon the performance on a test.

Furthermore, if groups are to be compared it is essential that they be equally motivated and that they approach the test in the same frame of mind. Now competition and rivalry are well established in our culture, and children soon learn that it is highly desirable that they excel their fellows. It is not so with all peoples, however. Elsewhere, cooperation may be emphasized at the expense of competition, being "first" may be a dubious privilege, and being with the group may be more desirable than being ahead of the group. Klineberg, in testing Dakota Indians, learned that it was considered very bad form for one of them to answer a question in the presence of others who did not know the answer, for Dakotas have no respect for the show-off. Similarly Porteus had difficulty in testing the intelligence of Australians, for they were in the habit of openly debating every problem of their tribal life until a unanimous decision was reached, and they could not understand why they should not discuss the problems presented to them in the atmosphere to which they were accustomed. They could not see why Porteus, who was administering the test and who obviously knew the answers, would give them no assistance, even though he had recently been accorded the honor of admission to membership in their tribe.

Similarly, it has been clearly shown by psychologists that performance on intelligence tests is affected by one's educational opportunities, one's social and economic background, the rapport between the experimenter and the subject, and various other factors totally unrelated to the hereditary capacities of the individual. Many, accordingly, have doubted the validity of the scores as indicators of the innate abilities of racial and ethnic groups.

Not all people, however, have been convinced that the evidence from the intelligence test scores has been adequately refuted by the explanations mentioned above. Recently a psychologist, Dr. Frank C. J. McGurk, reviewed some of the research bearing on this problem which has appeared since 1939.[25] He insists that "there is ample evidence that there are psychological differences between Negroes and whites." These differences, he continues, are apparent even when every precaution is made to compare only those from similar socioeconomic backgrounds. Moreover, he maintains that the factual evidence "com-

---

[25] F. C. J. McGurk, "A Scientist's Report on Race Differences," from a copyrighted article in *U.S. News and World Report*, September 21, 1956, pp. 92ff.

pletely denies the theory that improving the social and economic status of the Negro improves his capacity for education." He concludes:

> Regardless of our emotional attachment to the school-desegregation problem, certain facts must be faced. First, as far as psychological-test performance is a measure of capacity for education, Negroes as a group do not possess as much of it as whites, as a group. This has been demonstrated over and over. . . .
>
> The vast improvements in the social and economic status of the Negro have not changed his relationship to the whites regarding capacity for education. . . .
>
> The improvements in the social and economic opportunities have only increased the differences. . . . This is because such improvements have been given to both racial groups — not only to the Negro — and the whites have profited the more from them.

Another psychologist, Dr. Audrey M. Shuey, has more recently made an exhaustive analysis of the data from standard intelligence tests, and reaches the following conclusion:

> The remarkable consistency of the test results . . . ; the fact that the colored-white differences are present not only in the rural South and urban South, but in the border and northern states; the fact that relatively small average differences are found between the IQ's of northern-born and southern-born Negro children in northern cities; . . . the evidence that the tested differences appear to be greater for abstract than for practical and concrete problems; the evidence that the differences obtained are not due primarily to a lack of language skills . . . ; the fact that differences are reported in all studies in which the cultural environment of the whites appeared to be no more complex, rich, or stimulating than the environment of the Negroes; . . . all point to the presence of some native differences between Negroes and whites as determined by intelligence tests.[26]

The question of the inferiority and superiority of races, accordingly, is still moot. For a period, in the 1940's and 1950's, the proponents of white supremacy and segregation were inclined to base their position, not upon the supposed inherent superiority of the white race, but rather upon the doctrine of states' rights, the cultural gulf which separates the races, the unconstitutional encroachment of the Supreme Court upon the responsibilities of the legislative branch, the undesirability of encouraging racial amalgamation, the claim that Negroes do not want integration unless aroused by outsiders, and the doctrine that the mores take precedence over law in the governing of society.[27]

The 1960's, however, have witnessed a revival of the idea that races are inherently different in their intellectual capacities. One of the most articulate spokesmen has been the New Englander, Carleton Putnam, whose book, *Race and Reason: A Yankee View*, has had wide circulation. There have been numer-

[26] *The Testing of Negro Intelligence*, p. 318.
[27] Cf. T. R. Waring, "The Southern Case against Desegregation," *Harper's Magazine*, Vol. 212, No. 1268, January 1956, pp. 39–45; H. R. Sass, "Mixed Schools and Mixed Blood," *The Atlantic Monthly*, Vol. 198, No. 5, November 1956, pp. 45–49.

ous others.[28] No new evidence is offered, but they insist that the supremacy of the white race is proved by anatomical features, historical achievements, and intelligence tests.

Sociologists, in the early part of the present century, accepted the prevalent belief that some races were by nature intellectually superior to others. Later they reacted to such a view, and began to espouse the doctrine of equality in natural endowments and to denounce "the myth of white superiority." Among the first was H. A. Miller, who wrote, "Inherent racial inferiority is a myth. . . . It has no basis in fact."[29] In the sociological literature this theme has been the popular one for a long time, often expressed in such positive fashion as follows: "Modern science holds that all races are biologically equal so far as their mental and emotional potentialities are concerned."[30]

Such statements, for all their good and democratic intentions, can hardly be supported.[31] Science, indeed, has not been able to prove any race superior to the others; but it does not follow that races are therefore equal. Nor has science been able to prove that races are equal in their innate abilities, but this failure does not justify one in concluding that they are therefore unequal. The following would seem to be the safest conclusions we can reach on the matter:

1. Races and racial and ethnic groups possibly do differ in innate ability. Group differences do invariably appear in any measurable characteristic.

2. It can hardly be denied that there are significant psychological differences between racial and ethnic groups. The numerous life histories, the reports of ethnologists, and the studies of "national character" all point in that direction. Groups do have many of the characteristics with which they are popularly charged, such as aggressiveness, mediocrity, shiftlessness, and so on. Stereotypes are not entirely without foundation.

3. Differences, however, are always matters of degree, and not of kind.

4. Differences are slight, and on the average.

5. Overlappings far outweigh the differences.

6. Most of the differences are not innate, but are almost certainly the product of historical and environmental factors.

---

[28] Cf. W. C. George, *The Biology of the Race Problem*, prepared by Commission of the Governor of Alabama, 1962; *The Anatomy of a Controversy*, Mankind Monographs, published by *The Mankind Quarterly*, 1 Darnaway St., Edinburgh 3, Scotland, 1963.

[29] H. A. Miller, *Races, Nations and Classes*, pp. 129ff.

[30] Arnold and Caroline Rose, *America Divided*, p. 275.

[31] See J. W. Woodward, "Some Implications from Our Present Knowledge Concerning Prejudice, "*American Sociological Review*, Vol. 11, No. 3, June 1946, pp. 344–356.

4

Mankind in Motion

. . . race relations and all that they imply are generally the products of migration and conquest.

ROBERT E. PARK
Race and Culture

Race problems are a consequence of the movement of peoples over the earth. If societies were content to live to themselves, in isolated, self-sufficient communities, there would be no interracial conflict, no clash of cultures, no race prejudice, and no necessity for ethnic groups to adjust their differences. They would have their problems, to be sure, but *not* the so-called racial problems which afflict our heterogeneous modern nations.

No doubt, in years past, there were many such isolated societies, and even today they have not entirely vanished. Explorers periodically report the discovery of primitive tribes which have had little or no contact with the outside world. The following is one example:

WASHINGTON, June 12 (AP) — Two primitive Brazilian tribes — reported today to have been contacted by white men for the first time — still jealously guard the "military secret" of a forgotten civilization.

Dr. Kalervo Oberg of the Smithsonian Institution told today of his visits to the Nambiguara and Terena tribes deep in the Amazon jungles, and said they are suspicious of white men and of neighbors who have white contacts.

"Curiously, one of their major worries is that their 'military secret' will be revealed," Dr. Oberg said. "When a stranger approaches, their bows and arrows are hidden."

They believe man was created out of blocks of wood, and hold religious ceremonies regularly, attired principally in feather headdresses, their bodies painted with complicated red and black designs. At other times they go naked.

They live in a relatively unexplored area in dense forests bordering the banks of rivers which form the headwaters of the Amazon. This, the Smithsonian ethnologist said, has enabled them to remain almost completely cut off from civilization — making them "probably the world's supreme isolationists."[1]

Eskimos, until recent times, lived entirely to themselves, quite oblivious of the fact that other human beings also inhabited this planet. Redfield has described a village in Yucatan whose inhabitants have few and infrequent contacts with outsiders;[2] and Junek has written about a similar situation in Labrador.[3] One will find equally isolated groups living in various parts of Asia, in Africa, and on the islands of the Pacific.

We need not look very far, however, for examples of isolated communities. In the middle of Chesapeake Bay there lie Tangier and Smith Islands, whose inhabitants have preserved a surprising degree of independence from cultural entanglements with their neighbors on the nearby shores of Virginia and Maryland.[4] There are remote and isolated communities in the mountains of Kentucky, Virginia, and Tennessee, and in the Ozarks of Missouri and Arkansas, where the disrupting influences of modern technology, science, and urbanization have barely been felt. One such community, Colvin Hollow, is almost unbelievably

[1] The St. Louis *Post-Dispatch*, June 12, 1950.
[2] R. Redfield and A. Villa R, *Chan Kom, A Maya Village.*
[3] O. W. Junek, *Isolated Communities: A Study of a Labrador Fishing Village.*
[4] S. W. Hall, III, *Tangier Island: A Study of an Isolated Group.*

primitive.[5] It is located deep in a pocket of the Virginia mountains, less than a hundred miles from Washington, D.C. The authors of the study found there an illiterate folk, of almost pure Anglo-Saxon stock, living in mud-plastered log cabins, supporting themselves by a simple type of agriculture. There are no roads to the outside world, no cattle or poultry, no church, no organized government, and no school; and prior to 1928, the children had never seen the American flag or heard the Lord's Prayer. For better or for worse, however, such isolation, as a result of modern means of travel and communication, is rapidly coming to be a thing of the past.

Antiquity of Intergroup Contact

It must not be supposed, however, that contact between racial and ethnic groups is a phenomenon only of the modern world. We may be certain that ever since our distant ancestors descended from the trees, a million years ago, more or less, ours has been a restless, roving species. We need not assume that man is by nature nomadic, or that he inherits a "wanderlust." The contrary would seem to be true, namely, that most people are disposed to pass their lives in the locality where they are born, unless some force motivates them to migrate. It is the causes of *migration,* not the causes of immobility, that scholars have sought to find.

Throughout most of his career on Earth man has subsisted by gathering the wild products which nature provided, or by hunting, or by fishing. There are not a few societies today whose economy is still built upon these ancient practices, and even the most civilized societies preserve these activities either for commercial or for sentimental reasons. It was only a few thousand years ago that men learned to domesticate animals and to practice agriculture, thereby making a more settled life possible. Of course, there have been societies which depended upon hunting and fishing and which managed to avoid a nomadic existence. On the other hand, pastoral nomads are quite a familiar type, and even agricultural nomads are not unknown. However, the hunting-fishing-gathering type of economic activity, which has been most characteristic of human existence, makes it almost necessary for men to keep on the move.

There are abundant reasons for believing that preliterate, prehistoric peoples roamed widely over the earth and came into contact and conflict with strangers who differed from themselves both racially and culturally. The evidence for these prehistoric migrations is of several types.

1. *Archaeological evidence.* Just as we leave behind on our city dumps and refuse piles the evidences of our type of civilization, so have prehistoric peoples left behind material witnesses to their cultures. These the archaeologist digs up, and with them he seeks to reconstruct the history of ancient and departed societies. By studying the distribution of various types of artifacts, designs on

[5] M. Sherman and T. R. Henry, *Hollow Folk.*

pottery, ruins of dwellings, forms of art, and so on, he is often able to trace a people to its original home, follow their routes of migration, and make inferences as to their contacts with other civilizations. Archaeology offers indisputable evidence that, long before the dawn of history, primitive man was continually on the move, invading the territory of others, borrowing ideas from his enemies and from strangers, constructing his dwellings in order to insure his safety from marauders, and often mixing his blood with that of his conquerors or of his victims.

2. *Linguistic evidence.* Similarities in languages also reveal to the philologist the fact that certain peoples have migrated. Thus in North America most of the Athabascan-speaking Indians lived in Canada, but some of them had gone elsewhere. The Navajo and Apache of New Mexico and Arizona reveal in their speech the fact that they came originally from Canada. In all parts of the world, similarities of speech reveal to the trained ear the evidences of human migrations.

3. *Folklore.* The oral traditions of primitive peoples often include stories about their migrations and their conflicts with strangers. Long before the Hebrews were able to record their history, they passed on by word of mouth the stories of their origin in Ur of the Chaldees, of their years of slavery in Egypt, of their wanderings over the Sinai Peninsula, of their eventual entrance into the Promised Land and their wars with the tribes already settled there. Other preliterate peoples similarly transmitted their traditions. The Aztecs, for instance, told stories of their place of origin "in the North," of their invasion of Mexico, and of their conquest of the native tribes they found there. Incidentally, linguistic evidence gives support to these traditions.

4. *Biological evidence.* To the biological scientist, the presence of blond hair, blue eyes, or other racial features, in a population not generally possessing those features, is evidence of migration and contact. Too, the racial features of the American Indian indicated his Asiatic origin and his kinship to other Mongoloid peoples; the blondness found among certain Berbers of North Africa suggests an early migration of Nordics from Europe; and the Hottentots of South Africa give evidence of their migration from northeastern Africa, where they had mixed with the Hamitic peoples of that region.

5. *Cultural evidence.* The possession of certain traits of culture by a preliterate society often suggests that group's origin in some distant place. For example, certain customs of cattle-raising observed by the Yakuts of northeastern Siberia indicate to the anthropologist that these people migrated from farther south; and the wide distribution of Inca pottery in South America testifies to the expansive habits of that tribe. This type of evidence, however, must be used with caution, for culture traits are able to diffuse apart from the migration of peoples. The smoking of tobacco spread quickly over the earth and was

adopted by people who had never seen American Indians, who invented the custom; and we ourselves take delight in many a feature of our civilization which we owe to far-away peoples with whom we have never come into direct contact.

The story of prehistoric man's migrations over the earth has yet to be written; but, with the types of evidence discussed above, there can be no doubt that the phenomena which we nowadays refer to as racial and cultural contacts are very ancient.

The dawn of the historical period furnishes additional support to the theory that migration and intergroup contact are ancient phenomena. We know that the Germanic tribes migrated from Asia Minor into western and southern Europe, that the Greeks invaded the Mediterranean region at the end of the second millenium before the Christian era, that the Magyars moved into Hungary, Slavs superseded the Finnish people of Russia, Mongolians invaded Europe, and the Bulgarians migrated from the region of the Black Sea into the Balkan Peninsula. Our knowledge of the African continent is by no means comparable to our knowledge of Europe, but linguistic, traditional, and anatomical evidences point to the frequency of population movements there also. Abyssinia was peopled by Semitic invaders, the Arabs swept over northern Africa, and the Bantu tribes spread over the greater part of the continent, and presumably supplanted an old pygmy population.

The Case of the Jews

To illustrate the phenomenon of migration, no better group could be selected than the Jews, for theirs has been a migratory existence throughout history. "The Wandering Jew" is indeed an appropriate designation for these people. When first encountered in the dim and legendary past, they were a tribe of desert-dwellers, seeking a more comfortable homeland for themselves in that pleasant strip of land known as "The Fertile Crescent," lying between the Persian Gulf and the Mediterranean Sea. They eventually succeeded, after much conflict, in winning a foothold in that portion of the Crescent called Canaan. This was not for long, however, for famine struck and they were forced to move on to Egypt. There they lived through several unhappy centuries until, under the leadership of Moses, they set out once again for Canaan. Before reaching their destination they endured many years of wandering around the Sinai Peninsula; but eventually they reached their "promised land," only to find other claimants settled there, against whom they had to wage a series of bloody wars. In time, however, they established themselves, and for a while they flourished as a united nation. Then came conquering armies from the East, destroying their cities and carrying away the Hebrew people as captives. From these captivities many never returned; but in 538 B.C. some did find their way back to Jerusalem, which they proceeded to rebuild.

The years following were by no means free from contacts and conflicts with other peoples and cultures, for the Greeks came, under Alexander the Great, and later the Romans; but these incidents, while they had profound effects upon the psychology and the culture of the Jews, did not force them to leave their homes. In 70 A.D., however, came the Great Dispersion, when the Roman Titus captured and burned Jerusalem, slaying more than a million Jews in the process. Many of the survivors were enslaved and sent to labor in the mines of Egypt; others were taken as captives to march in a triumphal procession through the streets of Rome; and still others were driven to the corners of the earth. Even before this time the Jews were a widely scattered people; there were large communities of them in Alexandria, Rome, Athens, Antioch, Babylon, and many other ancient cities. But after 70 A.D., with the destruction of their temple, Jerusalem ceased to function as the Mecca of their pilgrimages and the bond of unity for the group, and they have continued to this day widely dispersed.

It is not possible here to trace their subsequent migrations, nor even to enumerate the most significant events. Suffice it to say that their expulsion from Palestine accentuated the migratory nature of their lives. Frequently they were offered inducements to settle in this land or that, but more often persecution forced them to leave the country in which they resided and seek a new home, if one could be found. The triumph of Mohammedanism, for instance, in the eighth century sent many a Jew scurrying, for the Moslems turned upon those people who steadfastly refused to accept the new faith. The Crusaders of the eleventh, twelfth, and thirteenth centuries presented many Jewish communities with the alternatives of flight or death. In 1290 every Jew was ordered to leave England, and between sixteen and seventeen thousand had to flee. It was not until 1654, when Oliver Cromwell rescinded this order, that Jews were permitted to return. They were expelled from France in 1306; and at one time or another they were ordered out of Vienna, Cologne, Nuremberg, Hamburg, and Wittenberg, and many another city, province, or state. In 1492, the very day before Columbus set sail for America, the Jews were expelled from Spain.

Occasionally some monarch would invite them to settle in his realm, but seldom for reasons of tolerance or pity. The King of Denmark, for instance, observing the commercial talents and wealth of the Jews in the Netherlands, opened the doors of his kingdom to them. In the fifteenth century, the Jews found a welcome in Poland. The rulers of that region looked with favor upon their coming, for theirs was a barbaric, sparsely-settled land, and they coveted a population of educated, urbane, commercial people such as the Jews.

The eighteenth century ushered in an era of tolerance which gave promise of marking the end of Jewish persecution and expulsion. In America, political leaders were saying that all men are created free and equal, and in France they were shouting, "Liberty, Equality, and Fraternity." In 1782 Joseph II of Austria issued his famous "Edict of Toleration"; in 1791 France abolished all laws directed against Jews; Holland and Prussia followed in granting civil liberties to their Jewish citizens.

These hopes for a brighter day for the Jews, however, were soon shattered. A reaction occurred, and the nations of Europe began to slip back into their old ways. In Germany there were massacres and expulsions. Some countries repealed the laws which had granted freedom to the Jews. In Russia they were made the scapegoats for the assassination of Alexander II, and suffered ghastly cruelties. In France the resurgence of anti-Semitism found its expression in the famous Dreyfus case.

Once again migration loomed as the only alternative to slow death. In Russia the harassed Jews had revived their ancient hope of finding a homeland in Palestine; but it remained for one of their number in Western Europe, Theodore Herzl, to translate this dream into the actuality of modern Zionism. His efforts met with well-nigh insurmountable obstacles and considerable opposition, even from many Jews, who felt that Zionism was a step backward. But the homeland in Palestine finally became a reality, and hundreds of thousands of the Wandering People began to wend their way back toward Jerusalem. Not all of them, however; for there are some 13 million Jews in the world, most of whom prefer to remain where they are.

The Expansion of Europe

An entirely different type of migratory movement is that known as the Expansion of Europe. One of the most amazing spectacles of history is the way in which the people of Europe began, in the fifteenth century, to overflow their boundaries and set out to explore, convert, conquer, and colonize every corner of the earth. For the student of race relations, no other historical event can compare in importance with this movement of white Europeans into other continents, their coming into contact with members of other races and different cultures, and creating problems of conflict and adjustment. As a migratory movement the expansion of Europe differs radically from the wanderings of the Jews.

It is customary to date this movement from the early fifteenth century, when Portuguese sailors began to venture forth upon the uncharted seas, or from the discovery of the New World in 1492. Also, it has not been uncommon to attribute the initiation of the movement to some individual, to the genius of Prince Henry the Navigator or the courage of Christopher Columbus; or to seek its cause in some incident, such as acquisition of the compass by European navigators. The fact is, however, that the Expansion of Europe was the result of a combination of factors, personal, social, technological, and economic. Its roots may be traced back long before the fifteenth century.

Europeans in ancient times had been in touch with the peoples of the East, but these contacts were broken by the barbarian invasions and, somewhat later, by the incursions of the Moslems. In the ninth century, however, adventurous seamen from the ports of southern Italy began to trade with the cities of the eastern Mediterranean, and soon other Italian cities, such as Venice, Pisa, and Genoa, entered this lucrative commerce. Europeans began to acquire a taste for the fabulous products of Asia, and the Crusades provided a great stimulus to the development of these new wants.

The wealth of the East was, indeed, dazzling to the European. His was a monotonous diet, and the spices from Asia made a world of difference to him in the enjoyment of his meals. Then there were the precious stones, the silks and satins, the beautiful rugs, the shawls and tapestries, the glass and porcelain. In return for these, the European had little to offer, other than rough woolen cloth, copper, lead, tin, and a few other base materials. He needed gold and silver, therefore, to pay for his imports, and his supply of these precious metals was inadequate. Small wonder, then, that he seemed greedy for the gold which he later discovered in the possession of Aztecs and Incas, and which he suspected other Indian tribes of having.

The eastern shores of the Mediterranean were the gateway for most of the trade with the East. The Spanish and Portuguese, accordingly, were not well situated to participate. They had developed the same tastes as their fellow Europeans, but they resented the high prices they were forced to pay. They were eager, therefore, to discover some new route to the East. They had reasons for believing that there were routes to the "Indies," for their knowledge of geography and navigation were not as primitive as many suppose. Their learned men knew that the world was round, and had even made a fairly accurate guess at its size, and the navigators of that century were familiar with the compass, the astrolabe, and other instruments which made their vocation less hazardous.

In 1415 the Portuguese began to expand by capturing Ceuta, across the Strait of Gibraltar, in Morocco. Then, under the leadership of Prince Henry the Navigator, and with the support of the King, they began their explorations of the western coast of Africa. Fifty years later they had reached the Guinea coast; in 1488 Bartholomew Diaz sailed to the southern tip of Africa; and before the close of the century Vasco da Gama had rounded the Cape and sailed on to India. In the meantime the Spanish, under Columbus, had discovered the New World; the British, under John Cabot, had reached the Canadian coast; and the Italian, Amerigo Vespucci, had made a voyage to Brazil and had written a letter in which he referred to "the new world." Others who participated in this initial expansion of Europe are familiar to all and too numerous to mention.

Exploration and trade, however, were not the only interests of the Europeans. They went out sometimes to conquer and subdue the native peoples and sometimes they went as settlers. They laid claim to all the lands they touched, and fought among themselves for their possession. They despoiled and exploited the peoples they met, and set about to supplant what they regarded as heathen customs with their own civilization. Missionaries introduced the Christian religion and traders developed a market for European products. The population of Europe increased at an incredible rate, and fifty million people crossed the seas to find a better place to live. This expansion of Europe has continued to the present day, with the result that the English-speaking peoples of North America and Australia far outnumber those in England, Spanish-speaking peoples of South and Central America are more numerous than those of Spain, and people of European descent are found living in every quarter of the globe. The "Europeanization" of the whole world has proceeded apace and continues today.

Nearly two million Iranian tribesmen still migrate with the changing seasons, as has been their custom for centuries

Types of Migrations

It is apparent from the cases reported thus far that many different kinds of movements of people are included under the term "migration." To understand race relations it is necessary to recognize the fact that contacts between different racial and ethnic groups occur under a wide variety of circumstances. Often they are made at the point of the sword, while at other times they are entirely peaceful; they may be voluntary or involuntary, on the part of either or both of the races; the motives leading to the contact may be selfish or altruistic; the interests of the two groups may be antagonistic or complementary. Our language contains a great many terms which indicate the variety of circumstances under which different peoples come together. The following classification of the types of migration is based upon the study of H. P. Fairchild.[6]

Dispersion

This type of migration was especially characteristic of the prehistoric period. Whether he originated in Asia or in Africa, man lost little time in moving from

[6] H. P. Fairchild, *Immigration: A World Movement and Its American Significance*, pp. 1–29. For a somewhat different typology, see W. Petersen, "A General Typology of Migration," *American Sociological Review*, Vol. 23, No. 3, April 1958, pp. 256–266.

his birthplace, and primitive peoples for thousands of years have continued to spread out whenever population pressure or adverse economic conditions have impelled them to do so. Migrations of this type have certain features. They are incredibly slow; consider the time it must have taken the American Indian to creep from Alaska to Tierra del Fuego. They are, for the most part, unconscious and irrational. A primitive band, when it disperses, has no destination in mind, for a migration of this type is a movement *away from*, not a movement *to* a particular place. Usually it is peaceful and unopposed, for it is a venture into uninhabited country.

Nomadism

This involves the repeated shifting of the habitat of a people in its search for subsistence. Nomads do not wander blindly or aimlessly; their movements are focused on certain centers of operation and vary according to climatic and topographic conditions and depending upon the methods employed in obtaining food. Some nomadic people rely upon hunting and gathering, others follow their domesticated animals, and there are some agricultural nomads.

Invasion

This term is commonly applied to any hostile or warlike encroachment upon the rights, possessions, or domain of another; but for our purposes we restrict it to those cases where a simple but virile people leaves its home and overruns the territory of a more highly developed society. An invasion has some of the characteristics of a dispersion; it is a mass movement, involving a large portion, if not the whole, of the tribe; a particular destination is lacking; there is a certain irrationality in the process. The Gothic migration from Asia into the Roman Empire, the Aztec into Mexico, the Hun and Magyar into Europe, and the Mongol into China are examples of invasions.

Conquest

This is almost the reverse of an invasion, involving the expansion and domination of a highly developed society over a simpler people. Fairchild describes conquest as follows:

> It is an overflow of civilization, of manners, of organization, of government, — not to any extent, of population. Conquest occurs when a well-developed state, full of vigor, sends its armies over the territory of less advanced peoples, imposing its political system upon them, and laying them under tribute, but not slaying the people or destroying their wealth more than is necessary to secure subjection. It is an enterprise of the state, seeking its own glory and aggrandizement. . . . The movement of population to the conquered territory may be insignificant, and in this, conquest differs from all other forms of migratory movements. Consequently the effects on the racial stock of the conquered people may be very slight,

and in most cases are. The effect on the mores, on the other hand, including language, may be profound and lasting.[7]

Colonization

This type of population movement occurs when a well-established society sends out bodies of its citizens to settle in certain specified localities. Such a transplanted fragment remains closely tied to its mother country, politically, economically, and culturally. The migration is often an undertaking of the state itself; but sometimes private groups have established colonies in pursuit of their interests as they see them. In these latter cases, however, the sanction of the state is usually involved, though not always.

Colonization is an ancient type of population movement, practiced by the Chinese, Greeks, Romans, Phoenicians, and many other peoples. It has taken a variety of forms, too; and many classifications of colonies have, accordingly, been made. Keller[8] distinguishes between the farm type and the plantation type. The farm colony arises where the soil and climatic conditions are similar to those of the country whence the settlers came, rendering acclimatization easy, permitting the migration of whole families, promoting independence and individual enterprise, and ultimately often resulting in the colonists' transferring their primary allegiance from their old home to the new. Such, for instance, was the settlement of Canada, most of the United States, South Africa, New Zealand, Tasmania, and Australia. The plantation colony, on the other hand, arises where the geographical conditions are quite different from those of the homeland. The colonizers are predominantly male, and their ties with the mother country remain strong. Agriculture takes the form of a highly specialized crop, produced by a large operating unit. Labor is a major problem, for the native populations can seldom be induced to work for wages and some system of forced labor must be resorted to. Many of the most crucial problems of race relations have arisen under such conditions. This type of colonization has been characteristic of the Portuguese in Brazil, the Dutch in Java and Sumatra, and the British in the Malay Peninsula and the Caribbean.

Forced Migration

This occurs when groups of people are compelled against their choice to leave their native land and go elsewhere, either with or without a specific destination. Thus, the Moors were expelled from Spain in 1609; the Jews, as we saw, have been forced to leave one country after another throughout their history. Huguenots were driven from France in the seventeenth century; Gypsies were expelled from England by Henry VIII; and the Acadians, heroes of Longfellow's *Evangeline,* were uprooted and scattered among the English colonies of North

[7] Fairchild, *op. cit.,* pp. 17–18.
[8] A. G. Keller, *Colonization,* p. 4. See also M. K. Knight, "Colonies," in *Encyclopedia of the Social Sciences,* Vol. 3, pp. 653–663.

America. The Governor of Missouri, in 1838, issued an order expelling the Mormons from that state. The slave trade, which we shall discuss presently, and the penal colonies, which have been established in Australia and elsewhere, are also examples of forced migration.[9]

Lest we conclude that forced migration is a cruel relic of the past, we might be reminded that the twentieth century has already witnessed a forcible expulsion of peoples on a scale hitherto unapproached. Today we know these people as "refugees" and "displaced persons." On the eve of World War I tens of thousands of Bulgarians had to flee from Turkey, and an equal number of Turkish Moslems had to flee from Bulgaria. Later on, thousands of persons in the Balkans were more or less forcibly removed under a program known euphemistically as the "transfer of minorities." To be sure, most of this transfer of populations was done under high-sounding treaties, supervised by commissions "to insure justice"; but the fact remains that most of the victims were reluctant to emigrate, and they were not happy to exchange their property for the redeemable government bonds they were forced to accept, and which, not surprisingly, promptly declined in value. Consequently, no small amount of compulsion had to be applied.

World War I cut millions adrift. During the war Turkey embarked upon a mass expulsion of its Armenian minority, sending many refugees into Europe, the Middle East, and the United States. Half a million found refuge of a sort in Russia. Between the two world wars the stream of refugees continued. The civil war in Russia stimulated a mass emigration, estimated at two million.

When Hitler came to power he declared that he would gladly give a thousand marks to any Jew who would leave the country. Soon, however, he adopted more effective methods of promoting emigration, with the result that some 365,000 Jewish refugees fled in the 1930's. To this figure, which represents only those of Jewish faith, must be added the so-called "non-Aryans" (i.e., Christians of Jewish or partly Jewish origin) and the innumerable "Aryans" who fled for political reasons.

The victory of Franco in Spain led to a mass flight across the border. The Republican army, together with a throng of civilians, retreated into French territory. Some of these eventually found their way to North Africa or to Mexico, while 200,000 remained in France.

World War II set in motion a refugee flood of astronomical proportions. When the Germans overran Poland, they pushed 300,000 refugees out of the country. Shortly thereafter the Soviet government insisted upon the transfer of some 400,000 German ethnics from the Baltic states, on which the Soviets had designs, and Hitler obligingly "recalled them to the Fatherland." When the Germans moved westward, hordes of Dutch and Belgian civilians streamed into France. The same sort of thing happened when the Germans invaded Russia and the Balkans. Finally, when the tide of battle turned, hordes of fearful Russians,

[9] J. J. Senturia, "Mass Expulsion," *Encyclopedia of the Social Sciences*, Vol. 10, pp. 185–189

Major Intercontinental Migratory
Currents in Modern Times

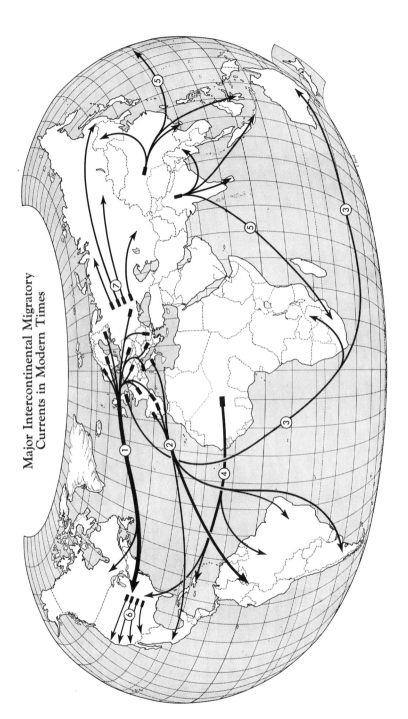

"The main currents of international migration since the begin-
ning of the sixteenth century have been: (1) from all parts of
Europe to North America; (2) from Latin countries of Europe
to Middle and South America; (3) from Great Britain to
Africa and Australia; (4) import of slaves from Africa to
America. Another current (5), partly intercontinental, partly

intracontinental, has flowed from China and India. The most
important internal migration has been (6) westward in the
United States and (7) eastward in Russia." (Source: W. S.
and E. S. Woytinsky, World Population and Production [New
York: The Twentieth Century Fund, 1953], p. 68.)

Ukrainians, and Balts joined the retreating Germans. Thirty millions, they say, were displaced. Many of these, of course, subsequently returned to their homes; but there were millions who, for one reason or another, dared not return.

Elsewhere in the world, in the years following World War II, the phenomenon of forced migration was apparent. Israel, a nation of refugees, faced the problem of absorbing masses of Oriental Jews who came bringing their strange customs with them. Refugees from Communist China flocked into Hong Kong and Formosa. Thousands fled from North Viet Nam to South. Following the partition of the country, eight million Hindus fled from Pakistan, and an equal number of Moslems fled from India to Pakistan. Some 800,000 Arabs fled from Israel, when that nation was established, and today they huddle along the borders in poverty and idleness. The abortive revolution in Hungary in 1956 sent thousands fleeing into Austria, and Castro's revolution drove great numbers of refugees from Cuba. In 1964 the Watusi, the tallest people in the world, were sent scurrying from Rwanda, when the Bahuta, after centuries of vassalage, suddenly acquired political control of the country. Indeed, forced migration is more characteristic of the twentieth century than of any other in history, and presents one of the major social problem of our time.[10]

Immigration

This type of population movement involves the entrance into an alien country of persons intending to take part in the life of that country and to make it their more or less permanent residence. It is largely a phenomenon of the modern world, especially of the nineteenth and twentieth centuries. It is a peaceful movement, between well-established countries which are on friendly terms or at least are not hostile; and one of which is old and densely populated while the other is new and less thickly settled. Immigration, unlike the movements described heretofore, is primarily an individual undertaking, or a "collective drift," rather than the organized movement of an integrated group, although whole villages have been known to migrate piecemeal to another country, and although governments do control, regulate, direct, and encourage or discourage the process.

Internal Migration

Still another form of movement which is often significant in race relations is that known as internal migration. There have been times, of course, when there was very little movement of people within the borders of a state. Under serfdom, for instance, one did not have the right to move; and, even with the disappearance of serfdom, the individual was still not endowed with independence of action, for he was a member of the commune, which regulated many aspects of

---

[10] The most complete account of the refugee situation will be found in J. Vernant, *The Refugee in the Post-War World*. See also D. R. Taft and R. Robbins, *International Migrations*, Part 2.

his life.[11] Nowadays, however, internal migrations are going on continually in all civilized countries. One of the most important of these is the drift of population from the country to the city. Internal migration has been a conspicuous feature of American society, profoundly affecting its history, its institutions, and its culture, as well as the relations between racial and ethnic groups. First, there were the migrations of the Indians, both before the arrival of Columbus and since. Then there was the westward march of the American people, expanding the young nation from the Atlantic to the Pacific.[12] Other important internal migrations in our country were the flight of the Mormons from New York to Utah, the rush of gold-seekers to California in 1849, the interstate migrations of recent years, the seasonal migrations of labor, and, especially, the great migration of Negroes from the rural South to the industrial cities of the North and the West.

TABLE 4.1

*Growth and Distribution of the Negro Population**

State	1910	1930	1960
Alabama	908,282	944,834	980,271
Alaska			6,771
Arizona	2,009	10,749	43,403
Arkansas	442,891	478,463	388,787
California	21,645	81,048	883,861
Colorado	11,453	11,828	39,992
Connecticut	15,174	29,354	107,449
Delaware	31,181	32,602	60,688
District of Columbia	94,446	132,068	411,737
Florida	308,669	431,828	880,186
Georgia	1,176,987	1,071,125	1,122,596
Hawaii			4,943
Idaho	651	668	1,502
Illinois	109,049	328,972	1,037,470
Indiana	60,320	111,982	269,275
Iowa	14,973	17,380	25,354
Kansas	54,030	66,344	91,445
Kentucky	261,656	226,040	215,949
Louisiana	713,874	776,326	1,039,207
Maine	1,363	1,096	3,318
Maryland	232,250	276,379	518,410
Massachusetts	38,055	52,365	111,842
Michigan	17,115	169,453	717,581
Minnesota	7,084	9,445	22,263
Mississippi	1,009,487	1,009,718	915,743
Missouri	157,452	223,840	390,853

[11] M. L. Hansen, *The Atlantic Migration*, pp. 5–8.
[12] M. L. Hansen, *The Immigrant in American History*, pp. 53–76.

TABLE 4.1 (continued)

Growth and Distribution of the Negro Population

State	1910	1930	1960
Montana	1,834	1,256	1,467
Nebraska	7,689	13,752	29,262
Nevada	513	516	13,484
New Hampshire	564	790	1,908
New Jersey	89,760	208,828	514,875
New Mexico	1,628	2,850	17,063
New York	134,191	412,814	1,417,511
North Carolina	697,843	918,647	1,116,021
North Dakota	617	377	777
Ohio	111,452	309,304	786,097
Oklahoma	137,612	172,198	153,084
Oregon	1,492	2,234	18,133
Pennsylvania	193,919	431,257	852,750
Rhode Island	9,529	9,913	18,332
South Carolina	835,843	793,681	829,291
South Dakota	817	646	1,114
Tennessee	473,088	477,646	586,876
Texas	690,049	854,964	1,187,125
Utah	1,144	1,108	4,148
Vermont	1,621	568	519
Virginia	671,096	650,165	816,258
Washington	6,058	6,840	48,738
West Virginia	64,173	114,893	89,378
Wisconsin	2,900	10,739	74,546
Wyoming	2,235	1,250	2,183
Total	9,827,763	11,891,143	18,871,831

* Source: Bureau of the Census

Causes of Migration

Apart from forced migrations, where the individual has no choice in the matter, what is it that motivates people to leave their homes and to set out to invade, to conquer, to colonize, or to settle in a strange land? The motives must of necessity be overpowering, for the hazards and discomforts attendant upon migration have always been great. Accustomed as we are nowadays to means of transportation which are rapid, cheap, safe, and convenient, we are likely to overlook the dangers and difficulties the emigrant of a century ago had to endure. Nor was transportation his only obstacle. Often there were legal barriers to be overcome, and by no means unimportant is the fact that most people have sentimental ties, not lightly broken, to bind them to their native soil.

Many myths and legends have arisen to explain the motives underlying migration. We have been led to believe that our own land was settled by persons who were impelled by a desire to worship God as they pleased, or by a love of freedom, or by rebellion against the oppressive Old World society. Such lofty motives were dominant at least with the earlier settlers, we are told, while less worthy motives of an economic nature prompted the later immigrants. Far less admirable were the interests of those who conquered and settled the Latin American countries, obsessed as they were with a greed for gold.

The real causes of migration (as of all social phenomena) are difficult to determine and are extremely complex. Hansen says:

> The truth is that an emigrant's motives were usually mixed. Before leaving home, when making application to local officials for permission to depart, he emphasized the material: the difficulty of providing a living for his family and the fear that they might be thrown upon the community for support. If the parish clergyman urged him to hesitate before risking everything in such a perilous adventure, the father pointed to his sons who were becoming lazy and shiftless in a country that could give them no work. Hence emigration was represented as a moral tonic. When he met his friends in the village tavern, where everyone grumbled about taxes and unsympathetic officials, he spoke of freedom as his purpose.
>
> Upon arriving in America, however, two of the three motives were likely to be forgotten, and the third emphasized. No longer did he mention material incentives. To do so would confirm the belief of the natives that the foreigner was a dangerous economic competitor, and their welcome would curdle into suspicion. Nor did he say that his sons needed moral discipline, for this would give point to the argument that immigrants were depraved and worthless. But one sentiment the American loved to hear. Still affected by the colonial's sense of inferiority, he believed that in culture and in wealth his country did not compare with the older nations of Europe. He did have his Constitution, however, and that was his constant boast. Hence, when the newcomer said, "I came to the United States to enjoy the blessings of your marvelous government and laws," the native warmed to him. . . .
>
> Immigrants soon learned the magic charm of this confession of faith.[13]

Even so, economic factors are certainly of greatest importance in stimulating migration. Anthropologists are of the opinion that the movements of primitive tribes are induced by some kind of economic pressure — changes in climate, desiccation of the country, depletion of the soil, overpopulation, or exhaustion of natural resources. The magnificent ruins in Mesa Verde National Park, in Colorado, bear witness to the fact that years of drought forced the inhabitants of those cliff-side cities to abandon the region they and their ancestors had inhabited for many centuries.[14] The folk tales of many primitive peoples relate how, when their numbers increased to the point where game and other resources

[13] *Ibid.*, pp. 77–78.
[14] For a somewhat different interpretation, see S. C. Jett, "Pueblo Indian Migrations," *American Antiquity*, Vol. 29, No. 3, January 1964, pp. 281–300.

were taxed, some of the tribe were forced to wander off in search of new sources of food. The Missouri, Iowa, and Oto Indians used to account in this manner for the fact that their ancestors, centuries earlier, had split off from the Winnebago tribe in Wisconsin.

Economic factors were of primary importance in the expansion of Europe and in the peopling of the United States. The phenomenal growth of Europe's population, doubling its size between 1700 and 1800, not only aroused the concern of Robert Malthus and other thinkers, but undoubtedly helped to put the idea of emigration into the popular mind. So too did the series of crop failures and the famines which afflicted one section of Europe or another from time to time. Similarly, economic conditions in America reflected themselves in the fluctuations of immigrant tides, decreasing in times of depression and mounting in times of industrial activity. This fact has been clearly demonstrated by Jerome, who noted a close correlation between immigration and business conditions. Says he:

> Whatever may be the basic causes of migration, there is a close relation between the cyclical oscillations of employment and those of immigration and emigration, and a moderately close resemblance in the respective seasonal fluctuations, with considerable reason to believe that this similarity, particularly in the cyclical oscillations, is due to a sensitiveness of immigration to employment conditions.[15]

From the settlement of Jamestown in 1607 down to the present day, it has been economic advantages and opportunities which have motivated most of the immigrants to these shores.

This is not to say that there have been no other motives. Religious persecution has unquestionably been a factor in promoting emigration. Jews have often had to flee in the face of intolerance; the Germans who came to Pennsylvania in 1683 were religious refugees; Huguenots were driven from France; the Armenians, who were Christian, suffered at the hands of the Mohammedan Turks, and sought refuge elsewhere. William Penn advertised his colony as a home for those who wanted to escape religious persecution, with the result that Quakers, Presbyterians, Mennonites, and many others came in considerable numbers to settle there.

Political and social conditions have also served as stimuli for migrations. In 1866, when Sweden established high property qualifications for voting, considerable discontent appeared among those who were disfranchised, and interest in emigration was aroused. Letters from Swedes who came to the United States in that period make frequent and favorable reference to the social and political equality they enjoyed. The failure of the revolutionary movement of 1848 gave the stimulus to the pioneers of the Bohemian immigration to America. Political discontent looms large in the history of Irish emigration, and operated also in the migrations of Russians, Poles, Finns, Hungarians, and many others.

[15] H. Jerome, *Migration and Business Cycles*, p. 243.

Discontent with the rigidity of Old World society or the class and caste systems, and desire to escape compulsory military service have motivated many to seek homes in another land.

But migration is not adequately explained in terms of impulses spontaneously aroused by conditions in the immigrant's homeland. Stimuli have also been artifically induced and introduced from the outside. The transportation of immigrants grew into a lucrative business, and agents for the steamship companies used to go about planting the idea of emigration in the minds of credulous peasants, often with little concern for the welfare either of the individual or of the nations affected. Labor agents, too, despite the fact that their operations were illegal, were responsible for considerable migration. Most important of all influences from the outside, however, were the immigrants themselves, whose letters to relatives and friends in the Old World were eagerly devoured, were circulated throughout the village and beyond, and were often printed in local newspapers. When they returned to their native communities, as they often did, boasting of their success and displaying their wealth, these fortunate ones encouraged many another to emigrate who would otherwise have resisted the temptation.

The motives for migration would doubtless run the whole gamut of human interests, and one must avoid the tendency to oversimplify them. Says W. C. Smith:

> The causes were complex and usually no one factor impelled the migrant to leave his country. In this mass movement certain general or fundamental causes operated but there were also many personal elements peculiar to individuals. A son or daughter left because of friction with unsympathetic parents; a girl went away to avoid marriage with the man her parents had chosen; a youth who had lost status because of a petty misdemeanor sought a new start far from the venomous tongues of local gossips; a girl fled to avoid scandal; a young man, grown weary of working for his father without compensation and with less freedom than a hired hand, yet loath on account of sharp class distinctions to hire out in the neighborhood where he was known, hoped to lose himself in America.[16]

Human migrations, accordingly, are the result of a variety of motivating factors; but, the *closer we keep our eyes to the soil,* as Hansen warns us, the better the chance of understanding the phenomena.

Migrations and American Society

A large and important portion of the history of the United States is concerned with the migrations of various peoples to these shores; and most of what the sociologists have regarded as the study of race relations has dealt with the meeting, the conflicts, the adjustments, and the amalgamation of the heterogeneous groups which have gone into the making of our nation. The United

---

[16] W. C. Smith, *Americans in the Making*, pp. 3–4.

States has experienced all the types of migratory movements we have described. Let us take a look at a few of the most significant.

The American Indian

We have been guilty of virtually ignoring the Indian in our histories. Artists, novelists, and showmen have not neglected him; but many students of the American scene have dismissed him with a few paragraphs. The truth is, however, that the presence of the Indian has profoundly affected our history and our culture. He played a part in the sheer matter of survival; for many a struggling colonial settlement would have been wiped out by starvation had not friendly Indians proffered aid. The Europeans had neither the knowledge nor the experience to found successful colonies. The Indians taught them what to plant and how to cultivate it; they shared with the white man their knowledge and skills of woodcraft; they blazed the trails which were later to become roads and highways. They have participated in all our wars. They even played a role in the development of American democracy; for many of the colonists had hopes

Arabian refugees who have fled from Palestine wait in line for their daily food ration in a refugee camp

of planting on this continent the European system of castes and classes, only to find that the rugged and dangerous life of the frontier was not conducive to such a social system.

The Indians were objects of mystery and speculation for the Europeans from the very beginning of their contact. It was once widely believed by the white man that the Indians were the descendants of the Ten Lost Tribes of Israel. Another legend held that Modoc, a Welsh prince, sailed westward in 1170 A.D. and discovered the New World. He returned to his homeland, outfitted a second expedition, and set sail, but was never heard from again. Some Indians, it was thought, were descended from Modoc's colony. Still other theories derived the Indians from the Egyptians, the Japanese, the Irish, the Polynesians, refugees from the "lost Continent of Atlantis," or from the continent of Mu, which is supposed to have existed once upon a time in the Pacific. These theories were based upon the flimsiest kinds of evidence, such as similarities in language, myths, or customs.

Considerable research has been done on the problem of the origin of the American Indian, and there is little doubt now that he came of Mongoloid stock and that he wandered into the Americas from Asia. The time of his coming is more difficult to determine; but few scientists doubt that he was living here at the close of the last glacial epoch, and there is a growing body of data pointing to the fact that he was here 15,000 to 25,000 years ago.[17] We may be certain that America was not originally settled by a single group of people, nor within a short span of time. This was no sudden, or mass migration, but was a migration which we have designated as of the Dispersal Type. Primitive bands of Asiatic hunters presumably came over in successive waves, probably across Behring Strait, and remained. As they multiplied, they continued to spread, until eventually they were living in the greater part of both American continents.

The Negro

The Negro's presence in the New World is the result of a series of events entirely different from those which operated in the case of the Indian; and his relations with the other races which he encountered have always been affected by the circumstances under which the contacts occurred. For centuries the relationship was one of slavery, the consequences of which are still felt, long after the institution itself has been abolished.

The Negro, as a matter of fact, was among the first to arrive in America in modern times. Tradition has it that the pilot on Columbus' flagship was "Alonzo, the Negro"; and history testifies that Negroes accompanied Balboa,

---

[17] E. B. Howard, "An Outline of the Problem of Man's Antiquity in North America," *American Anthropologist*, Vol. 38, No. 3 (Part 1), July–September 1936, pp. 394–413; F. H. H. Roberts, Jr., "Developments in the Problem of the North American Paleo-Indian," in *Essays in Historical Anthropology of North America*, Smithsonian Miscellaneous Collections, Vol. 100, 1940, pp. 51–116; H. E. Driver, *Indians of North America*, pp. 1–5.

Cortes, Velas, Pizarro, and many other conquistadores. One of them, Estevanico, was a distinguished explorer in his own right. These Negro pioneers, however, had little effect upon subsequent trends in race relations.

When Europeans began to exploit the New World they had discovered, their greatest problem was to secure a labor supply. At first they attempted to make use of the Indian. Enslavement and a variety of other devices were used in the effort to place the yoke upon the shoulders of the natives, but these attempts were failures. The English, accordingly, began to look eagerly upon the hordes of poor whites in their own country, inducing them to cross the Atlantic as indentured servants and to pay for their passage with a term of service. They also raided the jails and even resorted to kidnapping children, women, and drunken men. None of these sources proved satisfactory, and it was at this juncture that Africa seemed to offer what appeared to be an adequate and inexhaustible labor supply.

The Negro was not a total stranger to the inhabitants of Europe. That he was known to the ancient Greeks and Romans is proved by objects of art portraying negroid features and by references in the literature.[18] But there is no indication that the white peoples of ancient Europe had a prejudice against the Negro or that they attached any social significance to his racial features. It is probable that Negroes from Africa occasionally found their way into Europe throughout the historical period. Their numbers were small, and they were not looked upon as a solution to any of the problems of the time.

The story of modern Negro slavery, and of the Negro's transportation to America, begins in 1433. In that year, a Portuguese ship exploring the coast of Africa brought back two natives from Rio de Oro. Successive explorations resulted in the purchase or capture of other slaves, so that within five years 1000 Negroes had been taken to Portugal, and by 1460 seven or eight hundred were being imported annually. In the fifteenth and sixteenth centuries the Portuguese were confronted with a manpower shortage. The long wars with the Moors had depleted their population, and colonization and exploration were making serious demands upon them. Too, their growing commerce attracted rural people to the cities, with the result that agricultural labor was in short supply. Negro slaves, therefore, were especially welcome to the Portuguese. Spain was not long in following the example of Portugal.

Negro slaves were employed as early as 1502 by the Spanish settlers in the West Indies, but they were not regarded as the solution to the labor problem in the New World. Instead, the Indian seemed at first to be the answer. An institution known as the *encomienda* was established. This was a grant of land, with accompanying unpaid, forced, Indian labor for life. Another Spanish institution designed for the proper development of the colony was the *repartimiento*, which was a grant of Indian forced labor for use either on the land, or in mines, fac-

[18] F. M. Snowden, "The Negro in Ancient Greece," *American Anthropologist*, Vol. 50, No. 1 (Part 1), 1948, pp. 31ff.; and "The Negro in Classical Italy," *American Journal of Philology*, Vol. 68, No. 3, 1947, pp. 266–292; G. H. Beardsley, *The Negro in Greek and Roman Civilization: A Study of the Ethiopian Type.*

tories, monasteries, or for public works. Since the labor supply was supposed to be unlimited, the Indians were worked to death. So terrible was their life that they were driven to mass suicide and infanticide, with the result that their numbers declined with disastrous rapidity.

The Indians had one friend, Bartolome de Las Casas, Bishop of Chiapas. We cannot here recount his many labors on their behalf, and the opposition which he encountered from the Spanish colonizers and even from his own clergy. In a desperate effort to halt the annihilation of the Indians, Las Casas went to Spain in 1517, appeared before Charles V, and pleaded the cause of these unfortunate people: "At my first arrival in Hispaniola, it contained a million inhabitants, and now (twenty years later) there remain scarce the hundredth part of them." He urged that Negro slaves, whom he regarded as more robust and better adapted to agricultural operations, be sent out to provide the necessary labor. His suggestion met with approval; and thus a tremendous impetus was given to the African slave trade. One European country after another entered this new and lucrative occupation.

In the present United States, the beginnings of Negro slavery go back to the year 1619, when a Dutch ship unloaded "twenty Negars" at Jamestown. The Virginians, like the Spaniards in the Indies, were desperate for laborers. These Negroes, however, were not purchased as slaves, but were accepted as indentured servants — a status with which the English were more familiar. The institution of slavery in the 13 colonies was the product of a long, continuous development. Africa came to be regarded by them, too, as the most satisfactory source of workers for the task of developing a new continent.

After this beginning, the African continent was raided to supply the demand for laborers in the New World for nearly four centuries. No accurate figures are available on the number of Negroes transported to the Americas, and the estimates vary widely. The demand was certainly not uniform over the four centuries, and the restrictions upon the traffic were more severe at one time than another. Some scholars have thought that thirty million Negroes were brought from Africa to America in the course of the slave trade. For Brazil alone the estimates vary from three to eighteen million, with five million being a reasonable and conservative guess. No one doubts that the total figure would run into many millions. When we consider that, for every slave who succeeded in crossing the Atlantic, there were a number who were killed in the raids or who died in passage, the impact of the traffic upon the African continent assumes enormous proportions.

The Atlantic Migration

Yet neither the wanderings of the primitive Indians nor the forced migration of Negroes from Africa equals in magnitude or importance the flood of European emigrants who came to the United States to settle. Biologically, historically, and culturally the people of the United States are European. We are one of the results of the Expansion of Europe. Most of us, if we could trace our complete ancestry, would come upon Irish, German, English, and numerous other antecedents. Our American civilization itself is a patchwork quilt composed largely of the contributions of the various European peoples. Sociologists and historians have long been interested in the background of the heterogeneous groups which crossed the Atlantic to settle this nation, and in the conflicts and adjustments which resulted from their meeting here.

More than forty million people have left their homes in Europe, crossed the Atlantic, and come to settle in the United States. We cannot quote the precise figure, for it was not until 1820 that records began to be kept. Possibly two million came as colonists before the Revolutionary War, and it is estimated that another 250,000 came between 1776 and 1820. With the beginning of World War I in 1914 a sharp decline in immigration occurred, and shortly thereafter Congress placed drastic restrictions upon the number of persons permitted to enter the country. The Atlantic Migration, accordingly, reached its greatest proportions in the century between the close of the Napoleonic wars in 1815 and the opening of the World War in 1914. During that period more than thirty million immigrants entered the United States from Europe.

The flow of immigration was not uniform throughout this period, however, but fluctuated from year to year. Periods of economic distress in Europe would force large numbers to seek a home across the seas; at other times political disturbances or religious persecution would stimulate emigration. On this side, periods of industrial activity and prosperity would create a demand for labor, while depressions and wars would divert the flow of emigration elsewhere. There were times when other countries proved to be more attractive to the European emigrant than did the United States. The tropics always held a certain appeal, and in the decade of the 1820's Brazil loomed as the land of greatest opportunity. Hence the flow to this country varied greatly. We find that in 1816 about 8000 immigrants entered the United States, while in the following year the number jumped to 22,400. In 1820 only 8385 came, but in 1832 there were 60,482. The year 1891 saw more than half a million enter the country, but in 1898 there were only 229,299. The peak year was 1907, when 1,285,349 arrived; and we received more than a million also in the years 1905, 1906, 1910, 1913, and 1914. Not all of these immigrants, of course, were from Europe; but approximately 85 per cent were, while another 11 per cent entered from other American countries, principally Canada; and relatively few from the rest of the world.

Not only did the number entering the United States vary from time to time, but the ethnic composition also changed. For nearly three centuries most of our immigrants and colonists came from the countries of northern and western Europe — Great Britain, Ireland, the Scandinavian countries, Germany, the Netherlands, France, and Switzerland. This is known as the "Old Immigration." In the 1880's, however, immigrants from southern and eastern Europe, belonging to what is referred to as the "New Immigration," began to arrive in noticeable numbers. In 1896, for the first time, the latter outnumbered the former, and they held to their numerical superiority until 1921, when Congress deliberately set about to reverse the trend. This is not to say that people from

Immigrants from Europe disembarking at Rio de Janeiro, accepted by the Brazilian government as settlers

eastern and southern Europe were not among the earliest settlers. The fact is that in the colonies there were persons of Italian, Greek, and Russian ancestry,[19] and many of them played conspicuous roles in the Revolutionary War. The New Immigration, however, was relatively light until the last quarter of the nineteenth century. Italian immigrants, for example, numbered only 439 in the decade of the 1820's and 9231 in the 1850's, but there were 307,309 in the 1880's, and 2,045,877 in the first decade of the twentieth century. A similar trend is characteristic of the Greek, Russian, Austrian, Hungarian, and other eastern and southern European nationalities.

Much of the history of the United States is intertwined with the arrival and settlement of these multitudes, and the nation today is biologically and culturally the product of the meeting and mixing of these diverse peoples. America has, indeed, been a melting pot; but the process whereby the melting has taken place is by no means as simple and automatic as we have been led to suppose.

Refugees and Displaced Persons

The people of the United States like to think of their country as a haven of refuge, where those who are persecuted for racial, religious, or political reasons might find freedom and security. While we recognize that most immigrants have

[19] L. Adamic, *A Nation of Nations*, especially pp. 20–26, 147–151, 235–239, 267.

come for economic gain (which we regard as less praiseworthy), we recall with pride that many peoples, from the Pilgrims on down, have sought these shores for the sake of their spiritual ideals.

We even overlook the fact that certain other countries also have opened their doors to the victims of religious, racial, and political persecution. Great Britain, despite her periodic economic difficulties, has frequently welcomed refugees. So have Switzerland, Austria, West Germany, Greece, Belgium, the Netherlands, and the Scandinavian countries. France, especially, has long served as a magnet for refugees from every part of the world, and probably, more than any other nation, deserves to be called the "Land of Asylum." France has never taken steps for the systematic assimilation of her foreign population, nor has she opposed their formation of ethnic colonies nor the expressions of their national cultures. Yet, the psychological climate of France being what it is, experience has shown that foreigners, including refugees, tend to become assimilated.

Nevertheless, since World War I the United States has received hundreds of thousands of refugees and displaced persons. Unlike the immigrants of the nineteenth century, these people have reluctantly and unwillingly left their homes, not for economic gain, but because of the ravages of war, or because their political opinions or their religious or ethnic affiliations made them the objects of persecution.

Between 1933 and 1945 millions fled from the wrath of the Nazis and Fascists. How many of these reached the United States is not definitely known, though Davie supposes that there were between 250,000 and 300,000. For the most part they were middle- and upper-class persons; and, unlike most emigrants, their migration was not motivated by a desire to improve their economic condition. The majority were Jews, but many were Christians of long standing who were accused by the Nazis of having a Jewish ancestor, and not a few belonged to the approved race but refused to bow to the dictates of Hitler. Most of them came from Germany and Austria, but large numbers fled also from Poland, Italy, Czechoslovakia, Russia, and Hungary. In some respects the problems of adjustment these refugees faced were similar to those of all immigrants, but there were also many differences, due to their educational and economic background, the social status to which they had been accustomed and which they valued highly, the talents and skills they brought with them, and their attitudes toward the countries of their adoption.

During and after World War II, when millions of homeless people posed a problem of staggering proportions, the United States had to face her responsibilities. Our military forces made tremendous contributions toward caring for war victims, and we established the War Refugee Board, which rendered assistance to thousands. We were instrumental in establishing UNRRA (United Nations Relief and Rehabilitation Administration). When, toward the end of the war, it became evident that the refugee problem would remain with us for some time, we sponsored the formation of IRO (International Refugee Organization) and contributed generously to its support. In 1945, President Truman issued a directive which gave preference to refugees under our immigration

TABLE 4.2

The World's Refugees, 1963*

Hong Kong and Macao	1,270,000	from Mainland China
Mainland China	2,500	Europeans still awaiting exit
Southeast Asia	250,000	Chinese (including 50,000 in North Burma)
	900,000	Vietnamese
	35,000	Laotians in Cambodia and Laos
	1,000,000	Koreans from North Korea
India (1)	45,000	Tibetan refugees
Nepal	20,000	Tibetan refugees
Bhutan and Sikkim	5,000	Tibetan refugees
Pakistan	3,000,000	refugees from India
Africa	200,000	from Angola in the Congo
	160,000	from Ruanda in Burundi, Congo, and Tanganyika
	5,000	in Togo from Ghana, Ivory Coast
Europe	9,000	UNHCR mandate still in camp
	70,000	UNHCR mandate out of camp
	4,000,000	from East Germany
	150,000	refugees not benefiting from international programs, who may receive help from voluntary agencies
	30,000	Spanish Republican refugees in France
	750,000	Europeans fleeing Algeria, mostly in France
	180,000	Jewish refugees from Tunisia, Morocco, Algeria, and Egypt, mostly in France
	37,000	Algerian Moslems in France
	3,500	ethnic Greeks
	5,000	Cuban refugees in Spain
	5,000	Belgian returnees from Congo
	60,000	Dutch from Indonesia
	15,000	Italians from Egypt and Tunisia
Middle East	1,100,000	Palestinian Arabs in Jordan, Syria, Lebanon, and Gaza
	1,800	Russians in Turkey
	1,250	Armenians and Europeans in Lebanon
	5,000	Turkic refugees in Iran
Western Hemisphere	195,000	Cuban refugees; more than 150,000 in the United States, the others scattered throughout Latin America
Total	13,510,050	

(1) Approximately 3,000,000 refugees who fled Pakistan to India have now been almost completely resettled, according to the Indian government.

* Source: The United States Committee for Refugees

quotas, making it possible for more than 42,000 displaced persons to enter the country.

At the same time, our rigid, restrictive immigration laws prevented our opening the door, even a little, to refugees. Numerous bills were introduced into Congress, designed to modify the provisions of the law, but none passed. It was even proposed that refugees be used in the colonization of Alaska, but that suggestion fell on deaf ears.

In the meantime pressure for American participation in the resettlement of refugees began to build up. Various newspapers and magazines demanded, in their editorials, that legislation be enacted that would enable some of the war's displaced persons to come to America. Pressure to that end was also applied on Congress by such organizations as the National Catholic Welfare Conference, the National Council of Churches, the YWCA, and labor organizations. There was opposition, to be sure, from certain "patriotic" organizations and from some of the press.

Finally, after a bitter fight in Congress, the Displaced Persons Act was passed on July 19, 1948. It contained many bad features. President Truman, in signing it, condemned certain aspects of it as discriminatory. The *New York Times* declared, "The DP bill . . . is a sorry job." An ingenious feature of the bill was the way in which it ostensibly adhered to our sacrosanct quota system, and at the same time faced up to the realities of the world situation. It permitted countries to "mortgage" their immigration quotas, with the result that certain nations (Latvia, for example) are saddled with these mortgages for decades, even centuries, to come.

The Displaced Persons Act, however, did make it possible for more than 300,000 refugees to enter the United States between 1948 and 1952.

This act expired in 1952, but the following year, at the insistence of President Eisenhower, Congress passed another, the Refugee Relief Act of 1953. This, on the surface, was a more magnanimous bill than its predecessor. It would admit 214,000 persons, above and beyond the immigration quotas, over a period of three years. This bill, too, contained many features that made its administration difficult; and when it expired on December 31, 1956, somewhat less than the permissible number of refugees had actually arrived in the country.

Many persons, in Congress and without, had bitterly opposed the admission of refugees and displaced persons. They insisted that these fugitives from communism, fascism, and the ravages of war were degenerates, cowards, subversives, and criminals, and that they could never become assimilated. Such evidence as we have been able to amass, however, proves quite otherwise. The refugees of World War II are apparently becoming assimilated with remarkable speed and success. In fact, they seem to adjust and assimilate even more rapidly than did immigrants of earlier years. This is not too surprising, however, for the circumstances under which they enter the country are different from those for other immigrants. In the first place, these refugees and displaced persons, unlike immigrants of the nineteenth century, do not come cherishing the hope that, when a modest fortune has been laid by, they will return home. Some do;

Home for Chinese refugees: roof-shacks in Kowloon, Hong Kong

but most of them know full well that here they will live out their days, and here their children will remain. They are therefore motivated to acquire as quickly as possible the culture of their new home. In the second place, they are stateless people. Therefore, they seek to acquire citizenship at their earliest opportunity. Third, the system of sponsorship, embodied in the legislation, resulted in their wide geographical distribution, discouraging their concentration in ethnic colonies. A high degree of concentration draws attention to a group, often arouses prejudicial attitudes against it, and retards its assimilation. The refugees settled in all the states, and in cities, towns, and rural communities. Fourth, the refugees, sponsored for the most part by local churches and church organizations, had a unique opportunity quickly to establish primary relations with the native population. Such was not the case with immigrant groups in the past, who were seldom admitted to face-to-face relationships with the Old Americans. Instead their contacts were formal and impersonal — with government agents, school teachers, tax gatherers, policemen, and employers. It is otherwise with the refugees who have come to America since World War II, and it is not surprising that studies which have been made point to their rapid assimilation and adjustment.[20]

Problems of race relations, then, arise from the fact that peoples move from place to place, and in so doing they come into contact with others who differ from them racially and culturally. Such contacts almost invariably lead to a conflict of interests, to hostility, prejudice, and a struggle for dominance or survival. That is not all, however. Despite their disagreements, groups who are in contact will have a mutual effect upon each other, and seldom if ever do they fail to interbreed. Eventually they may succeed in reaching some sort of *modus vivendi*. In this whole process, however, the circumstances under which the groups came into contact are of utmost importance. It makes a world of difference whether they come together as conquerors and conquered, as masters and slaves, or as immigrants and hosts. People's memories are long, and the pattern of race relations which emerges from the contact never fails to reflect the fact that the initial meeting was a voluntary or an involuntary one, an invasion or a conquest, or that the newcomers were met with a welcome rather than a sneer.

[20] There is a rapidly growing body of literature dealing with the refugees and displaced persons in the United States. In addition to the two volumes mentioned in fn. 10, the reader is referred to M. R. Davie, *Refugees in America*; L. C. White, *300,000 New Americans: The DP Story*; H. B. M. Murphy, *et al.*, *Flight and Resettlement*; Nancy M. Krueger, *Assimilation of Post-War Immigrants in Columbus, Ohio*; D. P. Kent, *The Refugee Intellectual*; D. E. De Groot, *Assimilation of Post-War Immigrants in Atlanta, Ga.*

5

Conflict

Conflict consists in a test of power between antagonistic parties.

LEWIS COSER
The Functions of Social Conflict

Seldom have the members of diverse races met under more favorable circumstances than those which surrounded the initial contacts of white Europeans and brown Hawaiians. It was on the morning of the eighteenth of January, 1778, that the natives of the island of Kauai awoke to find Captain James Cook's two vessels, *Discovery* and *Resolution,* standing off shore. Accustomed to nothing more than small canoes, they were greatly impressed. "These are forests that have drifted out to sea," they exclaimed, as they marvelled at the lofty masts. They called the strange objects *moku,* islands, not knowing that they were but small ships, of less than five hundred tons.

The men aboard impressed them no less than the ships. They thought Captain Cook was their god Lono, and they accorded him royal honors and prostrated themselves before him as he passed. They were eagerly curious about their visitors and all they possessed, and were desirous of obtaining, by hook or crook, anything they could lay hands on.

Word spread rapidly about the mysterious creatures who had come on their huge, floating islands. "Fire and smoke issue from their mouths," so the rumors ran. "They have openings in the sides of their bodies into which they thrust their hands and draw out iron, beads, nails, and other treasures; and their speech is unintelligible." Natives on the other islands, of course, were properly skeptical of these wild tales, but they lost no time in taking to their canoes and setting out to glimpse these remarkable beings. They were convinced, too, when they actually saw smoke coming from the mouths of the sailors, and saw and heard the fire belching from the portholes of the ships with a noise like thunder.

Captain Cook did not take undue advantage of their credulity. As a matter of fact, he was a humane and tolerant man, especially so if we compare him with other explorers of that era. He commented upon the Hawaiians' pleasant dispositions, and admired them for their neatness and ingenuity. His intentions were honorable. He had come not to enslave or exploit them, but only to advance knowledge of geography and astronomy. Sometimes he would capture a few of the natives, take them aboard ship, treat them well, load them with presents, and set them ashore. He was determined that they not misunderstand his good intentions. Before he reached the Hawaiian Islands he had had some unfortunate experiences with the natives of other islands in the Pacific, and had been forced to shoot a few. But he always deplored such occurrences, and justified them on the grounds that he had to convince the savages that he intended them no harm. In short, he was a man of good will, and he had come to a land of friendly, curious people.

The records agree that relations were most cordial. The old king gave Cook a beautiful featherwork cape, and received in return a linen shirt and the Captain's own sword. The Hawaiian priests were especially generous, and sent to the ships endless supplies of meat and vegetables, for which they demanded nothing in payment. The historian of the expedition records that the instances of kindness and civility on the part of the natives were too numerous to mention. So generous were they, in fact, that after a time the islands began to run short of food. The king, accordingly, was forced to inquire politely and tactfully when his white friends planned to depart. When they told him the date, huge quantities of tapa, hogs, and vegetables were presented as farewell gifts.

These idyllic relations, unfortunately, came to an end. Shortly before the whites took their leave, an Hawaiian stole a blacksmith's tongs and chisel, and dived overboard with them. Pareah, a chief, went ashore at once to recover them, and he returned, not only the two articles, but other stolen goods as well, which had not been missed. An officer of the expedition insisted, however, on taking a canoe as additional punishment for the theft, and to this Pareah objected. A scuffle ensued, and the hostility of the Hawaiians began to mount. The next night one of the *Discovery's* boats was stolen for the nails it contained, which the Hawaiians highly prized. Captain Cook thereupon resolved to make use of one of his favorite expedients, seizing the king and making him a hostage until reparation should be made. So he went ashore, accompanied by a band of marines, and demanded that the king return with him to the ship. Cook failed to appreciate the loyalty which the natives felt for their king, and a battle ensued. As the party retreated to its boats, Cook received his death blow from a club in the hands of one of the chiefs. The whole affair was a tragedy of misunderstanding.[1]

Small wonder, then, that there are many who insist that conflict is an *inevitable* consequence of the meeting of peoples. Says Donald Young: "Group antagonisms seem to be inevitable when two peoples in contact with each other may be distinguished by differentiating characteristics, either inborn or cultural, and are actual or potential competitors."[2] Bogardus, Park, and Brown, who posit a natural cycle of steps or stages in race relations, invariably include conflict as one of them. We saw in Chapter 4 that even before the dawn of history primitive bands were moving over the face of the earth, encountering strange peoples, and trespassing upon their lands. Archaeologists suspect that these prehistoric contacts resulted in wars and bloodshed, and in the destruction and displacement of one group by another. Historic evidence supports such guesses, and indicates that conflict of some sort is a common occurrence when unlike peoples meet. There are many today who regard as the very essence of the race problem the elimination, reduction, and control of these persistent tensions. Certain it is that conflicts, especially in such violent forms as riots and lynchings, are the phases of the race problem which make the headlines and force upon people's minds the subject of race relations.

Contact Without Conflict

There are reports, however, of unlike groups that dwell together in peace and harmony. Let us consider some of these, for they may offer a clue to the way

---

[1] For accounts of the discovery of the Hawaiian Islands, see A. Kippis, *Narrative of the Voyages round the World Performed by Captain James Cook*; A. Kitson, *Captain James Cook, the Circumnavigator*; S. D. Porteus, *Calabashes and Kings*.
[2] *American Minority Peoples*, p. 586.

conflict might be reduced or prevented. At the least, they will cast doubt upon the generalization that conflict is an inevitable and universal accompaniment of the contacts of racial and ethnic groups.

Tungus and Cossacks

On the western border of Manchuria two unlike groups live together, trade and associate with each other, and for generations have managed to avoid conflict. They have been visited by Miss Ethel John Lindgren, who has published a report on what is unquestionably a remarkable situation.[3] She declares that during her period of residence among these peoples (1) she never heard a Tungus or a Cossack indicate that he regarded the other group with hatred, contempt, or fear; and (2) she was unable to discover any tradition or record that the relations between the two groups had ever been other than amicable, although she searched for such evidence in the memories of the oldest living persons in both groups. The Tungus, she says, will criticize the Cossacks for their thieving habits but will commend them for their sobriety, while Cossacks will extol the scrupulous honesty of the Tungus while deploring their acts of violence committed while under the influence of drink. The Tungus, moreover, will frankly confess that they prefer to live in their tents in the forest rather than in the Cossack village with its stuffy homes which they consider injurious to health. In brief, here is no blind and sentimental love of neighbor, for each group prefers its own way of life and regards that of the other with a critical but realistic tolerance.

Racially and culturally the two groups are quite different. The Tungus have Mongoloid physical features, while the Cossacks are Caucasoid. Apparently, however, they attach no significance whatsoever to the color of their skins or the type of their hair, and it never occurs to either group that the Tungus ought to have some fellow-feeling for the Chinese simply because they share certain superficial physical characteristics with them.

Culturally the Tungus and the Cossacks are far apart. The Tungus are an illiterate, nomadic, primitive people, dwelling in tents, depending upon their domesticated reindeer and on hunting for their subsistence. Nominally they are Christians, and they used to pay an annual visit to a church for baptisms and weddings; but lately they have been cut off from priests and churches, and their Christian affiliations have been limited to hanging ikons in their tents and placing crosses on graves. Their ancient primitive religious beliefs are persistent, and their medicine men enjoy great prestige for their skill in curing disease, predicting the future, and communicating with the spirits.

The Cossacks are proud of their Russian background. In all probability they are the descendants of Russians who invaded and conquered Siberia early in the seventeenth century. Later some of them left Siberia for Manchuria, where

[3] "An Example of Culture Contact without Conflict," *American Anthropologist*, Vol. 40, No. 4, October–December 1938, pp. 605–621.

they founded agricultural settlements and where they were visited by Miss Lind-gren. Christianity has deeper roots in their culture than in that of the Tungus, and they zealously participate in the ceremonies of the church. At the same time they are not without their superstitions and folk beliefs. They are village-dwellers, and their homes are more substantial and impressive than the rude shelters of the Tungus. It is their practice on cold nights to close doors and windows and keep their stoves hot, much to the amusement and discomfort of the Tungus, whose practice it is to sleep in partly open tents, lightly covered, and let the fire go out. The Cossacks rely for their subsistence upon agriculture and stock-raising, though hunting squirrels and wapiti assumes some impor-tance in their economy, and they carry on an extensive trade with the Tungus.

The Cossacks speak Great Russian, and never bother to learn the Tungus lan-guage. On the other hand, the Tungus are bilingual, and all the men and most of the women understand Russian quite well. This would seem to give the Tungus a distinct advantage in their trade relations, for they can consult together in the markets in a language which no trader can understand. The Cossacks, however, have one asset which tends to compensate for their linguistic limitations. They alone can read, write, and reckon. The Tungus culture is sadly deficient in mathematical skills, and even the simplest problems of addition are too difficult for most of them. Thus the advantage in trade which the Cossacks gain through their literacy and their monopoly on arithmetic is partly counterbalanced by the superior linguistic talents of the Tungus. In this sphere of life, as in others, the inequality between the two groups is not so great that respect ceases to be mutual.

Miss Lindgren points out that contacts between these two are numerous and frequent, and there are ample opportunities for clashes. First, there are markets. During the winter months, when the Tungus are busy hunting squirrels, Cossack traders will travel up the frozen rivers on horse-drawn sledges in order to trade; and in summer the Tungus will come with their reindeer to the Cossack village for the same purpose, at which time they are often entertained in the homes of their trader friends. Second, there are chance encounters in the forests. Both Tungus and Cossacks enjoy hunting, and frequently their trails cross. Third, there are extended visits, for one reason or another. Young Tungus men will often remain for a time in the Cossack village after the close of the summer mar-kets. Then, some years ago, when an epidemic took their reindeer, the Tungus migrated to the Cossack settlements, and became hired laborers in homes and fields, until they had saved enough to purchase new herds. Clearly, the absence of conflict is not to be explained on grounds that the two groups are strangers to each other.

How, then, can we account for these halcyon relations? The cause cannot be found in the temperament of the peoples, for both have contacts of quite a different sort with other groups. Among the plausible reasons suggested by Miss Lindgren's report are the following:

1. The numbers of the two groups have always been small and about equal in size. Some 50 years ago the Tungus numbered about 850, and the Cossacks

approximately the same. At the time of Miss Lindgren's visit (1932) smallpox had reduced the Tungus to 160. The Cossacks with whom they traded numbered about 150 individuals, though there were other Russians in the region.

2. There has been no competition for land and resources. The Tungus nomadize over a territory of 7000 square miles, giving the very low population density of about .02 per square mile. Only the fringes of this large area have been invaded by Russians, Chinese, and others.

3. Outside influences have been of such a nature that they tended to draw Tungus and Cossacks together, rather than drive a wedge between them. About 1908 the Chinese government became interested in the frontiers as possible sources of tax revenues, but the Tungus proved too elusive. Later they imposed taxes upon the fur trade of the Cossacks, thus tapping both groups in one stroke. This oppression by people whom they regard as outsiders has served to strengthen the bonds between Tungus and Cossack.

4. In many respects the two cultures happened to be supplementary rather than antagonistic. Economically, the trade in furs has been highly profitable to the Cossacks, and has brought to the Tungus many new items they have learned to prize. Furthermore, the attitudes they held with regard to religion, marriage, land, and property could harmonize rather than clash; and neither group brought to the contact situation beliefs in his own racial superiority. Miss Lindgren thinks that the social organization which characterized the two peoples, emphasizing values of freedom, individualism, and equality, goes far toward explaining the absence of conflict.

Whether these conditions still prevail, or will continue, we cannot say. It is not inconceivable that certain developments, such as depletion of the game supply, population changes, or interference with the fur trade, might operate to destroy the amicable relations between the Tungus and the Cossacks, and to promote discord and strife.

Indians and Ladinos

Another instance of race relations without conflict has been reported by Dr. John Gillin.[4] The community he describes is the town of San Luis Jilotepeque, in eastern Guatemala. The population of more than three thousand is composed of *ladinos*, who make up about one-third of the total, and Indians of the Mayan stock, who make up the remainder. Dr. Gillin maintains that these two "racial" groups are quite different, are in close physical contact, practice a mutual tolerance of each other's mode of life, and are remarkably successful in avoiding overt conflict, even though there is a good deal of "contempt" on the part of the *ladinos* for the Indians.

[4] "Race Relations without Conflict: A Guatemalan Town," *American Journal of Sociology,* Vol. 53, No. 5, March 1948, pp. 337–343. Cf. R. Redfield, "Culture Contact without Conflict," *American Anthropologist,* Vol. 41, No. 3, July–September 1939, pp. 514–517. This article draws some interesting comparisons between the Guatemalan and the Tungus-Cossack situations.

Differences between the two groups are great, though not as great as those separating Tungus and Cossack. The *ladinos* are lighter in color, and some are blonds, but many of them are as dark as the Indians. Consequently, physical features are not reliable as symbols of status, and resort must be had to such items as dress and mannerisms. Indian women wear a picturesque costume consisting of a wrap-around skirt, embroidered blouse, bright beads, and head shawl. The men wear the typical peon costume of white shirt and short white trousers which stop slightly below the knee. Neither wears shoes, although the men, on dress occasions, when they adopt clothes of European design, may put on sandals. The dress of the *ladinos* follows European patterns, even including neckties, which Indians never wear.

The two groups show innumerable other cultural differences, so that it would not be incorrect to think of them as distinct ethnic groups. *Ladinos* speak only Spanish, while the Indians are bilingual. While both are nominally Catholic, religion is rather superficial for the *ladinos*, while for the Indians it is an important and integral part of their lives and includes many aboriginal features and ceremonies which have been grafted onto the Christian faith. Dr. Gillin shows that *ladinos* and Indians are different not only on the surface but even in deeper matters of beliefs and attitudes. Regarding such things as the value of money, the soil, work, family, and relatives, the two groups have distinct cultures. For example, the *ladino* measures prestige by money and wealth, and the things that money will buy; but in the Indian community one achieves prestige through wisdom, experience, and character, none of which can be bought. Even so, the *ladinos* constitute the upper class of the village. They own most of the land, hold most of the important political posts, occupy the desirable residential sites, and they demand and receive from the Indians the respect and courtesies due to their superior social position.

One would expect, under such an unjust and inequitable system, that there would be continual strife and bickering. However, just one act of violence is recorded, and even this came about only when a *ladino* politician plied the Indians with liquor and incited them to attack his *ladino* rival. The fact is that the Indians are not seething with resentment and do not feel that they suffer from exploitation and discrimination. Rorschach tests indicate that aggression is far less characteristic of the Indian than of the *ladino*.

Dr. Gillin's explanation of this surprising absence of conflict is that the Indians have developed a culture which adequately satisfies their drives, wants, and desires, and they do not therefore feel that the pressure from the *ladino* is onerous or unendurable. Their kinship system gives them a feeling of social security and of belonging. Their religion, though it may seem superstitious to the outsider, does serve to reduce their worries and anxieties. Their medical folklore, while it may not cure, does bring peace of mind to the sufferer. Work on the land they regard as honorable rather than degrading, as the *ladinos* do. Finally, the Indian enjoys a certain freedom. He may, if he feels oppressed, cease to be an Indian and become a *ladino* by abandoning the Indian customs, adopting the clothes and manners of the upper class, putting on shoes and a necktie, and, if necessary, moving to another village. Thus in many ways the lot of the Indian is more enviable than that of the *ladino*. Frustration and boredom are virtually unknown to him, while they are the major problems of the *ladino* community.

The Basques of Idaho

Coming nearer home, we have reports of intergroup contacts here in the United States from which the element of conflict is lacking. One such recent report concerns the Basques of Idaho.[5] The author of this report states that he is a native of Idaho, attended the schools and colleges there, and had many Basques as fellow students. Later, as a businessman he had many relations with these immigrants; and, finally, as an instructor in a college in Boise, he had several Basque students in his classes. He insists that from the earliest days of the Basque immigration there has been "an almost complete absence of prejudice and conflict."

The Basques are an ancient, proud, and independent people whose native land is in the Pyrenees region of Spain and France. Their origin is clouded in mystery, and their language unique. Some of them came to America in the 1860's and early 1870's, settling in the Nevada area. Others followed, migrating to Oregon and Idaho in the 1880's. There are no accurate statistics as to their number in the United States at the present time, though estimates are placed as high as 15,000. There are approximately 3000 in the state of Idaho.

When the Basque newcomers began to arrive in Idaho, says Edlefsen, they attracted little attention except for the fact that they used a language totally unintelligible to the other residents of the area. Sheep owners and ranchers gave them employment. This was their traditional occupation, and they readily proved their worth. Their industry and dependability immediately resulted in an economic welcome being extended to others of this strange group, and their numbers grew. Those who had been married before emigrating arranged for their families to come, while others married young Basque women who came to the area with relatives and friends.

The Basques, however, tended to segregate themselves by establishing their own communities. Edlefsen maintains that such segregation was not forced upon them, for the older American residents did not regard the Basques as inferior, nor did they persecute them or discriminate against them in any way. He thinks that their segregation resulted from their strong racial pride, their determination to preserve their traditions, the nature of the occupation in which most of them engaged, the fact that they were Catholics in a predominantly Protestant environment, and most important, their fierce pride in and stubborn retention of their language.

Even so, they began to mix more and more and to become assimilated. Some of them moved into other occupations. Many established themselves as inde-

[5] J. B. Edlefsen, "Enclavement among Southwest Idaho Basques," *Social Forces*, Vol. 29, No. 2, December 1950, pp. 155–158.

pendent sheepmen and earned the reputation as leaders in the industry. Most achieved economic security and high status in the area. The men began to learn English, and their children, attending the local schools, became rapidly Americanized. Then they began to move out of their segregated residential areas, and to purchase homes wherever they chose, for there was no opposition to their doing so. As a matter of fact, says Edlefsen, they were welcomed as equals. Soon they abandoned their separate church and affiliated with the other Catholic group in the community. Increasingly they became naturalized citizens. Second- and third-generation Basques are tending to marry non-Basques, and the author says there is little doubt that, in time, amalgamation and assimilation will be complete.

There are still other accounts of intergroup relations which have not magnified the element of conflict. There are Indian tribes which boast that their relations with the white man have never been other than friendly. Dr. Irving Goldman has described the coming of the whites to the country of the Alkatcho Carrier Indians of British Columbia and concludes, "There seems to have been not the slightest physical conflict."[6]

Patterns of Conflict

One who insists upon the inevitability of conflict when unlike groups enter into relations with one another will be critical of the cases we have reported. He will say, for instance, that the hostility between whites and Indians was nowhere more severe than in Guatemala, if we look back into the records to the early days of contact. The present peaceful arrangements, he will say, are simply an instance of accommodation which follows conflict. He may say, too, that the seeds of conflict are present, and the probability of their blooming is neither impossible nor remote. Miss Lindgren, as a matter of fact, suspects that the harmonious relations between Tungus and Cossacks are a delicate adjustment which may be upset if there should be a depletion of the natural resources, or if the population ratio should become distorted. In the case of the Basques, Edlefsen drops the hint that the notorious hostility of cattlemen and sheepmen might on occasion have been directed toward these newcomers.

The crux of the matter really lies in our definition of conflict. Many instances of race relations without conflict might be discovered if we choose to define conflict narrowly, so as to include only its violent, overt forms. But if we recognize the fact that conflict involves also those subtle, restrained forms of interaction wherein one seeks to reduce the status of one's opponent, and not to eliminate him entirely from the conflict, then perhaps it is true that conflict invariably occurs when unlike peoples meet. Reuter has defined conflict as "a mutually destructive relationship of individuals or groups. It involves a clash of interests or values and the effort of persons or groups to make one set prevail over another. The objective is defeat, subjection, or annihilation of the opposing

---

[6] "The Alkatcho Carrier of British Columbia," in R. Linton (Ed.), *Acculturation in Seven American Indian Tribes*, p. 372.

person or group."[7] According to Lasswell, "Social conflict results from the conscious pursuit of exclusive values. In the widest sense of the word conflict is conscious competition, and the competitors become self-conscious rivals, opponents or enemies."[8] In a broader sense, then, conflict includes, in addition to wars and riots, such peaceful activities as picketing, boycotting, ridicule, laughter, and "insolence." These patterns of conflict change from place to place and from time to time, and each has its own history. Some are ineffective and futile, while others succeed remarkably in achieving their objectives. They are not limited, of course, to race relations, but occur also in the conflicts between other groups — labor and management, nation and nation, class and class, sect and sect. Let us consider now some of the forms conflict between racial and ethnic groups has assumed.

Lynching

Lynching is a pattern of conflict which has undergone considerable change in the course of its history. It involves execution by a mob, without trial and regardless of the existence of regular courts of law, of an individual who is suspected, convicted, or accused of a violation of laws or mores. It is a form of violence which has been especially characteristic of the United States throughout the past hundred years. It tends to be most prevalent in the South, in rural and small town communities; the victim is usually a Negro, and the participants lower-class whites.

It has not always been so, however. The origin of lynch-law is clouded in mystery, but it is commonly believed to have originated with a certain Charles Lynch, a Virginia Quaker, whose religious scruples forbade his taking human life even during wartime. Charles Lynch was born near the present city of Lynchburg, Virginia, in 1736. Although his sympathies were with the colonists in the Revolution, he was unwilling himself to participate in the fighting. In his frontier community the Tories were active, especially in stealing horses for the British armies; and the officers of the law, and the courts of justice, were totally incapable of coping with the situation. Lynch and several of his compatriots therefore decided to take the matter into their own hands. They apprehended the thieves, held court in the Lynch home, brought witnesses and accusers face to face with the suspects, and meted out punishment to the guilty, usually to the tune of 40 lashes across the bare back; but they did not resort to execution. They came to be respected as loyal patriots, and in October, 1782, the Virginia Legislature passed an act completely exonerating Lynch and his associates.[9]

Following the Revolutionary War, the pattern of lynching spread over the country. Especially on the frontier did the custom take hold of using extra-legal

[7] E. B. Reuter, *Handbook of Sociology*, p. 98.

[8] H. D. Lasswell, "Conflict, Social," *Encyclopedia of the Social Sciences*, Vol. 4, pp. 194–196.

[9] F. Shay, *Judge Lynch: His First Hundred Years*, pp. 20–25.

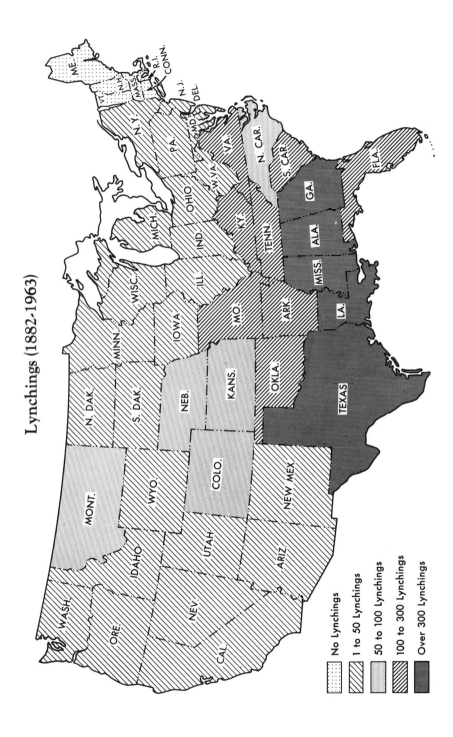

Lynchings (1882-1963)

No Lynchings
1 to 50 Lynchings
50 to 100 Lynchings
100 to 300 Lynchings
Over 300 Lynchings

procedures in dealing with horse thieves, wife-beaters, protectors of runaway slaves, gamblers, and murderers. Often there was a semblance of a trial, sometimes resulting in the acquittal of the accused. Punishment in the form of execution was far exceeded by fines, flogging, and tarring and feathering. Negroes were seldom the victims.

It was in the decades immediately preceding the Civil War that lynching began to acquire its modern character. White people in the cotton states grew desperately afraid of slave revolts, and resorted to lynch-law to suppress abolitionists, agitators, and rebellious Negroes. Finally, the period of the Civil War and the Reconstruction saw the pattern of lynching firmly established: courts of law, though in full operation, are circumvented; no effort is made to determine the guilt of the accused; punishment is invariably death, often accompanied by torture; and the victim is usually a Negro.

Statistics on the extent of lynching are not reliable. There is some difference of opinion as to just when a homicide should be classified as a lynching; and the laws of the various states are not in agreement. Minnesota, for example, defines it as the killing of a human being by the act or procurement of a mob, while in Kentucky and North Carolina the victim must first have been in the hands of the law. The *Chicago Tribune* made an annual summary between 1882 and 1917; and Tuskegee Institute has attempted to keep accurate statistics since 1889. From these data it appears that lynching has claimed more than 5000 victims since 1882.[10] What the number would be if we included the years prior to that date, and the victims of mobs in the Wild West, is anybody's guess.

Nine-tenths of the recorded lynchings have occurred in the Southern states, and four-fifths of the victims have been Negroes. Only the six New England states can boast of no lynchings. The victims, other than Negroes, have included Indians, Mexicans, Italians, Swiss, Japanese, Chinese, Jews, Bohemians, and Filipinos.[11] The crimes with which they have been charged are as varied as the racial groups victimized. Homicide leads as the crime for which most victims of lynching mobs have been accused, while rape takes second place. When we consider, however, the relative frequency of these two offenses, we find some basis for the general belief that there is a relationship between sex and lynching, and that violation of a white woman is a major incentive to mob action, as well as the commonest rationalization given by white people for lynching. While murder, rape, arson, and assault are the principal grounds for lynching, many others abound, including some most trivial. Among these are theft, insulting a white man, writing insulting letters, poisoning cattle, throwing stones, drunkenness, circulating radical literature, jumping a labor contract, organizing sharecroppers, asking a white woman in marriage, and refusing to give way to white persons.[12] These, of course, cannot be regarded as the *causes* of lynching; they

[10] Cf. Shay, *op. cit.*, pp. 7–8; F. W. Coker, "Lynching," in *Encyclopedia of the Social Sciences*, Vol. 9, pp. 639–643; G. B. Johnson, "Patterns of Race Conflict," in E. T. Thompson (Ed.), *Race Relations and the Race Problem*, pp. 142ff.
[11] J. E. Cutler, *Lynch-Law*, pp. 171–172; Young, *op. cit.*, pp. 252ff; Shay, *op. cit.*, pp. 153ff.
[12] Shay, *op. cit.*, pp. 79–81; Coker, *op. cit.*, p. 641; Johnson, *op. cit.*, pp. 144–145; G. Myrdal, *An American Dilemma*, Vol. 1, pp. 560ff.

are but the occasions, the excuses, or the incidents that arouse the mob. The causes lie much deeper, and would include the frontier heritage in American culture and the general attitude toward the law as well as various other complex social and economic factors.[13]

Lynching as a pattern of conflict between racial groups has definitely been declining. Since 1882, when something approaching reliable statistics has been available, there has been a sharp decline, though not a steady or a consistent one. In that year there were 114 deaths at the hands of mobs. The peak was reached in 1892, when 235 lynchings occurred. Lynching was especially prevalent during the 1890's, when there was an annual average of 154.1 executions. In the decade of the 1920's there were 315 lynchings, 33 in the 1940's, and 6 in the 1950's. One lynching was reported in 1961, but none in 1960 or 1962.

The credit for this decrease cannot be properly assigned. Many organizations of Southern whites have been active in condemning the practice, and many newspapers have taken a courageous stand against it. Some people who have faith in the efficacy of the law to change the mores point to the fact that since 1922, when the Dyer Anti-Lynching Bill was introduced into Congress, there has been a very sharp decline, even though the bill did not become law. Those who question the possibility of abolishing lynching by legislation point out that 20 states already have anti-lynching laws, while others have statutes which punish participation in mobs and riots generally.[14] Many Negroes feel that, even though a federal law would probably not insure the abolition of lynching, the agitation and discussion are themselves effective in turning public opinion against the practice.

There are those, on the other hand, who feel that the decrease in lynching is only apparent, that lynching has been "driven underground," and that certain substitutes have arisen to take its place, such as "quick justice," killing of accused persons by police officers, and murder by quiet, small groups, rather than by noisy mobs.[15] Perhaps the truth is that lynching as a form of conflict is simply giving way to other forms more in keeping with the times.

Race Riots

Unlike lynching, rioting is an ancient and universal form of conflict. Riots occurred in the Greek city-states, and throughout the Roman Empire they were a familiar phenomenon. They are a conspicuous feature in the history of all modern nations. A riot is an outbreak of temporary, spontaneous, violent mass disorder. Racial antagonisms are by no means the principal occasions for inciting riots; political, economic, religious, and other types of dissatisfaction have been far more important. Labor disputes, anti-clericalism, royalism, anarchism, socialism, strikes, unemployment, and poverty have produced infinitely more

[13] Myrdal, *op. cit.*, Vol. 1, pp. 563.
[14] C. S. Mangum, *The Legal Status of the Negro*, Ch. 9, and especially pp. 290–291.
[15] Myrdal, *op. cit.*, pp. 566, 1350.

riots than has race prejudice. The race riot, however, is a pattern of conflict which causes serious concern to the residents of all the biracial and multiracial areas in the world today.

A race riot is different from a lynching in that the action is two-way. A lynching is a one-sided form of conflict, in which the victim is hopelessly overpowered. A riot, on the other hand, sees the opposing forces more evenly matched; the minority fights back, inflicts damage upon the aggressors, and feels that it has some hope of defending itself. Whereas in this country lynching tends to be a Southern, rural type of conflict, the riot is an urban phenomenon, and tends somewhat to be more Northern than Southern. Riots are different, too, from insurrection, rebellion, and revolution, in that they involve no intention of overthrowing the existing political order, though they are often preliminary to social movements of greater scope.

A typical race riot is the one which occurred in South Africa in January, 1949, and which was described as follows:

> On January 13 hate and fear coalesced and exploded in Durban. Over the "bush telegraph" came a rumor that a young Negro had been attacked and injured by an Indian in Durban's downtown market. Some of the city's 100,000 Negroes, most of them Zulus, did not wait to verify the report (later proved untrue). Chanting Zulu war songs and hurling bricks and stones, they moved against the sections where about 120,000 Indians live and work. In four days, while the savage cry of *bulala!* (kill!) resounded through Durban, 83 Negroes, 53 Indians and one European died by violence.
>
> The riots grew out of an old complex of racial hates and abuses. The Union of South Africa's 2,300,000 white "Europeans" mortally fear and sternly repress the country's 7,750,000 Negroes, and the 280,000 expatriate Indians fare little better. The Indians, in turn, often exploit the helpless Negroes, creating a crisscross of enmities which have been intensified by the extremist racial policies of Dr. Daniel Francois Malan's new nationalist government. Fearing the whites, Durban's Zulus had struck blindly at the more vulnerable Indians.
>
> The Indians killed some Negroes; before the outbreak was crushed, even more were killed by white police and troops. . . .
>
> The Durban riots began in the heart of the city and then spread to the suburbs as police attacked the Zulus with clubs and whips. In an outlying Indian colony the frustrated rioters burned blocks of Indian homes, seven of the eleven occupants dying in one flaming house. Repeated volleys from machine guns, which killed many Negroes, finally ended the uprising. . . .
>
> Hunted Indians fled from Durban to a wooded valley near the city, looking only for a place to hide from the enraged mobs. The government posted guards around the area while troops and the police fought the pillagers in the city.
>
> In the week following the Durban riots there were racial flare-ups in other South African cities, but there was no indication that the government would modify its repressive measures against "non-Europeans."[16]

[16] *Life*, February 7, 1949, pp. 27–31. Copyright Time Inc. This story accompanies some vivid photographs of the riots. Other pictures illustrating the racial situation in South Africa can be seen in *Life*, March 10, 1947, and Sept. 17, 1950.

The riot has long been a feature of interracial conflict in the United States. In 1837 there was one in Boston in which the Irish were involved and in which 15,000 persons participated. The three decades prior to the Civil War witnessed many in Northern industrial centers, growing out of the competition between Negroes and various immigrant groups for jobs. Abolitionist riots were frequent also during the same period. At the time of World War I a wave of rioting swept through a number of cities. One of the worst was in 1917 in East St. Louis, Illinois, in which 39 Negroes and eight whites were killed and hundreds were estimated to have been more or less seriously injured, 70 having received treatment at one hospital alone. The year 1919 was an especially bitter period, prompting W. E. B. DuBois to say:

> That year there were race riots large and small in twenty-six American cities including thirty-eight killed in a Chicago riot of August; from twenty-five to fifty in Phillips County, Arkansas; and six killed in Washington. For a day, the city of Washington, in July, 1919, was actually in the hands of a black mob fighting against the aggression of the whites with hand grenades.[17]

There was a flare-up of rioting also during World War II. On February 27 and 28, 1942, a riot occurred in Detroit over the occupation of the Sojourner Truth Homes. a federal low-rent housing project designed for Negro defense workers. The Ku Klux Klan burned crosses the night before the tenants were to move in, and the following day the project was picketed by whites who lived nearby and a mob of 1000 sought to prevent moving vans from delivering furniture. Before the riot ended, 25 had been seriously injured and 110 Negroes arrested.[18] The next year there was another riot in Detroit, in which 34 were killed and more than 1000 wounded, the details of which have been given by two sociologists who made their observations on the scene.[19] Widely publicized also was the notorious "zoot-suit riot" in Los Angeles on June 7, 1943. Although local newspapers and authorities denied that this constituted a race riot, subsequent reports established the fact that the participants were white service men and civilians, on the one side, and Mexican and Negro youths on the other. Other serious riots of the 1942–1944 period occurred in New Orleans, Mobile, Beaumont, Newark, Seattle, and elsewhere.

Quite possibly other race riots would have occurred had not many cities taken steps to prevent them. Much has been learned about the techniques of locating danger spots in advance, of exposing the rumors which precede every riot and help to keep it going, and of handling rioting crowds.[20] There is little doubt

---

[17] *Dusk of Dawn*, p. 264.
[18] Photographs in *Life*, March 16, 1942, pp. 40–41.
[19] A. M. Lee and N. D. Humphrey, *Race Riot*.
[20] E. A. Gray, Jr., "Race Riots Can Be Prevented," *Harper's Magazine*, Vol. 191, No. 1147, December 1945, pp. 489–495; E. Brown, *Why Race Riots? Lessons from Detroit*; A. M. Lee, *Race Riots Aren't Necessary*; Winifred Raushenbush, *How to Prevent a Race Riot in Your Home Town*; R. Ottley, "A Barometer to Warn of Racial Tension," *The New York Times Magazine*, April 20, 1947, pp. 17ff.

that Superintendent Kelly, of the Washington police department, prevented a riot in his city in May, 1943, by his deft handling of a tense situation; and Mayor LaGuardia and Police Commissioner Valentine were able to quell a disturbance in Harlem on August 1 and 2, 1943, by applying the lessons learned from the mishandling of previous race riots. The danger, however, cannot be entirely removed other than by a determined attack upon the inequities of the social order.

Certainly all the ingredients for race riots were present in the United States in the 1960's, when Negroes began pressing their demands for full citizenship rights. Their impatience with the slow pace of integration had reached its limits, and their spokesmen were shouting, "We want it now." By means of demonstrations, sit-ins, and picket lines they proceeded to make their grievances known. They were often rebuffed with fire hoses, police dogs, mass arrests, and physical abuse. Much property was damaged and some blood was shed. However, the leaders of the Negro protest never forsook their commitment to non-violence, and so effective was their control over their followers that nowhere did the conflict take on the proportions of a full-fledged race riot. When, in August, 1963, the massive March on Washington began to take form, dire predictions were made. The Washington (D.C.) *Post* deplored the march, and warned of "catastrophic outbreaks of violence, bloodshed, and property damage." Despite the fears and warnings, however, some 160,000 Negroes and 40,000 whites assembled in the nation's capital, marched, and gave forceful expression to their demands, without explosion.[21]

Pogroms

This pattern of inter-group conflict has been especially associated with the Jews of Russia. Pogrom literally means *destruction*. The Jews, of course, have long been the victims of massacres, riots, and persecutions of all sorts; but pogroms are somewhat different. They often appear to have started spontaneously, but actually they are organized from above. Fearing revolutionary movements of peasants and workers, unscrupulous governments attempt to divert the grievances of the people from political and economic affairs and direct them against the Jews. The first pogrom occurred in 1881. The Czar Alexander II had been assassinated, and the bureaucracy and the landed aristocracy were afraid that the widespread discontent with the government might get out of hand. Although there were no Jews among the murderers of the Czar, the Jews were chosen as the scapegoat. Rumors were circulated, and people were even told that it was the imperial wish that on Easter the Jews be punished for their many faults. Peasants and city rabble, motivated by a desire for loot as much as by their prejudices, joined in the attack. The facts that these outbursts occurred simultaneously in many cities, and that the police and the military stood by until the third day, proved that the pogroms were organized and directed from above. Others were to

[21] For a report on the March on Washington, see M. P.. Brooks, "The March on Washington in Retrospect," *Journal of Human Relations*, 12 (First Quarter) 1964, pp. 73–88.

follow. After a few months of calm, the "summer pogroms" began, spreading to many cities which had been spared at Easter, and in March, 1882, they began again. After some years of peace, the Minister of the Interior, Von Plehve, organized an appalling number of pogroms, beginning with that of Kishinev in 1903. The Jews were attacked in more than 600 towns, villages, and cities. Thousands were killed, and the damage to property was tremendous. The Jews fled from Russia in droves, many of them coming to the United States, others going to South America, Africa, or Palestine, while penniless ones sought refuge in the various cities of Europe.[22]

Other Forms of Violence

There are many other patterns of violence which human conflict has assumed, among them wars, insurrections, rebellions, and revolutions. They are sufficiently different to warrant our having all of the words in our vocabulary, though distinctions between them are not easily made. *War* is defined nowadays as armed conflict between sovereign states, but the term is used metaphorically in many other connections, and in times past, conflict between any groups regarded as organic unities has been so designated. An *insurrection* is a movement involving the use of armed force against the established order; and such a movement, should it enlarge its scope, would be called a *rebellion* or a *revolution*.[23]

Whatever the differences, however, all these forms of conflict have characterized the relations between racial groups. The struggles which formerly prevailed between the whites and the Indians in the present United States are properly referred to as *wars*, for the Indian tribes were theoretically treated as though they were sovereign powers.[24] The so-called Sepoy Mutiny was in reality an *insurrection* on the part of Hindus and Mohammedans against British domination and British disregard for the mores of the native peoples. The uprising in Haiti under Toussaint L'Ouverture, whereby the Negroes succeeded in driving out their white masters, is properly designated a *revolution*, for it was directed toward a radical modification of the political and social order.[25]

Insurrections

Insurrections have been frequent in the history of the relations between racial groups. Contrary to the popular belief that the Negro stoically accepted his slave status, the truth is that he was continually taking up arms against his masters. There were numerous slave insurrections in Brazil,[26] and hardly an island in the

[22] J. Parkes, *The Jewish Problem in the Modern World*, pp. 63–66, 70, 74.

[23] F. L. Schumann, "Insurrection," *Encyclopedia of the Social Sciences*, Vol. 8, pp. 116–118.

[24] C. Wissler, *Indians of the United States*, passim, but especially pp. 65–69, 164–169, 203.

[25] See below, pp. 395–398.

[26] D. Pierson, *Negroes in Brazil*, p. 7.

Caribbean fails to show in its record at least one serious revolt of Negroes against slavery and the plantation system. In the United States the Negroes were continually plotting rebellion; and while these risings never seriously threatened the institution of slavery, they did put fear and trembling into the white population and some of them assumed considerable proportions.[27] Most notable were the insurrections led by Denmark Vesey and Nat Turner.

Denmark Vesey purchased his freedom in 1800. He established himself as a carpenter in Charleston, South Carolina, and for 20 years lived as a respectable "free Negro" and enjoyed a relatively comfortable existence. He was, however, a sensitive person, and he was unhappy over his own freedom and success while others of his race were in slavery. He therefore set about to plot a revolt. His plans were carefully laid, and his associates were chosen with utmost scrutiny. Over a period of years they collected their weapons — daggers, bayonets, and pike heads. The second Sunday in July, 1822, was set as the date for the revolt. The whites, however, were informed, and Vesey hastily moved the date ahead one month. His assistants, scattered as they were for miles around Charleston, did not all get the word, and the insurrection was readily quashed. Estimates of the number of Negroes involved in the plot ran as high as 9000. About 139 were arrested, 47 of whom were condemned. Four white men were imprisoned and fined for implication in the plot and for encouraging the Negroes.

Nat Turner was a slave who belonged to a Virginia planter, Joseph Travis. He was a mystical, superstitious person, who felt a divine call to free his people. The solar eclipse of February, 1831, convinced him that the time had come for him to deliver the Negroes from bondage. The date was to be the Fourth of July; but Turner became ill, and he postponed the date until he should see another divine sign. On August 13, 1831, it seemed to him that the sun turned "a peculiar greenish blue," and he therefore chose August 21 as the date for the revolt. He and his followers began by killing their master and his family, and then roamed the countryside destroying other whites. Within 24 hours a total of 60 whites had been killed. State and federal troops were called, and the Negroes were speedily overwhelmed. More than 100 slaves were killed in the encounter, and 13 slaves and three free Negroes were immediately hanged. Turner himself was captured two months later and was promptly executed.

Strikes and Boycotts

These weapons, long used the world over in labor disputes and by indignant consumers, have also been employed by ethnic groups in their conflicts with each other. Instances are continually reported in the press. For example, in April, 1949, students at the City College of New York went on strike against the administration for upholding two members of the faculty who had been accused of anti-Semitism and discrimination. Often white factory employees have gone

---

[27] J. H. Franklin, *From Slavery to Freedom*, pp. 66–67, 73, 79ff., 209–211; H. Aptheker, *Negro Slave Revolts in the United States, 1526–1860*; J. C. Carroll, *Slave Insurrections in the United States, 1800–1860*.

on strike in protest against the hiring or promotion of Negroes. The boycott, too, has occasionally been employed as a weapon in racial and ethnic conflict. In October, 1946, *Harper's Magazine* published an article by Kermit Roosevelt entitled "The Arabs Live There Too" in which the author outlined the Arabs' case against Zionism. Letters of protest were written to the editor, one of which follows:

> To the Editors:
> The Zionist organization in which I am proud to claim membership has passed a resolution to boycott your periodical.
>
> Esther Peltz,
Philadelphia, Penna.

American Negroes have often resorted to the boycott as a weapon in their struggle for job opportunities. During the depression of the 1930's large numbers rallied to the slogan, "Spend Your Money Where You Can Work," refusing to patronize merchants and institutions which refused to employ Negro labor. More recently they have used the boycott with great effect in Montgomery, Alabama. The incident began on December 1, 1955, when Mrs. Rosa Parks, a Negro seamstress employed by a downtown department store, refused to give up her seat when told to do so by the bus driver. At the time, there were 26 Negroes and 10 white persons seated in the 36-passenger bus. Bus drivers were, at that time, required by Alabama law to segregate passengers, but they could use their discretion in determining where the line should be drawn. When the driver asked Mrs. Parks and three other Negroes to give up their seats, a number of white persons were about to board. He declared later in court that he was trying to "equalize" seating facilities. Seeing that Mrs. Parks was adamant, the driver called a policeman who led her off the bus and escorted her to the police station. There she was booked on a charge of violating the city's segregation law. Subsequently the charge was changed to read a violation of state law, which gives the bus drivers the power to assign and reassign seating. The law makes it a misdemeanor for anyone to disobey the driver's orders. Mrs. Parks, when asked why she had refused to move to the rear of the bus, said, "It was a matter of dignity; I could not have faced myself and my people if I had moved." She was found guilty in the City Recorder's Court and fined $10. Her attorney filed notice of appeal.

In the meantime a movement on the part of the Montgomery Negroes to boycott the buses had begun. On the day of the trial three-quarters or more of the usual Negro riders stayed off the buses. The extent of the protest was noticeable, for the 50,000 Negroes who live in Montgomery constitute about 40 per cent of the city's population and made up nearly 75 per cent of the bus passengers. There was no widespread absenteeism from work that day; Negroes went to their jobs by taxis, wagons, or on foot over long distances.

That evening, after the court had rendered its judgment, a mass meeting was held in a local church. The 5000 persons, including 47 Negro ministers, who attended this meeting were urged not to ride the buses. A resolution was adopted to continue the boycott indefinitely; those present were urged to make their cars available in assisting others to get to work; the Montgomery Improvement Association was formed, and the Rev. Dr. Martin Luther King was elected chairman; and the three following proposals were addressed to the Montgomery City Lines as a basis for ending the boycott: (1) More courteous treatment of Negro passengers; (2) seating on a first-come, first-served basis, with Negroes continuing to sit from the rear of the bus and whites from the front; and (3) Negro bus drivers to be employed on predominantly Negro runs.

The following morning Negro patronage was estimated to have been down 90 per cent and subsequently it approached 100 per cent.

The boycott continued month after month. When the boycott moved into its second month the bus company declared that it was operating at considerable loss, curtailed its services, and petitioned for an increase in fares, which the City Commission granted. Negotiations were attempted, but were broken off when it became apparent that compromise was impossible.

On February 21, 1956, the grand jury returned eleven true bills, indicting 90 Negroes, including 24 ministers. The indictments were based on an Alabama law, enacted in 1921, which states, "Two or more persons who, without a just cause or legal excuse for so doing, enter into any combination, conspiracy, agreement, arrangement or understanding for the purpose of hindering, delaying or preventing any person, firm, corporation or association of persons from carrying on any lawful business, shall be guilty of a misdemeanor." On March 22, 1956, Dr. King was found guilty of leading an illegal boycott against the bus company. He was fined and sentenced to 386 days in jail, but notice of appeal suspended the sentence.

The boycott continued, and the case moved slowly through the courts. On November 13, 1956, the United States Supreme Court rendered its decision, declaring invalid the Alabama law and the city ordinance requiring segregation of races on interstate buses. The Supreme Court affirmed a ruling by a lower court which had held that the challenged statutes "violate the due process and equal protection clauses of the Fourteenth Amendment to the Constitution of the United States." Officials of several Southern states, where there are segregation statutes, indicated that they would continue, by some means or other, to enforce segregation on buses despite the court's decision. The Negroes of Montgomery, feeling their case had been won, voted to end the boycott on December 21, 1956.

Following the Montgomery affair Negroes in many cities and towns, in both the North and the South, have been encouraged to employ the boycott (sometimes referred to as "selective patronage"). The technique is not infallible. In many instances it has failed miserably, but frequently it has succeeded in winning major concessions from the dominant group.

White Citizens' Councils

White people in the South have also made use of the boycott in their efforts to prevent integration in the schools and similar encroachments upon the traditional pattern of race relations. Following the ruling of the United States Supreme Court in 1954 that segregated schools are unconstitutional, organizations calling themselves White Citizens' Councils began to be formed in Mississippi, whence they spread throughout the South. Their slogan is "Segregation or Economic Boycott." The National Association for the Advancement of Colored People has accused the movement of being a "dressed up Ku Klux Klan," but its leaders, many of whom are prominent citizens, insist that they do not believe in violence, and deny that there is any idea of reviving the methods of the old Klan. One who was instrumental in promoting the movement explained the plan of operation as follows:

> If I had a Negro working for me, and he belonged to the NAACP or some similar group, I'd do the same thing I'd do to any Negro working for me who wanted to cause trouble — I'd just let him go. . . . When the Negro tried to obtain work elsewhere in the region, he would find no jobs available. When he tried to borrow money, or even buy food in the stores, he would be met with a curt, "We don't have any money to lend," or "That item is not in stock." No law will be broken. There are volumes of court cases to back up every move that will be taken.

There can be no doubt that the economic sanctions employed by these Councils have had considerable effect. Negro teachers have lost their jobs, farmers have been boycotted by wholesalers, signers of desegregation petitions have had their names published in newspapers. Even white people who hold unorthodox racial views have been threatened, and white ministers who have been outspoken on racial matters have lost their pulpits.

White people of the South have not unanimously supported the Citizens' Councils. For example, the Montgomery *Advertiser*,[28] in an editorial entitled "Economic Lynch Law," declared:

> The manicured Kluxism of these White Citizens' Councils is rash, indecent and vicious . . . rash because the Negro himself holds a powerful and growing economic power of his own. The merchants, the bankers, the grocery stores and the auto dealers could find that they have grasped a two-edged sword that cuts wickedly in two directions. . . . What is proposed is indecent and vicious because we find a dominant group standing in the shadows threatening to confiscate the meat, drink, and shelter of dissenters.

Whatever may be the ultimate outcome of this economic tug-of-war, it is apparent that the boycott is not to be lightly dismissed but has become a weapon of considerable force in racial conflict.

Non-violence

The Rev. Dr. King, who served as leader of the Negroes of Montgomery in their contest with the bus company, is committed to the technique of non-vio-

[28] December 1, 1954.

lence. He is not the first in America, however, to espouse this weapon. Other individuals and organizations here in the United States operating in the area of race relations have long advocated and employed peaceful methods. To cite a few, there is the Congress of Racial Equality, which declares as its purpose, "to eliminate discrimination and segregation through methods of direct, non-violent action; to investigate the facts carefully before determining whether racial injustice exists in a given situation; to harbor no malice or hate toward any individual or group; to refuse to use violence in any form; to refuse to cooperate with racial injustice; and to seek a change in existing practices by direct action in picketing, boycotting, etc." Similarly the Fellowship of Reconciliation gives as its stated policy "to develop non-violent techniques for dispelling racial antagonisms and eliminating discrimination." Dr. King, however, has espoused and employed the technique of non-violence with astonishing success. He exhorts his followers, "Face violence if necessary, but refuse to return violence." He insists that they display no attitude and commit no act that would give offense to the whites. He concludes his mass meetings with the injunction, "Let us pray that God shall give us strength to remain non-violent though we may face death."

This method of non-violence, or non-cooperation, or passive resistance, as it is sometimes called, is especially associated with the name of Mohandas K. Gandhi, and Dr. King and others who proclaim it frankly acknowledge their indebtedness to him. It is, however, far older than Gandhi. Its origins go back to the ancient religions and philosophies of the East; it entered Europe as an aspect of Christianity; there is an element of it in stoicism; Tolstoy, Thoreau, and many others have espoused it in one form or another. Gandhi was certainly influenced by all of these. He was a keen student of the Bible and the Hindu scriptures; he read Thoreau's essay on *Civil Disobedience* when he was a young man, and he corresponded with Tolstoy.

By 1890 some 150,000 Indians had migrated to South Africa, most of whom had settled in Natal. The whites were strongly prejudiced against them, had imposed upon them numerous discriminations, and sought to prevent further immigration. In 1893 Gandhi was called to Pretoria on an important case. He was a young lawyer, having recently returned to India from three years of study in England. He was a person of some importance, and was accustomed to being treated with courtesy and respect. In South Africa, however, he suffered all the insults and indignities to which the members of his racial group were habitually subjected. He resented such treatment bitterly, and looked forward to the completion of his mission so that he might return to India.

When he was ready to leave, however, he learned that a bill was being proposed which would deprive the Indians in South Africa of the franchise. He resolved, accordingly, to remain there and to take up the cause of his unorganized, demoralized people. This meant the sacrifice of a lucrative law practice, which was bringing him at that time about $25,000–$30,000 a year. Nevertheless, Gandhi espoused a life of poverty, and for the next twenty years remained in South Africa fighting the battle for his fellow Indians.

He first used his legal talents to prove the illegality of the Exclusion Act. He founded a newspaper, organized the Indians, sought to promote education, taught the doctrine of non-resistance, and urged his followers to remove themselves from the society of the whites, to boycott all public services, to eschew violence altogether, and to return good for evil. Gandhi himself was the embodiment of this ideal. When the whites faced a crisis, Gandhi would come to their aid. During the Boer War he organized an Indian Red Cross; and when a plague broke out in 1904, he organized a hospital. For these services he was rewarded with medals and honors, which he subsequently returned in protest against the actions of the government. He met with some measure of success in relieving the oppression of the Indians in South Africa, and in 1914 he returned to India to champion the cause of his people against the British. His career there and his success in winning independence for his country are too well known to bear repeating.[29]

Gandhi's method of non-violence has had tremendous influence upon minorities throughout the world. If the Indians, without resort to arms, can prevail against the mighty British Empire, who is to say what other subordinate people may not hope to achieve? Many others have taken a lesson from Gandhi's techniques, eschewing violence, and relying upon peaceful methods to achieve their ends.

Art as a Weapon in Conflict

Conflict between racial groups is not limited to those violent and militant forms which we have been discussing, though they receive the greatest attention. There are subtle weapons which are no less effective than insurrections, riots, strikes, and boycotts to which oppressed peoples in their despair frequently resort. The fiction and autobiography of Richard Wright, for instance, doubtless deliver telling blows to the discriminatory system under which the Negro suffers. Other artists, too, have used their skills. Poets, painters, sculptors, actors, and musicians, too numerous even to list, have joined in the protest.[30] The American Negro, deprived of other weapons and appreciating the futility of armed conflict, began very early to employ the arts. Many of the famous spirituals gave voice to his defiance, and the last few decades have seen a great multiplication of protest art. This weapon, like all others, is more skillfully handled by some than by others. Consider the motion pictures in recent years which have had as their theme some phase of race relations — "Gentleman's Agreement," "The Outsider," "Lilies of the Field," "Raisin in the Sun," and "Sayonara," for instance. There are times when the artist goes so far in subordinating the artistic qualities of his work to his message that the sophisticated are repelled rather than attracted to it. Sinclair Lewis's novel *Kingsblood Royal* was a case in point. Consider, too, the wide variety of literary forms, devices, and styles which artists employ. James Weldon Johnson, Richard Wright, and James Baldwin may be in agreement on their basic purpose, but their literary products are quite dis-

[29] R. Rolland, *Mahatma Gandhi* (tr. by Catherine D. Groth); H. N. Brailsford, "Passive Resistance and Non-cooperation," *Encyclopedia of the Social Sciences*, Vol. 12, pp. 9–13.
[30] A summary appears in Franklin, *op. cit.*, Ch. 26.

similar. Langston Hughes and Paul Robeson both use art as a weapon of protest, but their techniques are worlds apart. None has been more effective in so using his artistic talents than Claude McKay, a Jamaica Negro who came to the United States in 1912, and who has given eloquent expression to his bitterness through fiction, autobiography and poetry, one example of which is his sonnet "If We Must Die":

> If we must die, let it not be like hogs
> Hunted and penned in an inglorious spot,
> While round us bark the mad and hungry dogs,
> Making their mock at our accursed lot.

> If we must die, Oh let us nobly die,
> So that our precious blood may not be shed
> In vain; then even the monsters we defy
> Shall be constrained to honor us though dead!

> Oh, kinsmen! we must meet the common foe!
> Though far outnumbered let us show us brave,
> And for their thousand blows deal one death-blow!
> What though before us lies the open grave?
> Like men we'll face the murderous cowardly pack,
> Pressed to the wall, dying, but fighting back![31]

This practice of using the fine arts as weapons of protest is not, of course, limited to the American Negro. Perhaps all oppressed peoples do so, as well as the dominant races who employ their arts in supporting the status quo. Even the preliterate peoples of the earth have sought, through their arts, to deliver a blow to those who dominated and exploited them. In a brilliant volume, *The Savage Hits Back*, Julius Lips has shown how primitive artists in all parts of the world, through wood carvings, paintings, masks, and other media, have ridiculed and denounced their foreign overlords. We have reproduced in the plate on the following page one of the objects of art with which the book is profusely illustrated, and quote Dr. Lips's interpretation of it:

The central figure is that of a Negro who has disdained giving his body the outward attributes of the white man, a Negro without hat or umbrella — things which he now knows to be ridiculous. His body is painted as it was painted thousands of years ago, his face is tattooed, his front teeth filed in native fashion. He stands ready to attack, with a weapon in his right hand. This weapon is not the white man's once adored rifle; it is the native's ancient lance, forged of iron melted in African furnaces, furnaces which had been in use long before the white man had fathomed the secret of metal alloys. On his body this savage wears

[31] From *Harlem Shadows* by Claude McKay, copyright, 1922, by Harcourt, Brace and Company, Inc. See S. A. Brown, A. P. Davis, and U. S. Lee (Eds.), *The Negro Caravan*, for many poems, novels, stories, and essays illustrating the literature of protest.

the container of the sacred magic medicine, and his lower limbs are clothed with an apron of native material. His left hand is holding the upper end of a European rifle, but it is not ready for firing. Its butt is resting on the black man's foot. Possibly it has been retained as a precaution in case the trusty ancient weapon fails, in case the spear does not suffice. It is a subordinate reserve arm, but it is no longer a firearm of magic power. And there, in European dress, stands a small figure between the black man's legs, a figure seeking protection.

Is it only a Negro dressed as a European, or is it actually the white man himself? And this creature who is seeking protection is small and insignificant; he is fleeing to the black warrior who seems to incarnate the ancient power of the dark continent, and to be calling to the attacking white world: "Halt! white man — whither bound?"[32]

Humor

A misconception has often prevailed that a sense of humor is more highly developed with some groups than with others, and that certain unfortunate ones are altogether devoid of it. The fact is, however, that humor is universally appreciated and is commonly used by racial and ethnic groups in their conflicts with one another. Those who have lived among a strange people long enough to appreciate the nuances of their language testify to the fact that all peoples have their humor and that they use it not merely for amusement but also to vent their hatreds. American Indians enjoy many laughs at the white man's expense, and anthropologists report that primitive people delight in mocking and ridiculing the customs of missionaries, traders, and colonial administrators.

Professor John H. Burma has analyzed the role of humor in race relations.[33] It is his thesis that in any conflict it is gratifying to make an opponent appear ludicrous to himself, but where that is not possible much satisfaction is still to be derived from making him ludicrous in one's own eyes. This is one of the functions of humor in conflict situations. Witness the innumerable jokes about Jews, Negroes, Italians, Irish, Chinese, Japanese, and Mexicans. An examination of Negro periodicals will reveal a plethora of jokes and cartoons, most of

[32] *The Savage Hits Back*, pp. 27–28.
[33] "Humor as a Technique in Race Conflict," *American Sociological Review*, Vol. 11, No. 6, December 1946, pp. 710–715. See also M. L. Barron, "A Content Analysis of Intergroup Humor," *American Sociological Review*, Vol. 15, No. 1, February 1950, pp. 88–94.

them, to be sure, having no relation to the racial struggle, though many of them bear witness to the fact that the Negro derives pleasure from seeing the white man get the worst of it. Dr. Burma observes that many jokes which are uproariously funny to a Negro would not appear humorous at all to a white person, the following being examples:

A Negro woman was asked by a white acquaintance, "Can you tell me where I can get a maid?"
The woman replied, with amazing aplomb, "I get mine at the Swedish agency. Have you tried there?"

The Negro cook was ready to go to work after the lady of the house had agreed on her terms for wages and hours. Then the "madam" said: "Sometimes my husband brings home unexpected guests for dinner. I would suggest that you always be prepared for such an emergency."
"Yes, ma'am," the cook nodded. "I'll keep my bags packed."

Two domestic employees were talking over their individual problems in connection with their work. Said one to the other: "The lady I work for says I should always warm the plates for our dinner guests. But that's too much work, so I just warm hers and she never knows the difference."

White people, on the other hand, have shown a fondness for stories which lampoon the ignorance and pomposity of Negro preachers, the Negro's fondness for chicken and watermelons, the hardness of his skull or the blackness of his skin, and the easy virtue of his women. Needless to say, these hold little or no humor for the Negro. But it comes as a surprise to whites when they learn that the Negro humor lampoons them. To the Negro a story is particularly humorous if it shows Jim Crow "backfiring," or if it holds up to ridicule the K.K.K., the D.A.R., the Eastlands, and the Talmadges. Share-cropping, the poll tax, segregated schools, Southern "crackers," and politicians are the butt of many a Negro joke. Dr. Burma demonstrates that "humor is one of the mechanisms rather frequently pressed into use in the racial conflicts of America."

Litigation

In many parts of the world, where racial groups smart under the domination of others, the privilege of fighting for justice in courts of law is not enjoyed by the minority. If they resent their status and wish to change it, or if they are simply driven to take out their resentment upon their oppressors, the only weapons at their disposal are the various forms of violence or the subtler methods of propitiation. It was formerly so in the United States. The Negro could not fight the institution of slavery by argument in the courts, nor could the Indian take out an injunction against the invasion of his territory or his removal to a reservation. All these disabilities, however, have been ostensibly removed in this country. The Fourteenth Amendment to the Constitution declares that "all persons born or naturalized in the United States . . . are citizens" and that they are entitled to the privileges of life, liberty, and property, and to the protection of the laws of the country.

In spite of this nominal equality, it has frequently been pointed out by students of race problems that Negroes, Japanese, Chinese, Mexicans, and European immigrants fall short of enjoying the ideal of American justice. One of the most flagrant violations was the treatment accorded American citizens of Japanese descent during World War II, when thousands of them were forcibly expelled from the Pacific Coast states, suffering great financial losses, and were herded into relocation centers. The only charge against them was the fact that they were of Japanese ancestry. Moreover, the wide prevalance of discriminatory laws, the biases of the police, miscarriages of justice, especially in the lower courts, and the devices for circumventing the law are well known.

Despite these shortcomings, however, it cannot be denied that minority groups in the United States have increasingly turned to litigation as a highly effective weapon in their struggle for equality. Consider, for example, the Negro's fight for educational opportunity. Repeatedly he has taken his case to the courts. In 1933 a Negro brought action against the University of North Carolina in an effort to gain admission to the school of pharmacy, but he lost his suit on a technicality. Two years later another succeeded in his attempt to enter the University of Maryland law school. In 1936 Lloyd Gaines attempted to enter the law school of the University of Missouri, and when his application was refused he took his case to the courts. He lost in the state courts, but the United States Supreme Court decreed that a state must provide equal education for all of its citizens *within the state*. This decision caused reverberations throughout the South. Maryland and West Virginia thereupon permitted Negroes to enter institutions which had theretofore been restricted to white students, while other states set about to provide graduate and professional education for Negroes.

On June 5, 1950, racial segregation in the United States received a deadly blow in three memorable decisions by the Supreme Court. On that day the Court: (1) outlawed the Jim Crow segregation of Negroes in railroad dining cars on interstate trips; (2) ordered the University of Texas to admit Herman Sweatt, Negro, to its law school, on the ground that the Negro law school that Texas had set up was not the equivalent of the school for whites; and (3) ordered the University of Oklahoma to stop segregating Negro graduate student G. W. McLaurin in its classrooms. In the Sweatt case the Court served notice that segregated law schools, however lavish their facilities, are inadequate; and it declared, in effect, that segregation and equality are incompatible:

> The law school to which Texas is willing to admit petitioner excludes from its student body members of the racial groups which number 85 per cent of the population of the State and include most of the lawyers, witnesses, jurors, judges and other officials with whom petitioner will inevitably be dealing when he becomes a member of the Texas Bar. With such a substantial and significant segment of society excluded we cannot conclude that the education offered petitioner is substantially equal to that which he would receive if admitted to the University of Texas Law School.

In the McLaurin decision the Court insists that Negro students, once they have been admitted to graduate schools, must be treated with complete equality. McLaurin had been admitted to classes with whites, but had at first been put in a little anteroom. Later, along with other Negroes at the University of Oklahoma, he had been simply seated in a different row from the whites. The Court declared that such practices impair the student's "ability to study, to engage in discussions, and exchange views with other students," and ordered that a Negro student "must receive the same treatment at the hands of the State as the students of other races."

Negroes continued to use the nation's courts in their fight for educational equality, with the result that on May 17, 1954 the United States Supreme Court ruled that "in the field of public education the doctrine of 'separate but equal' has no place. Separate educational facilities are inherently unequal." This ruling, however, has not brought an end to the matter, for an infinite number of obstacles have arisen in the implementation of the Court's decree. The important fact is that the courtroom has been chosen as the arena in which the contest will be waged and decided, and that argumentation is the principal weapon.

Similarly in their struggle for equality in other areas of life American Negroes have employed the weapon of litigation with increasing success. They have gone into the courtroom in order to win the right to play on municipal golf courses, to eat in restaurants, to travel on trains and buses, to sleep in hotels, to register and vote, to obtain employment, to use swimming pools, and even to be addressed as Mr., Mrs., or Miss.

Nor are Negroes the only minority group who use legal processes in their struggle for justice and equality. American Indians have been finding that the courts are more effective than guns and tomahawks in settling their grievances against the white man. Choctaws, Chickasaws, and Navajos have been eminently successful of late in securing their claims for millions of dollars from the American government, but most spectacular of all have been the Colorado Utes, who were awarded more than $31,000,000 for lands which they proved had been illegally taken from them. *Time* reported the case as follows in its issue of July 24, 1950:

> The Colorado Ute Indians (pop. 3,000) are not exactly hostile to the Government of the U.S.: they accept it as stolidly as Chicago accepted the Capone gang. But since 1868, when the U.S. designed a treaty guaranteeing them a 15 million acre reservation in western Colorado, they have put little faith in the Great White Father in Washington. They have reasons: after the Indians agreed to drop other claims in return for the land, the white man grabbed the reservation back and herded most of the tribesmen into an arid corner of Utah.
>
> The grabbing was a catch-as-catch-can business at first: gold seekers and homesteaders just moved in and made themselves at home. In 1880, after the angry Utes killed twelve whites, the Government officially took away all their land.
>
> The impounded reservation made a rich haul. Today it includes shale oil beds, vanadium and uranium deposits, 500,000 acres of coalfields, and a big chunk

of the Wilson Creek and Rangely oilfields. The Government promised to pay for all the Utes' land, but never got around to it. . . .

A Washington lawyer named Ernest Leroy Wilkinson took the Utes' case over in 1935, toiled at it for 15 years. Seven weeks ago he was finally able to go to Utah with big news: the day of reckoning was at hand.

The Indians postponed their annual spring Bear Dance for a day, poured across the reservation in battered cars, in wagons and on horseback to meet the attorney in a dilapidated school at Fort Duchesne. After they had filled the folding chairs, and squatted in impassive lines along the walls, Lawyer Wilkinson rose, took off his coat, and launched into recital of his triumphs.

Finally, he delivered his punch line: if the Utes agreed to the terms he had worked out, the U.S. court would award them between $31 and $32 million — bigger judgments than the court has ever awarded against the Government. He paused, faced his audience with a look of pardonable expectancy. Not an Indian flickered an eyelid. An interpreter repeated the statement. Dead silence still reigned.

After a few minutes, a long-haired Ute ancient named John Powinnee rose majestically, costumed in dark sunglasses, yellow shirt and dress pants. "We won't be able to decide until after the Bear Dance," he said. The audience shouted approvingly, "Hou! Hou!" Said another old man: "The land is worth more." . . . The Indians retired to a grove of cottonwood trees to powwow. It was not until sundown, three days later, that the rest of the tribesmen outvoted the old men.

Last week the court of claims awarded the Utes their record-breaking judgments — $31,700,000, or about $10,000 for every man, woman and child. Grunted a long-haired old Ute, still dissatisfied with the bargain, . . . "The Colorado land is richer than this money."[34]

The Ballot

Among the most powerful weapons in interracial conflict is the ballot. Leaders of minority groups recognize this fact, and bend every effort to win for their members the right to vote, and then to put it to use, once it has been won. At the same time, the dominant races appreciate the importance of keeping this weapon out of the hands of those whom they wish to control. In South Africa, where three million whites seek to maintain their superior status over twelve million colored people, the privilege of voting is zealously guarded.

In his study of colonialism,[35] Dr. Raymond Kennedy observes that one common feature of all the systems, be they British, French, Japanese, or any other, is the retention of political control by the possessing power, leaving the natives with little or no share in the government of their own land. The administration of colonies is directed from the mother country, all important positions being held by her representatives. Natives are often permitted to participate in ad-

[34] Courtesy of *Time*, copyright Time Inc. 1950.
[35] "Colonial Crisis and the Future," in R. Linton (Ed.), *The Science of Man in the World Crisis*, pp. 306–346.

African natives in Urundi go through voting procedures for the first time under the direction of a Belgian government representative

visory councils, and sometimes in legislatures, but the powers of such bodies are so circumscribed that decisions on all important matters remain with the home government or its agents. Whenever native leaders do try to organize their people for effective political action, they are denounced as radicals, imprisoned, or exiled.

In Guatemala, according to Dr. Gillin,[36] the *ladinos* have managed to retain control of the political machinery. For a time, local officials were appointed by the central government, and it was only *ladinos* who were chosen, not only for the higher offices, but for all paid political jobs as well. A new democratic government, however, has come into being, under which municipal officials are elected, and the Indians may vote. They have not taken full advantage of the opportunity, but candidates for office have learned to pay respect to the wishes of the Indians. This development has split the *ladinos* into two factions — conservatives, who deplore the gains made by the Indians and predict dire consequences should they get out of hand, and liberals, who believe in playing the political game with the Indians.

The political history of the United States is replete with the struggles of minority groups to use the ballot in advancing their cause. The Irish very early mastered the technique, while the Polish and Italian groups have met with considerable success, at least on the state and local levels. The epic struggle,

---

[36] *Op. cit.*, p. 339.

however, has been that of the Negro. Prior to the Civil War the Negro was disfranchised throughout the South, and most of the North as well.[37] The Fifteenth Amendment gave the ballot to the Negro, who set about immediately to make the best possible use of this new weapon. The whites were equally determined to curb its use; and by means of a variety of devices, such as the "grandfather clause,"[38] the poll tax, literacy and character tests, property requirements, and, above all, the white primary, succeeded in virtually disfranchising the Negro.

The Negro, in the meantime, has sought to regain the ballot. The Supreme Court declared the "grandfather clause" void in 1915; and that bulwark, the white primary, has been successfully assaulted and declared illegal after a great many test cases were taken to the courts. The poll tax was continually under fire for many years, until in 1964 the requisite number of states approved the Twenty-fourth Amendment to the Constitution, which states:

> The right of citizens of the United States to vote in any primary or other (federal) election . . . shall not be denied or abridged by the United States or any State by reason of failure to pay any poll tax or other tax.

Especially since the 1930's have the Negroes learned to make their political influence felt, and the major parties reveal in their platforms that they appreciate the strength of the Negro vote, especially in such crucial states as New York, Ohio, Michigan, Pennsylvania, and Illinois.

Direct Action

The Montgomery bus boycott convinced many Negroes of their power to effect social change. At the same time impatience with the slow processes of litigation and the ballot began to mount. Especially did the younger Negroes begin to resent the snail-like pace of desegregation and to long for active participation in the struggle. Accordingly, on February 1, 1960, in Greensboro, N. C., a group of Negro students took their seats at a lunch counter from which they had hitherto been barred, and they continued to sit quietly despite the fact that they were denied service. The affair received wide publicity in the press, and the sit-in movement spread rapidly to other communities throughout the country. Not only were lunch counters the objects of such demonstrations, but also churches, libraries, skating rinks, swimming pools, beaches, and parks, with the result that the public began to hear of kneel-ins, wade-ins, pray-ins, walk-ins, and lie-ins. The picketing of stores, city halls, construction projects, schools, churches, and offices of boards of education became daily occurrences.

In February, 1964, the members of CORE in San Francisco inaugurated a novel type of direct action which came to be known as the shop-in. The demonstrators would enter a supermarket, fill shopping carts with groceries, wheel them to the counter, have them checked, and then walk out, leaving the sacks and

[37] Mangum, *op. cit.*, pp. 371–372.
[38] See below, p. 190.

boxes piled in front of the clerks. The tactic aroused bitter resentment on the part of both Negroes and whites. The local Negro newspaper denounced it as "a malicious idea," and many Negroes declared that they would sever their connection with CORE if the practice continued.

It is difficult to evaluate the success of the direct-action technique. Daniel C. Thompson, who has studied the racial situation in New Orleans, says, "This strategy shocked the established leadership in New Orleans — both Negro and white. Individually, Negro leaders at first tended to criticize such methods of direct action and to underestimate their potential effectiveness. After the initial shock passed, most Negro organizations endorsed the strategy as appropriate in the Negro's struggle to break down Jim Crow laws."[39] At the same time, CORE, which initiates most of the action, is "condemned by all white organizations." Many whites, who had been sympathetic toward the Negroes' cause, or at least neutral, were made hostile. In a public opinion survey conducted in 1963,[40] in response to the question "If you were in the Negro's position, do you think you would be justified in lying down in front of trucks at construction sites to protest hiring discrimination?" 91 per cent of the whites replied, "No." Sixty-seven per cent disapproved sit-ins at lunch counters, and 74 per cent felt that Negroes were trying to move too fast in changing social patterns.

On the other hand, within two years after the Greensboro incident, sit-ins, or the threat to begin them, had brought about the desegregation of lunch counters in more than 100 Southern cities. They served to arouse many Negroes from their traditional apathy and passivity. And they dramatized for the whole nation the Negro's dissatisfaction with discrimination and segregation.[41]

Those sociologists who maintain that conflict is an inevitable and universal consequence of the meeting of unlike peoples certainly have abundant evidence to support their thesis, especially if they include those subtle and shadowy forms in which hostility often manifests itself. It is apparent, moreover, that the members of minority groups have sought in various ways to improve their lot and to subdue their oppressors. Some of the techniques which they have used have a long record of failure; yet even so they continue to be employed. Subordinate peoples have occasionally chosen their weapons with great care, and have recognized the importance of adopting the wisest possible strategy and the most promising techniques. Others, however, have struck out blindly, with little thought for the weapons they would use — if, indeed, they had any choice.

[39] *The Negro Leadership Class*, p. 116.
[40] *Newsweek*, October 21, 1963, pp. 44–57.
[41] On the strategies of the Negro revolution, see Thompson, *op. cit.*, Ch. 7; L. Killian and C. Grigg, *Racial Crisis in America*, pp. 18–26, 130–144; Jacqueline J. Clark, "Standard Operational Procedures in Tragic Situations," *Phylon*, (Fourth Quarter) 1961, pp. 318ff.

6

Steps, Stages, and Cycles

In no two instances have the inter-relations of different ethnic groups run exactly the same course.

R. T. LA PIERE
Sociology

R elations between racial and ethnic groups may seem to include an infinite variety of human experiences, to run the whole gamut of emotions, to involve all possible behavior patterns, and to be utterly unpredictable, capricious, and irrational. They seem to engender attitudes that range from curiosity and hospitality, at the one extreme, to the bitterest hostility at the other. They include friendly cooperation and serious conflict. They may be highly emotional today, and tomorrow may betray cool and calculating deliberation. The motives which bring peoples together range all the way from selfish to altruistic, and include love of freedom, desire for economic gain, religious devotion, and sheer adventure.

This is all very disturbing to a scientist, who looks for order, consistency, and uniformities so that he may better understand a problem. Is it possible, however, to reduce the phenomena of race relations to any kind of order, to discover consistent patterns, or to make valid generalizations?

Race Relations Cycles

Some sociologists profess to have found a pattern of race relations. They deny that each situation where unlike groups have come together is a law unto itself, but insist that there are recurring phenomena and that these have a natural, chronological relationship. They maintain that there is a succession of events or processes, a series of steps or stages, certain uniformities and similarities in all situations where the races have met. They have expressed their generalizations in the form of a "race relations cycle." We must bear in mind that the cycles these scholars have constructed are not the products of wild speculation, but were developed from observation and analysis of many concrete situations.

The Cycle of Robert E. Park

One of the greatest students of race relations was Professor Robert E. Park of the University of Chicago, who traveled widely and observed closely the behavior of various groups in their relationships with others. He reached the conclusion that "in the relations of races *there is a cycle of events which tends everywhere to repeat itself.*" First, he believed, groups come into *contact;* there invariably follows *competition;* eventually some kind of adjustment or *accommodation* is reached; and, finally, there is *assimilation* and *amalgamation.* Said Dr. Park:

> The race relations cycle which takes the form, to state it abstractly, of contact, competition, accommodation, and eventual assimilation, is apparently progressive and irreversible. Customs regulations, immigration restrictions, and racial barriers may slacken the tempo of the movement; may perhaps halt it altogether for a time; but cannot change its direction; cannot, at any rate, reverse it. . . . It does not follow that because the tendencies to the assimilation and eventual amalgamation of races exist, they should not be resisted and, if possible, altogether inhibited. . . . Rising tides of color and oriental exclusion laws are merely

incidental evidences of these diminishing distances. . . . In the Hawaiian Islands, where all the races of the Pacific meet and mingle . . . the native races are disappearing and new peoples are coming into existence. "Races and cultures die — it has always been so — but civilization lives on."[1]

Many a person who never heard of Dr. Park has reached similar conclusions. One frequently hears expressed the idea that, in the long run, the American Indians and the Jews will be completely absorbed and will disappear as distinct groups. Some even maintain that the Negroes will, centuries hence, become fused into the general population. "A thousand years from now," said one anonymous philosopher, "we will all be a shade darker, sing better, and be ten per cent more human." Under such simple, superficial predictions is the conviction that assimilation and amalgamation are inevitable results of the meeting of peoples.

The Cycle of E. S. Bogardus

Somewhat different is the cycle constructed by Professor Bogardus of the University of Southern California. He had in mind especially the relations of white Americans with the Chinese, Japanese, Filipino, and Mexican immigrants in California; and he believed that there were "sufficient recurrences in each case, as well as similarities in the behavior recurrences, to justify the label of a race-relations cycle."[2] The stages in this cycle are as follows:

1. *Curiosity.* First arrivals are invariably the objects of amazement and curiosity. Their strange habits and customs invite passing comments, and a certain sympathy is generated for the lone stranger far away from his home. The host group at first is not aroused or disturbed, and mechanisms and mores of defense do not make their appearance.

2. *Economic welcome.* Employers are quick to tap these new sources of labor, and either directly or indirectly encourage further immigration.

3. *Industrial and social antagonism.* Suddenly there arises a wave of opposition to the newcomers. At first there are sporadic outbursts of prejudice, followed by organized movements. Labor has usually taken the lead in protesting on grounds of unfair competition and the lowering of the American standard of living. Patriotic societies, protectors of the nation's traditions, offer their prompt cooperation to combat the alien threat. These two organized groups win the support of the native stock, whose fears can be easily aroused at the thought of the country's being overrun by foreigners. Neighborhoods resent the invasion of the conspicuous member of a strange radical or ethnic group, who seeks to find a better home by moving into a more desirable residential area.

4. *Legislative antagonism.* Opposition rises to the next level, when bills are introduced into state legislatures and into Congress that would restrict the

---

[1] R. E. Park, "Our Racial Frontier on the Pacific," *Survey Graphic*, Vol. 9, May 1926, p. 196. Reprinted in R. E. Park, *Race and Culture*, p. 150.

[2] E. S. Bogardus, "A Race-Relations Cycle," *American Journal of Sociology*, Vol. 35, No. 4, January 1930, p. 613.

movements of the immigrants. The newcomers are openly, publicly, and viciously denounced. Politicians make capital of these attacks against the foreigners, who cannot vote, and courageously campaign in the defense of the community, the state, and the nation.

5. *Fair-play tendencies.* Eventually, but invariably, a movement in behalf of tolerance and fair-play will develop. Certain citizens, either because of friendship for the immigrants or because they recognize the injustice of the attacks, will initiate a countermovement. Such movements are seriously handicapped, are not well organized, lack financial support, and are embarrassed by dreamers and zealots. However, they do serve to help the harassed immigrant retain his confidence in the American tradition, and preserve the nation's democratic reputation in the eyes of the rest of the world.

6. *Quiescence.* After the opposition has succeeded in obtaining the restrictive and prohibitive legislation which it desired, there is a slowing down of antagonistic activities. Those organizations which have been in the forefront of the attack, assuming that the danger has been removed, will modify their attitudes, will profess beliefs in tolerance and sympathy for the immigrants, and will espouse programs to secure justice for their erstwhile enemies.

7. *Second-generation difficulties.* Finally, problems of the second generation emerge, when the American-born children of the immigrants begin to react to their social situation. Their problems arise from the fact that they have lost touch with the culture of their parents, and are not entirely accepted by the Americans, with the result that they become a "lost generation," cultural hybrids, uncertain and insecure.

The Cycle of W. O. Brown

Even more cautious in the construction of a cycle has been Professor W. O. Brown of Boston University, who recognized the fact that "not all cases of race conflict fit the pattern," but who believes, nevertheless, that race relations do have a natural history, do pass through a series of stages, and do manifest a certain cycle of development. He proposes the following:[3]

1. *Initial contacts of a symbiotic, categoric sort.* At this stage there is some exchange of goods and services, a minimum of actual social contact, very little overt hostility, and some uncertainty, fear, and curiosity.

2. *Emergence of conflict.* Clashes at first are concerned, not with status, but with land, resources, and physical survival.

3. *Temporary accommodations.* Occasionally, but rarely, the conflict of the preceding stage will result in the destruction of the weaker group; but usually the two opposing groups will come to terms, the conquered accepting subordination or isolation in preference to destruction. If its numbers are small, it may even be absorbed into the dominant group, thus bringing the cycle to an end.

---

[3] W. O. Brown, "Culture Contact and Race Conflict," in E. B. Reuter (Ed.), *Race and Culture Contacts*, pp. 34–37.

In the event, however, that the weaker group continues to threaten the stronger, or the latter effectively resists fusion, the accommodations will be only temporary, and the fourth stage of the cycle will appear.

4. *Struggle for status.* The culture of the conquered group begins to disintegrate, for seldom can a social system live through conquest, domination, and forced isolation. The members of the subordinate group have no choice, therefore, but to try to penetrate the society of their masters, to adopt their culture, and to seek to satisfy their needs and interests in terms of the civilization of the dominant group. Such an invasion, of course, by a supposedly inferior people is resisted, with the result that there emerges a conflict for rights, for status, and for the privilege of participation in the social order.

5. *Mobilization.* As the struggle for status grows in intensity, each group mobilizes its forces. The dominant ones develop myths and ideologies to support the status quo, and formulate policies and programs to defend it. The subordinate race begins to manifest race consciousness and race pride, and supports movements and organizations calculated to win status and rights for the underprivileged. Race prejudice emerges and race becomes an obsession with both groups.

6. *Solution.* Theoretically, Brown thinks, there are three possible outcomes of racial conflict. Complete isolation of the races would be a perfect solution; but this is not practicable, for isolation menaces the interests of the stronger group and arouses the anger of the weaker. Subordination is another possibility; but this becomes increasingly difficult, for the diffusion of democratic ideals rouses subordinate peoples and makes them unwilling to "keep their places" meekly and peacefully. The third possible solution is assimilation and fusion. Brown thinks this last is "perhaps ultimately inevitable, but immediately improbable." Hence, he predicts that "race problems will continue to harass mankind and intrigue sociologists."

The Cycle of Clarence E. Glick

One of the more recent attempts to present race relations as a series of steps or stages is that of Professor Clarence E. Glick of the University of Hawaii.[4] He is aware that in each situation where unlike groups are brought together there are unique features, but feels that it is possible and useful to abstract from the many situations certain common and recurrent elements, and "to look at race relations as typically involving a sequence of phases."

1. *The precontact phase.* Prior to the expansion of Europe there existed in most parts of the world folk societies characterized by a slow rate of social change but a high degree of cultural integration and institutionalization.

2. *The contact and predomination phase.* This period is characterized by contacts between members of the indigenous folk society and persons, such as traders, from the invading "foreign" society. The native society often becomes

4 C. E. Glick, "Social Roles and Types in Race Relations," in A. W. Lind (Ed.), *Race Relations in World Perspective*, pp. 239ff.

severely disrupted, especially when the invaders attempt to establish domination over it. Normal modes of life and conduct are abandoned. New types of native leaders may arise, including persons who under the traditional system had no prospects of rising to positions of leadership, and who express more realistically than the hereditary leaders the feelings of resentment, hope, and despair which the members of their society share.

3. *The domination phase.* The conflict of the second period generally gives way sooner or later to some form of accommodation, wherein the invading group establishes itself as the dominant political power in the area. The native may become a peon or a landless squatter, working for his new master; or he may become an apathetic "ward" in a native reserve. Some of them accept the new power pattern and "cooperate" with the dominant group, and some become "professional natives," dancing and singing for the tourists. Assimilation proceeds apace. Missions or government agencies establish schools and health centers, and the cities attract natives as a source of labor. The values of the dominant group enjoy prestige, while those of the native group lose their appeal. Here we have the genuine beginnings of *race relations,* for the "educated native" appears, and feels his inferior status in the new society is determined by his race, not by his culture which he shares with the dominant group.

4. *The post-domination phase.* When the status system established during the domination phase begins to break down we come to the post-domination phase. In this period two types of challenges may be identified. (1) Nationalistic movements. Increasing numbers of natives seek to remove the members of the dominant group from their position in the top stratum of the hierarchy. A variety of organizations make their appearance, either actually or ostensibly set up for other objectives. If the dominant group permits these organizations to function openly, they provide the "native intellectual" with a niche for himself. (2) Integration. Under certain circumstances, especially where there has been extensive assimilation of the dominant culture by the natives, movements toward integration will appear. Those in the subordinate group will seek to solve the status dilemma by bringing the whole society to the point where it will eliminate race or color as the categorical basis for determining status. The phase will also see the establishment of interracial movements, drawing their support from both the dominant group and the minority, and affording members of the minority an opportunity to enjoy a status approximating equality with members of the dominant group who are participating in the movement. At the same time a cleavage appears in the dominant group, some still thinking in terms of a superior racial group and others thinking in interracial or non-racial terms.

The Cycle of Stanley Lieberson

The most recent cycle of race relations to be proposed is that of Professor Stanley Lieberson of the University of Wisconsin.[5] He recognizes the fact

[5] S. Lieberson, "A Societal Theory of Race and Ethnic Relations," *American Sociological Review,* Vol. 26, No. 6, December 1961, pp. 902–910.

that there are "wide variations between societies in the nature and processes of race and ethnic relations," and admits that a multiplicity of factors operate to produce these differences. He is critical of the cycles other sociologists have constructed. As for Park's, he insists that "neither conflict nor assimilation is an inevitable outcome of racial and ethnic contact," and regarding those of Bogardus and others, he says they were "narrowly confined to a rather specific set of groups or contact situations."

Lieberson maintains that the most crucial factor in determining the course of race relations is that of the relative power of the groups involved. When two populations, he says, begin to occupy the same habitat, but do not share a single economic-political-social order, each group endeavors to preserve that order with which it was familiar prior to the contact. Events will largely depend upon which group dominates, newcomers or indigenous people.

When a people migrating to a new territory is superior to the indigenous population in technology (especially weapons) and more tightly organized, warfare and conflict are likely to appear early, the local inhabitants suffer a numerical decline, their economic and political institutions are undermined, they may come slowly to participate in the institutions of the dominant group, racial consciousness and a sense of unity often arise, and, in some instances, they succeed in dispossessing their overlords. Africa offers numerous illustrations.

On the other hand, when the newcomers are subordinate and the indigenous people wield the power, the course of race relations is quite different. There is less conflict in the early stages of contact, and it is limited and sporadic when it does occur. Threats of demographic and institutional imbalance are reduced, for the host society is able to control the numbers and character of the migrants. Hostility is minimized, for the migrants usually fare better in their new home than they did in their old, and they have the option of returning if they wish to do so. The host society places great emphasis upon assimilation, pressure even is exerted, and the newcomers tend to become integrated with relative ease and rapidity. Even here, however, differences appear, as in Australia with her Italians and Germans, depending upon the conditions prevailing at the time of their entry.

Each Situation Unique

If it is true that the relations between racial and ethnic groups follow some universal and inevitable pattern, it would be well for us to know it; and the sociologist who discovers the cycle would indeed perform a useful service. We should then be able to predict the course of events, perhaps to control it, and certainly to mitigate some of the painful features of the process. At the present stage of our knowledge, however, it hardly seems possible even to sketch the bare outlines of such a race relations cycle. Dr. Bogardus makes no claim of universality for the cycle he has constructed; Dr. Brown confesses that his does not fit all situations; and Dr. Glick offers his cycle as merely a "heuristic device"

A variety of Brazilian types, gathered at a Salvador "snack bar"

for understanding various social roles and types. Dr. Park's theory is open to doubt, for assimilation and amalgamation may not be inevitable, and certainly there are instances of racial contact where conflict and competition have been conspicuously lacking. Some scholars, therefore, question the existence of any universal pattern, and incline rather to the belief that so numerous and so various are the components that enter into race relations that each situation is unique, and the making of generalizations is a hazardous procedure. As LaPiere has expressed it, *"In no two instances have the interrelations of different ethnic groups run exactly the same course."*[6] Let us look at some of the evidence upon which this statement is based.

Race Relations in Brazil

In many respects the components that went into the making of the racial situation in Brazil were similar to those present in the United States, but the resulting patterns have been quite different. Brazil, like our own nation, was colonized by a heterogeneous mass of Europeans. Early in the sixteenth century Portuguese adventurers, shipwrecked sailors, and deserters began to settle there. They were followed by undesirables banished from Portugal for religious or political reasons, or for crimes they had committed. Among the early settlers, also, were impoverished noblemen who hoped to recoup their fortunes in the

[6] R. T. LaPiere, *Sociology*, p. 429.

New World, and ambitious young men who, because of their physical fitness, were chosen to man the colonial garrisons. Orphan girls were sent over by the Crown to become the wives of the settlers. To complete the picture, there were prostitutes and clergymen, Jews and Jesuits, Gypsies and government officials, and a few hardy peasant families.

These white Europeans were met in Brazil by an Indian population. Bloody wars ensued, in which many of the Indians were killed, some were enslaved, and others were driven westward into the interior. Indian women were appropriated by the white men, first as concubines, later as legitimate wives; and eventually a large mixed-blood element arose. The trend has been toward the absorption of this *mestizo* population by the dominant white group.

At an early date the importation of Negro slaves from Africa began. Sugar came to be recognized as the principal crop, and the plantation system was eminently suited to its production; but inexpensive labor was needed, and neither the white Europeans nor the Indians proved equal to the demands. Accordingly the Negro slave, in Brazil as in North America, came as the answer to the problem, and millions of Negroes were imported before 1877, when slavery was abolished.

Brazil, then, like the United States, has been the meeting place of white, red, and black peoples. The adjustments of these groups to one another, however, have been quite different in the two countries. In the United States color prejudice has been very strong, discrimination and segregation have prevailed, and a system of color-caste has emerged. In Brazil, on the other hand, amalgamation has been the dominant policy and has become firmly fixed in the mores of the people. Pierson states, "To individuals from all classes of the population this eventual amalgamation and assimilation of diverse ethnic units is a matter

Agricultural education in Brazil includes 4-S Club work with coffee seedlings

of pride and self-commendation."[7] The racial problem, as the Brazilian sees it, is *not* one of "preserving racial purity," but rather one of overcoming the resistance which a group occasionally offers to absorption. Hence there has been some opposition to Japanese immigration, for fear that these newcomers might constitute a group difficult to assimilate. Furthermore, Brazil has not followed the practice of racial segregation. Pierson reported that in Bahia, which city was the basis of his study, families of whites, of mixed-bloods, and of relatively unmixed blacks dwell side by side. Nor is one excluded from professions, occupations, or social clubs on account of his racial features. This is not to say that Brazil offers to underprivileged groups a democratic utopia, for Pierson himself confesses that prejudice exists there, and he points out that the upper classes are predominantly light in color while the lower classes are black. He is supported in these observations by Brazilian sociologists, one of whom declares that "color prejudice and discrimination exist to some extent," but who presents evidence to prove that "public opinion is always on the side of the opponents of any kind of racial discrimination."[8] In these, and in many other details then, the course of intergroup relations has moved along quite different lines in Brazil and the United States.

Students of the Brazilian pattern of race relations have suggested the following factors as especially influential in shaping the events in that country:

1. In the early days of the colony relatively few European women came to Brazil, with the result that the Portuguese men took Indian woman as mates and wives. Both state and church gave approval to these unions. A century later, when women did begin to migrate from Europe, the process of race-mixing had become too firmly established to be readily checked.

2. The Portuguese themselves brought to Brazil a certain tolerance of color which facilitated interracial marriage. Pierson has the ingenious theory that Portugal, having been dominated by the Moors for 500 years, had come to regard dark skin as a symbol of prestige, and to consider it an honor and an improvement of status to have a mate darker than oneself.[9]

3. Portuguese folkways of sex and marriage have contributed to the continued amalgamation of the races. Among these customs is that of concubinage, or *mancebia*. This is a rather common type of union, the men often having a legal family at the same time, and the women involved are usually mulattoes, rarely blacks. Too, family ties are tenacious, transcending the loyalty one feels for church or state. Strong attachments hold parents to their offspring.

The future of race relations in Brazil cannot be predicted with complete assurance. The probability is that amalgamation and assimilation will proceed; the blacks will continue to be absorbed by the mixed-bloods, who, in turn, will continue to be absorbed by the predominantly European population. There are some indications, however, that Brazilians are growing more race-conscious.

[7] D. Pierson, *Negroes in Brazil*, p. 344.

[8] E. Willems, "Racial Attitudes in Brazil," *American Journal of Sociology*, Vol. 54, No. 5, March 1949, pp. 402–408.

[9] *Op. cit.*, pp. 116–117.

Closer contacts with other nations, where color prejudice holds high value, may conceivably affect the existing attitudes. Pierson reports[10] that large-scale European immigration of the past century, especially into the southern states of São Paulo, Santa Catharina, and Rio Grande do Sul, has had a modifying influence upon the racial opinions which formerly prevailed in those areas. He notes also that the rise of prejudice in the city of Rio de Janeiro was responsible for the organization in 1935 of "The Brazilian Movement against Race Prejudice"; and the fact that Negroes in São Paulo are becoming race-conscious and are resentful of discrimination is attested by the establishment of Negro literary and recreational clubs, women's organizations, and several Negro journals.

The Hawaiian Islands

Race relations on the Hawaiian Islands have followed a course quite different from that either in Brazil or in the United States. There are similarities in all three of these areas, to be sure, but the total Hawaiian configuration has been amazingly distinctive. A heterogeneous population of more than six hundred thousand makes its home on the 6449 square miles of these volcanic islands. A more variegated aggregation could not be found anywhere, for Hawaii includes among its citizens persons of American, British, Norwegian, German, Spanish, Puerto Rican, Portuguese, Negro, Chinese, Korean, Japanese, Filipino, Hindu, Danish, Micronesian, and Polynesian stocks, plus many other lesser groups, and an infinite variety of mixtures of all of these.

Bringing together peoples of such different racial and cultural backgrounds would seem to be an invitation to endless strife and hatred, but the remarkable fact is that Hawaii has gained a reputation as a "polyracial paradise." The islands have been referred to as "the world's most successful experiment in mixed breeding," and as a "melting pot, unmatched in today's world for inter-racial tolerance and affection." This reputation is certainly not without good foundation; but more discerning and objective writers have insisted that tensions do exist there, that upper-class whites often pay mere lip service to tolerance, and that beneath the calm surface one will find instances of inequality, prejudice, bitterness, and discrimination.[11]

Granted, however, that race relations in Hawaii have not been without blemish, there is no denying that the mores of equality have prevailed. Discrimination and segregation, as we know them on the mainland, have been conspicuously absent there. Titles of respect are given to persons of all races. There are no restricted sections in the theatres, and hotels and restaurants will not refuse service to anyone because of his color. If one visits the schools, one may perhaps find that the principal is a Negro or an American Indian. The police force

[10] Op. cit., pp. 342–343.

[11] W. C. Smith, "Minority Groups in Hawaii," The Annals of the American Academy of Political and Social Science, Vol. 223, September 1942, pp. 36–44. R. Adams, "The Unorthodox Race Doctrine of Hawaii," in E. B. Reuter (Ed.), Race and Culture Contacts, pp. 143ff; L. L. Lee, "A Brief Analysis of the Role and Status of the Negro in the Hawaiian Community," American Sociological Review, Vol. 13, No. 4, August 1948, pp. 437ff.

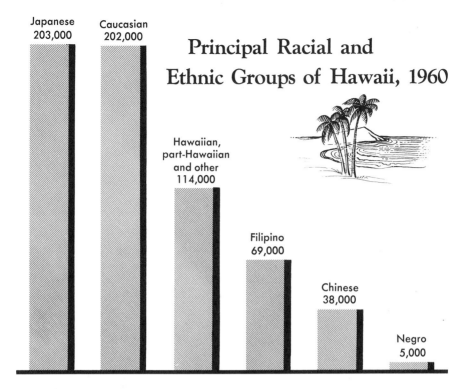

Principal Racial and
Ethnic Groups of Hawaii, 1960

Japanese
203,000

Caucasian
202,000

Hawaiian,
part-Hawaiian
and other
114,000

Filipino
69,000

Chinese
38,000

Negro
5,000

includes members of many racial stocks, and one may see a dark-skinned officer arrest a white offender. At social functions persons of all ethnic groups can be seen shaking hands and engaging in friendly conversation with one another. White men will be found working for employers of darker complexion, and taking orders from them, without feeling that such behavior is improper. A man's status depends more upon his ability and character than on his racial antecedents. Intermarriage is quite common, as it has been from the earliest days of contact, and persons of pure ethnic stock are becoming fewer and fewer. The prediction, based upon careful analysis of vital statistics, has been made that "by the end of the century, it may well be that a majority of the inhabitants will be persons of mixed blood, and Hawaiian blood will be found probably in the majority of these."[12] However one feels about all this apparent equality and tolerance, and about the racial intermixture, in Hawaii it is considered a breach of good manners to voice one's disapproval.

How did all these diverse peoples find their way to this tiny spot in the Pacific? To begin with, a thousand years ago primitive Polynesians paddled their canoes to the islands and settled there. Centuries later, in the middle of the 1500's, two Spanish ships were wrecked nearby, and those among the crew who survived took native wives, remained there, and left numerous progeny. It remained, however, for Captain James Cook to "discover" Hawaii on his third Pacific

[12] B. L. Hoormann, "Racial Complexion of Hawaii's Future Population," *Social Forces*, Vol. 27, No. 1, October 1948, p. 71.

voyage in 1778. Thenceforth close contact was maintained between the islands and the rest of the world. For a time Honolulu served as a way station in the international fur trade. Soon the sandalwood trade with China assumed commercial importance, until the islands were stripped of this natural resource. Then whalers began to use the islands as a supply station. Finally, when the whaling industry began to decline, the inhabitants turned more and more to agriculture. Sugar cane had long been known there. As early as 1802 a Chinese resident had found that the soil was eminently suited to cane production, and in 1835 American settlers had planted it extensively. But in the 1850's, the commercial possibilities of sugar loomed in the islanders' minds.

These economic activities of course brought in people from many lands. White people came from far and wide, many of them took native women for wives, and reared families. Missionaries arrived from New England in 1820. Negroes are known to have been there early in the nineteenth century,[13] as were representatives of many other races and nations.

The cultivation of cane, however, greatly stimulated immigration, for the planters soon faced the problem of a labor supply since the native Hawaiians were not disposed to perform the monotonous tasks demanded by the cane fields. Too, their numbers had been declining seriously following their contacts with the world. There were probably 300,000 of them at the time of Cook's discovery, but they were rapidly decimated by mumps, measles, and whooping cough, until they had dropped to the all-time low of 57,000 in 1872. The Hawaiians sought to rebuild their native stock by inducing Polynesians to come from other islands of the Pacific, and some few responded. The sugar planters, however, were more interested in cheap labor than they were in racial homogeneity, and they turned to Chinese coolies, large numbers of whom were imported as contract laborers. Toward the end of the nineteenth century the residents began to fear that Hawaii would become a Chinese colony, and a different source of labor was sought. Several thousand Portuguese were recruited, with other European peoples, but the demand could not be satisfied.

Then it was that attention was directed to Japan. A few Japanese had been brought in as early as 1868, but thousands were introduced in the years following 1885. The Japanese government shrewdly insisted that each shipment include a sufficient number of women. The fear then arose that Hawaii would become a Japanese community, and still other sources of labor were explored. Early in the twentieth century 5000 Puerto Ricans and approximately 7000 Koreans came to the islands. More Portuguese were induced to come, and eventually Filipinos were imported to work on the plantations.

How can we account for the fact that, with such diverse and numerous ethnic groups, and such keep competition for status, conflict has been kept to a minimum, tolerance and amity have been amazingly conspicuous, and assimilation has proceeded apace? The reputation the islands have won for interracial harmony and equality is richly deserved. What factors, then, have contributed to the development of such a situation?

[13] Lee, *op. cit.*, p. 422.

Without professing to know *all* the significant factors, we may say that certain characteristics of the native Hawaiians were decisive. Unlike the aborigines of Brazil and the United States, the native peoples of Hawaii were never enslaved, confined to reservations, driven into the interior, or reduced to subservient status. Instead, they maintained their position and actually set the pattern race relations would take.

The Hawaiians, at the time of their "discovery," were a simple preliterate people, carefree and tolerant. They had no knowledge of such an institution as slavery, had no feeling of inferiority, and were not averse to marrying outsiders. Although their culture was of a primitive, Stone Age type, they did possess the skills which enabled them to produce an abundance of vegetables, meat, fruit, timber, and salt — articles highly desired by the trading vessels plying the Pacific in the eighteenth and nineteenth centuries. Moreover, they were immediately attracted to the iron implements and weapons, the cotton goods, and various other articles the Americans and Europeans had to offer. Thus, trade was possible and quite acceptable to all parties concerned.

The Hawaiians, moreover, were not loosely and inadequately organized, as one might expect a primitive people to be, but throughout most of the contact period were united under strong and shrewd rulers. The white traders who came to the islands found it expedient to respect the authority of these chiefs, and to deal with them and their subjects as equals. These rulers, too, were able to secure the services of a number of white men, who took up their residence on the islands, and who brought to the Hawaiians the technical knowledge of the civilized world. These men were accorded positions of honor, were regarded as chiefs, married women of high rank, and set about to give the islands their mixed-blood population. Thus in Hawaii the hybrid from the beginning has enjoyed an enviable status, being descended from men and women of good position, of socially approved unions. It has been quite otherwise in other areas where the races have met, and where miscegenation occurs on the fringes of the population and among the least respectable members of the two groups.

This pattern of tolerance and respect, established early in the period of contact, was accepted by the later arrivals. Thus, when the New England missionaries appeared in 1820, they were doubtless shocked by many of the customs of the natives, and they certainly came with a desire to convert the benighted heathen to their own superior moral code. They were forced, however, to make compromises. Permission to settle on the islands had to be obtained from the king, and he was somewhat reluctant to grant it. Finally he referred the problem to one of his advisers, a white man who had lived in Hawaii 30 years, and who had a native wife and a family of half-breed children. His advice to the king was that they be allowed to remain, and the missionaries, accordingly, could hardly forget their indebtedness to him, however much they disapproved of his conduct. The arrival of these strait-laced New Englanders, with their own wives and children, might very well have introduced into the situation traditions of racial superiority and inferiority. Instead, the missionaries were impelled to accept the local mores of equality, to treat the natives as equals, and to show respect to those in authority. Somewhat later, when the white residents and transient sailors on the islands had grown numerous and strong, and were in a position to challenge the local authorities and to overturn the social system, it was the missionaries who came to the support of the natives and helped them to preserve order and to defend themselves against their would-be exploiters.[14]

No doubt there were many other factors which operated in the development of the unique pattern of race relations which we find in Hawaii today. W. C. Smith[15] believes that the multiplicity of ethnic groups has been an important influence, making it difficult for any group to single out another as a target for a long and concerted attack. He holds also that the large hybrid population, enjoying the prestige that it does in Hawaii, has played a significant role. Most important, however, was the character of the natives and the features of their culture at the time of the early contact, and the peculiar circumstances under which the first relations with the outside world occurred.

Race relations in Hawaii have many features in common with those in Brazil. In both regions we have a meeting of peoples widely different physically and culturally. There was the same mixing of blood and blending of cultures. There was a struggle for dominance, the efforts on the part of some to exploit the others, a show of resistance by the subordinate groups. In both areas we find evidences of the existence of prejudice, discrimination, inequities, and conflict.

At the same time it is apparent that the course of race relations has not been identical. Where the Indians were annihilated or driven into the interior, the Hawaiians held their own, in status if not in numbers. The plantation system was introduced very early into Brazil, but it was generations after the initial contacts before the plantation made its appearance in Hawaii. Slavery was quickly adopted by the Portuguese to solve their labor problem, and Negroes were forcibly transported to Brazil; but Hawaii never resorted to the institution of slavery to meet its demand for manpower. Certainly the story of race relations as it unfolds in Brazil is not duplicated in Hawaii.

The factors that entered into the two situations were quite unlike. For one thing, the Hawaiians presented to the whites upon their arrival a much more united front than did the Indians in Brazil. Too, the motives leading to the contact of the races were quite different. Brazil's Indians faced a heterogeneous group of adventurers who came to conquer and colonize, while the Hawaiians' first contacts were with sailors whose interest lay in trade and who were not bent upon dominating, exterminating, or dispossessing the natives of the islands. Of major importance, however, were the values and traditions the various racial and ethnic groups brought into the situation. The value the Portuguese attached to pigmentation, their familiarity with the institution of slavery, and their attitude toward concubinage were certainly important in shaping the events which were to follow in Brazil; and the value system of the native Hawaiians, as well as that of the whites, helps explain the course of race relations in the islands.

[14] An interesting account of the coming of the missionaries is given in Ruth E. McKee, *The Lord's Anointed: A Novel of Hawaii.*

[15] *Op. cit.*, p. 41.

Thus while some similarities between the two cases can be found, the differences make it clear that it is dangerous to generalize narrowly.

American Indians

To illustrate the thesis that "in no two instances have the interrelations of different ethnic groups run exactly the same course," we cannot do better than to consider the contacts between the white man and the various Indian tribes in our own country. Such a comparison has been made in a volume edited by Professor Ralph Linton[16] which describes the effects that the coming of the white man had upon the Puyallup, Shoshoni, Ute, Arapaho, Fox, Carrier, and San Ildefonso Indians. The story is quite different for each of these groups, as two extremes will illustrate.

The Puyallup

This tribe, for instance, was a loosely organized people living on Puget Sound, near the site of the present city of Tacoma. Fishing was the basis of their economy, but important also were hunting and the gathering of berries and other wild products. A high degree of specialization of labor had been developed in the pursuit of their various economic, religious, artistic, and military activities. They lived in large communal dwellings, but it was custom and necessity that dictated this practice rather than any strong group feeling. In fact, their society was highly competitive, characterized by intense jealousies and suspicions.

The whites descended upon the Puyallup in an avalanche. Prior to 1832 contacts had been few and indirect, and the influences of the white man upon the Puget Sound Indians were negligible. In that year, however, retired employees of the Hudson's Bay Company established a permanent settlement on Nisqually Bay at no great distance from the Puyallup, and whites began moving into the region, taking up land and engaging in agriculture. The discovery of gold in California in 1849 gave a tremendous impetus to the influx. Here was a ready market for building materials and food, and the homesteaders on Puget Sound set to work busily to meet that demand. The white population grew rapidly.

This was no country for white women, however. The bachelors who migrated thence, accordingly, took Indian wives. This arrangement proved quite satisfactory, for the Puyallup had long been accustomed to seeing their women marry outside the tribe, and the girls, in turn, were prepared to find that marriage called for a complete change in the way of life. They took readily, therefore, to the customs of their white husbands, and reared their half-breed children in much the same manner as other pioneer children were reared. Puyallup men, too, were not averse to doing manual labor for their white neighbors. They were good and skillful laborers, and quickly learned to use the tools and to perform the tasks demanded by their employers. The whites were extremely

[16] *Acculturation in Seven American Indian Tribes.*

careful to deal with the Indians justly, making no distinctions in the wages they paid for labor and the prices they charged for goods. The Puyallup continued to fish and to gather berries, and their new neighbors offered a ready and eager market for their products. Under such conditions, where the Indian and the white dealt with each other on a basis of equality, amalgamation and assimilation moved along rapidly, with a minimum of overt conflict.

Such was the situation prior to the 1860's. Says Linton:

> It would be hard to imagine better conditions for the acculturation of a native people than those which existed during the early part of Puyallup-white contact. The Indians were accepted on terms approaching social equality, with many legal intermarriages and the mutual recognition of relationship claims in both groups. Indians and whites worked side by side at the same tasks and for the same wages, and the only direct attempts to change the native culture were those connected with the abandonment of the communal houses and the introduction of Christianity. Even the latter seems to have been in the hands of intelligent and sympathetic missionaries. The individualistic patterns of the native culture made it easy for certain Indians to take on white habits without waiting for the rest of their group to assume them. The result of all this was the rapid assimilation of the Indians into the white population, and all distinctions would probably have disappeared if it had not been for certain later developments.[17]

Following the American Civil War, however, great numbers of white people flocked to the region. Between 1880 and 1886 the population of the state of Washington increased nearly 300 per cent. The cities around Puget Sound witnessed a mushroom growth. Tacoma flourished, and the Puyallup were right in the center of this development. Moreover, the newcomers did not share the attitudes toward the Indians which the pioneers had displayed. On the contrary, they were reluctant to intermarry with them and were disposed to discriminate sharply. The Indians became addicted to liquor, which they could now purchase easily, and which contributed greatly to their demoralization. The most significant change, however, was the sudden wealth which came to the Puyallup, as their lands skyrocketed in value and the white settlers and the railroad companies scrambled to purchase them.

The Indians were not prepared to cope with the wealth which had so unexpectedly fallen into their hands. Their scale of values became upset and distorted. They would see a fellow tribesman whom they had never respected suddenly acquire this new power, while a leader whom they had always revered was passed by in this new dispensation. In their earlier introduction to the white man's money, it was the able and industrious who succeeded in acquiring it, just as success had always been the lot of the deserving one in aboriginal times; but it was no longer so. Money was flowing freely and easily, and the undeserving were sharing equally in it. Disputes arose over the ownership of the land and the disposal of estates, and cases were taken to the courts. The age-old

---

[17] *Ibid.*, p. 37.

suspicions and jealousies were fanned into flame. Feuds and murders took a heavy toll. The Puyallup declined rapidly, and the small remnant left today will doubtless be absorbed into the white community eventually.

The Fox

A complete contrast is offered by the experiences of this group. Theirs has been one long struggle against absorption and domination by the whites, and against the adoption of the white man's culture. In these efforts they have met with a surprising degree of success.

The contacts of these Indians with Europeans date back to the early part of the seventeenth century. Father Allouez visited them in 1669, and found them using metal tools, testifying to their familiarity with the traders. At that time they were living near Green Bay, in what is now Wisconsin. Formerly they had inhabited southern Michigan, and subsequently they were to dwell in various places in the upper Mississippi Valley. These were village Indians, subsisting by hunting and cultivating their crops of corn, beans, squash, and pumpkins. They tapped the maple trees and made sugar, and gathered berries, nuts, and numerous other wild plants. Part of the year they lived in their permanent villages, and part they spent in roaming the country on long hunting expeditions.

War was one of the major interests in the life of a Fox man. The tribe had to fight, of course, to protect their hunting grounds against trespassers, and to acquire new territory as their numbers increased. They would fight, also, to avenge the death of one of their own group. More especially, though, they fought because they enjoyed warfare and because of the prestige it brought them. Older warriors would continually boast of their exploits, and martial success brought honor and respect. Fox boys could hardly restrain themselves until they were 15 or so, when they could join a war party.

The Fox were continually at war with other Indian tribes. During the historical period they numbered among their enemies, at one time or another, the Ojibwa, Sioux, Pawnee, Winnebago, Ottawa, Menominee, and many others. Hostility to the French also arose at an early date. Tradition attributes this antipathy to their dislike for the beards Frenchmen wore, but the truth probably is that some of their tribesmen were mistreated by the French in Montreal in 1671, and the Fox never forgave them for it. They were continually preying upon the French, frustrating all their plans, and disrupting their trade. The French, in fact, so despised the Fox that they determined to annihilate them, and made numerous efforts to do so. The British, to be sure, nurtured this hostility between the French and the Fox. They offered bribes to the Indians, and gave them a better price for their furs than the French were disposed to offer. In the Revolutionary War, the Fox took the side of the British, but subsequently came to terms with the new government of the United States.

Eventually, after many unwilling cessions of their lands and the signing of numerous treaties, they settled in what is now Iowa. They were determined to have as little as possible to do with the whites, but they were unable to isolate themselves. Settlers pushed into their territory and poached on their lands or took lead from their mines. Finally in 1842 they reluctantly ceded their Iowa lands to the whites and agreed to migrate to Kansas.

They loathed Kansas, however. The flat, treeless plains had no attractions for people who loved the green hills, woods, and water. Their kinsmen, the Sauk and Kickapoo tribes, had also been removed to Kansas, and they were no happier there than the Fox. These three groups, however, reacted to their new situation in different ways. The Kickapoo moved on to Mexico, where some of their descendants have remained to this day. The Sauk decided that the proper course for them was to adopt the ways of the white man, which they proceeded to do. The Fox, though, determined to return to Iowa and to continue their resistance to assimilation. Accordingly, they took a step without parallel in the history of Indian-white relations — *they purchased land from the whites.* They began by selling their ponies, which brought sufficient funds to enable them to buy 80 acres in central Iowa. They added to this, as other funds became available, until at the present time they own more than 3000 acres. There they have continued to live, shutting themselves off from their white neighbors as completely as possible, perpetuating their Indian culture insofar as they could.

Compromises, of course, have been inevitable. They have had to suppress their warlike traditions. Farming, formerly a repugnant idea to the men, has become the mainstay of their existence. They have learned to appreciate the white man's money. Some of them can speak English. They do not hesitate, moreover, to take over from the whites any items of culture which they feel will suit their purposes. Thus they have adopted automobiles, tractors, and other farm machinery. The men shave with razors, and the women have learned to can food, though they continue to preserve much of it by the ancient Indian methods. When they go to town they patronize the moving pictures and the pool rooms. They borrow from the banks when they need credit to run their farms. Insofar as possible, however, they have remained faithful to the Fox culture. Christianity has never succeeded in gaining a foothold among them. Their native language is used by all. Old ceremonies are still preserved. The ancient social organization still functions. At one time there was considerable infiltration of white blood, but this has virtually ceased. In short, the Fox have made certain necessary adjustments to the surrounding white community, but have been amazingly successful in their determination to resist amalgamation and assimilation.

The Gay Heads

Take one more case, the Indians of Martha's Vineyard, Massachusetts, as reported in the following news item:

> For an idea of the type of Indians who were neighbors of the first New England settlers, the best place to hunt for full-blooded survivors is at Gay Head, at the western end of Martha's Vineyard Island, off the southern coast of Massachusetts. Dr. Henry B. Collins, Smithsonian Institution ethnologist, found in this remnant

of the old Wampanoag tribe individuals with features more characteristic of the general American Indian type than of the traditional picture of the Algonquian stock, to which most of the natives of the Northeast belonged. Other Indians in the East today have been so mixed with other stock that they no longer "look like Indians."

The Gay Head Indians have been able to hold their own, Dr. Collins states, largely because of the square deal they got from one white man nearly 300 years ago. A severely righteous Puritan, one Thomas Mayhew, leased the whole island of Martha's Vineyard from the Earl of Stirling, to whom it had been granted by the crown.

He left the 3,000 Indians on the island in possession of all their rights, including the rich fishing waters adjacent, and he paid them fairly for all the produce they sold him. As a result, they remained loyal to him during King Philip's War in 1675–1676, which was terribly costly to the white settlements on the mainland and in the end disastrous to the Indians.

Relics of their original culture are now hard to find, Dr. Collins states, due partly at least to Thomas Mayhew's efforts to convert the tribe to the white man's religion and culture. . . . The present group at Gay Head is beginning to revive some of the old handicrafts.[18]

Reasons for the Differences

How may we account for the fact that the various Indian tribes, in their relations with the whites, have not followed any common pattern, nor gone through a similar process of steps and stages, but instead have displayed a wide variety of reactions and experiences? No doubt there are innumerable factors responsible for these differences, but the following have certainly been instrumental:

1. *The initial contacts.* Some tribes came suddenly to feel the full impact of European culture, while others had the good fortune to learn about it gradually. Those who inhabited the Atlantic coastal regions, for instance, were almost overnight confronted by a host of strange peoples and even stranger gadgets and customs, while those who lived farther inland, such as the Cherokees, were spared this traumatic experience. The former were overwhelmed by the multiplicity of new ideas, habits, and material objects, to say nothing of devastating diseases, while the latter were able to become acquainted with a few at a time, to ponder them, to accept or reject, and to integrate into their own culture those they chose to adopt. Moreover, the initial contacts were in some instances honest, equitable, and friendly, and a pattern of harmonious relationships was established; while in other instances the first knowledge the Indians had of the whites was acquired through dealings with dishonest, brutal, and unscrupulous individuals, leading inevitably to the formation of hostile and prejudicial attitudes.

2. *Tribal solidarity.* Some Indian tribes were closely knit, politically united, and possessed a strong sense of solidarity. The Indians of the Southwestern Pueblos, for instance, maintain themselves as "closed groups," admitting few aliens and censuring their own members who do not strictly conform. Various

[18] *The New York Times,* October 19, 1947.

mechanisms are used to preserve the exclusive character of the society. Rituals are employed for initiating members into the in-group; cleansing ceremonies are performed to re-introduce members to the group after an absence; there are secret activities for members only; and knowledge of the group's customs and values, and participation therein, are shielded from aliens. Tribes in which these conditions prevailed were in a better position to withstand the encroachments of white people and their culture. On the other hand there were tribes which were loosely organized, with only tenuous systems of leadership and authority. Strangers were not infrequently "adopted" into the tribe, and there were few secrets from which outsiders were guarded. The Puyallup, for instance, were highly individualistic, and felt no need to wait for others in the group to join in the adoption of the white man's folkways.

3. *Natural resources.* The effect of the coming of the whites upon the natural resources which the Indians relied on differed from tribe to tribe. Often the result was complete destruction of the economic base of tribal life, as by the depletion of buffalo herds; or the Indians were forcibly removed to a new and strange environment. In either case, established ways of life were radically altered and difficult new adjustments had to be made. Other tribes, for one reason or another, were not subjected to so painful an ordeal. The Indians of San Ildefonso, for example, suffered no important changes in their natural environment through the arrival of the whites. True, there was some destruction of the game, but agriculture, rather than hunting, was the foundation of their economic life, and this was not disturbed by either the Spaniards or the Americans.

4. *Values.* Each tribe had its own hierarchy of values, and these conflicted sharply with the values of the whites in some instances, whereas in other situations the two systems were complementary or at least compatible. Thus those who made warfare a virtue and regarded martial glory as the only avenue to the achievement of status inevitably found themselves at odds with the whites, who were bent upon the establishment of peace and order. Those who cherished a nomadic life, too, could not avoid conflict with the sedentary whites. Not all Indians, however, were nomadic, and many of them regarded war as a nuisance or a calamity. Some tribes placed highest value upon religion, or the acquisition of wealth, or the performance of ceremonies, and these values could be carried over easily into a world dominated by the whites.

5. *Attitudes of the whites.* The attitudes of the white people who came into contact with the Indians were of crucial importance in determining the course of race relations. There were traders, who had no desire to see the Indian way of life radically changed, but who had, instead, a vested interest in the perpetuation of the prevailing culture. Others came as permanent settlers, determined to take or to purchase the land. Missionaries, of course, were primarily concerned with changing the Indian; but some of these were tolerant, sympathetic, and patient, while others had no appreciation for the Indians' virtues and sought to produce a complete and immediate change. Then there were those whites who approached the Indians with preconceived ideas of racial superiority and aloofness, while others were devoid of such attitudes.

6. *Marriage and sex mores.* The various Indian tribes, as well as the whites, differed widely with respect to their mores on sex and marriage. Some were strictly endogamous, while others had traditions of tribal exogamy. Some placed high value upon chastity, and others did not. The Fox and the Puyallup illustrate the two extremes. It can be readily seen that under one system of sex mores assimilation and amalgamation would be accelerated, while under another system they would be prevented or retarded.

These are not the only variables, of course, which served to make the course of race relations different from one tribe to another. We cannot overlook the role played by certain outstanding individuals, some of whom were hospitable to the white man while others were adamant in their resistance. Important, also, was the fact that certain tribes were strongly ethnocentric, glorifying their own history and customs, while others had slight regard for their simple culture and readily acknowledged the superiority of the whites. Tribes differed, too, in their power structures. There were those, for instance, who bestowed great respect and authority upon the aged, the very ones who would be most inclined to manifest fear and suspicion of the new and unfamiliar ways of the invaders.

Uniformities

Even though the course of race relations is not identical in any two situations, we must not conclude that there are no similarities. As a matter of fact, certain phenomena are virtually universal in those areas where racial and ethnic groups have come together. Conflict, though perhaps not inevitable, is certainly a well-nigh universal accompaniment of the meeting of diverse peoples. Biological mixture is another, for there seems to be no exception to the rule that, when peoples come into contact, a mixture of blood results. The give and take of elements of culture is still another consequence, though wide differences occur in the rate of such exchange and the length to which it goes. The domination of one group over the other usually follows when peoples meet, and those in the subordinate group react in certain familiar ways. In the succeeding chapters we consider these widespread, if not universal and inevitable, phenomena.

7

Annihilation
and
Expulsion

Scientists studying the culture of Australian aborigines believe that the native population of the commonwealth
is fast disappearing.

THE NEW YORK TIMES
May 7, 1950

Among the several ways in which a conflict between races may be resolved is for one group to exterminate the other, and that has been the fate of less fortunate groups. Annihilation, to be sure, is not always, or even usually, a consequence of the meeting of peoples. Contact with strangers has often had a stimulating effect upon a society, both numerically and culturally. One student of the problem has reached the conclusion that, except in those cases where native peoples are destroyed by the initial and early contacts, "the population growth of native peoples is an inevitable resultant of European cultural incursion." He cites, in support of his thesis, the population statistics from Japan, India, China, Ceylon, Java, Egypt, Formosa, Algeria, and the Philippines.[1] Here in the United States the Navajo Indians are a notable case. Today they number more than 80,000, whereas they were but a small and insignificant band at the time of the white man's arrival in this hemisphere.

Hoormann has looked into this phenomenon, and has come up with the theory that societies which experience downward trends after contact with the white man are those which are based upon a subsistent, self-sufficient, non-trading type of economy, such as food gatherers and shifting agriculturalists. Those which experience upward trends, on the other hand, are the so-called peasant peoples.[2] He believes, moreover, these differences arise, not from any "racial" susceptibility or immunity to disease, nor some innate breeding propensity, nor exploitation and abuse, nor to ill-advised programs for natives such as insistence upon wearing clothes, but rather from the precontact situation of the groups involved, the way of life and the demographic equilibrium attained before contact. For example, isolated folk peoples have few or no endemic diseases, for the reason that the organisms causing such diseases need large human populations in order to remain viable. It is otherwise with the larger, relatively dense populations of the peasant societies, where disease-inducing organisms remain virulent by virtue of the fact that they can keep moving; that is, they are endemic, and periodically become epidemic. Moreover, isolated folk peoples "see" their population problem as one of keeping their numbers within those absolute numerical limits which their experience tells them will mean extinction or survival for the group, while peasants see their problem as one of increasing or guaranteeing the food supply available to them. The former seek to control population; the latter, food supply. Hoormann investigates still other aspects of folk and peasant societies which might account for the fact that the former usually decline and disappear under the impact of Europeans, while the latter seem to thrive. The extinction of native peoples following contact with European civilization is a phenomenon which has been widely noted and discussed, but Hoormann insists that the phenomenon is "not quite as universal as is frequently assumed."

Nevertheless, the number of societies which have disappeared altogether remains a tragic fact. Many tribes of American Indians became extinct soon

[1] E. N. Palmer, "Culture Contacts and Population Growth," *American Journal of Sociology*, Vol. 53, No. 4, January 1948, pp. 258–262.
[2] B. L. Hoormann, "Rigidity and Fluidity in Race Relations," in A. W. Lind (Ed.), *Race Relations in World Perspective*, pp. 25ff.

after the arrival of the Europeans, often within a few years. Such was the fate of the Missouri.[3] They were a proud and numerous people when they first came to the attention of the whites in 1673. Within a century smallpox had reduced them to a helpless little band, and forced them to seek the protection of their kinsmen, the Otoes, farther west. In 1907, the last full-blooded Missouri died in Oklahoma. Today the Indian has virtually disappeared from the eastern United States, eastern Brazil, Uruguay, most of Argentina, and the West Indies. Tribes once numerous and flourishing have left no trace of their former presence, other than a name for some river, lake, state, or mountain. Contact with the white man has brought a similar fate to societies in other regions, as the following item indicates:

> Scientists studying the culture of Australian aborigines believe that the native population of the commonwealth is fast disappearing.
> When the white settlement of Australia began in 1788, the native population was estimated at 300,000. Now it is 60,000 or lower, an Adelaide correspondent of *The Manchester Guardian* says.
> The race already is extinct in the states of Victoria and Tasmania, and forces at work in the other states may have profound effect on the surviving aborigines there.
> Contact with the white race has doomed the black wherever it has taken place, it is pointed out. Under the impact, the highly complex social life of the aborigines has disintegrated. The prospect of easily-won food at centers of white settlement has undermined the skill and morale of the Australian semi-civilized black man, for he has been accustomed to obtaining his sustenance under conditions in which the white man could not have survived.
> Every advance of the railway, the automobile highway and the airplane route into the center of the continent speeds the extinction of the native race. Many observers believe that even the British Commonwealth long-range weapons establishment, with its chain of observation stations across the western part of the continent, will hasten the detribalization, degeneration, and disappearance of the aborigines.
> In view of this condition, scientists are speeding the work of collecting firsthand data about the aborigines. The University of Adelaide, in conjunction with the South Australian Museum, has sent several expeditions of doctors, anthropologists, photographers, and linguists to isolated places in the center of Australia. There, with the help of missionaries, the scientists have made contact with hundreds of "uncontaminated" natives and placed observations on record.[4]

Disease and Vice as Decimators

As implied above, annihilation need not be deliberate and malicious. Accounts of the contacts between the white man and other races abound in testimonials to the ravages of disease. It is a familiar story how tuberculosis and measles deci-

[3] B. Berry, "The Missouri Indians," *Southwestern Social Science Quarterly*, Vol. 17, No. 2, September 1936, pp. 1–12.
[4] *The New York Times*, May 7, 1950.

mated the Polynesians, destroying whole villages, and how smallpox wiped out tribes of American Indians. Stefansson has reported on the destruction which was wrought in the Arctic area by one of the white man's diseases:

> Few men know the country better than Father Giroux. . . . He says it is true in the Mackenzie district, as it is among the Arctic Eskimo, that measles is the deadliest of all diseases. There have been several epidemics, so that it might be supposed that the most susceptible had been weeded out, and yet the last epidemic (1903) killed about one-fifth of the entire population of Mackenzie Valley.[5]

He tells, also, about the tragedy which befalls the Canadian Indians when they are exposed to tuberculosis and when they learn to desire "civilized-looking dwellings," for both of which they have only the white man to blame:

> No dwelling could be more sanitary and more likely to forestall tuberculosis than the tipi of the Indians of the Mackenzie Valley. It is not only always filled with fresh air, but it never becomes filthy, because it is moved from place to place before it has time to become so; but when a house is built, it cannot be moved. The housekeeping methods which are satisfactory in a lodge that is destined to stand in one place only two or three weeks at a time, are entirely unsuited for the log cabin, which soon becomes filthy and remains so. Eventually the germs of tuberculosis get into the house and obtain lodging in it. The members of the same family catch the disease, one from the other, and when the family has been nearly or quite exterminated by the scourge, another family moves in, for the building of a house is hard work and it is a convenient thing to find one ready for your occupancy; and so it is not only the family that built the house that suffers but there is also through the house a procession of other families moving from the wigwam to the graveyard.[6]

The great destroyer, then, has been those diseases against which no immunity had been built up, and with which the afflicted peoples had neither the knowledge nor the skills to cope. George Catlin, the distinguished artist and ethnologist, has given us a picture of how the Indians were overwhelmed when smallpox struck:

> Terror and dismay are carried with it [the disease]; and awful despair, in the midst of which they plunge into the river when in the highest state of fever, and die in a moment; or dash themselves from precipices; or plunge their knives into their hearts, to rid themselves from the pangs of slow and disgusting death.[7]

Only slightly less important as exterminators of peoples have been heavy drinking, prostitution, and other vices which followed contact with Europeans. Disease would reduce the population to a fraction of its former size, and vice served to demoralize those who managed to survive. In many parts of the world even the primitive peoples have long had an acquaintance with alcohol, but American In-

[5] V. Stefansson, *My Life with the Eskimo*, p. 26.
[6] *Ibid.*, p. 23.
[7] *The North American Indians*, Vol. 2, p. 28.

dians had but slight knowledge of it, and they easily fell a prey to its inducements.[8] Some of them did possess fermented beverages, and it is possible that a few even had acquired the skill of distilling liquor. For most, however, alcohol introduced them to a new experience, one for which their culture provided no folkways of control. White settlers soon realized that liquor was a dangerous article in the hands of the Indians, and even the traders, morally lax as they were, knew that too much rum made a poor customer. Consequently, though there were even fewer prohibitionists in colonial times than there are today, laws regulating the sale of liquor to Indians were promulgated as early as 1670. The first explorers, however, unlike settlers and traders, felt no responsibility for the behavior of the Indians, and they took delight in getting them drunk. A story has it that Henry Hudson invited several Indians aboard the *Half Moon*, gave one of them a potent drink which sent him reeling, so that when he recovered he recounted to his companions his experiences in the spirit world. One myth has it that the very name Manhattan means "the place of the first big drunk."[9] Be that as it may, the Indians soon acquired a taste for drink, and it played havoc with them.

Indian leaders recognized the evil and sought to eliminate it. The pitiful plea of the Delaware to the white colonists in 1698 is typical of many which were made, but to no avail:

> We know it to be hurtful to us to drink it. We know it, but if people will sell it to us, we so love it that we cannot refuse it. But when we drink it, it makes us mad; we do not know what we are doing; we abuse one another; we throw one another in fire. Through drinking, seven score of our people have been killed.[10]

Even in the journals of hardheaded fur traders we find reports on the devastating effects of alcohol upon the Indians, of the noisy fighting, the injuries and deaths, children neglected and abused by drunken mothers, the debauchery and theft the victims resorted to in order to procure liquor.

What has been said here about the ravages of disease and vice among the American Indians is not unique, and similar stories could be told of primitive peoples in many parts of the world who had the misfortune to be "discovered" by civilized Europeans.

Even where extermination has *not* been a conscious and deliberate policy, the surviving group or race has often regarded these natural processes of destruction with favor. The Pilgrims, for instance, felt this way about the plagues which struck the Indians. When they arrived at Plymouth in 1620, they found the deserted Indian village of Pautuxet, with its corn fields cleared and fertile, and

---

[8] For a discussion of the Indians' knowledge and use of alcohol prior to the arrival of Columbus, see J. H. Steward (Ed.), *Handbook of South American Indians*, Vol. 5, pp. 539–546; and H. E. Driver, *Indians of North America*, pp. 93–97.

[9] An amusing translation, but highly dubious. The probability is that Manhattan means "island of hills." See F. W. Hodge (Ed.), *Handbook of American Indians North of Mexico*.

[10] Quoted in Clark Wissler, *Indians of the United States*, pp. 267–268.

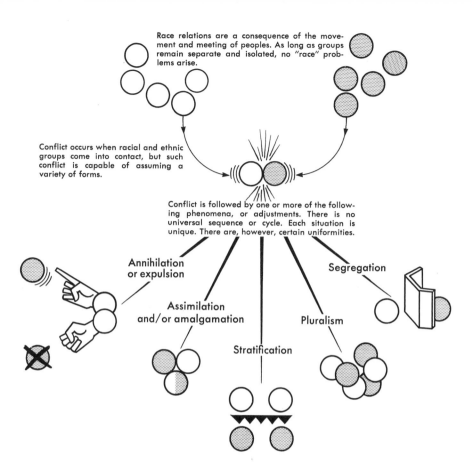

Race relations are a consequence of the movement and meeting of peoples. As long as groups remain separate and isolated, no "race" problems arise.

Conflict occurs when racial and ethnic groups come into contact, but such conflict is capable of assuming a variety of forms.

Conflict is followed by one or more of the following phenomena, or adjustments. There is no universal sequence or cycle. Each situation is unique. There are, however, certain uniformities.

Annihilation or expulsion

Segregation

Assimilation and/or amalgamation

Pluralism

Stratification

Race relations constitute a theme played upon these five "strings." In a sense, each is a "solution" of race problems.

one lone survivor to tell them the tragic story. They learned that a plague, presumably smallpox, had swept through the New England tribes in 1616. The disease had been introduced either from the French settlements to the north or from the English fishing and lumber ships which had been plying the New England coast for a decade or more prior to the arrival of the Pilgrims. The toll in lives had been ghastly. An English trader, Morton, who traveled through the hinterlands in 1622, seeing the ghost villages and the quantities of bones and skulls, said that the place "seemed to me like a new Golgotha." The Massachusetts tribe was reduced from 10,000 to 1000 souls. *The Pilgrims were delighted with all of this,* and regarded it as a justification for their taking the Indians' lands without payment. One of their early historians expressed the viewpoint in these words:

> There befell a great mortality among them; the greatest that ever the memory of father or son took notice of; desolating chiefly those places where the English afterward planted; sweeping away whole families, but chiefly young

men and children, the very seeds of increase. . . . Their wigwams lie full of dead corpses. . . . By this means, Christ, whose great and glorious works throughout the earth are all for the benefit of his churches and chosen, not only made room for his people to plant, but also tamed the hearts of these barbarous Indians.[11]

Genocide

But not all have had such faith that Providence would exterminate the com petitive racial group; or, alternatively, they have become impatient with the slow pace at which the divine plan moved and have, accordingly, taken the matter into their own hands in many instances. A new word, *genocide*, has rather recently been introduced into the language to designate this practice of de liberately exterminating a whole race or ethnic group. Concerning the origin of the word, the *New York Times* several years ago had this to say:

> Proceedings will soon begin at Nuremberg to establish the guilt or innocence of Nazi physicians who inoculated prisoners in concentration camps with various diseases. No doubt the defendants will plead that they were engaged in im portant scientific research for the benefit of society. For this reason it is im portant to charge the defendants with genocide, a term which was coined by Professor Raphael Lemkin of Duke University to designate the crime of which Goering and his colleagues were convicted.
>
> The term was used in the indictment of the Nazi leaders and also during examination. Adopting Professor Lemkin's reasoning the delegates of Cuba, India, and Panama have defined genocide as "a denial of the right of the ex istence of entire human groups in the same way as homicide is the denial of the right to live for individual human beings." That the outrages perpetuated in the name of science in the concentration camps fall within this definition there can be no doubt in the light of the evidence.
>
> In October, 1941, Professor Pokorny, a dermatologist and syphilologist, wrote to Himmler that since "the enemy must not only be conquered but exterminated" it was important to consider the work that a Dr. Madous had been doing in permanently sterilizing male and female animals by the injection or oral ad ministration of a drug obtained from the juice of a plant . . . known as . . . *Dieffenbachia seguine*. . . .
>
> He suggested that . . . the plant be cultivated in greenhouses; that immediate experiments be made on human beings to establish the dosage and duration of treatment; that chemical research be conducted to isolate the effective ingredient of the plant juice, so that synthetic production could be undertaken.[12]

It was without doubt the deliberate policy of the Nazis to exterminate the Jewish people in their midst, and they came very near to succeeding. When the high-ranking Nazi government officials, generals, and admirals were being tried

11 W. C. MacLeod, *The American Indian Frontier*, p. 50.
12 *The New York Times*, November 17, 1946.

at Nuremberg, Mr. Justice Jackson, in making his charges against the defendants, delivered the following accusation:

> The most savage and numerous crimes planned and committed by the Nazis were those against the Jews. These in Germany, in 1933, numbered about 500,000. . . . They were few enough to be helpless, and numerous enough to be held up as a menace.
>
> What we charge against these defendants is not those arrogances and pretensions which frequently accompany the intermingling of difficult peoples and which are likely, despite the honest efforts of government, to produce regrettable crimes and convulsions. It is my purpose to show a plan and design, to which all Nazis were committed, to annihilate all Jewish people. . . . The persecution of the Jews was a continuous and deliberate policy. . . . The plan to exterminate the Jewish people was so methodically and thoroughly pursued that despite the German defeat, this Nazi aim largely succeeded. Only the remnants of the European Jewish population remain in Germany, in the countries which Germany occupied, and in those which were her satellites. Of the 9,600,000 Jews who lived in Nazi-dominated Europe, 60 per cent are authoritatively estimated to have perished.

While the term "genocide" may be of recent origin, the practice itself is an ancient one. The Bible records many instances of a stronger group exterminating its rival. The Hebrews, fighting centuries ago for a foothold in Palestine, came into conflict with various peoples. We are told with complete candor in the third chapter of Deuteronomy:

> Og the king of Bashan came against us, he and all his people . . . and we smote him until none was left to him remaining. And we took all his cities at that time . . . and we utterly destroyed them . . . with the women and the little ones. But all the cattle, and the spoil of the cities, we took for a prey unto ourselves

And also, in II Kings 15:16:

> Menahem smote Tiphsah, and all that were therein, and the borders thereof, from Tirzah: because they opened not to him, therefore he smote it; and all the women therein that were with child he ripped up.

It must not be supposed that the Hebrews were abnormally brutal; they were simply following the practices of their time. The Assyrians and Babylonians were every bit as ruthless, and used to delight in a certain amount of torture as well; and Egyptian monuments show their monarch butchering his defeated enemies with his own hands. In fact, the Hebrews usually killed only the males, taking the women and children as captives.[13]

We have no right to console ourselves with the thought that genocide is a practice limited to ancient peoples, like the Hebrews, or to latter-day fanatics

[13] H. N. Brailsford, "Massacre," *Encyclopedia of the Social Sciences*, Vol. 10, pp. 191–194; "War," in J. Hastings (Ed.), *The Dictionary of the Bible*, pp. 964–965.

like the Nazis. The fact is that the prospect of solving a "race" problem by extermination has appealed to many modern minds. Arnold J. Toynbee maintains that it has characterized "the English method of overseas settlement."[14] A clear case in support of Toynbee's thesis comes from the island of Tasmania, where the British succeeded in wiping out the native population in the brief span of 73 years. The gruesome tale has been summarized as follows:

> The colonists regarded the aborigines as a degenerate race, not so much human beings as wild beasts to be ruthlessly exterminated. Even more barbarous in their treatment of the natives were the bushrangers, convicts who had escaped into the bush where they lived a life of brigandage. These outlaws hunted the blacks for sport. They stole their women, chaining them up, outraging them, and in the end killing them. One . . . used regularly to hunt natives in order to provide his dogs with meat.
>
> The aborigines, though naturally disposed toward peace and friendship with the whites, were roused to fury by these outrages, and retaliated in kind. But spears and waddies were no match for firearms. The blacks were driven steadily back as the settlements advanced, and their numbers were decimated. . . .
>
> Finally Governor Arthur, realizing that the depredations of the natives were acts of vengeance for the injuries they had received, resolved to put an end to the prevailing anarchy. To discourage killing the natives, he offered a reward of £5 for every adult captured alive and £2 for every child. This plan had unanticipated consequences. It sanctioned and encouraged the formation of capture parties. . . . Arthur then turned to another plan. Nearly five thousand soldiers, police and civilians, armed with guns and handcuffs, were formed into a cordon stretching across the island. In October, 1830, this line started to move southward to drive all the natives into the Tasman Peninsula and pen them there. But when this human dragnet had closed in, it had caught only one native man and a boy. The others had all slipped through the line "like a sunbeam through a butterfly net."
>
> What this great drive had failed to do was accomplished singlehanded by a Methodist bricklayer, George Robinson, who had a warm sympathy for the natives and was one of the few white men they trusted. Unarmed and accompanied by only a few friendly natives, he went into the bush to reason with the aborigines and to explain that, however the settlers and bushrangers might treat them, the government desired to protect them. At the imminent risk of his life he tramped hundreds of miles from one secret retreat to another. Through his unaided efforts all the surviving blacks — now only 203 in number — were gathered together in 1835 on Flinders Island in Bass Strait. Thus the "Black War" came to an end.
>
> Though kindly treated from then on, the natives could not withstand the changed conditions of life. Unsuitable food, catarrhal disorders, and pneumonia, aggravated by close confinement and the wearing of clothes and the restrictions of captivity, caused them to pine and sicken and die. Twelve years later, in 1847, when their numbers had been reduced to forty, they were transferred to a reservation near Hobart. But they were already doomed to extinction. The last

[14] *The Study of History,* Vol. 1, p. 465.

*A West African Hottentot
musician plays on
a reed flute*

aboriginal male died in 1869, and in 1876, with the death of the woman Truganina,
. . . the Tasmanian race became finally extinct. This in brief is one chapter in
the history of the triumph of "civilization" over "savagery."[15]

Instances of this sort could be recited indefinitely, and no race or nationality
can show itself innocent of the charge. The Dutch who first settled on the Cape
of Good Hope, and especially those who pushed as pioneers into the interior,
were bent upon exterminating the native blacks. Dr. I. D. MacCrone, who has
written an account of these racial contacts,[16] states that in the eyes of the European stock farmer in South Africa the natives were held in utter contempt, and
were regarded as an inferior race with no rights of their own to speak of. Bushmen and wild animals were bracketed together as dangerous vermin to be shot
at sight whenever the opportunity presented itself. It seems never to have occurred to any of the whites that the Bushmen might be the injured party, being
deprived of their means of existence by the encroachments of the Europeans;
and that in preying upon the frontiersmen, and stealing and crippling their cattle,
natives were simply reacting to an invasion of their territory as would any other
people the world over. Such a suggestion, say Dr. MacCrone, would have been

[15] G. P. Murdock, *Our Primitive Contemporaries*, pp. 16–18.
[16] *Race Attitudes in South Africa.* See especially pp. 89–136.

quite incredible to the Dutch stock farmer, who insisted that "the only good Bushman is a dead Bushman" — an expression, incidentally, not unlike one familiar to American ears.

Genocide is not always practiced with the blatancy of the Nazis, or the ruthlessness of the British in Tasmania or the Dutch in South Africa. It can be done with a certain finesse. Pierson tells us that the Portuguese in Brazil were intent upon exterminating those Indians who offered any resistance to their settlement, and one of the popular means for achieving that goal was to plant in the Indian villages clothing taken from recent victims of the smallpox. The Indians, strangers to this malady, quickly succumbed.[17] Bacteriological warfare is an old story to the student of race relations and is encountered in many other situations than the Portuguese. Again a convenient and inexpensive device is to take advantage of the cleavages within the enemy's camp, to pit faction against faction and tribe against tribe, and encourage them to kill each other. This policy was deliberately advocated and pursued in the United States. As early as 1717 a prominent citizen of the colony of South Carolina was insisting: "We must assist them in cutting one another's throats. . . . This is the game we intend to play if possible . . . for if we cannot destroy one nation of Indians by another, our country must be lost."[18] Governments have often seen advantages in encouraging their citizens to take the initiative in annihilating the troublesome minority. All our colonies followed the practice of paying bounties for Indian scalps. Shrieke says[19] that the policy was first adopted in 1641 by the Dutch in New Amsterdam, following the lead of their compatriots in the East Indies who had earlier learned that it is cheaper to encourage individuals to destroy the enemy on a commission basis than to maintain an army for the purpose. The other colonies soon adopted the ingenious policy of the Dutch, paying scalp bounties as an "encouragement to the enterprise and bravery of our fellow citizens." This is not to say that scalping was a Dutch invention. As a matter of fact a good many Indian tribes had followed the practice before the arrival of the whites; but the introduction of the rifle, and of iron and steel knives, greatly facilitated the process, and the paying of bounties raised it to a major interest with both Indians and whites. The Puritans, as early as 1637, had made a practice of giving rewards for Indian heads, since the more convenient practice of merely removing the scalp lock had not occurred to either the Puritans or the Indians.

Genocide, then, is a new word, but it refers to a very ancient practice. Long before the rise of modern science and the development of our present-day weapons of destruction, men had discovered that extermination is one way of solving so-called race problems.

Nowadays, however, the conscience of the world has been aroused, and steps to eliminate genocide, howbeit faltering, are being taken. Hardly had the

[17] *Op. cit.*, p. 6.
[18] Quoted in D. D. Wallace, *The History of South Carolina*, Vol. 1, p. 213.
[19] B. Shrieke, *Alien Americans*, p. 5. On the subject of scalping, see also A. Locke and B. J. Stern, *When Peoples Meet: A Study in Race and Culture Contacts*, pp. 165–170; Wissler, *op. cit.*, pp. 302–303.

United Nations been established before the problem of genocide began to be discussed in the Assembly and in the various councils and agencies of that body. On December 11, 1946, the General Assembly passed by unanimous vote a resolution affirming that genocide is a crime under international law, which the civilized world condemns and, for the commission of which, principals and accomplices are punishable. Thereupon the Assembly called for the preparation of a "convention"[20] on genocide which would define the offense more precisely and provide enforcement procedures for its repression and punishment.

After two years of study and debate the draft of the *Convention on Genocide* was presented to the General Assembly, where it was adopted. The *Convention* came into force January 12, 1951, after it had been ratified by the requisite 20 nations. Subsequently, more than 20 other nations accepted the *Convention*. The United States is not among those which have signed.

The *Convention* defines genocide as follows:

> Genocide means any of the following acts committed with intent to destroy, in whole or in part, a national, ethnical, racial or religious group as such:
> (a) Killing members of the group;
> (b) Causing serious bodily or mental harm to members of the group;
> (c) Deliberately inflicting on the group conditions of life calculated to bring about its physical destruction in whole or in part;
> (d) Imposing measures intended to prevent births within the group;
> (e) Forcibly transferring children of the group to another group.

The *Convention* furthermore provides that any of the contracting parties may call upon the United Nations to take action, under its Charter, for the "prevention and suppression" of acts of genocide. Too, any of the contracting parties may bring charges before the International Court of Justice.

Since the adoption of the *Convention* charges have been brought from time to time. In 1956, for example, Cuba introduced a resolution accusing Russia of having committed genocide, especially because of her intervention in Hungary and the suppression of the revolt in that country. Communists angrily denied the charge; but in the course of the debate it was charged that the Russians had deported large numbers of Hungarians, including women and children, to Siberian slave-labor camps. It was further charged that in 1943–1944 Russia deported wholesale several national minorities of the Caucasus because of their supposed collaboration with the Germans; that she deported to Siberia half a million Soviet nationals of German stock who lived in the region of the Volga River; and that hundreds of thousands of the population of Lithuania, Latvia, and Estonia had suffered a like fate.

It is too much to hope that the United Nations will be able to eliminate geno-

---

[20] The word "convention" has many meanings. In common practice it means only an assemblage of people or some kind of social custom. In international law the term refers to an agreement between sovereign nations. It is more than a resolution or an expression of opinion. It is a legal compact which pledges the several signatory countries to accept certain obligations. Broadly speaking, it is a treaty between a number of nations.

cide; but the world's attention has been focused upon it, and a powerful public opinion can be aroused against the nation suspected of the crime. The *Convention on Genocide* is but one of many achievements of the United Nations promoting universal respect for basic human rights and establishing a world rule of law.

Mass Expulsion

Racial and ethnic conflicts are often resolved when one group expels another from the territory in which it resides. For the victors the end result is comparable to that attained by annihilation, but the process is somewhat more humane. We say "somewhat" more, because mass expulsion is often carried out in an atmosphere of massacres, riots, and other forms of violence, though there are instances where the dominant group has manifested a degree of consideration for those who were being expelled, permitting them to convert their properties into movable wealth and affording them protection from mob attack. Mass expulsion, moreover, has often been resorted to when other methods have failed. There are instances where a minority group has been driven from a country only after a policy of extermination has failed, for one reason or another. On the other hand, mass expulsion has been adopted after concerted efforts to assimilate a minority have proved fruitless. Thus at the dawn of the modern era, when Spanish rulers were determined to promote homogeneity in their realm, they tried to convert the Jews to Christianity; when that failed, they expelled them.

So it was with the Moors. Those who embraced Christianity came to be known as Moriscos (that is, "little Moors") and stayed on in Spain. They were subjected to strict supervision, and from time to time efforts were made to change their foreign habits. Landlords liked them, for they were docile and industrious tenants; but their competition weighed heavily on the Spaniards and excited their envy. In 1568 the government of Philip II ordered them to renounce all their Moorish ways of life and to give up their children to be educated by Christian priests. One result of this policy was a rebellion in the city of Granada which was put down only with great difficulty. The Moriscos were expelled from the city and scattered throughout Spain. In 1608 it was decided to expel the whole body of them from the country, when it became evident that their forcible conversion had produced only superficial conformity. The edict of expulsion was published on September 22, 1609, and was carried out with the greatest cruelty. The number driven from Spain is variously estimated from 120,000 to 3,000,000. The loss to Spain was irreparable, for it deprived the country of a substantial portion of its labor force. It was worse, however, for the Moriscos, for their return to Morocco was bitterly resented by their kinsmen there, from whom they had been estranged so long and from whom they had grown far apart. It is estimated, moreover, that less than a fourth of those who were so cruelly expelled succeeded in surviving the ordeal.[21]

[21] H. C. Lea, *The Moriscos of Spain: Their Conversion and Expulsion.*

There are innumerable instances in history of the mass expulsion of minority racial and ethnic groups. The empires of the ancient world, and the traditions of preliterate peoples, afford many examples of this practice. The Jews have been subjected to this kind of treatment more times than could be counted. Henry VIII drove the Gypsies from England. The Acadians, who lived in what is now Nova Scotia, and who have been immortalized in Longfellow's *Evangeline*, were expelled by the British because they refused to take up arms against the French, and were scattered among the colonies on the Gulf of Mexico and the Atlantic Coast. The Huguenots were driven from France, and Mennonites and Dukhobors have suffered a similar fate from time to time.

For instances of mass expulsion of racial, religious, ethnic, and national minorities, however, one does not have to look at the past. The twentieth century more than any other has witnessed this phenomenon on a scale hitherto unequalled, especially if we include along with those deported or expelled the millions of refugees and displaced persons who have fled their native lands because of fear, threats, or persecution.[22]

The Trail of Tears

A classic example of mass expulsion, taken from our own history, is that of the forced removal of the Cherokees from their homeland in the East. The magnitude of the injustice and the toll of lives have caused the Indians to call this incident "The Trail of Tears."[23]

The Cherokees were a powerful people who lived in that region where Georgia meets Tennessee and North Carolina. Their first contact with the whites came in 1540, when DeSoto marched through their country; but there was nothing in the conduct of the Spaniards to make the Indians regard them as superior, and they hoped they would see no more of such people. A century and a half later the whites came again, this time the British. The initial contacts were friendly, for the Indians were far removed from the settlements and the white visitors were bent upon establishing cordial relations for reasons of trade and security. But as the frontier advanced, the Cherokees began to feel the encroachment of the land-hungry Europeans. There was friction; the Indians lost some of their territory; but in the meantime they had learned many things from the whites which had made them a stronger, more prosperous, even a civilized people.

By 1825 there were more than 13,000 Cherokees living in their Eastern home, while approximately 7000 others had been induced to migrate across the Mississippi. Contact with the whites, then, had greatly stimulated the growth of their population. They had willingly received into their group many white men and women who had taken Cherokee spouses. They still owned seven million acres

---

[22] J. J. Senturia, "Mass Expulsion," *Encyclopedia of the Social Sciences*, Vol. 10, pp. 185–189.

[23] G. Foreman, *Indian Removal*, pp. 229–314; Marion L. Starkey, *The Cherokee Nation*, pp. 282–301; Wissler, *op. cit.*, pp. 126–131; J. Collier, *The Indians of the Americas*, pp. 117–125.

of land. Schools and churches had been established, their farms were prosperous, they managed their political affairs well, the nation was out of debt, they were at peace, and they owned more than 1000 Negro slaves. One of their number, Sequoya, among the truly great men of American history, had invented a Cherokee alphabet, and he was on his way to turning them into a literate people.

The tide was turned when gold was discovered in the Georgia hills, for the whites were determined to get possession of it. On December 19, 1829, the legislature of Georgia passed an act appropriating a large area of the Cherokee lands. It provided, also, that the laws of the Cherokees would henceforth be null and void in that area, and all persons living therein would be subject to the laws of the state of Georgia. Finally, the act provided that "no Indian or descendant of an Indian . . . shall be deemed a competent witness in any court of this state to which a white person may be a party." The Governor warned the Indians that they would be liable to punishment if they mined the gold on the lands the state had appropriated. A lottery system was set up to distribute the Indian lands among the whites.

The Cherokees appealed to President Andrew Jackson; but he was no friend of theirs, old Indian fighter that he was. In fact, it was he who had been responsible for having Congress enact the Indian Removal Act, which placed upon his shoulders the task of driving all Indians to lands beyond the Mississippi. The Cherokees then appealed to the Supreme Court, but the Court declared that it was not its function to meddle in such affairs. The various branches of the government, far from seeing justice done to the Indians, actually connived in the theft. The President's commissioners, in fact, illegally persuaded a handful of the tribe's members to sell all of its seven million acres to the government, and the Senate quickly ratified this "treaty." The Cherokees, however, denounced the treaty, and remained on the land.

General Winfield Scott moved in with 7000 troops and an unruly rabble of civilians. Men, women, and children, the Indians were rounded up; homes and barns were burned; cattle and household goods were seized by the mob. Even graves were opened, and the silver and other valuables, which by Indian custom were buried with the dead, were taken with the loot. The captives were herded into stockades, conducted under guard down the Tennessee, Ohio, and Mississippi Rivers and up the White, and shoved into the territory which is now Oklahoma. The cost of all of this was charged to the Indians.

The details of this mass expulsion and of the westward trek are revolting. The suffering was intense, and the toll of life staggering. More than 10,000 Cherokees were driven west, and of that number it is estimated that 4000 perished along the way. One who is interested in reading the wretched story will find it in Grant Foreman's *Indian Removal*.

President Van Buren, in his address to Congress on December 3, 1838, was able to report: "The measures for Cherokee removal authorized by Congress at its last session have had the happiest effects. . . . The Cherokees have emigrated without any apparent reluctance."

A more recent case of mass expulsion occurred during World War II, when some 110,000 persons of Japanese ancestry were forcibly evacuated from the area bordering the Pacific Ocean, and including parts of Washington, Oregon, California, and Arizona. Ostensibly this was nothing more than a wartime measure undertaken in the interest of national security. But actually, as we gain the perspective of time, it appears to be simply one more chapter in the long conflict between whites and Japanese. Let us review that conflict.

The Japanese are among the most recent immigrants to enter the United States. For a long time Japan was opposed to its citizens leaving their own country. Prior to 1854 emigration was a crime punishable by death, and the construction of ocean-going vessels was forbidden by imperial decree. Then an occasional shipwrecked sailor or a stowaway found his way to these shores. Their numbers were negligible, however, for there were only 55 Japanese here in 1870, and 148 in 1880. But the Hawaiian Sugar Planters' Association, in 1884, prevailed upon the Japanese authorities to reverse their traditional opposition to emigration, and immediately the numbers of Japanese in other countries began to swell. They went to Hawaii in droves, and many came to Canada, the United States, and South America. There were 2039 here in 1890; and in the first decade of the present century some 55,000 arrived from Japan, and another 37,000 from Hawaii.

They were never warmly received in the United States, even though their labor was needed in the West where they settled. At the time they began to arrive in large numbers, Japan was emerging as a world power; and many Californians regarded the Japanese immigration as the spearhead of invasion. An anti-Japanese meeting was held in San Francisco on May 7, 1900; and in 1905 the Hearst newspapers launched a major attack upon them. Various repressive and discriminatory measures were adopted. In 1907 President Roosevelt, by executive order, stopped Japanese immigration from Hawaii, Canada, and Mexico; and he negotiated the famous Gentleman's Agreement with the Japanese government, putting an end to immigration from that source, except for the so-called "picture brides." These measures, however, did little to halt the tide of anti-Japanese prejudice. Hostile bills and resolutions were introduced in a number of state legislatures, California placed restrictions upon ownership of land by Japanese, and several other states followed her example. The culmination of the struggle came in 1924, when Congress passed a law barring the immigration of persons "ineligible for citizenship," which was intended, and interpreted, as a blow to the Japanese.

The Japanese have never been one of our large minorities, being greatly outnumbered by the Negro, Jewish, Mexican, and even the Indian groups. On the eve of World War II there were only 126,947 in the continental United States, two-thirds of whom, by virtue of their having been born on American soil, were citizens. They were concentrated, however, and this was a factor contributing to the misfortune they later suffered. At the outbreak of the war, 43 per cent of

*Japanese-American citizens work
in their own established
business in Los Angeles*

those gainfully employed were in agriculture, more particularly in the production of vegetables and fruits for the local urban markets; 23 per cent were engaged in the wholesale and retail trade, chiefly the distribution of Japanese-grown products; 17 per cent were employed in service industries — domestic service, cleaning and dyeing, and the operation of hotels, barber shops, and restaurants; and others owned stores or were engaged in the professions. In these latter areas, as a result of discrimination and boycotts, the patrons and clients were chiefly Japanese.

The attack upon Pearl Harbor gave the anti-Japanese forces their great opportunity. They began to clamor for expulsion. The Hearst newspapers took up the cry. Rumors of espionage and sabotage began to circulate, entirely without foundation in fact, for Japanese-Americans, both in Hawaii and in the United States, have a clear record on that score. Lobbyists went to work, and West Coast representatives in Congress recommended to the President "the immediate evacuation of all persons of Japanese lineage." Accordingly, the War Department was authorized in an executive order to set up military areas and to exclude from such areas any persons regarded as dangerous. Mr. Stimson, Secretary of War, delegated this authority to General J. L. DeWitt, who was commanding officer of the Western Defense Command.

The naïve racial beliefs and prejudices of General DeWitt are clearly manifested in his various public utterances, reports, and his testimony before Congressional committees. Said he, "The Japanese race is an enemy race and while many second and third generation Japanese born on United States soil, possessed of United States citizenship, have become 'Americanized,' the racial strains are undiluted." And he declared before the House Naval Affairs Subcommittee that Japanese-Americans "are a dangerous element, whether loyal or not. There is no way to determine their loyalty. . . . It makes no difference whether he is an American; theoretically he is still a Japanese, and you can't change him. . . . You can't change him by giving him a piece of paper."

In a series of orders General DeWitt called for the evacuation of all persons of Japanese ancestry from the area of the West Coast. President Roosevelt, realizing that some agency other than the Army would be needed to perform the task of removal, created the War Relocation Authority. At the outset, evacuation was on a voluntary basis and some 10,000 did depart. But it took money to leave, which many of them did not have; and those who did move suffered many unpleasant experiences. Many of them had substantial investments and businesses, and they could not bring themselves to believe that their rights as American citizens would be so lightly dismissed. The policy of voluntary evacuation, therefore, gave no promise of succeeding, and a shift to compulsory evacuation was made.

On the date fixed by the Army all persons of Japanese lineage reported to control stations, whence they were escorted to improvised assembly centers — race tracks, fair grounds, parks, and pavilions. Within about four months more than 100,000 persons had been transferred to these centers and placed under guard. Next they were moved to the relocation camps, of which there were ten, situated in Utah, Arizona, California, Idaho, Wyoming, Colorado, and Arkansas. Here, housed in barracks and surrounded by barbed wire, the inmates carried on as best they could. Attempts were made to estimate the loyalty of the Japanese, and those found disloyal were shipped away to the camp at Tule Lake in California. As a matter of fact, the overwhelming majority of them gave every evidence of loyalty, and even most of those who, on the basis of tests, were classified as disloyal hardly deserved that stigma.[24]

Originally it was intended that these camps would become actual relocation centers, but the Japanese did not remain there long. Employers needed labor to meet the manpower shortage, and the evacuees were issued work permits and were assisted in finding jobs in various parts of the country outside the prohibited zone. Students were granted leave to attend college and high schools. Though the evacuees had been declared "ineligible for military service," this decison was rescinded in 1943, and thousands entered the Army, where they distinguished themselves for their valor and where their knowledge of the Japanese language enabled them to play an indispensable role in the war as interpreters and intelligence officers. In 1944 the ban on their returning to the Pacific coast was lifted; and in March, 1946, the last relocation center was closed. Many of the Japanese have returned to their former homes, but large

[24] G. Eleanor Kimble, "The 'Disloyal' at Tule Lake," *Common Ground*, Vol. 6, No. 2, 1946, pp. 74–81.

numbers of them have chosen to settle in other states, and start new lives.[25]

This mass expulsion of the Japanese from the West Coast has been called "our worst wartime mistake." In the first place, the necessity for their removal for reasons of national security had no basis in fact. There were enemy aliens of German and Italian extraction in the country at the time who were not subjected to such treatment. While there were dangerous and disloyal persons among the Japanese, these were well known to the authorities, who had been checking on them for years, and they were promptly arrested at the beginning of the war. Other suspicious ones were under constant surveillance. General DeWitt's defense of his action, which he based upon "military necessity," "the threat of sabotage," "the necessity of protecting the Japanese from the violence of mobs," is supported neither by reason, fact, nor subsequent developments.

In the second place, the injustice inflicted upon these hundred thousand persons was colossal. Neither the Army nor the W.R.A. was in a position to act as custodian for the property of the Japanese, who had to move with haste and who suffered great losses in the process. Radios and refrigerators were sold for a pittance, and cars were disposed of for a fraction of their value.[26] No estimate can be placed upon the intangible losses which the Japanese suffered — the businesses and professions, products of years of effort, which were wiped out, and the humiliation and shock which expulsion gave to their pride and status.

Finally, this treatment of persons holding American citizenship presents a threat to certain basic principles of our society. It involved a sweeping deprivation of citizens of their civil rights, and it was done on a racial basis. It dealt a blow to the sacred principle that men are presumed innocent until they are proved guilty, that all citizens stand on an equal footing before the law, regardless of race, color, or previous condition of servitude; and it came dangerously near upsetting the traditional principle of the subordination of the military to the civil authority. Eugene V. Rostow, Professor of Law at Yale University, gives the following estimate of the gravity of the affair:

> The original program of relocation was an injustice, in no way required or justified by the circumstances of the war. But the Supreme Court, in three extraordinary decisions, has upheld its main features as constitutional. This fact converts a piece of wartime folly into national policy — a permanent part of the law — a doctrine enlarging the power of the military in relation to civil authority. . . . As Mr. Justice Jackson has said, the principle of these decisions "lies about like a loaded weapon ready for the hand of any authority that can bring forward a plausible claim of an urgent need." All in all, the case of the Japanese-Americans is the worst blow our liberties have sustained in many years. Unless repudiated, it may support devastating and unforeseen social and political conflicts.[27]

[25] The social and economic losses suffered by the Japanese-Americans are documented convincingly in L. Bloom and Ruth Riemer, *Removal and Return*.

[26] B. Smith, "The Great American Swindle," *Common Ground*, Vol. 7, No. 2, 1947, pp. 34–38; "Legalized Blackmail," *Common Ground*, Vol. 8, No. 2, 1948, pp. 34–36.

[27] "Our Worst Wartime Mistake," *Harper's Magazine*, Vol. 191, No. 1144, September 1945, p. 194.

One way to be sure of solving the problems of race relations is for the stronger group to annihilate the weaker, or, if that be too reprehensible a device, to drive it out of the country. Instances of both these practices are commoner than we like to think. Oftener, no doubt, racial and ethnic groups which are brought together in the course of events learn to adjust to each other and to live side by side more or less satisfactorily. It is to these less frightful consequences of the meeting of peoples that we must next turn our attention.

8

Stratification

The black man occupies the lowest
rung on the American ladder.

WILSON RECORD
Race and Radicalism

The island of Jamaica, 90 miles south of Cuba, holds a certain fascination for sociologists. British colonists settled this territory, as they did the United States, and they imported Negro slaves to perform the labor on their plantations; but quite a different pattern of race relations has emerged.

Jamaica was occupied first by the Spaniards in 1509. The Indian population gradually withered away, and eventually became extinct. The British acquired the island in 1670, and took over the operation of the sugar plantations which flourished there. At the end of the century there were in Jamaica approximately 10,000 whites and 40,000 Negro slaves. Seventy-five years later there were 18,000 whites and a quarter of a million slaves. By 1844 the number of whites had fallen to about 16,000, and it has remained at approximately that level ever since. In that year there were 68,500 colored (mixed-bloods) and 293,000 Negroes. The census of 1943 reported 13,400 whites, 216,000 coloreds, and nearly a million blacks. The white population includes a community of Jews, and there are also smaller, but important, groups of Syrians, Chinese, and East Indians.

Broom, who spent the year 1950 on the island and has written about the racial situation there,[1] maintains that the *drain of the white population out of the area* was a crucial fact in the developing social system. Many of the white plantation owners preferred to live comfortably in England rather than on the island; others sent their children to Europe for their education, whence they often failed to return. The sex ratio of the white population was, accordingly, heavily masculine, and the practice of concubinage was common. In consequence of the continual departure of the dominant whites, a vacuum was created in positions of intermediate responsibility, and the free mixed-bloods moved into this vacuum. Thus a differentiation developed between the colored and the black, and lightness of skin color came to be valued as a promise of higher status, and status itself came to be equated with lightness. In 1950, Broom found that the whites were far ahead of the other racial groups in education, wage earnings, and farm land tenure; the colored population came next; and the blacks were in a very disadvantageous position. These groups, to be sure, are not rigid castes; there are Negro lawyers and doctors, but their numbers, in proportion to the Negro population, are small in comparison to those of lighter skin. The whites dominate polite society, and control most of the large estates, the finance, and the shipping activities.

The whole society has somewhat the characteristics of a layer cake, though the layers are not so precisely distinguished, and the situation is manifestly a fluid one.

The color line is not sharply drawn, and a code of racial equality prevails. Speaking of the Caribbean in general, and not specifically of Jamaica, Williams has this to say:

[1] L. Broom, "The Social Differentiation of Jamaica," *American Sociological Review*, Vol. 19, No. 2, April 1954, pp. 115ff.

The racial situation in the Caribbean is radically different from the racial situation in the United States, and is thus rather incomprehensible to the native of the United States, white or black. It should first be clearly understood that there is no overt legal discrimination. The islands know neither Jim Crow nor lynching; there are neither separate schools, separate theaters, separate restaurants, or special seats in public conveyances. . . . White, brown, and black meet in the same churches in which pews, at a price, can be obtained by one and all. Graves of whites, browns, and blacks are side by side in the cemeteries.[2]

TABLE 8.1

Color and Ethnic Identity of the Population of Jamaica, 1943*

	Number	Per cent
Black	965,960	78.1
Colored	216,348	17.5
White (unlisted below)	12,550	1.0
Jewish	1,259	.1
Chinese	6,879	1.0
Chinese colored	5,515	
East Indian	21,393	2.1
East Indian colored	5,114	
Syrian	834	.1
Syrian colored	171	
Others and unspecified	1,040	.1
Total	1,237,063	100.0

* L. Broom, "The Social Differentiation of Jamaica," *American Sociological Review,* Vol. 19, No. 2, April 1954, pp. 115ff.

So much for public segregation and discrimination. In intimate social relationships and personal intercourse, color is all-important. Williams says, "A white skin is an indication of social status and the best passport to political influence. . . . It is this high market value of a white skin . . . which is responsible for those color distinctions for which the islands are notorious." This all-pervasive color-consciousness not only isolates whites from blacks, but erects a barrier between Negro and mulatto, and within the mixed group itself it prevents any development of cohesion and group loyalty. The hybrid, accordingly, despises his Negro ancestry, covets the status of whites, is more prejudiced against a black skin than is the white person, and is anxious to receive what recognition he can from white society.

[2] E. Williams, *The Negro in the Caribbean,* pp. 62–63.

The situation on Jamaica, therefore, has more the features of flexible, open social classes than of rigid castes and strict segregation. It is possible for an able and ambitious black man to marry a white or mulatto woman, to enter the high-status occupations and professions, to accumulate wealth, and thereby to climb the social ladder. A former Governor of Jamaica, Lord Olivier, was well aware of the advantages of such a social structure when he declared:

> It is unquestionable that the coloured people of blended race as they at present exist form a valuable and quite indispensable part of any West Indian Community, and that a colony of black, coloured, and white people has far more organic efficiency and far more promise in it than a colony of white and black alone. . . . The graded elements of mixed race in Jamaica and in other West Indian colonies contributed very valuably and very wholesomely to making an organic whole of the community.[3]

This principle of subordination manifests itself wherever peoples come into contact. In South Africa the relationships between white and black are clearly those of domination and subjection, as MacCrone describes them in the following sketch:

> We have here two communities who have lived side by side for several generations and established relations of many kinds with one another. . . . Our present economic, political, and social structure tends to lay upon the black the stigma of inferiority. From early childhood the white man is accustomed to look down upon the black as a member of the servant class, as one who definitely occupies an inferior status in the social system. The black man is at the beck and call of anyone with a white skin, his freedom of movement is restricted by pass laws, and all the menial, unpleasant and irksome tasks are performed by his labour. From the point of view of the white man, his one supreme function is to perform the "dirty" work of the white community. . . . There can be no question of comradeship, for that implies a feeling of equality, which is rendered impossible by the present social system, while any pretension of such equality on the part of individual members of the black community is either regarded as ridiculous . . . or excites excessive hostility. . . . Any kind of manual or menial work is "Kaffir" work, unfit for the individual who has the good fortune to be born with a white skin. In the same way and by the same process of association, a "dirty" stroke in a game of tennis is called a "Kaffir" stroke, while a decent person who "plays the game" is a "white" man even if he is a "nigger."[4]

Burlington, Vermont

Relationships between the various ethnic groups in Burlington, Vermont, are quite unlike those in South Africa, but differences of status are present nonetheless.[5] In this community of 25,000 there are no less than 35 distinct ethnic

[3] Quoted in E. V. Stonequist, *The Marginal Man*, p. 32.
[4] I. D. MacCrone, *Race Attitudes in South Africa*, pp. 259–261.
[5] E. L. Anderson, *We Americans, passim*, and especially Ch. 3.

groups; and, while status is an elusive social phenomenon and its measurement extremely baffling, it is very real and enters prominently into the consciousness of everyone. At the top of the status hierarchy stand the Old Yankees. They, of course, regard themselves as the best people; and Anderson says that newcomers "accept the Old Americans at their own evaluation." Although they may condemn them as snobbish, they frankly recognize their ability, shrewdness, prestige, and leadership. It was the ancestors of the Yankees who founded the city in 1763, set up the first institutions, and placed their stamp upon the culture of the community. Today their descendants have an abiding love for the place, and have a certain feeling of possessiveness toward it. They are proud of their English origin, conservative in political and economic philosophy, Protestant in faith, and committed to the preservation of the status quo — or, preferably, the status quo ante. There is widespread agreement about which groups occupy the opposite position in the system of rank — the Negroes and the Chinese vie for that unenviable position. And it is interesting to note that there are very few of either, so that the prejudice against them does not arise from any fear that they may some day dominate the community. English and English-speaking Canadians enjoy a high status, being more acceptable to the Yankees than other ethnic groups. The Irish have witnessed a great change in their position within the space of a century. When they first came to the city in 1849, they took a position on the lowest rung of the social ladder. Today, however, their status is much higher. They are the leaders of the opposition, the champions of the less fortunate ethnic groups, the critics of all things English. Their economic condition has immeasurably improved, and they participate actively in the political and civic affairs of the community.[6] The French Canadians are the largest group, being 10,000 strong; but their status is very low. They are among the oldest groups in the community, too, having been represented there almost as long as the Yankees. In fact, they regard Burlington as *their* city, cherishing the tradition that it was the French who first explored the region, and regarding the Old Yankees as virtually intruders. Even so, they are poor, docile, unaggressive, and concerned primarily with maintaining their customs, language, and religion. As one of their own number expressed it, "The French don't stick together; they act as if they felt inferior and ashamed of their nationality." There are many other peoples represented in Burlington's population — Jews (mostly Polish and Russian), Germans, Italians, Syrians, Greeks, Norwegians, Swedes, Finns, Armenians, Turks, and others — and each ethnic group has a certain position in the status hierarchy, which, though not rigid and permanent, is nevertheless apparent to all.

These differences of status manifest themselves in numerous ways. Certain occupations, for example, are highly regarded, and others are held in low esteem. Labor in mills and factories carries little prestige, and it is in this area that the French Canadians have well-nigh a monopoly. At the other extreme are the

[6] For an interesting analysis of the status of the Irish in the United States, see M. L. Barron, "Intermediacy: Conceptualization of Irish Status in America," *Social Forces*, Vol. 27, No. 3, March 1949, pp. 256–263.

professions, in which Old Americans take the lead. Thirty-one of the 44 lawyers are Old Americans, which is far more than their proportionate share. The medical profession is almost entirely in the hands of the Yankees, the Irish, and the English Canadians. The Old Americans have to a large extent retreated from the commercial life of the city, but they still control the banks, most of the city's manufacturing, and the University.

Status differences, too, are seen in residential locations. Most desirable is the hilltop in the vicinity of the University, and here the Yankees predominate. Least desirable is the waterfront, and it is there that the most recent arrivals settle, and there also remain the failures when the more successful in their group move on. Miss Anderson also interviewed many of the residents of Burlington, and put this question to them, "Whom do you prefer as a neighbor?" Almost invariably a preference was expressed for the members of one's own ethnic group. Newcomers, however, usually stated that their second choice would be Old Americans, and their third choice the Irish. The Yankees, on the other hand, chose the English-Canadians next to themselves. Last choices, for all groups, were Negroes and Chinese. While there are Jews living in the better residential sections, there is usually considerable opposition to their renting or buying property there, with the result that, when they moved from their original settlement on the waterfront, they formed a compact, wedge-shaped community of their own on the northern edge of the city. Thus, the meeting of racial and ethnic groups in Burlington has resulted in a pattern of stratification; though the lines between the various levels are not sharply drawn, the strata themselves are neither permanent nor precise, and vertical mobility is not utterly precluded.

"Elmtown"

The situation is somewhat the same in the Middle-western Corn Belt community, "Elmtown," according to Hollingshead, who studied the system of social classes prevailing there.[7] Elmtown is a city of some 6000 people, 93 per cent of whom are native born, and almost all of whom are white. There is but one Negro family in the town, and only a few Orientals and Mexicans.

Elmtown was settled in 1825, when pioneers from Ohio, Pennsylvania, New York, Massachusetts, Connecticut, Virginia, and Kentucky pushed into the region and dispossessed the Indians. Their descendants, as well as later settlers whose lineage can also be traced through four or five generations in the United States, regard themselves as the "real" Elmtowners, and like to refer to themselves as the "native stock," "real Americans," and "old American stock." Soon after the town had been established Irish laborers were brought in to dig a canal. They were a "hard-working, hard-drinking, hell-raising lot," and the local people hoped that they would dig the canal and promptly move on. Many of them did, but some remained behind to form the nucleus of an "Irish element" which is still a part of the community. A second wave of immigration occurred

[7] A. B. Hollingshead, *Elmtown's Youth.*

around 1850, when several well-to-do German families, fleeing from the Revolution of 1848 in their Fatherland, came to Elmtown. They established a foundry, a brewery, and a tannery, and induced other Germans to join them. Following the Civil War a third immigration occurred, bringing in a considerable number of Norwegians. They purchased what was supposed to be worthless land, and proceeded to tile, drain, and ditch it, with results that astonished the "Americans." Though the Norwegians originally settled as farmers in the outlying districts, many of them subsequently moved into Elmtown. The last migration consisted of a Polish group, imported early in the 1900's as strikebreakers. These Polish laborers enabled the owners of the local industries to break the strike, and then stayed on as an important element in the town's labor force. This so-called Polish group, as a matter of fact, is far from homogeneous itself, including persons whose ancestry is Hungarian, Ukrainian, Italian, or Slovenian, as well as Polish.

Elmtown has its stereotype for each of these groups. The Irish are described as Catholics, Democrats, fighters, cheap politicians, philanderers, and troublemakers. The Germans are regarded as good, thrifty people, hard workers, and moneymakers. The Norwegians are said to be clannish, sexually cold, religious, thrifty, but uninterested in education. The Poles are believed to be scabs, filthy, ignorant, "dumb," law-breakers, unable to learn American ways, and a problem in the schools. These stereotypes probably originated with the "Americans," but were adopted by the others. Thus the Germans hold the stereotypes of the Irish, Norwegians, and Poles; the Poles voice the usual derogatory remarks about the Irish and the Norwegians; and the Norwegians believe what they have been told about Irish, Germans, and Poles. These stereotypes enable the Elmtowners to assign individuals to their proper place in the social structure, and they function, too, as a mechanism of control to disparage the person who would climb out of his place. Mobility, however, is not precluded; and when an individual does display virtues which do not conform to the stereotype, Elmtowners readily explain the deviation on personal grounds.

Hollingshead discovered five distinct social classes in Elmtown. Class I is composed of families of wealth and lineage. They live in the most exclusive sections of town, own two or three cars per family, are conservative in their political and economic views, and are the owners of the banks, the large industries, extensive farm lands, and all the town's business buildings. Leisure, not labor, is dignified; travel is avidly followed as a leisure-time pursuit; and as little effort as possible is spent in making a living, a fact that is facilitated by the possession of inherited wealth. Class II consists of the leaders in civic and economic affairs. The men follow the professions, operate family-owned businesses, or serve as salaried executives in enterprises owned by Class I families. They are the leaders in the Chamber of Commerce, the Rotary Club, the Masonic Lodge, and the veterans' organizations. Almost half of the families in this class have achieved their positions through their own efforts; the others have inherited them, but their origins are too well known, or not enough time has elapsed, to enable them to enter the ranks of Class I.

Class III is made up of families who have sufficient income for the conveniences and comforts of life, but little surplus to invest in productive, wealth-producing enterprises. More than half of the men in this class are employed in offices, banks, mills, mines, and the public service, though many of them own small businesses, are salesmen, or have modest professional practices. Many of the women are gainfully employed, largely as teachers, beauticians, music teachers, secretaries, nurses, or seamstresses. They strive to live in the better residential areas, and many have succeeded in doing so. Class IV consists of those whom their superiors in the community regard as "hard workers, who pay their taxes, raise their children properly, but never seem to get ahead financially." Its members are wage earners, working on the farms, or in the mines, mills, and shops of Elmtown. Their income is large enough to provide the necessities of life and a few comforts, but few if any luxuries. Most of them neither own nor are in the process of buying their homes, and many of them do not even own an automobile. Formal education is limited almost exclusively to public elementary and high schools. Class V, finally, is regarded by the rest of the community as "the scum of the city," and its members themselves realize that they are "on the bottom" and believe that they can do nothing to improve their position. They may desire money, possessions, education, and prestige, but they do not know how to go about achieving them. Their earnings are meager. Most of the men are unskilled or semi-skilled laborers, and the women are dishwashers, cooks, laundresses, and domestic workers. Their employment is uncertain, and employers do not like to hire them, for they will leave a job casually, often without notice, and for flimsy reasons. They live in the least desirable sections of town, "north of the tracks," "below the canal," in "squatters' paradise," "Irish heaven," or Frog Hollow.

The factors which determine one's social position in Elmtown are numerous, subtle, and various. Wealth, of course, is important; but wealth alone is insufficient. (The operator of the local brothel has an income of $10,000 a year, but enjoys no social prestige.) How one makes his living is of considerable import. Among the other criteria are family background, place of residence, church affiliation, education, dress, behavior and mannerisms, physical appearance, and political opinions. Very important, too, is one's ethnic background.

To come of old "'American stock" is a distinct social advantage. It does not insure one's inclusion in the upper classes, however. Class IV, which regards itself as "the backbone of the community," includes all the major ethnic groups in about the same proportion in which they are found in the general population. Even in Class V, 58 per cent of the families trace their ancestry to "American stock" that came to Elmtown before the Civil War. The Irish, contrary to popular belief, are not unduly represented in this lowest class, and the Germans and Norwegians are found only one-third as frequently as we should expect if chance factors alone were operating. There are twice as many Poles, however, as their proportion of the general population would warrant. In Class III, on the other hand, a majority of the families trace their ancestry to some European stock. Norwegians make up 30 per cent, Irish 20 per cent, and Germans 10 per cent. No Poles, however, have succeeded in achieving Class III status. Four out of five of the families in Class II are of "American" stock. Others are of Norwegian, German, or Irish background, and can point to two or three generations who have lived in the area.

To illustrate how attitudes toward ethnic groups operate in determining one's status in Elmtown, Hollingshead cites the case of Cog Wheel, the elite men's club. Before the middle of the 1930's, no person of Irish extraction had been elected to membership. Needless to say, no Pole has ever been elected, and only a few of Norwegian and German ancestry. An Irish clergyman, however, maneuvered himself into a position where he was invited to become a member; and, once in, he worked to have several Irish leaders in the community admitted. They were members of families which had resided in Elmtown three or four generations. Having won his objective, the clergyman resigned from the club. Thereupon certain anti-Irish members proceeded to rid the organization of its Irish element. By 1942, Hollingshead reports, the campaign had succeeded; the Irish had dropped out, and no additional ones had been elected.

In Elmtown, then, the several ethnic groups which make up the town's population are somewhat stratified, though perhaps less rigidly than in Burlington, Vermont. The system of stratification operates to the distinct advantage of the "old Americans," penalizes slightly the Germans and Norwegians, discriminates more severely against the Irish, and proves quite burdensome to the Poles, Mexicans, Negroes, and Orientals.[8]

Forms of Stratification

Stratification is the process of dividing society into ranks, grades, or positions, and involves the unequal distribution of privileges, duties, responsibilities, power, prestige, and influence. Quite apart from the area of race relations, this process of arranging the individuals and groups of a society on horizontal levels operates wherever people try to work out a common life together. Perfect equality prevails nowhere, except in the dreams of utopian philosophers. The fact is that in every society there are various jobs that have to be done, and very early in human history it was discovered that specialization and division of labor resulted in greater efficiency. Furthermore, some of the functions which had to be performed were more difficult than others, some more appealing, and some downright repulsive. The problem, therefore, which every society has to solve is this: How is it possible to distribute these various functions; how assign people to their special roles? Nature helped to answer the problem by dictating that only the female members of the society should bear the children, but she did not go very much beyond that. Man had to figure it out for himself. Now there are

---

[8] The classic study of this nature is that of "Yankee City," conducted by W. L. Warner, in which it is shown to what extent "ethnicity" operates as "one of the several characteristics which modify the social system and are modified by it." See W. L. Warner and P. S. Lunt, *The Status System of a Modern Community*, and W. L. Warner and L. Srole, *The Social Systems of American Ethnic Groups*.

TABLE 8.2

Employed Workers Age 14 and over, By Race and Sex, United States, 1940, 1950, 1960*

Occupation group	Negro						White	
	Male			Female			Male	Female
	1940	1950	1960¹	1940	1950	1960¹	1960	1960
All occupations: Number (thousands)	2,937	3,501	4,005	1,542	1,875	2,624	39,462	18,549
Percent	100.0	100.0	100.0	100.0	100.0	100.0	100.0	100.0
Professional, technical and kindred workers	1.7	2.2	3.9	4.2	5.4	7.5	11.0	13.8
Proprietors, managers, and officials, except farm	1.4	2.1	2.3	.7	1.1	1.2	11.5	4.0
Clerks, sales workers	2.6	4.3	6.5	1.4	5.4	10.2	14.5	41.4
Skilled workers, foremen	4.4	7.7	10.2	.1	.6	.7	20.5	1.3
Semiskilled, operatives	11.7	21.0	23.5	13.5	14.6	12.8	19.5	15.7
Unskilled laborers	22.9	23.3	19.4	.8	1.5	1.0	5.6	.5
Service workers	13.7	14.4	14.4	63.4	60.7	55.0	5.3	16.5
Private household	(2)	1.1	.7	(2)	41.8	34.3	.1	4.1
Other	(2)	13.3	13.7	(2)	18.9	20.7	5.2	12.4
Farm workers	41.5	23.7	11.5	15.9	8.9	3.6	7.9	1.4
Farmers, farm managers	21.1	13.4	4.4	3.0	1.7	.7	5.6	.5
Farm laborers	20.4	10.3	7.1	12.9	7.2	2.9	2.3	.9
Occupation not reported	....	1.2	8.4	....	1.6	8.1	4.3	5.3

¹ All nonwhite
² Not available

*Source: U.S. Department of Labor, Bureau of Labor Statistics.

Percent of White and Non-white College Graduates, by Age Group.

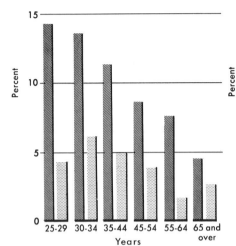

Percentage of White and Non-white High School Graduates, by Age Group.

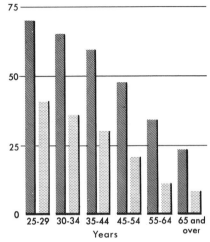

Percent of White and Non-white Unemployed Workers, 1954-63.

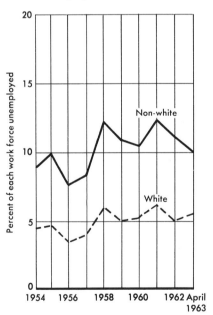

White and Non-white Life Expectancy in the United States, 1920-61.

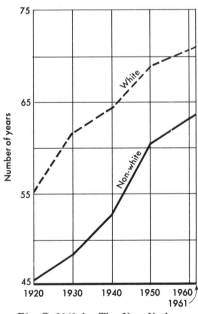

(Source: The New York Times, June 16, 1963, p. E3. © 1963 by The New York Times Company. Redrawn by permission.)

only two ways in which to meet the problem: (1) permit everyone to *compete*, in the hope that each would thereby come to perform the functions for which his interests and abilities fitted him; and (2) *assign* everyone to some societal role or roles, using as a basis for the assignment some easily ascertainable characteristic such as sex, age, family, or skin color. Both these methods have been widely employed, and both have proved equal to the task of getting a society's work done. The former is the essence of *democracy* — equal opportunity for each individual to compete for the role and status he desires, regardless of his race, religion, sex, or family. The second method, carried to its logical extreme, is that of *caste*, wherein the individual's status, role, and various other aspects of his life, are determined by birth and remain fixed throughout his life. The fact of the matter is that no society operates entirely on either of these principles. Even the most democratic, like our own, makes a practice of ascribing some roles and statuses; and the most caste-ridden societies have a certain amount of plasticity.[9]

Whenever racial and ethnic groups come into contact, the process of stratification operates in order to resolve the conflicts that arise and to adjust the disturbing differences. The *form* the stratification takes, however, varies widely from one situation to another, and from time to time. The relations between groups may assume the chasmy features of *slavery*, the arrogance of *caste*, the craftiness of *peonage* or other forms of *forced labor*, the flexibility of *class*, or the subtlety of *discrimination*. Stratification may result in the creation of wide and impassable barriers between racial and ethnic groups, or it may involve a pattern of differentiation so slight that it is readily overcome and ofttimes imperceptible.

An example of the latter type of stratification is found in a rural community in the state of New York, studied by H. F. Kaufman.[10] The community covers a township and has a population of approximately 1500, of whom 600 live in the village and the remainder in the open country. Most of these people come of old American stock and have long been resident in the vicinity; but there are 257 Finnish immigrants, called "Oldlanders" in the study, with whose status we are primarily concerned. Of these Finns 45 per cent are native born; two-thirds of them have lived in the community ten years or longer; almost all are American citizens; and, of the foreign-born, half of them speak English poorly or not at all.

Kaufman's report on this community reveals a certain degree of stratification and discrimination. Says he, "No doubt being an Oldlander lowers one's status in the eyes of many Yankees." No Finns were included in the highest prestige class of the community; none was included in the township and village governments; several organizations refrained from voting them in as members; many Yankees regarded them as "clannish," and were critical of their economic, political, and religious beliefs; and "the two ethnic groups, in both their formal and informal contacts, associated largely among themselves." Certain of the upper-class Yankees were definitely aware that some discrimination did exist;

[9] For a further elaboration of these principles, see R. Linton, *The Study of Man*, Ch. 8.
[10] *Prestige Classes in a New York Rural Community.*

and a few of the upper-class younger Finns recognized this discrimination to which they were subjected and resented it sharply.

Many evidences of a contrary sort were also apparent. While no Finns were included in the highest prestige class, there were none in the lowest; and some of them did enjoy a very high status in the community. The attitude of the Yankees toward the Finns was decidedly favorable; and Kaufman found that the higher prestige classes were more favorable toward them than the lower. The Finns were frequently described as "thrifty, honest people," "clean and industrious," and the Americans were greatly impressed by their ability to "purchase abandoned farms and make them into productive enterprises." While some of the Yankee organizations had not made it a practice to admit Finns to membership, a few Finns belonged to the Dramatic Club, the Men's Club, the Women's Club, and the Masonic Lodge, all of which carried high status in the community. Kaufman found also that the great majority of the Finns themselves were not aware of the fact that they suffered any discrimination or serious injustice. On the matter of intermarriage, which is perhaps the clearest indication of assimilation and acceptance, he found that "intermarriage between the two ethnic groups is extensive." Apparently the handicaps which one suffers by virtue of being a Finn are not onerous, and the barriers which mitigate against complete assimilation and acceptance are temporary and tenuous.

The Caste System in India

Seldom, however, does the process of stratification deal so gently with a minority group. The subcontinent of India is a case in point. For untold centuries the country has experienced wave after wave of invaders and conquerors, each seeking, often with success, to set itself up in a dominant position over the peoples already there. Within historic times there have come Persians, Greeks, Scythians, Arabs, Huns, Portuguese, and British; and long before the dawn of history there were invasions of Negritos — pygmies with dark skins and "peppercorn" hair — Australoids, and many other nameless peoples. The earliest invasion of India of which we have any sort of record was that of the "Aryans," somewhere about 1500 b.c. These people are known to have used an Indo-European language, and probably had fair hair and blue eyes. They first occupied and settled the northwest portion of India, and later established colonies elsewhere on the peninsula. They were desirous of maintaining their dominant position and of preserving their fair color; and it is supposed that soon after their invasion of India they prohibited intermarriage with the aborigines. Their efforts to prevent amalgamation did not succeed, though to this day the higher castes of India generally have lighter skins and narrower noses than the lower castes, though there are many exceptions to the rule.

This is not to say that the "Aryans" *invented* and superimposed the caste system, or created it out of whole cloth. It was, as a matter of fact, the product of a long period of development which has never ceased, and it grew out of a body of customs, taboos, ideologies, and patterns of social organization already present both among the Aryans themselves and among the native peoples they conquered. Long before the invasion the inhabitants of India had surrounded themselves with many food and occupational restrictions, were characterized by strong tribal cohesion, and had learned to follow their own customs and to manifest a spirit of compromise and tolerance for strange ideas and practices. Into this situation the Aryans brought their own social organization, consisting of a class system which included the ruling or military class, the priestly, and the commonality. Out of these ingredients, and others, the system of caste was formed, and it gave to the relationships between the ethnic groups of India a rigid, stable, immutable character that is unmatched in other biracial and multiracial situations.[11]

Forced Labor

Elsewhere dominant peoples have resorted to some form of *forced labor*. When the Spaniards arrived in the New World they imposed upon the Indians two institutions — *repartimientos* and *encomiendas* — both of which placed the natives under a peculiar type of bondage and resulted in the rapid depletion of the native population. When these institutions were abolished toward the end of the colonial period, the whites contrived new methods of holding Indian and *mestizo* labor under some form of involuntary servitude. One of the most common was that of *peonage*, whereby members of the subordinate group were encouraged to become deeply involved in debt. It then became necessary to render service in order to discharge the obligations incurred; but by means of low wages and high interest rates, it has frequently been possible to make of peonage a system of perpetual debt bondage, the indebtedness even being passed on from father to son.[12] Various other methods of forced labor have been and still are employed whereby native peoples and minority groups are maintained in a subordinate position.[13] Among them is the device used by the whites of South Africa in order to make available the black manpower needed on the plantations and in the gold, coal, and diamond mines. Theoretically the Europeans and the natives have chosen *segregation* as the basic form of accommodation to govern their relations with each other. Political parties declare their loyalty to a policy of *apartheid* or "separateness" and set up as a goal an "absolute territorial division between European and native so that ultimately there would be in South Africa a region in which no native, and another in which no European, would be regarded as a permanent inhabitant." However, poll taxes and "hut taxes" have been levied on the natives, and the poverty of their territories and

[11] For a good summary discussion of the complex origin and nature of the Indian caste system, see M. Olcott, "The Caste System of India," *American Sociological Review*, Vol. 9, No. 6, December 1944, pp. 648–657. Literally thousands of publications on the Hindu castes are available, but the student will find a brief but excellent account in J. H. Hutton, *Caste in India*. It must be borne in mind, however, that India is currently undergoing rapid and profound social changes, and the caste system is losing its hold on the people.
[12] G. M. McBride, "Peonage," *Encyclopedia of the Social Sciences*, Vol. 12, pp. 69–72.
[13] R. L. Buell, "Forced Labor," *Encyclopedia of the Social Sciences*, Vol. 6, pp. 341–345.

Employment and Earning Patterns of Whites and Non-whites

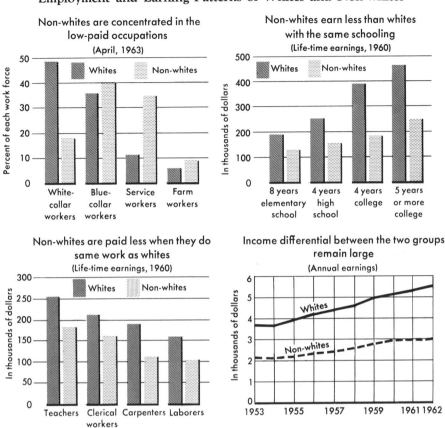

Charts are based on a study released by the Census Bureau. (Source: The New York Times, August. 4, 1963, section 4, p. 10E. © 1963 by The New York Times Company. Redrawn by permission.)

the pressure of population force many of them to leave home and work in mines and on farms to earn enough to pay the taxes. The whites frankly admit that the chief purpose of this system of taxation is to obtain native labor.

The Negro: Indenture and Slavery

The Negro in the United States has had more than three centuries' experience with stratification, and has been subjected to almost every form of it. In 1619, when the first 20 Negroes were unloaded from a Dutch man-of-war at Jamestown, Virginia, they were given the status of indentured servants, as we have seen, since apparently it did not occur to the Virginians at the time to make slaves of them. Slavery, of course, is a very old institution, can be traced back to prehistoric times, and has had a world-wide distribution. Many preliterate peoples have been familiar with it, and the ancient civilizations of Sumeria, Egypt, Greece, Carthage, and Rome regarded it as a natural and normal phenomenon.[14] In the early part of the seventeenth century slavery was well established among the Portuguese, Spaniards, and Arabs, but it had not taken firm hold upon the British. The Virginians, therefore, had no precedent for enslaving these 20 Negroes. They were familiar with the institution of indenture, a system whereby an individual would contract to serve a number of years in return for his ocean voyage. Unlike slavery, servitude under indenture was neither lifelong nor hereditary. The British settlers were desperately in need of labor; but in a region where resources are abundant and population is scanty, it is impossible to induce a sufficient number of people to work for wages. At the same time, there were in the British Isles great numbers living in "penurie and want," who were not unwilling to try to improve their lot in the New World if someone would pay their passage. It is estimated that half of those who settled in the 13 American colonies came as indentured laborers.[15] Even so, the demand for labor could not be met by this system.

The first Negroes, then, were assigned to the status of indentured servants, the presumption being that after they had performed the service called for in their contracts, they would be free. They did not enjoy this status very long, however, and soon they began to be treated with more severity than were other indentured servants. The punishment meted out to them for violations of laws and customs was greater than that for others in the servant class, and sexual relations with Negroes were regarded as especially debasing. Gradually, by a series of laws enacted, court decisions rendered, and attitudes and mores developed, the Negro's status changed to one of hereditary, lifelong servitude, or slavery.[16] The change had come about well before the close of the century. The underlying factor, of course, was the demand for a labor supply. The Negro was preferable to white indentured servants for several reasons. For one thing, his ineradicable racial features made it difficult for him to escape; his women could be put to work in the fields, which was not the custom for white women; his services were available for life, while white servants were available only for a few years; and his children, unlike the children of whites, were also valuable property. All things considered, the Negro slave was well worth the additional cost. Negroes, therefore, eventually displaced white indentured servants in the cotton and tobacco colonies.

For years the relations of most Negroes and whites in the United States were those of masters and slaves. There were, to be sure, free Negroes, and their number rose to nearly half a million by 1860. Most of these had been set free by their owners, for reasons of sentiment or ideals, or because of some meritorious service performed while in slavery. Others were the descendants of free

[14] B. J. Stern, W. L. Westermann, *et al.*, "Slavery," *Encyclopedia of the Social Sciences*, Vol. 14, pp. 73–92; B. Berry, "Slavery," *Encyclopedia International*, Vol. 16, pp. 532–536.

[15] C. Goodrich, "Indenture," *Encyclopedia of the Social Sciences*, Vol. 7, pp. 644–647.

[16] The process whereby this came about is described in E. F. Frazier, *The Negro in the United States*, Ch. 2.

mothers (white or black), or of Indians and Negroes; and some, by their own thrift, had earned enough to purchase their freedom.[17] There were few of them in the regions of the large plantations, but they were numerous in the tidewater sections of Virginia and Maryland and in the Piedmont of North Carolina and Virginia. For the most part, however, they were an urban people, being concentrated in the seaboard cities of New Orleans, Mobile, Charleston, Boston, New York, Philadelphia, Baltimore, and Washington. Their status was a peculiar one. Some amassed considerable wealth and even owned slaves themselves. In the southern cities they engaged in the skilled trades, and followed a wide range of occupations. Among them were hotelkeepers, milliners, storekeepers, teachers, clerks, architects, and so on. In the North they had a more difficult time gaining a foothold in the economy. Frazier says:

> The free Negroes in the North did not form an intermediate stratum in a stable stratified society as did their brothers in the South. They were concentrated in cities where a great industrial civilization was coming into existence. They saw themselves disfranchised where universal suffrage was extended to the male population. They were generally excluded from public education which was becoming the right of all citizens. More important still, they were restricted in their efforts to make a living.[18]

The status of the free Negroes suffered many changes throughout the period of slavery and varied greatly from place to place; it is therefore difficult to generalize. For the most part, however, it was precarious and inhospitable. They found considerable discrimination in the courts, at the polls, in education, in industry, and in freedom of movement. Franklin speaks of them as "quasi-free Negroes" and says that "toward the end of the slave period the distinction between slaves and free Negroes had diminished to a point that in some instances was hardly discernible";[19] and Johnson says, "Altogether they constituted a most unfortunate and uncomfortable group."[20]

The Negro: After the Civil War

The Civil War marked the end of slave status for the Negro, but a new status was not immediately forthcoming. For 30 years a bitter conflict raged to determine just what the new "place" of the Negro would be. There were those who were determined to give him a status in no wise different from that of other American citizens; but such an objective was abhorrent to the South and had slight appeal to the North. Even President Lincoln never formulated a clear conception as to what the status of the Negro should be. The South, however,

[17] E. H. Fitchett, "The Origin and Growth of the Free Negro Population of Charleston, South Carolina," *The Journal of Negro History*, Vol. 26, No. 4, October 1941, pp. 421–437.
[18] Frazier, *op. cit.*, p. 79.
[19] J. H. Franklin, *From Slavery to Freedom*, p. 215.
[20] W. D. Weatherford and C. S. Johnson, *Race Relations*, p. 253.

had its own ideas; and immediately after the war one state after another enacted laws, known as Black Codes, which practically re-enslaved the Negro. Limitations were placed upon his ownership and rental of property, possession of firearms, testimony in court, freedom of speech and movement, choice of occupation, and voting privileges. Heavy penalties were levied for vagrancy and breach of contract which were tantamount to a system of forced labor. The North, motivated more by political and economic considerations than by concern for the Negro's welfare, used the Black Codes as an excuse for imposing military rule upon the South for the ostensible purpose of insuring the Negro's citizenship rights. Historians have debated and recounted at great length the events of the succeeding decade, the Reconstruction Period, and its final culmination in the Compromise of 1876, when the question of the Negro's status was discarded as a national issue and turned back to the South.[21] There followed several decades of further conflict, and finally a new pattern of accommodation emerged. This new pattern is commonly spoken of in the South as "white supremacy," and Negroes refer to it as "second-class citizenship." Its features are well known. The Negro was virtually disfranchised. His economic opportunities were severely limited, many occupations being closed to him, and a "job ceiling" established in those areas where he was allowed to work. The educational facilities provided for him were definitely inferior to those provided for whites. He was barred from most hotels, restaurants, theaters, barber shops, auditoriums, parks, and playgrounds; the accommodations provided for him on trains, street cars, and buses were separate, but seldom equal. He was restricted and exploited as a homeowner or tenant. The medical facilities available to him were limited, with the result that he suffered high mortality rates. In courts, and at the hands of the law, he did not enjoy the same treatment accorded whites.

Sociologists have been in the habit of using the term "caste" to describe the stratification pattern which developed following the Civil War. Early in the present century W. I. Thomas and Charles H. Cooley were pointing out the caste-like nature of race relations in the United States;[22] and in recent years a great many studies of the American race problem have given a prominent place to the concept of caste in their analyses.[23] Several scholars have challenged this popular use of the term "caste," and have questioned its utility and its validity as a description of the stratification pattern which developed in the United States. Brooks maintains that *segregation system* would more adequately describe the nature of racial accommodation in America;[24] and Frazier objects

[21] Frazier, *op. cit.*, Ch. 7 & 8; Franklin, *op. cit.*, Ch. 17 & 18.
[22] W. I. Thomas, "The Psychology of Race-Prejudice," *American Journal of Sociology*, Vol. 9, No. 5, March 1904, pp. 609 ff; C. H. Cooley, *Social Organization*, p. 218.
[23] W. L. Warner, "American Caste and Class," *American Journal of Sociology*, Vol. 42, No. 2, September 1936, pp. 234–237; J. Dollard, *Caste and Class in a Southern Town*; W. L. Warner and W. A. Davis, "A Comparative Study of American Caste," in E. Thompson (Ed.), *Race Relations and the Race Problem*, pp. 219–245; W. A. Davis, B. B. Gardner, and Mary R. Gardner, *Deep South*; B. B. Gallagher, *American Caste and the Negro College*.
[24] M. R. Brooks, "American Caste and Class: An Appraisal," *Social Forces*, Vol. 25, No. 2, December 1946, pp. 207–211.

Diagrammatic Representations of the System
of Negro-White Classes and Castes in the United States

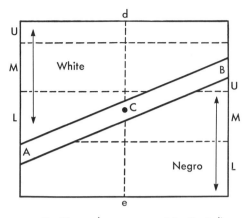 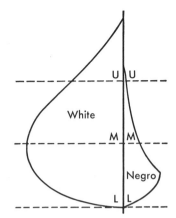

U — Upper class   A B — Caste line
M — Middle class   de — Ultimate position of caste line
L — Lower class   C — Axis of caste line

*The left-hand figure is Warner's diagram, presented in the Introduction to
A. Davis, B. B. Gardner, and M. R. Gardner, Deep South. The diagonal lines
separate the Negro caste from the white caste; the broken horizontal lines in
each segment separate the classes in each caste from one another. The double-
headed arrows indicate that movement up and down the class ladders does
occur. There is no movement or marriage, however, across the caste lines. Since
slavery (and to some extent even before) the caste line has swung on its
axis (C), so that the top Negro group is higher in class traits than the lower
white group. Will this swing continue, resulting in a horizontal arrangement,
or "parallelism," which many Negro and white leaders expound as a "solution"
of the race problem?*

    *The right-hand figure is from Myrdal, An American Dilemma, p. 692, and
represents the absolute numbers of whites and Negroes at each level of social
status.*

on the ground that there is no consistent pattern of Negro-white relations, even
in the South, but that the taboos and restrictions vary according to areas and
classes, between rural and urban environments, and the Negroes themselves are
continually fighting for their abolition. The most persistent opponent of the
caste concept, however, has been Oliver C. Cox,[25] who takes the position that
India alone has a developed caste system, and we must look there for the proper
criteria. Negro-white relations in the United States, he insists, differ from those
in India in that they are dynamic rather than static, are not accepted by the
Negroes are not occupationally restricted, and are not justified by a sacred

[25] O. C. Cox, "The Modern Caste School of Race Relations," *Social Forces*, Vol. 21, No.
2, December 1942, pp. 218–226; "Race and Caste: A Distinction," *American Journal of
Sociology*, Vol. 50, No. 5, March 1945, pp. 360–368; *Caste, Class and Race: A Study in Social
Dynamics*.

philosophy. Not many sociologists and anthropologists, however, would agree with Cox that India's system must be accepted as the norm for caste, and that the criteria he has chosen are the essential ones. Kroeber defines caste as "an endogamous and hereditary subdivision of an ethnic unit occupying a position of superior or inferior rank or social esteem in comparison with other such subdivisions";[26] and most social scientists, in their use of the term, would agree that hereditary status and endogamy are the essential features. It may be noted, further, that the Hindus themselves have never placidly accepted the caste system, nor has it been as static as Cox assumes.[27] Students of Hinduism have frequently referred to the continuous changes going on, and one of them says, "Throughout all the centuries since the caste system reached its full form, changes have occurred. . . . Groups of low-caste men have occasionally been able to secure recognition as belonging to higher castes. . . . Even now the process of caste formation has not ceased, and the modification of caste rules is still possible in any of the castes."[28] Cox's criticisms of the sociologists' use of the concept of caste in the American situation have not been convincing; and, while there are doubtless many differences between the caste systems of the various societies in which it has prevailed, there are basic similarities.[29]

The Negro: Revolt against the Caste System

There have been many changes over the years, and indeed the Negro's condition has never remained static, even during the period of slavery. Nor is it correct to say that the Negro meekly accepted his subordinate status. There have always been rebels among them, though for 300 years their efforts bore little fruit, and those who rallied behind them were few and far between.

During World War I, however, Negroes began to break the barriers of the caste system. Their horizons were lifted when some 400,000 of them moved from the rural South to the urban North to fill the employment vacuum created by the cessation of immigration from Europe. President Wilson's stirring assertions about democracy doubtless had their effect. Nearly 350,000 entered the Armed Services, and 100,000 served overseas. Negroes from various parts of the country were brought together, creating new insights and aspirations. They began to demand their rights as citizens, with the result that during and immediately following the war there were outbreaks of race riots in Washington, Chicago, Omaha, Knoxville, and scores of other cities and towns throughout the country. The Negro not only made demands, he was prepared to fight for them.

[26] A. L. Kroeber, "Caste," *Encyclopedia of the Social Sciences*, Vol. 3, pp. 254–256. See also *Dictionary of Sociology*, and E. B. Reuter, *Handbook of Sociology*, p. 89.

[27] Some of the historical cases of caste mobility are noted in J. H. Hutton, *Caste in India*, pp. 45, 107.

[28] J. H. Farquhar, *The Crown of Hinduism*, pp. 162–163.

[29] For a criticism of the Cox thesis, see N. D. Humphrey, "American Race Relations and the Caste System," *Psychiatry: Journal of the Biology and Pathology of Interpersonal Relations*, Vol. 8, No. 4, November 1956, pp. 379–381; E. W. Pohlman, *Hindu Social Class Organization and the Concept of Caste.*

The United States Supreme Court, too, which had long sanctioned the "white supremacy" and "separate but equal" philosophy, began to render verdicts favorable to the Negro's cause. In 1915 it invalidated the Oklahoma "Grandfather Clause," one device which had been employed for the disfranchisement of the Negro. In 1917 the Court ruled that a Louisville, Kentucky, ordinance providing for racial residential segregation violated the Fourteenth Amendment. Beginning in 1927 with the case of *Nixon v. Herndon* there was forthcoming a long series of rulings which destroyed the white political primary device; and in 1938 in the case of *Gaines v. Canada* the first crack appeared in the wall of school segregation.

The Great Depression of the 1930's weighed heavily upon the Negro, as it did upon the entire country, but many of the New Deal measures provided opportunities which had never existed before. Some received cash benefits under the various agricultural acts, and Negroes and whites voted together on the establishment of marketing quotas. Electricity was brought to many homes for the first time through T.V.A. and R.E.A. Many were assisted in purchasing farms through F.S.A., and others became home-owners with the assistance of H.O.L.C. Public housing projects enabled some to escape from the slums, and many learned skills and continued their education with the assistance of N.Y.A. In 1935 there was organized the Congress of Industrial Organizations (C.I.O.) which adopted membership policies more liberal than those of its rival organization, the American Federation of Labor.

World War II saw an acceleration of the movement toward equality. The number of Negro officers in the armed services grew from five to 7000. President Roosevelt's Executive Order No. 8802 forbade racial discrimination in defense industries and inaugurated the Fair Employment Practices Committee. The Supreme Court, too, continued to hand down decisions favorable to the Negro's cause.

Changes have come continually since World War II. President Truman in 1947 established the Committee on Civil Rights, and the following year saw the publication of its significant report, *To Secure These Rights*. Executive Order No. 9981, in 1948, led to the integration of the armed services. In 1945 New York State adopted a Fair Employment Practices law, and many other states followed in passing similar legislation. The Supreme Court continued to render decisions favorable to the Negro in the areas of voting, interstate travel, restrictive covenants, and education. Finally, on May 17, 1954, and on May 31, 1955, the Court handed down its historic decisions pertaining to separate educational facilities.

The Negro's changing status was manifested, also, by his acceptance into Big League baseball, football, and basketball, and by his prominence on Olympic teams, and in radio, television, and the movies. Negro novelists, poets, and artists were winning international acclaim, and Negro scholars began to receive appointments in the leading universities. His political power began to be used effectively, and the major parties vied for his vote. Big business became aware of his economic importance and began to compete for his patronage.

Congress passed new civil rights legislation in 1957, 1960, and 1964. The Negro's health and longevity showed significant gains, and illiteracy all but disappeared. Indeed, changes in the Negro's status in the 50 years between 1914 and 1964 far exceeded anyone's expectations or predictions.

Even so, there remains a broad hiatus between the Negro's position in society and that of the white.[30] His wages are lower, his unemployment rates higher. He has less formal education, and its quality is poorer. While his life expectancy has improved, so has that of other groups. He is still excluded from hotels, motels, restaurants, and places of amusement. It has been virtually impossible for him to break out of his ghetto. In many parts of the country he still finds insurmountable obstacles placed in the way of his registering and voting. He is still confined, partly by his own educational inadequacies and partly because of discrimination, to the low-paying service and semi-skilled occupations.

The Negro's demands for equality grew more insistent than ever in the 1960's. He grew impatient with the slow pace of school integration. He became disillusioned when he observed how the rulings of the courts and the acts of Congress were circumvented. Unemployment, brought on by increasing automation, fell heavily upon him. His leaders grew more aggressive. The older organizations, the N.A.A.C.P. and the Urban League, adopted bolder techniques; CORE (Congress of Racial Equality), which arose in 1942, gained in prominence; and new movements — Student Non-violent Coordinating Committee (SNCC or "Snick") — came into being. "Freedom Rides," demonstrations, marches, sit-ins, boycotts, and numerous other forms of protest became daily occurrences throughout the country. The American Negro had finally become aroused to destroy the caste system and to end his second-class status.

The Status of Hybrids

The process of stratification, operating as it does when racial and ethnic groups come into contact, invariably encounters the problem of the hybrid. What shall be the status of those of mixed blood, one of whose parents comes from the dominant group and the other from the subordinate? The problem arose very early in colonial America. In the hope of avoiding it, Virginia levied heavy penalties for miscegenation; but as we have seen, these did not prevent the rise of a mulatto element in the population. In 1662, accordingly, a law was passed which imposed the mother's status upon her children — that is, the children of a Negro woman slave and a white man would be slaves for life, and the father would pay a fine double that for other fornication. Other laws quickly followed. One specified that, should a white woman marry a Negro or a mulatto, she would be condemned to five years of servitude, if a servant, and if she were free, would be banished from the colony. Their children were classed as bastards, and

[30] See Marion Hayes, "A Century of Change: Negroes in the U.S. Economy, 1860–1960," *Monthly Labor Review*, December 1962, pp. 1359–1365; M. A. Kessler, "Economic Status of Nonwhite Workers, 1955–62," Special Labor Force Report No. 33, U.S. Department of Labor, July 1963; H. P. Miller, "Is the Income Gap Closed? No!" *The New York Times Magazine*, Vol. 11, 1962, pp. 50–58.

were bound, as other bastards were, to a term of apprenticeship until they were 30 years of age. In due course, further laws of a similar nature were passed; and Virginia was followed by Maryland, Massachusetts, Connecticut, Pennsylvania, New York, and the other colonies, in an effort to prevent miscegenation and to fix the status of the offspring of mixed unions. It became the practice to regard a person as a Negro who had any known Negro ancestry; and that is still the American policy, manifested in the decision of courts, the Census, and in social relations. Sinclair Lewis made this the theme of his *Kingsblood Royal*, a novel, incidentally, which would seem utterly incredible to those in other societies where the mulatto holds a status quite different from that assigned him in the United States. Within the Negro group, the person of mixed blood may enjoy a certain prestige; but as far as the dominant whites are concerned, no distinction is made between the status of the mulatto and the full-blood Negro. The whites, outnumbering the Negroes nine to one, have no need to drive a wedge between the mixed and the unmixed.

The status of the hybrid is quite different in other societies. Often it is distinctly lower than that of either of the parent stocks. Reference has been made repeatedly to the Anglo-Indian, who is rejected alike by his British and his Indian forbears, and who has been condemned to an anomalous and unenviable status. It was not always so, however, and need not remain so in the future. In the early days of contact, the Anglo-Indian stood much higher in the social system, and enjoyed many privileges denied to the natives. Another area where the hybrid has low status is East Africa. Dr. E. Kalibala, a native of Africa and a member of the Grasshopper clan of the Ganda tribe, told the author several years ago that there are mulattoes among his own people, and that they are regarded with condescension and contempt and are considered something of a problem. At one time the plan was discussed of relegating them to an island in Lake Victoria, where they might live out their lives in complete isolation.

Elsewhere the hybrid has been assigned a position intermediate between the dominant and subordinate groups. So it is in South Africa, where there are over a million mixed-bloods, known as the Cape Coloured. They are a mixture of Portuguese, Hottentot, Dutch, Malay, Bantu, and of Negro slaves imported from West Africa and Mozambique. Thousands of them over the years have passed into the white group, but most have some tell-tale racial features which make passing impossible. Some are agricultural laborers or farmers, but the majority live in the cities where they are engaged in the less desirable occupations. They take pride in their white blood, but despise their colored. They identify themselves in every possible way with the dominant whites, who are careful not to accept them as equals, and continually try to place as wide a gulf as they can between themselves and the natives, who doubtless would accept them if they chose to cast their lot with them. In the meantime they constitute an intermediate caste, a buffer group, separating whites and natives; and the former, so greatly outnumbered by the latter, appreciate the support of the Cape Coloured.

The status of the hybrid, therefore, varies greatly from place to place. In some situations he is a despised outcast, and in some he is forced into the status

‚As the Orthodox religious rituals show, many Jews cling to established customs and a feeling of group consciousness.

of the subordinate group from which he is descended. Often, however, he is assigned to an intermediate position — as in South Africa, the islands of the Caribbean, and Java — but even this intermediate status may be barely superior to the lower one, and may mean merely clinging to the fringes of the dominant group. And in Haiti, to cite only one instance, the elite of the society are mulattoes. These differences in the status of hybrids are the result of a complex of economic, demographic, historical, and cultural factors.

American Mestizos

Stratification, as a form of accommodation between racial and ethnic groups, is a continuous process, and does not result in a permanent, precise form of adjustment. Classes, castes, and other types of prestige groups are seldom drawn with exact lines, and never with inflexible ones. This is especially true of hybrid peoples. To illustrate the anomalous, unstable product of the stratification process as it operates in race relations, we shall consider a little-known group of Americans whom we call, for want of a better term, *mestizos*. As we have seen, *mestizo* is a word commonly used in Latin America to refer to the offspring of Indians and Europeans, but it is sometimes used for other mixtures also. The term has been rarely used in the United States, and with varying connotations.

Throughout the Eastern states there are numerous "islands" of people whose blood is mixed, but the nature of the mixture is a matter of dispute. Most of their ancestry is white, and their physical features are predominantly those of white people. There is probably some Indian blood in them also which traces back to colonial times. The crucial question revolves around the presence of Negro blood. The whites almost invariably suspect that there is some in the mixture, and occasionally there are racial features, such as skin color or hair form, to give a basis for their suspicions. The members of these isolated groups, however, vehemently deny any Negro ancestry.

Groups of such people are numerous and widespread. Gilbert has made a compilation, which gives some idea of their distribution, but which is by no means complete.[31] In South Carolina there are many communities, where they are known as Brass Ankles, Red Bones, Red Legs, Turks, or Yellow-hammers; in Alabama and Mississippi they are called Creoles or Cajuns; in North Carolina, where there are 45,000 of them, they are called Croatans; in West Virginia and Maryland, Guineas; in Virginia, Issues; in New Jersey and New York, Jackson Whites; in the Southern Appalachians, where Virginia, Kentucky and Tennessee meet, they are known as Melungeons; in Delaware they are Moors and Nanticokes; in Louisiana, Red Bones; in Southern Maryland, Wesorts; in Ohio, Carmel Indians.[32]

Most of these groups have a long history, generously interspersed with legend and myth. Their origins are generally unknown, but most of them have some story to account for their presence. Those in North Carolina, for instance, profess to be the descendants of Sir Walter Raleigh's Lost Colony; others think they are derived from the Acadians immortalized in Longfellow's *Evangeline*. Though these stories are doubtless fiction, there is evidence to prove the existence of these groups of free, hybrid peoples as far back as colonial times.

The status of these people is ill-defined. The whites, in accordance with their theory that a drop of Negro blood makes one a Negro, are disposed to regard them as Negroes and to subject them to the customary forms of segregation and discrimination. The *mestizos*, however, deny any Negro ancestry, and rebel against being forced into the Negro caste. They strive, therefore, to achieve the status of whites — or, at least, to avoid being classified as Negroes. Their problem is more difficult in the South, where strict segregation is the rule in schools, churches, trains, buses, theaters, jails, hospitals, and restaurants.

For generations the *mestizos* met their problem by isolating themselves, by forming compact rural communities removed from the whites and Negroes alike. Recently, with the shrinking of distances, their isolation has been breaking down; and they have been forced to seek other adjustments. Some of them fight their way into the white race; they migrate to nearby cities or to other parts of

[31] W. H. Gilbert, Jr., "Memorandum Concerning the Characteristics of the Larger Mixed-Blood Racial Islands of the Eastern United States," *Social Forces*, Vol. 24, No. 4, May 1946, pp. 438–447.
[32] Cf. B. Berry, *Almost White*.

the country, where they are not known and where they have little or no trouble in being accepted. Others have sought to win for themselves recognition as Indians, deeming that preferable to Negro status. Those in North Carolina and Delaware, especially, have followed such a policy, and with some success, though most whites say they are not "real Indians," and Johnson says they are "Indians by courtesy."[33] Some have followed the line of least resistance and have become absorbed by the Negroes; but many still continue, in spite of the mounting obstacles, to solve their dilemma by segregation and isolation.

One consequence of the meeting of peoples, then, has been the subordination of the one and the assumption by the other of a position of authority, power, and domination. This has been so at least since the dawn of history, and probably long before; and it has occurred on all continents and among all races. The form that such stratification takes, however, admits of wide variability, from a loose and flexible system of class to a rigid and immutable institution of caste. The members of a subordinate group may accept for a time their inferior status, and may devise ingenious and satisfying rationalizations for it, but they will not indefinitely submit to its injustice. Accordingly, race relations take on a dynamic character, and astute students of race problems have insisted that they are basically and essentially a struggle for status.

[33] G. B. Johnson, "Personality in a White-Indian-Negro Community," *American Sociological Review*, Vol. 4, No. 4, August 1939, p. 516.

9

Segregation

Segregation is a wall, erected by our fears, against certain real or supposed dangers.

JAMES MCBRIDE DABBS
The Southern Heritage

The late Senator Theodore Bilbo of Mississippi, beloved of the Ku Klux Klan and despised by most liberals and other minority groups, used to insist that he was a great friend of the Negro. As evidence of his sincerity he would periodically propose that the Negroes be sent "back to Africa." This theme was a popular one with the Senator's constituents, and, curiously enough, won the support of many Negroes, as the following shows:[1]

Mississippi's Theodore ("The Man") Bilbo arose in the Senate one day last week to display a bulky petition. It bore, he said, the names of 2,500,000 U.S. Negroes who would prefer to live in Africa. For three-and-a-half hours and 26 pages of the *Congressional Record*, he expanded on a way to make this possible: let the Government establish a Greater Liberia for "repatriated" blacks.

Mr. Bilbo thus returned to a favorite theme and revived an idea older than the U.S. itself. By subsidizing a Negro exodus to Africa, he maintained, the U.S. would rid its whites of a depressed and depressing race, save itself from racial "amalgamation."

"By this separation," droned little Mr. Bilbo, "the blood stream of the white race shall remain uncontaminated and all the . . . blessings of the white man's civilization shall forever remain the priceless possession of Anglo-Saxons. . . ."

In support of his bill to create Greater Liberia, Senator Bilbo . . . declared that 20,000 mulattoes annually "cross the color line" (pass for whites). If miscegenation goes on unchecked, he predicted the U.S. will become a land of decadent mongrels, "a yellow race yet to come."

Listening in the Senate gallery was Mrs. Mattie Maude Lena Gordon, a portly mulatto from Chicago. Mrs. Gordon raises her coffee-cream arms, shouts to her audiences: "There's amalgamation for you." Most of the signatures on Mr. Bilbo's petition were gathered from 45 states by her Peace Movement of Ethiopia, a repatriationist cult which has its headquarters at her apartment on Chicago's South Side. . . . Last week some 300 of her followers . . . arrived in Washington by truck and car, so fagged that they could hardly drag themselves up the Capitol step to hear their friend from Mississippi. . . .

Senator Bilbo vows that 8,000,000 . . . Negroes would hop at the chance to escape the white man's yoke, live on the white man's subsidies until they establish farms and businesses. . . .

Mrs. Gordon, and her Peace Movement of Ethiopia, still preach their doctrine from their headquarters in Chicago, despite the passing of their champion, Senator Bilbo; but today the call for segregation is sounded in louder and clearer notes by the Black Muslims. The Muslims deplore the trend toward integration, ridicule Martin Luther King and his philosophy of non-violence, profess contempt for the white man, and laud and glorify the history and achievements of the Black Man (they reject the term "Negro"). They disclaim any desire to be accepted by white society, for, they insist, the days of the white man are numbered. They long for the time when American Negroes will return to their homeland in Africa, and in the meantime they demand that one or two of the 50 states be set aside for Negroes only, where they might live in isolation.

[1] Courtesy of *Time*, Copyright Time Inc., May 8, 1939.

The Nature of Segregation

Segregation means the act, process, or state of being separate or set apart. It is a form of isolation which places limits or restrictions upon contact, communication, and social relations. Many people regard segregation as a form of partial ostracism, superimposed upon a minority by the dominant group; and it is often treated as though it were synonymous with discrimination. Usually it does indeed involve unequal treatment, and it is commonly a condition forced upon one group by another. It need not, however, include either coercion or discrimination. Segregation is essentially a pattern of accommodation, which assumes a wide variety of forms and is the product of many complex motives.

Voluntary Segregation

Segregation may be either voluntary or involuntary. The former process is illustrated by the Mennonites, who have striven to isolate themselves from the general population in their determination to resist the forces of assimilation. They began migrating to America from Central Europe in the Colonial period, when William Penn promised them religious tolerance in his colony; and from Pennsylvania they have moved on to a number of other states. A second wave of Mennonite immigration, this time from Russia to Canada and the United States, began in 1871. It was prompted by the inauguration of a new Russian policy which threatened to break down the isolation of these people and to foster assimilation. Accordingly, they fled to the New World, where they proceeded to establish their remote communities, to exclude all outside influences, and thereby to safeguard their social heritage.[2] They have not been as successful as

[2] E. K. Francis, "The Russian Mennonites: From Religious to Ethnic Group," *American Journal of Sociology*, Vol. 54, No. 2, September 1948, pp. 101–107.

they hoped in rejecting the culture of their neighbors, but they have, to an amazing degree, remained a distinct ethnic group. Among their many colonies are two in Yamhill County, Oregon, which have been the subject of sociological study.[3] In these communities many of the old features of Mennonite culture have been retained — the headship of the bishop, the ban against exogamy, the taboo of secret societies and labor unions, the disapproval of commercial insurance, the refusal to participate in elections and to use the courts, the simplicity of dress, the wearing of beards but not mustaches (they shave the upper lip because the mustache was formerly the badge of a soldier). The Amish,[4] the more conservative of the two communities, even forbid the automobile, the telephone, moving pictures, and secondary and college education. They do, however, accept electric lights, the daily newspaper, and tractors. The authors of the study suspect that, in this selection and rejection of new culture traits, there is a disposition to interdict those which facilitate communication with the out-group and which threaten solidarity. Thus automobiles are forbidden, but not tractors; the moving picture is undesirable, but baseball is admitted; the telephone is feared, but not electric lights. The newspaper is recognized as a danger, but they subscribe nevertheless in order that they may "follow news events as they are related to Biblical prophecy."

Involuntary Segregation

The segregation of the American Negro, on the contrary, is not of his own volition. Unlike the Mennonite, he wants to attend the theater, join labor unions, participate in elections, escape residential restrictions, use the public services, acquire all the education possible, enter any occupation, and face the same dangers in time of war that other citizens are called upon to face. In all these areas of life, however, he finds himself circumscribed and excluded; and he accordingly wages an incessant war against the restrictions which isolate him and prevent his full participation in the culture.

There are other racial and ethnic groups whose segregation partakes of both voluntary and involuntary features. Consider the heterogeneous population of a typical American city, with its Chinatown, "Little Tokyo," "Dago Hill," "Kilgubbin," "Little Poland," and "Swede Town." In the case of some of these groups, of course, there is a conscious and deliberate effort at segregation, and public opinion and restrictive covenants have been effectively employed to that end; but often the ethnic colonies which have arisen in the cities are the result of a competitive process, mostly economic, of which both the dominant and the minority group are but dimly aware. Such was the Persian colony of Chicago, described by Zorbaugh.[5] At the time the study was made it was estimated that there were

---

[3] W. C. Smith, Victoria Fugua, and P. Louie, "The Mennonites of Yamhill County, Oregon," *Research Studies, State College of Washington*, Vol. 7, 1940, pp. 33–38.

[4] The most thorough account of the Amish is to be found in J. A. Hostetler, *Amish Society*.

[5] H. W. Zorbaugh, *The Gold Coast and the Slum*, pp. 142–145.

approximately 3000 members of the group. They were concentrated for the most part, but not entirely, for there was a scattering of Persians elsewhere in the city. It was not pressure from the outside which forced them into the colony, nor a burning desire on their part to perpetuate their culture. Instead, their segregation might have been more properly attributed to their economic status, their preference for their own kind, and the enjoyment of the coffee house, where they gathered in the evenings to eat, talk, smoke, and play cards. In Seattle, Schmid found great differences between the various racial and ethnic groups in their tendency toward segregation.[6] English, Welsh, Danes, Canadians, Scotch, Irish, and Germans were well scattered over the city, and showed no appreciable tendency to become segregated; while the Norwegians, Swedes, Russians, Austrians, and Greeks showed a marked tendency toward concentration. The Finns were segregated, but in two widely separated communities; and the Italians were the most concentrated of all the foreign-born ethnic peoples. The *racial* groups in the population — Japanese, Chinese, Negroes, and Filipinos — showed a pronounced tendency to segregate, which Schmid attributed to "pressure of public opinion, internal cohesion, and relatively low economic status."

A sharp distinction, accordingly, cannot be drawn between voluntary segregation on the one hand and involuntary segregation on the other. As a matter of fact, Professor Werner J. Cahnman of Rutgers finds the two processes so unlike that he chooses to call the former "congregation" and the latter, only, "segregation." And Professor D. Y. Yuan of Louisiana State has proposed a "scale of intensity" as follows:

Voluntary Segregation: (1) Strict voluntary
(2) Voluntary
(3) Voluntary involving involuntary factors
Involuntary Segregation: (4) Involuntary involving voluntary factors
(5) Involuntary
(6) Strict involuntary.[7]

Universality of Segregation

Our illustrations thus far in this chapter have all come from the United States, but one must not suppose that segregation is a peculiarly American pattern of interracial adjustment. The fact is that wherever unlike peoples have come into contact and have attempted to live together, they have hit upon the device of setting themselves apart and restricting their contacts. Centuries ago the Chinese built a great wall — one of the wonders of the world — in an effort to save

[6] C. F. Schmid, *Social Trends in Seattle*, pp. 4–5. Cf., also, C. F. Schmid and W. W. McVey, Jr., *Growth and Distribution of Minority Races in Seattle, Washington*.
[7] "Voluntary Segregation: A Study of New York Chinatown," *Phylon* (Fourth Quarter) 1963, pp. 255ff.

themselves from contacts with foreigners; and more recently, when Jews and Arabs were at odds over their relations in Palestine, the policy of dividing the country between them appeared the only feasible solution.

And today, on the island of Cyprus, where Greeks and Turks seem unable to live side by side, it is being proposed that the island be divided, each ethnic group being assigned a territory from which the other group would be excluded.

In the Republic of South Africa a pattern of segregation has long been in effect. The population of the republic is nearly 16 million, of whom approximately 19 per cent are known as Europeans, 68 per cent are Natives (Bantus), 9 per cent are Coloureds (hybrids), and 3 per cent are Asiastics. These figures, however, barely suggest the heterogeneity of the population. The Europeans, for instance, include 100,000 Jews, and, of the remainder, about 40 per cent are of British descent, and 60 per cent Afrikaners (formerly known as Boers, and themselves a mixture of Dutch, Huguenot, and several other strains). The Asiatics are represented by Chinese and others, but are mostly second-generation Indians, whose parents were brought over to work on sugar plantations. In addition, there is a substantial minority of Cape Malays, as well as a few odd groups such as Griquas, Hottentots, Bushmen, St. Helenians, and others. Small wonder, as MacCrone says, that

> In South Africa racial prejudices of all kinds find a happy hunting-ground. . . . Contacts between English and Dutch, between Jew and Gentile, between white and black, between Bantu, Cape Coloured, and Indian, have all, without exception, proved to be fertile breeding-grounds for those social attitudes which are so inadequately described as "race" or "colour" prejudices.[8]

The major problem, as the white Europeans have always defined it, is that of maintaining their position of dominance with respect to the far more numerous natives, and they have met the problem in part by establishing a rigid system of segregation. Prior to 1948 nearly half the natives lived on Reserves, or Native Areas, which had been set aside for them, and where they were permitted to carry on their tribal life in some fashion, free from contacts with whites. Half a million lived in compounds belonging to the gold and diamond mines and to other industrial concerns. Three quarters of a million lived in segregated districts in the suburbs of cities, known as *locations*, or in servants' quarters in the rear of Europeans' homes. The remainder were employed as laborers on the farms of Europeans.

The fears of the Europeans, however, were not allayed by these arrangements. In the elections of 1948 one of the chief campaign planks of the National party was one known as *apartheid*, or segregation. It was proposed to divide the Republic of South Africa into separate compartments, each reserved for one racial group. One was to be for Europeans only, another for Natives, and another for those who are neither European nor Native (chiefly Asiatics, Indians, Pakistanis, and so on). Segregation, under the plan, would be compulsory.

[8] I. D. MacCrone, *Race Attitudes in South Africa*, p. vi.

Once the government had ordered, say, Indians, to evacuate an area reserved for whites, there could be no appeal. Nor would compensation be provided for expropriated property. Nor did the government obligate itself to provide land or housing for uprooted persons.

The National party won the election, and the policy of racial segregation, advocated in the campaign, has been vigorously promoted both by Prime Minister Malan and by his successors in office. The program has aroused bitter protests, especially from the Africans and Asiatics most adversely affected by it, but also from many whites.

Segregation, nevertheless, has been extended and enforced. The courts severely punish any kind of race mixing, and advocates of integration find themselves accused of treason. With few exceptions, Negroes in South Africa are denied the right to vote or to live in white neighborhoods. They may not hold public office, attend schools with whites, ride the same buses, or hold the same kinds of jobs as whites. They must carry passes when they move around; and they may not buy homes outside their reservations. Interracial marriages are strictly prohibited. Negroes are forbidden to belong to a union, or to strike; they may not buy liquor, patronize the same theaters or hotels that whites use, or sit on benches in parks and stations which are reserved for Europeans. Segregation, in short, has been extended to cover every aspect of life, and has the full force of the government behind it.

Elsewhere in the world one finds the pattern of racial segregation in effect. For example, in the city of Brazzaville, in what was formerly French Equatorial Africa, Europeans and Negroes were in the habit of segregating themselves. Comhaire, who studied the situation, maintained that it was an entirely voluntary arrangement. Africans had the privilege of living anywhere in the city they chose, even in the European areas, but they apparently preferred to live with others of their own race and culture.[9] Gist maintains that segregation prevails in the cities of India, but such segregation reflects caste, occupation, religion, and economic status.[10] One finds, he says, areas occupied mainly or exclusively by Brahmins, others by "untouchable" castes, and still other areas occupied by those of intermediate castes. Most of the larger Indian cities have fairly large Moslem populations which reside, for the most part, in Moslem districts. Christians, too, manifest the same tendency. "Segregation in Indian cities," says Gist, "is essentially voluntary; certainly it is not legally compulsory, although the dictates of custom are strong, prejudices do exist, and there is undoubtedly some discrimination."

Spatial and Social Segregation

In most instances of segregation the isolation and social distance between the racial groups are based upon physical separation. Thus the American Indians

[9] J. L. L. Comhaire, "Urban Segregation and Racial Legislation in Africa," *American Sociological Review*, Vol. 15, No. 3, June 1950, pp. 392ff.

[10] N. P. Gist, *Urban Society*, p. 184.

are removed to reservations, the natives of South Africa are confined within the reserves, the Negro is restricted to residence within the Black Belt, the Chinese are driven into Chinatown, or the Amish withdraw to their own rural community. But segregation does not depend upon physical separation. Custom and tradition may erect barriers between groups which serve to isolate them as effectively as stone walls or miles of open space. Gillin observed such a situation in the Guatemalan town of San Louis Jilotepeque.[11] A spot map of the community shows that residential segregation is not practiced at all; Indians and *ladinos* live side by side in all quarters of the town, and their interdependence is such that neither could live without the other. Even though they are not separated physically and spatially, there are insurmountable cultural barriers. Custom regulates their social intercourse so effectively that the two groups virtually have different civilizations; and Gillin says, "It may properly be asked if this situation can rightly be considered a community, or whether it is actually two communities."

An even better example of social segregation comes from the Southern states, where etiquette and mores serve to isolate Negroes and whites, even though physical contacts are numerous and frequent, and residential segregation is not pronounced. Custom not only decrees that the races be separate in their schools and churches, but it forbids their eating and drinking together or jointly participating in recreational activities, and even regulates such behavior as conversation, sitting and standing in each other's presence, handshaking, the tipping of the hat, use of titles and terms of address, bodily postures to be assumed, the tone of the voice, proper approaches in public, and entrance into a home.[12]

The chief function of interracial etiquette is no doubt social control but it operates effectively also to keep the races apart. Myrdal comments upon the "remarkable lack of correct information about the Negroes" which he found among white lawyers, physicians, ministers, and educators in the South, and says:

> The ignorance about the Negro is the more striking as the Southerner is himself convinced that he "knows the Negro," while the Yankee is supposedly ignorant on the subject. The insistence on the part of the Southern whites that they have reliable and intimate knowledge about the Negro problem is one of the most pathetic stereotypes in the South.[13]

It was Myrdal's contention that segregation is growing so complete that the white Southerner has no opportunity to know the Negro except as a servant or in other standardized and formalized situations.

[11] J. Gillin, "Parallel Cultures and the Inhibitions to Acculturation in a Guatemalan Community," *Social Forces*, Vol. 24, No. 1, October 1945, pp. 1–14.

[12] B. W. Doyle, *The Etiquette of Race Relations in the South*; G. Myrdal, *An American Dilemma*, pp. 608–618. The interracial etiquette is well portrayed in Richard Wright's *Black Boy* and *Uncle Tom's Children* (especially the autobiographical sketch, "The Ethics of Living Jim Crow").

[13] *Op. cit.*, p. 41.

How completely isolated the races are is especially apparent to northern Negroes when they experience the segregation system of the South for the first time. A. R. King has investigated some of these cases.[14] One was a young Doctor of Philosophy, a descendant of Negroes who had lived in the North for generations. He had always associated with whites, and had been subjected to a certain amount of discrimination both in high school and at the small New England college from which he had graduated. Nor was he entirely unfamiliar with the southern situation, having learned much about it from a brother who had taught in the South, and having discussed the problem frequently with his family. When he finished his college work he accepted a teaching position in the Deep South, and felt that he was able to adjust to the segregation pattern. The realities of the situation, however, were worse than he had anticipated. Upon arrival in the city, no white taxi driver would take him to his destination; he was unprepared for the thorough-going segregation which he found in public conveyances, stores, and theaters; he was humiliated by the treatment accorded him on one occasion by the police. Although there was a white university in the same city in which his own institution was located, he felt cut off from his fellow scientists there. His feelings were expressed in the following words:

> The fact that my association with whites has been taken away does not matter so much. The real fall in my status is the fact that the professional contact has been lost. I have only my associate here at the college and a high school teacher to really discuss things with. I only go to the white university for a specific purpose, not to talk and discuss in an informal way. . . . Around here my training forces recognition from my white contemporaries in my field. They are willing to accept me on a professional level. However, I have lost most of my contacts . . . and I find myself being left out in the cold.[15]

The etiquette of race relations in the South is a highly complex ritual, and is not mastered overnight. There are even occasions when the rules are set aside, if one knows how, when, and where. Violations of the ritual on the part of whites are an invitation to reproach, ranging from ridicule and gossip to ostracism and even bodily harm. Negroes who fail to observe the etiquette are not dealt with so lightly, and lynchings have often been defended, if not caused, by a Negro's being "too uppity," "insulting a white man," or "not turning out of the road for white boy in auto." Ignorance of the etiquette is no excuse, and northern Negroes who are unacquainted with its details have often paid the penalty for their inexperience. Making the matter even more complicated are the variations in the etiquette from place to place, a fact which has been well substantiated by Charles S. Johnson, who has shown that "the ubiquitous color line in the United States traces a varied and complex pattern . . . irrational and

---

[14] "Status Personality Change in Northern Negroes in Southern United States," *Social Forces*, Vol. 26, No. 2, December 1947, pp. 153–166.

[15] *Ibid.*, p. 158.

intangible . . . devoid of defensible logic . . . nevertheless one of the most positive realities in American life."[16]

When Johnson wrote his book, *Patterns of Negro Segregation*, in 1943, none would have disputed his contention that there is a "ubiquitous color line" dividing Negroes and whites in the United States, and that the system of social segregation was so complete and effective that communication between the races was reduced to a bare minimum. Negroes, especially in the South, lived in their restricted neighborhoods, attended their own schools and colleges, had their own churches, rode in separate sections of buses and street cars, sat in restricted seats in movie theaters, were limited to their own recreational facilities, had their own clubs and associations, and commonly used separate drinking fountains, toilets, elevators, waiting rooms, stairways, and entrances.

Many changes have come about, however, since World War II. Courts have ruled against restrictive covenants, have declared segregation illegal in housing developments receiving direct or indirect aid from tax sources, have gone on record against segregated schools, have ruled against segregated swimming pools and golf courses, have ordered integration on common carriers, and in various other ways have dealt mortal blows to the segregation pattern. In addition to these formal steps, there has been occurring what some have described as "creeping desegregation." Negroes, by virtue of their increased purchasing power and their improved educational status, find that merchants, the press, professional people, and the general public are less insistent than they formerly were on the rigidity of the color line and on the subtleties of interracial etiquette. The end of social segregation is not in sight certainly, but cracks, even wide gaps, are apparent in the structure.

Many and Mixed Motives for Segregation

The motives have been numerous. Even altruism has not been absent, as when the Danish government isolated its Greenland Eskimos to protect them against the ravages of white contact. Ethnocentrism has often prompted a group to isolate itself in order to preserve what it regards as the purity of its racial stock, or to avoid assimilation, or to perpetuate and protect a way of life which is highly valued. Isolation has frequently been chosen by an ethnic group as preferable to competition and conflict. An equally wide variety of motives has operated within the dominant groups which have imposed segregation upon unwilling minorities. In some instances a policy of segregation has been adopted only when efforts at assimilation have failed. At other times it has been imposed for fear of the disruptive effects the minority might have upon the society, or simply because of deep prejudice and antipathy toward the isolated group. Most often, perhaps, segregation has been adopted as a technique of controlling the minority, and of protecting the dominant group's status. Segregation, too, is a device which facilitates exploitation of one group by another.

[16] *Patterns of Negro Segregation*, p. 227.

Patterns of Segregation

Conflict between racial and ethnic groups is as old as the human race itself, and the practice of resolving those conflicts by separation, isolation, or segregation is equally ancient. The Bible and other early records afford many illustrations, and even preliterate peoples have frequently resorted to it. Thus the primitive Ainus, faced with annihilation or absorption when the Japanese invaded their territory, chose to withdraw to the less hospitable islands at the northern end of the archipelago; the pygmy Semang retreated to the jungles to avoid contact with the numerous hordes which for centuries have swept over the Malay Peninsula; and the Bushmen, driven by one people after another, finally found refuge in the unwanted Kalahari Desert of Africa. Indian tribes in the Americas, too, have often chosen withdrawal and segregation in preference to annihilation, assimilation, or subordination. Segregation, operating as it has done over so wide a range and under such a variety of circumstances, has assumed a multitude of forms, a few examples of which we now consider.

Chinatown

There are some 230,000 persons of Chinese ancestry living in the United States today, the great majority of whom are native-born American citizens. They are a highly urbanized people, many of them being squeezed into the Chinatowns of our major cities. The largest of these is in San Francisco, with more than 17,000, and second is that in New York with 11,000. Chicago, Oakland, and Los Angeles have two, three, and four thousand respectively; Chinatowns of more than 1000 are found in Stockton, Brooklyn, Boston, Seattle, Portland, and Sacramento; and many other cities have colonies of several hundred. The Chinese were once the objects of bitter prejudice but are so no longer. Instead, they are looked upon with a certain tolerance and indifference by the whites. Many a city considers its Chinatown a commercial asset — an attraction for tourists, a perfectly safe spot where one may go for an exotic meal, for curios, or for a glimpse of a quaint and mysterious people. Though the Chinese live in the very heart of our cities, so great is the gulf which separates them from the rest of society that they are indeed a strange and unknown minority. Those who crossed the Pacific to America have had quite a different experience from those who stopped off at Hawaii.

The records show that only one Chinese was admitted to the United States in 1820, and in 1850 there were only 758 in the country. But they began arriving in great numbers with the discovery of gold in California. About 20,000 were admitted in 1852, and 13,000 in 1854. While they were never welcomed with open arms, there was a place for them in California in those days. The miners, intent upon finding gold, did not relish any foreign competitors at all; but there were menial jobs that had to be done, food to be cooked and clothes to be laundered, and the Chinese were not unwilling to perform these lowly tasks. Their presence, accordingly, was somewhat appreciated; and they were spoken of as "thrifty," "orderly and industrious," "sober and law-abiding." Governor Mc-Dougal even recommended that further immigration be encouraged by land grants, since they were "one of the most worthy of our newly adopted citizens."[17] The gold fever began to subside by 1856; but after the Civil War the transcontinental railroads were being constructed, and there was a demand for labor which the Chinese were called upon to fill. The Union Pacific, moving from the East, relied largely upon the Irish and other European immigrants; but on the Central Pacific, pushing from the West, nine out of ten of the laborers were Chinese. The final joining of these two roads at Promontory, Utah, on May 10, 1869, marked an historic moment for America, but catastrophe for the Chinese. It meant that they would have to look for other jobs, and there was a business depression at the time.

The Chinese were willing to do anything. They began as miners, but when the whites resented their competition, they moved into other fields. They worked as domestics and common laborers; they were available for seasonal work; they operated stores and hotels; they engaged in fishing; they became cooks and carpenters; they were employed in the first manufacturing enterprises on the West Coast — cigars, shoes, clothing, soap, and candles. At one time most of the agricultural laborers in California were Chinese.

Conflict appeared whenever the whites moved into those occupations in which the Chinese were engaged.[18] First it was mining. The California legislature in 1852 imposed a special tax upon all aliens engaged in mining, and the tax was increased in succeeding years, until it was declared unconstitutional in 1870. There was agitation against the Chinese cigar makers in 1859; and in 1867 there was a race riot, when whites engaged in the boot and shoe industry blamed a reduction in their wages on Chinese competition. A smallpox epidemic in 1870 was attributed to the Chinese. Anti-coolie clubs were organized; mass meetings, parades, riots, and destruction of property prevailed; and political parties pledged themselves to rid the state of the Mongolian menace. The Chinese, once praised for their industry and cleanliness, now found themselves condemned as filthy, deceitful, "moon-eyed lepers."

The Californians made a national issue of their prejudice against the Chinese. They were clever in the way they proceeded, tying up the Oriental problem with that of the Negro whenever possible, and pressing the issue especially on the eve of elections, when political parties were eager to please anyone who could cast a vote. In 1868 the Burlingame Treaty was negotiated, recognizing the right of immigration between the United States and China, but hedging on the matter of naturalization. This treaty pleased the railroads, which still wanted cheap labor, but incensed white workmen. Finally, after much pressure had been applied, Congress passed the Chinese Exclusion Act in 1882, which suspended all immigration from that source for ten years. The ten-year extension was renewed in

[17] Mary R. Coolidge, *Chinese Immigration*, pp. 21–22.
[18] For accounts of this conflict, see B. Shrieke, *Alien Americans*, pp. 8ff; C. McWilliams, *Brothers under the Skin*, Ch. 2; L. G. Brown, *Immigration*, Ch. 14; D. Y. Yuan, "Voluntary Segregation: A Study of New York Chinatown," *Phylon* (Fourth Quarter) 1963, pp. 255ff.

1892, and indefinitely extended in 1902. Many other acts of discrimination against the Chinese were passed; and in 1924 all immigration was suspended for those ineligible for citizenship. As a gesture of friendship to our wartime ally, in 1943 the Chinese were placed under the same quota system as the Europeans, making it possible for 105 to enter the country annually.

How did the Chinese react to all this discriminatory legislation, and to the incessant vilification and abuse to which they were subjected? First, they fought back in the courts, but to no avail. Second, many of them returned, though some unwillingly, to China. Third, numbers of them moved away from the Pacific Coast to New England, the Middle West, and the South. Fourth, they migrated to the large cities, congregated in tight colonies, and proceeded to segregate themselves insofar as possible from the general population. They withdrew socially, politically, and economically, as well as physically. They turned from those occupations which brought them into competition with whites, and developed art and curio shops, restaurants specializing in unusual atmosphere and large servings of Chinese food, and hand laundries. They settled their disputes among themselves, deeming it a disgrace to be haled before the white man's court. In their Chinatowns they made a concerted effort it preserve their ancient institutions.[19] They established their temples, published newspapers and periodicals, celebrated their Old World festivals (Ching Ming, Dragon Boat, Moon, Winter Solstice, and so on), and emphasized their clan and family organizations. They developed new institutions, too, to help them adjust to the New World conditions — tongs, Chinese schools, benevolent societies, and political organizations. In spite of their isolation, however, assimilation did occur; and the Chinese learned to observe Christmas, Thanksgiving, and Easter, and especially Father's Day and Mother's Day; and they joined the American Legion and the Girl Scouts, attended the moving pictures, and acquired American culture.

Not all Chinese crowded into the cities. A Mr. Wong, for instance, migrated to Mississippi in 1875, and settled in the rich farming area known as the Delta. He was followed by others, with the result that in 1940 some 900 Chinese were living there.[20] They did not develop the usual Chinese occupational specialties (laundries, chop suey restaurants, and the like) but became independent merchants. During the first 50 years of their residence in the Delta they were not the victims of segregation, as their fellow nationals were in the cities, and their assimilation proceeded rapidly. They joined the white Baptist Church and participated in its services, and their children attended the white public schools. Then a trend toward segregation set in. One of their children was expelled from the white school. The case was fought vigorously, but the court ruled for segregation, on the ground that its purpose was "to preserve the purity and integrity of the white race, and prevent amalgamation." As a compromise, special schools

[19] Rose Hum Lee, "Social Institutions of a Rocky Mountain Chinatown," *Social Forces*, Vol. 27, No. 1, October 1948, pp. 1–11.

[20] See R. W. O'Brien, "Status of Chinese in the Mississippi Delta," *Social Forces*, Vol. 9, No. 3, March 1941, pp. 386–390.

for Chinese were established in two Mississippi towns. At the same time, segregation made an appearance in the church; while still members of the white church, and permitted to use its facilities for weddings and other functions, the Chinese now had to attend special services. Mr. O'Brien, who reported on the situation in the Delta, suspects that the trend is toward the formation of a third caste, intermediate between those of the white and the Negro. This means, of course, that the assimilation of the Chinese will be retarded, perhaps even reversed, which is not the choice of the Chinese themselves, who would prefer to become absorbed into the life of the community.

There are indications that the Chinatowns are on the wane, and that the assimilation of the Chinese proceeds in spite of the obstacles which have been placed in its way.[21] The younger generations are indifferent toward the preservation of the Chinese culture, and are bent upon breaking through the wall which isolates them. World War II gave them an opportunity to find employment in many occupations from which they had long been excluded. The Chinese, like the Jews, are a people who have a high regard for learning, and they make sacrifices to educate their children. The children, when they acquire an education, are disposed to turn away from the traditional occupations, to enter the professions, and to move out of the Chinese community.[22] Dr. Rose Hum Lee has analyzed the trend with respect to the Chinatowns of America, and her conclusions are:

> No new Chinatowns will be created. . . . It is probable that, as the Chinese reside longer in this country and the Chinese-Americans increase in population, another redistribution of their numbers may occur, with settlement in cities under metropolitan status. Where only a few Chinese reside in a community, they are socially well accepted. Acculturation and assimilation are more rapid for "marooned families" and isolated individuals than for concentrated populations. . . .
>
> It appears that the number of Chinatowns in this country will decrease almost to a vanishing point. Only those of historical or commercial importance, as in San Francisco and New York, will remain. . . . As Chinese-Americans become acculturated and strive for higher status . . . this dispersion will be similar to that of any other small minority group already an integral part of American society. With acculturation and settlement among the members of the larger society, amalgamation will increase, and in time assimilation will be attained.[23]

The Ghetto

Segregation is an old story to the Jewish people, who have experienced it in all its forms — voluntary and involuntary, social and spatial. Even in that distant

[21] Patricia Page, "Chinatown: Not East, Not West," *The New York Times Magazine*, December 15, 1946.

[22] Beulah Ong Kwoh, "The Occupational Status of American-Born Chinese Male College Graduates," *American Journal of Sociology*, Vol. 53, No. 3, November 1947, pp. 192–200.

[23] "The Decline of Chinatowns in the United States," *American Journal of Sociology*, Vol. 54, No. 5, March 1949, p. 432.

period, where history and myth can hardly be distinguished, we are told that the Hebrews, during their four-hundred-year sojourn in Egypt, lived apart from the others "in the land of Goshen." From that time to the present day, segregation has been an inseparable feature of their existence.

The word "ghetto" applies strictly to the Jewish quarter of a city, but it is often used nowadays to refer to the Chinatowns, the Black Belts, or to the segregated areas occupied by any racial or ethnic minorities. The origin of the term is in dispute. It seems doubtful, as some have supposed, that it is derived from the Hebrew *get*, meaning separation or segregation. Others have suggested that it came from the German *gitter* (bars of a cage), or from the Italian *borghetto* (a small, negligible section), or from the Italian *guetto* or *guitto* (a filthy creature). The probability is, however, that it derives from the Italian *gietto*, the cannon foundry at Venice near which the Jewish settlement was located.[24] The word, whatever its origin, came much later than the practice of Jewish segregation. In medieval Germany there were separate Jewish quarters bearing such designations as *Judenstrasse, Judengasse*, or *Judendorf*; in Portugal it was *Judiaria*; in France, *Juiverie*; in England, *Jewry*; in North Africa, *mella*. These names indicate that in many European cities of the fourteenth century there existed clearly defined areas inhabited by the Jews. No doubt the Jews dwelt together in the cities of the ancient world, long before the fourteenth century, and even before the Christian era, a fact to which the New Testament bears witness.

The first formal recognition of a Jewish area in a city dates from 1084 A.D. In that year Rudiger, Bishop of Speyer, granted the Jews the right to have a separate residential section of their own. He was eager to attract Jews to his city, in order, he said, "to add to the honor of our place"; and he was constrained to permit their segregation so that "they might not readily be disturbed by the insolence of the populace." The fact is that segregation, far from being a badge of infamy, was a privilege enjoyed and appreciated by the Jews. Not only did it afford them protection, but, as Wirth points out,[25] it was a convenient administrative device, and it facilitated the observance of various religious customs, such as the proper preparation of food, attendance at the synagogue, and participation in community affairs. In one city the Jews annually commemorated the establishment of their ghetto with a special ritual, indicating that they recognized the privilege that was theirs; and several communities, upon losing their ghetto charters, went to the expense of repurchasing them.

In the course of time, however, the ghetto became transformed from a voluntary to a compulsory institution, and from a privilege to a symbol of discrimination and persecution. This transformation did not come about suddenly. Here and there a temporal ruler or a church council would go on record as insisting upon the separation of Jews and Christians, or Jews and Moslems. Among the early steps in the direction of compulsory segregation was the following decree issued by an ecclesiastical synod held at Breslau in 1266:

[24] "Ghetto," *The Jewish Encyclopedia*, Vol. 5, pp. 652–655; Wirth, *The Ghetto*, pp. 1–2; J. Lestschinsky, "Ghetto," *Encyclopedia of the Social Sciences*, Vol. 6, pp. 646–650.
[25] *Op. cit.*, pp. 18ff.

Since the land of Poland is a new acquisition in the body of Christianity, lest perchance the Christian people be, on this account, the more easily infected with the superstition and depraved morale of the Jews dwelling among them . . . we command that the Jews dwelling in this province of Gnesen shall not live among the Christians, but shall have their houses near or next to one another in some sequestered part of the state or town, so that their dwelling place shall be separated from the common dwelling place of the Christians by a hedge, a wall, or a ditch.[26]

In 1311 the provincial council of Ravenna, disturbed by the commingling of Jews and Christians which was apparently the vogue in that section, decreed that "Jews shall not dwell longer than a month anywhere, except in those places in which they have synagogues." The Council of Valencia, in 1388, insisted that Christians dwelling in the Jewish quarter should immediately move out; and the Venetian senate, in 1516, placed compulsory residential restrictions upon the Jews. Decrees of this sort were made in country after country in Europe, in Turkey, and in Morocco, between the thirteenth and the sixteenth centuries.

The compulsory ghetto, however, did not become general throughout the Christian world until 1555, when Pope Paul IV called for segregation in a papal bull. It is absurd, the bull declares, for accursed Jews to live openly among Christians, to own real estate, and to employ Christian servants. They should be compelled to live within an enclosure set apart for them, and not to appear outside that quarter unless they wear some distinguishing mark, such as a yellow hat for men and a yellow veil for the women. The Roman ghetto, created at that time, was one of the filthiest examples of the institution. It was situated on a low bank of the Tiber, surrounded by a brick wall, subject to annual floods, an incredibly unhealthy and impoverished community. It was not, however, too unlike hundreds of others throughout Europe.

The motives which brought into existence the compulsory ghetto were often stated in the numerous edicts, and Wirth apparently accepts these as valid.[27] It was feared that the presence of the Jews would weaken the faith of the Christians, that they would make converts, that they would be a source and a stimulation for heresy. Lestschinsky, however, who looks upon the compulsory ghetto as a product of the sixteenth century, thinks these religious arguments were but the rationalization of a more basic conflict.[28] The bourgeoisie, he thinks, were out to eliminate and cripple their competitors. The Jews were playing an important role in trade, commerce, money-lending, and certain handicrafts, and into these fields the bourgeoisie were edging their way. At the same time, the bourgeoisie were endeavoring to obtain greater mutual autonomy from the feudal barons, bishops, kings, and emperors — the very ones who furnished protection to the Jews and who profited so handsomely from them in the form of taxes, loans, and

[26] Quoted in Wirth, *op. cit.*, p. 30.
[27] *Op. cit.*, pp. 33–34.
[28] *Op. cit.*, Vol. 6, p. 648.

"gifts." Any handicap that could be placed upon the Jews, therefore, in the way of restricting their movement, limiting their economic activities, or impoverishing them, would return to the bourgeoisie in the form of greater profits and greater freedom from their feudal overlords. The truth probably is that a complex of motives underlay the development.

The compulsory ghetto began to dissolve and to disappear in the eighteenth century. This was a result of forces operating both within the ghetto and without. The movement known as the "Enlightenment" did not pass the Jews by, but served to liberate them from the provincialism of the ghetto. The German philosopher, Moses Mendelssohn, was the embodiment of this trend; and he, in turn, had no small part in modifying the prejudices of the Christians and in broadening the outlook of his fellow Jews. The inhabitants of the ghettos, thus stimulated, began to speak the language of the country in which they lived, to read French and German books, to shave their beards and cut off their earlocks, to wear short coats, and "to swear by the name of Moses Mendelssohn." Wirth mentions, among the other social movements which had profound influence upon the dissolution of the ghetto, the growth of socialism, the revival of interest in Hebrew, the birth of Zionism, and the Reform movement which favored cultural assimilation with the general population.[29]

At the same time there were forces stirring on the outside. The people of western and central Europe, and their governments, began to manifest a change in their attitudes toward the Jews. Up to this time the Jews were virtually aliens in the countries where they lived, were denied the rights of citizenship, excluded from participation in political affairs, barred from schools and many occupations, denied the privilege of owning land, restricted as to dress and residence, and subject to insult and violence. The first to advocate the mitigation of these handicaps was the Englishman, John Toland, who published a book in London in 1714 under the title *Reasons for Naturalizing the Jews in Great Britain and Ireland, on the Same Foot with All Other Nations.* Forty years later Parliament did discuss a bill to facilitate the naturalization of Jews, but public opposition to it was insurmountable. Other bills were subsequently introduced, several of them passing the House of Commons only to be rejected by the Lords. In 1858 Lionel de Rothschild was permitted to take his seat in Parliament, and in the years following, Jews were admitted to the highest offices in the government and in the universities. The British colonies had even earlier removed restrictions on Jewish citizenship; and the Constitution of the United States, and the First Amendment, established equality without mentioning Jews. The philosophers of the French Revolution were ardent advocates of Jewish emancipation, and toward the end of the eighteenth century there began a gradual removal of the restrictions under which the Jews in France had been living.

The nineteenth century witnessed the emancipation in one country after another. Belgium emancipated her Jews in 1815; Denmark in 1849; Sweden in

---

[29] *Op. cit.,* pp. 97–110. See, also, S. Baron, "Jewish Emancipation," and S. Dubnow, "Jewish Autonomy," *Encyclopedia of the Social Sciences,* Vol. 8, pp. 391–399.

1865. It was not a steady and continuous movement, for there were periods of reaction. In Germany and Austria the Jews won some rights in the eighteenth century, but these were withdrawn after the fall of Napoleon. Emancipation came in Austria-Hungary in 1869, and in Germany with the formation of the Empire in 1870. In eastern Europe the dates were much later. The rise of Hitler, of course, brought on a catastrophic reversal of this long trend. The fact is, however, that within a century the walls of the compulsory ghetto were leveled, and the Jews had everywhere achieved formal and legal equality, except in out-of-the-way places like Yemen and Ethiopia.

There is a difference, however, between formal equality and social equality; and the abolition of the compulsory aspect of the ghetto did not mean the end of segregation. There are still barriers which isolate the Jews and keep them from participating fully in the life of the larger society. Discrimination prevails regarding the holding of public office, in employment, in place of residence, in social intercourse, and in admission to educational institutions. The Jews are still highly concentrated; 60 per cent of the five million Jews in the United States live in Boston, Philadelphia, Chicago, and New York. As Wirth says:

> There is scarcely a city of any considerable size in Europe or America that does not have a ghetto. Even in towns containing only a score of Jews, there is to be found in all parts of the world some more or less organized Jewish community.
> Just as the ghetto arose before formal decrees forced the Jews into segregated areas, so the ghetto persists even after these decrees have been annulled.[30]

The Jews are almost unanimously in favor of *legal* emancipation, though some conservatives among them have foreseen the effects and have been suspicious of it. When Holland granted equal rights to her Jews in 1795, a petition bearing a thousand names requested that such rights be revoked. As for *social* emancipation and the dissolution of the ghetto, the attitudes of the Jews vary. Those who accept the philosophy of assimilation are, of course, in favor of it; but those who desire the perpetuation of their group and the preservation of their three-thousand-year-old social heritage are faced with the difficult problem of maintaining some sort of balance between the forces that would absorb them and those that would isolate them.

Racial Islands

The American Negro, too, has had a long and varied experience with segregation. The restrictions placed upon his residential choice, of course, subject him to a degree of spatial isolation; but for the most part the segregation of the Negro is of a social and symbolic sort. Negroes may be seen anywhere — in

---

[30] *The Ghetto*, pp. 117–123. For a description of these communities, see T. Shafter, "The Fleshpots of Maine," *Commentary*, Vol. 7, No. 1, January 1949, pp. 60–67; J. Graebner and S. H. Britt, *Jews in a Gentile World* (Chapters by L. Bloom on "The Jews of Buna," and S. Koenig on "The Socio-economic Structure of an American Jewish Community"); A. I. Gordon, *Jews in Transition;* J. R. Kramer and S. Leventman, *Children of the Gilded Ghetto.*

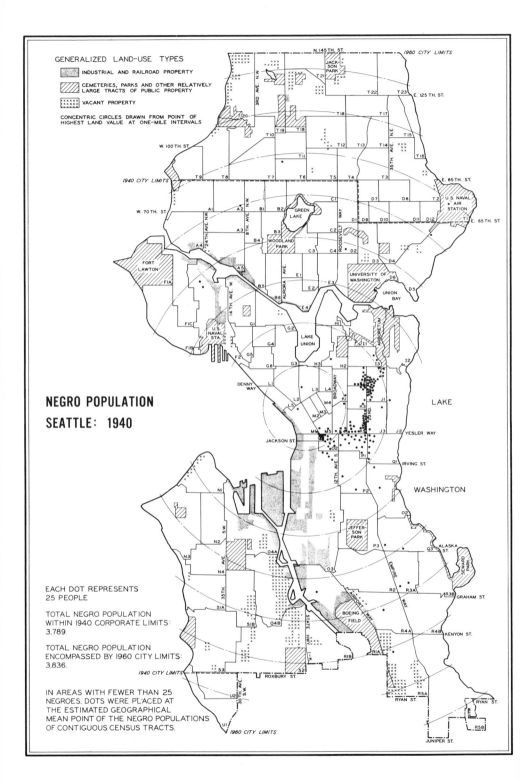

GENERALIZED LAND-USE TYPES

INDUSTRIAL AND RAILROAD PROPERTY

CEMETERIES, PARKS AND OTHER RELATIVELY
LARGE TRACTS OF PUBLIC PROPERTY

VACANT PROPERTY

CONCENTRIC CIRCLES DRAWN FROM POINT OF
HIGHEST LAND VALUE AT ONE-MILE INTERVALS

NEGRO POPULATION

SEATTLE: 1940

EACH DOT REPRESENTS
25 PEOPLE

TOTAL NEGRO POPULATION
WITHIN 1940 CORPORATE LIMITS:
3,789.

TOTAL NEGRO POPULATION
ENCOMPASSED BY 1960 CITY LIMITS:
3,836.

IN AREAS WITH FEWER THAN 25
NEGROES, DOTS WERE PLACED AT
THE ESTIMATED GEOGRAPHICAL
MEAN POINT OF THE NEGRO POPULATIONS
OF CONTIGUOUS CENSUS TRACTS.

214

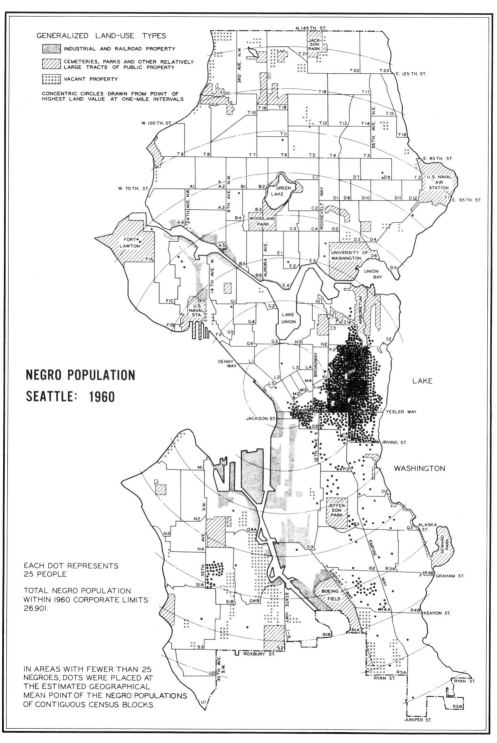

NEGRO POPULATION
SEATTLE: 1960

EACH DOT REPRESENTS
25 PEOPLE

TOTAL NEGRO POPULATION
WITHIN 1960 CORPORATE LIMITS:
26,901.

IN AREAS WITH FEWER THAN 25
NEGROES, DOTS WERE PLACED AT
THE ESTIMATED GEOGRAPHICAL
MEAN POINT OF THE NEGRO POPULATIONS
OF CONTIGUOUS CENSUS BLOCKS.

GENERALIZED LAND-USE TYPES

INDUSTRIAL AND RAILROAD PROPERTY

CEMETERIES, PARKS AND OTHER RELATIVELY
LARGE TRACTS OF PUBLIC PROPERTY

VACANT PROPERTY

CONCENTRIC CIRCLES DRAWN FROM POINT OF
HIGHEST LAND VALUE AT ONE-MILE INTERVALS

Maps are from Calvin F. Schmid and Wayne W. McVey, Jr., Growth and Distribution of Minority Races in Seattle, Washington.

the homes of white people, in hotels, restaurants, and exclusive clubs — provided they wear some garment which indicates lower status. Especially in the South are they in close contact with whites, preparing their food, nursing their children, cleaning their homes, and laundering their clothes. The two races jostle each other in the buses, on the streets, and in the stores. Despite these intimate relations, however, there is a barrier between them which isolates no less effectively than did the iron bars and stone walls of the ancient ghetto. The common expression "Jim Crow" implies social discrimination more than spatial isolation; and it is the former, rather than the latter, which arouses resentment.[31]

Spatial segregation has also entered into the Negro's experience. As far back as 1714 it was proposed that Negroes be sent back to Africa, and though nothing came of it at the time, the idea has never been dropped. In 1777 Thomas Jefferson headed a committee which explored the possibilities of exporting the Negroes. Many organizations interested in the problem of slavery included in their program some scheme of resettlement. In 1815 one Paul Cuffe, at his own expense, took 38 Negroes to Africa. Thereupon the American Colonization Society was organized, including many prominent names among its members, and soon won widespread support for its plan to establish a colony, choosing Liberia for its purpose. There were other proposals, too. Haiti, Canada, South America, and even the American West were considered as possibilities. No less a person than Abraham Lincoln at one time entertained the idea that some such plan of segregation offered the best solution for the problem of Negro-white relations. He once invited a group of free Negroes to the White House, urging them as follows to support his colonization scheme:

> Your race suffer greatly, many of them, by living among us, while ours suffer from your presence. In a word, we suffer on each side. If this is admitted, it affords a reason why we should be separated.[32]

These various attempts to solve the race problems by a sort of "Negro Zionism" have been conspicuous failures. The American Colonization Society, in its palmiest days, succeeded in transporting only some 12,000; places other than Liberia have attracted no more than a trickle. Among the Negroes themselves, some have received these schemes with mild approval, some with bitter opposition, but most have shown utter indifference. But the proposals continue to sprout. A generation ago Marcus Garvey, who called himself "The Black Moses," was able to hypnotize many credulous people and to attract a tremendous following with his Back-to-Africa Movement.[33]

Negroes, however, have often succeeded in withdrawing from the society of whites and establishing segregated communities of their own. There are today no less than 50 all-Negro communities in the United States, functioning so quietly

---

[31] See H. H. Smythe, "The Concept 'Jim Crow'," *Social Forces*, Vol. 21, No. 1, October 1948, pp. 45–48; C. V. Woodward, *The Strange Career of Jim Crow*.

[32] Quoted in J. H. Franklin, *From Slavery to Freedom*, p. 277.

[33] R. Ottley, *New World A-Coming*, Ch. 6; Franklin, *op. cit.*, pp. 481–483.

and so unobtrusively that their presence is hardly suspected by the greater society. Some of these segregated communities were established many years ago. Frazier, who calls them "racial islands," has visited and described a number of them.[34] Among them is the Gouldtown settlement near Bridgeton, New Jersey, concerning the origin of which we have well-authenticated records. It seems that a certain John Fenwick, having been granted a tract of land, came to America in 1675. One of his granddaughters, Elizabeth Adams, became enamoured of a Negro by the name of Gould, much to the distress of John Fenwick, who threatened to disinherit her

> unless the Lord open her eyes to see her abominable transgression against Him, me and her good father, by giving her true repentance and forsaking that Black which hath been the ruin of her and becoming penitent for her sins.

This couple and their children formed the nucleus of the Gouldtown settlement. They were joined by others of mixed Negro, Indian, and white blood, who together formed a community which maintained itself for more than two centuries but has recently been dwindling. Some of its members have moved away, intermarried with whites, and lost themselves in the white population, while others have identified themselves with the Negro race. All of the "islands" which Frazier describes, most of them tracing back to colonial times, were formed by hybrids who were reluctant to be classed with Negroes and were not acceptable as whites, and who therefore chose this form of segregation as a feasible escape from their dilemma.

Other Negroes have turned to the segregated community, not to escape their racial identification, but as preferable to assuming a subordinate position in the white community. Such all-Negro settlements are found today in Oklahoma, Ohio, Kansas, California, Arkansas, Illinois, Michigan, Pennsylvania, West Virginia, and in all the Atlantic and Gulf states from New Jersey to Texas. Among them is Mound Bayou, Mississippi.[35] This community was established in the late 1880's by a remarkable Negro, Isaiah T. Montgomery, who had been a body servant to Jefferson Davis, President of the Confederacy. Following the Civil War, Davis sold his Mississippi plantation to his former slaves, who managed the estate with outstanding success. Then the falling price of cotton, and legal difficulties with the Davis heirs, forced the Negroes to abandon the plantation. A few years later a railway company acquired a large tract of land it wanted to develop, and hearing of Montgomery's success as a cotton planter, proposed that he establish a Negro colony. With the help of his cousin, Ben Green, Montgomery enlisted a band of Negroes in the project, and together they purchased 840 acres. The experiment met with success, and other Negroes joined them. Fifty years later the community had grown to the size of 8000, 1000 of whom lived in the town of Mound Bayou, the others farming the adjoining territory covering 30,000 acres. Schools, stores, churches, sawmills, and political institu-

[34] E. F. Frazier, *The Negro Family in the United States*, Ch. 11.
[35] W. Waldron, "All Black: A Unique Negro Community," *Survey Graphic*, January 1938, pp. 34ff.

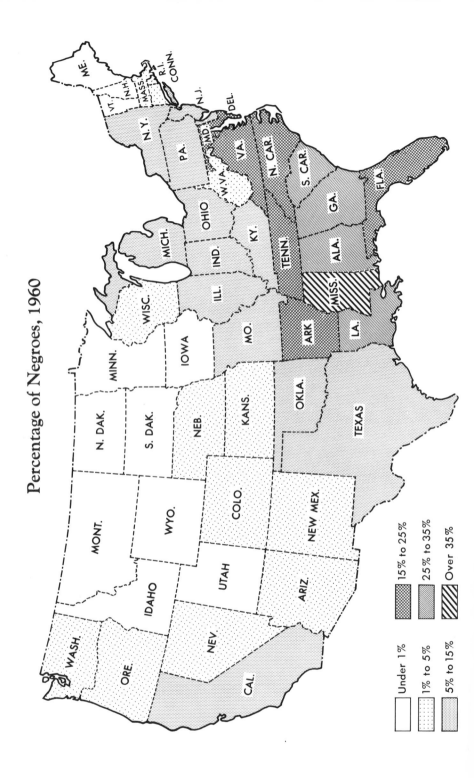

Percentage of Negroes, 1960

Legend:
- Under 1%
- 1% to 5%
- 5% to 15%
- 15% to 25%
- 25% to 35%
- Over 35%

tions resemble those of other southern towns, with the exception that they are owned and operated by Negroes; and as one of the citizens said, "Here we can hold our faces up."[36]

Segregation, regardless of the form it takes and of the racial groups which adopt it, is a problematical and ephemeral pattern of adjustment. Regarding the all-Negro community, Charles S. Johnson, one-time President of Fisk University, had this to say:

> The all-Negro community is an interesting cultural enclave in the American society, but in my judgment it has very limited possibilities for bringing about permanent racial adjustment. . . . It may, indeed, preserve its members from the disturbing shocks of race prejudice, and permit them to participate fully in the life of the segregated community. But, like other types of culturally isolated communities, the group disadvantages often outweigh the shadowy advantages of individual escape. . . .
>
> It is exceptionally difficult, if not impossible, for any American community to survive except through successful integration in the American economic system, and within the cultural framework of the larger society. . . .
>
> Of the two evils it seems better for Negroes in America to direct their energies toward normal participation in the life of American communities, even though this involves more frequent personal disappointment and much disorganization during the gradual process of acculturation.[37]

It appears, then, that in all parts of the world and for untold centuries racial and ethnic groups have sought to resolve their conflicts by some form of segregation, by restricting their contacts and relations with one another. There are few who would deny to any group the right to withdraw unto itself, if it chooses to do so. Most of us would doubtless grant the Jews the right to establish a homeland of their own, or the Amish to live to themselves in isolated communities, or the people of Canada and the United States to restrict the numbers of immigrants whom they will admit as citizens. It is a different matter, however, when a strong group forces segregation upon a weaker group which does not wish it, especially when such segregation involves discrimination and exploitation, as it invariably does. The wisdom of segregation and isolation is also debatable, but the judgment depends upon one's scale of values. From the practical standpoint, however, segregation as a pattern of intergroup accommodation grows increasingly difficult. With the increase in mobility, the growth of interdependence, improvements in communication and transportation, the spread of democratic ideals, and the diffusion of education and literacy, the possibility of a group's living unto itself, whether or not it chooses to do so, becomes less and less feasible.

---

[36] For accounts of similar communities, see M. C. Hill, "A Comparative Analysis of the Social Organization of the All-Negro Society in Oklahoma," *Social Forces*, Vol. 25, No. 1, October 1946, pp. 70–77; C. L. Spellman, *Elm City: A Negro Community in Action.*

[37] C. S. Johnson, "A Footnote on Isolation," *Survey Graphic*, January 1938, p. 36.

10

Pluralism

*Our national character is too histori-
cally famous, and in spite of every
degradation, too fine to make its annihilation desirable.*

THEODOR HERZL
The Jewish State

The survival of the Jewish people is certainly one of the most amazing phenomena of all history. For 2000 years they have been scattered over the face of the earth, speaking many different languages, acquiring a variety of cultures, having no unique racial features (despite the popular stereotype), adopting as their own now this nation and now that, engaging in a multitude of occupations, and adjusting to every kind of physical environment. Could any other human group have survived so variegated a series of experiences, or retained its identity in the face of such harassing obstacles? People, unlike the other social animals, are not held together in groups by instinct. If they are to survive, therefore, they must resort to artificial bonds, such as flags, kings, and other symbols, or loyalty to a common culture, history, religion, or tradition. Among the most powerful bonds which hold human groups together are a common language, concentration in and an attachment to a certain geographical spot, or the possession of a government of their own. The Jews have long been without many of these unifying forces.

In addition to all these disuniting influences, the Jews have had to cope with the continual hostility of the out-group. The gentiles, however, have never fully known just what they wanted to do with the Jews. They have expelled them from a country at one time and refused them permission to migrate at another; they have dispersed them and confined them to pales and ghettos; they have persecuted them and given them special privileges; they have tried to force them to assimilate and erected barriers against them; they have imposed isolation upon them and criticized their clannishness; they have adopted much of the Jews' culture and deplored their influence. The gentiles are agreed that there is a Jewish problem; but there is no consensus on the nature of the problem or the desired solution.

For that matter, the Jews themselves are not of one mind either. To be sure, none of them wants to be annihilated; none approves of anti-Semitic onslaughts; and none craves a subordinate status in the social system. When it comes to positive goals, however, there is wide divergence. The distinguished author, Lewis Browne, has one answer.[1] His gentile friends, says he, keep asking him, "What are you Jews going to do about it?" He tells them that the Jews would readily disappear and cease to be if they were not continually hounded and reminded that they are Jews. In short, they would quickly and easily become assimilated and amalgamated. He says:

> We are not so much voluntary Jews as involuntary gentiles. . . . Millions of us no longer know the ways of our fathers. . . . Millions more consider those ways outworn and unappealing. . . . Let us be, and in time we shall actually cease to be. Our history proves that. . . . Wherever we have been least hounded, there we have been most prone to disappear. . . . It is commonly imagined that we never assimilate with the people among whom we dwell. This is simply not true. . . . In the time of Jesus there were at least 1,000,000 Jews in Egypt. Three centuries later hardly a sign of them remained. . . . Similarly a large settlement be-

[1] "What Can the Jews Do?" *The Virginia Quarterly Review*, Vol. 16, No. 2, Spring 1939, pp. 216–226.

came absorbed in China. . . . In Italy, once a great center of Jewish population, not 40,000 survive today. Were they expelled or massacred? On the contrary, thanks to Papal influence, medieval Italy was relatively tolerant of the Jews. As a result, most of them became assimilated.

In answer to the question, "What can the Jews do?" Browne would throw the question back, "What do you gentiles have in mind?" Assimilation is clearly what he wants, if he is permitted to have it.

Assimilation, however, is precisely what many Jews do *not* want. The Orthodox, who constitute the majority, certainly are not assimilationists. The Zionists, even though they may have no wish to make their homes in the Holy Land, believe that there are values in their culture which ought to be preserved; and those who have settled in Palestine are not solely concerned with saving their skins.

Is there no other alternative between assimilation and disappearance on the one hand, and segregation and isolation, either in ghettos or in Israel, on the other? Rabbi Milton Steinberg believes there is.[2] Assimilation, he thinks, is impossible. An occasional Jew may succeed in losing himself in the non-Jewish world; but most will have to remain Jews, no matter how hard they struggle against their fate. Most assimilatory effort in the past, he says, has resulted in the dejudaizing of the Jew without winning for him gentile acceptance. Nor does he believe in isolation or "self-ghettoization." "I do not now envisage, nor have I practiced, withdrawal from the general life of America." He insists, instead, that one may be loyal to Jewish religion and tradition without its militating in the least against full participation in the common political and spiritual life of the country. He calls this "cultural dualism," and says of it:

Is it practicable, this prospectus of two civilizations, the primary American and the secondary Jewish? . . . Can a person live happily, without stress and strain, in two cultures?

If I may judge from my experience — and that of many Jews who share my viewpoint — the program is amazingly undifficult of execution. To me the American tradition is my primary heritage. I acknowledge only one political allegiance — to America. English is my first language, and that of my children. I was educated in the public schools of my community. The history of America is my history. . . .

But Jewish history is my background, too. Lincoln and Jefferson are my heroes together with Rabbi Akiba and Moses Maimonides. The four get along in my imagination most companionably. . . .

The process is immensely facilitated by the essential sympathy in spirit between the two traditions. . . .

Any program for the Jewish group must meet a two-fold test of acceptability: the welfare of the Jewish group, and the welfare of America. I am convinced that the pattern I follow measures up better than all its alternatives. . . . America is best served by its Jews when they strive to exploit the special resources of their group.

2 M. Steinberg, "To Be or Not To Be a Jew," *Common Ground*, Vol. 1, No. 3, Spring 1941, pp. 43–50.

Not only the Jews, but many other ethnic groups as well, have believed that it is possible for peoples who are different to live together on a basis of equality, tolerance, justice, and harmony. This involves, of course, a degree of voluntary segregation, but without the prejudices and discriminations that usually come with segregation. Accommodation, according to this doctrine, need not result in a relationship of dominance and submission, of subordination and superordination, but may also occur on a plane of equality. This fact has long been recognized in sociological theory, and political scientists and social philosophers have devoted much thought to it. It is discussed under many different labels. Rabbi Steinberg, as we have seen, calls it "cultural dualism"; some prefer "cultural democracy"; and Berkson uses the term "community theory." Milton M. Gordon, who has furnished us with the most penetrating analysis of the concept, makes a valuable distinction between "cultural pluralism" and "structural pluralism."[3]

Its advocates are not entirely in agreement as to its definition, implications, and ultimate objectives. Many Jews who subscribe to the pluralistic position also support Zionism, on the ground that an autonomous Jewish community with a territorial basis in Palestine is indispensable for the preservation of Jewish groups and the Jewish culture in various other parts of the world. Berkson has written:

> Indeed the Zionist idea becomes even more urgent in view of the type of adjustment, admittedly precarious for the ethnic group, demanded by the democratic conditions. Even the possibility of maintaining a vital ethnic culture in the diaspora is dependent upon the existence of a cultural center to serve as a source of spiritual replenishment. . . . The "Community" theory becomes a hopeful solution only if there will be established an autonomous Jewish center in Palestine.[4]

Rabbi Elmer Berger, speaking for a minority of American Jews, takes the opposite position, namely, that the existence of an autonomous Jewish state will militate *against* the democratic and tolerant accommodation of the Jewish and gentile groups. Says he:

> Jewish nationalism is not now and never has been the expression of the real hopes of Jews of America or anywhere else. . . . We reject a program that makes of Jews a separate, unintegrable, segregated minority. . . .
> What alternative do we offer? . . . Jews are citizens of those countries in which they live and those lands are their homelands. . . .
> Emancipation and integration *vs.* nationalization is the issue. . . . No matter what persecution in the middle ages may have *forced* us to be, we *wish* to be free individuals in the modern world, fully integrated into the societies in which we live, and distinctive only in our religious faiths.[5]

[3] M. M. Gordon, *Assimilation in American Life*, pp. 132–159. Gordon maintains that "structural pluralism is the major key to the understanding of the ethnic makeup of American society."
[4] I. B. Berkson, *Theories of Americanization*, p. 109.
[5] *Emancipation: The Rediscovered Ideal.*

The fear that tolerance and equality may simply mean rapid assimilation is no doubt warranted. M. R. Davie, who advocates cultural pluralism for all the ethnic minorities in the United States, regards it as an effective and painless means toward the end of national unity and homogeneity. He says:

> Cultural democracy . . . implies cooperation rather than conflict between majority and minority groups, appreciation of the cultural heritages of minorities, preservation and incorporation of some of [their] . . . elements rather than complete repression, and realization that modification must take place slowly in order to avoid cultural disintegration and social maladjustment. . . .
>
> There appears to be an irresistible pressure toward assimilation, which may eventually result in complete cultural integration. Cultural pluralism then will have disappeared, but it will have served the useful purpose of contributing to the final culture pattern.[6]

Those who advocate pluralism as the most desirable pattern of ethnic group accommodation recognize the fact that there are limits beyond which cultural freedom cannot go. Any society, if it is to survive, must have a considerable agreement among its members as to basic ideals, goals, values, mores, folkways, and beliefs. An aggregation of individuals, or of groups, each speaking its own language, worshiping its own gods, practicing its own sex mores, following its own peculiar customs with respect to food, dress, recreation, and government, would not be a society at all. Ethnic groups which differ radically in their fundamental value systems could hardly become accommodated on a plane of equality and tolerance. Rabbi Steinberg is aware of this fact when he points out that "cultural dualism" is possible for the American Jew because of the "essential sympathy in spirit between the two traditions." Both, he says, are democratic; both emphasize the worth of the individual and his right to freedom; both have a devotion to the ideal of social justice; and both have a vision of the more abundant life. Stewart G. Cole, also a proponent of pluralism, comments upon the responsibilities of citizenship in a society committed to such an ideal:

> A good citizen of this country may retain a measure of loyalty to the racial, religious, ethnic, or socio-economic group in which he enjoys membership. . . . Should the bonds eventuate in a chauvinistic temper of the group, as they may if a policy of cultural pluralism is carried to the extreme, then there is the clearest evidence that a privilege of in-group nurture is being overworked to the neglect of out-group obligation. The individual's pleasure in sharing one of the multiple group cultures needs to be balanced by his assumption of responsibility to keep his primary allegiance to the people of the United States of America soundly enlisted. National cultural unity must not be jeopardized by an exaggerated development of the forces of cultural diversity.[7]

[6] Reprinted by permission from *One America*, rev., edited by Francis J. Brown and Joseph Slabey Roucek. Copyright 1937, 1945 by Prentice-Hall, Inc., New York. Pp. 550–551.

[7] Reprinted by permission from *One America*, rev., edited by Francis J. Brown and Joseph Slabey Roucek. Copyright 1937, 1945 by Prentice-Hall, Inc., New York. P. 564.

*Two deacons of the
Old Order Amish at a barn
construction project
for one of their group*

Pluralism, as a method of resolving the conflict between unlike groups inhabiting the same territory, has a special appeal for those who are committed to the ideals of democracy and tolerance. At the same time the *language* of pluralism is frequently employed by those whose purposes are quite otherwise. For instance, the white American who enthusiastically espouses the doctrine of "separate but equal" may be sincere in his belief, but likely as not he is more concerned with the "separate" than with the "equal." For half a century, under that doctrine, schools, medical facilities, transportation, and recreation were rigidly separated for whites and Negroes, but little or no effort was made to have them equal.[8] So it is in South Africa, where many a white man defends his belief in *apartheid*, not on the grounds that it will facilitate his control over the Negro, but rather on grounds that suggest a belief in a pluralistic society. This discrepancy between the *theory of apartheid* and *apartheid in practice* has been pointed out by Anthony H. Richmond.[9] In theoretical discussions of racial problems in the Republic, he says, the concept of *apartheid* places emphasis upon separation of the races as a means of obtaining social autonomy and minimizing conflict. Its advocates profess a deep interest in preserving the way of life of the natives, and of wanting them "to develop along their own lines." A policy of strict separation, according to its advocates, would enable each racial group to

[8] Cf. L. R. Harlan, *Separate and Unequal, passim.*
[9] *The Colour Problem,* pp. 81–137.

preserve its biological purity, to own its own territory, to practice the customs it prefers, to educate its children as it wishes, and ultimately to achieve complete self-sufficiency and sovereignty. Actually, Richmond insists, the practical politicians do not support any such ideal, but rather regard *apartheid* as an instrument for continued domination of the African, Coloured, and Asiatic communities by the European.

Pluralism is not merely an ideal, a theory, or a goal toward which its advocates hope that race relations might move; it has been a matter of public policy on numerous occasions. Let us consider some of these.

The Swiss

Switzerland is a small nation of 15,000 square miles — hardly large enough to make a fair-sized American state — and has a population of four million. It is a country of great diversity, with high mountains and deep valleys, glaciers and sunshine. Its people, also, are anything but homogeneous. There is no Swiss language serving to bind these four million together as a nation. Instead, a majority of them speak German, or rather a variety of German known as Schwyzerdütsch, which itself varies from canton to canton. French is spoken by 19 per cent of the people; Italian is the language of 9 per cent; and slightly less than 1 per cent speak an ancient language known as Romansh. These language differences are barely indicative of the deep cultural diversities found in the country. Almost every valley in the high Alps has retained its very distinct characteristics; and there are regional differences in costume, dialect, ways of thought, and ways of acting. Nor does religion serve to bind the people together, for 57 per cent are Protestant and 41 per cent Catholic. These religious and linguistic cleavages, which are subject to statistical presentation, are indicative of the conflict between latinity and teutonism. This conflict has deep roots, and rests on differences of temperament, manners, customs, sense of humor, and other subtle characteristics. In short, Switzerland is composed of very diverse ethnic groups, having all the potentialities of bitter antagonism.

As a matter of fact, throughout most of her history, Switzerland has been a battleground. Far from being isolated and protected by her high mountains, she is actually astride several highways, and every conqueror from Caesar and Hannibal to Napoleon and Hitler has had to reckon with her. The Swiss have had every opportunity to learn about war; and until recently, the word "Switzerland" brought to most people's minds not milkmaids, yodelers, watch-makers, and hotel keepers, but professional soldiers, and ferocious ones at that. The Swiss, in addition to having their own domestic difficulties, participated as mercenaries in most of the wars of other European nations, and the Swiss Guard at the Vatican today is a picturesque survival of an ancient profession.

Despite all this diversity, the Swiss have succeeded in combining these ethnic groups into a national unit. Conceivably it might have been done on a basis of subordination and superordination, or on a basis of segregation — neither of which, however, would have produced the national loyalty which the Swiss now

TABLE 10.1

Percentage Distribution of the Swiss Population
by Language, 1850–1960*

Years	German	French	Italian	Romansh	Other
1850	70.2	22.6	5.4	1.8	...
1880	71.3	21.4	5.7	1.4	0.2
1888	71.4	21.8	5.3	1.3	0.2
1900	69.8	22.0	6.7	1.2	0.3
1910	69.1	21.1	8.1	1.1	0.6
1920	70.9	21.2	6.2	1.1	0.6
1930	71.9	20.4	6.0	1.1	0.6
1941	72.6	20.7	5.2	1.1	0.4
1950	72.1	20.3	5.9	1.0	0.6
1960	69.3	18.9	9.5	0.9	1.4

* Source: Consulate of Switzerland, Cleveland, Ohio

possess. Instead, an accommodation in the nature of cultural pluralism was reached during the nineteenth century. As to Catholic and Protestant, the principle of complete religious freedom was adopted, and liberty of conscience prevails. As for the linguistic differences, German, French, Italian, and Romansh were designated in the Constitution as "national languages," and the first three were declared to be "official languages" — a distinction difficult for an outsider to comprehend. At any rate, all federal documents are translated into the three official languages, all versions being equally authoritative. In the political sphere, cultural pluralism found expression in granting to each of the cantons a large measure of local autonomy and sovereignty, somewhat greater than that enjoyed by the several American states.[10] Other political devices, such as proportional representation and initiative and referendum, were adopted with the view to safeguard the integrity and the interests of the various ethnic groups. This is not to say that ethnocentrism was suddenly eradicated and a spirit of tolerance instantly engendered. After all, the Swiss are human; and the prejudices of Latin and Teuton, Papist and Calvinist, have deep foundations. Nevertheless, these people have learned to live with their differences and to develop common loyalties. Switzerland does afford an example of diverse ethnic groups dwelling together in harmony and equality, and with a high degree of national feeling. One writer, attempting to explore the mind of the Swiss, has this to say:

> It is difficult to believe that a nation should suddenly reform its habits merely because such action would be to its best advantage. Even if the Swiss were wise enough to mend their errors in the nick of time, it still would be interesting to know why they were so wise, while other nations, hardened in their sins despite their better knowledge, have foundered.

[10] For an account of the political structure, see W. E. Rappard, *The Government of Switzerland.*

Yet, does a Swiss really feel Swiss? The question cannot be answered simply. . . .

A Swiss feels more Swiss on certain days than on others. He feels very Swiss when he stands on a mountain top and looks upon his land; he feels very Swiss when he serves in his army, when he commemorates old battles, when he compares his country with the rest of the world. . . . In his everyday life, he is more likely to feel Argovian, Neuchatelois, or whatever he may be. In his intellectual life he may feel more affinities with the French, the Germans, or the Italians than with those among his fellow Swiss who speak a tongue different from his own. . . .

Now anyone who unites so many levels of loyalty within his person is unlikely to be swayed overmuch by any particular loyalty. A German Swiss, for instance, will sympathize with Germany — but only culturally, as it were. . . . He will feel strongly for his canton most of the time. But when the question of being Swiss is involved — well, he is a Swiss, and he intends to stay one. What is more, on all levels of loyalty he is equally faithful to his national traditions.[11]

Sociologists, as well as statesmen and political scientists, have tried to determine how the Swiss learned to blend their cultural differences into a national unity. One piece of research has inquired into the demographic basis for this unity.[12] The national languages of Switzerland — German, French, Italian, Romansh — are recognized by the constitution as equal, but they are not actually equal in importance. Table 10.1 shows that German-speaking Swiss greatly outnumber the other three, and over the years they have been gaining slightly. The explanation lies in differences in fertility, the French-speaking cantons having considerably lower birth rates than most of the German-speaking cantons. These differences in fertility, however, have been offset by internal migrations. The French regions of the country have proved much more attractive to German-speaking migrants than the German regions have to the French-speaking Swiss. Furthermore, the migrants tend to become rapidly assimilated, especially so when they have children who can use only the official language of the region in school. High mountains mark off the boundaries between the Italian-speaking region and the rest of Switzerland, thus preserving the Italian language intact. Mayer, who made this study of Swiss equilibrium, maintains that no effort whatsoever is made by the German-Swiss, who constitute an overwhelming majority, to impose their language upon the nation. This linguistic equilibrium, which represents one of the foremost stabilizing and integrating influences in modern Switzerland, originated at a time before language was made a symbol of national and ethnic identification, and the demographic factors have kept it so. To be sure, this fortunate circumstance has been consciously reinforced by wise political measures designed to prevent language from becoming a focus of division and conflict, as it has elsewhere. Those who embrace the ideal of cultural pluralism would do well to give close attention to the Swiss, for they have been without peers in putting into practice this rare and difficult pattern of accommodation in ethnic group relations.

[11] C. Herold, *The Swiss without Halos*, p. 135.
[12] K. Mayer, "Cultural Pluralism and Linguistic Equilibrium in Switzerland," *American Sociological Review*, Vol. 16, No. 2, April 1951, pp. 157–163.

The Russians

Soviet Russia is another heterogeneous modern nation which has reputedly adopted a policy of cultural pluralism toward her numerous ethnic minorities. That is no easy task for a nation of peoples so diverse as are the citizens of the U.S.S.R. The largest group are the Russians, who make up about half of the population; but others, numbering millions each, are the Ukrainians, Jews, Armenians, Georgians, Poles, Tartars, and many more. Altogether there are about 185 distinct ethnic groups, speaking approximately 147 different languages. The cultural differences are incredibly wide. At one extreme are literate, civilized, urbanized, industrialized moderns, and at the other preliterate, nomadic primitives. There are Moslems, Jews, and many varieties of Christians, to say nothing of the non-religious and the anti-religious.

The conflicts between these diverse groups were long utilized by the dominant Russians in their efforts to exploit and control the country. Anti-Semitism was fostered, and pogroms were launched from time to time to deflect popular discontent from the government. Ethnic groups other than the Jews fared no better. Periodically they were the objects of a policy of ruthless Russification; steps were taken to cripple their cultures, to restrict the use of their native tongues, and to suppress their religions. Ignorance and illiteracy were condoned. It is estimated that in 1914 only 40 per cent of the population nine years of age and older were literate. The utter isolation of masses of the people is suggested by that grim expression, "the deaf villages." The Czars were committed to a policy of "divide and rule." The Armenians were set against the Georgians, and Germans against the Letts. In promoting such a policy the government would frequently extend special privileges to one minority group solely for the purpose of creating enmity and jealousy among its neighbors. In short, the czarist program for the numerous minorities had one overall purpose — domination; and, in pursuit of that end, segregation, isolation, forced assimilation, and mass expulsion were employed as the occasion arose.

The revolution saw a complete reversal in this policy. In fact, Stalin himself gave much attention to the problem of minorities, and as early as 1913 wrote:

> In the Caucasus there are a number of peoples each possessing a primitive culture, a specific language, but without its own literature; peoples, moreover, which are in a state of transition, partly becoming assimilated and partly continuing to develop. . . .
>
> What is to be done with the Mingrelians, the Abkhasians, the Adjarians, the Svanetians, the Lesghians, and so on, who speak different languages, but do not possess a literature of their own? . . .
>
> The national problem in the Caucasus can be solved *only by drawing the backward nations and peoples into the common stream of a higher culture.* . . .
>
> A minority is discontented not because there is no national union, but because it does not enjoy liberty of conscience, liberty of movement, etc. Give it these liberties and it will cease to be discontented. Thus *national equality in all forms (language, schools, etc.) is an essential element* in the solution of the national

problem. A state law based on complete democracy in the country is required, prohibiting all national privileges without exception and all kinds of disabilities and restrictions on the rights of national minorities.[13]

Within one week after the Revolution had broken out, in 1917, the new government issued a Declaration of the Rights of Peoples of Russia, which proclaimed, over the signatures of Lenin and Stalin:

1. Equality and sovereignty for the peoples of Russia;
2. The right of the peoples of Russia to self-determination even to the point of separation from the state and creation of a new independent government.
3. Abolition of all religious and nationality group privileges;
4. Free development of national minorities and ethnic groups inhabiting the territories of Russia.

These principles have been given expression on numerous occasions in the years since 1917. They have been reiterated in the pronouncements and speeches of prominent Soviet officials. They were incorporated in the constitution of July 10, 1918, as well as in the constitutions of the Soviet Republics of the Ukrainians, White Russians, Azerbaijans, Armenians, Georgians, and others, as they were organized and admitted to the Union. Stalin specified that each ethnic group should operate its own courts and governmental agencies, utilize its own language, and be helped to establish its own newspapers, schools, theaters, clubs, and other institutions. These principles were incorporated in the first Union constitution, adopted in 1924. The next 12 years witnessed a great revival of ethnic sentiment, even to the point where it endangered Soviet unity. The largest group, the Great Russians, began to display considerable ethnocentrism, with the result that Stalin had to denounce the arrogant attitude of Russians toward the other ethnic groups. However, these other peoples themselves, under the encouragement shown them by the government, began to manifest an aggressive nationalistic spirit, and to discriminate against minorities within their territories. Thus the Armenians, Ossets, and Adjarians, dwelling within the Georgian Republic, were the objects of abuse on the part of the dominant Georgians; and the same thing was occurring in the other Soviet Republics. Cultural pluralism, as far as the U.S.S.R. sought to adopt it as a policy, was not to be easily achieved. When the Constitution was revised in 1936, however, the same principles were again incorporated, including the following:

Any direct or indirect restriction of the rights, or conversely any establishment of direct or indirect privileges for citizens on account of their race or nationality, as well as any advocacy of racial or national exclusiveness or hatred and contempt is punishable by law.

These Soviet efforts, which were not limited to speechmaking, toward the establishment of equality between the various racial and ethnic groups within their borders, won the admiration of liberals all over the world.

[13] Quoted in B. J. Stern, "Soviet Policy on National Minorities," *American Sociological Review*, Vol. 9, No. 3, June 1944, pp. 230–231.

At the same time, the Soviet minority policy has come in for a great deal of condemnation, and the motives behind it have been regarded with suspicion. Max Boehm thinks it is only a "sham solution" of national and cultural problems, that there is no sincere concern for the welfare of minorities, and that the whole program serves merely to mobilize the illiterates of these groups against their own upper classes. Others have regarded it as simply a product of expediency, as a technique for maintaining power and extending control.

Others maintain that, despite their professions of cultural and ethnic toleration and autonomy, the Soviets have followed no such policy at all. Dr. Solomon M. Schwarz, who was born and educated in Russia, and who came to the United States in 1940, maintains that anti-Semitism has continued throughout the Soviet period to be severe and virulent.[14] He cites many instances to prove that Yiddish journals have been suppressed and publishing houses closed "for serious manifestations of Jewish bourgeois nationalism," meaning Zionism; outstanding Yiddish authors have been arrested; Jews have suffered disproportionately in the several purges; they have been removed from responsible government posts; anti-Semitism flourishes in the Russian Army; and now a campaign is under way to squeeze the Jews out of the Soviet bureaucracy. Dr. Schwarz declares that anti-Semitism has penetrated the urban middle classes, the upper strata of industrial workers, university students, the Communist Youth, and even the Communist Party itself. The government's attitude has wavered. In the middle 1930's, when Communism and Nazism were bitter enemies, the Soviets put themselves forth as the champions of the Jews and openly and firmly attacked anti-Semitism; but when the Hitler-Stalin pact was formed, the ideological fight was toned down. With the coming of peace, Dr. Schwarz is convinced, there has arisen among Soviet officialdom a "creeping, half-heartedly disguised anti-Semitism," bent upon relegating Jews to the background of Soviet life.

Russia's professions of pluralism and tolerance for ethnic minorities has nowhere been punctured more forthrightly than in an article by Rabbi Joseph Miller, of Brooklyn, N.Y.[15] Dr. Miller was one of seven rabbis chosen by the New York Board of Rabbis to pay a visit to Russia in 1956 and to report upon the Jews' condition there. He wrote:

There are many ways of killing people. You can shoot them. You can starve them. You can gas them in chambers. Or, if you want to be more subtly effective, you can do what the Politburo is doing to the Jews in Russia — you can make them forget who they are.

As a result of 40 years of post-Czarist anti-Semitism, which reached its bloody peak during Stalin's time, two and a half million Russian Jews face cultural and religious extinction — not to mention in some cases, actual physical extinction or imprisonment in Siberia. Plainly and simply, the Red leaders want to destroy the Jew as a Jew. . . . The fear, the sense of hopeless alienation, the futility that permeated the Jewish communities I visited were enough to make me weep. . . .

[14] "The New Anti-Semitism of the Soviet Union," *Commentary*, Vol. 7, No. 6, June 1949, pp. 535–545.

[15] Rabbi Joseph Miller, "The Plight of the Jews in Russia," *Look*, Nov. 27, 1957.

We learned many things from our brethren in Moscow. . . . We learned that no city, no matter how big, has more than one synagogue. We learned that no schools are allowed wherein the beliefs and traditions of the Jews can be inculcated into the young. Furthermore, there are almost no rabbis or teachers left to do any teaching even if it were permitted. We were told that virtually no religious marriage ceremonies are performed any more for fear that the people involved would be reported to the government as religious fanatics. . . .

In community after community . . . we discovered that such situations as this had developed among the Jews a gnawing fear of informers — or *kookers* — in their midst. . . .

Before leaving Russia, we were given an interview with a member of the Ministry of Religious Cults, whose name was Prychodkov. . . . He explained that no religious schools are permitted in the Soviet Union. . . . "If we permit the Jews to set up their own publications and religious institutions, then all the other denominations will ask the same thing. We can't permit this."

"Mr. Prychodkov," I said, "please tell me if Jews will be allowed to emigrate."

"Why not?" he replied. "Jews are citizens like all others. But why should they want to leave? They live in a free country."

As for the other non-Jewish minorities, the prospects are none too bright. Dr. Jacob Robinson, who also has had ample opportunity to know the situation, reports that "Soviet policy is, in some measure, reminiscent of the imperial policy of Czarist Russia," and says:

> Soviet theoreticians speak of the Soviet Union as a multi-national socialist state. It would be more correct to define it as a multi-lingual state. Even after the shifts which have occurred, Soviet policy does not recognize national traditions, in the full sense, as worthy of perpetuation. While fostering customary folk dances and folk lore, the Soviets impose a deadening uniformity on the national literatures. In principle the cultures of all the nationalities in the Union are supposed to be national in their form only — that is in language — but "socialist in content." . . . A new expression, now being widely used, speaks of the Soviet people, instead of the peoples of the Soviet Union.[16]

Thus it seems doubtful that the Soviets, in spite of all their talk, have ever been committed to a policy of pluralism for their numerous ethnic minorities. Assimilation is their ultimate goal and pluralism, insofar as they have promoted it, is but a temporary and expedient step toward the goal of a monolithic society. As Lenin put it, "We must divide in order to unite"; and Stalin, even before the Revolution, declared:

> Regional autonomy in the Caucasus is acceptable because it draws the backward nations into the common cultural development; it helps to cast off the shell of isolation peculiar to small nationalities; it impels them forward and facilitates access to the benefits of a higher culture.[17]

16 "The Soviet Solution of the Minorities Problem," in R. M. MacIver (Ed.), *Group Relations and Group Antagonisms*, p. 192.
17 Quoted in Stern, *op. cit.*, p. 231.

The American Indians

Pluralism might be said to have been the policy of the United States government toward its Indian wards in the period 1933-1950. Historically, the attitudes of the whites toward the Indians in the area now the United States illustrates any and all of the phenomena of race relations. Conflict, for example, has been intermittent, assimilation and amalgamation and mass expulsion have been employed from time to time, segregation and stratification have been practiced, and we find an expression of tolerance and sympathy, even of sentimental idealization, which partakes of cultural pluralism. While all these policies have prevailed, and have even run concurrently, we may recognize particular periods when one or the other has been dominant in Indian-white relations.[18]

From the very beginning the policies of the Spaniards differed from those of the English, Dutch, and others who settled north of the Rio Grande. The Spaniards regarded the Indians as subjects of the crown and the church. To be sure, the Indians were relegated to the inferior status of forced laborers, and were mercilessly exploited; but at the same time, assimilation and amalgamation were deliberately fostered. The Spaniards seldom dealt with the Indian tribes as though they were sovereign powers, and did not resort to the purchase of lands and other rights from them; instead they established missions, and set about Christianizing and "civilizing" them.

The Dutch, British, Swedes, and others who settled our Atlantic Coast did not deliberately depart from the Spanish precedent; but conditions were so different that a new policy did emerge. For one thing, the Indian population was not nearly so large, and did not pose the danger that the Spaniards faced. More important, however, was the fact that colonization in non-Spanish North America was not a function of the crown, but was a business proposition, undertaken by private enterprise, for the purpose of economic gain. Much to the disappointment of the entrepreneurs who backed them, the colonies never gave much financial promise, and never attracted enough capital to warrant military conquest of the natives. Accordingly, the policy developed was one of dealing with the various tribes as though they were independent, sovereign powers, of recognizing their title to the land and paying them for it, and of negotiating with them by treaties. This policy, of course, led to interminable conflict, for the Indian's conception of land and property was entirely different from the white man's. Moreover, the treaty as an instrumentality assumes a degree of social organization and centralization of authority which certainly did not prevail in Indian society, and hardly prevailed in the colonies. All the while there were missionaries and humanitarians who worked for the education and assimilation of the Indians; there were fur traders who preferred to leave them as they were; and there were hard-headed realists who advocated their extermination and were assisted in their endeavors by disease, vice, and intertribal wars. The major policy, however, was one of removal or mass expulsion. Thomas Jefferson enter-

[18] For an account of these various policies, see W. T. Hagan, *American Indians;* D. Mc-Nickle, *The Indians of the United States: Ethnic and Cultural Survival.*

tained the idea of moving the Indians across the Mississippi River, and the purchase of Louisiana, he thought, would provide land for them. Presidents Monroe and Adams insisted that the Indians could not be removed without their consent, and often this could not be obtained. Whatever the Indians felt, however, the frontier kept pushing them westward. Treaties depriving them of their land were forced upon them by one means or another; worse still, the provisions of many of these treaties have never been satisfied to this day, much to the bitterness and disillusionment of the Indian.

In the middle of the nineteenth century a change in policy developed. The Indian, it was decided, would have to be segregated and isolated. Between 1850 and 1880 most of the reservations, of which there are now more than 200, were created. This change from annihilation and expulsion to segregation was a product of gradual development, interrupted briefly by the Civil War. As a matter of fact, many of the Indian tribes, in ceding their lands to white conquerors, had "reserved" a portion for their own use. By a series of laws and court decisions the status of the Indians was changed from that of sovereign nations to that of wardship. In 1834 the western portion of the old Louisiana Purchase was set apart as solid Indian territory; but in the same year Indian sovereignty was invaded by the extension of federal criminal law to cover all crimes on Indian territory where a white person was either the victim or the criminal. Just prior to the Civil War many treaties were made extinguishing Indian title to certain lands; and after the war penalties in the form of land cessions were exacted from those tribes which had gone on the warpath and those which had fought on the side of the Confederates. Again, a decision of the Supreme Court held that a treaty with an Indian tribe had no greater force than an act of Congress, and that Congress had the right to abrogate the terms of such treaties. Finally, on March 3, 1871, an act was passed which put an end to the use of treaties in dealing with Indians and of recognizing Indian tribes as independent, sovereign nations. Henceforth they would be controlled through segregation on reservations and special legislation by Congress.

Segregation, however, was not successful as a solution to the problem. Nomads did not readily take to a settled life. Hunters could not easily change themselves into farmers. Proud and independent warriors did not appreciate the status of wards and the ministrations of a guardian. To tide them over until they could make the necessary adjustments, and to make them contented with their lot, the government issued rations, but this served only to pauperize them. It became evident that the policy of segregation was a failure; and those who had a genuine interest in the Indian's welfare (and some who hoped to do him out of what little he had left) clamored for assimilation and "Americanization."

In the 1880's, accordingly, another shift in policy occurred. The Indian was to be "civilized," assimilated, "Americanized." This meant the destruction of his tribal organization, suppression of his pagan religion and ceremonies, cutting his hair short and teaching him to dress like the whites, making him speak English, emancipating him from his ancient customs, developing in him the ideas and values of white society, making of him a rugged, go-getting individualist. As Mr. John Collier, later Commissioner of Indian Affairs, put it, "To smother, to exterminate the entirety of the Indian heritage became the central purpose." The chief instrument of this new policy was the General Allotment Act, passed by Congress in 1887. This act provided for the destruction of the reservations by giving to each Indian a share of the reservation lands. This share was to be held in trust for a period of 25 years, during which time it could not be taxed or sold. After that the Indian would be given a fee patent and be declared competent to manage his own affairs. The sponsors of the bill believed, quite correctly, that destroying the communal ownership of the land would break the backbone of the Indian culture. The Secretary of the Interior of that era remarked, "The enjoyment and pride of the individual ownership of property is one of the most effective civilizing agencies"; and Senator Dawes, whose name is attached to the act, insisted that it would create in the Indian that spirit of selfishness which, in the Senator's opinion, was the main motivation of white civilization.

The breaking up of the reservations was only a part of the program to force and accelerate the Indian's assimilation. His children were placed in boarding schools, where they were weaned away from their Indian culture, and indoctrinated with the standards of the whites. Indian languages were systematically suppressed, the ancient arts were allowed to wither, and Indian religion, ceremonies, and traditions were discouraged and often forbidden.

No adequate provision was made, however, for the Indian's assumption of the role of citizen. In World War I many non-citizen Indians served in the armed forces; and a law was passed in 1919 conferring citizenship upon any honorably discharged soldier who requested it. By 1924 about two-thirds of the Indians had become citizens, in one way or another; and in that year Congress declared that all who were born in the United States were citizens. This, however, did not confer upon them the right to vote, which is regulated by the states. In some states Indians were denied this right on the grounds that they were not taxpayers, and in Arizona they were barred by a law which forbade persons under guardianship from voting. Some years ago the Arizona Supreme Court rendered a decision in favor of the Indian's franchise, and a federal court declared New Mexico's restrictions upon them unconstitutional. Now, for the first time, all Indians in the country can vote.

The policy of compulsory and rapid assimilation, which prevailed from the middle of the nineteenth century until the 1920's, proved a miserable failure. The boarding school nearly destroyed the Indian's family institution, and the concerted attack upon his culture had a devastating effect. Economically it ruined him. When the Dawes Act was passed in 1887, Indians owned some 140 million acres of land, an area larger than the state of California. Within 45 years they had lost all but 48 million acres, and a large part of what remained had never been good land and much of it had become worthless through overgrazing. An investigation made in the 1920's[19] revealed that only 2 per cent

[19] L. Meriam and Associates, *The Problem of Indian Administration.*

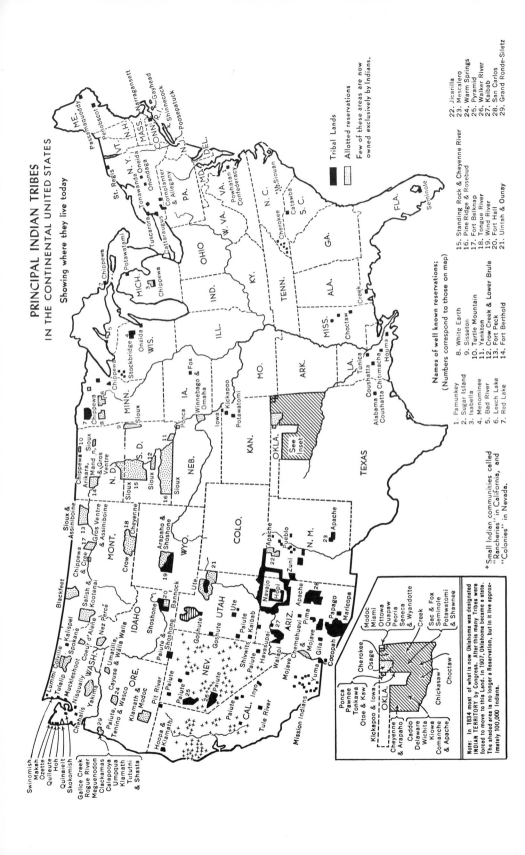

PRINCIPAL INDIAN TRIBES
IN THE CONTINENTAL UNITED STATES
Showing where they live today

Tribal Lands

Allotted reservations

Few of these areas are now owned exclusively by Indians.

Names of well known reservations;
(Numbers correspond to those on map)

1. Pamunkey
2. Sugar Island
3. Isabella
4. Menominee
5. Bad River
6. Leech Lake
7. Red Lake
8. White Earth
9. Sisseton
10. Turtle Mountain
11. Yankton
12. Crow Creek & Lower Brule
13. Fort Peck
14. Fort Berthold
15. Standing Rock & Cheyenne River
16. Pine Ridge & Rosebud
17. Fort Belknap
18. Tongue River
19. Wind River
20. Fort Hall
21. Uintah & Ouray
22. Jicarilla
23. Mescalero
24. Warm Springs
25. Pyramid
26. Walker River
27. Kaibab
28. San Carlos
29. Grand Ronde-Siletz

+ Small Indian communities called "Rancherias" in California, and "Colonies" in Nevada.

Note: In 1834 most of what is now Oklahoma was designated INDIAN TERRITORY by Congress. After this many Tribes were forced to move to this Land. In 1907, Oklahoma became a state. The shaded area is no longer a Reservation, but it is live approximately 100,000 Indians.

Swinomish
Makah
Ozette
Quileute
Hoh
Quinaielt
Skokomish

Galice Creek
Rogue River
Meguendon
Clackamas
Calapooya
Umpqua
Klamath
Tututni
& Shasta

Lummi
Muckleshoot
Tulalip
Nisqually
Chehalis

Colville
Kalispel
Spokane
Coeur d'Alene
Kootenai
Salish &
Kootenai

Blackfeet
Chippewa
& Cree

Sioux &
Assiniboine

Gros Ventre
& Assiniboine

Chippewa
Arikara, Sioux
Mand n,
&Gros
Ventre

2 Chippewa

Potawatami

Chippewa

Stockbridge

Oneida

Chippewa

Chippewa

Fox

Winnebago &
Omaha

Ponca

Iowa

Kickapoo
Potawatomi

St. Regis

Tonawanda Oneida
Tuscarora
Onondaga
Cattaraugus
Complanter
& Allegany

Passamaquoddy
Penobscot
Gayhead
Narragansett
Shinnecock
Poosepatuck

Powhatan
Confederacy

Pamunkey

Cherokee
Catawba

Seminole

Yakima
Muckleshoot
Paiute,
Cayuse & Walla Walla
Umatilla &
Wasco
Nez Percé

Klamath &
Modoc

Crow
Cheyenne

Arapaho &
Shoshone

Sioux

Sioux

Sioux

Apache

Pit River

Paiute
Paiute
Shoshone
Shoshone
Bannock

Goshute
Goshute
Ute
Ute

Arapaho &
Shoshone

Paiute

Paiute

Shiwits

Kaibab

Havasupai
Walapi
Chemehuevi
&
Mojave
Mojave
Yuma

Navajo
Hopi

Zuni
Pueblo

Apache
&
Pima

Gila
Papago
Maricopa
Cocopah

Apache

Apache

Mission Indians

Tule River

Hoopa &
Klamath

Paiute &
Klamath

Tunica
Coushatta
Alabama
Coushatta Chitimacha
Houma

Creek

Choctaw

Inset (OKLA.)

Ponca
Pawnee
Tonkawa
Otoe & Kaw
Kickapoo & Iowa

Cheyenne
& Arapaho
Caddo
Delaware
Wichita
Kiowa
Comanche
& Apache

Cherokee
Osage

Modoc
Miami
Ottowa
Quapaw
Peoria
Seneca
& Wyandotte

Creek
Sac & Fox
Seminole
Potawatomi
& Shawnee

Chickasaw
Choctaw

of the Indians had incomes of over $500 a year, death rates and infant mortality were extremely high, tuberculosis and trachoma were widespread, housing conditions were appalling, sanitary provisions were lacking, diet was poor, and the reservation, far from disappearing, was the only friendly refuge for children leaving the boarding schools and the center of existence for those who never went to school. In short, the policy had failed to assist the Indian in making the transition to the American culture.

Another change in policy then had to be made. All along, it had been tacitly assumed that the Indians were a "vanishing race"; that the particular policy did not matter very much anyway; and that time would solve the problem. Instead, they proved to be very hardy, increasing in spite of conditions which would have eliminated others; and the realization dawned that the Indian would be with us for a long time to come. Under President Herbert Hoover, accordingly, a new policy of cultural pluralism and gradual assimilation was inaugurated. In place of "deserving politicians" who had neither knowledge nor sympathy for their tasks, competent persons were appointed to the Indian Bureau, who were pledged to a program of reform. Thus the groundwork was laid for a new policy, but it remained for the next administration, under President Roosevelt, to put that policy into operation. John Collier, who became Commissioner of Indian Affairs, summarized the new principles:

1. Civic and cultural freedom and opportunity for the Indian;
2. Organization of the Indian tribes for managing their own affairs;
3. Economic rehabilitation of the Indian.

This new policy was put into operation on June 18, 1934, with the passage of the Indian Reorganization Act, which provided for the following:

1. Prohibiting the alienation by sale or foreclosure of land still owned by Indian tribes;
2. Prohibiting individual allotting of lands now in tribal status and lands to be purchased for Indian tribes;
3. Providing for the purchase of new lands for those tribes in need of land;
4. Providing credit for the use of Indians in financing their farming and other business enterprises;
5. Permitting consolidation of Indian lands which had become split up through inheritance;
6. Encouraging the organization and incorporation of Indian tribes for the political and economic management of their resources and affairs;
7. Providing loan funds for Indian students seeking higher education; and
8. Giving preference to Indians for employment in the Indian Service.

The act was to be permissive, not mandatory. The tribes were asked to vote on whether they would accept or reject the new law. Most chose to accept it, but some preferred to operate otherwise. The underlying philosophy was stated by Collier as the "simple principle of treating the Indians as normal human beings capable of working out a normal adjustment to and a satisfying life within the framework of American civilization, yet maintaining the best of their own culture and racial idiosyncrasies." The Indians, accordingly, were encouraged to revive and develop their ancient arts and crafts, to use their own languages, to worship as they pleased, to practice their ceremonies, and to observe their customs and traditions.

This policy, which we regard as one of pluralism, came under attack from many sources. Critics maintained that it was retrogressive, that it aimed to "re-Indianize the Indian," and to perpetuate a permanent bureaucracy for controlling Indian Affairs. Others, of unquestionable good will toward the Indians, regarded this policy as "mystical and exotic," and insisted that the sooner integration and assimilation could be achieved the better. One, who certainly had the interests of the Indians at heart, wrote:

> I need hardly add how deeply I sympathize with the efforts of the present administration. I must however say, to my regret, that I do not share the implied optimism as to the possibility at this late date of saving the culture and the creativeness of the Indians along the old lines. The material aspects of the situation can certainly be relieved and built up, and the self-respect of the Indian can be restored, but the idea of native cultures existing safely, happily, and creatively in our midst somehow does not fit into my view of the nature and possibilities of our civilization. I hope that I am wrong. . . ."[20]

It appears that the official policy of pluralism, with respect to the Indian and his culture, began, around 1950, to shift back to one of assimilation.[21] This came about, not with a repeal or repudiation of the Indian Reorganization Act, but through a change of the top administrative personnel, bringing with it a different philosophy. Many who are responsible for the shift in policy doubtless believe sincerely that the only hope for the Indian lies in his becoming completely integrated into the economic, political, social, and cultural life of the United States. They believe that the Indian, as long as he remains isolated on reservations, will be the victim of poverty, disease, overpopulation, and hopelessness. These, who sincerely believe in assimilation, are supported in their efforts by others whose motives are selfish, who are eager to get their hands on the land, timber, and mineral resources the Indians now possess. To them, perpetuating the Indian's culture and social organization is abhorrent.

This trend continued under the administration of President Eisenhower. On July 27, 1953, Congress, upon the advice of the Department of the Interior, passed Joint Resolution 108, announcing a change in policy toward the Indian. In pursuance of this resolution, Public Law 280 was enacted, permitting any state government to substitute itself for the federal government in civil and

---

[20] A. A. Goldenweiser, *Anthropology*, p. 439. Copyright 1937.
[21] See J. B. Gittler, *Understanding Minority Groups*, pp. 33–57; Dorothy Van de Mark, "The Raid on the Reservation," *Harper's Magazine*, Vol. 212, No. 1270, March 1956, pp. 48–53; J. Collier, "Letter to General Eisenhower," *The Nation*, Vol. 176, No. 2, January 10, 1953, pp. 29–30; Dorothy Bohn, "Liberating the Indian — Euphemism for a Land Grab," *The Nation*, Vol. 178, No. 8, February 20, 1954, pp. 150–151; J. Collier, "Back to Dishonor," *The Christian Century*, Vol. 71, No. 19, May 12, 1954, pp. 578–580; H. E. Fey, "Our National Indian Policy," *The Christian Century*, Vol. 72, No. 13, March 13, 1955, pp. 395–397.

TABLE 10.2

American Indian Population By States*

State	1950	1960	State	1950	1960
Alabama	928	1,276	Montana	16,606	21,181
Alaska	14,089	14,444	Nebraska	3,954	5,545
Arizona	65,761	83,387	Nevada	5,025	6,681
Arkansas	533	580	New Hampshire	74	135
California	19,947	39,014	New Jersey	621	1,699
Colorado	1,567	4,288	New Mexico	41,901	56,255
Connecticut	333	923	New York	10,640	16,491
Delaware	0	597	North Carolina	3,742	38,129
District of Columbia	330	587	North Dakota	10,766	11,736
Florida	1,011	2,504	Ohio	1,146	1,910
Georgia	333	749	Oklahoma	53,769	64,689
Hawaii	?	472	Oregon	5,820	8,026
Idaho	3,800	5,231	Pennsylvania	1,141	2,122
Illinois	1,443	4,704	Rhode Island	385	932
Indiana	438	948	South Carolina	554	1,098
Iowa	1,084	1,708	South Dakota	23,344	25,794
Kansas	2,381	5,069	Tennessee	339	638
Kentucky	234	391	Texas	2,736	5,750
Louisiana	409	3,587	Utah	4,201	6,961
Maine	1,522	1,879	Vermont	30	57
Maryland	314	1,538	Virginia	1,056	2,155
Massachusetts	1,201	2,118	Washington	13,816	21,076
Michigan	7,000	9,701	West Virginia	160	181
Minnesota	12,533	15,496	Wisconsin	12,196	14,297
Mississippi	2,502	3,119	Wyoming	3,237	4,020
Missouri	547	1,723	Total	357,499	523,591

* Source: Bureau of the Census

criminal matters involving Indians. This means, in effect, that the states are free to destroy and pulverize tribal organizations and cultures. President Eisenhower signed the bill, though he termed it "unChristian" and expressed the hope that Congress would amend it and correct its abuses. Other bills followed, designed "to end as quickly as possible individual trust protection and federal services to Indians," and "to liquidate all tribal organizations and dispose of their assets."

The following news item is a typical result of this policy:

SAN FRANCISCO, Feb. 9, 1957 — New steps toward solution of an American Indian "problem" are being taken by Congressional committees.

Involved is the Klamath Tribe and its 867,000-acre timber-studded reservation in Southern Oregon. The tribe members must be put on their own, freed from nearly a century of Federal supervision, by mid-August of 1958 if provisions of a termination law adopted in 1954 are followed. . . .

Estimates in the last two years have put a valuation of about $80,000,000 on the property, which has rich stands of ponderosa and sugar pine. . . .

The Klamath Termination Law gives to all adult members of the tribe the right to say, on behalf of themselves and their minor children, whether they will leave the tribe and get their rightful shares of the tribal property or stay in the tribe and participate in a management program to be operated by or for those who remain. . . .

The prospective choices have not only led to factional strife in the tribe but have aroused Southern Oregon to alleged dangers inherent in any wholesale withdrawal of tribal members. . . .

Specialists say reports to them indicate that 70 per cent of the tribe members will choose to withdraw. . . . If 70 per cent withdraw, about 2,660,000,000 board feet of timber would have to be sold to pay them their shares. . . . These "forced sales," the specialists argue, would mean depressed prices, with resultant losses not only to the tribe members who withdraw but also to those who remain to participate in the management of whatever resources are left.[22]

22 The *New York Times*, February 10, 1957.

*American Indians show
an interesting combination
of segregation
and assimilation*

Seldom have the Indians themselves been asked what they wanted. However, in June, 1961, a conference was held in Chicago, attended by some 450 representatives of 90 tribal groups. The conference adopted a "creed" which included:

> We believe in the inherent right of all people to retain spiritual and cultural values, and that the free exercise of these values is necessary to the normal development of any people. . . .
>
> We believe that . . . the Indian has been subjected to duress, undue influence, unwarranted pressures, and policies which have produced uncertainty, frustration, and despair.

They enumerated their demands and aspirations, among which were:

(1) Revocation of Joint Resolution 108 of the 83rd Congress, which inaugurated the policy of termination.
(2) Economic assistance looking toward the establishment upon the reservations of industries and other activities to provide employment for Indians.
(3) Participation of Indians in all programs.
(4) Revolving loan funds.
(5) Better health services and facilities.
(6) Improved housing conditions.
(7) Provision for retaining, consolidating, and acquiring land.
(8) Great expansion in educational facilities, including vocational and on-the-job training, adult education, guidance and counseling.

And so our government's policies toward the Indian swing to and fro. Our predecessors sought to exterminate them, or at least to drive them into the hinterland. Later, efforts were made to assimilate them, or to segregate them. For two decades in the recent past we undertook to live with them, to accept them, and to permit them to be themselves. Through it all the Indian, miraculously, has survived. As a matter of fact, he thrives. Those who insist that assimilation is inevitable find little support here. The safest prediction would seem to be that for many years to come we shall have with us Indian tribes, Indian communities, and Indian cultures.

Pluralism, as a form of adjustment for the differences of racial and ethnic groups, has a special appeal to those who subscribe to democratic ideals and processes. It is very congenial to those who place high value upon good sportsmanship, fair play, freedom, and the sacredness of human personality. It attracts those who hold that "variety is the spice of life," and who deplore the modern trend toward uniformity, homogeneity, and standardization. At the same time it must be admitted that pluralism is a delicate form of accommodation, difficult to achieve, applicable only in rare circumstances, and demanding a high degree of mutual tolerance and sympathy.[23]

[23] Some of the problems and difficulties inherent in a pluralistic society are analyzed in Gordon, *op. cit.*, Ch. 8.

11

Assimilation

The melting pot does not always work.
ROBIN M. WILLIAMS, JR.
Strangers Next Door

Conflict is no doubt the phase of race relations which most easily catches the public's attention. Riots, lynchings, insurrections, and mass expulsions make the headlines and create the impression that racial and ethnic groups are naturally and continually at each other's throats. But race relations also include interactions of a very different sort, which are less conspicuous than conflict but in the long run more significant. Annihilation or expulsion of the weaker group by the stronger is not the usual outcome of the contact of races. More common by far is the fusion of the two (assimilation and amalgamation) or the reaching of some *modus vivendi* (accommodation). We are concerned here with assimilation as one of the consequences of intergroup contact. The following autobiographical sketch written by a young American of Chinese ancestry illustrates most of the processes and problems involved:

My parents came from China in 1900. Father was a herbalist. . . . In China herb doctors are very much in demand. . . . When Father settled in Los Angeles, he continued his profession. He was successful almost from the start. He dealt exclusively with "Americans." His knowledge of English was woefully inadequate. "R's" he never could pronounce, and my brothers and I always laughed when we heard him advise his patients to eat "lice."

But my mother doesn't even speak English, although she has been in California now for forty-one years. She lives the protected life of a Chinese lady in China. Except for infrequent Sunday afternoon drives, she seldom leaves the house. . . . Mother has tiny bound feet, wears Chinese gowns always, and drinks nothing but tea, which she has on hand in a thermos bottle, hot, twenty-four hours a day. She loathes milk and cheese, and will refuse anything cooked with butter. . . .

Being China-born, my parents were excluded from American citizenship; and I believe this fact prevented Father, at least, from making a serious effort to adopt American ways. And yet Father was grateful to America too. He named all his sons for American Presidents. . . . He named his first-born Taft . . . the next two William and Howard. . . . Two more became Monroe and Lincoln. . . .

From early childhood, I, with my brothers and sisters, lived a double life. We drooled over ice cream cones at the corner store, we ran wildly over school grounds shouting English insults at our classmates, we played American baseball. . . . We generally spoke English to each other. . . . But to our parents we spoke only Chinese. Father was strict about our learning the language properly. . . . But we'd absentmindedly divide not only a sentence into Chinese and English words, but the words themselves into Chinese and English syllables. . . .

During all my early youth, and in many respects even now, the American way was more attractive. . . . I use chopsticks, but not to the exclusion of knives and forks; I play mah jongg, but I enjoy contract bridge as well.

Only toward my parents was I uncompromisingly Chinese. Our relationship was formal and reserved. . . . Father was the head of the family, and no one doubted his authority; while Mother had her respected function as matriarch and ruler of the domestic system. . . . To us they were always respectfully "Father" and "Mother," never "my old man" and "my old lady."

Christmas was a big day in our household, which seems odd considering that my parents were not Christians. To this extent Father and Mother became

Americanized. They knew how important this day was for children all over America. So they had the tallest and bushiest tree our living room could hold; and all their gifts to us were always labelled in Father's own hesitant scrawl, "From Santa Claus." This holiday was one of the few occasions when the whole family sat down to dinner and ate with knives and forks. Except for such holidays we always used chopsticks. . . .

The Thanksgiving celebration was a more elaborate occasion. The Chinese love any excuse for a feast, and even with their scant knowledge of American history my parents knew that the big idea of Thanksgiving was to have a huge feast. . . . Mother and Father presided, he in his American tailor-made dark suit, and Mother in a beautiful jade and gold lace Chinese gown, wearing her jade earrings and jade pins in her shining black hair.

When we were older, Father let us celebrate New Year's Eve, too. . . . There was dancing for the young crowd and mah jongg and Chinese dominoes for Father's and Mother's friends. . . . Ice cream and cake for us and gai chuk or chicken porridge for the oldsters. . . . But there was no differentiation when it came to ringing in the new year; and it was my Father, it seemed, who always made the loudest toot on his horn come midnight.

Then on every Fourth of July we'd have the biggest demonstration of fireworks on our block. . . . To passersby it must have seemed incongruous that when it came to celebrating the independence of this country, the Chinaman's family always made the biggest noise. . . .

Just before the conclusion of our college years, many of us Chinese-Americans began to face the problem of the future — how to earn a living in a country which was native to us by birth, yet alien in many ways. One girl . . . graduated with high honors, but could not find a job. . . . Another friend who finished an engineering course *magna cum laude* . . . now works as a waiter in a chop suey restaurant. Another . . . today is clerking at a fruit stand.

I decided that my best possibility was to secure a position with some American company doing business in the Orient. . . . That was when I thanked my Father for his insistence on Chinese-language school. . . . Without Chinese it would have been impossible. . . . I wrote letters to three large American companies. . . . I received an offer from two. The company I accepted assigned me to its Hawaiian office. . . . Future work will take me to China. . . . My knowledge of Chinese is not so complete as my knowledge of English, nor do I feel as much Chinese as . . . American. But at least I understand both.[1]

This interesting autobiographical sketch by Lincoln Leung brings out a number of aspects of the assimilation process. Note how eagerly and easily the youngsters in the family adopted American customs, language, and values, and how difficult it was for their parents. The father, to be sure, did accept some of the customs of his adopted home; he tried to learn English, he wore American clothes, and he celebrated the holidays of this strange land, even though he grasped only the external features of those occasions. The mother, on the other hand, clung tenaciously to her Chinese ways, though even she learned to appreciate the advantages of the thermos bottle. Both parents, however, agreed upon

[1] L. Leung, "The Twain Meet," *Common Ground*, Vol. 2, No. 2, Winter 1942, pp. 100–103.

certain values in their old culture which they were determined to transmit to their children — the Chinese language and the Chinese insistence upon respect for elders. No doubt they looked with some misgiving upon their children's fondness for ice cream cones, baseball and dancing, and tried to inculcate in them a taste for mah jongg, gai chuk, and chicken porridge. But their efforts were certainly doomed to failure. They could see their children growing up more American than Chinese; and one does not have to be a prophet to foresee that their grandchildren are likely to have little knowledge about, nor interest in, the language and customs of China. There were obstacles aplenty in their way — their Oriental racial features, their limited contacts with Americans, the fact that the parents could not become citizens — but even these formidable barriers could not long delay the trend toward assimilation.

It is not always this way, however. Chinese have migrated to many parts of the world other than the United States, and the story has been quite different. Long before the Leung family came to America Chinese were leaving the southeastern provinces of Fukien and Kwangtung and taking up residence in Burma, Thailand, Malaya, the Philippines, and elsewhere in Southeast Asia. With the advent of European colonialism this migration greatly increased, with the result that today there are some ten million "Overseas Chinese" living in that area. The original emigrants certainly had no intention of founding permanent settlements abroad, nor did they have any desire to become citizens of those outlandish countries. They simply hoped that by engaging in some kind of legitimate business they might amass a reasonable fortune and eventually return to their homeland. For most of them, however, their plans went awry and they never returned to China. Today, generations later, we find their descendants still living in those foreign parts; and, while they have made an excellent economic adjustment, they are unassimilated, socially distinct, and not identified politically or psychologically with the countries in which they reside.

Maurice Freedman, of the London School of Economics, has made extensive studies of these Overseas Chinese,[2] and he raises the question as to why they have failed to become assimilated. Race is certainly not a factor. In British Malaya, he says, little stands in the way of a Chinese who wishes to become a Malay. Anyone who becomes a Moslem can easily find a place and a spouse in Malay society. It is sometimes said that the failure of the Chinese to assimilate was the direct product of deliberate colonial policies of divide and rule; but Freedman, while recognizing some truth in this assertion, points out that in Thailand, which never fell under European control, there is found also this unassimilated Chinese minority. There is, to be sure, a certain degree of assimilation. In Malaya there are Chinese who have acquired at least the formal characteristics of the native culture, and they are known as "Straits Chinese," or "Baba"; and in Indonesia one finds the "Peranakan," Chinese who speak no Chinese (at least as their mother tongue) and have adopted Indonesian habits to a considerable extent.

2 "The Chinese in Southeast Asia," in A. W. Lind (Ed.), *Race Relations in World Perspective*, pp. 388ff.

And yet, says Freedman, "It is still the case that every Overseas Chinese community to a greater or lesser degree has the characteristics of a subsociety oriented toward a homeland across the seas."

The Chinese of Thailand have been the object of a special study by Richard J. Coughlin.[3] He says that Chinese were residing there as early as the sixteenth century, but that immigration reached substantial proportions only within the past 80 years. He estimates that today there are two million Chinese in Thailand, or approximately 10 per cent of the population. "Judged by any material standards, the Chinese have made an unusually successful adjustment. . . . Yet the Chinese in Bangkok have not been assimilated. They remain distinct from the Thai people in their occupations, in their voluntary associations, in political interests and activities, and in the educational facilities they utilize. The two groups are not racially different, for they are both Mongoloid people; but Coughlin finds few cultural similarities between them. There are fundamental differences in language, music, literature, drama, religion, and family organization. For the Chinese, life is centered in the family, which is cooperative and male-dominated, and status is largely determined by financial success. Thai society, on the other hand, is characterized by a loose family system, considerable freedom for women, and adherence to Buddhist values which encourage individualism and the estimation of one's worth in terms of spiritual development. Hence, the Thai fear and distrust the Chinese and discriminate against them, and the Chinese, in turn, effectively resist assimilation and do not become identified with their adopted homeland.

[3] "The Chinese in Bangkok: A Commercial-Oriented Minority," *American Sociological Review*, Vol. 20, No. 3, June 1955, pp. 311–316.

Several Chinese-language newspapers are published in San Francisco's Chinatown

The Nature of Assimilation

By assimilation we mean *the process whereby groups with different cultures come to have a common culture.* This means, of course, not merely such items of the culture as dress, knives and forks, language, food, sports, and automobiles, which are relatively easy to appreciate and acquire, but also less tangible items such as values, memories, sentiments, ideas, and attitudes. Assimilation refers thus to the fusion of cultural heritages, and must be distinguished from *amalgamation,* which denotes the biological mixture of originally distinct racial strains. It must be distinguished, too, from *naturalization,* a political concept denoting the act or process of admitting an alien to the status and privileges of a citizen. *Americanization,* of course, is simply a special case of assimilation, and refers to the process whereby a person of some foreign heritage acquires the customs, ideals, and loyalties of American society, just as Europeanization, Russianization, and Germanization denote a similar process with respect to those cultures.

These terms are related but are not interchangeable. Assimilation and amalgamation, for example, usually go together. As people acquire the habits and attitudes of another society they are less reluctant to choose their mates from that society; and, on the other hand, the biological intermingling of different groups usually leads to cultural exchange. It need not be so, however. Full-blooded Indians have acquired the values, loyalties, and skills of our society to such a degree that they made excellent soldiers in our recent wars; while, at the same time, there have been Indian tribes into which considerable white blood has found its way, but little of the white's culture. So with naturalization. Lincoln Leung's father could never hope for naturalization, regardless of how thorough his assimilation might be or how sincere his Americanization. On the contrary, many a one has completed the process of naturalization whose familiarity with American ways was extremely casual and whose loyalty to American society highly dubious. Prior to 1906 the admission of aliens to citizenship was a function of the various states, operating under the general provisions of the federal law. There was, consequently, a great lack of uniformity in the procedure, and in many places naturalization was more or less a farce. Prior to an election immigrants were herded in droves before judges who created new citizens at the rate of hundreds per day, and all who came along would be sworn in. Needless to say, many were naturalized whose assimilation had barely begun.

Misconceptions

Few people appreciate the difficulty one faces when he tries to adjust himself to a strange civilization. An American, even when he visits England, where the culture is so very similar to his own, confronts innumerable obstacles. The monetary system is hard to comprehend, the food is different, the utensils with which he is expected to eat are somewhat unfamiliar, and even commonplace objects (elevators, thumb tacks, street cars, subways, and so on) are called by strange names. Here at home the failure of an alien to conform to our ways is often attributed to his ignorance, backwardness, stubbornness, or stupidity. Assimilation, according to the popular view, is easy, simple, and speedy, if one has a mind to discard his primitive customs and adopt our own superior practices. In the United States these misconceptions of the process of assimilation have found their expression in two widely accepted theories: (1) the melting pot; and (2) Americanization.

Prior to World War I the philosophy which prevailed with respect to the various ethnic elements in the population was symbolized by the phrase "the melting pot."[4] Negroes, Indians, and Orientals, of course, were not included, but the multitudes who had been crossing the Atlantic were supposed to be undergoing a process of fusion which would eventually produce a great civilization and a race of supermen. William Jennings Bryan eloquently voiced the faith in these words:

> Great has been the Greek, the Latin, the Slav, the Celt, the Teuton, and the Saxon; but greater than any of these is the American, who combines the virtues of them all.[5]

It was even more eloquently expressed by Zangwill:

> America is God's Crucible, the great Melting Pot where all the races of Europe are melting and reforming! — Here you stand good folk, think I, when I see you at Ellis Island, here you stand, in your fifty groups, with your fifty languages and histories, and your fifty blood hatreds and rivalries. But you won't be long like that brothers, for these are the fires of God you come to — these are the fires of God. A fig for your feuds and your vendettas! German and Frenchmen, Irishman and English, Jews and Russians, into the Crucible with you all! God is making the American! . . . The real American has not yet arrived. . . . He will be the fusion of all races, perhaps the coming superman . . . . Ah, what is the glory of Rome and Jerusalem, where all races and nations come to worship and look back, compared with the glory of America, where all nations come to labour and look forward![6]

There is, of course, a large element of truth in this conception. The error lay in its assumption that the process was easy, rapid, natural, and inevitable, and that it would invariably produce a superior type of person. Assimilation, it was thought, would take care of itself. The melting pot theory represented the doctrine of laissez faire applied to the realm of race and culture contact.

World War I gave a rude shock to this comfortable theory. It became apparent that assimilation had not been working as automatically as had been supposed. When the nation began to take stock of itself, the startling fact emerged that there were millions in the country who could neither read, speak, nor write the English language; less than half the foreign-born white males of voting age

---

[4] For a history and analysis of the concept, see M. M. Gordon, *Assimilation in American Life*, Ch. 5.

[5] Quoted in R. E. Park and E. W. Burgess, *Introduction to the Science of Sociology*, p. 734.

[6] I. Zangwill, *The Melting Pot*, pp. 33ff.

were citizens; there were thousands of organizations flourishing among the foreign element, and hundreds of newspapers and periodicals published in foreign languages; immigrants were concentrated in "colonies" in the cities; and foreign governments were in the habit of encouraging their nationals to retain their old allegiance, not without some success.

As a result of these disclosures a new philosophy of assimilation came into being, and a program, known as the "Americanization Movement," was inaugurated.[7] No longer would the assimilation of alien peoples be left to the operation of natural forces. No longer would assimilation be regarded as an inevitable outcome of the meeting of cultures. Deliberate, organized efforts would be made to divest the immigrant of his foreign heritage, to suppress his native language, to teach him English, to make of him a naturalized citizen, and to inject into him a loyalty to American institutions. Many agencies participated in the movement — public schools, patriotic societies, chambers of commerce, women's clubs, public libraries, social settlements, and even industrial plants where foreigners were employed.

The movement itself was based upon a misconception of the process of assimilation, and, as a result, the term "Americanization" (older, of course, than the movement) fell into a certain disrepute from which it has never recovered. It made the mistake of ignoring the values in the cultures of the immigrants and assuming that these must, and could, be discarded as though they were old garments. It involved tacit implication that American culture was a finished product, in an Anglo-Saxon pattern, that it was superior to all others, and that aliens should promptly acquire it. Implicit in the movement was a spirit of coercion, condescension, and suppression, which aroused the resentment of those at whom it was directed and in the end served to defeat its purpose.

It is not only in the United States, of course, that the problems and complexities of the assimilation process have been misunderstood. Wherever racial and ethnic groups have met, the same misconceptions have arisen. At one extreme is the viewpoint of laissez faire and at the other is coercion. Between these two poles our own policies have fluctuated, not only with respect to the immigrants from Europe, but with respect also to Indians, Negroes, Mexicans, and Orientals. The great imperialist countries of Europe have also revealed this same ambivalence and variability, as an examination of their native policies will reveal.[8] The English always held themselves aloof from the native peoples of British colonies, and neither encouraged nor facilitated their acquisition of British culture. The Dutch more or less followed the lead of Britain. The French, on the contrary, were wont to display an intolerance and lack of sympathy for the native cultures over which they exercised domain, but approved of their colonials' acquiring the French language and culture and regarding themselves

---

[7] Gordon (*op. cit.*, p. 85) uses the term "Anglo-conformity," which theory, he says, "demanded the complete renunciation of the immigrant's ancestral culture in favor of the behavior and values of the Anglo-Saxon core group."

[8] Jose Ots y Capdequi, W. C. MacLeod, and S. H. Roberts, "Native Policy," in *Encyclopedia of the Social Sciences*, Vol. 11, pp. 252–282; R. Kennedy, "The Colonial Crisis and the Future," in R. Linton (Ed.), *The Science of Man in the World Crisis*, pp. 306–346.

as citizens of France. Spain, Portugal, Belgium, Italy, Russia, and all other nations which have, or have had, colonial empires have been driven to develop policies which fall somewhere between compulsory assimilation, at the one extreme, and opposition or indifference to assimilation at the other.

Principles of Assimilation

The process whereby groups with different cultures come to share a common culture is not too well understood. Much thought and study has been given to the more conspicuous aspects of race relations (conflict, lynchings, riots, discrimination, segregation, and demonstrations), while those phenomena which are quiet and elusive go unnoticed. Even so, one of the first great sociological classics, *The Polish Peasant in Europe and America*, by W. I. Thomas and Florian Znaniecki, dealt with the problems of assimilation, and in the early years of the present century American sociologists did concern themselves with the problems of immigration. Today the social scientists of Israel, confronted with the great influx of Oriental Jews, are giving serious study to the subtleties of "absorption." A generation ago anthropologists began to turn their attention to preliterate peoples whose cultures had suffered from the impact of European civilization. There are, accordingly, a few principles which are supported by a considerable body of empirical evidence.

Assimilation Not Inevitable

It is reasonable to suppose that ethnic groups in contact with each other will, in spite of themselves, take on some of the customs of their neighbors; accordingly, a certain degree of assimilation will occur, even though the two groups never merge into one. There is evidence for believing that this is exactly what happens, and there is some basis for the predictions of those sociologists who insist that, given sufficient time, complete assimilation will take place. There are the Fox Indians, described in Chapter 6, who long ago turned their backs upon the white man's civilization and determined to have none of it, and who have been very successful in carrying out their resolve. And yet the Fox today are using automobiles and tractors, their tipis are covered with canvas instead of buffalo hides, they consult white physicians when certain diseases strike, they understand money quite well, and in many other ways, where they least suspect it, the effects of their contacts with the whites can be seen. Who would dare predict that the Fox will continue to hold out indefinitely against the forces of assimilation?

So it is with the Tungus and the Cossacks, described in Chapter 5. These two groups have manifested no interest in adopting each other's customs, and each regards his own culture as quite satisfactory. But the Tungus have acquired from the Cossacks a taste for flour, tea, sugar, tobacco, and alcohol; have grown dependent upon them for lead, gunpowder, and cotton materials; and have learned from them the value of iron pots and pans, needles, scissors, thread, spoons, and forks. The Cossacks, in turn, have learned to build the Tungus type of conical shelter for use during the harvest, to wear leather garments of the Tungus fashion when they go hunting in winter, and have acquired a taste for bread baked, Tungus style, without an oven. Centuries hence, if they continue to live in close contact with each other, perhaps their differences will be entirely obliterated.

These, and many similar cases, lend support to the theory that assimilation is an inevitable consequence of the meeting of groups. There are instances, however, where ethnic groups have been in contact for long periods of time, where the assimilation has been at a bare minimum, and where one would have to posit a very long time indeed for the fusion of the cultures.

Handman has reported such a situation on the Transylvanian Plateau in Central Europe.[9] Here, he says, is a population of four and a half million, 55 per cent of them Rumanian, 34 per cent Magyar, and 9 per cent German. Originally the Magyars and Germans came into the region as conquerors and colonists, and they have retained their position of dominance in economic and political affairs. These three ethnic groups, Handman tells us, have been living in fairly close contact for *nearly 1000 years*, and yet have remained culturally distinct. The Magyars are Roman Catholics, Calvinists, and Unitarians; the Germans are Lutherans; and the Rumanians are Greek Catholics and Greek Orientals. Their costumes are different; they have different diets, the food preferences of one group are regarded by another as nasty habits; each has its own language, to which it is passionately devoted; and each has its own peculiar folkways and traditions pertaining to courtship, marriage, births, funerals, amusements, art, songs, and dances. Handman recognizes the fact that there has been a certain amount of cultural interchange; the Rumanian language contains a few words of foreign origin, the houses show the German influence, and the architecture of the Magyar peasant betrays Rumanian influence. These are minor considerations, however, in view of a thousand years of contact; and their paucity gives little basis for predicting that the future will see any appreciable assimilation.

From Guatemala comes another suggestion that contact between groups does not invariably lead to their assimilation.[10] The Indians in Guatemala are organized into local groups, known as *municipios*, somewhat comparable to our townships, but actually very important ethnic units. The members of a *municipio* think of themselves as a distinct people, biologically and socially. Each *municipio* has its own typical costume, which identifies its wearer wherever he goes and sets him apart from other groups. The various *municipios* differ, also, in their etiquette, types of houses, food and cooking, and in their customs pertaining to birth, baptism, marriage, burial, kinship, and family organization. In short, they are in reality distinct ethnic groups. Though they are in constant contact, they have virtually no wish to adopt one another's customs.

[9] M. Handman, "Conflict and Equilibrium in a Border Area," in E. B. Reuter (Ed.), *Race and Culture Contacts*, pp. 86–111.

[10] S. Tax, "World View and Social Relations in Guatemala," *American Anthropologist*, Vol. 43, No. 1, January–March 1941, pp. 27–42.

Their failure to become assimilated, however, is not due to isolation. On the contrary, the *municipios* are not far apart, and the Indians frequently travel from one to another. Public markets are a common feature of all the towns, and the Indians gather from near and far to exchange their products on market-days. There are ample opportunities for the Indians of one *municipio* to become acquainted with the customs of another; and, as a matter of fact, they do know a great deal about the cultures of their neighbors. Neither isolation nor ignorance, therefore, can explain their failure to assimilate. There does seem to be a minimum of culture borrowing. New remedies which have proved their worth are likely to be adopted by persons from the other *municipios*, when they learn about them; and so with new crops and new techniques for growing them. The Indians are not so likely to display conservatism when the new item can be translated readily into dollars and cents. There are not many items of such a nature, however, and the process of assimilation, accordingly, moves at an incredibly slow pace.

Dr. Tax, who made the study of Guatemala here cited, accounts for the situation on two grounds. One feature which runs through all the cultures of the various *municipios* is the emphasis placed upon the impersonal character of social relations, whether they be economic, religious, or familial. It is possible, therefore, for one to establish frequent and widespread relations with his neighbors with a minimum of the kind of intimate contacts which are most conducive to the exchange of cultural items. Second, and more important, is the fact that cultural variability is regarded by the Indians as a perfectly natural and normal condition, and this makes for great tolerance of differences and no strong wish to imitate each other's practices. Cultures vary, they think, from place to place just as do flora and fauna, and that is the way it should be. "That is their custom; it is all right for them," is their general attitude. It is not surprising, then, that one's neighbors in a nearby *municipio* should dress, eat, or worship after a fashion which is not evaluated as either good or bad, desirable or undesirable. Such a philosophy, which conceives of culture as so closely tied to geography and biology, would indeed retard the assimilative process.

A third case of ethnic contact which did not result in assimilation has been reported from the continent of Asia.[11] In the southern part of India, high in the Nilgiri Hills, there live four groups, or tribes: the Todas, a pastoral people; the Badagas, agriculturalists; the Kotas, artisans and musicians; and the Kurumbas, sorcerers, food-gatherers, and dwellers in the jungle. A century ago the British discovered the plateau on which these peoples live, built roads and developed it as a place of refuge from the summer heat of the plains below. Prior to that time, however, and for many centuries, these four tribes had the plateau entirely to themselves.

They were in close contact with one another. Each was highly specialized, and they traded among themselves extensively. The Todas furnished the dairy prod-

[11] D. G. Mandelbaum, "Culture Change Among the Nilgiri Tribes," *American Anthropologist*, Vol. 43, No. 1, January–March 1941, pp. 19–26. See also G. P. Murdock, *Our Primitive Contemporaries*, Ch. 5.

ucts; the Badagas traded their grain and other farm produce; the Kotas specialized in the manufacture of pottery and ironware, and their musicians were called in by the other tribes to perform on important occasions; and the primitive Kurumbas, whose sorcerers were feared and respected, were sought out in times of crisis to practice their magic. Yet in spite of these close and constant contacts, the four cultures had little in common.

Mandelbaum, in his study of the situation, says, "There was some cultural give and take among the tribes; the great wonder is that it amounted to so little." In explaining the failure of these peoples to become assimilated, he points to three facts: (1) the totally different economic base upon which each society operated, giving each a focus of interest to which the others could make little contribution; (2) the contacts, though frequent, were narrowly defined, strictly regulated by custom and tradition, and intimacy was stringently tabooed; and (3) the resistance each offered to another's adopting its customs. He cites the occasion when a few Kotas began imitating the Badagas by wearing turbans. The Badagas ambushed and beat up the offenders, and thereby prevented the spread of that particular custom.

The arrival of the British, bringing with them Hindus and Moslems, created a new problem for these people. They have not been as successful in resisting the influence of these new civilizations, nor in coping with them, as they had been before. Consequently, rapid and disruptive social changes have been occurring in the Nilgiri Hills during the past century, but the four tribes have reacted differently to this impact, and the effects have been more disastrous for some than for others.

In most instances, when racial and ethnic groups come together, there is considerably more cultural interchange than in the three cases we have cited, and even in these three there is a certain amount of borrowing one from the other. The process of assimilation, then, does seem to operate whenever peoples meet; but there are many situations, in addition to those discussed here, in which the interchange is so restricted and so retarded that one must hesitate to conclude that cultural fusion is an inevitable consequence of intergroup contact. Certainly there are peoples who have lived in close contact for very long periods without any appreciable degree of cultural fusion having taken place.

A Reciprocal Process

The view is widely held that assimilation is a one-way process, that it involves the discarding of the traditional culture of one group and the adoption of the culture of the other group. As one wag puts it, "Assimilation means your total absorption into my culture." This was essentially the philosophy which dominated the Americanization Movement which came into being during World War I. The problem was that of forcing the immigrants to divest themselves of their Old World civilization, to sever their allegiances, to abandon their loyalties, and to take upon themselves the culture of the United States. It was believed, furthermore, that this American culture which the immigrant was to acquire was a finished product, in substance essentially Anglo-Saxon. This interpretation of assimilation is not confined to misguided patriots and chauvinists, but has been advanced by sociologists of the caliber of Dr. H. P. Fairchild. Says he:

> The great question is, Is social assimilation a one-way process? . . . The whole problem virtually narrows down to the proposition, Do nationalities blend? Can they blend? . . . Some light on this vitally important set of queries may be derived from reviewing some of the major elements of nationality, and trying to discover whether they are of such a character that they can be blended. . . . First of all, take language. . . . Under modern conditions languages simply do not mix. . . . Once a language becomes well solidified and embodied in a printed literature, it can hardly be blended with another. . . . How about religion? . . . It is obvious that religion presents the same situation as language. . . . The case is no different when we turn to the family institution. . . . In minor matters of fashion, dress, decoration, sports, etc., there can be an unlimited amount of borrowing, but there is little of blending of basic patterns. Without attempting to run through the entire list of nationality items . . . it appears that in social assimilation, as in physiological, . . . the receiving body sets the pattern. . . . And the process of assimilation does require that all foreigners . . . must be adapted to fit into an integrated whole without friction or disturbance.[12]

Fairchild is correct in insisting that assimilation involves the *integration* of new elements with the old. The transferring of a culture from one group to another is a highly complex process. It is not a simple matter of addition and subtraction. It often involves the rejection of ancient ideologies, habits, customs, language, and sentiments. It involves, also, the elusive problem of *selection*. Of the many possibilities presented by the other culture, which will one adopt? Why did the Indians, for instance, when they were confronted with the white man's civilization, take avidly to guns, horses, rum, knives, and glass beads, and manifest no interest in certain other features to which the whites themselves attached the highest value? And, when new items of culture are selected for adoption, the problem of integration is presented, for assimilation means more than the superficial addition of another folkway or the acquisition of another gadget.

Fairchild is correct, also, in perceiving that in the process of assimilation one society "sets the pattern," for the give-and-take of culture seems never to operate on a "fifty-fifty" basis. Invariably one group receives more than it gives. Various factors interact to make this so. Usually one of the societies enjoys greater prestige than the other, giving it an advantage in the assimilative process; or one is better suited to the environment than the other; or one enjoys greater numerical strength than the other. Thus, the pattern for the United States was set by the British colonists, and to that pattern the other ethnic groups have adapted themselves — German, Italian, Greek, Negro, and Chinese.

This is not to say, however, that assimilation is a one-way process. Most sociologists, anthropologists, and historians who have studied the problem of

12 *Race and Nationality*, pp. 109–112.

race relations would disagree with Fairchild and insist that assimilation is re-ciprocal.[13] The Tungus learn much from the Cossacks, but they also teach them certain things; the Leung family, while it proceeds to acquire a taste for every-thing American, from thermos bottles to Santa Claus, introduces Americans to a variety of ancient Chinese herb remedies.[14]

The cultural contributions of the various ethnic groups which have migrated to the United States are difficult to trace, but that they have been numerous can-not be doubted. Most of these contributions have become so thoroughly inte-grated into our culture that we do not suspect that they are relatively recent additions. Grimm alfalfa was introduced into Minnesota by an immigrant who brought the seed with him from Germany; it was Germans who did so much to develop pure-bred horses, cattle, and hogs; Mennonites who came from Russia to Kansas brought with them hard wheat; Russian and Ukrainian farmers brought Kherson oats; Hungarians planted the first Tokay grapes in Cali-fornia; Danes developed the dairy industry; Germans introduced sauerkraut and frankfurters; Italians, spaghetti. Much of our interest in music can doubt-less be attributed to the influence of German, Jewish, and Italian immigrants.

It is much easier to determine the extent to which the Indian, in the course of his assimilation, has influenced our civilization.[15] Everyone knows, of course, that it was the Indian who discovered, utilized, and developed tobacco and maize; but it is not so generally known that we are indebted to the Indian, also, for our knowledge of the potato, the kidney bean, the tomato, the peanut, chocolate, squash, maple sugar, the pineapple, the avocado, and about 35 other food plants. Had the Indian not learned to cultivate these plants it is doubtful that the whites ever would have, for they would probably have introduced the crops with which they were already familiar in the Old World. This alone is no small contribution, but it does not begin to exhaust the list. It was from the Indian that the whites learned about the art of woodcraft, various medicinal plants (cas-cara, witch hazel, cocaine, quinine), canoes, snowshoes, toboggans, moccasins, hammocks, and rubber. Finally, he has had an influence upon our art, architec-ture, and literature; and no less than 500 words in our language were appropri-ated from Indian tongues. There can be no doubt that, in the course of our attempts to assimilate the American Indian, the process has been reciprocal.

Even in the case of the Negro in the United States the assimilative process has been reciprocal. This, however, has not been the accepted theory. Scholarly opinion has long inclined to the view that the Negro, in the course of his en-slavement and transportation to the New World, lost every vestige of his African culture. It would have been impossible, the scholars have said, for people to preserve their cultural heritage when they were captured and sold into slavery, when their tribal and family units were broken up and they were widely dispersed

[13] Linton, *op. cit.*, p. 512; M. L. Hansen, *The Immigrant in American History*, Ch. 3–6; W. C. Smith, *Americans in the Making*, pp. 393ff.

[14] The extent to which our culture has been affected by the Chinese is well demonstrated by P. F. Cressey in "Chinese Traits in European Civilization: A Study in Diffusion," *American Sociological Review*, Vol. 10, No. 5, October 1945, pp. 595–604.

[15] Cf. H. E. Driver, *Indians of North America*, Ch. 26.

in their new environment. Moreover, the slave owners themselves deliberately encouraged the destruction of the African culture, for they realized that the problem of control would be immeasurably greater if their slaves spoke a strange language, retained their old religion, and were permitted to cherish their ancient customs and traditions. Every effort was made, therefore, to destroy the African culture and put in its place a simple version of the white man's civilization. Frazier has expressed as follows the opinion which has been shared by many another:

> Probably never before in history has a people been so nearly completely stripped of its social heritage as the Negroes who were brought to America. Other conquered races have continued to worship their household gods within the intimate circle of their kinsmen. But American slavery destroyed household gods and dissolved the bonds of sympathy and affection between men of the same blood and household. Old men and women might have brooded over memories of their African homeland, but they could not change the world about them. Through force of circumstances, they had to acquire a new language, adopt new habits of labor, and take over, however imperfectly, the folkways of the American environment. Their children, who knew only the American environment, soon forgot the few memories that had been passed on to them and developed motivations and modes of behavior in harmony with the New World. Their children's children have often recalled with skepticism the fragments of stories concerning Africa which have been preserved in their families. But of the habits and customs as well as the hopes and fears that characterized the life of their forebears in Africa, nothing remains.[16]

Herskovits has challenged this widely held theory, which would make assimilation a distinctly one-sided affair as far as the American Negro is concerned.[17] Many suspect that Herskovits, in his zeal to discover a cultural heritage for the Negro, has overstated the case; but, in the face of the evidence he has presented, no one can longer insist that the Negro's contribution to American civilization has been negligible. It has long been suspected that African influence may be seen in the Negro's music, dancing, and folklore (tales, riddles, proverbs, and jokes), and Herskovits finds considerable support for this view. He maintains, moreover, that Africanisms of many other kinds have survived, such as in methods of planting, codes of polite behavior, conceptions of time, habits of cooperative labor, fondness for lodges and societies, family organization, beliefs and attitudes concerning personal names, customs and superstitions associated with death, and customs and beliefs centering on children. In short, a considerable body of African culture has survived to this day among American Negroes, and no small part of it has found its way into the thought and behavior patterns of the whites.

The reciprocal character of assimilation is more clearly seen in Brazil, where contacts between white Portuguese and their Negro slaves were especially close,

[16] E. F. Frazier, *The Negro Family in the United States*, pp. 21–22.
[17] M. J. Herskovits, *The Myth of the Negro Past*.

and where the opportunities for the preservation of African culture were greater than they were in the United States. Freyre and Pierson have both reported innumerable items in the Brazilian culture whose origin may be traced back to Africa, including many words in the language, articles of food, methods of cooking, manner of speaking, practices connected with cattle-raising and agriculture, folk tales and folk medicines, gestures, names, costumes, superstitions, music, and dancing.[18]

A Slow Process of Uneven Pace

One fact stands out in bold relief in all the studies of assimilation which have been made, and that is the unhurried pace at which the process moves. Even under the most favorable circumstances it takes a long time for two cultures to fuse. An individual who is reared in one society and has acquired its culture could not possibly, in his lifetime, completely divest himself of all that he has learned and succeed in taking on the customs, language, beliefs, ideals, attitudes, and skills of another society. Even his children are not likely to do so, nor even his grandchildren, unless the numerous obstacles to assimilation which are usually present have been removed. No time limit can be given for the assimilative process, because it varies so much from place to place, from group to group, and from one item in the culture to another.

The tangible objects of a culture are usually the ones most readily adopted. W. C. Smith records a great number of these.[19] He tells of the Mexican boy who entered a school in Texas and had the harrowing experience of being laughed at by the others because he wore suspenders, following the custom of his people. "After a while," he said, "I got some money and bought me a belt, so I would not have to wear the suspenders." Rumanian immigrants soon realized that their attire was arousing the curiosity, and sometimes the scorn, of people on the streets, and hastened to adopt the dress of Americans. A Puerto Rican in New York grew self-conscious because people looked at him and laughed, until a friend told him that the trouble was with the hat he wore.

Pihlblad, describing the assimilative process as it operated with the Swedes who settled in central Kansas, says:

> In matters of making a living and in economic organization adjustment to American conditions was most rapid. The style of farming in Sweden of the sixties was entirely unadapted to Kansas conditions. . . . It would be difficult to find any essential differences in economic organization of these Swedish communities from any pioneer American settlement on the Kansas plains. In clothing and shelter the Swedes were quick to take on the patterns which they found. The early homes were log cabins or dugouts common to all pioneer settlements. . . . In matters of clothing also the prevailing modes of dress were not different from

[18] G. Freyre, *The Masters and the Slaves*, pp. xviii, 78ff., 100ff., 155, 170; and D. Pierson, *Negroes in Brazil*, pp. 94–107, 237–274.
[19] *Op. cit.*, pp. 126ff.

those worn by non-Swedish people. The desire to be like an American in matters of clothing is manifested by the experiences of the writer's grandmother. Her last dollar, on arriving in Kansas City, was spent for the purchase of a hoop skirt in the American style. Pictures from the early period indicate that there was little to distinguish the Swedish immigrant from non-Swedish people.

In general, it may be said that in seeking food, shelter, and clothing the Swedish immigrant immediately adopted the patterns he found in America.[20]

It is a different story, however, when it comes to other items. Pihlblad reports that the Swedes clung to the paternalistic family, looked with disfavor upon marriage with non-Swedes, opposed the introduction into their community of movies and pool halls, held to the Lutheran faith, and were slow to replace the Swedish language with English.

Even the adoption of the external, tangible features of the new culture is not without problems. The costume of the Amish has a religious significance and cannot be readily discarded for the prevailing style; and the beard of the Jew is not shaved off without an inner struggle, even when he knows that it is an obstacle to him economically. A Greek woman said about American food:

> I almost starved before I could learn to eat American food. It seemed to me painfully tasteless. . . . As for the potatoes, I had never seen such quantities in my life. We had them for breakfast, for luncheon and for dinner, in some form or other. Just before we sat down to the table the principal said grace, in which were the words, "Bless that of which we are about to partake." To my untrained ear "partake" and "potatoes" sounded exactly alike, and I wrote home that the Americans not only ate potatoes morning, noon, and night, but they even prayed to the Lord to keep them supplied with potatoes, instead of daily bread.[21]

The assimilation process has run its complete course when the newcomers (or their children, or grandchildren) cease to think of themselves as either aliens or hyphenated Americans but simply as Americans, and are so regarded by the host society. Gobetz maintains that the acid test of assimilation is "reciprocal identification."[22] Gordon believes that the assimilation process involves a series of steps or subprocesses which he has outlined in Table 11.1.

It is Gordon's thesis that American society is, and will remain for a long time to come, a congeries of ethnic subcommunities, where a high degree of behavioral assimilation is taking place, but where there is much less structural assimilation.

The various racial and ethnic groups, too, differ widely in the rapidity with which they become assimilated. It is a commonplace observation that British immigrants to the United States are quickly and readily melted and lost, and

[20] C. T. Pihlblad, "The Kansas Swedes," *The Southwestern Social Science Quarterly*, Vol. 13, No. 1, June 1932, pp. 4–5.
[21] Demetra V. Brown, *A Child of the Orient*, pp. 275–276.
[22] G. E. Gobetz, "Adjustment and Assimilation of Slovenian Refugees." Unpublished doctoral dissertation, Ohio State University, 1962.

TABLE 11.1

The Assimilation Variables*

Subprocess or Condition	Type or Stage of Assimilation	Special Term
Change of cultural patterns to those of host society	Cultural or behavioral assimilation	Acculturation
Large-scale entrance into cliques, clubs, and institutions of host society, on primary group level	Structural assimilation	None
Large-scale intermarriage	Marital assimilation	Amalgamation
Development of sense of peoplehood based exclusively on host society	Identificational assimilation	None
Absence of prejudice	Attitude receptional assimilation	None
Absence of discrimination	Behavior receptional assimilation	None
Absence of value and power conflict	Civic assimilation	None

* Milton M. Gordon, *Assimilation in American Life*, p. 71, reprinted by permission of Oxford University Press.

that others become adjusted more slowly. Louis Adamic has related in an interesting fashion the stories of a number of immigrants (Croatian, Finn, Greek, Armenian, Japanese, Mexican, and so on), and one striking contrast is the ease with which some have fitted into their new environment and the towering difficulties which stood in the way of others.[23] Prejudiced persons make much over this fact, and infer that some groups possess an innate quality of "assimilability" while others are "unassimilable," and that the ease with which one assimilates is proof positive of superiority. Let us hope they are wrong, for among the most culturally "indigestible" groups under the sun are substantial Americans who take up their residence in foreign countries, form their tight little colonies, worship in American churches, send their children to American schools, and in devious and ingenious other ways resist "going native."[24]

Occasionally nations have become impatient over the time it takes immigrant groups to become assimilated, and have attempted to speed up the process. This has occurred in the infant nation of Israel. The pioneers who conceived and established that state were mostly from European countries, and it was their

[23] *From Many Lands.*
[24] Ethelyn Davis, "The American Colony in Mexico City." Unpublished doctoral dissertation, University of Missouri, 1942.

desire to transplant Western civilization in the new nation. However, on the very day when the people of Israel declared their independence, they opened their gates to Jewish immigration from the four corners of the earth. Immediately immigrants began to pour into the country, coming from all six continents and from 70 to 80 nations. The entire Jewish communities of Yemen and Bulgaria, and almost all the Jews of Libya, Tripolitania, Yugoslavia, and Iraq came to Israel. The sheer magnitude of the migration created huge problems of employment, housing, education, and health. An even more startling challenge to the new nation came from the diversity of the cultural backgrounds represented. It was feared by many that Israel might become more Oriental than European in its cultural complexion. Teachers, government officials, social workers, and social scientists began to concern themselves with the problem of assimilating (or "absorbing," to use their word) this flood of non-European Jews. Nor did they think they could afford the luxury of allowing time to take its course. Consequently, a variety of measures was taken, and institutions were created, to "Westernize" the Oriental Jews who were arriving in such huge numbers. Schools were utilized to the fullest extent, youth organizations undertook tasks of assimilation, methods of foster-placement of children were employed, and even the army took on the additional function of introducing immigrants to a new culture.[25]

As a matter of fact, it began to be apparent that the process was being accelerated to a dangerous degree, as indicated by the following item:

ISRAEL CUTS PACE OF WESTERNIZING

Flame Under the Melting Pot Lowered, Taking Account of Oriental Cultures

TEL AVIV, ISRAEL, March 1 — The flame under the Israeli melting pot has been turned down. The Government is moving away from the "pressure cooker" method of Westernizing immigrants from Oriental countries.

New villages are no longer made up by mixing immigrants from all countries. The trend now is to populate new settlements not only with immigrants from the same country, but as far as possible from the same village.

Nurses no longer snip amulets from Oriental patients, even if the black threads or herbs that are supposed to protect the wearer from the "evil eye" are a little dirty. The nurses now recognize that the amulets may reinforce the patients psychologically in time of illness.

In many such ways, social workers, nurses, doctors, trade union officials, educators and others whose job it is to help integrate the immigrants are showing more understanding for their traditions and prejudices.

There is no formal announcement of a shift in policy, but a clear indication of the change of attitude was the appointment of a Government anthropologist to brief officials dealing with immigrants on the different cultures. The anthropologist is Mrs. Phyllis Palgi.

"You can't integrate cultures or raise the standard of living of immigrant groups without a knowledge of the basic patterns of their cultures and their subjective ethnical values," Mrs. Palgi says. . . .

[25] Cf. S. N. Eisenstadt, *The Absorption of Immigrants*; C. Frankenstein (Ed.), *Between Past and Future*; R. Patai, *Israel between East and West*.

Mrs. Palgi said that all Government and Legislative activities here had been based on the view that immigrants must be given a Western civilization as quickly as possible.

The ethnocentric attitude, which assumed the mission of molding all people in the Western image, has defeated its purpose, the anthropologist continued.[26]

Problems of assimilation, according to Joseph W. Eaton,[27] have been handled rather wisely by immigrants of a religious sect known as Hutterites, who came to the United States and Canada some 90 years ago, and settled in the provinces of Manitoba and Alberta, and the states of Montana and South Dakota. The Hutterites consider themselves a people chosen by God to live the only true Christian way of life. They originated in Switzerland in 1528, where they were persecuted by both Protestants and Catholics, and were nearly exterminated. In 1770 some of them went to Russia, where they had been promised religious freedom. A century later they fled, because of attempts to enforce Russification upon them, and crossed the Atlantic.

The Hutterites are ardent pacifists, and emphasize simplicity in every aspect of living. Their isolated, self-sufficient rural communities are said to be virtually free of crime, divorce, suicide, insanity, lonesomeness, friendlessness, uncertainty, and insecurity. The aged, the ill, and the infirm are generally well protected and cared for. Even quarreling is very rare. They have a communal system of sharing property and products of labor. They have their own schools, and children are indoctrinated systematically so that they grow up to believe and act in accordance with the group's traditions.

They do, however, have some contacts with their American and Canadian neighbors, whom they refer to as "the outside," and there are pressures for change and assimilation. Some of these pressures come from "the outside." Their communities are visited occasionally by salesmen, government officials, teachers, and doctors. They have business contacts with nearby villages. Modern means of transportation place them within an hour or two of Winnipeg, Sioux Falls, or some other city. The women, who in the past seldom left their colonies, now accompany their husbands on trips to town.

There are pressures for change also from the "inside." The younger Hutterites frequently learn to want some of the things they see their neighbors possessing and enjoying. They desire more individual freedom and initiative, and they come to regard as necessities certain items which their elders insist are luxuries.

This situation could very well lead to discord, dissatisfaction, family conflict, cleavage between older and younger generations, and community disorganization. The Hutterites, however, according to Eaton, have developed techniques for bringing about gradual social change, and for holding in check the speed of the assimilative process.

"By bending with the wind," says Eaton, "Hutterites have kept themselves from breaking." Believing as they do that man is born to sin, they do not expect

[26] *The New York Times*, March 2, 1955.
[27] "Controlled Acculturation: A Survival Technique of the Hutterites," *American Sociological Review*, Vol. 17, No. 3, June 1952, pp. 331–340.

perfect and complete compliance with all the rules and traditions of their sect. They do not expel or punish a person for deviating *slightly* from the narrow path of custom. Nor do they possess a body of written rules covering systematically and comprehensively the whole of life. They are governed, rather, by their ancient traditions, which are transmitted to each succeeding generation through example and oral instruction.

They do enact formal rules from time to time. When some innovation or deviation becomes widespread in one or more of their communities, the leaders are likely to decide that a formal and official statement is required. A new rule, accordingly, will be proposed at an intercolony meeting of elected lay preachers. If such a formal rule is adopted by this body, it is read to the governing assemblies of male members in every colony. Adoption or rejection is by majority vote of all baptized males. New rules are not lightly and carelessly proposed. The leaders keep their ears to the ground, and never adopt a new rule unless they are convinced that public opinion is solidly behind them. Nor do they repeal a rule that has grown obsolete; they simply refrain from enforcing it. In this manner the Hutterites accept cultural innovations before the demand for them becomes so great as to threaten the group's harmony and cohesiveness.

A few examples will illustrate how this occurs. The Hutterites insist upon simple and unostentatious dress for men and women. However, through their contacts with those on "the outside," they become aware of styles and fashions, and some of them succumb to the pressure. Boys and young men began buying grey hats and pith helmets until a rule was adopted stipulating black hats only. Tradition demanded that clothes be fastened with hooks and eyes; but a rule was made that buttons "could be retained," indicating that their use had become common. Sweaters began to be worn, until a rule was forthcoming requiring that they be "summarily gotten rid of." Members began wearing shoes which they bought in town, in preference to the home-made ones, and finally the purchase of all types of shoes was authorized, but only in certain approved styles. In similar manner they came to adopt fur linings for winter clothes, mattresses, motor vehicles, refrigerators, and a host of other once-forbidden items. Thus the process of assimilation moves, but is well controlled.

Both a Conscious and an Unconscious Process

The immigrant who adopts American dress, of course, knows precisely what he is doing and why he is doing it. When he studies the new language, builds a home like his neighbor's, buys a new implement and learns to use it, he is consciously participating in a culture which he hopes to make his own. Missionaries, teachers, and foreign representatives of business concerns are deliberately seeking to produce changes in a people's culture and to promote assimilation, whether or not they describe their work in sociological terms. Governments have frequently initiated programs and policies for the stated purpose of promoting homogeneity among their citizens. Many sociologists, however, have been impressed by the relative paucity of these conscious and deliberate changes.

Panunzio goes so far as to define assimilation as the process by which "individuals or groups of varying cultures *more or less unconsciously* exchange and fuse culture traits or complexes,"[28] and Park states that "assimilation in any case takes place gradually and by degrees so slight that they are not open to observation or measurement."[29] Changes in one's pronunciation, gestures and mannerisms, attitudes, values, sentiments, loyalties, and tastes do indeed come about by a slow and imperceptible process of which the individual himself is hardly aware. Jonassen comments upon the fact that Norwegians become Americanized without their realizing it; and it comes as a shock to them when, returning to the Old Country, they discover that they have lost the mastery of the language (which they had no desire to do) and have grown so far away from the old culture that they no longer feel happy in its presence.[30]

The Rate of Assimilation

Differences in the rate of assimilation, as reflected by various racial and ethnic groups, have received a great deal of attention from sociologists. Certainly there is no single explanation, but rather a number of interacting factors must be taken into consideration in order to understand the phenomenon.

Attitudes of the Dominant or Host Group

The attitudes of the dominant group in a society toward the newcomers in its midst are subject to wide variation, but whatever they be, they profoundly affect the process of assimilation. Among many primitive and ancient peoples there was a *general* hostility toward strangers, and their presence was not tolerated. This was true of many medieval communities of Europe; and Japan was a thorough-going isolationist nation until 1853, when Commodore Perry opened her up, against her will. An ancient Japanese proverb had it, "When you see a stranger, count him a robber." In most cases, however, the attitude of hostility is directed toward certain *specific* racial or ethnic groups, while toward others there may be shown sentiments of hospitality, or at least of tolerance.

In the United States certain ethnic groups have consistently been accepted by the host society, while others have had every possible obstacle to social participation and assimilation thrown in their way. The following story of a second-generation American of mixed English and Irish ancestry indicates a process of adjustment which has been relatively painless:

> I seldom think of myself as other than American. Neither I nor any other member of my family, so far as I know, has ever had an un-American thought. If, in my youth, I ever gave the seemingly spontaneous Americanization of my

[28] C. Panunzio, *Major Social Institutions*, p. 525.
[29] R. E. Park, "Assimilation, Social," in *Encyclopedia of the Social Sciences*, Vol. 2, pp. 281–283.
[30] C. T. Jonassen, *Norwegians in Bay Ridge: A Sociological Study of an Ethnic Group*.

parents a thought, it probably seemed natural to me that, speaking the same language, my people adjusted themselves naturally and painlessly. It was, therefore, quite a shock to me to hear the statement that the English are the hardest people to Americanize. . . .

My father ran away from home at an early age. He enlisted as a seaman and served many years in the English navy. He participated in petty warfare in India and Africa, all the while accumulating a disgust for the attitude of England for her colonies. When his vessel sailed from an especially desirable port, he was not on board. In cold print the word "deserter" seems very dishonorable; certainly it does not fit the fine character of my father as I knew him, silent, unemotional, and the most patriotic American I ever knew.

Mother came to this country from Ireland when she was eighteen. Four years later she and father were married. By dint of hard work and thrift, they saved enough to buy a farm in Ohio, and here they raised a large and patriotic family. . . . Although they spent their early lives in poverty, my parents never complained of their lot. They have often expressed themselves as grateful to have had the opportunity of establishing their home and raising their family in America.

Among our early neighbors were many Scandinavians and Germans. The children spoke the language of their parents. We, in contrast, felt ourselves to be outstanding Americans because we spoke the language of the United States. Our father was a citizen; theirs were not. Our parents could read and write; theirs could not. . . . With the exception of a pleasing, almost indiscernible brogue, my mother speaks excellent English. My father's enunciation is free from any noticeably broad *a*; it is entirely devoid of any cockney expressions common to so many Londoners — his *h*'s are in the correct place. He talks good "United States" without the slang. . . .

My husband, now dead, came of a family so long Americanized that there is a difference of opinion as to when the break was made. I could not see that his ideas toward the United States differed essentially from my own. His son by a previous marriage early developed a love of music, and has become an exceptional musician. . . . My daughter also, to the fond eyes of her mother, seems worth working for and with. Life is full, busy, and very much worth while.[31]

The Chinese, on the other hand, are a people whose assimilation has been retarded by the prejudices and discriminations to which they have been subjected. The following story is evidence of that fact:

I was born in Portland forty-nine years ago. My father was merchant in Portland. I went to Chinese school little time in Portland, not very long. I go to American school also. My mother tell me when I eight year old that I have to go to China. I go to China and stay there until eighteen year old. When I first come back I go to my father's business. I stay with him about ten year. After this I go to San Francisco. . . . Then I go to Denver. . . . I go back to Portland. . . . I come to Seattle and open up same kind of business. . . .

My father born in China, Canton Province. All my brothers and sisters born in this country. . . . I do business with many; black, brown, white, any color just the same. . . .

[31] H. G. Duncan, *Immigration and Assimilation.* Reprinted by special permission of D. C. Heath and Company, Boston, Mass. Pp. 709–713.

A grandfather at Santa Clara Pueblo helps his grandson put on his boots

Lots of people insult me. Once I remember I go barber shop. I sit one hour no ask me what I want. Pretty soon barber say, "What you want?" I tell him I want hair cut, how much? He say $3. That make me mad, but I make him cut my hair just same. I say, "All right, I have my hair cut." He give me good hair cut. When he through I pay him $3.50. He very surprised. He tell me come again. I never go to white bastard again.

Once I go to restaurant; they refused to serve me. I no want to cause trouble; so I just walk out. Whole lot of things like this happen, but I forget. Now when I want to eat I go to chop house. No trouble there. . . .

When I in Portland I want to live in residential district, but they make lots of trouble if you try to live outside Chinatown. One friend he buy $6000 house in select city district. White people make hell lot trouble for him. They take it to court. He fight it. Just the same they kick him out. He can own house but no live there. Those people very uncivilized. Have no regard for humanity. So when my friend have so much trouble I decided to stay in Chinatown. Nobody care there. . . .

Me being citizen, I vote in all election. Sure I vote every time I get chance. When I young fellow I felt that I American; I no Chinaman. Now I get more sense. I know I never be American, always Chinaman. I no care now any more. . . .

Some day I think maybe I go back to China. Maybe I stay, maybe not. Not sure about going back because I own lots of property here, have lot of building to look after. Maybe I cannot find anybody to buy or take care of it for me. City grows. Property be more valuable all the time. Some day I think worth lots of money.

I hope this survey do lot of good for Chinese people. Make American people realize Chinese people are human. I think very few American people really know anything about Chinese. Maybe this survey help them to know more. I hope so.[32]

Some groups, like the Irish, have seen a great change in attitude manifested toward them. Hansen says that when the Irish first began to pour into New England, they were regarded by the residents as stupid, dirty, diseased, superstitious, and untrustworthy.[33] Farmers would give them jobs only when forced by a labor shortage to do so, and then they complained; and the factories would take them on if no other employees were available, but would give them only the lowest positions. The Yankee's attitude toward the Irish has undergone something of a metamorphosis, and while Irish ancestry may not be an asset to a social climber, it certainly does not carry the stigma that it once did, nor does it prevent one's elevation to the presidency of the United States.[34]

It must be pointed out, however, that a favorable attitude on the part of the dominant group toward a minority is no assurance of rapid assimilation. Useem has shown that the Norwegians in North Dakota have retained much of their Old World culture even though they have never been persecuted by their neighbors, or been assigned to an inferior status socially or economically, or been forced to study and imitate the customs of their neighbors in order to cater to or compete with them.[35]

Attitudes of the Minority Group

The case of these Norwegians suggests that the rate of assimilation is affected by the attitudes of the minority as well as by those of the dominant group in the society. There are, of course, many instances of subordinate groups whose overwhelming wish is to become completely assimilated, even amalgamated. The American Negro wages a perpetual battle against segregation, discrimination,

[32] H. G. Duncan, *Immigration and Assimilation*. Reprinted by special permission of D. C. Heath and Company, Boston, Mass. Pp. 811–814.

[33] Hansen, *op. cit.*, pp. 156ff.

[34] M. L. Barron, "Intermediacy: Conceptualization of Irish Status in America," *Social Forces*, Vol. 27, No. 3, March 1949, pp. 256–263.

[35] John and Ruth Hill Useem, "Minority-Group Pattern in Prairie Society," *American Journal of Sociology*, Vol. 50, No. 5, March 1945, pp. 377–385.

and "second-class citizenship." What he wants is "integration" or "full participation" in American life. So with the Japanese-Americans. But there are
groups which fear assimilation and resist it to the utmost, while others want it
only to a certain degree.

The case is reported from one of the islands of Micronesia, where the chief of
the Kanaka, confronted with all the marvels of white civilization, would have
none of them. When told of the benefits to be derived from an acceptance of
Western culture, he replied:

> Benefits! Too many benefits! Before the foreigners came we lived in peace.
> The forest fed us — simply but sufficiently. We did not work. Is work a virtue
> when there is nothing to be gained by it? Neighbors were friendly, children were
> obedient. Life was a trade wind without gusts or squalls. But now comes struggle
> — struggle to make money. Money for what? We do not need clothing — the
> sunshine clothes us. We do not need an iron roof to carry rain water into a
> cement tank. The water that streams down the trunk of a tree can be turned into
> a jar. We do not need farming tools of iron and steel. We can make our own
> from the shell of the giant clam. We do not need alarm clocks and phonographs
> and electric lights. They spoil the sounds of the forests and the light of the moon.
> We do not need the telephone — we can talk to those on faraway plantations
> through the shell trumpet. We do not need schools. The father can teach his
> children all that is necessary for our manner of life. We do not need hospitals.
> This is a small island — if some did not die there would soon be too many people,
> too little food. But our young men are upset by the idea that they must do some-
> thing, even if it is something useless. On the athletic field near the school a track
> has been made where boys may run around in a circle. That is what civilization
> is — running around in a circle.[36]

The mere desire on the part of an ethnic group to retain its traditional culture
is not, of course, sufficient to insure it against the forces of assimilation. The
Russian Molokans, who migrated to Los Angeles,[37] were determined to perpetuate their way of life but have found the task too great for them. The Amish
and Mennonites, on the other hand, have met with considerable success in their
determination to keep their identity.

An interesting case of resistance to assimilation comes from Brazil.[38] At the
close of our Civil War several thousand Southerners, convinced that they could
not live in a country dominated by Negroes and Yankees, emigrated to South
America. They went with every intention of perpetuating the culture that they
valued. They chose Brazil, in fact, because it was ruled by a rural aristocracy,
still had the institution of slavery, and possessed the climate and soil suitable to
the cultivation of cotton, tobacco, sugar cane, and watermelons. They had visions
of carving out large plantations, building mansions of Southern style, maintaining retinues of slaves, and carrying on as though the war had never been fought.

[36] W. Price, *Japan's Islands of Mystery*, pp. 171–172.
[37] Pauline Young, *Pilgrims of Russian Town*.
[38] J. A. Rios, "Assimilation of Emigrants from the Old South in Brazil," *Social Forces*,
Vol. 26, No. 2, December 1947, pp. 145–152.

They made a desperate effort to realize their dream, but the obstacles were greater than they had supposed. The process of assimilation began to operate immediately upon their arrival. Most of them had to compromise on their homes, and settle for dwellings more Brazilian than Southern. Indian and Negro women, whom they engaged as domestics, taught them about the local foods and how to prepare them, so that one of them, writing to the editor of the New Orleans *Times* in December, 1867, could say, "We have already learned to love it." Other features of the Brazilian culture were more distasteful to them. The language was an obstacle; the labor force, unaccustomed to continuous work, was exasperating; slavery in Brazil was not the same institution that they had known in the South; roads were non-existent; they had difficulty in establishing schools and churches; and the operations of the government were disappointing and disheartening. Most difficult of all, however, was the racial situation. Color was not the dominant criterion of status, and the relations between the races were incredibly shocking to them.

Some of them could not take it, and returned to the United States. Others put aside their pride, refused to regard manual labor as degrading, and sought to make the necessary adjustments. Some, failing to make a go of their farms, migrated to the cities, married Brazilians, and their descendants today are doubtless completely assimilated. As far as is known, Vila Americana, in São Paulo, is the only one of their communities remaining. One may see there an occasional American flag, plantation houses of Southern style, and hear English spoken with a Portuguese accent and Portuguese with an English accent; but the crucial fact is that the grandchildren of the pioneers feel that they are Brazilians, and are so regarded.

Cultural Kinship

The rate of assimilation is greatly affected by the similarity or dissimilarity of the two cultures in contact. Schermerhorn comments upon the fact that the Czechs in the United States have become assimilated much more rapidly than their fellow nationals, the Slovaks, and inquires into the reasons.[39] He finds that a differentiation between these two peoples can be traced to their historical backgrounds in the Old World. Their experiences were such that the Czechs became more literate than the Slovaks, they enjoyed a period of political tutelage which fostered democratic tendencies, they acquired a higher standard of living, they became skilled as workmen and professionals, and they developed a familiarity with the highly respected German culture. All these characteristics stood them in good stead when they migrated to the United States, and gave them a distinct advantage over the Slovaks, who possessed them all in less degree.

Among the aspects of culture which facilitate assimilation none is the equal of language. It has been pointed out repeatedly that the rapidity with which the Irish were assimilated into American society can be largely explained by the

[39] *Op. cit.*, pp. 316ff.

fact that they already had upon arrival a command of English. So important is language, both as the carrier of culture and as the tool for acquiring a culture, that many sociologists regard statistics on the mother tongue as the best index of a group's assimilation.

Religion, too, may serve either to retard or to accelerate the assimilation of a people. Huguenots who came to the United States quickly appreciated the fact that their Protestant faith made them more acceptable as citizens; and the widely publicized fact that the Armenians are a Christian people has mitigated the difficulties of their adjustment. On the other hand, those who have brought with them their Buddhist or Moslem faith have simply encountered one more obstacle to their assimilation.

It is so with all the other items and values of the culture. American society places great emphasis upon thrift, foresight, and diligence, and accords a readier welcome to those whose social heritage includes these same virtues than it does to those, say, the Mexicans, who relegate them to a minor position. In the American hierarchy of values a high place is accorded to literacy, cleanliness, speed, wealth, competition, indulgence of wife and children, and so on. In other societies entirely different scales of values prevail. The rapidity and the ease with which assimilation occurs depend largely upon the similarity in the rank order of values held by the groups in contact.

Race

The rate of assimilation may be seriously affected by the racial features of the peoples in a contact situation. Societies differ, of course, in the social significance they attach to such characteristics as skin color, hair form, eyes, lips, and width of nose. Among some, no significance whatsoever is attached to these racial traits. The Tungus and Cossacks pay no attention to them at all. In Brazil some weight is attached to them, but not a great deal. In many societies, however, such as those of South Africa and the United States, these biological features are regarded as of prime importance. They profoundly affect the status and role of the individual and largely determine the neighborhood he will live in, the church he will worship in, the friends he will have, the organizations he will belong to, even his health and longevity. Needless to say, racial features will play a very important role in the assimilative process in societies of this latter type, determining how long the process will take and even whether or not it will occur at all.

Other Factors

Many other factors affect the rate of assimilation, either favorably or adversely, and have received the attention of sociologists. Among these are: (1) the relative numbers of the groups involved in the contact situation; (2) the rate of entrance of the minority group; (3) the manner of settlement, whether rural or urban, and the extent of its isolation; (4) the age and sex composition of the groups; (5) the influence of certain personalities, either in opposing or encouraging assimilation. Not to be overlooked, too, are the crises which arise, sometimes stimulating the assimilative process and sometimes reversing the trend altogether. One of the first great motion pictures was entitled "The Birth of a Nation," and had as its theme the Civil War. The title was not inappropriate, for that crisis did much to weld together the various ethnic groups in America. Hansen has made much of this fact, assessing its role as follows:

> The United States in 1860 was made up not merely of two nations — the North and the South — as is sometimes said, but of many. The North comprised a dozen different peoples who without qualifying their adopted political allegiance lived in the cultural environment of some European nation. What might have been the outcome if the course of development had been uninterrupted no one knows, for the Civil War altered the face of events for both the alien and the native. . . . The poor immigrant of 1857 was the rich farmer of 1865; and his ardent interest in the culture of the country he had left was cooled by the knowledge that the culture of his adopted country now lay within reach. . . .
>
> His son entered the army. Almost five hundred thousand foreign-born volunteers helped to fight the battles of the Union. No longer could the newcomers be taunted about enjoying the benefits of a government which they had no hand in creating, for now they were helping to save it. The Civil War begot a body of tradition in each foreign stock. . . . The past in Europe was overshadowed by the future in America. Four years of anxiety, binding the immigrant family to the fortunes of the struggling nation, created a new attitude toward the society which their sons were fighting to preserve. . . .
>
> The earlier immigrants had desired to perpetuate a social minority in the American environment; the newer comers, whatever their individual inclinations, were obliged to accept the idea that ultimately their distinctive features would disappear. All they could hope for was to add a bit of their own culture to the amalgam formed by the mingling of many peoples.[40]

It is thus a well-established fact that when groups of people who differ culturally come into contact there tends to be some interchange of ideas, customs, beliefs, and material objects. In short, the *process* of assimilation seems to operate invariably when peoples live side by side. Even when one group is most reluctant to adopt the ways of its neighbors, and is incredibly adept at erecting barriers against such importations, the forces of assimilation make themselves felt. If assimilation be thought of as a process of cultural give and take, there is good reason for regarding it as an inevitable consequence of the meeting of peoples.

If, however, we think of assimilation as a *condition* — as the end result of the process — wherein groups once dissimilar in their beliefs, customs, and attitudes have become similar, then we may well doubt that it is an inevitable consequence of contact. We may insist that eventually the Jews and Indians in the United States will lose their identity and become completely assimilated, but it

---

[40] Hansen, *op. cit.*, pp. 140–142.

will be a statement of faith, not of scientific fact. Certainly there are instances where unlike groups have lived together for very long periods without such fusion.

Sociologists have learned a great deal about the process of assimilation, so that many blunders of the past are no longer excusable. The folly of coercion seems well established. A certain Polish priest is credited with the wise remark that "the Germans tried to make Germans of us, and we remained Poles; the Americans do not care; we will soon be Americans." Sociologists have amply demonstrated that assimilation is a long, slow, often painful process.

Much remains to be learned, however, about the process of assimilation. What are the agencies responsible for the transfer of culture from one group to the other? How effective are the various agencies — the public schools, for example? Why are certain items of the strange culture chosen for adoption more readily than others? What elements of the old culture are clung to most tenaciously, and why? What about the time needed for the acceptance and integration of new traits? What happens to old ideas when new ones are introduced? These and a host of other questions remain to be answered before we can say that we fully understand the assimilative process.

12

Amalgamation

The whole history of man has been characterized by the crossing and re-crossing of races.

E. V. STONEQUIST

The Marginal Man

Beneath a captivating picture of husky, smiling children in the August 23, 1948, issue of *Life* magazine appeared the following cheerless story:

The seven half-Negro children in the picture above were conceived in war and orphaned by peace. They are illegitimate children of colored American troops and white English mothers — seven of 552 born of such unions during the war. Their fathers have returned to the U.S. Their mothers have given them up, in most cases reluctantly, because of ostracism by village neighbors. . . . They are wards of the Somerset County Council, and indirectly of the British Home Office, which has tried without success to establish parental responsibility. Since this has failed, British authorities are now considering offers of adoption received from U.S. Negro families.

Although it is more dramatic, the dilemma of the half-Negro children is only a small part of a worldwide problem of illegitimacy. In Britain alone, 22,000 children were born out of wedlock to white U.S. soldiers. There have been no surveys in France, Italy and many other countries, but it is estimated that U.S. forces have been responsible for 30,000 to 50,000 illegitimate births in Germany; for 1,000 to 4,000 in Japan; and for 2,000 to 4,000 in the Philippines.

Uncle Sam has shown virtually no interest in the problem. Marriage has been made difficult for troops everywhere. In Japan, with permission of the Army, a U.S. soldier may marry an enemy national, but one discouraged GI wrote home, "only under unusual circumstances, and pregnancy is not considered unusual." . . . Nor will the Army consider romantic damage claims, although it has paid out $9 million for broken palm trees, soil damage, and even miscarriages among English sheep unnerved by American artillery fire.

Efforts made in behalf of young half-Americans have come entirely from private and voluntary agencies . . . but until some official U.S. agency recognizes the validity of the problem, Japanese mothers will continue to seek a solution in abortion or infanticide, and more and more little European-Americans will become public wards.[1]

The surprising thing is that the editors of *Life* should have regarded such a story as newsworthy, for it deals with one of the commonest phenomena in all history. Biological mixing, legal or otherwise, seems invariably to accompany the meeting of racial and ethnic groups. Soldiers are no more guilty than travellers, explorers, settlers, traders, and colonial administrators. Not even missionaries are exceptions. One of the first to carry Christianity to the heathen of South Africa was the heroic Dutchman, Dr. Jacobus Theodorus Vanderkemp, who married a native woman in order to identify himself more completely with the people to whom he devoted his life. His story is doubtless not unique. Gertrude Millin's novel, *God's Stepchildren,* has as its theme the struggle of the children of such a union to achieve the status of white people. In earlier chapters we have seen that when races meet, conflict usually appears, and the process of assimilation usually sets in, though by combing the literature carefully we are able to find possible rare exceptions. Not so with amalgamation. According to Reuter, "there seems to be no historical exception to the rule that when peoples

[1] Courtesy of *Life,* copyright 1948, Time Inc.

come into contact and occupy the same area there is a mixture of blood."[2] Wirth and Goldhamer say, "It is doubtful whether two races have ever lived within the confines of a single society without the process of race mixture setting in."[3] In Fairchild's judgment, amalgamation "is a process that takes place almost automatically when two or more racial groups are brought into juxtaposition,"[4] and Stern says, "Whenever history brought together two or more races in the same territory, unions of persons of different races have occurred."[5]

Apparently it has always been so. Coon finds ample evidence for race mixture in prehistoric times, even describing the "Neanderthaloid hybrids of Palestine"; and when *Homo sapiens* appeared on the European scene, there was no reversal of the process.[6] In fact, the meeting and mixing of racial types is a recurring theme in his book, evidence for which is found throughout the Paleolithic, Mesolithic, Neolithic, Bronze, and Iron Ages. Hooton doubts that Neanderthal man was completely annihilated by the *Homo sapiens* invaders of Europe, for he says, "Whenever men meet they mingle their blood." He suspects, therefore, that the large brow ridges and the retreating foreheads which one sometimes encounters in modern individuals, neither prove the survival of Neanderthal man nor are they the results of chance variation, but testify instead to some miscegenation in the distant past.[7] It is this ancient human proclivity to interbreed which makes the racial classification of modern man so difficult and which casts doubt upon the existence of "pure" racial types.

The expansion of Europe gave a great boost to the process of amalgamation. Wherever the Europeans went they left behind a trail of half-castes and mixed-bloods. In his *History of Carolina*, published in London in 1709, John Lawson, who himself travelled among the Indians and knew whereof he wrote, had this to say:

> The English trader is seldom without an Indian female for his bedfellow, alleging these reasons as sufficient to allow of such familiarity. First, they being remote from any white people, that it preserves their friendship with the heathens, they esteeming a white man's child much above one of their own getting. . . . And lastly, this correspondence makes them learn the Indian tongue much the sooner.

The Portuguese, who were in the vanguard of European expansion, always mixed freely with the people they came in contact with. They first reached India in 1498 and established themselves in Goa, on the Malabar coast, whence they proceeded to govern their colonial empire and where they sired a hybrid population, the Goanese. Within 20 years they were on the Chinese coast. These

---

[2] E. B. Reuter (Ed.), *Race and Culture Contacts*, p. 7; "Amalgamation," *Encyclopedia of the Social Sciences*, Vol. 2, pp. 16–17.

[3] L. Wirth and H. Goldhamer, "The Hybrid and the Problem of Miscegenation," in O. Klineberg (Ed.), *Characteristics of the American Negro*, p. 263.

[4] H. P. Fairchild, *Race and Nationality*, p. 88.

[5] C. Stern, *Principles of Human Genetics*, p. 563.

[6] C. S. Coon, *The Races of Europe*.

[7] E. A. Hooton, *Up from the Ape*, 1st ed., p. 336.

pioneers were truculent fellows, for the most part, but they finally rented a strip of seacoast at Macao, near Canton, and promptly begat a mixed people known as the Macanese. The process of amalgamation is well nigh complete in the case of the Goanese and the Macanese, and even the assimilation process has virtually run its course. They are reported to be much closer to the native peoples among whom they live than are other Eurasians, though they are devout Christians; and today they are found up and down the coast of Asia, and as far south as Mombasa, in Africa, where they function as intermediaries between the Oriental and Occidental worlds.[8] And, of course, centuries before the Portuguese reached India, the light-skinned Aryans invaded the country, made war upon the dark Dravidians whom they found there, and proceeded to amalgamate with them. The story is much the same wherever we look and whoever be the people whose fortunes we trace. This is not to say that amalgamation occurs with equal facility in all biracial situations. There are ethnic groups which have strong feelings of endogamy, while others are indifferent to, or even favorably disposed to, mating with strangers. Amalgamation, accordingly, displays variations both in the extent to which it is carried and the rate at which it takes place. To some degree, however, it apparently occurs whenever racial and ethnic groups are brought together. Those sociologists, anthropologists, and geneticists who have made generalizations about the universality of race mixing seem to be on solid ground.

Amalgamation and the Mores

Miscegenation occurs whether or not the mores of the society approve the practice. The social attitudes, as a matter of fact, cover the widest possible range, from encouragement at one extreme, through tolerance and indifference, to the opposite extreme of grim determination to prevent it. The Jews from about 400 B.C. were strict in their prohibitions against marriage with non-Jews, and yet, says Wirth, "There is a great deal of evidence to support the contention that the Jews, even in the dark ghetto days, frequently intermarried with non-Jews."[9] As a consequence of this interbreeding on a world-wide scale the Jewish physical type has become so variable that it is manifestly absurd to refer to the Jews as a race at all.[10] The British, when they first moved into India, looked with approval upon intermarriage with the native peoples, and an official communication dated April 8, 1687, stated:

The marriage of our soldiers to the native women of Fort St. George formerly recommended by you, is a matter of such consequence to posterity, that we shall be content to encourage it with some expense, and have been thinking for the future to appoint a pagoda to be paid to the mother of any child that shall here-

[8] R. E. Park, *Race and Culture*, pp. 122–123.
[9] L. Wirth, *The Ghetto*, p. 67.
[10] Coon, *op. cit.*, pp. 432-444, gives an account of the biological background of the Jewish people.

after be born of any such future marriage, on the day the child is christened, if you think this small encouragement will increase the number of such marriages.[11]

The British policy met with some success, with the result that there are today in India more than 150,000 Anglo-Indians. In the early days of the conquest these mixed-bloods enjoyed a certain prestige. They were useful to the English as intermediaries, their services were appreciated, and sometimes they even married into the British nobility. But as the conquerors became firmly established, and as improved means of transportation tied them closer to home, they began to disapprove of miscegenation. The status of the Anglo-Indians thereupon rapidly deteriorated, until they became a pathetic minority, ostracized alike by English and Indians. They tried desperately to identify themselves with the Europeans, wore British clothes exclusively, and would speak of England as "home" though they had never been there; but all to no avail. They despised their Indian blood, and were despised, in turn, by the Indians. As the spirit of nationalism developed in India, their position grew more and more precarious, for the native leaders suspected that their sympathies lay with the British. Their plight was portrayed in these words:

> The British disown them as half-breeds and treat them with contempt. They are not admitted to membership in European clubs or other social organizations, save in rare cases. From the Hindu point of view there is no place in the system of caste for persons of mixed blood. . . . Thus the Anglo-Indians are refused admittance into either European or Hindu society, and are caught between the currents of antagonistic cultures. They are a people "without a country."[12]

The anomolous position of the Anglo-Indian has been well portrayed by John Masters in his novel, *Bhowani Junction*. In this story, Victoria Jones, part Scottish and part Indian, fails to identify herself completely with either of the heritages of which she is a product. This uncertainty of status became acute for the Anglo-Indians as India moved toward independence. Many fled to England. Many, whose racial characteristics were sufficiently Caucasoid to make them acceptable there, migrated to Australia. Most of them, however, remained in India, and the indications are that they decided that their best future lay in identifying themselves with India. Mr. Frank Anthony, President of the Anglo-Indian Association, issued the following statement on October 7, 1946: "Our position in India has been made difficult merely because of our past services to the British administration. . . . Our bitterness is steadily increasing. . . . The Anglo-Indian community has now decided that their future lies with the Indian people."[13] Their ultimate outcome may well be their absorption by the native stock.

[11] Quoted in Park, *op. cit.*, p. 130.
[12] P. F. Cressey, "The Anglo-Indians: A Disorganized Marginal Group," *Social Forces*, Vol. 14, No. 2, December 1935, p. 264. An excellent portrayal of the Anglo-Indian is to be found in E. V. Stonequist, *The Marginal Man*, pp. 12–18.
[13] Information Cables, Government of India Information Services, Washington, D.C., October 8, 1946.

The British, as they have migrated over the earth, have adhered to a rigid color line, holding themselves aloof from the darker peoples. While it has not been their policy to make use of legislation to prohibit intermarriage, a severe public opinion has usually served as an effective check. Nor do they relax their caste barriers in the case of the mixed-bloods, as some nations are in the habit of doing. There are exceptions, to be sure. In the British West Indies the mulattoes occupy a somewhat favored position. Sir Conrad Reeves was a poor mulatto boy who rose to be one of the most famous Chief Justices of Barbados; and in Trinidad a colored man recently became a dominant figure on the island — a prominent lawyer, King's Counsel, and a Knight of the British Empire. Even so, the British have frowned upon miscegenation, and have discriminated against the offspring of mixed unions. Nevertheless amalgamation, chiefly on an extramarital basis, has proceeded apace, as witness the large mixed-blood populations in all those areas where the British have moved — Africa, India, Jamaica, Trinidad, Barbados, and elsewhere.[14]

Attitudes of other peoples toward miscegenation have differed from those of the British. The Portuguese, as we have seen, have mixed freely wherever they went; but even they were not without some prejudices in the matter. Those who settled in Brazil did not hesitate to take Indian women as wives and concubines, and both church and state placed the stamp of their approval upon mixed marriages. It was not the same with the Negroes. Marriages with Negroes were frowned upon at first, and most of the sexual unions were extra-legal — a distinction, of course, which has no bearing upon the amalgamation process. But whereas marriages of Portuguese men to Indian women were held to be "convenient and noble," one would be condemned as "staining one's self" to marry a Negro or a Jew.[15] The Spaniards, when they first came to America, forbade marriage with the Indians, but the prohibition was removed in 1514 in the hope that intermarriage would win the friendship of the Indians and at the same time serve as an inducement to permanent settlement on the part of the immigrants. Marriages continued to be rare, however, though concubinage was common. Also, the Spaniards mixed with the Negroes they imported, though marriage was neither favored nor widespread.

The French, too, have always taken a liberal attitude toward miscegenation. As Toynbee says, "In the seventeenth and eighteenth centuries of our era, in North America, when the English settlers were expelling and exterminating the Red Indians, the French settlers were intermarrying with them and assimilating them."[16] In 1685 the French did promulgate their famous *Code noir* which stipulated a fine of 2000 pounds of sugar as punishment for concubinage between a white man and a Negro which resulted in issue; but, if the man married the woman, the fine was remitted, the woman set free, and the children declared legitimate. In 1724 Louis XV decreed that no marriages between whites and

---

14 E. Williams, *The Negro in the Caribbean*, passim; Stonequist, *op. cit.*, passim.
15 D. Pierson, *Negroes in Brazil*, pp. 115ff; G. Freyre, *The Masters and the Slaves*, pp. 84ff., 407ff.
16 A. J. Toynbee, *The Study of History*, Vol. 1, p. 225.

blacks in Louisiana should take place, but the prohibition did not apply to Indians. Ideally, the policy of the French has been one of assimilation and amalgamation, but the realities have fallen far short of the ideal.[17]

Here in the United States we have the supreme instance of a society's attempt to halt the process of amalgamation by legislative means. The fact that miscegenation occurred from the time of the earliest intergroup contacts is indicated by the kinds of problems reported in the historical records. When Negro women who were slaves had children by white men who were either indentured servants or free, could the children be held in slavery? Or when free white women bore children by Negro men, what would be the status of the children? These and a multitude of other problems arising from miscegenation had to be taken into the courts, and legislatures set to work to deal with them. Virginia soon passed laws providing special penalties for illicit intercourse between blacks and whites, and calling for the banishment of any white person who married a Negro, mulatto, or Indian. Massachusetts followed with a law punishing fornication on the part of Negroes and whites, and prohibiting marriage between them; and other colonies were not slow in passing similar legislation. Following the Revolutionary War one state after another either placed upon the statute books or wrote into its constitution prohibitions against miscegenation, although they were disregarded in some states and subsequently repealed in others.

At the present time 19 states seek by legislative enactment to forbid miscegenation.[18] The laws vary considerably, and great confusion has arisen in the interpretations which the courts have placed upon them. In the first place, they differ as to the racial groups toward which the prohibitions are directed. All 19 forbid intermarriage of whites and Negroes; but, in addition, whites are forbidden in 13 states to marry members of the Mongolian race; and in six, Indians and their descendants. North Carolina and Louisiana forbid Indians and Negroes to marry, and Oklahoma has a prohibition against the intermarriage of Negroes, Indians, and Mongolians. Other states specify such groups as "Malayan and Korean races," *mestizos*, Kanakas, and half-breeds. The penalties provided by these laws vary. Fines range up to $2000, and terms of imprisonment vary from a few months to ten years. In the second place, the definitions of these so-called "races" differ widely in the statutes, and some of them are scientifically indefensible. Georgia seeks to prevent the marriage of a white and a person with "any ascertainable trace" of "African, West Indian, Asiatic Indian, or Mongolian blood." Quite understandably, the exact provisions of the law are not enforced. Some state their prohibitions in the most general terms (African descent, Negro blood, etc.) while others resort to precise fractions (one-fourth, one-eighth, one-sixteenth). Finally, the difficulties which the courts have had

[17] R. Kennedy, "The Colonial Crisis and the Future," in R. Linton (Ed.), *The Science of Man in the World Crisis*, pp. 328–330.

[18] Alabama, Arkansas, Delaware, Florida, Georgia, Indiana, Kentucky, Louisiana, Maryland, Mississippi, Missouri, North Carolina, Oklahoma, South Carolina, Tennessee, Texas, Virginia, West Virginia, Wyoming.

with the interpretation of these statutes, the kinds of evidence which are admissible in attempting to prove the race of anyone accused of miscegenation, the grounds on which the decisions have been based, and the moot question of their constitutionality make a long story, the telling of which is beyond the scope of this chapter.[19]

The United States Supreme Court has never ruled directly on the question of the constitutionality of laws barring mixed marriages, but many authorities predict that, when the issue is presented, the Court will find them invalid.

All the while, the process of amalgamation has continued, oblivious of the presence of these legal prohibitions. The Indian Service estimates that about 60 per cent of the Indians in the United States are full-bloods, but its definition of full-blood allows for a certain degree of admixture. It is doubtful that the statutes have had any effect upon the retardation of the Indians' amalgamation. In the case of the Negroes a conservative estimate is that 70 per cent of them now have some white or Indian blood.[20]

If amalgamation has proceeded thus far in three centuries, what of the future? Linton says, "Most anthropologists agree that there will be no Negro problem in another two hundred years; by then there will not be enough recognizable Negroes left in this country to constitute a problem."[21] He bases his prediction upon three considerations: (1) that the proportion of Negroes to whites in the population is steadily declining; (2) that the Negro is no longer concentrated in the South, but is distributed more evenly over the country, facilitating his absorption; and (3) that the Negro is growing lighter, not through an evolutionary process, but from steady infiltration of white blood. Linton's position has been attacked by Kephart,[22] who denies that the proportion of Negroes in the population is declining and questions the assumption that the Negro is becoming lighter as a result of the steady infiltration of white blood. It is generally thought by students of race problems that, whatever may have been the extent of Negro-white miscegenation during the periods of slavery and reconstruction, there has been a great decrease in recent years.[23] The truth of the matter is, as Blue has pointed out,[24] that predictions are hazardous and unreliable because there are too many gaps in our knowledge. We have no data on the amount of miscegenation, and there are many genetic problems which

---

[19] Cf. C. S. Mangum, *The Legal Status of the Negro,* pp. 236–273; J. Greenberg, *Race Relations and American Law,* pp. 397ff.; "When Negroes and Whites Intermarry," *U.S. News and World Report,* Oct. 7, 1963, p. 63.

[20] M. J. Herskovits, *The Anthropometry of the American Negro,* p. 279; *The American Negro,* p. 10; Wirth and Goldhamer, *op. cit.,* pp. 268–273; G. Myrdal, *An American Dilemma,* pp. 132–133.

[21] R. Linton, "The Vanishing American Negro," *American Mercury,* Vol. 64, No. 178, February 1947, p. 133.

[22] W. H. Kephart, "Is the American Negro Becoming Lighter? An Analysis of the Sociological and Biological Trends," *American Sociological Review,* Vol. 13, No. 4, August 1948, pp. 437–443.

[23] Myrdal, *op. cit.,* p. 133; Wirth and Goldhamer, *op. cit.,* pp. 272ff.

[24] J. T. Blue, Jr., Letter to the Editor, *American Sociological Review,* Vol. 13, No. 6, December 1948, pp. 766–767.

would have to be answered before we could predict with any assurance. Nor do we know the extent of interracial marriages, although the *New York Times* reports that they have increased in number in recent years,[25] and Burma, in a study conducted in Los Angeles and covering the years 1948–1959, reports that their number tripled over that eleven-year period.[26] Even so, the extent of interracial marriage in the United States remains very small indeed.[27] Amalgamation, like assimilation, does not move at a steady, consistent, and uniform pace.

Biological Consequences

Despite the fact that some — notably the protagonists of the melting-pot theory — have espoused the mixing of peoples, the opinion has often been expressed that the biological consequences of miscegenation are harmful, even disastrous. The man on the street has defended this thesis, and scholars have been fascinated by it. Many who have had first-hand contact with the American Indian have often testified to the treachery of the half-breed, while at the same time extolling the virtues of the full-blood. Many a Southerner insists that the mulatto is the troublemaker, while the "pure" Negro "knows his place." Stonequist says that in India the Anglo-Indians "have been the subject of much comment concerning the adverse consequences of race mixture; mentally, morally, and physically they have been cited to prove the contention that mixed-bloods inherit the vices of both parent races."[28] Historians have used the mixture of races as the key to the understanding of the past. Some have attributed the greatness of Egypt, Greece, and Rome to the purity and high quality of the racial stock, while their decline is explained as the consequence of their unwise mixing with peoples of lesser breed. Other scholars, however, have accounted for the very greatness of certain nations — Greece, Rome, England, the United States, and others — by their being the products of diverse strains, and point out that the most backward peoples of the earth are those of purest racial stock — the Southern mountaineers, the Australian aborigines, and the Ainu of Japan, for instance.

There have been several scientific studies of mixed peoples, but much more needs to be done before positive conclusions can be drawn.[29] Some of these support, and some contradict, the contentions of those who take a dim view of amalgamation. It is said, for example, that *disharmonious combinations* result from the promiscuous crossing of diverse races. An investigation of the Negro-white hybrids of Jamaica is one of the bases for this conclusion.[30] Jennings,

25 F. Powledge, "Negro-White Marriages on Rise Here," *The New York Times*, October 18, 1963, p. 1.

26 J. H. Burma, "Interethnic Marriage in Los Angeles, 1948–1959," *Social Forces*, Vol. 42, No. 2, December 1963, pp. 156ff.

27 Cf. J. W. Vander Zanden, *American Minority Relations*, p. 287; M. M. Gordon, *Assimilation in American Life*, pp. 165ff.

28 Stonequist, *op. cit.*, p. 16.

29 For a summary of these studies, see Wirth and Goldhamer, *op. cit.*, pp. 320–329.

30 C. B. Davenport and M. S. Steggerda, *Race Crossing in Jamaica*. For a criticism of this publication, see Wirth and Goldhamer, *op. cit.*, p. 328.

relying partly upon this study, points to the disadvantages of miscegenation:

> In the mixture of races found in the United States . . . some of the stocks differ greatly in physique from others. . . . When such divers races are crossed, the offspring, receiving genes from both sides, may well develop combinations of parts that lack complete harmony. If a large body is combined with small kidneys, the latter may be insufficient for the needs of the individual. Or a large body might be combined with a small heart . . . [or] large teeth in a small jaw. In consequence the teeth decay. Partly to it, Davenport ascribes the prevalence of defective teeth in the United States. . . . Since inharmonious combinations of physical characteristics that are thus open to precise study are shown to occur as a result of race crossing, it appears probable that similarly inharmonious combinations of a more serious character may likewise occur. Davenport expresses it tersely, "A hybridized people are a badly put-together people."[31]

Meanwhile, other studies have indicated a relatively high degree of homogeneity in hybrid peoples. Williams,[32] who measured a great many Spanish-Maya hybrids in Yucatan, found a low variability; and a similar conclusion has been drawn from the studies of the Polynesian-white inhabitants of Pitcairn Island,[33] and the Boer-Hottentot hybrids of South Africa.[34] Most frequently cited, as evidence for the homogeneity of the hybrid, is Herskovits's investigation of American mulattoes,[35] leading to the conclusion that a definite new physical type, with low variability, is in the making. These investigations, however, have not gone unchallenged, either because of the smallness of their samples, or because of the physical traits selected for measurement and comparison. Miscegenation, it appears, need not result in the harmonious blending of racial types, as occurs when colored liquids are poured together, nor does it result in the production of monstrosities. But exactly what does occur has not been definitely and conclusively determined.

It has also been alleged, even by persons of scientific repute, that race-crossing is tantamount to race suicide, for it leads to sterility, debility, and demoralization. Sometimes these startling conclusions have been reached by the dubious practice of comparing human beings with mules, or with hybrid rabbits whose reproductive capacity showed some diminution. Fischer, however, found large families among the Boer-Hottentot people; Shapiro saw no evidence of the loss of fecundity among the hybrids of Pitcairn Island; and Boas found half-breed Indian women outstripping their full-blood cousins in the bearing of children. Herskovits disposes of the sterility argument in these words: "As far as has been ascertained, there are no crosses between human groups which carry lethal determinants for the offspring."[36] In fact, some scientists have gone to the

[31] H. S. Jennings, *The Biological Basis of Human Nature*, pp. 280–282.
[32] G. D. Williams, *Maya-Spanish Crosses in Yucatan*, Harvard University, Peabody Museum Papers, Vol. 13, No. 1, 1931.
[33] H. L. Shapiro, *The Heritage of the Bounty*.
[34] E. Fischer, *Die Rehobother Bastards und das Bastardierungsproblem beim Menschen*.
[35] Herskovits, *op. cit.*
[36] "Race Mixture," in the *Encyclopedia of the Social Sciences*, Vol. 13, pp. 41–43.

A group of Brazilian elementary school children, watching a puppet show, display a great variety of racial intermingling.

opposite extreme in asserting that mixed peoples possess a certain "hybrid vigor." Jennings, who deplores "disharmonious combinations," counts this enhancement of vigor as one of the advantages of race-crossing, and he is supported by the reports of Fischer, Shapiro, and others.

The intellectual and personal characteristics of hybrids have also entered into the debate on the consequences of miscegenation. Davenport said that the hybrids of Jamaica did not do so badly on the intelligence tests, but that many of them were "muddled and wuzzle-headed," whatever that means. The Norwegian scientist, Mjen, in his study of Lapp-Norwegian hybrids, professes to have found among them an unusually large number of prostitutes and persons who were "unwilling to work" and who "lacked balance."[37] His explanation of these facts is biological, not social. Much has been written about the personality of the hybrid, even though scientific study of the problem is beset with difficul-

[37] Quoted in O. Klineberg, *Race Differences*, pp. 214–215.

ties. There are many reasons for believing that the person of mixed blood does indeed have unique experiences which leave their marks upon his personality, but these can better be explained by the social situation than by the blood mixture within him. The intellectual qualities of hybrids, too, have received a great deal of attention, and with contradictory results. Some have shown the mulatto superior to the dark Negro, or the half-breed superior to the full-blood Indian. Other studies, and usually those more carefully designed, show no relation between color and intelligence.[38]

The truth of the matter seems to be that the biological consequences of miscegenation are in themselves neither good nor bad, but depend upon the qualities of the individuals who enter into the mixture. The ill effects of race-crossing, which have been so frequently noted and written about, are social rather than biological in character. Curt Stern, a geneticist, has summarized the present state of our knowledge of the biological consequences of race-crossing in the following words:

> Miscegenation is frequently regarded as undesirable. In so far as it focuses attention on sociological problems arising from unsolved difficulties in the attitudes of races toward one another, the question of undesirability of unions between members of different major racial groups does not fall into the scientific field of the human biologist. It also does not lie in the domain of the geneticist to evaluate the historical consequences of a gradual disappearance of the diversity of cultures as a result of possible extensive mingling of races. Nor are the unusual psychological conflicts which may confront an individual whose parents belong to two racial groups with widely different cultures of primary genetic concern. The opinion is often expressed, however, that biological reasons exist, which make hybridization between human races undesirable. . . .
>
> Differences between human races seem to be dependent, not on a few genes which independently determine striking properties of parts, but rather on numerous multiple factors each of which affects slightly one or more characters and whose recombinants are able to direct development toward a reasonably harmonious system. This seems to be the explanation for the fact that hardly any well-substantiated examples of disharmonious constitution resulting from miscegenation have been reported. . . .
>
> There is no fully proven case of heterosis [hybrid vigor] following miscegenation in man. . . . Heterosis . . . may have played a role everywhere, but a rigid proof of this contention is lacking. . . .
>
> Confronted with the lack of decisive evidence concerning the genetic consequences of miscegenation in regard to physical and mental traits, the conservative will still counsel abstention, since the possible ill effects of the breakdown of races formed in the course of evolution will not be reversible; while the less conservative will regard the chance of such ill effects as negligible and will not raise his voice against the mingling of races which, from a very long-range point of view, is probably bound to occur in any case.[39]

[38] Klineberg, *op. cit.*, pp. 219–222; Wirth and Goldhamer, *op. cit.*, pp. 330ff.
[39] From Curt Stern, *Principles of Human Genetics*, W. H. Freeman and Co., 1949, pp. 567–579.

Social Consequences

Nature, it would seem, is quite indifferent to the whole problem of miscegenation. She neither punishes such unions with monstrous and inferior offspring nor blesses them with supermen. Man, however, has shown much more concern in the matter, and he has produced laws and mores for coping with it. Nature replies to the question of miscegenation with a shrug of the shoulders; man speaks out, but he falters and contradicts himself and talks from both sides of his mouth.

The social consequences of miscegenation, then, cannot be understood apart from the cultural setting. There are many places where racial and ethnic groups have met and mixed and where there have been no serious social consequences. Pitcairn Island is such a place. In 1789 sixteen of the officers and crew of the British naval vessel, the *Bounty*, mutinied, cast the skipper adrift, and sailed away to a hiding place on the little-known island of Pitcairn in the South Pacific. On the way there, they stopped at Tahiti, and persuaded a number of Polynesian men and women to join them. Landing on Pitcairn, all the phenomena of race relations manifested themselves. Conflict between the whites and the browns was fierce, until finally all the Polynesian men, and most of the British, had been killed. Assimilation, in the usual reciprocal manner, occurred, with the result that the present culture of the island is a blend of English and Polynesian, with the former predominating. Amalgamation, too, has been complete, all of the islanders being of mixed blood. Miscegenation in this case has certainly not resulted in any biological disaster; and Shapiro, who studied the population, was impressed by the high mental and physical quality of the people.[40] The social consequences of amalgamation have been negligible. The fact that its population is a mixed people plays no part in the social structure of the island and has no perceptible effect upon personality. It makes the people feel neither inferior nor superior. Some of them are much darker than others, but this apparently is not used on the island as a basis for discrimination and status. They pay as little attention to skin color as we pay to the color of the eyes or the width of the foot. Isolated as they are from the outside world, the attitudes of others toward the hybrids is of no consequence to them.

The isolation of the Pitcairn Islanders, and the fact that all are hybrids, do not in themselves account for this indifference to racial features. Another community, equally mixed and isolated, has followed a different course.[41] Tristan da Cunha consists of three small islands in the South Atlantic. They were uninhabited when first discovered by the Portuguese in 1506, but the British took possession of them in 1816, and a small garrison was established there. Their nearest neighbors were on St. Helena, 1400 miles away. The garrison was removed the following year; but three men — a Scot and two

[40] Shapiro, *op. cit.*, pp. 10–11.
[41] P. A. Munch, "Cultural Contacts in an Isolated Community — Tristan da Cunha," *American Journal of Sociology*, Vol. 53, No. 1, July 1947, pp. 1–8.

Englishmen — requested that they be permitted to remain. The Scot, who had formerly served in Cape Colony, had married a hybrid woman of part-Boer stock, and he brought his family to Tristan da Cunha. In the years following others came to the island — mostly shipwrecked sailors of English, Scottish, Dutch, Italian, and Scandinavian nationalities. Some of them remained, but most left as soon as they had the opportunity. In 1827 the Scot's wife was the only woman on the island; but in that year five of the bachelors paid an American whaling captain to bring them women from St. Helena, which he did. These women were all hybrids of uncertain ancestry, but Munch suspects that they were white-Negro-Malay. He says, further, that in 1938 all the residents had some Negro and Malay blood with the exception of two, neither of whom were natives. Today most of them look Caucasian, even Nordic, but some are dark, betraying Negroid or Malayan features.

Unlike the Pitcairn Islanders, who have attached no social significance to their mixed racial character, those on Tristan da Cunha do show some concern, even though slight. They have a preference for the lighter skin. When it comes to marriage, fair girls have an advantage over the darker ones in making a desirable match; and the upper stratum of the society is made up largely of the lighter shades. A dark skin does not doom an individual to low status, but it is a handicap which can be surmounted only by exceptional zeal and industry. Munch thinks that this color prejudice "is due to an indoctrination of European ideas, either as a survival of the social heritage of the settlers or as a more recent indoctrination through European visitors."

The Marginal Man

Usually, however, in those areas where racial and ethnic groups have lived together, miscegenation has not been ignored, as on Pitcairn, or lightly regarded, as on Tristan da Cunha. Instead, it has been looked upon as a serious matter, and the innocent offspring of such unions have felt the full force of the society's attitude. The mores regarding miscegenation and the hybrid offspring vary both in form and intensity from one society to another. In most parts of the United States one may boast of Indian blood without loss of status, but not of Negro or Japanese; and a Norwegian grandparent may prove an asset, where a Greek grandparent would prove the reverse. Similarly, the problems the hybrid faces are quite different in India, Java, Jamaica, Hawaii, and the United States. Generalization is difficult. Sociologists, however, have been in the habit of discussing the *social* consequences of race-crossing under the concept of the *marginal man*. The marginal man, to be sure, need not be a product of diverse racial strains. Stonequist distinguishes the cultural hybrid and the racial hybrid, though both are considered types of marginal men. Examples of the former are Europeanized Africans, Westernized Orientals, second-generation immigrants, and denationalized Europeans; while examples of the latter are Eurasians, Indo-Europeans, Cape Coloured, and Jamaica "whites." Park, who first used the expression "marginal man," defined him as "one whom fate has condemned to live in two, not merely different but antagonistic cultures"; and Stonequist, who has given the fullest exposition of the concept, says:

> The marginal man . . . is one who is poised in psychological uncertainty between two (or more) social worlds; reflecting in his soul the discords and harmonies, repulsions and attractions of these worlds, one of which is often "dominant" over the other; within which membership is implicitly if not explicitly based upon birth or ancestry (race or nationality); and where exclusion removes the individual from a system of group relations.[42]

The concept of the marginal man, despite its wide acceptance by sociologists, has come in for criticism.[43] Certainly, the marginal type of personality is not limited to racial and ethnic hybrids. Many of the symptoms are seen in the hillbilly who migrates to the city, or in the Yankee who moves to the South. Stonequist includes in his analysis such diverse types as the "detribalized native" of Africa and the children of immigrant parents in the United States. Moreover, not all racial and ethnic hybrids display the personality traits of marginality. Some hybrids are simply more sensitive than others, and some, like the Pitcairn Islanders, are spared the experiences which call them forth. Wirth and Goldhamer question the applicability of the concept to the American mulatto; Goldberg shows that many a second- and third-generation Jew regards his mixed culture as normal; and Green contrasts college students of Greek and Polish ancestry, to show that differences in their cultural backgrounds tend to make marginal personalities of the former but not of the latter.

Despite these criticisms, the fact remains that frequently the process of amalgamation deeply affects the personalities of those who are going through it. According to Stonequist, the following are the personality traits commonly present in greater or less degree in the racial or cultural hybrid: a dual personality, a "double consciousness"; ambivalence of attitude and sentiment; divided loyalty; irrational, moody, and "temperamental" conduct; excessive self-consciousness and race-consciousness; inferiority complex; superiority complex, as a compensation for feelings of inferiority; hypersensitivity; withdrawal tendencies; egocentrism; tendency to rationalize; aggressiveness; day-dreaming; hypercritical disposition; skill in noting the contractions and hypocrisies of the dominant culture; mental activity, sometimes creative, but usually imitative and conformist.

The marginal man has been a popular theme with novelists, many of whom have portrayed with precision and understanding the emotions of the hybrid who is "neither fish nor fowl." John Masters, in *Bhowani Junction*, mentioned earlier, takes his reader into the mind of the Anglo-Indian and reveals the

---

[42] *Op. cit.*, p. 8.

[43] M. M. Goldberg, "A Qualification of the Marginal Man Theory," *American Sociological Review*, Vol. 6, No. 1, February 1941, pp. 52–58; A. W. Green, "A Re-examination of the Marginal Man Concept," *Social Forces*, Vol. 26, No. 2, December 1947, pp. 167–171; Wirth and Goldhamer, *op. cit.*, pp. 335–342; A. C. Kerckhoff and T. C. McCormick, "Marginal Status and Marginal Personality," *Social Forces*, Vol. 34, No. 1, October 1955, pp. 48–55; Gordon, *op. cit.*, pp. 54–59; Vander Zanden, *op. cit.*, pp. 281ff.

ambivalence, sensitivity, and frustrations found there. Diana Chang, in her novel *The Frontiers of Love,* does the same thing for the Eurasians of Shanghai, and Lyle Saxon, in *Children of Strangers,* deals realistically with the plight of the Negro-white hybrids of Louisiana. Playwrights and poets, too, have turned their talents to this universal theme. Langston Hughes gets right to the point in these rapier-like lines:

CROSS

My old man's a white old man
And my old mother's black.
If ever I cursed my white old man,
I take my curses back.

If ever I cursed my old black mother
And wished she were in hell,
I'm sorry for that evil wish
And now I wish her well.

My old man died in a fine big house,
My ma died in a shack.
I wonder where I'm gonna die,
Being neither white nor black?[44]

An Index of Assimilation

Amalgamation and assimilation are related both as cause and as effect. In the biological process of interbreeding, even when illicit, there is at least a minimum of cultural exchange; and, on the other hand, as people become assimilated, and their cultural differences disappear, they are less reluctant to intermarry. Apparently there is no group, *all* of whose members are unwilling to have sex relations with individuals in the out-group — a fact amply proved by the hybrid populations which have arisen wherever contacts have occurred. Inter*marriage,* however, is quite a different matter. Young records a great many comments made by the Russian Molokans of Los Angeles to show the intensity of their feelings with regard to out-marriage. A woman of this group had given a good deal of thought to it:

I had several chances to marry American fellows, but I would not forsake my people. . . . My parents would absolutely disown me. I could never come back to the Colony. Then I figure that not all marriages turn out right. I could never later marry a Russian man. I would be without a husband and without my people too.[45]

[44] *The Weary Blues,* p. 52. Reproduced by permission of the publishers, Alfred A. Knopf, Inc. Copyright 1926 by Alfred A. Knopf, Inc.
[45] Pauline Young, *Pilgrims of Russian Town,* p. 78.

One of the insights in Myrdal's study of the American Negro is his theory of the "rank order of discriminations." He maintains that the primary and essential concern of the white man, in his relations with the Negro, is to prevent amalgamation, and that he is determined to utilize every means to this end. Accordingly, he insists upon segregation and discrimination in nearly all spheres of life; but the closer the relationships come to threatening the anti-amalgamation doctrine, the greater are the limitations and restrictions. Myrdal maintains, therefore, that the force of the discriminations the whites place upon the Negroes takes on a rank order. He has worked out such a division, as follows:

Rank 1. Highest in this order stands the bar against intermarriage and sexual intercourse involving white women.

Rank 2. Next come the several etiquettes and discriminations, which specifically concern behavior in personal relations. These are the barriers against dancing, bathing, eating, drinking together, and social intercourse generally; peculiar rules as to handshaking, hat lifting, use of titles, house entrance to be used, social forms when meeting on streets and in work, and so forth. . . .

Rank 3. Thereafter follow the segregations and discriminations in use of public facilities such as schools, churches, and means of conveyance.

Rank 4. Next comes political disfranchisement.

Rank 5. Thereafter come discriminations in law courts, by the police, and by other public servants.

Rank 6. Finally come discriminations in securing land, credit, jobs, or other means of earning a living, and discriminations in public relief and other social welfare activities.[46]

Myrdal believes, further, that the Negro, too, has a rank order which is just about parallel, but inverse, to that of the white man. The greatest concerns of the Negro are with economic opportunity and injustice in the courts, while intermarriage with the whites "is of rather distant and doubtful interest."

Further indication of the significance which groups attach to intermarriage comes from the famous Bogardus social distance test, the results of which are given on page 292. This scale attempts to measure the reaction of native-born Americans to various racial and ethnic groups. Bogardus asked 1725 persons, mostly of North European descent, to indicate to what relationship they were willing to admit the members of various other groups. The English were most acceptable, not only as fellow citizens and neighbors, but as members of the family; while Hindus, Koreans, Turks, Filipinos, and others evoked quite different reactions. It will be noted, too, that intermarriage is the relationship to which all out-groups are most reluctantly admitted.

Such being the case, sociologists have regarded statistics on intermarriage as one of the best indices of a group's assimilation. Lowry Nelson has called it

[46] *Op. cit.*, pp. 60–61.

"the final test of assimilation,"[47] and Drachsler, who made a study of the problem in New York, said:

> A study of the facts of intermarriage offers a reasonably secure base from which to begin excursions into the elusive problem of assimilation. . . . Intermarriage, as such, is perhaps the severest test of group cohesion. Individuals who freely pass in marriage from one ethnic circle into another are not under the spell of an intense cultural or racial consciousness.[48]

Opposition to intermarriage, of course, may come from either or both of the groups involved; and some groups have developed much more effective techniques than others for enforcing endogamy. At the same time, the mere *frequency* of out-marriage is not alone proof of assimilation, for there are other factors involved. Anderson, in her study of the city of Burlington, Vermont, found that the Old Yankee stock showed a decided preference for marrying their own kind; the Irish and the Germans, who are well along in the process of assimilation, show a distinct tendency to marry outside their groups; the Italians, though far less assimilated, are forced to marry outsiders, as their numbers are small; and, finally, the French-Canadians are the most endogamous of all.[49] These differences obviously are not perfectly correlated with the groups' assimilability. Similarly, Adams in his investigation of intermarriage in Hawaii reports that the Chinese, when they first came to the islands, took Hawaiian women for wives simply because Chinese women were not available. Recently, however, they have developed an adverse attitude toward out-marriage and have shown a tendency to marry among themselves, now that the ratio of the sexes is more balanced, their own status has become enhanced, and they have developed a greater group consciousness.[50]

Many investigations of intermarriage, however, have clearly shown that assimilation and intermarriage are closely related, that some racial and ethnic groups far surpass others in their tendency toward out-marriage, and that frequency of intermarriage increases with succeeding generations. Pihlblad found that the percentage of Swedish-American children who reported mixed parentage was much greater in the lower grades than in the upper;[51] Hiller discovered a similar trend among the French-Canadians of rural Illinois;[52] and Wessel reported that, in Woonsocket, Rhode Island, the rate of out-marriage for the first generation was 9.6 per cent, for the second 20.9 per cent, and for the third 40.4 per cent.[53] Miss Wessel found, also, that the percentage of intermarriage

[47] "Intermarriage among Nationality Groups in a Rural Area of Minnesota," *American Journal of Sociology*, Vol. 48, No. 5, March 1943, p. 585.
[48] J. Drachsler, *Democracy and Assimilation*, p. 87.
[49] E. L. Anderson, *We Americans*, pp. 188ff.
[50] R. Adams, *Interracial Marriage in Hawaii*, pp. 142–159.
[51] C. T. Pihlblad, "The Kansas Swedes," *Southwestern Social Science Quarterly*, Vol. 13, No. 1, June 1932, pp. 1–14.
[52] E. T. Hiller, *et al.*, "Rural Community Types," *University of Illinois Studies in the Social Sciences*, December 1928.
[53] B. B. Wessel, *An Ethnic Survey of Woonsocket, Rhode Island*, Ch. 8.

was greater for the British, amounting to 32.4 in the first generation, and that the Irish, French-Canadians, Slavs, Italians, and Jews followed thereafter, in that order.

The Jews are something of a special case, though their record illustrates clearly the close relationship between assimilation and amalgamation. The Bible itself testifies to the fact that, from the earliest times, the Jews intermarried with the various ethnic groups around them, even though exogamy was frowned upon. We are told that Jacob went to his own people for his wife, while his brother Esau chose his from the local non-Jewish population. The practice of out-marriage must have been rather common, for a special ceremony is provided in the regulations of Deuteronomy 21:10–13:

> When thou goest forth to battle against thine enemies, and Jehovah thy God delivereth them into thy hands, and thou carriest them away captive, and seest among the captives a beautiful woman, and thou hast a desire unto her, and wouldest take her to thee to wife; then thou shalt bring her home to thy house; and she shall shave her head and pare her nails; and she shall put the raiment of her captivity from off her, and shall remain in thy house, and shall bewail her father and her mother a full month; after that thou shalt go in unto her, and be her husband, and she shall be thy wife.

Jewish intermarriage in more recent times has been studied by M. L. Barron, who reaches the conclusion that it "does not necessarily adhere to a pattern of increasing incidence. It varies in time and place according to the fluctuations of social conditions."[54] Until late in the nineteenth century, Barron says, European Jews rarely married outsiders, but from the latter part of the nineteenth century until the advent of Hitler, intermarriage increased steadily, even to the point of causing concern among some Jewish scholars for the survival of Judaism itself. In Switzerland the rate of intermarriage per 100 marriages increased from 5.39 in 1888 to 11.66 in 1920; in Hungary intermarriage almost quintupled in the 40 years up to 1935; in Sweden the twentieth century saw almost as many intermarriages as in-marriages, until the rabbis protested violently and refused to participate in the ceremonies; in Italy almost all Jewish families had acquired Christian relatives through intermarriage, but Italian legislation in 1938 prohibited marriage between Jews and Christians; in England, Jews of Spanish and Portuguese origin have almost disappeared through intermarriage. In the United States, Barron finds, Jews intermarried during the colonial period at a higher rate than they have since, with the result that Jewish pioneers in Kentucky, for instance, have disappeared; and in New York, Pennsylvania, Connecticut, and Massachusetts the early Sephardic Jews have virtually become lost through amalgamation. Elsewhere, and at other times, the rate of intermarriage has been very low, as in Lithuania where, in 1931, it was only 0.39 per cent.

[54] "Jewish Intermarriage in Europe and America," *American Sociological Review,* Vol. 11, No. 1, February 1946, pp. 6–13. See also W. J. Cahnman, *Intermarriage and Jewish Life.*

Sociologists whose special interest is the family institution, and persons engaged in marriage counseling, have long suspected that unions which cut across racial and ethnic lines are fraught with difficulties. The literature abounds with cases of family conflict arising from cultural differences between spouses. Anderson reports the following remarks of a Burlington citizen of German stock:

> I don't think we're ready for too much intermarriage yet. I think we've been too hasty in bringing people together. . . . I can see the difference in my brother's marriage and mine. I married a German girl. He married a Yankee. We both have difficulties. But whenever a troublesome situation arises, my wife and I can meet it from the same point of view, can measure it in terms of the same values; while he and his wife have to approach it from two different angles, and it is often difficult for them to get together.[55]

Many times the problems are more serious and the outcome of a mixed marriage is tragic, as in the case of the Molokan woman who said:

> I was twelve years old when we came to this country. When I went to school for a few years, I thought I was Americanized and married an Irishman. I had a miserable life with him, and was divorced. I realized then what it meant to be away from Russian-Town. A few years later I married a Molokan. . . . Slowly I began to return to *sobranie*. I felt as if I was a newborn person. I craved to hear the women talk, even though it was a sharp rebuke. . . . During our last holiday, on Judgment Day, I was so inspired by the service that I felt I must get up and say something. And say I did. I at once realized that I did the wrong thing, as I heard the people around me comment that a woman of my character should hold her tongue. . . . I was humiliated and broken up over it. . . . I just have to keep on trying until they accept me again.[56]

Marriages which cut across racial lines offer even greater difficulties than those which cross religious and ethnic lines. Drake and Cayton have made a study of Negro-white marriages in Chicago.[57] They recognize the fact that there is considerable miscegenation between the races, but very little intermarriage in spite of the absence of legal bars. The social pressures, however, are tremendous, and they are effective, too, so that the rate of intermarriage has probably been declining since the beginning of the present century. Nevertheless, they have been able to locate 188 such mixed marriages, and they suspect that there have been many others. Where interracial marriages have ended in divorce, the partners are hard to find, reluctant to be interviewed, and often will never admit that they had even participated in such an experiment. Accordingly, it is probable that the 188 mixed marriages which Drake and Cayton studied

[55] E. L. Anderson, *We Americans*, pp. 199–200.
[56] Pauline Young, *op. cit.*, p. 79.
[57] St. Clair Drake and H. R. Cayton, *Black Metropolis*, Ch. 7.

TABLE 12.1

Reactions of 1725 Americans to
40 Different Races by Percentages*

Regarding races listed below	To close kinship by marriage	To my club as personal chums	To my street as neighbors	To employment in my occupation	To citizenship in my country	As visitors only to my country	Would exclude from my country
English	93.7	96.7	97.3	95.4	95.9	1.7	0.
Americans (native white)	90.1	92.4	92.6	92.4	90.5	1.2	0.
Canadians	86.9	93.4	96.1	95.6	96.1	1.7	.3
Scotch	78.1	89.1	91.3	92.8	93.3	1.7	0.
Scotch-Irish	72.6	81.7	88.	89.4	92.	16.7	.4
Irish	70.	83.4	86.1	89.8	91.4	4.	.7
French	67.8	85.4	88.1	90.4	92.7	3.8	.8
Welsh	60.8	72.3	80.	81.4	86.	5.4	.3
Germans	54.1	67.	78.7	82.6	87.2	6.7	3.1
French-Canadians	49.7	66.4	76.4	79.3	87.	4.4	.8
Swedes	45.3	62.1	75.6	78.	86.3	5.4	1.
Dutch	44.2	54.7	73.2	76.7	86.1	2.4	.3
Norwegians	41.	56.	65.1	72.	80.3	8.	.3
Danes	35.	52.2	65.5	71.4	80.1	4.5	.9
Spaniards	27.6	49.8	55.1	58.	81.6	8.4	2.
Finns	16.1	27.4	36.1	50.5	61.2	12.8	2.8
Russians	15.8	27.7	31.	45.3	56.1	22.1	8.
Italians	15.4	25.7	34.7	54.7	71.3	14.5	4.8
Portuguese	11.	22.	28.3	47.8	57.7	19.	3.3
Poles	11.	11.6	28.3	44.3	58.3	19.7	4.7
Hungarians	10.1	17.5	25.8	43.	70.7	20.3	7.
Rumanians	8.8	19.3	23.8	38.3	51.6	22.	4.6
Armenians	8.5	14.8	27.8	46.2	58.1	17.7	5.
Czecho-Slovaks	8.2	16.4	21.1	36.	47.4	26.	9.5
Indians	8.1	27.7	33.4	54.3	83.	7.7	1.6
Jews, German	7.8	2.1	25.5	39.8	53.5	25.3	13.8
Bulgarians	6.9	14.6	16.4	19.7	43.1	21.9	7.
Jews, Russian	6.1	18.	15.7	30.1	45.3	22.7	13.4
Greeks	5.9	17.7	18.	35.2	53.2	25.3	11.3
Syrians	4.3	13.8	18.	31.	41.1	21.4	9.
Serbo-Croatians	4.3	10.4	12.	10.3	30.4	18.6	8.
Mexicans	2.8	11.5	12.3	77.1	46.1	30.8	15.1
Japanese	2.3	12.1	13.	27.3	29.3	38.8	2.5
Filipinos	1.6	15.2	19.5	36.7	52.1	28.5	5.5
Negroes	1.4	9.1	11.8	38.7	57.3	17.6	12.7
Turks	1.4	10.	11.7	19.	25.3	41.8	23.4
Chinese	1.1	11.8	15.9	27.	27.3	45.2	22.4
Mulattoes	1.1	9.6	10.6	32.	47.4	22.7	16.8
Koreans	1.1	10.8	11.8	20.1	27.5	34.3	13.8
Hindus	1.1	6.8	13.	21.4	23.7	47.1	19.1

* Emory S. Bogardus, *Immigration and Race Attitudes*, p. 25.

represent the more successful of them. Even so, the trials they undergo are severe. Mixed couples often experience difficulties in obtaining and holding jobs, in securing a place to live; they are subject to social ostracism, not only from society in general, but from friends and relatives as well; and, in the rearing of their children, they face a number of problems incomprehensible to those who have married within the conventional patterns.

A study made by Golden of Negro-white intermarriage in Philadelphia corroborates the findings of Drake and Cayton in Chicago.[58] In the first place, Golden found that intermarriage was not extensive, despite the fact that there are no laws forbidding it. About seven such marriages took place yearly during the period studied — 1922 to 1947. Golden had great difficulty in finding these couples, but he did succeed in interviewing 50 of them. He suspects, however, that these 50 might not constitute a representative sample of the Negro-white families, since some refused to be interviewed and others could not be located. It is Golden's judgment that the 50 he interviewed possibly represented the more successful of the interracial marriages. Even so, they had many problems. Prior to marriage, they had been forced to conduct a "sub rosa courtship," since most of the white parents and a great number of the Negro parents disapproved of such relations. The wedding ceremony itself continued the pattern of secrecy, being civil rather than religious. Frequently the white spouse's family was not notified about the marriage, and contacts with the family following the marriage were rare at most. The Negro family was usually willing to meet the white spouse, but approval of the match was by no means automatic. The Negro community, Golden found, tends to condemn Negro-white marriage in general, but is willing to receive the white spouse if her personal qualities are acceptable. The families Golden interviewed admitted to having difficulties in finding residential quarters, and usually lived in peripheral areas, on the border between white and Negro residential districts. There are not many children, and Golden ventures the guess that these families feel so insecure in their married life that they refrain from inviting the additional hazard of children. Other problems, peculiar to these mixed families, include their occupational adjustments, their relations with friends, churches, and the community generally. Even so, Golden concludes that "these marriages have a good chance of survival," despite the obstacles they have had to overcome.

It is not to be denied, however, that mixed couples often feel that there are compensations for their trials, and their marriages are often quite happy.[59] Nor should one jump to the generalization that interracial marriages, regardless of time, place, and race are unstable. In other countries, where attitudes toward race are different from those in the United States, interracial marriages

[58] J. Golden, "Characteristics of the Negro-White Intermarried in Philadelphia," *American Sociological Review*, Vol. 18, No. 2, April 1953, pp. 177–183; and "Patterns of Negro-White Intermarriage," *American Sociological Review*, Vol. 19, No. 2, April 1954, pp. 144–147. See also Powledge, *op. cit.*; Burma, *op. cit.*; Vander Zanden, *op. cit.*, pp. 285–290.
[59] See K. Eskelund, *My Chinese Wife*: R. L. Williams, "He Wouldn't Cross the Color Line," *Life*, Vol. 31, No. 10, September 3, 1951, pp. 81–94.

are doubtless regarded with no more concern than we regard marriages between Methodists and Presbyterians, or between Republicans and Democrats. Even in this country public opinion makes a distinction between the marriage of Jew and Gentile, white and Indian, American and Chinese, Yankee and Mexican.

Since World War II thousands of American soldiers have taken unto themselves Japanese wives, whom they subsequently brought back to America with them. It was widely predicted that such marriages were doomed to failure, and in both the newspapers and the popular magazines there have been stories about the prejudice, discrimination, and the tremendous adjustment problems these couples have faced. The few sociological studies that have been made, however, do not bear out these pessimistic reports. Walters studied 35 American-Japanese families in Ohio,[60] and found that they were making rather successful adjustments. None reported having encountered severe prejudice and discrimination, either on the part of the American families or of the communities. Their children are still too young to have been exposed to prejudicial treatment, but Walters doubts that they will be, for they bear their father's American surname and, in appearance, he found most of them not particularly Oriental.

Strauss has made a study of American-Japanese couples living in the Chicago area,[61] and he concludes that they do not support the assumption that interracial marriages are peculiarly subject to strains and instability. To be sure, there are difficulties and disagreements, but for the most part they are present also in endogamous marriages. As a matter of fact, Strauss maintains that circumstances may be such that certain kinds of stress are *less* likely to occur in mixed marriages than in non-mixed. For example, the Japanese girl is socialized in such fashion that she expects to leave her family and to transfer her allegiance and obligation to her husband; she is not career-minded; she is not likely to exert much pressure on her husband to improve himself occupationally; she does not make demands upon her husband to supply her with money for clothes and other status symbols. Hence, Strauss thinks, Japanese-American marriages may be quite "stable," and may involve fewer major stresses than many marriages between native Americans.

Nevertheless, the preponderance of data that we have suggests that marriages across racial, religious, and ethnic lines are faced with peculiar obstacles, in addition to those which all marriages face. An investigation of poorly adjusted families in Providence, Rhode Island, led to the conclusion that there was evidence of "a degree of maladjustment due to cultural conflicts between the European background and the American milieu and to conflicts of this sort within the family itself."[62] Baber, too, has gathered information on 325 mixed marriages and concludes:

[60] L. K. Walters, "A Study of the Social and Marital Adjustment of Thirty-five American-Japanese Couples," unpublished M. A. thesis, Ohio State University, 1953.

[61] A. L. Strauss, "Strain and Harmony in American-Japanese War-Bride Marriages," *Marriage and Family Living*, Vol. 16, No. 2, May 1954, pp. 99ff.

[62] R. R. Willoughby, "A Study of Some Poorly Adjusted Families," *American Sociological Review*, Vol. 7, No. 1, February 1942, pp. 47–58.

Comparing all three groups — inter-faith, inter-nationality, interracial — *the degree of happiness varied inversely with the degree of difference in culture or color.* This relationship held even in the racial sub-groups; the greater the color difference the lower the happiness rating.[63]

And so, even though interracial marriages in the United States are relatively few in number, marriages across ethnic and religious lines are increasing. Bossard, who made a study of 70,000 marriages in the state of New York, found that 48.7 per cent "crossed either a nativity or nationality line," which led him to say, "The melting pot bubbles actively, because there are so many diverse ingredients in it; it fuses somewhat less than one is apt to suppose.[64]

---

[63] R. Baber, "A Study of 325 Mixed Marriages," *American Sociological Review*, Vol. 2, No. 5, October 1937, pp. 705–716.
[64] J. H. S. Bossard, "Nationality and Nativity as Factors in Marriage," *American Sociological Review*, Vol. 4, No. 6, December 1939, pp. 792–798.

13

Prejudice

Prejudice, like race, has only marginal relevance to race relations.

CAREY MCWILLIAMS
Brothers under the Skin

J ohn Hunter never knew where he was born, nor when, nor who his parents were. In all probability his birth occurred in the last decade of the 1700's; as for the place, Illinois would be as good a guess as any. He supposed that his parents were pioneer settlers on the Western frontier, that they were massacred by the Indians, and that he was taken captive when he was only an infant. But he was never sure of it.

His earliest recollections went back to his childhood in a Kickapoo Indian village, somewhere in the Mississippi Valley. He remembered little of those early years, except that the Indian children used to tease him because his skin was white, and they insisted that all white people were squaws. That made him very angry, and led to frequent fights with the other boys in the village. As a consequence he became very skillful in all the manly arts, and he grew so adept at hunting that the Indians eventually gave him the name "The Hunter."

About this time traders and missionaries began to visit the village, and finding a white boy there they invariably tried to persuade him to return with them. "But," said he, "the accounts of the white people, which the Indians had been particular in giving me, were in no ways flattering to my color. They were represented as an inferior order of beings, wicked, treacherous, cowardly, and only fit to transact the common drudgeries of life. I was assured that my transportation from them to the Indians was for me a most fortunate occurrence, for now I might hope to become an expert hunter, a brave warrior, a wise counsellor, and possibly a distinguished chief. All this I considered true."

The traders proceeded to correct these errors. They told him white people were numerous, powerful, brave, generous, and good; that they lived in large houses, some of which even floated on the water; and they fought with great guns, and could kill many at a single shot. Hunter confessed that he partially believed these reports, and he was filled with wonder and curiosity, but he could not bring himself to accompany the traders on their return to their homes. Occasionally, when he did express a desire to go with them, his Indian friends had little difficulty in dissuading him. They told him that if he did undertake such a journey he would probably be taken captive and be forced to work in the fields *even after he had grown to the size of a warrior.* That was too much for him, and, said he, "After some reflection the prejudices imbibed in early life returned in their full strength, and I still thought the white people were what they had been represented, and even worse."

Hunter could not, however, permanently resist the impact of white influences, any more than could his Indian friends. After a time, and as a consequence of some traumatic experiences, he cast his lot with the whites. The transition was not easy. It was with greatest difficulty that he adopted the white man's style of clothing, learned to speak English, and mastered the intricacies of a monetary system. He often had feelings of guilt and regret for what he had done. Said he, "I looked back with the most painful reflections on what I had been and on the sacrifice I had made." Once especially did he feel so when a white man, taking advantage of his unfamiliarity with monetary matters, swindled him out of a considerable sum. His ancient prejudices returned, and he declared he was convinced again that all he had first been taught about the whites was essentially true, and fraud and deceit were invariable traits of their character.

One thing, more than any other, prevented his forsaking the society of whites. John Hunter (he adopted the name John) became, as he said, "literally infatuated with reading, and seldom went anywhere without a book." Books, rather than the various other features of their culture to which the whites pointed with so much pride, convinced him that he would prefer to live out his days in civilized society. He did just that, as far as we know; though he never ceased to recall the Indian way of life with nostalgia, nor to regard the civilization of the whites with critical, suspicious eyes.[1]

The Nature of Prejudice

Hardly anybody has a good word to say for prejudice nowadays, especially for that variety known as race prejudice. It is commonly denounced as an "enemy of society," or an "insidious disease," or a "canker undermining the body politic." H. G. Wells says of it, "There is no more evil thing than race prejudice. It holds more baseness and cruelty than any other error in the world." It is hard for us to examine objectively something which is so universally hated — and so widely indulged.

What do we have in mind when we use the word? Literally, of course, it simply means "a pre-judgment." Literal translations of Greek and Latin words, however, can be misleading. (*Sincere* means literally, "without wax," *salary* means "salt," and *electricity* means "phenomena associated with amber.") In the first place, prejudice is hardly a judgment, for a judgment is an operation of the mind which involves comparison, discernment, examination of facts, logical processes, and good sense. Prejudice is more emotion, feeling, and bias than it is judgment.

Nor is prejudice necessarily *pre* anything. To be sure, John Hunter did form his opinion of white people before he had seen any of them, and many others have done likewise with respect to other groups. Some scholars, as a matter of fact, have emphasized this feature in making their definitions of the term. Powdermaker, for instance, says "Prejudice means jumping to a conclusion before considering the facts";[2] and according to Frazier, "Prejudice is a pre-judgment in the sense that it is a judgment concerning objects and persons not based upon knowledge or experience."[3] These definitions themselves involve a subtle attack upon prejudice, for they imply that if one only knew the facts, and had some firsthand experience with the people whom he dislikes, his bias would disappear. There is some truth to this, and programs looking toward the eradica-

[1] John Hunter, with the assistance of friends, published *Memoirs of a Captivity among the Indians of North America*, London, 1823. For a brief summary, see B. Berry, "The Education of John Hunter," *Social Science*, Vol. 15, No. 3, July 1940, pp. 258–264. There were many such instances on the frontier of white persons being captured and reared by Indians. See C. C. Rister, *Border Captives*.

[2] Hortense Powdermaker, *Probing Our Prejudices*, p. 1.

[3] E. F. Frazier, *The Negro in the United States*, p. 665.

tion of prejudice have often been built upon that assumption. More often, however, attitudes of hostility arise *after* groups have come into contact, and presumably know something about each other. To cite only one instance, Biesanz reports[4] that today the natives of Panama have a great antipathy for the West Indian Negroes who were brought to that country originally to help the Americans dig the Panama Canal, and who, with their offspring, now number close to 50,000. Prior to that time, however, the Panamanians were a notably tolerant people, devoid of racial prejudice, ready to amalgamate with any who took up residence among them. They have grown hostile, however, toward these "undesirable immigrants" from the West Indies, who came speaking English instead of Spanish, boasting of their British culture, displaying pictures of the Royal Family in their homes, talking of pounds and shillings, dressing differently, and voicing contempt for Panamanian ways. The older stock, itself a mixture of Spanish, Indian, and Negro, now regards these newcomers with fear and resentment, and has fortified its bias with stereotypes, compounded of fallacies and half-truths. Oddly enough, the strongest prejudices are held by the most negroid of the native Panamanians, who do not at all identify themselves with the West Indians in spite of the fact that they have so many "racial" features in common with them.

Prejudice, according to Wirth, is "an attitude with an emotional bias."[5] Every one of us, in the process of socialization, acquires attitudes, not only toward the racial and ethnic groups with which we come into contact, but toward all the elements of our environment. We learn to have attitudes toward dogs, flowers, caviar, democracy, red hair, poetry, communism, television, Elks, chiropractors, news commentators, modern art, and even toward ourselves. How many of these have we formed after a careful, scientific study of the "facts"? These attitudes, moreover, run the whole gamut of feelings from love to hate, from esteem to contempt, from devotion to indifference. John Hunter's prejudices included both an unfavorable attitude toward whites and a most favorable one toward Indians. Biesanz says that while Panamanians in general dislike the West Indians intensely, the range of attitudes varies with individuals, from repulsion to easy-going tolerance. Usually, however, when we speak of *race prejudice*, we are thinking, not of friendly attitudes toward racial and ethnic groups, but of unfriendly attitudes. Allport is correct in insisting that "ethnic prejudice is mostly negative."[6] *Antipathy* would really be a more accurate term than prejudice to describe the phenomenon with which we are dealing. Antipathy, of course, covers a wide range of attitudes itself, including hatred, aversion, dislike, enmity, and various other hostile and unfavorable feelings.

Race prejudice, as the term is commonly used nowadays, includes still other elements which writers on the subject have emphasized. Many insist that the

[4] J. Biesanz, "Cultural and Economic Factors in Panamanian Race Relations," *American Sociological Review*, Vol. 14, No. 6, December 1949, pp. 772–779.
[5] L. Wirth, "Race and Public Policy," *The Scientific Monthly*, Vol. 58, No. 4, March 1944, p. 303.
[6] G. W. Allport, *The Nature of Prejudice*, p. 6.

prejudicial attitude, unlike most of our other attitudes, is essentially "irrational," "rigid," "without sufficient warrant," "immutable." Other attitudes we may change when they conflict with new facts, but prejudices resist change even in the face of knowledge and evidence. Thus, Marden defines prejudice as "an attitude unfavorable or disparaging of a whole group . . . based upon some elements of irrationality,"[7] and Simpson and Yinger say that it is "an emotional, rigid attitude toward a group of people."[8] Others point out that race prejudice implies a disposition to overgeneralize, to categorize too hastily and too readily, to "think of people in bunches, as though they were bananas," to overlook or ignore individual differences, and to assume that every person in a group possesses the objectionable qualities the prejudiced person ascribes to that group. Allport's definition, which follows, incorporates most of the features which scholars maintain inhere in the term:

> Ethnic prejudice is an antipathy based upon a faulty and inflexible generalization. It may be felt or expressed. It may be directed toward a group as a whole, or toward an individual because he is a member of that group.[9]

Prejudice and Discrimination

Prejudice (or attitudes of antipathy) must be distinguished from discrimination. The former refers to subjective feelings, the latter to overt behavior. Discrimination simply means differential treatment accorded individuals who are considered as belonging in a particular category or group. Old people, in many societies, are subject to considerable mistreatment, abuse, and indifference, while in other societies they are accorded privileges and respect. Women, too, have often been denied the rights and privileges enjoyed by the male members of society, and have been the objects of discrimination in economic, religious, political, and social affairs. Negroes, Jews, Japanese-Americans, and Mexicans, to mention only a few of our minorities, continually complain of the differential treatment to which they are subjected in this country.

Prejudice and discrimination, however, are not perfectly correlated. Nor can we say that one is cause, the other effect. Our attitudes and our overt behavior are without doubt very closely related, but are neither identical nor coextensive. One may have feelings of antipathy without expressing them overtly or even giving the slightest indication of their presence. For example, we may, without ever revealing the fact by word or deed, feel the greatest antipathy for women's hats, oily hair, pictures hanging aslant, people who "pop" gum or chew food audibly, and innumerable other annoyances. On the other hand we may, through our overt behavior, completely conceal the real attitude we hold. We may even flatter a woman for her unbecoming coiffure, or smile at the destructive antics of our guest's child, or smack our lips over some detestable delicacy which our host serves us.

[7] C. F. Marden, *Minorities in American Society*, p. 31.
[8] G. E. Simpson and J. M. Yinger, *Racial and Cultural Minorities*, p. 13.
[9] Allport, *op. cit.*, p. 9.

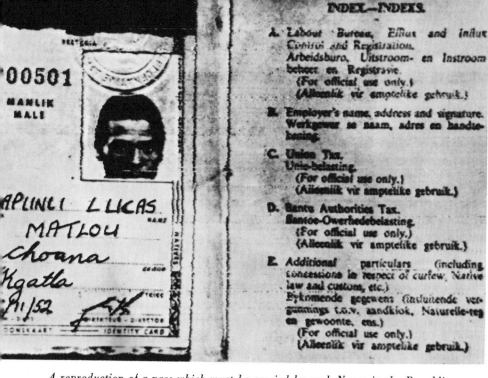

A reproduction of a pass which must be carried by each Negro in the Republic of South Africa. Without it, he cannot move between areas.

This simple fact, namely, that attitudes and overt behavior vary independently, has been succinctly applied by Merton to the problem of racial prejudice and discrimination.[10] There are, he thinks, four types of people, as follows:

The Unprejudiced Non-discriminator or All-Weather Liberal

In this category belong the confirmed and consistent liberals. They are neither prejudiced against the members of other racial and ethnic groups nor do they practice discrimination. They believe implicitly in the American creed of justice, freedom, equality of opportunity, and dignity of the individual. Merton recognizes the fact that liberals of this type are the ones who are properly motivated to diffuse the ideals and values of the creed and to fight against those forms of discrimination which make a mockery of them. At the same time, the all-weather liberals have their shortcomings. They "enjoy talking to themselves," engaging in "mutual exhortation," thereby giving psychological support to one another; they succumb easily to the illusion that the consensus which prevails among themselves is taking hold in the larger community; they confuse discussion with action; and since their own "spiritual house is in order," they do not themselves feel the pangs of guilt, and accordingly shrink from any collective effort to set things aright.

[10] R. K. Merton, "Discrimination and the American Creed," in R. M. MacIver (Ed.), *Discrimination and National Welfare*, pp. 99–126.

The Unprejudiced Discriminator or Fair-Weather Liberal

This type includes persons who think continually of expediency. Though they are themselves free from racial prejudice, they will keep the silence when bigots speak out. They will not condemn acts of discrimination lest they somehow lose status thereby, they will make concessions to the intolerant, and will acquiesce in discriminatory practices for fear that to do otherwise would "hurt business." It is these who suffer most keenly the pricks of conscience, and feel shame for their failure to harmonize their behavior and their beliefs.

The Prejudiced Non-discriminator or Fair-Weather Illiberal

This category is for the timid bigots, who do not accept the tenets of the American creed, but conform to it and give it lip service when the slightest pressure is applied. Here belong the man who hesitates to express his prejudice when he is in the presence of those who are more tolerant, the employer who hates certain minorities but hires them rather than run afoul of some Fair Employment Law, the labor leader who suppresses his racial bias when the majority of his followers demand an end to discrimination.

The Prejudiced Discriminator or All-Weather Illiberal

These are the bigots, pure and unashamed. They do not believe in the American creed, nor do they hesitate to give free expression to their intolerance both in their speech and in their actions. For them there is no conflict between attitudes and behavior. They practice discrimination, believing that it is not only proper that they do so, but is, in fact, their duty.

Dimensions of Prejudice

Race prejudice is not the simple, unitary attitude some have supposed it to be, but instead is complex and multidimensional. To be sure, there is some evidence to the contrary. The tolerant person seems to have friendly feelings, not only for Negroes, but for Mexicans, immigrants, Jews, refugees, and all other under-privileged groups, while the bigot — the person for whom the Ku Klux Klan has an appeal — is contemptuous of Negroes, Jews, Catholics, Mexicans, Puerto Ricans, and all foreigners. There are some data from research to support such an opinion. Hartley a few years ago undertook an investigation of the prejudices of college students. He asked them to express their attitudes toward 32 nations and races, using the Bogardus Social Distance Scale (see p. 292). However, he included with his 32 familiar nationalities and ethnic groups three non-existent groups — the "Daniereans," the "Pireneans," and the "Wallonians." It so happened that the students who proved themselves prejudiced against the familiar groups were also prejudiced against these imaginary ones, while the tolerant students indicated an open-mindedness toward these fictitious ones.[11] Allport

11 E. Hartley, *Problems of Prejudice*, p. 68.

goes so far as to say, "One of the facts of which we are most certain is that people who reject one out-group will tend to reject other out-groups."

Nevertheless, race prejudice is a phenomenon of many dimensions. Reference has already been made to the dimension of *intensity*. Antipathy toward a minority group may vary from mild aversion or indifference to the most violent animosity: while between these two extremes one encounters various degrees of unfriendliness, dislike, ill will, and abhorrence. Kramer has pointed out that, not only are there discrepancies between how people *feel* toward ethnic groups and how they *act*, but people differ also as to what they *think* about other groups, how they *talk* about them, to what extent they are averse to *contact* with them, and in the *intensity* of their hostility toward them.[12] Nor does one hold a single attitude toward Negroes, Jews, and foreigners, but varies his opinion with respect to their social, political, and economic aspirations. The same individual, too, will hold different degrees of prejudice toward the various minority groups, being bitterly hostile, say, toward Negroes, moderately hostile toward Greeks, but having no animosity whatsoever toward French Canadians.

Westie has studied still another dimension of prejudice.[13] It is a mistake, he thinks, to try to ascertain the white man's attitudes toward *the* Negro, for those attitudes vary with the Negro's occupational and social status. He took a sample of the white population of Indianapolis and, using an ingenious device, measured the antipathy, or "social distance," felt toward Negroes. Not just Negroes "in general," however, but toward Negro doctors, lawyers, bookkeepers, ditch-diggers, and so on. He found, among other things, that the prejudices of the whites varied significantly depending upon the Negro's occupation. "The higher the occupational status of the Negro, the less distance expressed toward him." Moreover, he found the whites most rigid in their antipathy toward Negroes when it comes to personal relations and residential proximity, and least rigid with respect to the Negroes' achieving positions of prestige and power in the community. He discovered still another dimension: "The higher the socio-economic status of the responding white, the greater the alteration of response with variations in the occupational status of the Negro."

It is a mistake, too, to regard prejudice as an attitude held only by members of the dominant group for their inferiors. Minorities, too, are not without their prejudices. American Negroes have an antipathy for whites; and they share with their native-born, white, Protestant fellow-Americans the usual prejudices toward other ethnic minorities. Jews, too, are guilty of anti-Gentilism, and some of them are even anti-Semitic. These latter express their disgust for the Jewish religion, or with the Yiddish language, or with Jews of particular nationalities; and they blame the orthodox, or recent Jewish immigrants, for the minority status to which all Jews are ascribed. Lundberg and Dickson have demonstrated

[12] B. M. Kramer, "Dimensions of Prejudice," *Journal of Psychology*, Vol. 27, Second Half, October 1949, pp. 389–451; E. L. Horowitz, "Race Attitudes," in O. Klineberg (Ed.), *Characteristics of the American Negro*, pp. 143–157.
[13] F. R. Westie, "Negro-White Status Differentials and Social Distance," *American Sociological Review*, Vol. 17, No. 5, October 1952, pp. 550ff.

that high school students representing various American minorities display *even greater* ethnocentrism than do native white Americans.[14] And if it is true, as none will deny, that whites have nourished deep antipathy for the Indian, it is also true that the Indian has been equally prejudiced against the whites:

> I grew up believing that whites are wicked, deceitful people. It seemed that most of them were soldiers, government agents, or missionaries, and that quite a few were Two-Hearts. The old people said that the whites were tough, possessed dangerous weapons, and were better protected than we from evil spirits and poison weapons. They were known to be big liars, too. They sent Negro soldiers against us with cannons, tricked our war chiefs to surrender without fighting, and then broke their promises. Like Navahos, they were proud and domineering — and needed to be reminded daily to tell the truth. I was taught to mistrust them and to give warning whenever I saw one coming.[15]

There are numerous other dimensions of prejudice which need to be explored. Are there regional differences in the degree of race prejudice? Are men more prejudiced than women? Are the better educated more tolerant than the uneducated? How do Catholics, Protestants, and Jews compare? Are there differences in the prejudices of the upper classes and those of the lower classes? Are older people more prejudiced than younger? We all have ideas on these matters, but to what extent can we support them with facts?

There has been some study of these questions, but the results are inconclusive. Some show that women are more prejudiced than men, while others show the reverse. Some indicate that Protestants are more tolerant than Catholics, but other studies, using a different sample, dispute this. Allport,[16] while recognizing that it is hazardous to draw sweeping conclusions on these problems, does venture a few generalizations: (1) Southern whites have less favorable attitudes toward Negroes than do those in northern and western states; (2) anti-Semitism is greater in the northeast and midwest sections of the country than in the South and West; (3) people with college education are somewhat less prejudiced than those with only grade school or high school education; (4) whites in the lower socio-economic brackets are, on the average, more bitterly anti-Negro than are whites in the higher brackets; and (5) anti-Semitism is more pronounced at the higher socio-economic levels than at the lower. Thus, race prejudice has many facets and dimensions, only a few of which have begun to be explored.

Theories of Prejudice

A generation or two ago reputable scientists and scholars maintained that race prejudice is an inborn, instinctive human characteristic. One can see how they came to such a conclusion. Antipathy for strangers, aliens, and members of the out-group is so widespread, so ancient, and so deep-rooted that it is no wonder that it was regarded by students of the subject as inherent in all people.

[14] G. A. Lundberg and Lenore Dickson, "Selective Association among Ethnic Groups in a High School Population," *American Sociological Review*, Vol. 17, No. 1, February 1952, pp. 23ff.

[15] L. W. Simmons (Ed.), *Sun Chief: The Autobiography of a Hopi Indian*, p. 88.

[16] *Op. cit.*, pp. 79ff. See also R. M. Williams, Jr., *Strangers Next Door*, pp. 257–275.

Somewhat later, when we grew more cautious about attributing human behavior to instinctive tendencies, there were those who still supposed that it was "natural" to look with fear and suspicion upon any who were different from us. Thus, Professor F. H. Giddings held that race prejudice originated as a sort of secondary or incidental manifestation of what he called "consciousness of kind." Things which are familiar to us, he thought, are congenial and comfortable, while those that are strange provoke in us reactions of hostility and fear. Park and Burgess supposed that it was based on "fear of the unfamiliar and uncomprehended,"[17] and Reuter and Hart attributed it to "the universal fear of things new and strange."[18]

These explanations, however, are subject to grave doubt. It is now apparent that we *acquire* all our attitudes, including our prejudices toward racial and ethnic groups. There are several lines of evidence pointing to the fact that our prejudices are not innate. In the first place, there is the evidence from history. White Europeans, prior to modern times, had no antipathy for mongoloid features or a black skin. The records testify to the frequency of marriages between whites and Negroes in Portugal, between whites and Indians in the New World, and even between whites and Negroes in Virginia, before slavery became the established form. In the second place, it is significant that racial prejudice manifests itself thus unevenly and inconsistently throughout the world. Finally, there are numerous studies of the prejudices of children which indicate clearly how we acquire our attitudes and how they grow and diffuse.[19] It is apparent from numerous studies that, in our society at least, children acquire their prejudices toward racial and ethnic groups at a tender age — usually before they enter the first grade, and often still earlier. At first these feelings are general and vague, but with the passage of time they become differentiated and increasingly well integrated, for the reasons people give for their prejudices change with age, eventually assuming the form of conventional, acceptable rationalizations. Moreover, it is not uncommon for people to attribute a prejudice to some unique and traumatic experience; but the truth seems to be that we acquire an antipathy, not so much from contact with the particular racial or ethnic group itself, as from other persons who already have the prejudice, especially our parents.

If prejudice, then, is so artificial a phenomenon, how can we account for its wide prevalence? There has been a paucity of facts but a plethora of theories, many of them purporting to account only for some special manifestation of prejudice, such as anti-Semitism or anti-Negro feeling. Among these are:

Economic Theories

So decisive are the economic factors in the life of man that some scholars have looked to intergroup competition and exploitation for an understanding of race prejudice. O. C. Cox, one of the proponents of this idea, says:

[17] R. E. Park and E. W. Burgess, *Introduction to the Science of Sociology*, p. 578.
[18] E. B. Reuter and C. W. Hart, *Introduction to Sociology*, p. 263.
[19] Cf. Horowitz, *op. cit.*, pp. 159–184; and Allport, *op. cit.*, pp. 297ff.

Race prejudice is a social attitude propagated among the public by an exploiting class for the purpose of stigmatizing some group as inferior so that the exploitation of either the group itself or its resources may be justified.[20]

It is natural, according to this theory, for us to develop feelings of antipathy for our rivals, for those who threaten our economic well being or our social position. We are reluctant to welcome new competitors in the struggle for the things we want; instead we seek to exclude, eliminate, or cripple those who would deprive us of our special privileges or force us to share with them our economic goods. Klineberg, who recognizes that "the economic motive may not be the only one," nevertheless believes that "prejudice exists because something is to be gained by it," and that the gain "which emerges most clearly and unmistakably is the economic."[21] Carey McWilliams has applied this theory to the Jews and the Japanese-Americans.[22] Prejudice against the latter, he thinks, is primarily a result of agitation by vested interests, and anti-Semitism he regards as "a mask for privilege."

There is much to be said for these economic theories. Tolerance has often turned to intolerance when the members of an ethnic group have begun to encroach upon the business of others. The Chinese in California were held in high esteem as long as they confined themselves to occupations whites had no desire to follow. Violent antipathy arose, however, as soon as they presented themselves as competitors; but it subsided again when the Chinese withdrew into their Chinatowns and confined their economic activities to "hand laundries," "curio shops," and "Oriental restaurants." The same thing occurred in Hawaii with both the Chinese and the Japanese. Here in the United States the intensity of the feeling toward immigrants has been closely related to economic conditions, and there are reasons for believing that racial prejudice is stimulated in periods of depression and economic unrest.

The theory, however, fails to reckon with many phenomena associated with prejudice. It does not account for the fact that antipathies fall so neatly and perfectly within racial and ethnic lines. Why is there greater hostility toward Japanese competitors than Scottish competitors? Why is there prejudice for a group whose numbers are so small as to present no economic threat at all? Anti-Negro and anti-Semitic feeling runs high in many an American community in which these groups are represented, if at all, by only a few members. The intensity of prejudice is not perfectly correlated with the size and strength of the minority group. Nor does the theory explain the fact that Quakers, Mormons, and other groups have, from time to time, been the objects of hostility, and certainly not for economic reasons. Furthermore, Myrdal contends that

20 Op. cit., p. 216. See also, by the same author, Caste, Class, and Race: A Study in Social Dynamics.

21 O. Klineberg, Social Psychology, pp. 391–392.

22 Prejudice. Japanese-Americans: Symbol of Racial Intolerance and A Mask for Privilege: Anti-Semitism in America. Cf. W. J. Cahnman, "Socio-economic Causes of Anti-Semitism," Social Problems, Vol. 5, No. 1, July 1957, p. 27.

it is the economic hopes and aspirations of the Negro which meet with the least opposition from the dominant whites. The fact is that people cherish a great many values, economic and otherwise, and they will undertake to defend them and will develop antipathies for individuals and groups who threaten them or who are suspected of so doing.

Symbolic Theories

There have been many theories, some utterly fantastic, which hold that our prejudices arise from the fact that we see in certain racial and ethnic groups a symbol of that which we hate, fear, or envy. Whites are prejudiced against the Negro, according to this theory, because the Negro is a symbol of natural, un-inhibited sex activity; and the whites, repressed and inhibited by their Puritanical codes, are jealous and envious.[23]

For the most part, however, symbolic theories of prejudice have been offered as explanations of anti-Semitism. The Jew, according to some, is the symbol of urbanism, a phenomenon which the predominantly rural Gentiles fear, distrust, and envy. Lewis Browne says, "The hostility between Jew and non-Jew . . . is essentially but an aggravated phase of the universal hostility between the towns-man and the rustic";[24] and Rose says, "Jews are hated today . . . primarily because they serve as a symbol of city life."[25] It is the impersonality, the pushi-ness, the sharpness of the city which arouse the hatred of the rustic (whatever be his place of residence). At the same time the haters of urbanism recognize the city as a necessity, and even admire and envy its many attractions. Torn thus between admiration and hatred, between fear and fancy, the Gentiles solve their dilemma by directing their hostility, not upon the city, but upon the Jews. For the Jews are indeed an urban people *par excellence*. In many minds "New York" and "Jew" are virtually synonymous. Long ago the Jews identified them-selves with cities, and they have succeeded in making a successful adjustment to urban conditions. Hence they serve as a perfect and ready symbol for that which disturbs those whose traditions and habits are of a rural character.

Others have attempted to account for anti-Semitism along similar lines.[26] Maurice Samuel was the first of many to assert that prejudice against the Jews is basically hatred of Christ. Bigots, according to this view, actually hate Jesus and the ideals for which he stood — peace, brotherhood, equality, pacifism, char-ity. Many of them, however, are professing Christians, and the mores prevent their speaking their minds, or even admitting to themselves their honest feelings. Instead, they vent their hatred on the Jews, who, because they gave Christ to the world, serve as a symbol for the Christ whom the bigots hate.[27] Other theories

[23] Cf. Arnold and Caroline Rose, *America Divided*, pp. 290–291.
[24] *How Odd of God*, p. 223.
[25] A. Rose, "Anti-Semitism's Roots in City-Hatred," *Commentary*, Vol. 6, No. 4, October 1948, p. 376.
[26] For a summary of these, see A. and C. Rose, *op. cit.*, pp. 285–292.
[27] *The Great Hatred*, *passim*, and especially Ch. 11.

of this type have seen in the Jews the symbol of internationalism, therefore hated by the chauvinists; or they serve as the symbol of capitalism, or of communism, or of "successful nonconformity," and become, in turn, the enemies of the communists, the capitalists, or those in authority.[28]

Psychological Theories

There have been a number of theories, several of them enjoying wide popularity, wherein racial prejudice is regarded as satisfying some psychic need of the individual, or as compensating for some defect in the personality. Prominent among these has been the "scapegoat" theory. Human beings, so it seems, have always been reluctant to blame themselves for their troubles, woes, and shortcomings. Instead, they look elsewhere for some object, some animal, some "force," or some evil spirit upon which they gladly lay the blame. Many primitive peoples have made a formal ceremony of thus "passing the buck."[29] The ancient Hebrews made it an annual event to load all of their sins on a goat, which they promptly chased into the wilderness,[30] and which has come to be known as the "scapegoat," or the goat allowed to escape. The term has come to be applied to any person or group forced to bear the blame for others.

Many minority groups have served as scapegoats. The Romans used to blame the Christians for all the troubles of the Empire, including the burning of their city. Said Tertullian, "If the Tiber rose to the walls of the city, if the inundation of the Nile failed to give the fields enough water, if the heavens did not send rain, if an earthquake occurred, if famine threatened, if pestilence raged, the cry resounded, 'Throw the Christians to the lions!'" Centuries later the English pounced upon a colony of French Huguenots living in their midst, and accused them of lowering the standard of living, depriving them of jobs, and reducing their wages. Italians, Norwegians, Irish, Japanese, Jews, and innumerable others have, at one time or another, been forced to play the unwilling role of the scapegoat. So have the Catholics, Protestants, atheists, deists, Quakers, and Baptists.

Racial and ethnic groups have been admirably suited for the role, some much better than others. According to one analysis,[31] a group, to be an acceptable scapegoat, ought to have the following characteristics. First, it should have distinguishing, salient features, and be "highly visible." Physical traits such as skin color or shape of nose best meet this demand, although distinctive names, gestures, language, food habits, or religious customs may serve instead. Second, it should not be too strong, nor be in too good a position to retaliate or to answer back. Preferably, a scapegoat is a safe goat, to use the words of Carey McWilliams. Third, it should be readily accessible, even concentrated in one

28 Cf. A. and C. Rose, op. cit., pp. 286ff.
29 For numerous illustrations, see J. G. Frazer, The Golden Bough, Vol. 2, pp. 182ff; W. G. Sumner and A. G. Keller, The Science of Society, Vol. 2, p. 1212.
30 Leviticus 16:5–22.
31 G. W. Allport, ABC's of Scapegoating, pp. 42–43.

Parental Education and Prejudice

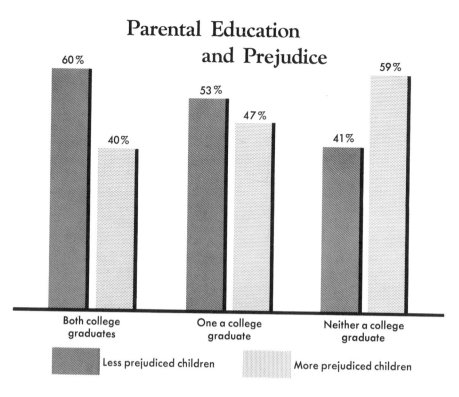

60%

53%

47%

40%

59%

41%

| Both college graduates | One a college graduate | Neither a college graduate |

Less prejudiced children   More prejudiced children

A study of 437 undergraduate students at Dartmouth, Harvard, and Radcliffe Colleges indicates that parents exert the earliest and probably strongest influence on the development of prejudice. (See Gordon W. Allport and B. M. Kramer, "Some Roots of Prejudice," The Journal of Psychology, Vol. 22, July 1946.)

locality, for a remote scapegoat would hardly serve the purpose. Fourth, it is well for the victim to have been a previous object of blame, and that there be a certain latent hostility against him. And, fifth, it should personify some idea which is disliked.

Some groups possess these characteristics in greater degree than others. The American Negro, it would seem, is well suited for the role. But, as Zawadski has pointed out,[32] the Negro's social and economic position has been so low that it is hardly plausible to offer him as a source of our troubles. The Jew is a better choice, for he is strong enough to be a convincing foe, yet not too strong to be formidable. While he is not nearly so "visible" as people generally suppose, visibility can be manufactured, and he has frequently been required to mark himself in some conspicuous manner, with peculiar garments or a badge, or by the adoption of distinctive names. The scapegoat theory, then, serves better as an explanation of anti-Semitism than it does for other manifestations of racial and ethnic prejudice.

[32] B. Zawadski, "Limitations of the Scapegoat Theory of Prejudice," *Journal of Abnormal and Social Psychology*, Vol. 43, No. 2, April 1948, pp. 127–141.

Another psychological theory of prejudice is that of frustration-aggression.[33] According to this theory, hostility for a racial group is a socially approved channel for the expression of the aggressive tendencies people acquire as a consequence of their being frustrated. All of us, simply in the process of growing up in a society, are subject to considerable inhibition and restraint, and these frustrations call for some outlet. There are many things, for instance, which a child wishes but is not permitted to do, and the resulting frustrations call into action an aggressive tendency. He seeks some legitimate object toward which his aggressiveness and hostility may be directed. Dollard suggests that much of this irrational, latent hostility may be drained off when society presents an object, such as the Negro, whom one may abuse and detest with a clear conscience. The frustrated individual, in other words, is given social permission to hate the members of a minority group. Thus, the poor white, kept down by the wealthy landowner or the industrialist, or even by his poor physical environment, finds relief from his frustrations through his anti-Negro prejudice. Or the Germans, frustrated by the instability of the government, the failure of their nationalist ambitions, and a runaway inflation, gave vent to their aggressive feelings in their persecution of the Jews. For that matter, any incompetent, unsuccessful, maladjusted person, whether he be a member of the dominant or the subordinate group, may find in racial prejudice a counterweight to his own failure and futility. This theory, however, fails to explain why one group rather than another is selected as the object of discrimination, and it fails to recognize that frustration need not manifest itself in aggression, and, especially, in aggression toward a minority group. The theory does, however, offer some explanation of the fact that prejudice and discrimination vary greatly in their intensity from one individual to another.

Still another psychological theory finds in race prejudice a refuge for the sick mind or a haven for the defective personality. As Ben Hecht put it:

> Prejudice is our method of transferring our own sickness to others. It is our ruse for disliking others rather than ourselves. We find absolution in our prejudices. We find also in them an enemy made to order rather than inimical forces out of our control. . . . Prejudice is a raft onto which the shipwrecked mind clambers and paddles to safety.[34]

Other investigators, without going so far as to say that prejudice is indicative of either psychosis or neurosis, nevertheless do maintain that it is a function of the personality. The intolerant individual, they say, does have a definite personality structure, and prejudice is a manifestation of, say, fear, and particularly fear for one's status. Hartley,[35] for example, believes that the relatively tolerant personality is likely to exhibit some combination of the following:

---

[33] See especially J. Dollard, *Caste and Class in a Southern Town*, pp. 474–480; J. Dollard et al., *Frustration and Aggression*, pp. 151–156.

[34] *A Guide for the Bedevilled*, p. 31.

[35] E. Hartley, *Problems in Prejudice*, pp. 62–63. Cf., also, R. M. Williams, Jr., *op. cit.*, pp. 78–114.

. . . a strong desire for personal autonomy associated with a lack of need for dominance, a strong need for friendliness, along with a personal seclusiveness, fear of competition, a tendency to placate others along with lack of general conformity to the mores. He is likely to be fairly serious, to be interested in current events, to have ideas about bettering society, to be a member of a political group and to have great need for personal achievement in the vocational area. He is likely to be an accepting personality, disliking violence, able to appreciate the contributions of others, conscious of feeling that people tend to be more or less alike and adopting a nurturant rather than a dominant attitude toward those younger than he. He is conscious of conflicts concerning loyalties and duties, he thinks very seriously about moral questions. His interests center about what commonly are called the social studies, reading and journalism. Although personally seclusive, he has a great need to be socially useful.

The relatively intolerant personality, Hartley finds, might be expected to combine the following characteristics in varying degrees:

. . . unwillingness to accept responsibility, acceptance of conventional mores, a rejection of "serious" groups, rejection of political interests and desire for groups formed for purely social purposes, absorption with pleasure activities, a conscious conflict between play and work, emotionality rather than rationality, extreme egocentrism, interest in physical activity, the body, health. He is likely to dislike agitators, radicals, pessimists. He is relatively uncreative, apparently unable to deal with anxieties except by fleeing from them. Often his physical activity has in it a compulsive component; it may be that this compulsion to be on the move, that is, constantly occupied with sports, motoring, travel, etc., serves for him the same function that studies and activities with social significance serve in the case of the individual with high tolerance. Both the tolerant and the intolerant individuals have anxieties, but there seems to be a distinct difference in the way in which they work them out.

A considerable body of subsequent research has given support to Hartley's theory that race prejudice, far from being an isolated and independent attitude, is in fact a symptom or a function of a basic personality structure. As Allport puts it: "Prejudice is more than an incident in many lives; it is often lock-stitched into the very fabric of personality."[36] The authors of *The Authoritarian Personality*[37] report that highly prejudiced persons are characterized by a rigidity of outlook, suggestibility, gullibility, dislike for ambiguity, anti-scientific and pseudo-scientific attitudes, and unrealistic ideas as to how to achieve their goals. Allport finds that the following are the "earmarks of a personality in whom prejudice is functionally important":

1. *Ambivalence toward parents.* The prejudiced person often insists that he likes his parents, but underneath there is jealousy, suspicion and hostility, and vigorous protest. A relationship of power, rather than of love, prevails.

[36] *The Nature of Prejudice*, p. 408.
[37] T. W. Adorno, Else Frenkel-Brunswik, D. J. Levinson, & R. N. Sanford, *The Authoritarian Personality.*

2. *Moralism.* Prejudiced personalities reflect the anxiety which haunts them by adopting a rigidity with respect to morals. They tend to place great stress upon cleanliness, good manners, and social conventions. Theirs is not a true moralism, which is more relaxed and integral, but instead is tense, compulsive, and projective.

3. *Dichotomization.* Prejudiced persons reject the sentiment expressed in this familiar bit of doggerel:

> There is so much good in the worst of us,
> And so much bad in the best of us,
> That it scarcely behooves any of us
> To talk about the rest of us.

On the contrary they tend to believe that there are two kinds of people, the good and the bad; a right way and a wrong way; the weak and the strong; the pure and the impure. Things are black or white — not varying shades of gray.

4. *Need for definiteness.* The prejudiced person is "intolerant of ambiguity." He clings to old and tried solutions of problems. He is reluctant to say, "I don't know." He always has an opinion when he is asked for one. He "knows all the answers." He demands a clear-cut structure for his world.

5. *Externalization.* The prejudiced person believes that things happen *to* him — they are not caused *by* him. He does not feel that he has very much control over his destiny. It is not one's actions or shortcomings that bring unhappy and undesired consequences, but rather fate, or the position of the stars, or some uncontrolled external agency.

6. *Institutionalization.* Prejudiced people are more devoted to institutions than are the unprejudiced. They are more "patriotic." They care more than their tolerant brothers for their fraternities and sororities. They manifest greater devotion to their lodges, schools, clubs, churches. Institutional membership helps them satisfy their need and hunger for safety and security.

7. *Authoritarianism.* The prejudiced person has no great fondness for individualism, freedom, democracy, indefiniteness, disorderliness, and social change. Instead he prefers authority, definite power arrangements, discipline, strong leaders, and an orderly society.

The tolerant person is just the opposite of all this. In the literature of social psychology dealing with this subject he is described as having come from a home where he was loved and accepted, where punishment was neither harsh nor capricious, where good companionship and wholesome fun were regarded as more important than correct manners and proper behavior. He does not bifurcate his world into the wholly proper and the wholly improper. His mind is flexible; he feels secure and self-sufficient; he does not feel that he must always blame others when something goes wrong. He is liberal in his political views, and feels a genuine sympathy for the underdog. The tolerant person has a high degree of self-insight, and is aware of his own capabilities and shortcomings. He has a sense of humor; and, since he is able to laugh at himself, he is less inclined to feel that he is superior to others.

These theories are no doubt flattering to those who regard themselves as free from prejudice and bias. It is comforting to be told that one is neither psychotic nor neurotic, but that one is, instead, well-balanced, urbane, self-sufficient, altruistic, democratic, sympathetic, intelligent, and high-minded. The evidence upon which the theory rests, however, is admittedly scanty. The samples studied have been small, and the individuals tested have themselves been extreme types. Hartley himself warns that his suggestions are "by no means conclusive," and that they are offered "solely as hypotheses." Allport recognizes various methodological weaknesses in the research to date, but insists that "we cannot possibly explain away the trends reported." Simpson and Yinger say: "One must be careful not to assume too quickly that a certain tendency — rigidity of mind, for example — that is correlated with prejudice necessarily causes that prejudice. . . . The sequence may be the other way around. . . . It is more likely that both are related to more basic factors."[38] There are those, too, who maintain that racial and ethnic prejudice is part and parcel of our American culture pattern, and that it is the rebellious individuals, the nonconformists, who tend to be more tolerant, while those who are normal, accepted, and well-adjusted tend to conform to, and abide by, the standards and conventions of their society, which include the norms of prejudice and discrimination.

The Social Norm Theory

Some scholars have insisted that antipathy for members of the out-group is neither an instinctive feeling nor a manifestation of a disturbed personality, but is, instead, a natural, normal development of group living. In a heterogeneous, multi-group society such as ours, it is inevitable that such prejudices be numerous and that their intensity cover a wide range. According to Fairchild:

> Is there any self-conscious people on earth that does not consider itself superior to its neighbors, or at least prefer its own character and ways to those of other people? Is there any people that does not have at least one foreign group upon whom it looks down with contempt, derision, and hatred? . . . From time immemorial it has been inherent in the very nature of human group identification that the members of any particular group should feel more warmly attracted to other members of their own group than to outsiders. It is the very essence of human association that persons who live together continuously in more or less intimate bonds of society should be characterized by many similarities of thought, feeling, and action, and moreover that they should regard their own ways as right and good and preferable to those of strangers. Moreover, if the members of a particular group also possess distinctive observable physical traits of skin, hair, eyes, or other features, it is also in the established order of things that these particular endowments should be regarded as correct, admirable, and beautiful. . . . Feelings of loyalty, devotion, and approbation, along with a comfortable sense of "belonging," are characteristic of practically everyone's sentiments toward the "in-groups" of which he is a member. . . . For the aggregate of these sentiments

[38] *Op. cit.*, p. 91.

there is probably no better comprehensive word than "sympathy." . . . The obverse is "antipathy," and this is the typical attitude toward the "out-group" and its members. . . . All of these things have been accepted without question from time immemorial, and it has been ordinarily taken as a matter of course that one's attitude toward the stranger should be one of dislike, suspicion, and hostility.[39]

Attitudes of antipathy for the out-group, then, are widely prevalent, and they represent the standard, normal, accepted form of behavior in many societies. It is natural and conventional under such conditions to think of people in terms of their racial or ethnic background, and on that basis to assign value to them and to differentiate among them. The young child, of course, begins life without these prejudices, just as he begins without an understanding of language and without the various other skills, understandings, and attitudes in his cultural environment. The process by which he acquires his prejudices is a subtle and gradual one. He is largely unaware of it; and when he reaches adulthood and finds that he has antipathetic feelings toward Negroes, whites, Jews, Gentiles, Irish, Italians, or Mexicans, he can seldom identify the forces and influences which made him the person he is. To be sure, individuals in any society vary in the extent to which they adopt the prevailing prejudices, and herein lies something of a mystery. The same thing holds, however, for the other aspects of a culture, which is entirely too broad and complex a phenomenon for anyone to embrace the whole of it. Individuals vary, not only in the intensity of their prejudices, but in the extent to which they adopt, understand, and adhere to all the other elements of their culture — language, food habits, laws, patterns of recreation, values, and modes of dress, to mention only a few.

Other Theories

Still other theories of prejudice have been proposed. It has frequently been attributed to ignorance, or to a lack of intelligence, or to the tendency of people to generalize about a whole group on the basis of an unpleasant experience with a single member of that group. Others have insisted that the minorities do actually possess those obnoxious characteristics of which they are accused, for which they are disliked, and of which the prevailing stereotypes are composed. As Fairchild says:

> No one can be expected to love his brother just because he is ordered to, and by the same token no one can be expected to love his brother if the brother is not lovable. The obligation to control group antipathy is matched by the duty of the object of that antipathy to remove any extraneous causes and to make himself as truly lovable as is consistent with his own legitimate group traits and sentiments.[40]

[39] H. P. Fairchild, *Race and Nationality*, pp. 4–6.
[40] *Ibid.*, p. 87. See also G. B. Johnson, "The Stereotype of the American Negro," in O. Klineberg (Ed.), *Characteristics of the American Negro*, pp. 3–22. See Allport, *The Nature of Prejudice*, pp. 87ff., for a discussion of the "Well-Deserved Reputation" theory of prejudice.

Others have suggested that racial antipathy thrives simply because conflict and antagonism are more exciting than friendliness and good will, just as war is more thrilling than peace, and malicious gossip more eagerly devoured than panegyrics. Still others have seen in race prejudice simply a fascist technique for weakening, and ultimately destroying, a nation.

Obviously there has been no dearth of theories to account for race prejudice. The fact is, however, that sociologists long ago abandoned their quest for the ultimate *origins* of social phenomena, when they discovered how hopeless and futile that quest proved to be. Moreover, social phenomena have a way of undergoing so drastic a change over the course of time that, even though we could learn how something originated, that information might contribute very little to an understanding of its present form and meaning. Racial and ethnic prejudice would be no exception to such a process. Furthermore, prejudice may very well be the product of a multiplicity of factors, and not of any single one.

Some sociologists have recognized the fact that prejudice is a complex phenomenon, and have wisely eschewed simple explanations of it. Frazier, for example, holds that "prejudice against another race is determined by the culture of one's group . . . is accentuated by competition . . . and affected by personal factors . . . the two most important being . . . the feeling of insecurity and frustrations."[41] MacIver and Page have presented an equally comprehensive interpretation.[42] Prejudice, as they see it, is a result of social indoctrination; it varies enormously from group to group, from time to time, and from person to person; it is rooted in the individual's failure to achieve a satisfactory integration in the group; its persistence is partly due to ignorance and irrationality; economic advantages for the dominant group, however, are important factors in its perpetuation; socio-psychological gains are no less important in its persistence; and minorities do perform the much-needed scapegoat function.

One is forced to conclude that race prejudice is a complex phenomenon, not to be explained by any single factor. Multiple causation is obviously at work. Most, if not all, of the theories discussed above contain at least an element of truth. Herman Melville once said, "It is vain to popularize profundities, and all truth is profound." Whether or not that observation is generally acceptable, it certainly applies to the problem of race prejudice.

Rationalizations

Whatever be the *real* reasons for racial antipathy and discrimination, they are seldom admitted by the guilty parties even when they are themselves aware of these reasons. Instead, plausible and socially acceptable explanations are offered for the prejudices and discriminatory practices which prevail in all biracial and multi-racial societies the world over.

[41] Frazier, *op. cit.*, p. 670.
[42] R. M. MacIver and C. H. Page, *Society: An Introductory Analysis*, pp. 407–416.

It is not only the dominant groups that rationalize their prejudices or seek to justify their exploitation of others. Subordinate peoples, too, feel the need for a satisfying explanation of their minority status, and they often succeed in developing rationalizations which enable them to bear the burden of discrimination, and to retain a measure of pride, hope, and self-respect. Observers have often commented upon the famous cheerfulness of the Bantus of South Africa, and their irrepressible humor in the face of trying circumstances, in spite of the fact that they live under incredible conditions of exploitation and discrimination. The explanation, says Cope,[43] lies in the fact that when the Bantus were finally defeated by force of arms, they looked upon their subjection not as evidence of their inferiority but as a natural disaster. It was interpreted as the work of a dark, mysterious, superior, magical power. It was, like a famine or a cattle disease, something entirely beyond their control, and for which they themselves were not responsible. Accordingly, they were not depressed, but proceeded to make the best of the situation. When they were abused by their white masters, forced to work against their will, taxed, whipped, and imprisoned, they regarded these as misfortunes to be borne rather than as injustices to be resented. Rationalizations, however, are never permanent. The Bantus have subsequently learned from the missionaries the concepts of justice and equality, and they have ceased to be the submissive people they formerly were. They have grown surly and bitter, where they were once loyal and cheerful. They are beginning to cherish the hope of liberation, to appreciate their own strength, and to place their reliance, no longer upon magic, but upon guns, riots, and political and physical force.

[43] R. K. Cope, "African Magic and White Science," *The Nation*, Vol. 169, No. 16, October 15, 1949, pp. 369–370.

Women pickets at an integrated school in New Orleans jeer a white student who had participated in sit-in demonstrations with Negroes.

Others, too, have taken refuge in the comfortable thought that racial domination and subordination are "natural," or "inevitable," or even non-existent. Thus Toynbee maintains that the very word "native" is "not a scientific term but an instrument of action," a convenient device which enables us in Western civilization to look indiscriminately upon the rest of the world. The word, he says, "is like a piece of smoked glass which modern Western observers hold in front of their eyes when they look abroad upon the world, in order that the gratifying spectacle of a 'Westernized' surface may not be disturbed by any perception of the native fires which are still blazing underneath."[44]

White Americans, and particularly Southerners, have sought either to deny the reality of the Negro's plight or to regard it as natural and inevitable. The following is but one example:

> The South has no problem in connection with its race relations. The South has a race situation but no race problem. . . . The South has been accused of being unjust to the Negro and discriminating against him whereas the rest of the country was not doing so. Why, then, haven't the Negroes during the past eighty years left that part of the country where they have been so badly treated and gone to those other parts of the country where they have received "equal" terms? . . . How does the South treat the Negro? In the only way under natural laws that they can be treated — by segregation. . . . Segregation is not discrimination, a fact that many people are prone to overlook. Segregation is best for both peoples. It permits the development of pride of race, without which no people can hope to progress.[45]

Most people, however, have not closed their eyes to the fact of discrimination, but have sought to justify it in some such terms as the following:

> "This is a white man's country."
> "What little they have, they have got it from the whites."
> "Actually, they live on the white people."
> "The whites pay all the taxes."
> "They couldn't sustain themselves a day if we gave them up."
> "Economic inequality has to be maintained, for it is the barrier against social equality."
> "If you gave the Negro more wages, he would stop working."
> "They are satisfied with very little."

Rationalizations of racial prejudice and discrimination by dominant groups, wherever encountered and whatever the terms in which they are expressed, invariably fall into four categories: (1) Self-defense. The dominant group maintains that its attitudes and policies are necessary if it is to defend itself, its values, its status, and its way of life. (2) Subordination and superordination are universal, natural, inevitable, normal phenomena. They have been regarded as sacred and divinely instituted. (3) The fault lies with the minority group itself,

[44] A. J. Toynbee, *A Study of History*, Vol. 1, pp. 151–153.
[45] T. Sensing, "The South Has No Race Problem," *Manufacturers' Record*, July 1944.

for it is either innately and biologically inferior, or it is addicted to immoral, filthy, dishonest, treacherous habits. (4) Prejudice and discrimination, or what appears to be so, are in reality but a manifestation of worthy, unselfish, altruistic motives. Differential treatment is in the best interest of the minority itself.

These rationalizations have been applied in one way or another to all minorities. Jews, Negroes, Mexicans, Italians, Greeks, Irish, and others have felt their force. In fact, Myrdal has pointed out that, in a society where adult males enjoy a privileged status, these same justifications are offered for the inferior status of women and children.[46] LaPiere has reported on a situation in Fresno County, California, where a colony of first- and second-generation Armenians has settled.[47] Some of the non-Armenians, he says, will go so far as to insist that the only cure for the "Armenian problem" would be the "importation of a few Turkish butchers"; but most of them say that the Armenian would be all right "if he would only stay in his place." LaPiere found that the reasons given by the non-Armenians for their antipathy revealed three distinct stereotypes: (1) They are dishonest, deceitful liars. The manager of the Merchants' Association said, "I can safely say, after many years of credit work, that the Armenians are, as a race, the worst we have to deal with." (2) They are parasitic; they do not contribute their fair share to community life and welfare. (3) They have a low moral code; they are "always getting into trouble with the law." LaPiere attempted to determine the truth of these accusations, and could find no support for them. Far from being dishonest, he found that the records of the Merchants' Association revealed that the credit standing of the Armenians was "remarkable." A study of admissions to the County Hospital and of the requests at the Welfare Bureau proved that the Armenians' demands for charity were very small, considering their ratio in the general population. As for their being a lawless group, LaPiere's analysis of the police records showed Armenians in only 1.5 per cent of the cases, yet they make up 6 per cent of the population.

Not infrequently the very people who voice these rationalizations come to doubt their validity. Usually, however, a dominant group will cast about for newer and better rationalizations when those to which they have adhered begin to give way under attack. Thus when the older theological and Biblical justifications Europeans offered for their exploitation of Negroes, Indians, and others began to crumble, they eagerly embraced the newer doctrine of evolution, with its emphasis upon the universality of struggle, and the "survival of the fit." When this, in turn, lost its force, the results of intelligence tests were offered as justification for discrimination and segregation. Even so, doubts continually arise in the minds of those who seek to justify their exploitation of their fellow man. This, as Myrdal maintains, constitutes the white man's "dilemma," for he believes only half-heartedly in the ground upon which he takes his stand. Thus the race problem becomes, in the last analysis, a moral problem, a conflict of values, and a burden upon the conscience.

[46] G. Myrdal, *An American Dilemma*, Vol. 2, Appendix 5, pp. 1073–1078.
[47] R. T. LaPiere, "Type-Rationalizations of Group Antipathy," *Social Forces*, Vol. 15, No. 2, December 1936, pp. 232–237.

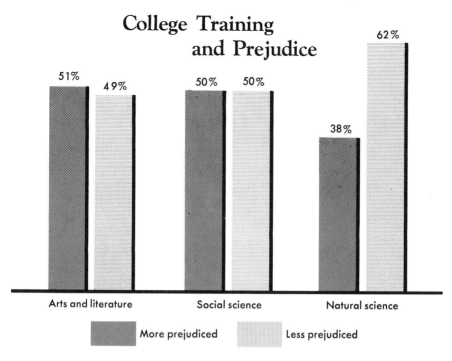

College Training and Prejudice

51%   49%   50%   50%   38%   62%

Arts and literature   Social science   Natural science

More prejudiced   Less prejudiced

A study of 437 undergraduate students at Dartmouth, Harvard, and Radcliffe Colleges indicates that students specializing in the natural sciences tend to be more free from prejudice than are students in social sciences and the humanities. (See Gordon W. Allport and B. M. Kramer, "Some Roots of Prejudice," The Journal of Psychology, *Vol. 22, July 1946.)*

The Reduction of Prejudice

Recent years have seen a growing concern, in the United States at least, with problems of race prejudice. Nor is it only the victims of prejudice — Jews, Negroes, and Japanese-Americans, for instance — who have spearheaded the movement to reduce, control, and perhaps eliminate it. Many white, native-born Protestants have been no less desirous than their less fortunate fellows to pull its fangs. They have grown acutely aware of the fact that prejudice and discrimination are incompatible with certain values they hold in highest esteem — democracy, justice, freedom, equality of opportunity, sacredness of human life, dignity of man, Christianity, and good sportsmanship. They have learned, too, that the strength of a nation lies as much in the unity and loyalty of its citizens as it does in armaments. We have realized that our domestic minority policies have world-wide reactions, that lynchings and riots cost heavily in good will, and those we sorely need as friends and allies scrutinize closely our treatment of our colored citizens.

There has arisen, accordingly, a multitude of organizations and movements bent upon reducing the racial and ethnic tensions which threaten our national welfare and make a mockery of our democratic Christian professions. Some of these are official commissions, appointed by governors or mayors, such as New Jersey's Good Will Commission, the Mayor's Interracial Committee of Detroit, and Cleveland's Post-War Planning Commission; others are the creations of churches, labor unions, educators, philanthropic foundations, or youth groups.

Not all these organizations, to be sure, are specifically concerned with the reduction of prejudice. Some direct their attack at discrimination, in the belief that it is more important to eliminate injustice than to undertake the dubious and desultory task of changing people's attitudes. Others are intent upon helping the members of minority groups meet the various practical problems which confront them day by day. And still others are concerned with the reduction of "tensions," the prevention of riots, lynchings, conflict, hostilities, and bloodshed. The National Urban League, for instance, has always been primarily interested in helping Negroes obtain better housing, employment, and social services, but it seeks also to influence public opinion. The truth of the matter is that every organization operating in the field of race relations is concerned with the reduction of prejudice, whether or not that is its primary or stipulated purpose.

At the same time there are skeptics who doubt that racial prejudice can be reduced, at least by any of the techniques currently employed; and there have always been bigots who insist that what we need is not less, but more racial prejudice. These latter have organized, too. The United States has had its full quota of societies for the promotion of intolerance, ethnocentrism, and discrimination — Native American Party, "Know Nothings," American Protective Association, Ku Klux Klan, America First Party, Mason-Dixon Society, Silver Shirts, Black Legion, Society of Forward Men, United Sons of America, Gentile Cooperative Association, Anglo-Saxon Federation, and innumerable others.[48] Seldom have these organizations been regarded as innocuous or ineffective, or accused of working at cross-purposes with one another.

It is not so, however, with the organizations interested in the promotion of tolerance. They differ widely in the goals they seek, the techniques they employ, the philosophy which motivates them, the speed at which they hope to move, the segments of the population toward which their efforts are directed, and the effectiveness of their programs. Some are concerned with education in the schools, some with adult education, some engage in serious research, some promote cultural and recreational activities, some act through the courts to secure legal redress, some are interested chiefly in promoting legislation, and some are engaged in action programs in their local communities. A certain degree of diversity is doubtless necessary and good, yet the most ardent proponents of tolerance deplore overlapping organizations and wasted effort.

In the last analysis, the theory of prejudice one adopts will determine his strategy in attacking it. Rose, as we saw earlier, believes that anti-Semitism stems from the fact that Jews are a symbol of urbanism, which phenomenon the Gentiles regard with a mixture of fear and envy. He maintains, therefore, that the cure for anti-Semitism lies, first, in dissociating Jews from urban life

[48] G. Myers, *History of Bigotry in the United States*; J. R. Carlson, *Under Cover*, and *The Plotters*.

in the minds of Gentiles, and, second, in developing among the Gentiles a less anti-urban attitude. On the other hand, Carey McWilliams, who places major emphasis upon the economic bases of prejudice, and who regards anti-Semitism as "a mask for privilege," recommends the inauguration of programs aimed at reducing the social, psychic, and economic gains which accrue from hostility toward the Jews, plus long-range efforts to reinforce the legitimacy and the binding effect of the American creed as the standard of our society. Cox maintains race prejudice is a product of our economic system, so deeply embedded that it can be eliminated only by a major alteration of the system:

> It is probable that without capitalism . . . the world might never have experienced race prejudice. Indeed, we should expect that under another form of economic organization, say socialism, the relationship between whites and people of color would be significantly modified.[49]

Contact and Acquaintance Programs

There are many who believe that people are inclined to be suspicious of, and prejudiced against, that which is strange and unfamiliar to them, that antipathy is increased by isolation and segregation, and that "contact brings friendliness." We find, accordingly, that many efforts are made to bring together the members of different groups, in the belief that tolerance and sympathy will result. Interracial contacts and cooperation have been established in housing projects, in camps and other recreational activities, in various work situations, in interracial churches, in student organizations, and on forums, councils, and committees. In Chicago the device has been employed of bringing together neighbors of various ethnic stocks for the purpose of improving the neighborhood in which they live. It is reported that when they unite thus in a common activity, tolerance and understanding begin to supplant suspicion and antipathy. The proponents of intercultural education in the schools maintain that imparting information is not enough to counteract prejudice, and that the students must make field trips into the neighborhoods where minorities live, must meet and talk with them, and participate with them in festivals and community projects.[50]

The Informational Approach

By and large, however, most organizations concerned with the reduction of prejudice seem to operate on the same assumption that antipathy arises from ignorance, that stereotypes are false, that hostility is unnatural and unrealistic, and that prejudice will disappear if people are only given the facts (skillfully presented, to be sure). The underlying philosophy was expressed by Ambrose Bierce, who said, "Prejudice is a vagrant opinion without visible means of support." The task, then, is to make this point crystal clear, to report the facts

---

[49] O. C. Cox, *Caste, Class and Race*, p. 345.

[50] For a description and evaluation of the numerous types of contact and acquaintance programs, see Allport, *The Nature of Prejudice*, pp. 261–282, 488–491; Vander Zanden, *op. cit.*

about minorities, to correct the misinformation, to destroy the stereotypes, and to expose the rationalizations. No channel of communication has been overlooked: schools, churches, radio, stage, television, motion pictures, the press, billboards, labor unions, and service clubs. Comic strips, sermons, slogans, leaflets, pamphlets, books, lectures, conferences, and workshops are used.

Evaluation

Just how effective are these various programs in reducing prejudice is a moot point. Those who teach in intercultural education, and those who engage in the numerous other programs of exhortation, education, and propaganda are no less uncertain than are the critics and cynics. It is suspected that they reach only a limited audience of those who are already convinced. Says Watson:

> The visitor going to a strange city to learn how problems of interracial and inter-religious tension are met, is likely to be struck at first with the large number of organizations that claim to be working in some way in this field. . . . The next discovery is that at each meeting, whatever its title or auspices, many of the same faces reappear. Despite the impressive paper structure, only a handful of citizens are really active.[51]

Merton has commented as follows upon the same fact:

> Ethnic liberals are busily engaged in talking to themselves. Repeatedly, the same groups of like-minded liberals seek each other out, hold periodic meetings in which they engage in mutual exhortation and thus lend social and psychological supports to one another. But however much these unwittingly self-selected audiences may reinforce the creed among themselves, they do not thus appreciably diffuse the creed in belief or practice to groups which depart from it.
>
> More, these group soliloquies in which there is typically wholehearted agreement among fellow-liberals tend to promote another fallacy limiting effective action. This is the *fallacy of unanimity*. Continued association with like-minded individuals tends to produce the illusion that a large measure of consensus has been achieved in the community at large.[52]

There are those, moreover, who doubt that prejudices can be changed by facts and logic, however cleverly presented. Alexander insists that "prejudices . . . cannot be touched by reason, argument, logic, sympathy, religion, or threats."[53] And there are others, like Fairchild, who regard in-group and out-group feelings as natural and inescapable, but who are not without hope of curbing their more destructive manifestations. Says he:

> What the world needs today is not an unrealistic, sentimental crusade to induce people to eliminate group preferences entirely from their personality equipment, but a campaign to convince people that group feelings are designed to be kept in

---

[51] G. Watson, *Action for Unity*, p. 5.

[52] *Op. cit.*, p. 104.

[53] C. Alexander, "Antipathy and Social Behavior," *American Journal of Sociology*, Vol. 51, No. 4, January 1946, p. 292.

restraint, firmly directed, and prevented from manifesting themselves in cruel and selfish behavior, just as is equally true with the equally natural feelings of hunger, sexual desire, love for beautiful things, the passion for admiration, or any one of the other myriad impulses that motivate human behavior.[54]

Finally, there are those who insist that the best way to handle the problem of intergroup tensions is to say as little as possible about them. Brameld, who made a study of intercultural education in the public schools, found this to be "more typical of American schools than any other single policy."[55] Even members of minority groups themselves often wish that people would stop talking about them as a "problem." Not a few Negroes insist that they have been "over-studied," and that well-meaning reformers merely accentuate their difficulties.

Some research has been directed toward evaluation of these programs. It is manifestly a difficult task to determine how effective, say, is the institution of "Brotherhood Week," or a series of lectures, or a summer workshop. Are one's prejudices affected by reading a book, scanning a comic strip, participating in a folk festival, hearing a sermon, or attending an interracial gathering?

Does contact with members of a minority group make one more tolerant? There are those who believe that merely by bringing together people of different races, nationalities, and religions friendly attitudes will emerge. However, instances readily come to mind where prejudice and conflict have increased, rather than diminished, when Negroes moved into a white residential neighborhood, when Irish invaded an Italian community, when public schools became desegregated, when different racial groups met at an amusement park or on an excursion ferry. Obviously contact itself does not automatically result in a reduction of prejudice.

On the other hand, there are many instances proving that contact does help to diminish prejudice.[56] Accordingly, we must take into consideration other factors than mere contact. We must consider the frequency and duration of the contacts, whether the persons involved enjoy equality of status or not, whether they meet in a competitive or a cooperative capacity, whether their meeting is voluntary or compulsory, the backgrounds of the persons in association, and whether they meet in a political, religious, occupational, residential, recreational, or casual situation. Trying to make allowances for all these possible variables, Allport comes to the following conclusion regarding the effects of contact:

> It would be fair, then, to conclude that contact, as a situational variable, cannot always overcome the personal variable in prejudice. . . . At the same time, given a population of ordinary people, with a normal degree of prejudice, we are safe in making the following general prediction: . . .
>
> Prejudice (unless deeply rooted in the character structure of the individual) may be reduced by equal status contact between majority and minority groups in the pursuit of common goals. The effect is greatly enhanced if this contact is sanctioned by institutional supports (i.e., by law, custom or local atmosphere),

[54] Fairchild, op. cit., p. 87.
[55] T. Brameld, Minority Problems in the Public Schools, p. 161. See pp. 14, 30, et passim.
[56] G. W. Allport, The Nature of Prejudice, pp. 261ff.; R. M. Williams, op. cit., pp. 150ff.

and provided it is of a sort that leads to the perception of common interests and common humanity between members of the two groups.[57]

Doubt also prevails as to the effectiveness of formal educational programs in reducing prejudice. Here, again, no small amount of research has been done in an effort to measure the effects of classroom teaching. The results are conflicting. Some evidence indicates that the student's attitudes and prejudices are changed, and that there is a positive correlation between knowledge and tolerance: but the results of other studies do not bear this out.[58] Moreover, there are differences of opinion as to the most effective teaching methods. Hardly anyone maintains that merely imparting specific information about minority groups has any effect upon prejudice. Pedagogical methods in better repute include the use of movies, dramas, fiction, field trips, area surveys, exhibits, pageants, discussion, socio-drama, and individual conferences. Many insist that it is more effective to approach the subject indirectly through literature, geography, history, and the like, rather than directly. The evidence suggests that knowledge itself does not automatically produce tolerance and understanding, *but* there is no evidence that sound factual information makes one more prejudiced. Moreover, in the long run it is probable that scientific facts about race and about minorities do have important consequences. They gradually penetrate people's attitudes and opinions; they puncture the stereotypes, the rationalizations, and the prejudices; and they furnish the bricks and mortar for other programs.

There is even more doubt about the effectiveness of the numerous other devices in common use — sermons, exhortations, comic strips, leaflets, spot announcements on radio, posters, slogans, "Brotherhood Week," movies, to mention a few. In fact, certain tentative principles emerge from the studies which have been made on such devices:

1. Auditory stimuli are more effective than visual.
2. Speakers are more effective than printed matter.
3. Emotional appeals are more effective than logical, though there are exceptions.
4. Oral propaganda is more effective in small groups than in large audiences.
5. The effectiveness of propaganda tends to be greater when linked with prestige symbols.
6. The use of several channels of communication simultaneously is more effective than the use of only one medium.
7. Pictures and cartoons are more effective in gaining attention than the written word, and in conveying a message, except in the case of complex and abstract ideas.[59]

---

[57] Allport, *op. cit.*, pp. 261ff.

[58] For the evidence for this statement, see R. M. Williams, *The Reduction of Intergroup Tensions*, pp. 27ff; G. W. Allport, *The Nature of Prejudice*, pp. 483ff.; C. M. Stephenson, "The Relation between the Attitudes toward Negroes of White College Students and the College or School in which They are Registered," *Journal of Social Psychology*, Vol. 36, 1952, pp. 197–204.

[59] Williams, *op. cit.*, pp. 31ff. Cf., also, A. Rose, *Studies in the Reduction of Prejudice;* Horowitz, *op. cit.*, pp. 228–243; G. W. Allport, *The Nature of Prejudice*, pp. 493–495.

The Attack upon Discrimination

Many persons believe that the wiser plan is to bypass the problem of prejudice and attitudes altogether and to set about promptly to minimize and abolish discrimination. Says Watson, "One of our most fundamental hypotheses, growing out of this survey, is that *it is more constructive to attack segregation than it is to attack prejudices.*"[60] MacIver concurs in this and declares, "*Wherever the direct attack is feasible, that is, the attack on discrimination itself, it is more promising than the indirect attack, that is, the attack on prejudice as such. It is more effective to challenge conditions than to challenge attitudes or feelings.*"[61] Not all sociologists, however, agree with Watson and MacIver. Williams distinguishes between conflict, prejudice, and discrimination, and points out that attempts to eliminate one may actually accentuate the others. "The attempt to eliminate discrimination often leads directly to increases in hostility and conflict; efforts to avoid conflict, conversely, may perpetuate or reinforce patterns of discrimination."[62]

The debate continues, then, as to just what the goals are (amalgamation, pluralism, assimilation, or what?), the possibility of achieving them, strategy and techniques, the weapons most likely to succeed, and the point at which the attack should be made. Unless we are prepared to see much time, money, and effort wasted, the thing that is obviously needed is more information. This is where the psychologist, the sociologist, and the anthropologist can make their contributions, and they have, as a matter of fact, been turning their attention to these problems. They have already learned something about the nature of prejudice. They know that our attitudes are acquired — not inherited — and that itself is a heartening discovery. They are delving into the causes of prejudice, and, despite the divergence of opinions, some promising results have been achieved. They are trying to learn just how attitudes function, and what effect they have upon behavior. Finally, they are tackling the most difficult problem of all, that of changing attitudes.

Frankly, we do not yet understand how best to proceed in reducing prejudice, in transforming antipathy into sympathy, in converting bigotry into benevolence. Attempts are continually being made to learn the answer to this most fundamental of all human problems. In the meantime, those who adhere to the American creed will continue to teach, to preach, and to propagandize, in the hope that their values may prevail, and with some reason to believe that their efforts are not entirely in vain.

[60] G. Watson, *Action for Unity*, p. 64.
[61] R. M. MacIver, *The More Perfect Union*, p. 247.
[62] *Ibid.*, p. 40n.

14

Techniques
of
Dominance

The sad truth is that whatever modifi-
cations have been effected . . . are due
to great and incessant pressure.

JAMES BALDWIN
Nobody Knows My Name

In 1670 a small band of Englishmen made the first permanent settlement in what was to become the state of South Carolina. Theirs was a perilous and precarious venture, and the foothold they gained on the coast was none too solid. The Indian tribes were justifiably suspicious, and the Spaniards to the south were anything but hospitable. For their own security, the English welcomed immigrants to their colony, and offered every possible inducement. Others from Britain soon joined them, and the settlement grew in numbers and strength. Presently there began to arrive groups of thrifty, pious French Huguenots, who were harried and persecuted at home, and who were attracted to Carolina by the promise of religious freedom. The English were glad to see them. There was land aplenty for all, and the Huguenots were skillful, hard-working citizens. But they spoke a strange language, their customs were queer, and their religion was not of the approved Anglican variety. There were no objections to their settlement in Carolina; but the English wanted it understood that they were to stay "in their place." They could own land, be wealthy, work and worship; they could not aspire to the status of the English, enter the government, or establish their language or faith.

Years later, when it was proposed that the Huguenots be permitted to send delegates to the Assembly, the English raised the cry, "Shall the Frenchmen, who cannot speak our language, make our laws?" The answer, obviously, was No.

Time healed the wounds, however. In 1696 the Assembly granted to aliens living in the colony "all the rights, privileges, powers and immunities whatsoever, which any person born of English parents may, can, might, could or of right ought to have, use and enjoy." Assimilation proceeded rapidly. The French language began to disappear. Huguenot clergymen sought ordination in the Anglican church, and most of the Huguenot churches were eventually placed upon the establishment. The process, to be sure, was not without discord. The Huguenots exploded when their English neighbors insisted that they had not been properly married and that their children were, therefore, illegitimate; and the British laughed at the awkward efforts of the French to speak English, and were shocked at their practice of receiving the sacrament sitting down, their dispensing with godparents, and their refusal to make the sign of the Cross. The historical records abound with numerous instances of conflict and misunderstanding. But all that was years ago. The Huguenots, as a group, have long since ceased to be. One of their churches, the only Huguenot church in the United States, still stands in Charleston. French surnames are not uncommon to this day, and the names of streets testify to their former residents. The processes of assimilation and amalgamation, however, have run their entire course.

Much the same thing happens whenever racial and ethnic groups come into contact. The group which enjoys the greater prestige and wields the power is invariably jealous of its status, will not surrender its prerogatives without a struggle, and is determined to defend its own values and its culture against competing and conflicting systems. The lesser group, at the same time, is no less attached to its traditions and values, is not satisfied with a subordinate "place," and is determined to improve its status. As Park puts it:

This struggle for status . . . is the very source and origin of the race problem as we know it. The man of lower caste, who is usually a man of different racial stock, is invariably "all right in his place." It is when he seeks to rise that his presence, his occupation, and his position in society — if it is one in which his superiors are not accustomed to seeing him — is resented. This resentment is naturally intensified when the intruder exhibits, as he is almost certain to do, the ignorance, arrogance, and bad manners of an upstart. To the extent that the individuals of a particular caste or class are identified with a particular racial stock, the conflict of races and nationalities tends to become involved with the conflict of classes.[1]

Here, then, is the very crux of the so-called race problem. The underprivileged minority conceives of the problem as one of achieving a more desirable status, of removing the stigma of inferiority, of casting off the disabilities and handicaps imposed upon it, of acquiring power and status equal to that of any other group. To the dominant group, on the other hand, the race problem is seen essentially as one of maintaining its position of dominance, of holding on to its power and prestige, and of preserving its way of life. A docile, subservient, industrious racial or ethnic minority can be most useful, even indispensable; but such a minority becomes a menace when it grows restless, seeks to change its status, and aspires to play new roles. Dominant groups, then, must devise techniques, agencies, and policies of social control. Indeed, they have often long foreseen the inevitable uprising, and have taken steps to prevent it.

Crude methods of physical force, important though they be in achieving dominance over others, are not in themselves adequate for maintaining a position of superiority. To be sure, force must always be held in reserve and be readily available in an emergency; but effective domination depends upon techniques more subtle and efficient than guns and bombs. As a matter of fact, dominant racial and ethnic groups are often greatly outnumbered by the peoples over whom they exercise control, and their power and prestige would be insecure indeed if they rested only on physical force. In South Africa, for instance, three million whites lord it over more than ten million natives; in Hawaii, the *haoles* (whites of American and European origin), who enjoy the greatest power and prestige, are decidedly outnumbered by those of other racial stocks; and in Jamaica, the whites, in control, are a mere 2 per cent of a population which consists of 78 per cent Negro, 18 per cent mulatto, and a scattering of East Indians, Chinese, and others. In many parts of the world, then, the dominant racial group cannot rely upon its numerical strength, but must look to other techniques to insure its dominance. Even where it does have the advantage of numbers, and where its power is undisputed, symbolic means of control are employed. In the United States, though the Negro is outnumbered nine to one, whites use many devices other than physical force to hold supremacy.

[1] R. E. Park, "The Nature of Race Relations," in E. T. Thompson (Ed.), *Race Relations and the Race Problem*, pp. 23ff.

Control of Numbers

Among the devices employed by dominant peoples is that of regulating the numbers of those who threaten to upset the status quo. The following news item illustrates such a policy in its most ingenuous form:

> In Bermuda the population consists of 18,000 Negroes and 12,000 whites, but suffrage is dependent on sex and property held. Because of this the voters of Bermuda number 1,387 whites, 963 Negroes (all males). Thus the white majority in any election is safe, but the basis on which this is accomplished may not last forever. The House of Assembly of Bermuda last week put through a budget providing ample funds for the Government to propagandize Bermuda in favor of birth control, and supply the necessary apparatus cheap to poor Negroes.[2]

Not infrequently, however, keener foresight has been shown, and a group has sensed the danger before it has assumed threatening proportions. Benjamin Franklin was disturbed by the thought of large numbers of foreigners flocking to Pennsylvania, and in 1750 he wrote to a friend asking

> why the Pennsylvanians should allow the Palatine Germans to swarm into our settlements, and by herding together to establish their Language and Manners to the exclusion of ours? Why should Pennsylvania, founded by the English, become a colony of Aliens, who will shortly be so numerous as to Germanize us instead of our Anglifying them?[3]

The fears expressed by Franklin were shared by others in his time, but many years were to pass before they would affect the immigration policy of the nation.

Elsewhere, however, the practice of regulating and restricting the number and type of immigrants has long been in force. Canadians, for instance, have never looked upon their country as a haven for the surplus population of foreign lands or a refuge for the poor, oppressed, and underprivileged. Immigration they regard as a purely domestic problem, and they definitely want their country to remain British in character and allegiance. They have so stated on numerous occasions, as the following official pronouncement reveals:

> Canadians usually prefer that settlers should be of a readily assimilable type, already identified by race or language with one or other of the two great races now inhabiting this country. . . . Since the French are not to any great extent an emigrating people, this means in practice that the great bulk of the preferable settlers are those who speak the English language. . . . Next in order of readiness of assimilation are the Scandinavians, Dutch and Germans. . . . Settlers from Southern and Eastern Europe, however desirable from a purely economic point of view, are less readily assimilable. . . . Less assimilable still are those who come to Canada from the Orient.[4]

[2] Courtesy of *Time*, Copyright Time Inc., November 16, 1936.
[3] Quoted in W. C. Smith, *Americans in the Making*, p. 394.
[4] *Canada Year Book*, 1932, p. 149.

Canada, nevertheless, is eager to see her population grow, and she continues to welcome — and to seek — immigrants. In the ten years following World War II she received more than a million newcomers, quite a feat for a nation of fifteen million, and she has accepted a goodly share of the world's refugees from Communism. Even so, a third of these newcomers were of British stock, and almost another third were from France, Germany, the Netherlands, Austria, and the United States. Her policy of keeping the numbers of immigrants manageable, and of insuring their assimilability, remains in force:

> Since the end of the Second World War it has been the policy of the Government of Canada to stimulate the growth of the population by selective immigration. Efforts are made to choose immigrants of prospective adaptability to the Canadian way of life and to admit them at such times and in such numbers as employment conditions warrant.[5]

The "White Australia" Policy

Australia, even more than Canada, is determined to keep itself a white British commonwealth, and racial and ethnic groups which would be likely to endanger such a goal have been consistently excluded. The result is that Australia's population is approximately 95 per cent British. When the United States adopted its quota system in the 1920's, Australia took immediate action and empowered its Governor-General to prohibit the entry of any person deemed undesirable because of his "presumed unassimilability." This action was aimed especially at immigrants from the South and East of Europe, and its purpose was to prevent their seeking a home in Australia when the United States had closed its doors against them. So effectively has the color bar been enforced that only 1 per cent of the population is non-white, and many of these are the offspring of persons in Australia when the rigid immigration laws were enacted.

This "White Australia Policy" has its critics, both within and without the commonwealth. The colored peoples of overpopulated Asia deeply resent the policy which excludes them from a continent almost the size of the United States, sparsely settled by a mere 10,000,000 people. Australia hopes to have a population of 20,000,000 within the next two decades, but insists that only whites be permitted to enter. Within the country also there is some criticism of this policy of racial exclusion. The Communists have adopted the issue as an ideal one for their purposes, and certain religious groups have sought to have the laws relaxed. Their efforts, however, have been of no avail. All governments — Labor, Liberal, and Conservative — have supported the policy since 1901, as have the press and public opinion. Australia frankly and officially states her policy in these words: "In pursuance of established policy, the general practice is not to permit persons of non-European descent to enter Australia for purpose of settling permanently."[6]

[5] *Ibid.*, 1963–64, p. 198.
[6] Official Year Book of the Commonwealth of Australia, No. 48, 1962, p. 311.

Hawaii

Hawaii affords another instance of a society in which the dominant element has attempted to protect its interests by controlling the influx of competitive groups. Early in the nineteenth century the sugar industry began to loom large in the economy of the islands, and the *haoles* readily gained control of this lucrative business. As we have seen, they desperately needed labor on their plantations, and the native Hawaiians were not disposed to engage in so monotonous a task. The *haoles*, accordingly, began to import large numbers of Chinese from Canton. The Hawaiians themselves, more interested in racial homogeneity than in sugar production, would have preferred to rebuild the shattered population of their islands by inducing other Polynesians to migrate thither; but the *haoles*, whose primary concern was a labor supply, preferred the Chinese and their preference prevailed. Before long, however, when many of the Chinese left the plantations, moved into the cities, and began to compete with the *haole* merchants and artisans, vociferous opposition to them arose. The royal cabinet investigated the issue and reported:

> The excessive proportion of Chinese in the kingdom, and their rapid encroachment upon the various businesses and employments of the country, require adequate measures to prevent the speedy extinction in these Islands of western civilization by that of the East, and the substitution of a Chinese for the Hawaiian and other population.

Chinese immigration, accordingly, was at first restricted and then stopped altogether. The demand for labor, however, was still pressing, and the *haoles* turned next to Portuguese and Japanese. When the Japanese, in turn, became dangerously numerous, the tension was relieved by the importation of Koreans, Puerto Ricans, Spanish, and still more Portuguese.

Immigration Policies of the United States

The policies of the United States with respect to immigration have undergone considerable change over the years. From its inception as a nation until 1882, its policy was almost one of free and unrestricted admittance. While this country has never made a practice of soliciting and assisting immigrants, as have British dominions and certain South American countries, the United States did encourage their coming during the first century of its history. This was regarded as the land of the free, a haven for those oppressed by tyrants, a place of opportunity for all who were willing to labor. The words of Emma Lazarus, inscribed on the Statue of Liberty, were indeed appropriate:

> Give me your tired, your poor,
> Your huddled masses yearning to breathe free,
> The wretched refuse of your teeming shore,
> Send these, the homeless, tempest-tossed to me:
> I lift my lamp beside the golden door.

Anti-Semitism in Chicago was indicated by destruction and defacements in a cemetery. About 40 gravestones were marked with swastikas and scribblings.

To be sure, there were those who had misgivings about foreigners. George Washington wrote to John Adams in 1794: "My opinion with respect to immigration is that except for useful mechanics and some particular descriptions of men or professions, there is no need of encouragement"; and Thomas Jefferson was even more emphatic in expressing the wish that there might be "an ocean of fire between this country and Europe, so that it would be impossible for any more immigrants to come hither." Such fears, however, were not widely felt. There was the West to be opened; railroads had to be built and canals dug; there was land to be had for the asking; people were pouring across the mountains; and the young nation was eager for population.

Opposition to immigration did begin to crystallize, however, in the 1830's. It was suspected, with good reason, that various European countries were in the habit of dumping their paupers and criminals onto these shores; and several of the states took steps to prevent the landing of "undesirables." The proper type of legislation, however, was difficult to frame. The states all wanted immigrants of good quality, and did not want to divert the stream elsewhere. It was no easy task, therefore, so to word the laws that they would exclude the undesirable types without discouraging the desirable ones also. In the end it became obvious to everyone concerned that state control of immigration was neither feasible nor constitutional, and the whole problem was turned over to the federal government.

There were other reasons, besides dislike of paupers and criminals, that lay back of the growing opposition. In the discussions of the time there appeared the familiar arguments about the dangers of a heterogenous population, the difficulty of assimilating certain ethnic groups, their tendency to segregate themselves in colonies, the congestion in the cities, and the political corruption to which the foreign-born, often unwittingly, lent themselves. Much was said, also, about the effect of immigrants upon the wages of native workingmen, their willingness to adopt a lower standard of living, to do more work for less money, and their readiness to function as strike-breakers. Finally, there was hatred and fear of the Roman Catholic religion, the faith to which the majority of the Irish and many of the Germans adhered.

From these circumstances there arose two political movements. One was the Native American party, centered largely in the cities of Massachusetts, New York, and Pennsylvania, and coming into prominence for the first time about 1835. Rioting, destruction of property, and anti-Catholic demonstrations were among the techniques whereby the adherents of the party gave vent to their opposition, but it was in politics that the movement sought to make its influence felt. The party held a national convention in 1845 and adopted a platform which called for repeal of the naturalization laws and the appointment of none but native Americans to office. They did succeed in electing eight members to Congress, where numerous bills and resolutions were introduced; but no positive measures can be traced to the party.

The other movement took the form of a secret organization, which probably started in New York City in 1850. Its name was "The Supreme Order of the Star Spangled Banner;" but since its members were in the habit of answering all questions about their organization by saying, "I don't know," it came to be known as the "Know Nothing" party. The society grew very rapidly, and by 1854 had discarded most of its secret character. It openly endorsed candidates for public office and even put forth candidates of its own. The following year the movement claimed to have among its members the governors of seven states, the majority in a number of state legislatures, numerous other public officials, and 43 representatives and five senators in Congress. In 1856 a national convention was held, and Millard Fillmore was chosen as its nominee for the presidency. The principles of the party, as embodied in its platform, were: Americans must rule America; only the native-born should hold office in federal, state, and municipal governments; the naturalization laws should be changed to require 21 years' continued residence as a prerequisite for citizenship; paupers and criminals should be excluded; Romanism and all papal influences should be resisted; all military organizations composed of foreigners should be forbidden. The Know Nothings, despite their political strength, had little influence on legislation. The events immediately before the Civil War diverted the public interest to slavery, immigration itself declined after 1854, and the Know Nothing party passed out of existence. In 1855 Abraham Lincoln wrote:

Our progress in degeneracy appears to me to be pretty rapid. As a nation we began by declaring that "all men are created equal!" We now practically read it, "All men are created equal, except Negroes." When the Know-Nothings get control, it will read, "All men are created equal, except Negroes and foreigners and Catholics." When it comes to this, I shall prefer emigrating to some country where they make no pretense of loving liberty — to Russia, for instance, where despotism can be taken pure, and without the base alloy of hypocrisy.[7]

After the Civil War immigration began once more to climb steadily. In fact, immigrants were actually in good favor for a time. The war had taken a shocking toll of life. Moreover, Congress had passed in 1862 a homestead act having liberal and generous features, and as a consequence many people were drawn to the West. Accordingly, nobody felt cramped by the presence of the immigrants. The first federal law dealing with immigration, passed in 1864, far from restricting it, actually gave it encouragement. Among other things, this law provided for the appointment by the President of a Commissioner of Immigration, to be under the direction of the Department of State; and it provided, further, for the protection of the immigrant from fraud and imposition, and for assistance in helping him reach his ultimate destination in this country. At the same time the steamship was supplanting the sailing vessel as a means of transportation. This greatly mitigated the perils and discomforts of the steerage passengers; and it contributed, also, to the great increase in immigration from southern and eastern Europe.

1882 is a crucial date in the history of immigration, for it marked a radical change in the American policy from one of freedom to one of *federal regulation*. This was not, however, a sudden or surprising transition. Decades earlier, as we have seen, there had been loud and organized opposition to the immigrant, but it had never succeeded in getting itself expressed in federal legislation. Congress did place a ban upon the entrance of convicts and prostitutes in 1875, and the following year the Supreme Court rendered a highly significant decision declaring unconstitutional all the state laws pertaining to the regulation of immigration. In the meantime the feeling had been growing that the United States no longer needed foreigners in its labor force, and competition between native workingmen and immigrants was ceasing to be regarded with equanimity. More pertinent, however, was the bitter antagonism which Californians were showing toward the Chinese.[8] On August 3, 1882, accordingly, Congress passed its first general immigration law, inaugurating a period of federal regulation, control, and selection which continued to 1921. A vast and complicated body of federal immigration laws came into existence. Chinese laborers were at first excluded for a ten-year period, and later, indefinitely; head taxes were imposed; defectives, idiots, lunatics, and convicts were excluded; provisions were made for deportation of undesirables; paupers, and persons suffering from loathsome diseases, were forbidden to enter; the doors were closed

[7] A. J. Beveridge, *Abraham Lincoln, 1809–1858*, Vol. 3, p. 354.
[8] See above, pp. 206ff.

to epileptics, anarchists, polygamists, professional beggars, chronic alcoholics, vagrants, stowaways, and persons who advocate overthrow of the government by force or violence.

The year 1921 is another landmark in the nation's immigration history, for it marks the inauguration of a policy of *restriction,* as distinct from the policy of selection which preceded it. In that year Congress passed an emergency measure, limiting the total immigration for any year to 358,803, and stipulating that "the number of aliens of any nationality who may be admitted under the immigration laws to the United States in any fiscal year shall be limited to three per cent of the number of foreign born persons of such nationality resident in the United States, as determined by the United States Census of 1910." This was a deliberate attempt to keep out immigrants from southern and eastern Europe, and to favor those from the countries of northern and western Europe.

This restrictive and discriminating legislation was the climax of a long period of agitation. For more than 20 years prior to the passage of the quota act, immigration had been a vital national issue. Woofter has analyzed the arguments as they were presented in the press.[9] Between 1900 and 1907, he found, immigration was debated primarily from an economic, and only incidentally from a racial or ethnic viewpoint. Restriction was urged in order to protect the American standard of living, and to prevent pauperism, crime, bossism, and the decay of democratic ideals. Between 1907 and 1914, Woofter discovered, the arguments shifted to racial and eugenic grounds. Immigrants from southern and eastern Europe were declared to be "unassimilable," doubts were cast upon the ability of the Anglo-Saxon stock to survive, and heterogeneity was accused of undermining the strength of the nation. Many bills designed to restrict immigration by imposing a "literacy" test were introduced into Congress. Several of these passed one house or the other, and some passed both houses only to be vetoed in turn by Presidents Cleveland, Taft, and Wilson. Cleveland characterized them as "a radical departure from our national policy relating to immigration," as indeed they were; and both Taft and Wilson rejected them on the grounds that their purpose was really restrictive, and not selective, as they professed to be. Nevertheless, Congress did enact a bill over President Wilson's veto on February 5, 1917. Its provisions, seemingly innocuous, would merely exclude "all aliens over sixteen years of age, physically capable of reading, who cannot read the English language, or some other language or dialect."

Actually, however, the literacy test was a deliberate attempt to limit the number of immigrants, to discourage the "new immigration," and to favor the "old." The act also included a "latitude and longitude test," forbidding immigration from the South Sea Islands and various parts of Asia not already covered by the Chinese Exclusion Act and the "gentleman's agreement" with Japan, and thereby allaying the fears of many Americans who envisioned a great influx of Asiatics to the Pacific Coast. Finally, this Act of 1917 designated so meticulously the various classes of persons who would be denied admission to the United

---

[9] T. J. Woofter, Jr., *Races and Ethnic Groups in American Life,* pp. 22ff.

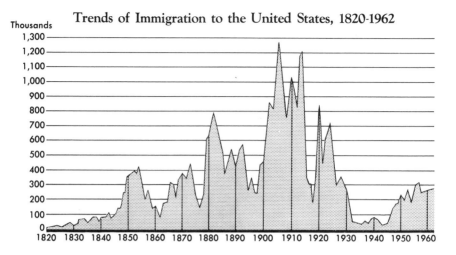

Trends of Immigration to the United States, 1820-1962

Thousands

1,300
1,200
1,100
1,000
900
800
700
600
500
400
300
200
100
0

1820 1830 1840 1850 1860 1870 1880 1890 1900 1910 1920 1930 1940 1950 1960

States that Fairchild described it as "the most inclusive catalog of human frailties to be found anywhere in the English language."[10] Thus, under the guise of individual selection, there were introduced into the American immigration policy the somewhat more questionable principles of group selection and restriction.

The Quota System

The Quota Act of 1921, in preparation for which the Immigration Act of 1917 had served as an entering wedge, was frankly a temporary measure, adopted to meet an emergency. When World War I ended, it became obvious that Europeans were on the verge of resuming the migration to the United States which had reached such tremendous proportions in the early years of the twentieth century. The Quota Act was an attempt to stem the tide, and at the same time to tip the scales in favor of those ethnic groups for which the American people had a preference. This temporary measure was superseded, finally, by the permanent Immigration Act of 1924. Under this law the number to be admitted each year was limited to 2 per cent of the population of such nationality resident in the United States according to the census of 1890, the total number under this plan not to exceed 164,667. Beginning in 1929 a new method of computing the quotas on the basis of *national origins* was put into effect. The total number to be admitted each year was 150,000, and the quota for each country would be based upon the proportionate number of that nationality living in the continental United States in 1920 in relation to the total population for that year, except that a minimum quota of 100 was established. Davie summarizes the procedure:

> To determine the quota for any given nationality it is necessary to find out what proportion that nationality contributed, by birth or descent, to the total American

[10] H. P. Fairchild, *Immigration: A World Movement and Its American Significance*, p. 390.

population in 1920 — a most difficult statistical problem — and then to apply this percentage to 150,000. If, for example, 10 per cent of the American people in 1920 were Irish by birth or descent, then 10 per cent of 150,000 or 15,000, would be the annual quota for Eire.[11]

Since the minimum quota for any country is 100, the total comes to slightly more than 150,000. In 1944 the Chinese, who had long been excluded altogether, were brought within the system, and were assigned a quota of 105; in 1946 India was assigned a quota of 100 and the Philippines were allowed 100.

On the surface, the quota system appears to be just and impartial. Actually it discriminates decidedly in favor of the "old" immigration, allotting about 25,000 annually to the countries of southern and eastern Europe, and more than five times that number to the nations of northern and western Europe. The quotas, however, give no clear indication of the realities of immigration to the United States since their adoption. During the 1930's immigration declined to a mere trickle. In fact, the year 1932 saw 35,600 arrivals and 103,300 departures; and 1933 saw 23,100 arrivals against 80,100 departures. During 1943 only 23,735 aliens entered the country as immigrants. In some years the greater part of the quotas go unused, while in other years the demand for admission far exceeds the number permitted to enter.

Moreover, those who hoped that this new policy would make for a more homogeneous population were in for disappointment. Under the provisions of the law certain parts of the world were subject neither to total exclusion nor to a quota. This unrestricted area included all the independent nations of North, Central, and South America, and the West Indies. There were no limits placed upon eligible native-born citizens of those countries who might choose to enter the United States. Therefore, when immigration from Europe was drastically reduced, there developed a partially, compensatory movement of peoples from Canada, Mexico, and other American countries, and from our own territories, especially Puerto Rico.

The McCarran-Walter Act

This highly controversial piece of legislation, enacted by Congress in 1952, did not appreciably change the country's immigration policy. The quota system, based upon national origins, remained intact. The bill was designed to bring thousands of piecemeal immigration statutes and regulations (accumulated since 1789) into one compact code. It removed some glaring inequities; e.g., all Asiatic immigrants would be eligible for citizenship, where previously Japanese and certain others were barred. It placed under the quota system certain nations whose citizens had hitherto been excluded. In short, it accepted the principles of quotas and national origins without reservation. Table 14.1 gives the normal immigration quotas provided for in the law.

[11] M. R. Davie, *What Shall We Do about Immigration?* Public Affairs Pamphlet No. 115, p. 9.

TABLE 14.1

United States Immigration Quotas, 1962*

Country	Quota
All countries	156,687
Europe	149,597
Austria	1,405
Belgium	1,297
Bulgaria	100
Czechoslovakia	2,859
Denmark	1,175
Finland	566
France	3,069
Germany	25,814
Great Britain	65,361
Greece	308
Hungary	865
Iceland	100
Ireland	17,756
Italy	5,666
Netherlands	3,136
Norway	2,364
Poland	6,488
Portugal	438
Rumania	289
Spain	250
Sweden	3,295
Switzerland	1,698
Turkey	225
U.S.S.R.	2,697
Yugoslavia	942
Other Europe	1,434
Asia	3,290
Africa	3,200
Australia, New Zealand and other Oceania	600

* Source: Bureau of the Census, *Statistical Abstract of the United States*

The McCarran-Walter Act has been the subject of considerable criticism and debate. President Truman, in vetoing it, took occasion to denounce its inequities and its discriminatory features, but Congress promptly passed it over the veto. In the political campaign of 1952 candidate Eisenhower and candidate Stevenson vied with each other in denouncing it and calling for its radical revision. They did so again in the campaign of 1956.

Critics of the law include most of the liberal members of Congress, much of the press, many pressure groups, churches, and nationality associations. The criticisms follow these lines:

1. The racist philosophy which underlay the restricting legislation of the 1920's remains as the basis of the McCarran-Walter Act. It implies that immigrants from northern Europe are inherently superior to those from southern and eastern Europe, assimilate more readily, and prove themselves better citizens.

2. The census figures of 1920 are retained as the basis for the determination of quotas, whereas 1960 would provide a more democratic base.

3. The law assigns large quotas to countries which do not use them, and small quotas to countries whose citizens would like to emigrate to America. Quotas ought to be pooled, and those that are unused ought to be transferred to those countries whose quotas become exhausted.

4. Despite the apparent impartiality in assigning quotas, Orientals suffer a special type of discrimination. Those who are naturalized citizens of Western nations (e.g., Hong Kong Chinese) may not come in under the quotas of their Western nationalities. The law puts all Orientals in the very small quotas of their ancestral countries.

5. Too much discretion is given to consuls and officers of the Immigration and Naturalization Service.

6. Naturalized citizens, and especially aliens, may be deported for most trivial reasons.

7. The law is overly "security-conscious," and excludes from the country many innocuous persons and many whose presence would be highly desirable.

The McCarran-Walter Act, however, with some minor amendments, remains the law of the land. Suggestions for its revision, even from the President of the United States himself, have gone unheeded. The attitudes of a majority of the members of Congress, and perhaps of the nation, were correctly reflected in the following editorial in the *Saturday Evening Post:*

> The national-origins system seems to us to represent pretty well the views of the average American on how new arrivals should be distributed among the various emigrating nations. Some people would like to see more Swedes or fewer Scotsmen admitted, but there is no universal demand for upsetting the present proportion of ethnic groups in our population. There is no demand to throw away a workable slide rule like the national-origins system in favor of a series of dog fights.[12]

Assimilation

Dominant peoples, jealous of their way of life and eager to preserve it, have often looked upon assimilation as the solution of their problem, and have sought to impose their culture upon the foreign elements in their midst. "Assimil-

[12] *Saturday Evening Post*, Vol. 225, No. 34, February 21, 1953, p. 10.

ability" has thus sometimes been regarded as the crucial test to be applied to those who would enter the society. Canada's policy of carefully selecting her immigrants is frankly based upon such an assumption, as is that of Australia.[13] Brazilians, according to Pierson,[14] are convinced of the eventual amalgamation and assimilation of the diverse ethnic units in their population, and take pride in the extent to which the process has already been accomplished in their country. The very essence of the race problem, as they conceive it, is the *resistance* which an ethnic group offers, or is thought to offer, to absorption. Thus opposition to Japanese immigration to Brazil has been largely motivated by the apprehension that the Japanese would constitute a difficult group to assimilate. The Japanese embassy, in an effort to refute such an imputation, issued in 1934 a pamphlet bearing the title *Intermixture among the Japanese: The Myth That They Do Not Interbreed with Other Races,* and included photographs of mixed Japanese-Brazilian families to prove the point.

In the United States

Assimilation has also been the policy of the United States, though not so consciously and systematically pursued as in Australia at present. As we have seen, for a long time in this country there prevailed the comfortable belief that assimilation was an inevitable, automatic process, and that the various ethnic minorities would of their own accord adopt the dominant English pattern of living if left to their own devices. Such optimism, however, was hardly justifiable, nor was it shared by all. As a matter of fact, there were certain ethnic groups in early nineteenth-century America who envisioned quite a different course. German intellectuals, for instance, pondered various schemes for concentrating their people and perpetuating their social heritage in the New World. Some of them even proposed that the Germans take over one of the American states and adopt German as the official language. At one time the Irish petitioned Congress for a land grant in the West on which they might settle certain of their fellow nationals. Congress wisely rejected the petition, on the ground that it would be undesirable to concentrate alien peoples geographically, and thereby encourage the formation of a nation which would be a patchwork of foreign settlements. Concerning this action Hansen has said, "Probably no decision in the history of American immigration policy possesses more profound significance,"[15] for it committed the nation to a policy of assimilation rather than one of Balkanization. Even so, there were times when the English language held but a scant advantage over the German. So important was the Teutonic element in Illinois before the Civil War that Abraham Lincoln, astute politician that he was, tried to master the German tongue, and for a time was the owner of a German-language newspaper. A great influx of British settlers, however, was sufficient to tip the scales.

[13] See above, pp. 329f.
[14] D. Pierson, *Negroes in Brazil*, p. 344.
[15] M. L. Hansen, *The Immigrant in American History*, p. 132.

America has indeed shown herself adept at molding into one nation a wide variety of peoples. Her motto, "E Pluribus Unum," is not altogether an idle boast. Some of her minority groups, however, have had insurmountable obstacles placed in their path, even when they themselves desired to become assimilated; and many other more fortunate groups have encountered no little discrimination. America's paradoxical and ambivalent attitude toward the assimilation of minorities has been described by Myrdal as follows:

> In spite of all race prejudice, few Americans seem to doubt that it is the ultimate fate of this nation to incorporate without distinction not only all the Northern European stocks, but also the people from Eastern and Southern Europe, the Near East, and Mexico. They see obstacles; they emphasize the religious and "racial" differences; they believe it will take a long time. But they assume that it is going to happen, and do not have, on the whole, strong objections to it — provided it is located in a distant future. . . .
>
> The Negroes, on the other hand, are commonly assumed to be unassimilable. . . . Negroes are set apart, together with other colored peoples, principally the Chinese and the Japanese. America fears the segregation into distinctive isolated groups of all other elements of its population and looks upon the preservation of their separate national attributes and group loyalties as a hazard to American institutions. Considerable efforts are directed toward "Americanizing" all groups of alien origin. But in regard to the colored peoples, the American policy is the reverse. They are excluded from assimilation.[16]

Discrimination

Dominant peoples everywhere have resorted to various devices for restricting economically, politically, and socially the racial and ethnic groups over whom they have set themselves. The term commonly applied to such practices is *discrimination*, which F. H. Hankins has defined as the "unequal treatment of equals, either by the bestowal of favors or the imposition of burdens." Discrimination touches upon every phase of life. Subordinate groups are often restricted in their use of hotels, restaurants, transportation, and such public facilities as parks, playgrounds, swimming pools, and libraries. Churches and hospitals are often closed to them; intermarriage is opposed; and social contacts between master and servant are hedged about with an elaborate system of etiquette.[17] In the economic realm members of minority groups are barred from trade unions and professional associations, they are effectively excluded from many occupations, they are the "last to be hired, and the first to be fired," and, where they are permitted to work, they are kept down by the imposition of a "job ceiling." One function of these discriminations is to isolate the dominant and subordinate groups and to limit contact and communication between them.

[16] G. Myrdal, *An American Dilemma*, Vol. 1, pp. 53–54.
[17] The role of etiquette as a means of social control has been most thoroughly described and analyzed in B. W. Doyle, *The Etiquette of Race Relations in the South*.

TABLE 14.2

Immigrants, by Country of Last Permanent Residence*

Country	Total, 143 years 1820–1962
All countries	42,396,068
Europe	34,787,153
Belgium	191,059
Bulgaria	66,406
Czechoslovakia	129,593
Denmark	353,261
Estonia	960
Finland	28,000
France	693,262
Germany	6,773,586
Austria } Hungary {	4,278,702
Great Britain	3,821,350
England	2,939,520
Scotland	789,261
Wales	92,569
Greece	494,721
Iceland	2,582
Ireland	4,687,263
Italy	5,001,450
Latvia	2,041
Lithuania	3,303
Luxembourg	2,167
Netherlands	334,636
Norway	841,933
Poland	444,225
Portugal	290,509
Rumania	159,371
Spain	186,005
Sweden	1,253,240
Switzerland	327,392
Turkey in Europe	160,097
U.S.S.R.	3,344,897
Yugoslavia	68,862
Other Europe	846,298
Asia	1,137,516
China	410,795
Japan	333,940
Turkey in Asia	207,047
Other Asia	185,734
America	6,048,140
Canada and Newfoundland	3,647,140
Mexico	1,235,936
Central America	132,481

TABLE 14.2 (*continued*)

Country	Total, 143 years 1820–1962
All countries	42,396,068
South America	276,406
West Indies	661,224
Other America	95,478
Africa	51,204
Australia and New Zealand	82,826
Other Oceania	21,997
All other countries	266,707

* Source: Bureau of the Census, *Statistical Abstract of the United States*, 1963, p. 100.

Isolation and segregation, accordingly, help to preserve the status quo, impede the process of assimilation, and, in fact, serve to *dull the appetite for status* on the part of the underprivileged group.

Reluctance to Educate "Inferiors"

More important, discriminatory policies make it difficult for oppressed groups to acquire the knowledge, skills, and tools with which to improve their status. Dominant peoples have often refused to place firearms in the hands of those beneath them. The Spaniards, for instance, sought to prevent the Indians from possessing guns and from learning to ride horseback.[18] Here in the United States, the whites, even when their backs were to the wall in the Revolutionary and Civil Wars, were reluctant to arm the Negroes. Among the colonial powers France alone imposed conscription for military duty on her subject peoples, although Great Britain did draw a fair proportion of her armed forces from her dependencies, especially India. The potential military manpower of colonial areas is vast, but, significantly enough, the ruling powers have avoided training many of their subjects in warfare. The truth would seem to be that they are afraid to do so, for fear the natives might turn their arms upon their masters. More dangerous than rifles, however, are two other weapons which dominant groups have jealously guarded or grudgingly and warily shared, namely, *education* and *the ballot*.

Colonial powers have been notoriously tightfisted in their support of education for their subjects. Even France, committed to a policy of assimilation, never developed an adequate system of schools; nor have the British, Dutch, Portuguese, Japanese, Belgians, or any other imperialistic power. Financial reasons are commonly offered as the excuse, although other social services, such as agricultural, veterinary, and public health programs, often receive a fair degree

[18] See H. J. Priestly, *The Coming of the White Man, 1492–1848*, p. 89.

*This segregated fountain
was erected in 1952
in Jacksonville, Florida.
(Ewing Galloway photo)*

of support. The simple truth is that ruling groups realize that education of the natives would blast the whole system of control. Even where there is some development of schools, emphasis is placed upon "practical," "useful," technical subjects — not upon the barren social sciences and the effete humanities.

It has been so in the United States. Prior to the Civil War there was strong sentiment against the education of Negroes, both slave and free. This was true even in the North, while in several of the states of the South, the teaching of Negroes was forbidden by law (though frequent violations are recorded). So effective were the barriers, however, that very few Negroes were literate when they were granted their freedom. Upon emancipation, accordingly, the Negroes manifested a keen desire for education, a fact which Booker T. Washington explained as their natural curiosity to discover just what there was about books which made them so dangerous.

Negro leaders have always realized that there were two keys that could open the doors to the Negro's advancement — education and the ballot. Some regarded the former as the more important, some the latter, and others insisted that both were essential. The whites, in the meantime, showed little enthusiasm for the education of their onetime slaves. However, their own value system would not permit them to deny educational opportunities altogether to the Negro, and they compromised by seeing to it that such opportunities be inferior and inadequate. Myrdal analysed the situation as follows:

> There is petty pressure on Negro education in the South, but the truth is that *Southern whites have never had the nerve to make of Negro education an accomplished instrument to keep the Negroes in their caste status.* It would have been

possible, but it has not been done. The Southern whites' caste policy has been halfhearted all through, but particularly so in education. The explanation is again that they are also good Americans with all the standardized American ideals about education. The interest in educating the Negroes to become faithful helots has been obvious, but the Southern whites have not even attempted to make it effective in practice. Instead, they have merely kept Negro education poor and bad. And even on that point they have been gradually giving up resistance.[19]

When Myrdal made his comment, and long before that, it was a matter of common knowledge that the education provided the Negro in the South was far below that of the whites. The difference was apparent whatever the criterion of measurement used. (1) The money spent per pupil was less for Negroes than for whites. (2) There was great discrepancy in the value of school properties. (3) The length of the school term was shorter for Negroes. (4) Less was spent for transportation. (5) The pupil-teacher ratio was more favorable in the white schools. (6) Teachers in the Negro schools were less well prepared, and their salaries were lower, than those of the whites.[20]

Discrimination against the Negro in education was not limited to the South, though the method whereby it was accomplished differed from one region to another. Some Northern cities practiced a type of extra-legal segregation in their school systems, gerrymandering of school districts was not unknown, and, most important, the residential segregation imposed upon Negroes resulted in virtually segregated schools. So it was at the higher levels. There was, for instance, a "quota system" which placed restrictions upon, not only Negroes, but Jews, Italians, and members of various other minorities as well. Some colleges and universities excluded them altogether, while others made it extremely difficult for them to enter, and accepted only a limited number from the many applicants. Thus in devious ways have dominant groups guarded the possession of the knowledge and skills requisite for acquiring and retaining prestige and power.

For many years the Negro's struggle to acquire educational equality was handicapped by the application of the "separate but equal" principle. This principle had been given legal sanction in the famous case of Plessey v. Ferguson (1896). In that case the United States Supreme Court *sustained* a Louisiana statute requiring separate railroad accommodations for Negroes and whites, and in support of the decision, referred to the accepted practice of segregation in the public schools. This action of the Court was interpreted as giving the green light to those who wanted separate schools for the two races. For two generations thereafter, accordingly, the philosophy of "separate but equal" prevailed in the South, even though it was obvious that the schools were indeed separate, but far from equal. Churches and philanthropic organizations attempted to equalize the educational opportunities by establishing schools of their own and providing

---

[19] *Op. cit.*, p. 896. See also Myrdal's discussion of "industrial" versus "classical" education for Negroes, *op. cit.*, pp. 896ff.

[20] Cf. L. R. Harlan, *Separate and Unequal*; E. Ginzberg, *The Negro Potential*; W. Mendelson, *Discrimination*, especially Ch. 2.

various kinds of subsidies, but the task was too great for them. Negro lawyers, in representing their clients, were often able to prove that the opportunities were not equal, and steps had to be taken to provide a semblance of equality. Finally, in the 1950's, the principle of "separate but equal" was itself challenged, and the Supreme Court handed down its shattering decision that "separate educational facilities are inherently unequal."

The Court's ruling, however, did not solve the problem. The proponents of segregation resorted to a variety of means to nullify or circumvent the decision. One device was that of giving county and city boards of education authority to assign pupils "so as to provide for the orderly and efficient administration of the public schools." The State of Georgia made it a felony "for any school official . . . to spend tax money for public schools in which the races are mixed," and South Carolina amended its constitution to provide for the elimination of the provision for a liberal system of free public schools. In the Northern states residential segregation, plus a certain amount of gerrymandering of school districts, accounted for a high degree of "de facto" school segregation.

The decade following the Supreme Court's decision witnessed many changes, but the end is not in sight. In May, 1964, it was reported that 90 per cent of the 3,408,688 Negro pupils in the District of Columbia, the eleven states of the Confederacy, and the six Border states were still attending segregated schools. Most of the progress toward integration had taken place in the Border states of Delaware, Maryland, Kentucky, West Virginia, Missouri, and Oklahoma. In the states which formed the Confederacy, however, there were only 34,110, or 1.18 per cent of the 2,814,563 Negro pupils, enrolled in desegregated classes; and approximately 18,000 of these were in the state of Texas.[21]

The movement toward educational equality for Negroes continues, however slowly; and the resistance, even in those states where it has been greatest, appears to be a delaying action rather than a determined, last-ditch stand. On the tenth anniversary of the Supreme Court's historic decision there were demonstrations, sit-ins, boycotts, and similar manifestations of the Negro's dissatisfaction with the slow pace of integration; and the civil rights bill, enacted into law in the summer of 1964, contained provisions for assisting and accelerating the process.

The Ballot

The ballot is still another weapon which dominant peoples have shared with others only under pressure. Kennedy[22] finds that one of the common features of colonial systems is the retention of political control by the possessing power, leaving to the natives little or no share in the government of their own land. There are many ways in which this can be done, even while giving the ap-

---

21 Cf. "Ten Years in Review," *Southern School News*, May 17, 1964; C. Sitton, "Since the School Decree; 10 Years of Racial Foment," *The New York Times*, May 18, 1964, p. 1.

22 R. Kennedy, "The Colonial Crisis and the Future," in R. Linton (Ed.), *The Science of Man in the World Crisis*, pp. 308ff.

pearance of a certain degree of self-government. Natives, for instance, are permitted to have advisory councils, but crucial decisions are always made elsewhere; local leaders are retained in office, but if they express opinions hostile to their real rulers, they are quickly spirited away to remote penal areas.

In the Caribbean, as we have seen, many of the familiar techniques of domination are absent. Jim Crow and lynching are not in evidence; segregation is not practiced in schools, theaters, restaurants, or public conveyances. White, black, and brown meet together in the same churches, and are buried side by side in the cemeteries. But when it comes to the ballot, the black man, until very recently, found himself deprived of it; and the mulatto joined with the white to see that he did not get hold of it. In 1942 Eric Williams, a Negro who has since risen to political eminence in that region, described the situation in which whites and mixed bloods conspired to withhold the ballot from the black man.[23] "The attitude of the majority of the colored middle class," he wrote, "is one of open contempt for the black workers." He insisted that they were adamant in their refusal to countenance any extension of the franchise to the "barefooted man," who, they declared, was not yet ready for such a boon. In Haiti, Williams wrote, the ruling mulatto elite dominated the country economically, politically, and socially; in the British West Indies high property qualifications disfranchised all but a handful of colored and white voters; and in Trinidad one had to earn a relatively high income to be permitted to vote, and, to be a candidate for the Council, one had to be a wealthy man, by local standards. There have been many changes since World War II and the Negro has made tremendous strides toward the acquisition of political power.

In the United States the whites have never lost sight of the fact that the ballot, in the hands of the Negro, would be a powerful instrument for social change. At the beginning of the Civil War even the free Negroes were disfranchised throughout the South, and in most of the Northern states as well. There were only six states, in fact, which did not discriminate against the Negro at the polls. After the war, the South lost no time in enacting discriminatory legislation, designed to perpetuate white supremacy. This legislation, the so-called Black Codes, was instrumental in bringing about the adoption of the Fourteenth and Fifteenth Amendments, which put an end to all the various constitutional and statutory provisions which the southern states had devised in order to limit the elective franchise to the whites.

The South thereupon set about to circumvent the Constitution, and to prevent by other means the Negro's using the ballot. The whites stooped to fraud, bribery, threats, and violence; they resorted to stuffing ballot boxes, to the employment of more boxes than were necessary, and to the surreptitious removal of the polls at the last moment. Such fraudulent and illegal devices, however, were not deemed adequate, and the whites began to cast about for some legal means of excluding the Negro from the suffrage. They adopted the famous "grandfather clause,"[24] subsequently declared unconstitutional; they

[23] See E. Williams, *The Negro in the Caribbean*, pp. 61ff.
[24] See above, p. 126.

excluded those who had been convicted of crimes of a kind to which Negroes were peculiarly vulnerable; they insisted that in order to vote one must be "of good character," or one should be able to read, understand, and explain the Constitution, and they administered these tests so as to discredit the Negro. Most effective of these devices, however, have been the poll tax and the white primary.

Both the poll tax and the white primary came under attack. The poll tax not only disfranchised most Negroes, but disqualified many of the whites also, and it played neatly into the hands of commercial and industrial interests, political machines, and demagogues.[25] Several Southern states proceeded to abolish it of their own accord, until, by 1964, it was retained only in Texas, Arkansas, Mississippi, Alabama, and Virginia. In that year the requisite number of states approved a measure to add the Twenty-fourth Amendment to the Constitution, according to which the right to vote in any primary or other Federal election may not be denied by reason of failure to pay a poll tax. This, however, is not likely to increase appreciably the number of Negro voters, for there are other obstacles far more difficult to surmount, such as intimidation, rigged "literacy" tests, and the like.

The white primary has taken a drubbing at the hands of the courts in a series of interesting cases initiated by the National Association for the Advancement of Colored People. In most of the southern states the Democratic primary has long been the decisive election, and Negroes were rigidly barred from participation. Then, in 1927, the United States Supreme Court heard a case which had been appealed from the Texas courts, and rendered the decision that the Texas law which excluded Negroes from the Democratic primaries was unconstitutional. Thereupon the whites of Texas tried various other devices, with more or less success, to prevent the Negroes from participating in elections. Finally, in 1944 the Supreme Court set aside the subterfuges Texans had been employing. In that decision, a majority of the Court, through Justice Reed, said:

> It may now be taken as a postulate that the right to vote in such a primary for the nomination of candidates without discrimination by the state, like the right to vote in a general election, is a right secured by the Constitution. By the terms of the Fifteenth Amendment that right may not be abridged by any state on account of race. Under our Constitution the great privilege of the ballot may not be denied a man by the state because of his color. . . .
>
> The United States is a constitutional democracy. Its organic law grants to all citizens a right to participate in the choice of elected officials without restriction by any state because of race. This grant to the people of the opportunity for choice is not to be nullified by a state through casting its electoral process in a form which permits a private organization to practice racial discrimination in the election. . . .

Not to be outdone by the Supreme Court, some states continued to cast about for schemes whereby the Negro might be disfranchised. South Carolina, for

---

[25] Cf. W. J. Cash, *The Mind of the South*, pp. 150ff.

example, repealed all of its laws which regulated the primaries and declared that the Democratic Party was a "private club," having the right to choose its own members. A Federal District Court, however, outlawed this device a few years later. Then in 1948 the Democrats adopted an oath to be required of all voters in the primary, according to which they would swear to their belief in "social and educational separation of the races," and to their opposition "to the Federal so-called F.E.P.C. law." The effect was to bar Negroes from the primary, but the same District Court issued a ruling prohibiting the oath requirement. Other Southern states have tried their own devices to keep the Negro from voting, but they too have run into difficulties. Some, following the court's decision, simply abandoned the white primary system; and throughout the South Negroes have been voting in increasing numbers in recent years.

The political power of the American Negro, however, is only beginning to be used.[26] In 1960 the Census Bureau estimated the population of voting-age Negroes at about 10,000,000. But in the eleven states which comprised the Old Confederacy only 1,500,000 were registered to vote, and in the rest of the country only 3,500,000 were registered. There has been some improvement. In the first five months of 1964, according to the Southern Regional Council, new Negro registrations amounted to 241,659 in the South, bringing the total Negro voters in that region to more than 2,000,000. The Commission on Civil Rights has found that racially restricted voting is now confined to eight states — Alabama, Florida, Georgia, Louisiana, Mississippi, the Carolinas, and Tennessee — and in these states "substantial discriminatory disenfranchisement of Negroes" exists in only about 100 counties. Neither the Civil Rights Act of 1957, nor that of 1960, was able to remove all the obstacles, and it remains to be seen how effective the Civil Rights Act of 1964 will be in correcting the abuses. However, it is not only fear, intimidation, and trickery on the part of the whites which stand in the way of the Negro's effective use of the ballot; there is also widespread apathy. Even in the cities of the North, where the Negro vote is often crucial and where no barriers are erected against his registering, barely 40 per cent of those eligible to vote have been doing so. Political apathy, however, is not a unique characteristic of Negroes, but is found among all lower-class, poorly educated peoples. The ballot is a powerful weapon, but knowledge and skill are prerequisites for its effective use.

[26] Mendelson, *op. cit.*, pp. 5–32; T. Wicker, "Negro Vote Gains Importance for '64," *The New York Times*, October 13, 1963; Freda H. Goldman (Ed.), *Educational Imperative: The Negro in the Changing South*, pp. 42–49, 85–87; B. Taper, *Gomillion versus Lightfoot, passim.*

15

Cleavages

The higher a coloured person rises in the social scale, the less he tends to associate closely with other coloured persons of lower social status.

SYDNEY COLLINS

Coloured Minorities in Britain

Domination is made all the easier by the fact that minorities do not present a united front, but are inevitably rent by cleavages, jealousies, and rivalries. As a matter of fact, dominant groups are not unknown to make use of such cleavages, and to encourage them, the better to maintain their own position. "Divide and rule" is a device well understood in the area of race relations.

Europeans who first settled this country were ably assisted in gaining a foothold by the fact that the Indians were continually at one another's throats. The Iroquois were a terror to other tribes for miles around, the Osage plundered Indian villages and white settlements alike, the Sac and Fox virtually wiped out the Missouri, and the Haida had no qualms about robbing and enslaving members of their own race if they happened to belong to hostile bands. It was the proud boast of the Pawnee that they never fought against the United States, but gladly joined with the whites on numerous occasions to annihilate other Indians. The English, Dutch, French, and Americans took advantage of these intertribal hatreds, pitting Indian against Indian, and easily winning red allies to help them destroy other red men. There were shrewd Indian chiefs who saw the folly of all this and attempted to bring about a union of the tribes to stem the flood of white men. Joseph Brant, a Mohawk chief, toured the country trying to persuade the Indians to band together in defense of their lands, as did King Philip, Pontiac, Black Hawk, Tecumseh, and many others. It need hardly be said that the gulf that separated tribe from tribe was too great to be spanned by the zeal and oratory of these prophets.

Minorities, to be sure, do occasionally close their ranks and present a solid front to their opponents. American Negroes, for all their differences, are not far apart in their hopes and aspirations. Moreover, they have occasionally identified themselves with colored minorities the world over. They displayed a great sympathy for the peoples of India in their struggle against the British, they championed the cause of the Indonesians against the Dutch, they were greatly aroused by the invasion of Ethiopia by the Italians, and they frequently rally to the support of Mexicans, Orientals, Indians, and other "colored" minorities in the United States. Drake and Cayton insist that the Negroes even felt a certain sympathy for the Japanese in the recent war, though they vigorously deny that the Negro was lacking in loyalty and patriotism. One informant, however, did make the following confession, which typified the feelings of many another:

> I was really ashamed of myself the day Pearl Harbor was hit. When I heard the news I jumped up and laughed. "Well, sir," I said, "I don't guess the white folks will say colored people can't fly airplanes from now on." Then I caught myself. I know the Japanese are a bunch of Fascists. I know this isn't a race war. I shouldn't have been pleased at anything the Japs did. . . . They may make the white man wake up to the fact that he can't shove the darker people around forever. Of course, we've got to lick the Japs.[1]

[1] St. Clair Drake and H. R. Cayton, *Black Metropolis*, p. 745.

As a matter of fact, the pressure exerted by a dominant group often has an integrating effect upon the minority. The persecution of the Jews has been a major factor in holding them together; and it is a familiar story that, where the Jew has failed to encounter prejudice and discrimination, he tends to be assimilated and to disappear. Miller[2] has observed how minorities have often become unified by directing their animosity toward some distinctive trait in their opponent's culture, or by adopting as a symbol something of their own which sets them off from their oppressors. Thus, the Poles made Catholicism the symbol of their nationalistic aspirations, for their enemies on one side were Russian Orthodox, and on the other, German Lutheran. Similarly, the Irish and the Czechs have used their opponents' religion as an object of their antipathy. The Koreans, who in 4000 years had never developed or adopted any national religion, and gave scant attention to missionaries, took eagerly to Christianity as a symbol for their Independence Movement, once the Japanese had conquered their country and attempted to force assimilation upon them. Language, too, has often served as a rallying point for an oppressed group, as Norwegians, Irish, Poles, and many other European minorities well illustrate. African natives, moreover, reacted to white domination by developing a "we-feeling" which had never existed before. Says Kidd:

> When white men first appeared in South Africa, the natives seemed to have no consciousness that they formed a class opposed to the white men. One tribe regarded the next tribe as its eternal enemy. The natives were intensely conscious of the tribal bonds, but it never occurred to them that they had a bond of "color." The effect of civilization and education has been to draw their attention to this racial conflict; the antithesis of black and white has had a most potent effect in awakening a sense of racial, as opposed to tribal, solidarity.[3]

Leaders of minority groups, appreciating the tremendous power which lies in unity, have sought from time to time to bring together, not only their own people, but others who also suffer discrimination. Appeals are made to all minorities to band together to defeat some bigoted candidate for office, to support a liberal one, to invalidate restrictive covenants, or to promote the passage of F.E.P.C. legislation. In Europe, minorities have often attempted to wring concessions from dominant groups by joining forces. It is a formidable task, however, to overcome the divisive forces which operate within and between racial and ethnic minorities and to get them to agree upon goals and establish a permanent and effective organization, however great the advantages may be.

The stereotypes we carry around in our minds, then, do not admit of the wide range of differences which actually prevail. The "typical" Negro, Jew, or Italian does not exist, except in the imagination, on the stage, and in fiction. Stereotypes persist, however, by virtue of the fact that, when we encounter an individual who departs radically from our mental picture of the "type," we dismiss him with the comfortable excuse that he is "not typical." The truth of

[2] H. A. Miller, *Races, Nations and Classes*, pp. 57–67.
[3] D. Kidd, *Kaffir Socialism*, pp. 156ff.

the matter is that minority groups reflect an infinite range of personalities, philosophies, values, roles, and statuses, and these differences help the dominant group, making it easier to maintain control and exercise power.

This is not to deny that dominant groups, too, are seldom of one mind. In the South today by no means all white people are committed to a policy of segregation, nullification of the Supreme Court, and white supremacy. There are many voices raised in favor of abiding by the law of the land, observing the decree of the Court, and moving toward the goal of integration. The Ku Klux Klan and the White Citizens' Councils do not include among their members all who are eligible, for there are many who condemn those organizations, their objectives, and their methods.[4]

It is so in South Africa, also. There, where the whites constitute so small a minority, numerically speaking, one would suppose that they might form themselves into one monolithic group the better to preserve their power and prestige. We are told, however, that there is a cleavage between Gentile and Jew; and between British, English-speaking subjects, on the one hand, and those of Dutch descent, who speak Afrikaans, on the other. There are differences, too, with respect to racial policy. While the great majority of the whites are firm believers in white supremacy, and are supporters of the government's policy of *apartheid*, there are also the Integrationists, who insist that the Natives must become Europeanized, their standard of living be brought up to that of the whites, and that they share political power with the whites. The Integrationists look forward to a South Africa where equal rights will be granted to all civilized persons within the same political structure, irrespective of race and color. This proposal, of course, elicits only revulsion from the advocates of *apartheid*.

No doubt it is true everywhere that racial and ethnic groups which enjoy power and prestige are rent with internal differences and divisions, but in this chapter we shall examine the bases of cleavage common to minority groups, and which prevent their offering a united front in their struggle for status.

Intergroup Cleavages

Minority status alone has seldom been an adequate reason for bringing unlike peoples together. On the contrary, it frequently happens that the hatred one minority bears for another surpasses even its hatred for its oppressors. African natives, for instance, will vent their rage on the helpless Hindus rather than on the domineering whites. Cape Coloured are no less prejudiced against black natives than are the whites; and Anglo-Indians have long shown a reluctance to identify their interests with those of the Indians.

Negroes and Immigrants

In the United States the problems faced by the European immigrant have much in common with those faced by the Negro. Both have been the victims

---

[4] J. McB. Dobbs, *The Southern Heritage*; R. McGill, *The South and the Southerner*.

of exploitation, segregation, and discrimination. They have been forced to reside in the blighted areas of our cities, and to earn their living at the least desirable occupations. One would think that common interests would have created within them a strong fellow-feeling. Instead, Negroes have traditionally manifested a bitter prejudice against foreigners, and the immigrants, in turn, have been quick to adopt the prevailing attitudes toward Negroes. Most of the early race riots in New York City involved the Negroes and the Irish. Drake and Cayton report that Chicago's Negroes, at the turn of the century, viewed the influx of European immigrants with mixed emotions.[5] True, they often lived side by side in the slums of the city, and sometimes in the same buildings; and the Negroes regarded the foreigners with a certain amount of understandable condescension. At the same time they were not oblivious to the fact that these aliens constituted a potential threat to their jobs as butlers, barbers, maids, janitors, bootblacks, and waitresses. They complained that "foreigners learn how to cuss, count, and say 'nigger' as soon as they get here." During the lean years of the depression the Negro press sounded the familiar note that it was unfair for "foreigners" to hold jobs while Negroes were unemployed. Myrdal's estimate of the situation is as follows:

> The European immigrant groups are the ones thrown into most direct contact and competition with Negroes: they live near each other, often send their children to the same schools, and have to struggle for the same jobs. Obviously attitudes among immigrants vary a good deal. Recent immigrants apparently sometimes feel an interest solidarity with Negroes, or, at any rate, lack the intense superior feeling of the native Americans educated in race prejudice. But the development of prejudice against the Negro is usually one of their first lessons in Americanization. Because they are of low status, they like to have a group like the Negroes to which they can be superior. For these reasons, it should not be surprising if now, since new immigration has been restricted for a considerable time, a study of racial attitudes should show that the immigrant groups are on the average even more prejudiced than native Americans in the same community.[6]

The Negroes' antipathy for immigrants is evident even when the immigrants themselves are members of the Negro race.[7] Recent years have seen thousands of Negro aliens entering the United States, chiefly from the West Indies. Theirs has been the peculiar task of adjusting, not only to a new culture, but to a new conception of the significance of race. Not the least of their problems is that of getting along with the native-born Negro, who regards these newcomers with suspicion. He sees in them a threat to his status, and complains that he finds it harder to get a job because the West Indians are so "clannish" that, when one succeeds in getting work, he proceeds to bring in a full crew of his fellows.

---

[5] Drake and Cayton, *op. cit.*, pp. 57, 83.

[6] *Op. cit.*, p. 603.

[7] Cf. I. de A. Reid, *The Negro Immigrant, passim*; Elena Padilla, *Up from Puerto Rico*, pp. 93ff.

The protest is made that "they" have ruined the Baptist Church, or captured the Episcopal, or monopolized politics. The foreign-born Negro, the native-born will say, undermines all concerted efforts to destroy segregation and discrimination by numerous surreptitious stratagems. He will use his British citizenship, for example, in order to circumvent the restrictions Negroes are customarily subjected to. While such devices may be to the personal advantage of the individual, they tend to weaken the American Negro's protest against discrimination. The native-born, accordingly, refer in contemptuous terms to these foreigners, calling them "monkey chasers" (all West Indian Negroes), "Spics" (Spanish-speaking Negroes, particularly Puerto Ricans and Cubans), or "Garveyites." The immigrants, in their turn, display resentment and hostility toward American Negroes.

Negroes and Jews

These are the two largest minority groups in the United States, and their leaders have often expressed the hope that they might join forces in their efforts to obtain their democratic rights. It does seem that a small degree of *rapprochement* has been achieved. On the one hand, the Jews are a notoriously liberal group, harboring less anti-Negro feeling than gentiles, and less given to the observance of Jim Crow practices. They have joined and supported liberal organizations, and were among the founders of the National Urban League and the National Association for the Advancement of Colored People. Jewish philanthropists, such as Julius Rosenwald, have generously contributed to the Negro's progress. Negroes, for their part, have often expressed a great admiration for the Jews, and frankly envy them their success in overcoming the obstacles which have been placed in their path. They have looked, sometimes with mixed feelings, upon the achievements of the Jews, and upon their success in becoming governors of states and justices of the Supreme Court. Negro intellectuals have frequently exhorted their people to study and emulate the Jewish techniques for fighting discrimination and prejudice.

At the same time, the Jews have shown a reluctance to identify their problem with that of the Negro, and have chosen instead to align themselves with the white gentiles. And the Negro of late has increasingly displayed anti-Jewish prejudices.

Anti-Semitism among Negroes has recently become a matter of some concern.[8] It has been especially virulent in the cities of the North, where it is a relatively new phenomenon. Negroes have engaged in boycotts of Jewish establishments, have disseminated anti-Semitic propaganda, have published vicious sheets like *Dynamite* and *Negro Youth,* and have flirted with such movements as the Christian Front. Negro businessmen have used anti-Semitism as a major weapon in their competition with Jewish merchants, and have made effective

[8] A. Rose, *The Negro's Morale*, pp. 128–140; R. Ottley, *New World A-Coming*, pp. 122–136; N. Glazer and D. P. Moynihan, *Beyond the Melting Pot*, pp. 71–73.

use of such slogans as "Spend Your Money Where You Can Work," "Sustain Negro Enterprise," and "Patronize Your Own." In Chicago they have organized the All-Negro Businessmen's Association, which voices the protests, bitterness, and aspirations of a large part of the business people of that community. The president of the association defended the policies of his organization:

> This situation boils down to the law of nature as the struggle of the survival of the fittest. And our slogans, our program, are a weapon in that struggle. The Jews' weapons are reputation, business contacts, controls of the best districts, and a good training in business. The Negro doesn't have these weapons and if he's going to survive and get ahead, then he's got to insist that his people patronize his store, and not the Jew's. After all, the Jew can open up a store outside the Black Belt, but can the Negro?[9]

Much of the Negro's anti-Semitism is essentially anti-white prejudice, for it so happens that in the urban North the Jew is the representative of the white race who comes into closest contact with the Negro. Ironically, as Rose points out, the fact that Jews are less prejudiced against Negroes than gentiles are makes them more willing to have business dealings with Negroes, and these relationships, in turn, give rise to suspicion and animosity. Jews, for instance, are not averse to renting residential properties to Negroes, or to serving as agents and collectors. Pawnshops owned and operated by Jews are a conspicuous feature of the Negro urban community. The Jew is often an employer of Negro labor, and Jewish merchants dominate the business of the Negro ghetto. Drake and Cayton found that in 1938 three-fourths of the merchants in Bronzeville, the Negro community in Chicago, were Jews, and Ottley reports a similar situation in Harlem. Formerly the urban Negro's contacts with whites were made through the Irish, whom they came to hate; and in New Orleans it was the Italians who served and exploited the Negro community. Recently, however, the Jew has assumed that role, and one result has been an increase of anti-Semitism among Negroes.

Old World Hates Transplanted

The bitter rivalries which have burned for centuries between the various nationalities of Europe are not extinguished by a passage across the Atlantic; and one finds, accordingly, a persistence of these age-old antipathies among the ethnic groups of the United States. As Schermerhorn says, "Often a prejudice retained from the European environment has continued in the American scene; residual Slovak hatred of Hungarians or Polish antagonism toward Germans and Russians has continued unabated for long periods and made it possible for employers to play these groups off against each other."[10] Witness, moreover,

[9] H. L. Sheppard, "The Negro Merchant: A Study of Negro Anti-Semitism," *American Journal of Sociology*, Vol. 53, No. 2, September 1947, p. 97.
[10] R. A. Schermerhorn, *These Our People*, p. 498.

the chronic hatred of the Irish for the English. Roberts even assigns to this traditional attitude an important role in fomenting the American Revolution. Because of oppressive laws enacted in Ireland in 1695, he says, a great number of Irish schoolmasters emigrated to America, where they continued to follow their profession, never losing an opportunity to add fuel to the smoldering fires of resentment for the English whom they found in the colonies.[11] Similar in effect is the prejudice of the Finns for their erstwhile oppressors, the Swedes and the Russians; the hatred of the Flemish for their fellow-Belgians, the Walloons; the Norwegians' jealousy of the Swedes; and the hostility of the Armenians toward the Turks. Czechs and Slovaks bear little love for each other, and insist that, if their names must be joined together, it take the form of Czecho-Slovakia rather than Czechoslovakia. Serbs, Croats, and Slovenes have never been on friendly terms, despite their political union into the nation of Yugoslavia, and those who have come to America have brought their ancient jealousies with them. It is even reported that Irishmen from County Cork, building railroads in America, quit their jobs rather than work alongside Irishmen from County Connaught.

Many of the prejudices which minorities bear for one another, however, are not imported, but are the product of the new environment. We have already described the cleavages present in Burlington, Vermont, where French Canadians, English Canadians, Irish, Russians, Poles, Jews, English, Germans, Italians, and 29 other ethnic groups, to say nothing of the Old Yankees, live side by side.[12] Those of Old American stock consider themselves the charter members of the community and its true aristocrats; and the newcomers on the whole take them at face value, though the Irish are the leaders of the opposition and are critical of all things English, while the Yankees tend to identify themselves with the English tradition. The French Canadians look upon Burlington — and all New England for that matter — as peculiarly their own. Was it not the French who first discovered, explored, and settled the region? Accordingly, they regard all other groups, including the Yankees, as intruders. The Jews, 800 strong, are making their presence felt, and the other ethnic groups are coming to look upon them as an irritating element in the community. These cleavages are not mere matters of friendly rivalry, for they cut deep into the life of the city, manifesting themselves in the schools and churches, in politics, family, social and community affairs.[13]

Intragroup Cleavages

However serious the enmities racial and ethnic groups bear for one another, they are no less an impediment to united action than are the cleavages within

---

[11] E. F. Roberts, *Ireland in America*, pp. 95–100.

[12] E. L. Anderson, *We Americans*. See pp. 173–175 above.

[13] Compare C. W. King, "Social Cleavages in a New England Community," *Social Forces*, Vol. 24, No. 3, March 1946, pp. 322ff.

such groups. The bases for such intragroup divisions are numerous and varied, but the principal ones follow the lines of color, status, age, and attitudes toward the dominant group.

Color

Williams reports that the islands of the Caribbean are notorious for the color distinctions their inhabitants recognize, and for the high market value they place upon white skin. He concludes that these distinctions have the greatest effect in the lack of cohesion which exists among the middle classes, and quotes a native of Trinidad, as follows:

> Between the brown-skinned middle class and the black there is continual rivalry, distrust, and ill-feeling, which, skillfully played upon by the European people, poisons the life of the community. Where so many crosses and colors meet and mingle, the shades are naturally difficult to determine and the resulting confusion is immense. There are the nearly-white hanging on tooth and nail to the fringes of white society, and these, as is easy to understand, hate contact with the darker skin more than some of the broader-minded whites. Then there are the browns, intermediates, who cannot by any stretch of the imagination pass as white, but who will not go one inch toward mixing with people darker than themselves. And so on, and on, and on. Associations are formed of brown people who will not admit into their number those too much darker than themselves, and there have been heated arguments in committee as to whether such and such a person's skin was fair enough to allow him or her to be admitted, without lowering the tone of the institution. Clubs have been known to accept the daughter and mother, who were fair, but to refuse the father, who was black. A dark-skinned brother in a fair-skinned family is sometimes the subject of jeers and insults and open intimations that his presence is not required at family functions. Fair-skinned girls who marry dark men are often ostracized by their families and given up as lost. There have been cases of fair women who have been content to live with black men but who would not marry them. . . . The people most affected by this are people of the middle class who, lacking the hard contact with realities of the masses and unable to attain to the freedoms of a leisured class, are more than all types of people given to trivial divisions and subdivisions of social rank and precedence.[14]

The cleavage between persons of various shades of color is not quite so bitter among American Negroes as it is in the Caribbean, but many sociologists have reported the fact that it does exist. "For the Negroes in Cottonville," says Powdermaker, "color is highly important. . . . A light skin is considered an asset."[15] Davis and Gardner found that among the Negroes of Natchez, Mississippi, color and hair form are among the most important bases for clique and class associations.[16] Drake and Cayton comment upon the prestige which ac-

[14] E. Williams, *The Negro in the Caribbean*, pp. 64–66.
[15] Hortense Powdermaker, *After Freedom*, pp. 175ff.
[16] A. Davis, B. B. Gardner, and Mary Gardner, *Deep South*, pp. 214ff.

crues in Chicago's Negro community to him who is blessed with caucasoid features, and they emphasize the tendency there to idealize "brownness" and to deprecate "blackness." The preferred name for that section of the city is "Bronzeville" — not "The Black Belt."[17] Johnson found among Southern Negro youth a decided preference for light color and says:

> Conflict situations may develop between families and arise within families. It often happens that darker children in families feel that their parents give preference to the children of lighter complexion. Even such inadvertent and casual comparisons as "better hair," "nicer complexion," "prettier skin," "nicer shade" affect the more sensitive young people and contribute to their feeling of inferiority. Children may apply color values unfavorably to one or the other parent or find themselves apologizing for the dark complexion of a parent. They may even harbor resentment against the parent who was biologically responsible for their own undesirable appearance. By far the most frequent instances of color sensitivity, however, occur outside the home as the child attempts to make adjustments to new groups.[18]

It is not universally true, however, that caucasoid features take precedence over negroid. In Africa it is the other way round, and the offspring of whites and Negroes find themselves handicapped in their tribal life.

Age

Sociologists have long been aware of the conflicts which rage between immigrants to the United States and their American-born children. It is quite under-

[17] Drake and Cayton, *op. cit.*, pp. 495–506.
[18] C. S. Johnson, *Growing Up in the Black Belt*, p. 267.

Great color distinctions are made in the Caribbean islands.

standable. Immigrants bring with them their customs, traditions, attitudes, and values. They make constant and desperate attempts to preserve and perpetuate them, and to inculcate them in their children. The new generation, however, often remains apathetic, or even antagonistic, preferring instead to adopt the ways of the dominant group. There are certain bases for conflict between parents and children even under the best of circumstances, but in the case of immigrant minorities the occasions for conflict and misunderstanding are greatly multiplied. Children come to regard their parents as "old-fashioned"; they despise them for their old world origin, their lack of education, their unfamiliarity with the English language, and their ignorance of American standards. They reject their advice and authority, and thereby reverse the usual relationship which prevails between the generations.

Strong reports a second-generation Japanese young woman as saying:

> In regard to the young people's socials where dancing is involved, our first generation usually disapprove by saying it is not becoming for respectable young men and women to be seen in each other's arms. . . . Since our parents have never experienced dancing themselves, and have never seen it in Japan, when they are exposed to it here they think dancing indecent.[19]

Brunner found a similar cleavage between the first and second generation of Poles. Says he:

> Harmonious relations between parents and children are exceptional. In these exceptional cases the parents have got away from traditional modes of behavior and show openmindedness in accepting new values. They have adopted a higher standard of living, speak the English language well, and are willing to disregard traditional standards of a religious and moral nature. They do not persist in holding to national solidarity as a duty, and are desirous of having business and social contacts with Americans. Wherever this is not the case, antagonism is inevitable. . . . It shows itself in a defiant attitude, a disrespect of the parents and repeated cases of friction. A girl said to her mother, who asked her not to go out so late at night, "The old lady is crazy; shut up!" Parents speak of their children as "these American children" with an air of resignation.[20]

Young found many bitter conflicts between the Molokan immigrants of Los Angeles and their American-born children. The situation was vividly illustrated in the remarks of one bewildered youngster, who said:

> You see, we young people live in two worlds, and learn the ways of both worlds — the ways of our parents and the ways of the big world. Sometimes we get mixed up and fight, we fight our parents and we fight the big world. Sometimes I feel I am not much of an American. I was raised by Russians, I understand Russians, I like Russians. At other times I think I am not much of a Russian. Except to my parents, I never speak Russian, and all my friends are Americans.

[19] E. K. Strong, *The Second-Generation Japanese Problem*, p. 259.
[20] E. de S. Brunner, *Immigrant Farmers and Their Children*, pp. 239–240.

*These children of Japanese-American
parents share interests
with other American children.*

Well, I am an American; we live in America — why shouldn't we take their ways?
When my parents object to my American friends, I say, "I work with them. I do
everything with them; why shouldn't I go out with them?" Then they come back
at me and say, "Why don't you sleep with them?" They think they would disgust
me with Americans, but I get mad and say, "Well, I will!" and they have nothing
more to say. . . . I have learned American ways. I can't go against my friends
and do the Russian way. . . .

Many times I get mad, and then I leave the house. You see, I don't want to
hurt my parents and still I want to live like I see is right — that is, right according
to American ways. They can't see it my way, and I can't see it their way.[21]

Old and New Settlers

A certain degree of prestige seems always to be derived from long residence
in a particular place. There are, to be sure, other determiners of status, but one
who can remember "way back when," or who can trace his lineage to the first
settlers, or who bears the surname of one of the old families, enjoys considerable
advantage in the struggle for social position. Thus the First Families of Virginia,
the Daughters of the American Revolution, the Mayflower Descendants, and
the Daughters of Texas Trail Drivers cherish the peculiar possession which is

[21] P. V. Young, *Pilgrims of Russian Town*, pp. 114–115.

theirs, and look with some condescension upon those whose forebears arrived at a later date.

It is not surprising to find similar attitudes prevailing among the members of ethnic minorities. The old settlers feel superior to newcomers, ridicule their awkward and ignorant ways, blame them for lowering the group's status, and are reluctant to become identified with them. Thus Drake and Cayton say that the Negroes who have lived in Chicago a long time, or who are descended from early settlers, are quite unhappy over the horde of southern rural Negroes who have been pouring into the city since the days of World War I. The Old Settlers look back with nostalgia to an earlier time when Negroes enjoyed greater opportunities and suffered less discrimination, and they blame these newcomers for the increase in prejudice and the erection of color barriers.[22]

A cleavage of the same sort prevailed for many years within the Cherokee Nation of Indians, producing a condition of smoldering civil war. On the one side were the "Old Settlers," including those who, early in the nineteenth century, had gone more or less voluntarily to the Indian Territory which is now the state of Oklahoma.[23] Opposing them was the other faction of the tribe, far more numerous than the "Old Settlers," known as the Cherokee National Party, under the leadership of a great chief, John Ross. This latter group was composed of those who had been forcibly expelled from their home in the mountains of North Carolina, Tennessee, and Georgia, and had been driven to Indian Territory. Both factions desired to heal this tribal wound; but the Army, which had jurisdiction over Indian Affairs until 1849, had a different idea. One of the Army's devices for controlling the Indians was the technique of "divide and rule." Lines of cleavage were carefully felt out in the various tribes, and these were aggravated so as to prevent any strong cohesion and resistance on the part of the Indians. In the case of the Cherokees, the Army prodded and encouraged the "Old Settlers," with the result that for a decade the tribe was split into two hostile camps.

American Jewry also manifests this familiar cleavage between early arrivals and later. Jewish immigration to the United States may be divided into four major periods. The first, corresponding roughly to the colonial period, brought Jewish immigrants chiefly of Spanish and Portuguese origin. As early as 1654 (34 years after the Mayflower brought the Pilgrims to Plymouth) a band of 23 Jews, under the leadership of Asser Levy, arrived in New Amsterdam, as New York was then called. It took some shrewd dealing to persuade the Governor, Peter Stuyvesant, to grant them permission to land. Four years later 15 Jewish families settled at Newport, Rhode Island. This latter community grew and prospered, and in 1763 it built a handsome synagogue, which is still standing. Jews are known to have been living in Pennsylvania in 1657; and in the same year the records of Maryland testify to the presence in that colony of "ye Jew Doctor," Dr. Jacob Lombrozo. Other colonial records establish the fact

---

[22] *Op. cit.*, pp. 66, 73–76.
[23] See above, pp. 163f.

that Jews were living in Virginia, South Carolina, Georgia, and Connecticut in the seventeenth and eighteenth centuries. The second wave of immigration, beginning in 1815 and reaching its peak around 1848, brought chiefly German Jews of a white-collar and professional class. The third and largest wave stemmed from eastern Europe and began in 1881, when the Jews in Russian Poland and the Ukraine were threatened with persecution and extinction. Others followed from Hungary, Rumania, Slovakia, and Bohemia, until nearly two million, mostly skilled and unskilled workers and tradesmen, had entered the country. The fourth period covers the years between the two world wars. In the 1920's many fled from Europe to escape the postwar economic dislocations, until their number was drastically reduced by the immigration laws of 1924; and in the 1930's many came from Germany, Austria, Poland, and other central European countries to escape the Nazi persecutions.

Rivalry between the Jews of western Europe and those of central and eastern Europe traces back many centuries. Says Wirth:

> Quite early in the medieval history of the Jews there grew up partisan camps in the larger Jewish community. On the one hand were the Spanish, or Sephardic Jews, who prided themselves on the purity of their stock and the superiority of their status; on the other hand were the German Jews, or Ashkenazim, whose ghetto history considerably lowered their status.[24]

The order of their arrival in America, far from allaying this attitude, served only to stimulate it. Those colonial pioneers of Spanish and Portuguese stock held themselves aloof from their co-religionists from Germany, and those from Germany in turn felt themselves superior to Jews from Russia. One of the earliest symptoms of this rift was seen in the secession of the Ashkenazic element from the Jewish community of Philadelphia in 1802, and the formation of a separate congregation and the establishment of separate benevolent and educational activities. This set the pattern for other communities. "The first Jewish settlers of Chicago," says Wirth, "were Bavarian Jews. . . . The Bavarians considered themselves the earliest settlers, and looked down upon the Poles as an inferior caste."[25] Barron found that the members of the various sub-groups of Jews refrained, until recently, from intermarrying with one another. His comment is:

> The earlier arrivals scorned the later ones as crude, superstitious, and economically indigent, and the latter despised the former as snobs and religious renegades. As recently as 1925, one student of immigrant groups asserted that "intermarriage between a Sephardic Jew and a Russian Jew, for instance, is as rare, if not rarer, than intermarriage between Jew and gentile." Even within each of these divisions of Jews there was at first aversion to marriage with some of the subdivisions. Bavarian Jews hesitated to marry with those German Jews

[24] L. Wirth, *The Ghetto*, p. 84.
[25] *Op. cit.*, p. 160.

who came from the area near the Polish border, derisively labelled "Pollacks." The Russian Jew looked down on the Polish and Galician Jews and refused to marry them or permit his children to do so. Although these intra-Jewish barriers to marriage have largely disappeared in recent times, first generation Jewish parents may still go through the motions of embarrassment when their children marry the sons and daughters of a ridiculed subgroup.[26]

This type of cleavage, however, is but one of many bases for disunity. As a matter of fact, American Jews are anything but a homogeneous group. Among them are reactionaries and progressives; Orthodox, Reform, and Conservative; employers and employees; rich and poor; capitalists and laborers; Republicans and Democrats; Zionists and anti-Zionists; assimilationists and anti-assimilationists; professional men and laborers. In short, they present a good cross-section of the American urban population; and all these differences of wealth, philosophy, occupation, and political leaning serve as bases of cleavage within the group.[27]

Social Classes

Minorities, too, have their social classes, which serve further to prevent cohesion and cooperation. To illustrate this fact we shall consider the American Negro, whose class structure has received far more attention from sociologists than that of any other racial or ethnic group.[28] The phenomenon of social class is admittedly a difficult one to study, for it is only in a few societies that people fall neatly and precisely into well-marked strata. Instead, class lines are usually vague and flexible, the criteria of status are numerous and subtle, and the demarcation of class lines is somewhat arbitrary. Accordingly, social scientists are not in complete agreement as to just how many classes there are, or just where to draw the distinctions between them. It is customary and convenient, however, to use a threefold classification of upper, middle, and lower.

The Negro lower class is far and away the largest of the three, including perhaps 70 or 80 per cent of the twenty million American Negroes. It is hazardous, of course, to generalize about so large a population, scattered as it is over North and South, and living under both rural and urban conditions. The various studies, however, do warrant some cautious descriptions of this class. It consists largely of unskilled laborers, farm hands and sharecroppers, household servants, janitors, porters, laundresses, and bootblacks. Extreme poverty is com-

[26] M. L. Barron, "The Incidence of Jewish Intermarriage in Europe and America," *American Sociological Review*, Vol. 11, No. 1, February 1946, p. 11.

[27] Cf. M. M. Gordon, *Assimilation in American Life*, pp. 173–195.

[28] For reports on the class system of Negroes, see Myrdal, *An American Dilemma*, pp. 689ff.; Drake and Cayton, *op. cit.*, pp. 495–715; M. R. Davie, *Negroes in American Society*, pp. 415–433; Powdermaker, *op. cit., passim*; Davis *et al., op. cit.*, pp. 228–251; E. F. Frazier, *Black Bourgeoisie*, and *The Negro Family in the United States*, pp. 295ff.; C. S. Johnson, *Patterns of Negro Segregation*, pp. 231–235; Gordon. *op. cit.*, pp. 166–173.

mon, there is little or no ownership of property, incomes are low and uncertain, standards of industry and honesty are not high, and in times of economic crisis many of this class are on relief. Family life is disorganized, sexual morals are lax, illegitimacy and desertion are common, and the family tends to be centered on the mother and is even matriarchal. There is little education, and the older members of the class are either illiterate or practically so. Books, newspapers, and periodicals play an insignificant role in their lives. Instead, religion and recreation are the interests, with Baptist, Methodist, Holiness, and Spiritualist churches predominating. Fighting and roistering are common, delinquency and crime rates are high, and aggression and violent behavior are neither rare nor disapproved. This class falls far below the American minimum standards in housing, food, and clothing. In color of skin, this class is the darkest of the three.

The Negro upper class presents an entirely different picture. It is a small group, about 5 per cent of the total. It includes the owners of sizable farms, professional men (doctors, lawyers, druggists, professors, artists, writers, and some teachers, ministers, and civil service employees), and the owners and operators of substantial businesses (banking, insurance, contracting, real estate, and service establishments). The income of this group is well above the average for Negroes, but it is not comparable to that of upper-class whites. Home ownership is important, and often there is ownership of other property as well. Family background is stressed, legal marriage is essential, illegitimacy and desertion are regarded as disgraceful, and the family tends to follow the paternalistic pattern. Education is highly important, more so even than wealth, and is much more a determiner of status than in white society. Members of the upper class will try to shield their children from contacts with lower-class Negroes and from humiliating experiences with whites. Adults themselves will keep their contacts with whites to a minimum, and to that end their recreational activities are centered in the home, including such diversions as dinner parties and bridge. The boisterous, "shouting" forms of religious expression are eschewed, and church membership, insofar as it prevails, tends toward the Episcopal, Congregational, and Presbyterian. This group insists that its ministers be men of refinement and education. In fact, decorous behavior is virtually an obsession with the upper class, great stress being laid upon good manners, strict morals, correct speech, cultural attainmennts, and respectability. In certain Southern cities, as a matter of fact, the Negro upper class adheres to a strict puritanical code. Light skin color and caucasoid features are disproportionately represented in this class, and a certain bias against Negro racial features has even been reported. The Negro class structure, however, is a dynamic, not a static, phenomenon; and both the criteria of status and the composition of the classes are undergoing constant change.

Between these two extremes stands the middle class. It is larger than the upper class, but considerably smaller than the lower, including perhaps 15 per cent of the Negro population. Here are found the small business men, professional men with limited practices, successful farm tenants, skilled and semi-skilled industrial laborers, schoolteachers, social workers, sales people, office workers, clerical employees in the civil service, well-paid servants, Pullman porters, dining-car waiters, policemen, and firemen. Theirs, in short, is regular but low-paying employment. For the most part this group has attained primary or secondary education, but few of them, other than teachers, have attended college. Education, however, they hold in high esteem, and they look forward to sending their children to college. Here is a group striving to better its condition and especially that of the children. Prominent among its social types are the "strivers" and the "strainers." It holds aloft the symbols of respectability and success. High among its values are thrift, independence, honesty, and industry. They are obsessed by a drive to get ahead, "to lay a little something by," to have a nice home, to wear good clothes, and to live in a decent neighborhood. It is a proud boast among them never to have had trouble with the law. Family life tends to be stable, though common law marriages are not unknown. They are the pillars of the Baptist and Methodist churches, and a large portion of lodge membership comes from this class. They are not so light as the upper class, nor so dark as the lower. Brown is the prevailing color.

Between these social classes there is not the best of feeling.[29] The upper class condemns the lower as black, boisterous, stupid, and sexually promiscuous. Its members are described as emotionally unstable crapshooters, engaging in liquor brawls, loud in their conversation, disgusting in public, without ambition, disposed to have large families they cannot support, without decent background, living in dirty homes, and rearing dirty children. The middle class is equally severe in its criticism of the lower, deploring its shiftlessness, dirtiness, and laziness. The lower class, in turn, is contemptuous of the upper, referring to them as "big shots," "dicties," "stuck-ups," "muckti-mucks," and accusing them of being disloyal to their race ("sellin' out to the white folks"), extremely selfish and snobbish, unbecomingly proud of their caucasoid features and light color, and ever ready to exploit their Negro patients and customers. The middle class they accuse of being sanctimonious, greedy, miserly, pretentious, and hypocritical. Those in the middle criticize the upper class for their card playing, lewd dancing, irreligion, and insincerity; and these, in reply, wound their inferiors with the "unkindest cut of all," saying that they are "nice, respectable, and honest — but nobody."

Thus the cleavage between the Negro social classes magnifies the difficulty for this racial minority, numerous though it be, to present a united front to its oppressors. The existence of social classes, furthermore, serves to disperse the Negro's discontent with his lower status, for if *some* have succeeded in acquiring wealth, education, and position, does it not follow that the way is open for *any* Negro to improve his lot, if he will but make the effort? If there is ignorance and poverty, is it not the individual who is at fault, rather than the system? Thus, dominant groups, in their own selfish interests, prove themselves shrewd when they temper their rule with a modicum of generosity and opportunity.

[29] Drake and Cayton, *op. cit.*, pp. 559–652; Davis *et. al.*, *op. cit.*, pp. 230–234; Myrdal, *op. cit.*, p. 703.

Minority groups, then, are invariably rent by cleavages of one sort or another, a fact which plays conveniently into the hands of dominant groups. Such cleavages, we have seen, follow many different lines. Of prime importance, however, are the differences in the attitudes the members of a minority have for the dominant group. Some are disposed to acquiesce, some to resist, and some to compromise. Even among those who would make a show of resistance there is disagreement on strategy and techniques. Here we have still another basis for cleavage, which we shall explore in the following chapter.

16

Reactions
to
Minority Status

*Negroes, regardless of station in life,
have a common cause — the abolition of racial inequalities.*

DANIEL C. THOMPSON
The Negro Leadership Class

How do the members of minority groups react to their subordinate status? How do they feel about discrimination, disfranchisement, segregation, and second-class citizenship? What are their attitudes toward the dominant group, which looks down upon them as inferiors and which jealously guards its prestige and its privileges?

The members of dominant groups like to feel that subordinate peoples regard them with admiration and respect, and even with gratitude for the favors they have received. Colonial powers insist that their subjects, except for disgruntled agitators, deeply appreciate the blessings which have been brought to them by their conquerors — peace and order, relief from tyrants, sanitation and medical care, commerce and industry, education, Christianity, and a higher standard of living. American whites insist that Negroes, if they were let alone, and not aroused by radicals, would be quite happy with their lot. It is said that they are childlike, simple, carefree people, not disposed to worry themselves with problems of government and finance, and incapable of looking very far into the future. Dominant peoples everywhere, it seems, comfort themselves with stereotypes of contented, unambitious, humble subordinates, blissfully ignorant of the cares and burdens of superiority.

Disorganization

Anthropologists have long said that contacts between racial and ethnic groups frequently result in disorganization and demoralization. This was put very well by a primitive, unlettered native of the Solomon Islands, who said:

> You white men give us orders; we no longer give orders to ourselves. . . . The white man has come and tells us we must behave like *his* father. Our own fathers, we must forget them. . . . In the olden days we did this thing, we did that thing. We did not stop and say to ourselves first, "This thing I want to do, is it right?" We always knew. Now we have to say, "This thing I want to do, will the white man tell me it is wrong and punish me?"[1]

The literature of ethnology abounds in reports of primitive tribes in all parts of the world which have been well-nigh shattered by the impact of European civilization. These are not the dismal travelogues of biased or myopic white men, but the careful descriptions of competent, sympathetic observers. They tell of onetime vigorous peoples who are now "dying of boredom," or who are "losing their zest for life," or who are "lazy, indolent parasites, devoid of all stamina and ambition." The story is much the same, whether the victims be the nonliterate peoples of Asia, the American Indians, Melanesians, Polynesians, Eskimos, African blacks, or the Australian aborigines. To cite one instance:

> Elderly informants look back to the old days with nostalgia, which is nothing uncommon with Indians. They do appreciate these times, however. . . . These times are at least peaceful. The ancient warriors are tired. Despite such injustices as the tribe claims to have suffered at the hands of the whites, they remember

[1] H. A. Hogbin, *Experiments in Civilization*, pp. 153–154.

that these suyapi pacified the land. One can trade, though warily, even with the Blackfoot. Battle, murder, and sudden death stalked the land in the old days. . . . The women particularly appreciate the fact that they can go to sleep at night and wake up free instead of as despised captives. Sometimes the old warriors will admit as much.

Intelligent informants do claim that the old days were busier and therefore healthier and happier. They deprecate the modern custom of living in houses, blaming this practice as bitterly as the smallpox for the decimation of their people. In those old days men hunted. Everybody fished. Women, children, and old men gathered berries and roots. The hunter carried the quarry to his lodge and dropped it. His work was finished. Women worked hides continually, pounded pemmican of deer, and, in season, of bison. Bones were boiled for succulent broth. Women packed in firewood. The industrious were respected and loafers despised. True, the men had the easier and more interesting work, but their constant danger was appreciated by their wives and mothers. The modern protected men still expect spoiling and hence cause bitterness among the women and scorn among the uncomprehending whites. But formerly a wife who had any affection for her husband at all was anxious to pamper her husband. The Blackfoot were indomitable. Should one's man die, a wife could be comforted that he died gloriously. . . . Chiefs were not sourly coughing their lives away with tuberculosis, and young men and women were something, not half white suyapi, and half of the people not anything at all entirely.[2]

Another account tells the tragic story of the Sioux Indians.[3] Two and a half centuries ago these Indians moved from the Eastern woodlands out onto the plains, and adapted themselves to the hunting of the buffalo. A century ago the white man began to encroach upon their territory, destroying their food supply and disrupting their way of life. The result was a series of struggles, which have found a prominent place in the folklore and history of America, and which ended in 1869 when the Sioux were removed to reservations. Thus, for nearly a hundred years these Indians have been reluctantly traveling the rough road leading to the white man's civilization. The victors were on hand to help, for it was their policy "to civilize" and "to humanize" them. Children were virtually kidnapped and placed in the government schools. Their hair was cut. Their Indian clothes were thrown away. They were forbidden to speak their own language. Punishment was meted out to those who ran away, or who persisted in clinging to their old ways. Even when the older policy of rapid and compulsory assimilation was abandoned, the hope remained that the Indian might be made over according to the social and economic ideals of white Americans.

It has indeed been a rough road, marked by one defeat after another, and ending finally with the loss of their cattle and their grazing lands. Even more tragic, however, has been the loss of their ancient virtues of honor, bravery, generosity, and moral integrity, all of which were prominent among them. Men have now lost the skill of leadership and the sense of responsibility.

[2] H. H. Turney-High, *The Flathead Indians of Montana*, Memoirs of the American Anthropological Association, No. 48, 1937, p. 149.
[3] G. MacGregor, *Warriors Without Weapons*.

The children, exposed on the one hand to the residue of the old Indian culture, and on the other to the confusion of an alien white culture, present a distressing picture. They are described by MacGregor as "immature, resigned, and apathetic." The total effect of such an environment upon them is the creation of personalities which are insecure, passive, without purpose, and without hope. Mac-Gregor insists that it is not too late to salvage this once-stalwart people; but a program, to be successful, must be focused, not only upon goals of material rehabilitation, but upon the restoration of pride, responsibility, and self-confidence.

Even missionaries, for all their good intentions, have often had a demoralizing effect upon the very people they desired to help. This is not to deny that their accomplishments have frequently, perhaps predominantly, been beneficial. Cultural diffusion is as old as human history. Long before missionaries appeared on the scene culture was being carried from place to place by soldiers, traders, captives, thieves, bootleggers, and nomads. Diffusion has a disconcerting effect, regardless of who be the bearers of the new item. Missionaries are no exception. They are, by their own admission, bent upon changing the lives of the people among whom they labor; but the changes are not always the ones they anticipate. Ako Adjei, himself a member of the Ga tribe of the Gold Coast, has this to say:

> The theory which supported the action of the early Christian missionaries in Africa was that everything African or indigenous was bad and contrary to the Will of God but that everything European or foreign was good and acceptable to the Will of God. The effect of this theory on African social institutions was great. Application of the theory brought about a great disruption of African social life. Nobody was baptized into the Christian Church until he . . . had agreed to abandon the African and follow the European way of life. For example, the missionaries changed even the traditional names of individual Africans — names which have deep meanings and spiritual significance in African culture. . . .
>
> The activities of Christian missionaries have brought about a great confusion and suspicion in the minds of many Africans. They have also brought about a conflict between the basic values that are dominant in African culture and the incipient European social ideals. One of the major effects of Western civilization upon African life is that many Africans have lost their respect for the traditional institutions of African society.[4]

Sociologists, too, have noted the bewilderment and disorganization which have so frequently characterized the initial reaction of immigrants in the United States. This fact is continually encountered in immigrant autobiographies, in letters, and in the records of legal aid societies, criminal courts, juvenile courts, and various welfare agencies. One immigrant to America wrote as follows:

> How can one find happiness in this Hell where people rush as though mad, over the ground and under the ground and even, God forgive them, through the air; where everything is entirely different from what one is accustomed to at

[4] "Imperialism and Spiritual Freedom," *American Journal of Sociology*, Vol. 50, No. 3, November 1944, p. 194. See also, in the same issue, R. E. Park, "Missions in the Modern World"; H. Stunz, "Christian Missions and Social Cohesion"; G. G. Brown, "Missions and Cultural Diffusion."

home; where it is impossible to distinguish to what social class a man belongs; where it is impossible to understand a single word of what they say; where baptized Christians are run after by street boys even as a non-Christian, a Turk, would be run after at home?"[5]

It was this problem of disorganization, as a matter of fact, which was a theme of one of the early sociological classics, *The Polish Peasant*.[6] The authors of this study attempt to explain the demoralization so common among Polish immigrants and their children. The Polish immigrant, they say, was born and reared in a permanent, coherent primary group, in an agricultural community, settled for many hundreds of years in the same locality, changing so slowly that each generation was able to adapt to the changes with little effort. His conduct was regulated by habit and custom, and by the immediate and direct suggestions and reactions of his associates. It was all quite different, however, when he crossed the Atlantic and settled in an American city. Here he was isolated and practically unknown, economically poor and insecure, surrounded by people who were indifferent, contemptuous, and often hostile, whose language he did not speak and whose ways he did not understand. This well-nigh insurmountable problem of adjustment, however, does not always lead to active demoralization and antisocial behavior. Many of these people, to be sure, made the transition with apparent ease, though Thomas and Znaniecki insist that "a certain lowering of moral level is inevitable," and that there is a "partial or general weakening of social interests, a growing narrowness or shallowness of the individual's social life." Many an immigrant family, however, found the adjustment more than it could manage, and the authors point to the wide prevalence of crime, economic dependency, divorce and desertion, delinquency, and prostitution as evidence of widespread disorganization.

W. C. Smith has made a good analysis of the process of disorganization through which so many immigrants have passed, with varying degrees of anguish.[7] The immigrant, he says, often misapprehends the life about him. He sees the new culture, not through intimate and personal contacts with the older residents, but through such secondary media as newspapers, moving pictures, politics, and business activities, where keen competition, graft, and misrepresentation are common practices. He finds himself in a totally different situation, where his old standards do not apply. He rubs shoulders with other groups, who have different customs and values, and he cannot easily and immediately organize a workable scheme from this tangled maze. Many of them suffer a loss of status, being forced to stoop to the lowest common labor, and being ridiculed for being "queer."[8] As one of them said:

---

[5] V. Korolenko, *In a Strange Land*, p. 52.
[6] W. I. Thomas and F. Znaniecki, *The Polish Peasant in Europe and America*, especially Vol. 5, pp. 165ff.
[7] *Americans in the Making*, pp. 61ff.
[8] This loss of status was an especially acute problem with the refugees of the 1930's, as pointed out by M. R. Davie in *Refugees in America*, p. 395. See also J. Kosa, *Land of Choice, passim*.

When I first came I thought I could not stand it here, so many people would refer to the southern European class and refer to the peasant class of people with great disdain. They seemed to look down upon Europeans from our land. I know that many have a serious misconception of class. Our peasant is a landholder, more nearly compared to the American farmer, and is far from the bottom of the social scale. We have classes of peasants, the half peasant, the quarter and even the eighth peasant with smaller holdings of land. Below them are still lower classes of laborers, cottiers, and other workers. As in America the standing is measured by the stock he holds. Our peasant is a link in a long line of family inheritance and tradition which oftentimes runs back many centuries with a name, a reputation to sustain and a posterity. So my blood would boil when many an uneducated person would look down upon me and speak in a condescending way. For a long time these sarcastic remarks hurt me, and worried me.[9]

The immigrant becomes torn by inner conflicts when he discovers that his moral codes and behavior are not applicable and are even ridiculed. If these sacred elements in his life are false, then what is dependable? Moreover, his language, dress, customs, and mannerisms are objects of sneers and disdain. With the breakdown of the old patterns of behavior there is an ever-increasing development of individualization. Group consciousness gives way to egoistic attitudes. He thinks only of himself, and tends to gratify his own wishes even at the expense of his fellows.

More Permanent Adjustments

Disorganization and demoralization, however, are not permanent conditions. Occasionally, as we saw in Chapter 7, the subordinate racial or ethnic group is annihilated, but more often some form of accommodation is reached. One of the groups achieves a dominant status, enjoying prestige, power, and privilege, while the other is relegated to a position of subordinate status. Let us consider now the various adjustments the members of the minority groups are obliged to make to the discriminations, segregation, and indignities to which they are subjected by the dominant group. The problem has been treated by many social scientists in a variety of ways.

Negro Social Types

The Negro's reactions to his status, Strong thinks, can be seen in the social types which he found in the Negro community of Chicago.[10] These types are

---

[9] W. C. Smith, *Americans in the Making*, pp. 67–68.

[10] S. M. Strong, "Negro-White Relations as Reflected in Social Types," *American Journal of Sociology*, Vol. 52, No. 1, July 1946, pp. 23–30. Robert Johnson also used the device of "social types" in reporting on the Negro community in an upstate New York city. See his "Negro Reactions to Minority Group Status," in M. L. Barron (Ed.), *American Minorities*, pp. 192ff.

thoroughly familiar to the members of the community, and Strong describes them as follows in the language which the Negroes themselves employ:

1. *The "white man's nigger."* Persons of this type, sometimes called "Uncle Toms," accept the superordination of whites as natural and inevitable. They are servile and affable, and they feel an allegiance to some group of whites which supersedes their loyalty to their own group.

2. *The "bad nigger."* He refuses to accept the place society assigns to him. He is prepared to fight the system; he fights, not intelligently, but blindly and recklessly.

3. *The "smart nigger."* He, too, protests against white supremacy, but his protest assumes a different form from that of the "bad nigger." He objects to kowtowing to the whites, but he is adept at handling them, without losing his dignity, and without assuming the role of "Uncle Tom."

4. *The "white man's strumpet."* This is the mistress of a white man. However, it is not the fact that she is a mistress which causes her to be so greatly disliked by other Negroes, but the fact that she is the mistress of a white man.

5. *The "mammy."* She is the female counterpart of the "white man's nigger," and is generally disliked by Negroes. She is a very familiar type in the South, but is not frequently encountered in the urban North.

6. *The "sheet lover."* This is the Negro who is particularly attracted to white, or at least light, women. This type is not so well recognized as the others, and is somewhat, but not greatly, disliked.

7. *The "race leader."* He is not simply an ardent racialist, but is a man of ability who has something to contribute to Negro advancement. He seeks no personal gain from his activities. He is adept in the arts of compromise, and moves with patience and caution. He is greatly admired.

8. *The "race man."* He is not held in such high esteem as the "race leaders," for it is suspected that his frequent expressions of loyalty to the Negro are a guise to further his own ends. Perhaps he does contribute to the advancement of the race, but he is regarded as wanting in either the sincerity or the ability of a "race leader."

9. *The "race woman."* She is the female counterpart of the "race leader," sincere, forceful, intellectual, educated. She is a fearless champion of the rights of Negroes. She is the object of great admiration by the Negro community.

These social types, Strong thinks, represent various forms of adjustment the Negro makes to the problem of discrimination. They serve other purposes, too. They function as symbols of racial solidarity and a growing race consciousness. And, to the extent that these various types are approved or disapproved, they reflect the Negro's temper and changes in attitudes toward whites.

It is a far cry from the modern Negro community of Chicago to the Jewish community of Palestine two millennia ago. Yet though widely separated in space and in time, these two communities have one thing in common — an oppressed minority faced with the necessity of adjusting to a dominant group. In the case of the Jews, the dominant group was first the Greeks and later the Romans.[11]

The Jews were not of one mind as to the proper adjustment, any more than are the Negroes of Chicago. They, too, had their "Uncle Toms," their compromisers, assimilationists, fighters, and isolationists. The labels they attached to these social types were unique and different, but the viewpoints have a familiar ring. The Jews, 2000 years ago, had their Sadducees, their Pharisees, their Essenes, and their Zealots.

The Sadducees were an aristocratic group who wished to see the Jews a nation among nations. Religion to them was a matter of some indifference. They were sympathetic with the culture of the Greeks and Romans, and were disposed to assimilate it, and to have a part in its diffusion. The Pharisees, on the contrary, were strictly religious. Foreign domination they regarded as God's punishment for the sins of the people. Their desire was to make of Judea an isolated religious commonwealth, removed as far as possible from contamination with the life and culture of the heathen. In the meantime they would withdraw from everything that might defile them. They were scrupulous in the observance of religious customs, traditions, and rules. To achieve their goal of an isolated Jewish commonwealth they were forced by circumstances to participate in the religious struggles rife in Palestine at the time. Growing sick at heart when their efforts to found a political kingdom met with no success, they began to look more eagerly to the coming of a divine Messiah who would drive out the Romans and bring in the Kingdom of God.

The Essenes went far beyond the Pharisees in their determination to separate themselves from contamination with the world. Whereas the Pharisees, driven by circumstances, were forced to participate in political affairs, the Essenes withdrew farther and farther into the loneliness of the wilderness and the region of the Dead Sea. They were ardent pacifists, and were among the first to condemn slavery as a violation of the ideal of the brotherhood of man. They turned their backs upon wealth and scholarship, and devoted themselves to meditation, prayer, and religious ceremonies. They supported themselves by agriculture and handicrafts, but would have nothing to do with trade, for fear that it would develop covetousness within them.

The Zealots, finally, were militant in their protest. In many respects they were akin to the Pharisees, and looked forward to complete political independence from Rome. They came to despair of the coming of a divine deliverer, grew tired of exercising faith and patience, and eventually resorted to arms and revolution. Their rebellion precipitated the catastrophic massacre of the Jewish people

[11] See S. Mathews, *A History of New Testament Times in Palestine.*

at the hands of the Romans in 70 A.D., and the dispersion of the remnant to the corners of the earth.

Sadducees, Pharisees, Essenes, and Zealots have long since passed out of existence, but their spiritual successors may still be found among the Jewish people in their varied reactions to the persecution and discrimination which have continually been their lot.

Japanese-Americans

An excellent opportunity to observe the reactions of a minority group to discrimination and domination was afforded when more than a hundred thousand Japanese-Americans were forcibly expelled from the Pacific Coast states soon after the United States entered World War II.[12] These people were sent to ten relocation centers in the West and Middle West. Most were American citizens by virtue of having been born in the country, and there were no charges of subversive activity laid upon them. Even though the authorities undertook to treat them with consideration, it is generally recognized now that the whole procedure was a momentous blunder, and that tens of thousands of innocent, loyal American citizens were subjected to deprivations, discomforts, and indignities which they did not deserve. They had every reason to feel resentful of such discrimination. "They can't do this to me!" many of them kept saying. But "they" did, nevertheless.

An excellent report is available on the relocation center at Poston, Arizona, where some 17,000 of these evacuees were stationed.[13] The author of the report discusses, among many other things, the reactions of the Japanese to the injustices they suffered. He classifies these reactions as (1) cooperation, (2) withdrawal, and (3) aggressiveness; and he believes, moreover, that these represent *"three universal kinds of behavior with which individuals react to authority when subject to forces of stress that are disturbing to the emotions and thoughts of the individual. . . .* They have been seen in every kind of human group that has ever been carefully studied. They are particularly evident in minorities where it is often possible to divide a community roughly into three parts in terms of those who show predominantly cooperation, withdrawal, or aggression in relation to the majority group. This has been noted in many American Indians, among Negroes, in Jewish communities, among Italian-Americans and among Spanish-Americans, and it was, of course, true of the Japanese in America long before the war."[14]

There were many at Poston who chose the path of cooperation. They carefully obeyed the regulations, worked enthusiastically in building the center, assisted in the maintenance of law and order, and offered their services as administrative aides. Especially in the early days of the center, there was much overcrowding, and there was a lack of equipment and material necessary for comfort and

12 See above, pp. 165–168.
13 A. H. Leighton, *The Governing of Men.*
14 *Op. cit.,* p. 263.

privacy. Even so, there were those cooperative souls who submitted quietly to these discomforts. Some would even insist that the food was satisfactory, even when it was inadequate by any normal standards.

Withdrawal, Leighton thinks, was perhaps the most widespread of all the reactions of the Japanese. This took many different forms. At one extreme was the individual who persisted in living alone out in the mesquite, coming in occasionally for a supply of rice to supplement the fish he caught in the nearby river. At the other extreme were patients who were brought to the hospital for "mental trouble," and who were apparently escaping from the stresses of life in the center by flight into fantasy worlds of their own. Between these two extremes were the many who stoically bore their tribulations, withdrew from painful contacts, refrained from "sticking their necks out," and followed a policy of "lying low." There were those, too, who found an escape from hard reality in magic, prophecy, and religious cults.

Finally, aggressive attitudes were present among the evacuees. There were those who heaped abuse upon the Administration, made inflammatory speeches, registered interminable complaints, and issued threats. They would disregard the regulations, refuse to work, and steal government property. They were continually clamoring for more living space, better food, more hospital facilities. They circulated petitions. They would make a flourish of Japanese nationalism. They would attack other evacuees suspected of being informers, whom they called "dogs." The culmination of their aggressive activities was a major strike, which virtually brought the operation of the center to a standstill.

Patterns of Reaction

The three cases we have cited may seem to have little in common. The minority groups themselves are about as different as human groups can be, the problems they faced were quite dissimilar, and their reactions and adjustments appear to be quite distinct. Basically, however, there is much similarity. After all, there is a limit to the ways in which an oppressed minority *can* react, and it is not surprising to find that subordinate peoples everywhere respond to dominance in somewhat the same manner. They will, of course, be influenced by the culture in which they live. If they choose to resist, for instance, they will invariably employ the weapons at their disposal — spears and tomahawks, bows and arrows, or guns and bombs. They will be influenced, too, by the intangible elements in their cultural environment — the beliefs, folkways, attitudes, and philosophies. Passive resistance comes readily to the Hindu mind, whereas it would be incomprehensible to a Zulu or a Sioux.

Glick's Social Types[15]

Clarence E. Glick, as we saw earlier (pp. 132 f.), believes that race relations move through a series of stages, and that each stage produces typical personal

[15] C. E. Glick, "Social Roles and Types in Race Relations," in A. W. Lind (Ed.), *Race Relations in World Perspective*, pp. 239ff.

reactions, or social types. It will be recalled that, according to Glick's theory, the phases through which race relations progress are (1) a precontact phase, (2) a contact and predomination phase, (3) a domination phase, and (4) a post-domination phase. Social types characteristic of race relations situations do not make their appearance in the first phase, nor in the early parts of the second phase. At first, contacts occur between persons from indigenous societies and "foreigners" (mostly Europeans, but also Chinese, Indians, Arabs, and so on). Roles and statuses have not had time to take form, and conduct tends to reflect the ways in which immediate situations are sized up by those involved in them. Under such circumstances a person's latent disposition manifests itself in ways that, in a more stable situation, would be subjected to social restraints. Traders, for instance, who had learned their roles in their own society might develop patterns of behavior which differ greatly from those which would have been tolerated at home, and native chiefs might develop self-concepts quite different from those which they would have held had not contact occurred. Similarly, new types of native leaders might arise, including some who under normal circumstances would never have risen to positions of leadership.

The domination phase produces a variety of social types. Some will become the "apathetic government wards," listless and lazy. There emerge the "cooperative natives," enjoying certain privileges by virtue of their attitudes toward their masters rather than from the support of their own group. There are also the "professional natives" — singers and dancers, hunting and fishing guides, tour assistants, ethnological "experts," and the like — who flourish on the tourist frontier. As the foreign power becomes more firmly planted and schools are established, there appears the "educated native," envied by some of his society, disparaged by others. Under the plantation system we find the familiar types of "the missus," the overseer, "the mammy," the field hand, the fugitive, the pensioner, the "toady," and many others.

Social types also make their appearance in the dominant group. There is the "empire builder," the *sahib* and the *mem-sahib*, the *tuan besar* and the *baas*. Early in the present century, in Hong Kong and Shanghai, there emerged the *tai-pan* (great manager), the *griffin* (somewhat wild junior executive), and the "old China hand."

Finally, we come to the post-domination phase, when the erstwhile masters begin to lose their power, and when the long-suffering native begins to make his demands either in the form of nationalistic movements or in movements for integration. Social types in the dominant group which formerly symbolized respected roles ("old master," *baas*, *mem-sahib*, and so on) are held up to ridicule by the nationalist leaders. The cooperative native is also the object of disparagement and contempt. Among the social types conspicuous in this phase of race relations are the "cracker," the "peckerwood," the "scared liberal," the "right guy," and the "dyed-in-the-wool liberal," the "straight-shooter," the "status quo conservative," the "racial demagogue," the "gradualist," the "radical reformer," the "left-wing revolutionary," the "color blind," and others.

Protest:
The March on Washington.

Generalizations

Attempts have been made from time to time to generalize about the reactions of the members of minority groups to the discrimination, prejudice, and inferiority which are their lot. Stonequist, for instance, maintains that there are three patterns of adjustment available to the racial or cultural hybrid: (1) the intermediary role, (2) the nationalist role, and (3) assimilation and passing.[16] Davie, discussing the Negro's reaction to his status, recognizes seven types of responses: (1) acceptance, (2) resentment, (3) avoidance, (4) overcompensation, (5) race pride, (6) hostility and aggression, and (7) protest.[17] Johnson, also thinking of the American Negro, makes a fourfold classification: (1) acceptance, (2) avoidance, (3) direct hostility and aggression, and (4) indirect or deflected hostility.[18]

Professor George E. Simpson of Oberlin College, who has made intensive studies of race problems in Jamaica and elsewhere in the Caribbean, maintains

[16] *The Marginal Man*, pp. 159–200.
[17] M. R. Davie, *Negroes in American Society*, pp. 434–455.
[18] C. S. Johnson, *Patterns of Negro Segregation*, pp. 244–315.

that members of minority groups make six types of adjustment to their disprivileged social position; and these adjustments, which are to be thought of as constituting a continuum rather than as a set of absolute categories, are:

Type I. Acceptance. Some members of subordinate groups embrace their disprivileged position and accept the dominant group's definition of their status and role.

Type II. Withdrawal through the invention of a symbolic Utopia. Certain persons solve the problems of their minority status by adopting a fundamentalist religious orientation which stresses preparation for the next world.

Type III. Political withdrawal combined with verbal aggression. This category includes those who hold the values of the dominant group but are convinced they cannot achieve them under existing institutions and conditions. Simpson feels that the members of the Ras Tafari cult of Jamaica fall into this type. This cult is a semireligious, semipolitical movement. Its adherents are violently antiwhite, regard Haile Selassie, Emperor of Abyssinia, as the living god, and see no hope for the black man in the British West Indies. They withdraw from such activities as voting and attending political meetings, and they expect no real achievements from labor unions. They look forward to their early "return" to their homeland in Ethiopia, and in the meantime they keep up their verbal attack on the white man.

Type IV. A type of adjustment between Ras Tafarianism and active participation in protest organizations in the United States. In this category belong those who are more optimistic and realistic than the members of Ras Tafari, but less sophisticated than are the members of politically active organizations such as the N.AA.C.P. in the United States. These are the somewhat less aggressive members of a racial or cultural minority. Simpson believes that, in the United States, the average small-town northern Negro, if not the average northern Negro, represents this type of adjustment.

Type V. Full acculturation to the values of the dominant society. This includes those who drop the withdrawal (supernatural, political or geographical) theme completely and work for full assimilation. Active participants in the N.A.A.C.P. exemplify this type of adjustment.

Type VI. Political withdrawal combined with physical aggression. In this category are those who renounce the values of the dominant group altogether and attempt to free themselves from its control. Here are the rebels and insurrectionists. The Mau Mau movement in Kenya included persons of this type.[19]

Simpson, Davie, Johnson, and Stonequist are fundamentally in agreement. For our purposes we shall borrow from all of them and distinguish *four patterns of reaction to dominance*, which seem characteristic of subordinate peoples everywhere: (1) *acceptance*, (2) *avoidance*, (3) *assimilation*, (4) *aggression*.

As a rule, one will find all these reactions manifested continually in a minority group. Every oppressed people seems to have its "Uncle Toms" and its "smart

---

19 G. E. Simpson, "The Ras Tafari Movement in Jamaica: A Study of Race and Class Conflict," *Social Forces*, Vol. 34, No. 2, December 1955, pp. 167ff.

niggers," its Pharisees and its Sadducees, its Scarlett O'Haras and its Melanie Hamiltons, its assimilationists and its survivalists. There are times and places, of course, where one or another of these responses is the prevalent and popular one. The Amish, for instance, have consistently followed a policy of avoidance, while the Cape Coloured and the Anglo-Indians, despite the barriers erected against them, have never wavered in their desire for assimilation. There are other instances where the dominant group has effectively suppressd certain patterns of reaction, or has been able to enforce the pattern it approved. Even so, one invariably finds rebellious ones who choose to react otherwise.

Of the Negro, Powdermaker believes that *age* is the most important factor in his reaction to his inferior status.[20] The older generation, she found in her study of a Mississippi community, accepts the doctrine of white supremacy, believes that Negroes are inferior, and manifests toward the whites the traditional respect and deference. Members of the next generation, those who are now middle-aged, are ambivalent. They do not believe whites are actually superior, but in their dealings with them they act as if they did. Finally, the young generation bears keen and outspoken resentment against the whites. Its members are in more or less open rebellion against a social system which relegates them to an inferior status.

Johnson, on the other hand, believes that the problem is much more complicated than that. The Negro's response to discrimination, he thinks, is a product of a number of factors, including the regional and cultural setting, the basic personality type of the Negro himself, his social class, his age, sex, education, appearance, occupation, and the degree of intimacy with whites he has experienced.[21] Johnson is inclined to regard social class as a major factor contributing to the differentiation of Negro responses to segregation and discrimination. Johnson does not attempt to estimate the relative strength of these various forces, but he does insist (1) that basic psychological factors play *some* part in the differential responses of Negroes to segregation and discrimination, and (2) that the role the individual has learned to assume during his formative years is most important in his total personality structure and in his behavior in subsequent contacts with the white world.

Banks has made a careful study of the Negroes in Columbus, Ohio, and has found that there are appreciable differences in their sensitivity to discrimination and segregation.[22] Attitudes of acceptance and accommodation he found to be exceedingly rare. Only 2 per cent of those he interviewed were disposed to regard the discriminations against Negroes as "not serious." All others he found to be "moderately or highly resentful" of them. Age itself proved to be of slight significance. Younger Northern Negroes are apparently less sensitive to discrimination than is generally believed. The highest degree of sensitivity he found to be characteristic of the age group between 35 and 44, a majority of

[20] Hortense Powdermaker, *After Freedom*, pp. 325ff.
[21] C. S. Johnson, *op. cit.*, pp. 231ff.
[22] W. S. M. Banks, II, "The Rank Order of Sensitivity to Discriminations of Negroes in Columbus, Ohio," *American Sociological Review*, Vol. 15, No. 4, August 1950, pp. 529–534.

whom were born in the South and had their introductions to Negro-white relations in a Southern setting. The Banks study reveals a significant correlation between occupation and sensitivity to discrimination in that the higher the occupational level, the lower is the sensitivity. A possible explanation of this fact is that Negroes in the professions and other high-status occupations enjoy a degree of economic security which makes it possible for them to circumvent or avoid those situations which involve flagrant discrimination; or, perhaps, they attempt to dissociate themselves from the general Negro community and to identify themselves with the middle or upper classes of white society. Banks found also, strangely enough, that the more years of schooling which had been completed the less was the sensitivity to discrimination. The one variable, however, which seems to be most directly correlated with sensitivity to discrimination, is the place of early exposure to Negro-white relations. Negroes who had acquired their basic conditioning in the South or who had spent several years in the South proved more sensitive than those whose conditioning had been acquired in the North. The Southern Negro, Banks thinks, has in his background many personal experiences with discriminatory practices which serve to accentuate his resentment and antagonism, while the northern Negro's reaction to the word "discrimination" is somewhat more abstract and intellectualized.

The observations of Banks, Johnson, Powdermaker, and others all point to the fact that Negroes react in different ways to their subordinate status in American society. These observers are not in agreement, however, on the nature or relative importance of the factors that go to make up these varied reactions. The answer to that problem calls for more information than we now have about the mysteries of human personality. In the meantime let us see *how* the members of minority groups react to domination, even though we cannot say *why* they react as they do.

How Do Minorities React?

1. Acceptance

It is an amazing fact, but one amply attested, that some human beings have an infinite capacity to endure injustice without retaliation, and apparently without resentment against their oppressors. Instances of this phenomenon are numerous, and they come from every part of the world where one group dominates another. Militant leaders of protest movements have been driven to despair by the apathy they have encountered among those they would lead to freedom; and members of dominant groups have often commented on the cheerfulness and loyalty they observe among those who would seem to have no reason for such sentiments.

Tulto, an Indian from the pueblo of Taos, has suffered much at the hands of the whites, but apparently he bears no grudge against them.[23] As a boy he lived the normal life of his pueblo, riding his pony, driving the cattle, and playing

---

[23] His story, summarized here, is recounted by E. R. Embree in *Indians of the Americas*, pp. 223–233.

shinny, mumblety peg, and leap frog. He hunted rabbits and deer, prayed to the Sun Father, and was thrilled by the religious dances on the plaza. His story has a charm all its own:

When I was about thirteen years old I went down to Santa Fe to St. Michael's Catholic School. Other boys were joining the societies and spending their time in the kivas being purified, and learning the secrets. But I wanted to learn the white man's secrets. I thought he had better magic than the Indian. . . . My father was sad but he was not angry. He wanted me to be a good Indian like all other boys, but he was willing for me to go to school. He thought I would stop soon. There was plenty of time to go into the kiva.

While I was there a white man — what you call an Indian Agent — came and took all of us who were in that school far off on a train to a new kind of village called Carlisle Indian School, and I stayed there seven years. . . . Seven years I was there. I set little letters together in the printing shop and we printed papers. For the rest we had lessons. I learned to talk English and to read. There was much arithmetic. It was lessons: how to add and take away, and much strange business like you have crossword puzzles only with numbers. The teachers were very solemn and made a great fuss if we did not get the puzzles right. There was something called Greatest Common Denominator. I remember the name but I never knew it — what it meant. When the teachers asked me I would guess, but I always guessed wrong. We studied little things — fractions. I remember that word too. It is like one half of an apple. And there were immoral fractions.

They told us that Indian ways were bad. They said we must get civilized. I remember that word too. It means "be like the white man." I am willing to be like the white man, but I did not believe Indian ways were wrong. But they kept teaching us for seven years. And the books told how bad the Indians had been to the white men — burning their towns and killing their women and children. But I had seen white men do that to Indians.

We all wore whiteman's clothes, and ate whiteman's food, and went to the whiteman's church, and spoke whiteman's talk. And so after a while we also began to say Indians were bad. We laughed at our own people and their blankets and cooking pots and sacred societies and dances. I tried to learn the lessons — and after seven years I came home. . . .

It was a warm summer evening when I got off the train at Taos station. . . . Here came my father and my mother and many brothers and cousins. They all began hugging me, and we all cried and were very happy. . . . Every time a new cousin would come we would all cry again. It was a happy night. . . .

But the chiefs did not want me in the pueblo. Next morning the governor of the pueblo and the two war chiefs and many of the priest chiefs came into my father's house. They did not talk to me; they did not even look at me.

The chiefs said to my father, "Your son who calls himself Rafael has lived with the white men. He has been far away from the pueblo. He has not lived in the kiva, nor learned the things that Indian boys should learn. He has no hair. He has no blankets. He cannot even speak our language and he has a strange smell. He is not one of us."

The chiefs got up and walked out. My father was very sad. I wanted him to be angry, but he was only sad.

And I walked out of my father's house and out of the pueblo. . . . I walked until I came to the whiteman's town. I found work setting type in a printing shop there. Later I went to Wyoming and Colorado, printing and making a good living. . . . I worked in some blacksmith shops and on farms. . . . All this time I was a white man . . . but I was not very happy . . . and after many years I came back to Taos.

My father gave me some land from the pueblo fields. . . . I took my money and bought some cattle. I built a house just outside the pueblo.

My father brought me a girl to marry. . . . She was a good girl and she came to live with me in my new house outside the pueblo. . . . When we were married I became an Indian again. I let my hair grow. . . . I put on blankets, and I cut the seat out of my pants. . . . I grew my farm like the other Indians, and my woman cooked Indian food. I wanted to be among my people. But I wanted to live in the kind of house I had learned to like.

When I settled with my woman in this new house, the chiefs came over from the pueblo, and they said I must burn my chairs and bed and break the glass out of my windows. And they thought my house was too large. But I said to them, "I have built outside the pueblo. You rule inside and let me alone here."

I want to live at peace.

It seems that minority peoples everywhere, either because they "want to live in peace," or for some other reason, learn to accept a social system which discriminates against them and bestows prestige upon some other group. Indeed it would be difficult, in fact impossible, for one people to dominate and exploit another if a substantial number of the minority did not more or less accept it.

Acceptance, however, as a type of response to domination, is capable of wide variation. On the one hand there are those who are completely accommodated, such as the Nashville Negro who said, "I know how white folks is and I understand their ways. I always stand fair with my white folks. They always been fair to me, and I been good to them."[24] Another said, "They've always been friends to me; they are nicer than colored sometimes. I am sick of colored people." Others accept the situation, but with resentment, such as the man who said, "I don't like it, but the best thing I can do is keep from worrying about it."

To some degree conformity to the prevailing etiquette of race relations is an unconscious matter, to which one becomes conditioned in the process of socialization. Much of it, however, is the conscious, rational acceptance of a role, which one may dislike but which one accepts as necessary for survival. In short, it is not uncommon for one to conform externally while rejecting the system mentally and emotionally.

Negroes who accept the caste system and abide by it will give a variety of reasons for their behavior. One woman said, "It's the law of the land," and let it go at that. Another said, "I don't like to associate with white folks. They's some good ones, but they ain't many." Others excuse themselves for reasons of economic necessity or personal security. "I work for them, get their change, and

24 This and the following comments from Negroes are taken from C. S. Johnson, *op. cit.*, pp. 244–266, and Powdermaker, *op. cit.*, pp. 325–353.

go right on." Some profess a desire for peace, and say, "Let the Negro stay to his self and the white man stay to they self, and they never be no trouble." Many have accepted the stereotype of the Negro as the inferior, and therefore interpret the status quo as natural and inevitable. "I ain't got no faith in a colored doctor." Some have even identified themselves with the whites, as did the woman who said, "Colored people done graduated me."

The foregoing rationalizations were given by members of the lower classes. There are also upper-class Negroes who assume the role of acceptance, and they too seek to justify their actions. Some even profess not to be aware of discrimination, and deny its existence. Johnson records a number of these. A Negro professional man in Houston said:

> I haven't seen anything special that a Negro is expected to do. If he is, I must have been wrong a number of times, because I don't even know what it is. . . . We do not belong to the same organizations as the whites, but they co-operate with us in anything that we attempt in our little organizations.

More often, however, those of the upper classes whose reaction to dominance is basically one of acceptance, comply under duress and with bitter hearts.

Negroes, of course, are not the only ones who stoically accept discrimination and even justify it by subtle rationalizations. Jews, too, have often defended second-class citizenship, on the grounds that it is persecution which has kept alive their individuality. Said Rabbi Joel Blau:

> But the Modern Pharisee knows that these dissimilarities hold the secret of Jewish individuality. Upon this knowledge he stands four-square, neither pleading nor apologizing. He has nothing to hide, nothing to gloss over. He calmly faces all attacks upon the citadel of Jewish personality, no matter whence they emanate: from foe or friend, from the Christian world, or from his own Sadducee brother. The broad way of assimilation he would not tread; he knows too well the egregious folly of assimilation. . . .
>
> This oriental soul the Modern Pharisee claims as his birthright, not to be traded away for the contents of any pot — even though it be the melting pot. What both the ill-wind of the world and the cowardice of his weaker brethren regard a reproach and a shame he considers a glory and an honor. And his highest aspiration is to bring the spirit he is made of to its highest flowering. His very name — Pharisee — means distinctiveness, separation, noble aloofness.[25]

There are many Jews today who, if the choice lay between discrimination and assimilation, would readily take the former.

2. Avoidance

Minority groups, from the beginning of time, have sought to solve their problem by running away from it. The Hebrews, under the leadership of Moses,

[25] Quoted in H. P. Fairchild, *Race and Nationality*, p. 144.

fled from Egypt, where they were slaves, and endured the hardships of the Red Sea, the wilderness, and implacable enemies. American Indians living on the Atlantic seaboard, overwhelmed by the influx of Europeans, sought refuge beyond the Appalachian Mountains; and when the inescapable whites followed there, they pressed on across the Mississippi River. Following the Civil War thousands of southern whites fled to Mexico and Brazil rather than submit to the domination of Negroes, Yankees, and "carpetbaggers." American Negroes, unwilling to accept domination, forbidden to assimilate, and sensing the futility of resistance, have often cherished the dream that they might flee from it all. Various schemes have been proposed, beginning in the 1700's.[26] Some have looked to Africa as a possible refuge, and considerable numbers have gone there. Others have cast hopeful eyes upon Central America, or Western Canada. Still others have proposed the establishment of a separate state for Negroes only, as do the Black Muslims today. A generation ago Marcus Garvey won a tremendous but temporary following by offering Africa to the Negroes as an avenue of escape. And there are in the United States today not less than 50 all-Negro communities.

The modern Zionist Movement is essentially an avoidance reaction. Many who are attracted by the prospect of a homeland in Palestine are motivated by a desire to flee from annihilation and persecution. Still others are fleeing from the equally-unwanted prospect of assimilation. Said Theodor Herzl, the great pioneer of Zionism:

> I referred previously to our "assimilation": I do not for a moment wish to imply that I desire such an end. Our national character is too historically famous, and, in spite of every degradation, too fine to make its annihilation desirable. We might perhaps be able to merge ourselves entirely into surrounding races, if these were to leave us in peace for two generations. But they will not leave us in peace. . . . Thus, whether we like it or not, we are now, and shall henceforth remain, a historic group with unmistakable characteristics common to us all.[27]

There are many devices for avoiding one's oppressors, however, other than fleeing to Africa, Palestine, South America, or to a self-contained ethnic community. Burrows correctly infers that "many and devious are the ways of withdrawing from an intolerable situation"; and he discusses some of those techniques which he observed among the minority peoples of Hawaii in their reactions to *haole* prestige.[28] He suspects, and with some reason, that insanity is one mechanism of escape, alcoholic intoxication another, and opium still another for those of Oriental ancestry. The Hawaiians, he thinks, take flight into the romantic past, much of it synthetic; and many of them have participated in a revival of the culture of their ancestors, upon which they had formerly been disposed to turn their backs. He quotes Romanzo Adams, an authority on Hawaiian affairs:

[26] J. H. Franklin, *From Slavery to Freedom*, pp. 234–238, 481–483.
[27] *The Jewish State*, pp. 38–39.
[28] E. G. Burrows, *Hawaiian Americans*, pp. 139ff.

It is easy for one who has been in contact with Hawaii's young people for a long time to note the beginning of a change in attitude toward the culture of their ancestors. Fifteen or twenty years ago one was impressed by the tendency of Hawaiian born and educated young people to deprecate the customs and ideas of their parents. As American citizens they were trying to win an economic status superior to what their parents possessed, and they felt that the persistence of old country traditions was burdensome and that it was an obstacle to achievement.

But in the more recent years young people of the same age — the younger brothers and sisters or, perhaps, the nephews and nieces — are undergoing a change of attitude. . . . They evaluate old country customs more discriminatingly. They find some things that seem to be permanently good and there is beginning to be a tendency to idealize the traditional ways followed by their ancestors.

The American Negro, however, is without a peer when it comes to improvising techniques for avoiding those he dislikes. Avoidance is indeed of major importance as a pattern of Negro response to white dominance. Investigators have recorded many such comments as the following:

> I found that the best way to get along with white folks is just to be pretty careful and come in contact with them as little as possible.
> I stay as far away from 'em as I can.
> The farther they is from me, the better I like it.

Avoidance is no easy task for the Negroes, bound as closely as they are, economically and politically, to the white population. They have, nevertheless, made that choice, and Johnson describes many of the subtle devices whereby they keep their contacts with whites to the barest minimum.[29] Some have found in farm ownership an effective means to maintain their independence. It is the proud boast of many Negroes that they have never ridden on a segregated street-car or bus. Indeed, it has been said that the automobile has been no less instrumental than Lincoln's Proclamation in emancipating the Negro. Those of the middle and upper classes will pay their bills by mail in order to avoid the necessity of contacts with white "collectors." They will do as much of their routine shopping as possible by telephone, since, as one cultivated woman said, her voice and diction get more consideration than her face. They refrain from attending theaters and auditoriums where they would be required to enter by the alley door and sit in the segregated balcony. They absent themselves from public gatherings where they suspect they will be subjected to insults and indignities. They patronize places of business where they are known, and their trade is appreciated, and avoid stores where they are rudely treated.

Nor is it only the gross forms of discrimination that they wish to avoid; they also want to escape the necessity of having to conform to the patterns of behavior prescribed by the caste system. And they want to preserve their dignity, to "save face." There are sly and subtle ways of doing this, too. Richard Wright tells how he did it on one occasion:

[29] *Op. cit.*, pp. 267–293.

There are many times when I had to exercise a great deal of ingenuity to keep out of trouble. It is a southern custom that all men must take off their hats when they enter an elevator. And especially did this apply to us blacks with rigid force. One day I stepped into an elevator with my arms full of packages. I was forced to ride with my hat on. Two white men stared at me coldly. Then one of them very kindly lifted my hat and placed it upon my armful of packages. Now the most accepted response for a Negro to make under such circumstances is to look at the white man out of the corner of his eye and grin. To have said: "Thank you!" would have made the white man *think* that you *thought* you were receiving from him a personal service. For such an act I have seen Negroes take a blow in the mouth. Finding the first alternative distasteful, and the second dangerous, I hit upon an acceptable course of action which fell safely between these two poles. I immediately — no sooner than my hat was lifted — pretended that my packages were about to spill, and appeared deeply distressed with keeping them in my arms. In this fashion I evaded having to acknowledge his service, and, in spite of adverse circumstances, salvaged a slender shred of personal pride.[30]

3. Assimilation

One may well insist that the happiest response for the members of minorities to make is that of merging themselves with the dominant group. "When in Rome do as the Romans do." "If you can't lick 'em, jine 'em." Economically, mentally, and emotionally there are advantages in being with the majority. According to the assimilationist philosophy, immigrants in a new land should transfer their loyalty to the country of their adoption, they should become citizens as quickly as possible, they should learn the language, discard their quaint costumes for the conventional dress, acquire the food habits, acquaint themselves with the nation's ideals, learn to like its sports and pastimes, conform to its laws, abide by its institutions, and, above all, rear their children in accord with the standards of the new culture. This is what the members of the dominant group like, generally speaking. They are ethnocentric, as nearly all people are, and are flattered to think that strangers recognize the superiority of their ways. Besides, it is a nuisance to have people around who do not understand the language, who are "queer," whose habits are "outlandish," and whose morals and ideals are "questionable."

Assimilation, however, it not a painless process. It is not easy to learn a new language, and to speak it without an accent. One does not immediately feel comfortable in strange garments, or acquire a taste for new foods, or enjoy baseball upon first exposure to it, or learn to handle new systems of weights, measures, and money. These are skills and tastes which take many years to acquire, and they are but a small part of any strange new culture. How much longer, then, does it take a person to absorb the intangibles — traditions, ideals, values, beliefs, attitudes, and loyalties? Sociologists have learned that it takes several generations, even under the most favorable circumstances.

30 *Uncle Tom's Children*, pp. 21–22.

The circumstances, moreover, are not always favorable. Members of minority groups are seldom prepared to discard their culture *in toto,* as one would trade in an old car for the latest model. They are strongly attached to it. They believe that most of it is good, and they want their children to have it. Assimilation, therefore, does not appear to them as the solution of their problem of adjustment. They may agree that assimilation is desirable, up to a point; but beyond that point they will resist it. The dominant group, on the other hand, may insist upon assimilation, may prate about "Americanization," may do its utmost to indoctrinate the alien, and may even try to accelerate the process at a dangerous speed, while at the same time it erects obstacles to the very thing it urges. For some groups the obstacles are well-nigh insurmountable — to the Negroes, Jews, Japanese-Americans, Mexicans, and Chinese-Americans, for instance. Complete assimilation, if they are to seek it, must be a surreptitious variety known as "passing."

Passing. Members of certain minorities, if they choose to identify themselves with the dominant group, will be commended for their wisdom. If a German immigrant, for instance, decides to Anglicize his name, he may do so openly, and will not be suspected of sinister motives. If he decides to transfer his church membership from the Lutheran, which is not represented in his community, to the Methodist, he will be welcomed with open arms. If he becomes a naturalized citizen and boasts of his preference for the progressive, democratic American society, he will be praised for his good sense. But suppose a Jew changes his name, and joins the Christian Science Church; will he not be under suspicion? And what of a Negro of light color who decides to join the whites? Or an Indian who, to make life easier for himself, declares that he is an American of swarthy European ancestry? Assimilation is an adjustment not permitted to all minorities, except to a limited degree; but some of them manage it:

I was a Jew, until a few years ago. Now, I am not!

Many of you, the Jews whom I address, as well as many gentiles, may scoff at the notion of a Jew ever becoming a non-Jew. And my former people may blame me bitterly for changing.

Fortunately, I cannot be reached. I have changed my name. I have changed my work. I have moved into a strange region and started afresh. My past is as finally sealed as though I had died and arisen with a new personality — for it is really necessary that a Jew change some important parts of his personality when he throws off his Jewishness.

Let me tell you how it was done. . . . I need not, in addressing Jews, enlarge on the pain of rebellion and self-exile, family love being so strong among the Jews. I, having no immediate family, gained freedom without keen heartaches.

It was at a Menorah Society organization meeting, in a great Eastern university that I arose and declared my convictions.

First, we were gravely addressed by a professor, a Zionist, who urged the importance of a homeland in Palestine. . . . Then came an excited student, a poor Polish Jew, who spoke English badly, to the amusement of some of our more cultivated members. . . .

Said he: "We are all Americans. Here we have good things. We are free. Soldiers do not spit upon us. Drunken bullies do not kick us publicly because we are Jews. This is my homeland. I am not a citizen of Palestine. I will never be. I am an American."

Poor fellow! He doubtless realized later how hard it is for a Jew to be an American like other Americans. . . .

I made my decision, declaring, "Very well — I choose to be an American," and walked out.

And, although I could not make my formal severance that day, or even that spring, I did make it the following summer, at the cost of abandoning my credits at that and other universities to enter, later, a new school, by examination, under my new name.

For, having made my decision, I went through with it determinedly — the more easily since I had no kin in America nearer than cousins and uncles and aunts. For young Jews, sheltered and dearly loved in a family, my course might be too hard.

So I changed my name, legally, and invented for myself a false history, claiming to be descended from non-Jewish Adrianople Turks. The dislocation of boundaries following several wars and the shrinkage of Turkey in Europe made it impossible to disprove my story. . . .

In a fervor of Americanism, I went west, into a new country, and tried a variety of callings, but shunned the Jewish favorites. . . . I was a garage mechanic, stake man on a survey gang, farmhand, cropshare farmer, laborer, and later foreman on a riprap gang along the Mississippi. . . . I have everywhere been accepted as an equal, despite my slight accent and rather dark complexion and the Balkan ancestry I claimed.

Then with two years of real work behind me and savings enough to carry me through school, I boned furiously, passed my exams, and entered a western university as an American — a simple, unclassified American. . . .

I graduated from the university and married shortly thereafter. I am now raising children who need never learn to endure snubs, who will never be tempted to retaliate against cruel discrimination. From this pleasant sunshine, I look back with horror at the somber world in which my race-proud kin persist on their ancient and unhappy course.

Life is good. I never regret my step.[31]

Passing is a phenomenon reported from many parts of the world, and is a type of reaction to dominance which is not unknown to any minority group. It has received considerable attention, however, in the United States, and especially in relation to the Negro. Passing has been a popular theme with novelists and playwrights.[32] So widespread is the folk belief in the "black baby" that writers

[31] Anonymous, "I Was a Jew," *Forum*, Vol. 103, No. 1, January 1940, pp. 8–10. See, along the same line, "I Changed My Name," *Atlantic Monthly*, Vol. 181, No. 2, February 1948. This latter article was followed, two months later, by another, "I Kept My Name," by D. Cohn.

[32] Among the moving pictures are "Pinky" and "Lost Boundaries." Novels and plays include J. W. Johnson, *Autobiography of an Ex-Colored Man;* D. Heyward, *Brass Ankle;* Fannie Hurst, *Imitation of Life;* L. Saxon, *Children of Strangers;* G. M. Shelby and S. G. Stoney, *Po' Buckra;* C. R. Sumner, *Quality;* C. Van Vechten, *Nigger Heaven.*

of fiction can rely upon it as a sure-fire climax, when a more substantial one is not forthcoming. Efforts to verify the innumerable rumors, however, have never been successful; and biologists themselves are extremely dubious about the scientific possibility of the complete throwback.[33]

The amount of passing which takes place among American Negroes has received some attention, although it is obviously a most difficult phenomenon to measure. Some of the difficulty arises from the fact that passing itself is not easy to define. Much of it is deliberate and intentional. On the other hand, it is quite common for members of minorities, including very light Negroes, to find themselves, through no fault of their own, mistaken for members of the dominant group. Students of race problems, accordingly, have made a distinction between *conscious* and *unconscious* passing, though one may question the advisability of including "mistaken identity" as a form of passing. There is a difference, however, between *temporary* and *permanent* passing. Quite often Negroes will pass as white in the work-a-day world, for the economic advantages to be gained thereby, while preferring to remain Negroes except when on the job. Many will pass temporarily in order to be admitted to a restaurant, to attend a theater, or to obtain service in hotels or on trains. Passing, moreover, is usually an individual matter, though there are instances of whole communities striving collectively to win acceptance as whites or Indians. Typical examples of the latter are the Croatans of North Carolina, the Brass Ankles of South Carolina, and similar peoples in many other eastern sections of the United States.[34]

Despite the difficulties of measuring so elusive a phenomenon, many estimates have been suggested and some effort has been made to determine the extent of it. Ottley maintains that between 40,000 and 50,000 Negroes "pass" into the white community yearly, and that "between 5,000,000 and 8,000,000 persons in the United States, supposed to be white, possess a determinable part of Negro blood."[35] Asbury has guessed that the yearly number who pass is 30,000.[36] Few would accept so high a figure, however. A generation ago, Hart concluded from a study of census data that approximately 25,000 annually change their racial identification from Negro to white.[37] More recently Hart's interpretation of the data has been criticized by both Burma and Eckard, who conclude that 2000 or 2500 would be a more accurate figure.[38] Day, using an entirely different approach to the problem, making a case study of 346 families of mixed blood,

[33] L. Wirth and H. Goldhamer, "The Hybrid and the Problem of Miscegenation," in O. Klineberg (Ed.), *Characteristics of the American Negro*, p. 239; G. Myrdal, *An American Dilemma*, pp. 1208–1209.

[34] B. Berry, *Almost White*.

[35] R. Ottley, "5 Million U. S. White Negroes," *Ebony*, Vol. 3, No. 5, March 1948, pp. 32ff.

[36] H. Ashbury, "Who Is a Negro?" *Collier's*, August 3, 1946.

[37] H. Hart, *Selective Migration as a Factor in Child Welfare in the United States, with Special Reference to Iowa*, pp. 28–29.

[38] J. H. Burma, "The Measurement of Negro Passing," *American Journal of Sociology*. Vol. 52, No. 1, July 1946, pp. 18ff.; E. W. Eckard, "How Many Negroes Pass?" *American Journal of Sociology*, Vol. 52, No. 6, May 1947, pp. 498ff.

suggests also this lower figure.[39] If this conservative estimate is correct, the prospect of the Negroes' amalgamation through the passing process is remote indeed. Robert Stuckert maintains, however, that more than 20 per cent of the white population of the United States "are descendants of persons of African origin."[40]

Why, then, do not more members of minority groups solve the problem of discrimination by passing? To be sure, Burma does maintain that "probably all Negroes who can pass do so." But he goes on to say that such passing is of a segmental and temporary nature, consisting of riding in the front section of a bus, eating in restricted restaurants, or in other ways making an opportune use of one's caucasoid features. He concludes that there is usually no disposition to become permanently identified with the white group. It does seem that passing makes no wide appeal even to those persons who would have little difficulty in doing so. The fear of exposure is doubtless effective in some cases; but loyalty to family and friends, and a normal pride in one's group, are usually sufficient to make passing a distasteful adjustment. It is also true that the individual who passes suffers a loss in status. This is especially so in the case of Negro women; for the very characteristics which would make it possible for them to slip into the lower levels of white society would give them high prestige among Negroes. Finally, minority groups themselves seldom look with favor upon the passing technique, though there is a certain ambivalence in their attitude. Says Myrdal:

> Most Negroes, particularly in the upper strata, know of many other Negroes, sometimes half a hundred or more, who pass as whites. As they usually do not expose them, this shows a significant degree between the two castes in the attitude toward passing. Many Negroes obviously take a sort of vicarious satisfaction out of the deception of whites. It is a big joke to them. Some show envy. This is particularly apparent among darker Negroes who cannot think of passing. Negroes realize, of course, that as a mass they cannot find an escape from the lower caste by passing. Further, they are increasingly brought to the compensatory feeling of race pride.[41]

All in all, passing is a dubious way of adjusting to dominance and discrimination. It is fraught with feelings of uncertainty, insecurity, guilt, and disloyalty. Even so, there are many who choose it, agreeing with the onetime Jew who said, "I never regret my step."[42]

4. Aggression

The members of minority groups have a fourth alternative — aggression. Not for long will people calmly accept subordinate status. Avoidance of contact with

[39] Caroline B. Day, *A Study of Some Negro-White Families in the United States*, Harvard African Studies, Vol. 10, 1932.
[40] "African Ancestry of the White American Population," *Ohio Journal of Science*, Vol. 58, No. 3, May 1958, pp. 155ff.
[41] *Op. cit.*, p. 687.
[42] See above, p. 390.

the dominant ones is less and less feasible in the modern world. Assimilation is distasteful to some, unobtainable for others, and difficult for most. From time immemorial, however, the members of oppressed minorities have taken the offensive, have asserted themselves, have resisted, opposed, attacked, and rebelled against their superiors. They have given vent to their resentment and hostility in innumerable ways. By the term "aggression" we mean any behavior whose goal is the destruction, injury, frustration, embarrassment, discomfiture, or annoyance of another person or group. Let us consider some of the variegated forms aggression has assumed.

The form of aggression which is most obvious and familiar to us is that manifested by most American Indians when they saw the white man moving into their territories, taking their land from them, destroying their game, disrupting their way of life, and challenging their power and sovereignty. The Indian, very understandably, struck back, and our histories abound with tales of that conflict. The leaders of the Indians' counterattack are legendary figures, not altogether forgotten nowadays, and among them one of the greatest was Tecumseh.

In the fall of 1811, 5000 Indians of the Muskogee tribes gathered on the banks of the Tallapoosa River in Alabama for their annual Grand Council. This was to be a special occasion, however, for the distinguished Shawnee warrior, Tecumseh, had sent runners ahead to announce that he would pay them a visit. Tecumseh, as almost everyone on the continent knew, was bent upon forming a confederation of Indian tribes to stem the advance of the white man. An Ameri-

Scene on a New York City construction job — a sit-in demonstration against alleged discrimination in the building trades.

can frontiersman, Sam Dale, was present at the time and has given us an account of the whole affair.[43]

On the second day of the council Tecumseh marched into the great square at the head of his band of 24 chosen Shawnee warriors. "They were the most athletic body of men I ever saw . . . austere . . . and . . . imperial," said Dale. Their faces were painted red and black, indicating that they had not yet made a choice between peace and war. They were approached in dead silence by Big Warrior, the colossal chief of the Creeks, who offered his pipe to Tecumseh, and then pointed to the lodge which had been prepared for them.

Several days passed, in which Tecumseh spoke not a word. He was apparently waiting for the Government Agent, Colonel Hawkins, to leave the grounds, which he eventually did. Whereupon, at high noon, Tecumseh and his retinue emerged from their guest cabin, their bodies painted black, and entirely naked except for loin cloths and war clubs. They marched in single file to the center of the square, where they sprinkled tobacco and powdered sumac leaves on the ground, saluted Big Warrior with a "diabolical yell," and proffered the Shawnees' pipe. Then for the first time since his arrival, Tecumseh spoke. Dale said, "I have heard many great orators, but never one with the vocal powers of Tecumseh, or the same command of the muscles of his face. Had I been deaf, the play of his countenance would have told me what he said. . . . Stern warriors shook with emotion. . . . Tomahawks were brandished in the air. Even Big Warrior, who had been true to the whites . . . was visibly affected. . . . More than once I saw his huge hand clutch, spasmodically, the handle of his knife." These were Tecumseh's words:

> In defiance of the white warriors of Ohio and Kentucky, I have traveled through their settlements, once our favorite hunting grounds. No war whoop was sounded, but there is blood on our knives. The palefaces felt the blow, but knew not whence it came.
>
> Accursed be the race that has seized our country, and made women of our warriors! Our fathers, from their tombs, reproach us as slaves and cowards. I hear them now in the wailing winds.
>
> You Muskogees were once a mighty people. The Georgians trembled at your war whoops. Now your very blood is white; your tomahawks have no edge; your bows and arrows are buried with your fathers. Oh, Muskogees, brush from your eyelids the sleep of slavery! Once more strike for vengeance. . . . Let the white race perish. They seize your land; they corrupt your women; they trample on the ashes of your dead. They must be driven back — back whence they came — on a trail of blood. Back, aye, into the great water. . . . Burn their dwellings! Destroy their stock! Slay their wives and children! The red people own the country. . . . War now! War forever! War upon the living! War upon the dead! Dig their very corpses from the graves; our country must give no rest to a white man's bones!

The Indians, to be sure, had their quislings and collaborators; there were assimilationists among them, who urged the adoption of the white man's ways;

[43] J. M. Oskison, *Tecumseh and His Times*, Ch. 11. Also C. Wissler, *Indians of the United States*, pp. 79–83; A. Britt, *Great Indian Chiefs*, pp. 126–155.

there were cautious souls who, when pressed on the frontier, advised withdrawal deeper into the wilderness. Tecumseh, however, was one of a long line — which included King Philip, Pontiac, Black Hawk, Sitting Bull, and others — who chose to resist the white man's advance by a show of arms. Apparently there were few, if any, who rose to positions of leadership, who were so naïve as to suppose that red men and white could live together in peace, harmony, and equality. One elementary fact of race relations was obvious to them all: when races meet, a well-nigh universal consequence is the domination of one and the subordination of the other. Most Indians, and especially the Shawnees, were proud people, who valued highly their independence and their status. To Tecumseh, certainly, death was preferable to subjection and submission. After the disastrous battle at Tippecanoe,[44] he allied himself with the British — not that he respected or trusted them, but he hated the Americans more — and he lost his life in the War of 1812. The Kentuckians who slew him scalped and flayed his corpse, and distributed his skin among them for razor strops.

Aggressive behavior, as manifested by Tecumseh, failed to resolve the problem with which the Indians were faced. It is not always so, however. For an example, with a very different outcome, let us turn to the island of Haiti.

Toussaint L'Ouverture. The island of Haiti was the first country in the New World to sweep away the institution of slavery, and this was largely the result of the efforts of an incredible individual by the name of François Dominique Toussaint L'Ouverture.[45] The date of his birth is not known, but it was presumably about 1744. Toussaint was one of more than a thousand slaves on the great Breda plantation. The owner of the plantation was Count de Noe, a benevolent man, who lived in France. He instructed the manager of his plantation to show consideration to his slaves, and his instructions were obeyed, for the Breda slaves were reputedly treated with comparative humanity.

It is difficult for us to realize today the enormous importance to Europe of the islands of the West Indies two centuries ago. Haiti (or Saint Domingue as it was then called) was by far the wealthiest of the French colonies, and it is small wonder that the French Government, and later Napoleon, showed constant interest and anxiety over the affairs of that distant island. The products of the island were at first cocoa, indigo, and tobacco; but in the middle of the seventeenth century sugar cane was introduced, bringing about a great economic revolution. Large plantations supplanted the small farms which had until then prevailed, and these plantations, with their own mills, became manufacturing as

---

[44] Tippecanoe was a noted Indian village site on the west bank of the Wabash just below the mouth of the Tippecanoe River, in Indiana. It was occupied successively by Miami, Shawnee, and Potawatomi. Tecumseh and his brother, The Prophet, made it their headquarters in 1808. When, in 1811, the Indian revolt had grown to threatening proportions, General William Henry Harrison marched with 900 troops against the town. Tecumseh was absent in the South at the time. Near the town, at daybreak on November 7, the whites were attacked by the Indians under the leadership of The Prophet. A desperate engagement ensued, resulting in the complete defeat and dispersion of the Indians.

[45] Among the many biographies of him, two recent ones are especially recommended: R. Korngold, *Citizen Toussaint;* and S. Alexis, *Black Liberator.*

well as agricultural establishments. The manufacture of sugar called for great outlays of capital. It called also for an abundant supply of labor, which could not be satisfied with indentured servants. Negroes, accordingly, were imported in great numbers from Africa.

By 1789 nearly a million Negroes had been transported to the colony. In that year some 30,000 whites sat in authority over 452,000 slaves. There were, in addition, 24,000 free Negroes and mulattoes living on the island.

The slaves were considered to be scarcely human. In theory the owner's power over his slave was limited. The law permitted the master to inflict corporal punishment only for laxness in a slave's work, and then only to a reasonable degree. All other offenses were to be punished by the authorities, who, it must be admitted, had no reputation for leniency. The law, however, was scarcely observed, for the plantations were far removed from the communities in which the authorities resided. Hilliard d'Auberteuil, who sought to reform the institution of slavery though not to abolish it, said:

> Negroes die daily in chains and under the lash. They are beaten, strangled, burned to death without any legal formality. Every act of cruelty against them remains unpunished. In St. Domingo any white man can ill-treat a Negro with impunity. The situation is such that the Negroes may be said to be the slaves not only of their masters, but also of the general public. An injury done to a slave is considered by the magistrates only from the point of view of the pecuniary damage suffered by the owners.[46]

It was commonly believed among the managers of the plantations that it was preferable to buy and import slaves than to breed them, and that it was profitable to amortize a slave in seven years. During that period the slave should be driven to the limit of his endurance. If, after that time, he became useless or died, it did not matter — a new slave could be bought to take his place. There were those, however, who insisted that greater efficiency could be employed in the management of plantations if slaves were exhausted in four years. It need hardly be added that the death rate among slaves in Haiti exceeded the birth rate.

The Negroes did not meekly accept this situation. Some of them fled to the mountains in the interior. There were occasional slave rebellions, but these were quickly and effectively suppressed. They did, however, continually resort to aggressive behavior. Many would hang themselves or cut their throats with the object of inflicting injury and loss upon their masters. They formed suicide pacts, and a dozen or more on a plantation would kill themselves simultaneously. Death was regarded by many of them as a form of migration back to Africa. Their most effective weapon for aggressive behavior, however, was poison. Arsenic was readily available on the plantations, since large quantities of it were used in combating the dreaded sugar ant. The Negroes also used ground glass, dogwood root, and black-eye. With these they frequently dispatched cattle, mules, other slaves, and the masters themselves. The whites lived in perpetual

[46] Quoted in Korngold, *op. cit.*, p. 30.

fear of such a fate; and it is said that many a planter who had nothing more than a stomach-ache imagined himself poisoned, and tortured a slave to force him to confess.

News of the French Revolution in 1789 caused great concern to the whites in Haiti; and its watchwords — liberty, equality, fraternity — fell on fertile soil among the slaves. Oddly enough, it was the whites themselves who were the principal disseminators of these ideas. Visitors to the island were astonished at the recklessness with which the whites discussed the revolution in the presence of their slaves. Says Korngold:

> Imagine a formal dinner party at a plantation house, with a slave in attendance behind every chair. Letters and newspapers have arrived from France, and the host describes with dramatic emphasis how his uncle or cousin has had to flee with his family because his scoundrelly peasants have burned down his castle, have looted his stores and will no longer recognize him as their lord. The narrator expresses the opinion that if the said uncle or cousin had made a liberal use of the whip such outrages could not have occurred. Others tell of similar misfortunes that have befallen their relatives. One asks if those present have read the shameful proclamation of the Rights of Man, which asserts that all men are created free and equal. Another remarks that if the *Amis des Noirs* had their way, this would even apply to Negro slaves! All join in denunciation of the National Assembly, and even of the King — who, if he were not utterly spineless, would have his soldiers arrest the whole pack of traitors and shoot them.
>
> The household slaves listen, standing barefoot behind each chair, passing the highly spiced Creole dishes and pouring the sparkling wines of France. Their expression does not change, but something in them has been kindled. Many have relatives among the field hands and mill slaves, to whom they pay an occasional visit. They sit with them around the fire and tell the exciting news they have heard. . . . The idea germinates in the minds of several that the black slaves of St. Domingo ought to follow the example of the white slaves of France.[47]

The revolt of the slaves began on August 22, 1791, at about ten o'clock in the evening. Men, women, and children on one of the plantations poured from their cabins, the men grasping their machetes with an air of resolution. The white overseers came running, whips in hand; but when they found that the Negroes would no longer bare their backs meekly to receive the lash, they retreated to the plantation house and barricaded themselves. They were not molested. The slaves, lighting their way with torches, moved from plantation to plantation, swelling their numbers as they marched. The revolution was orderly at first; buildings were not burned nor were the whites massacred. Trouble soon began, however, when on one of the plantations the mob killed the manager, swarmed into the house, and set about helping themselves to whatever struck their fancy. Presently someone touched a torch to the house, releasing a spirit of destruction. Building after building burst into flame, and other rebels ran with torches into the fields and set fire to the dry sugar cane.

[47] *Op. cit.*, pp. 63–64.

The movement spread rapidly. Within two months a hundred thousand slaves were in revolt, and more than a thousand plantations had ceased to exist. Atrocities were committed by both sides. The slaves, drunk with rum and thirsty for revenge, indulged in an orgy of violence. Thousands of whites were slain, and many more Negroes.

The Negroes had a number of shrewd leaders — Boukmann, Dessalines, Christophe, Chavannes, Rigaud, and Oge — but the greatest of all was Toussaint L'Ouverture. He was an able soldier, and certainly more humane than his followers. For six years he was the dominant figure on the island. He waged relentless war against the soldiers from France and emerged victorious. Napoleon regarded Toussaint as an obstacle to his dream of creating a French empire in the New World, and sent an army of 25,000 men under General Le-Clerc to subdue the island. Even this large and experienced force was unequal to the task of conquering the Negroes, ably assisted as they were by yellow fever, malaria, and the rains. But LeClerc by a ruse captured the intrepid Toussaint, who was shipped to France, where he died in prison on April 6, 1803.

The exploits of Toussaint and his successors had reverberations throughout the world. Americans were terrified at the news of what was happening in Haiti, and measures were taken in a number of states to discourage the further importation of slaves. The anti-slavery movement was intensified and defined. Quakers and other humanitarian groups took advantage of the situation to strengthen various aspects of anti-slavery legislation. Historians even suspect that the failure of the French to regain control of Haiti was a decisive factor in Napoleon's decision to sell the vast territory of Louisiana to the United States.

Wovoka and the Ghost Dance. Aggressive behavior of an entirely different character is exemplified in the Ghost Dance, which swept through the American Indian tribes in the last decade of the nineteenth century. The Indians by that time had sunk to the depths of despair, poverty, and discontent. The westward movement of the whites seemed destined to destroy what little of their ancient culture remained. The religion of the Ghost Dance was one way in which they struck back at the white man, whom they blamed for most of their woes.

Originator of the new faith was Wovoka, a Paiute, who was known to the whites as Jack Wilson. He was born in Nevada, and was probably the son of Tavibo, himself a mystic and a dreamer. Like most of his tribe, Wovoka had made what seemed to be a satisfactory adjustment to the white settlers. He worked on the ranch of a white man, David Wilson, from whom he received his nickname. He was making a good living, had acquired some knowledge of English, and had learned a little about Christianity. Until he was 30 he lived quietly and obscurely in an isolated valley in Nevada, surrounded by ice-capped sierras.

During an illness in 1888 Wovoka went into a trance and had a spiritual experience, from which he evolved his new teaching. It was not entirely new; inventions seldom are. Rather, it was obviously a composite of various beliefs and traditions long held by the Indians, plus a dash of Christian theology. Wovoka insisted that he had a message for the Indians which he had received from their departed ancestors. He urged them to do right, love one another and all men, live at peace with the world, pray and hope for a day of reunion in a state of everlasting happiness for all Indians, living and dead. A Messiah was coming very soon, he taught, and with him would come their ancestors in bodily form. There would arise a great whirlwind, and the whites would perish. The buffalo and other game would be restored, and the Indians would live together under the pristine conditions of the "golden age."

Wovoka taught that this day of deliverance was close at hand, but the Indians could hasten its advent by dancing the Ghost Dance, and by performing certain ceremonies. They should cast aside the white man's ways and his garments, and put on the clothes of the Indian again. Above all, they should dance, dance, dance!

Messengers went from tribe to tribe preaching this new religion and teaching the dance. The dance itself would begin in the middle of the afternoon, or later. No musical instruments were used, except those held by individual dancers. Some of them would wear a "ghost shirt," almost always made of white cloth, tailored in the Indian fashion. No metal was to be worn. The leader carried red feathers, red cloth, and a "ghost stick" about six feet long. Other articles used in the dance included arrows with bone heads, bows, gaming wheels, and sticks. The ground on which the dance was performed was consecrated.

The participants would shake with emotion and fall into hypnotic trances. They professed to see Indians in the beyond dancing too. They would see them playing games, gathering for war dances and the hunt, and joining together in their ancient societies and brotherhoods. On regaining consciousness they would relate to the others all that they had seen in their visions.

The Ghost Dance began to spread throughout the plains area, and it took on a hostile expression among the dissatisfied Sioux, where Sitting Bull and Red Cloud had long been the irreconcilable enemies of the whites. The dance so excited the Sioux that R. F. Roger, Indian Agent at Pine Ridge, South Dakota, wired for troops. Many settlers left their homes in fear of a major Indian War.

Troops arrived on October 19, 1890. General Nelson A. Miles, commanding officer in that area, ordered the apprehension of Sitting Bull, but the chief was killed while resisting arrest. Skirmishing followed in the Badlands. Finally, on December 28, American troops discovered the principal band of hostile Indians, under the leadership of Big Foot, camped on Wounded Knee Creek, South Dakota. The Indians were ordered to lay down their arms, which most of them promptly did. A few resisted, however, and general firing began, resulting in the slaughter of more than 200 Indian men, women, and children. White losses were 29 dead and 33 wounded. Many wounded Indians, left on the field, froze to death in a blizzard the following night. History refers to this incident as the Battle of Wounded Knee, but it was actually a massacre. At any rate it marked the climax of the Ghost Dance and the tragic attempt at resistance which it had called into being.

Nativistic movements similar to the Ghost Dance have been reported from many parts of the world.

In numerous other ways the members of minority groups have tantalized those who dominated them. Leighton tells how the Japanese-Americans in one relocation center expressed their hostility for the treatment they were accorded. Some of them, he says, "assumed a scornful air," they heckled the speakers who appeared before them, they taunted the administrators with charges of Fascism and violations of democracy, criticized the school program, and complained about the food, the living quarters, the enforced crowding, the furniture, the lack of privacy, the treeless environment, the hospital facilities, and the difficulty of obtaining proper food for babies and invalids. Finally, their aggressive reactions took the form of a general strike, which paralyzed the life of the center, but which led to a solution of the problems and tensions which had been the source of grievance.

Johnson has enumerated the countless and subtle ways in which American Negroes vent their hostility to whites.[48] In the South, he says, they will grasp any opportunity to "talk back" to a white man, they will commit acts of petty sabotage, will quit their jobs without giving notice or offering explanations, they will engage in telling jokes, spreading destructive gossip, and petty malingering. Those in better economic position will boycott merchants who discriminate against them and give their patronage to those who show proper courtesy. Some will indulge in sly retaliation by using exaggerated titles for whites, as described by a Negro porter in Houston:

> I usually say "judge," "lawyer," or "colonel," just like they do to us. I know that none of them are judges, and some of them I call lawyers are not lawyers. I just do it because they do us that way, and they like it. They think I am just fine. Where I work I call a lot of those fellows "editor." Some of them aren't any more than reporters or just office help; but I call them "editor" anyhow. They like to be flattered. We have some down there who belong to the National Guard, and I call them "captain." They like to be impressed that they are big shots.

Others ingeniously use courtesy itself as a weapon in a "war of nerves" as recounted by the Negro businessman who said:

> I come in contact with some of the toughest of them, but I always try to be courteous with them and nothing ever happens to me. That is the best thing that you can do to get the white man's nerves. If you can still be courteous and let him know where to get off and don't get all excited and scared when he blows up, you can handle him pretty well. They get all excited quick and if the Negroes do not get scared too, they think that they had better be careful.

In the North, Johnson says, the most common form of aggression is vehement verbal assertion of rights, some temperaments lending themselves more readily than others to this type of behavior. Another quite effective way of expressing aggression is to sue white offenders. He cites the instance of a Chicago

---

[48] C. S. Johnson, *op. cit.*, pp. 294–315.

Negro who purposely went into an "exclusive" bar in the Loop. The reluctant bartender gave him the drink he ordered, but charged him $1.25, which was considerably more than the established price. The Negro took issue with the bartender, and subsequently brought legal proceedings against the owner. Johnson says there are middle- and upper-class Negroes in the North who seek out opportunities to express their resentment of discrimination. One of these said:

> I wish I had nothing to do but float around and let myself in for it because I like to fight. They don't put a lot over on me. I don't care where I am or who is around. I know I am as good as anyone. I know my rights, even if I do belong to a minority group. I'll fight for them with anybody any time.

The 1960's have witnessed a profusion of new forms of aggression, including demonstrations, sit-ins, lie-ins, wade-ins, pray-ins, shop-ins, freedom rides, boycotts, selective patronage, marches, parades, and picket lines.

Organized Protest

Aggressive behavior is most likely to achieve its goal when it is organized, properly directed, and expertly led. Minority groups again and again have

A Birmingham riot scene

learned the value of organization, with the result that we find innumerable agencies operating in the area of race relations and having as their purpose the elimination of prejudice and discrimination and the assurance of justice and equality. American Negroes, during slavery, were deprived of the opportunity of meeting together and organizing their aggressive desires. There were, of course, slave revolts which called for a degree of organization, but which failed in their purpose. In the North there was some concerted action on the part of Negroes. They formed their separate church bodies, they protested against the colonization of free Negroes in Africa, and they took an active part in the abolition movement.

Organized Negro protest in the United States, however, assumed significant proportions early in the present century when certain of the Negro intelligentsia began to challenge the Booker T. Washington doctrine of industrial education, conciliation, and compromise. A group of men, under the leadership of W. E. B. DuBois, met at Niagara Falls, Canada, in 1905, and drew up a platform of aggressive action. Thus was launched the Niagara Movement, and a number of subsequent meetings were held at Harpers Ferry, West Virginia, Boston, and Oberlin, Ohio.

At the same time another organization was being formed by liberal whites, which eventually absorbed the Niagara Movement. In 1908 there occurred in Springfield, Illinois, a race riot which served to dramatize the insecurity of the Negro. The riot provoked considerable discussion in the press, including an article entitled "Race War in the North," by William E. Walling, which was published in *The Independent,* September 3, 1908. The author forcefully argued that the only alternative to race war was the treatment of the Negro "on a plane of absolute political and social equality." This article made an especial appeal to Miss Mary White Ovington, a New York social worker who had long been interested in the problems of the Negro. She, in consultation with others, decided to call a conference for Lincoln's Birthday, in 1909, to accept the challenge announced in Walling's article. The young radicals of the Niagara Movement were invited to the conference, and most of them accepted. A program was adopted, which included the following objectives:

Abolition of all forced segregation.
Equal educational advantages for colored and white.
Enfranchisement of the Negro.
Enforcement of the Fourteenth and Fifteenth Amendments.

From this conference there eventually emerged a permanent organization known as the National Association for the Advancement of Colored People.

The Association has become the most effective organization in this country fighting for the rights of Negroes. It set about immediately to open up industrial opportunities for Negroes, to insure them greater police protection, to abolish lynching, and to combat lawlessness. It has established an impressive record of successful court battles against discrimination in social, educational, legal, and political relations.[49] So effective has it been that the proponents of White Supremacy have come to regard the N.A.A.C.P. as their principal *bête noire*, and have sought by one means or another to outlaw it or to destroy it.

American Negroes have formed other organizations to give direction to their protest. The National Urban League, while chiefly concerned with meeting the social and economic problems arising from the mass migration of Negroes to northern cities, has also functioned as an agency for the elimination of prejudice and discrimination. Its methods have generally been more pacific than those of the N.A.A.C.P., and its program has tended to be but slightly more liberal than the prevailing attitudes in the communities in which it operates. Among the many other organizations formed for the purpose of expressing the Negro's protest are the Congress of Racial Equality, the Southern Christian Leadership Council, the Student Nonviolent Coordinating Committee, the Black Muslims, and others.

Not only the Negroes, however, but other minorities as well, and their sympathizers, have found that aggressive action can best be expressed through organization. To mention only a few, the Jews have their American Council for Judaism, the American Jewish Committee, the American Jewish Congress, and the Anti-Defamation League of B'nai B'rith. Working for the Indians are the Association on American Indian Affairs, the Indian Council Fire, the Indian Rights Association, and the National Congress of American Indians. The Japanese in the United States have their Japanese-American Citizens League; and the Mexican immigrants have their Mexican-American Movement.

What is the "best" solution for the problems of intergroup relationships? Certainly there is no simple answer, nor even a single one. Nor is there a permanent one. Too much depends upon the temperament of the individual and upon the values to which one is attached. Those who prize homogeneity will give one answer, while those who prize heterogeneity will give another. There are patient individuals who take a long view, and there are restless ones to whom time is the very essence of the problem. Those who exalt the unity of the state will differ from those whose concern is for human personality and individuality. Those who long for assimilation and integration will disagree with those who are interested in the preservation of traditions and values they hold dear. There are those to whom peace is priceless, and others who find conflict exhilarating, or at least preferable to discrimination. There are good reasons for believing, however, that whatever be one's disposition, and whatever his goal, the prospects for a happy solution of race problems are best in a society in which democratic ideals flourish, and in which social change is accomplished by the democratic processes of free discussion and free expressions of opinion.

---

[49] For information on the N.A.A.C.P., see Mary Ovington, *The Walls Came Tumbling Down*; E. F. Frazier, *The Negro in the United States*, pp. 523ff.; J. H. Franklin, *From Slavery to Freedom*, pp. 437ff.; Myrdal, *op. cit.*, pp. 819–938; Davie, *op. cit.*, pp. 449ff.

Bibliography

Abbott, Edith. *Immigration: Select Documents and Case Records.* Chicago: University of Chicago Press, 1924.

Abrams, Charles. *Forbidden Neighbors: A Study of Prejudice in Housing.* New York: Harper & Row, 1955.

Adamic Louis. *A Nation of Nations.* New York: Harper & Row, 1944.

Adamic, Louis. *From Many Lands.* New York: Harper & Row, 1940.

Adams, Romanzo. *Interracial Marriage in Hawaii.* New York: Macmillan Co., 1937.

Adorno, T. W., *et al. The Authoritarian Personality.* New York: Harper & Row, 1950.

Aikin, Charles. *The Negro Votes.* San Francisco: Chandler Publishing, 1962.

Alexis, Stephen. *Black Liberator: The Life of Toussaint Louverture.* New York: Macmillan Company, 1949.

Allport, Gordon W. *The Nature of Prejudice.* Cambridge: Addison-Wesley Publishing Co., 1954.

Anderson, E. L. *We Americans: A Study of Cleavage in an American City.* Cambridge: Harvard University Press, 1937.

Banton, Michael. *White and Coloured: The Behaviour of British People toward Coloured Immigrants.* New Brunswick, N.J.: Rutgers University Press, 1960.

Barron, Milton L. *American Minorities.* New York: Alfred A. Knopf, 1957.

Barron, Milton L. *People Who Intermarry.* Syracuse, N.Y.: Syracuse University Press, 1946.

Barzun, Jacques. *Race: A Study in Modern Superstition.* New York: Harcourt, Brace and World, 1937.

Beardsley, G. H. *The Negro in Greek and Roman Civilization.* Baltimore: Johns Hopkins Press, 1929.

Benedict, Ruth. *Race: Science and Politics.* New York: Modern Age Books, 1940.

Benson, A. B. *Americans from Sweden.* Philadelphia: J. B. Lippincott Co., 1950.

Berger, Elmer. *Emancipation: The Rediscovered Ideal.* Philadelphia: American Council for Judaism, 1945.

Berger, Morroe. *Equality by Statute: Legal Controls over Group Discrimination.* New York: Columbia University Press, 1952.

kson, Isaac. *Theories of Americanization.* New York: Teachers College, Columia University, 1920.

le, Beatrice B. *80 Puerto Rican Families.* New York: Columbia University Press, 958.

ry, Brewton. *Almost White.* New York: Macmillan Co., 1963.

telheim, Bruno, and Morris Janowitz. *Dynamics of Prejudice.* New York: Harper Row, 1950.

eridge, A. J. *Abraham Lincoln, 1809–1858.* Boston: Houghton Mifflin Co., 1928.

sanz, John, and Mavis Biesanz. *The People of Panama.* New York: Columbia niversity Press, 1955.

om, Leonard, and Ruth Riemer. *Removal and Return: The Socio-Economic Effects the War on Japanese Americans.* Berkeley and Los Angeles: University of alifornia Press, 1949.

ardus, Emory S. *Immigration and Race Attitudes.* Boston: D. C. Heath and Co., 928.

d, William C. *Genetics and the Races of Man.* Boston: Little, Brown and Co., 950.

meld, Theodore. *Minority Problems in the Public Schools.* New York: Harper & ow, 1946.

t, Albert. *Great Indian Chiefs.* New York: McGraw-Hill Book Co., 1938.

oks, Maxwell R. *The Negro Press Re-examined.* Boston: Christopher Publishing ouse, 1959.

om, Leonard, and John I. Kitsuse. *The Managed Casualty: The Japanese-American Family in World War II.* Berkeley and Los Angeles: University of California ress, 1956.

z, Howard. *The Black Jews of Harlem.* New York: Free Press of Glencoe, 1963.

wn, Demetra V. *A Child of the Orient.* Boston: Houghton Mifflin Co., 1914.

wn, F. J., and J. S. Roucek. *One America.* New York: Prentice-Hall, Inc., 1945.

wne, Lewis. *How Odd of God.* New York: Macmillan Co., 1934.

nner, E. de S. *Immigrant Farmers and Their Children.* New York: Doubleday, oran and Company, 1929.

gess, M. Elaine. *Negro Leadership in a Southern City.* Chapel Hill, N.C.: University of North Carolina Press, 1962.

ma, John H. *The Spanish-Speaking Groups in the United States.* Durham, N.C.: uke University Press, 1954.

ns, W. Haywood. *The Voices of Negro Protest in America.* New York: Oxford niversity Press, 1963.

rows, E. G. *Hawaiian Americans.* New Haven: Yale University Press, 1947.

man, Werner J. (Ed.) *Intermarriage and Jewish Life.* New York: Herzl Press, 63.

oll, Joseph C. *Slave Insurrections in the United States, 1800–1860.* Boston: hapman and Grimes, 1938.

er, W. A. *The Urban Negro in the South.* New York: Vantage Press, 1961.

, W. J. *The Mind of the South.* Garden City, N.Y. Doubleday & Co., 1954.

in, George. *The North American Indians.* London: Chatto and Windus, 1880.

d, Irvin L. *Italian or American? The Second Generation in Conflict.* New aven: Yale University Press, 1943.

Christie, Richard, and Marie Jahoda (Eds.) *Studies in the Scope and Method* *"The Authoritarian Personality."* New York: Free Press of Glencoe, 1954.

Cilliers, S. P. *The Coloureds of South Africa.* Cape Town: Banier Publishers, 19

Cleveland, Harlan. *The Overseas Americans.* New York: McGraw-Hill Book (1960.

Collins, Sydney. *Coloured Minorities in Britain.* London: Lutterworth Press, 1957

Coolidge, Mary Roberts. *Chinese Immigration.* New York: Henry Holt and Co., 19

Coon, C. S. *The Races of Europe.* New York: Macmillan Co., 1939.

Coon, C. S. *The Origin of Races.* New York: Alfred A. Knopf, 1962.

Coughlin, Richard J. *Double Identity: The Chinese in Modern Thailand.* H
Kong: Hong Kong University Press, 1960.

Cox, Oliver C. *Caste, Class and Race: A Study in Social Dynamics.* Garden C
N.Y.: Doubleday & Co., 1948.

Cronon, E. D. *Black Moses: The Story of Marcus Garvey and the Universal Ne*
Improvement Association. Madison, Wisc.: University of Wisconsin Press, 195!

Curry, J. E., and Glen D. King. *Race Tensions and the Police.* Springfield, ▮
Charles C Thomas, 1962.

Cutler, James E. *Lynch-law: An Investigation into the History of Lynching in*
United States. New York: Longmans, Green and Co., 1905.

Davenport, C. B., and M. S. Steggerda. *Race Crossing in Jamaica.* Publication
395 of the Carnegie Institution of Washington, 1929.

Davie, M. R. *Negroes in American Society.* New York: McGraw-Hill Book Co., 1!

Davie, M. R. *Refugees in America.* New York: Harper & Row, 1947.

Davie, M. R. *World Immigration.* New York: Macmillan Co., 1936.

Davis, A., B. B. Gardner, and Mary Gardner. *Deep South: A Social Anthropolog*
Study of Caste and Class. Chicago: University of Chicago Press, 1941.

Davis, Ethelyn. *The American Colony in Mexico City.* Unpublished doctoral
sertation, University of Missouri, 1942.

Davis, S. *Race-Relations in Ancient Egypt.* New York: Philosophical Library, 1!

Day, Caroline Bond. *A Study of Some Negro-White Families in the United Sta*
Harvard African Studies, Vol. 10, 1932.

Dean, John P., and Alex Rosen. *A Manual of Intergroup Relations.* Chicago: ▮
versity of Chicago Press, 1955.

Deasi, Rashmi. *Indian Immigrants in Britain.* New York: Oxford University Pr
1964.

DeGroot, Dudley. *The Assimilation of Postwar Immigrants in Atlanta, Geor*
Unpublished doctoral dissertation, Ohio State University, 1957.

Deutsch, M., and Mary E. Collins. *Interracial Housing.* Minneapolis: University
Minnesota Press, 1951.

Dollard, John. *Caste and Class in a Southern Town.* New York: Harper & R
1949.

Doyle, B. W. *The Etiquette of Race Relations in the South.* Chicago: Universit
Chicago Press, 1937.

Drachsler, Julius. *Democracy and Assimilation.* New York: Macmillan Co., 192(

Drake, St. Clair, and H. R. Cayton. *Black Metropolis.* New York: Harcourt, B
and World, 1945.

Driver, Harold E. *Indians of North America.* Chicago: University of Chicago Pr
1961.

Bois, W. E. B. *Dusk of Dawn.* New York: Harcourt, Brace and World, 1940.
ncan, H. G. *Immigration and Assimilation.* Boston: D. C. Heath and Co., 1933.

wards, G. Franklin. *The Negro Professional Class.* New York: Free Press of Glencoe, 1959.
enstadt, S. N. *The Absorption of Immigrants: A Comparative Study Based Mainly on the Jewish Community in Palestine and the State of Israel.* New York: The Free Press of Glencoe, 1955.
kins, Stanley. *Slavery: A Problem in American Institutional and Intellectual Life.* Chicago: University of Chicago Press, 1959.
bree, E. R. *Indians of the Americas.* Boston: Houghton Mifflin Co., 1939.
stein, Benjamin R., and Arnold Forster. *Some of My Best Friends.* New York: Farrar, Straus and Cudahy, 1959.
kelund, Karl. *My Chinese Wife.* Garden City, N.Y.: Doubleday & Co., 1945.
sien-Udom, E. U. *Black Nationalism: A Search for Identity in America.* Chicago: University of Chicago Press, 1961.

irchild, H. P. *Immigration: A World Movement and Its American Significance.* New York: Macmillan Co., 1926.
irchild, H. P. *Race and Nationality.* New York: Ronald Press, 1947.
rquhar, J. H. *The Crown of Hinduism.* London: Oxford University Press, 1920.
scher, Eugen. *Die Rehobother Bastards und das Bastardierungsproblem beim Menschen.* Jena: G. Fischer, 1913.
zhugh, George. *Sociology for the South: Or the Failure of Free Society.* Richmond, Va.: A. Morris, 1854.
ng, N. B. *The Chinese in New Zealand.* New York: Oxford University Press, 1960.
reman, Grant. *Indians and Pioneers.* Norman, Okla.: Oklahoma University Press, 1936.
reman, Grant. *Indian Removal.* Norman, Okla.: Oklahoma University Press, 1932.
ankenstein, Carl (Ed.) *Between Past and Future.* Jerusalem: Henrietta Szold Foundation for Child and Youth Welfare, 1953.
anklin, J. Hope. *From Slavery to Freedom.* New York: Alfred A. Knopf, 1948. Second edition, 1956.
azier, Sir James G. *The Golden Bough: A Study in Magic and Religion.* 12 vols. London: Macmillan and Co., Ltd., 1913–1915.
azier, E. Franklin. *Black Bourgeoisie.* New York: Free Press of Glencoe, 1957.
azier, E. Franklin. *The Negro Family in the United States.* Chicago: University of Chicago Press, 1939.
azier, E. Franklin. *The Negro in the United States.* New York: Macmillan Co., 1949.
azier, E. Franklin. *Race and Culture Contacts in the Modern World.* New York: Alfred A. Knopf, 1957.
eedman, Maurice (Ed.) *A Minority in Britain: Social Studies of the Anglo-Jewish Community.* London: Vallentine, Mitchell and Co., Ltd., 1955.
eyre, Gilberto. *The Masters and the Slaves: A Study in the Development of Brazilian Civilization.* New York: Alfred A. Knopf, 1946.

Galitzi, Christine. *A Study of Assimilation among the Roumanians of the Unit* *States.* New York: Columbia University Press, 1929.

Ghurye, Govind S. *Caste and Race in India.* London: Kegan Paul, Trench, Trubi and Co., 1932.

Ginzberg, Eli. *The Negro Potential.* New York: Columbia University Press, 1956.

Gittler, Joseph B. (Ed.) *Understanding Minority Groups.* New York: John Wi and Sons, 1956.

Glass, Ruth. *London's Newcomers: The West Indian Migrants.* Cambridge: Harva University Press, 1961.

Glazer, Nathan. *American Judaism.* Chicago: University of Chicago Press, 1957.

Glazer, Nathan, and Daniel Patrick Moynihan. *Beyond the Melting Pot.* Cambridg M.I.T. Press and Harvard University Press, 1963.

Glazer, Nathan, and David McEntire (Eds.) *Studies in Housing and Minority Grou* Berkeley and Los Angeles: University of California Press, 1960.

Goldenweiser, Alexander. *Anthropology.* New York: F. S. Crofts and Co., 1937.

Gordon, Albert I. *Jews in Suburbia.* Boston: Beacon Press, 1959.

Gordon, Albert I. *Jews in Transition.* Minneapolis: University of Minnesota Pre 1950.

Gordon, Milton M. *Assimilation in American Life.* Copyright © by Oxford Univers Press, 1964.

Govorchin, G. G. *Americans from Yugoslavia.* Gainesville: University of Flori Press, 1961.

Graebner, Isacque, and S. H. Britt (Eds.) *Jews in a Gentile World.* New York: M millan Co., 1942.

Greenberg, Jack. *Race Relations and American Law.* New York: Columbia U versity Press, 1959.

Greer, Scott. *Last Man In: Racial Access to Union Power.* New York: Free Press Glencoe, 1959.

Griffith, J. A. G., *et al. Coloured Immigrants in Britain.* London: Oxford Univers Press, 1960.

Hagan, William T. *American Indians.* Chicago: University of Chicago Press, 1961

Hall, S. Warren, III. *Tangier Island: A Study of an Isolated Group.* Philadelph University of Pennsylvania Press, 1939.

Handlin, Oscar. *Boston's Immigrants, 1790–1865.* Cambridge: Harvard Univers Press, 1941.

Handlin, Oscar. *The Uprooted.* Boston: Little, Brown and Co., 1951.

Hanke, Lewis. *Aristotle and the American Indian: A Study in Race Prejudice in* *Modern World.* Chicago: Henry Regnery, 1962.

Hansen, Marcus Lee. *The Atlantic Migration.* Cambridge: Harvard Univers Press, 1942.

Hansen, Marcus Lee. *The Immigrant in American History.* Cambridge: Harv University Press, 1942.

Hartley, Eugene. *Problems in Prejudice.* New York: King's Crown Press, 1946.

Harlan, Louis R. *Separate and Unequal.* Chapel Hill, N.C.: University of No Carolina Press, 1958.

Hawthorn, H. B. (Ed.) *The Doukhobors of British Columbia.* Vancouver: Univers of British Columbia and J. M. Dent and Sons, Ltd., 1955.

Hecht, Ben. *A Guide for the Bedevilled.* New York: Charles Scribner's Sons, 19

llman, Ellen (Ed.), assisted by Leah Abrahams. *Handbook on Race Relations in South Africa*. London: Oxford University Press, 1949.

nriques, F. M. *Family and Colour in Jamaica*. London: Eyre and Spottswoods, 953.

rold, J. Christopher. *The Swiss without Halos*. New York: Columbia University Press, 1948.

rskovits, M. J. *Acculturation: The Study of Culture Contact*. New York: J. J. Augustin, 1938.

rskovits, M. J. *The American Negro: A Study in Racial Crossing*. New York: Alfred A. Knopf, 1928.

rskovits, M. J. *The Anthropometry of the American Negro*. New York: Columbia University Press, 1930.

rskovits, M. J. *The Myth of the Negro Past*. New York: Harper & Row, 1941.

rzl, Theodor. *The Jewish State*. New York: Zionist Organization of America, 1941.

gbin, H. Ian. *Experiments in Civilization*. London: George Routledge and Sons, 939.

lley, J. W. *You Can't Build a Chimney from the Top*. New York: William-Frederick Press, 1948.

lingshead, A. B. *Elmtown's Youth*. New York: John Wiley and Sons, 1949.

ton, E. A. *Up from the Ape*. New York: Macmillan Co., 1931. Revised edition, 946.

stetler, John A. *Amish Society*. Baltimore: Johns Hopkins University Press, 1963.

rani, A. H. *Minorities in the Arab World*. London: Oxford University Press, 947.

ddleston, The Rev. Trevor. *Nought for Your Comfort*. Garden City, N.Y.: Doubleday & Co., 1956.

bener, Theodore. *The Germans in America*. Philadelphia: Chilton Company, 962.

ghes, Everett C., and Helen MacGill Hughes. *Where Peoples Meet: Racial and Ethnic Frontiers*. New York: Free Press of Glencoe, 1952.

ghes, Henry. *Treatise on Sociology, Theoretical and Practical*. Philadelphia: ublished by the author, 1854.

nter, John Dunn. *Memoirs of a Captivity among the Indians of North America*. London: Longman, Hurst, Rees, Orme, and Brown, 1823.

ton, J. H. *Caste in India: Its Nature, Functions and Origins*. Cambridge: Cambridge University Press, 1946.

xley, Julian S., and A. C. Haddon. *We Europeans: A Survey of "Racial" Problems*. New York: Harper & Row, 1936.

stitute of Race Relations. *Coloured Immigrants in Britain*. London: Oxford University Press, 1960.

nnings, H. S. *The Biological Basis of Human Nature*. New York: W. W. Norton and Co., 1930.

rome, Harry. *Migration and Business Cycles*. New York: National Bureau of Economic Research, 1926.

hnson, Charles S. *Patterns of Segregation*. New York: Harper & Row, 1943.

hnson, James Weldon. *Negro Americans, What Now?* New York: Viking Press, 935.

Johnson, Robert. "Negro Reactions to Minority Group Status," in M. L. Barr (Ed.), *American Minorities*. New York: Alfred A. Knopf, 1957.

Jonassen, C. T. *Norwegians in Bay Ridge: A Sociological Study of an Ethnic Grou* Ann Arbor, Mich.: University Microfilms, Inc., 1948.

Jones, Maldwyn Allen. *American Immigration*. Chicago: University of Chica Press, 1960.

Junek, O. W. *Isolated Communities: A Study of a Labrador Fishing Village*. N York: American Book Co., 1937.

Kardiner, Abram, and Lionel Ovesey. *The Mark of Oppression: A Psychologi Study of the American Negro*. New York: W. W. Norton and Co., 1951.

Kaufman, Harold F. *Prestige Classes in a New York Rural Community*. Itha Cornell University Agricultural Experiment Station, 1944.

Keller, A. G. *Colonization*. Boston: Ginn and Co., 1908.

Kent, Donald P. *The Refugee Intellectual: The Americanization of the Immigra of 1933–41*. New York: Columbia University Press, 1953.

Kephart, William M. *The Family, Society and the Individual*. Boston: Hought Mifflin Co., 1961.

Keur, John Y., and Dorothy L. Keur. *Windward Children: A Study in Human Ec ogy in the Caribbean*. Assen, Netherlands: Roual Van Gorcum, Ltd., 1960.

Kidd, Dudley. *Kafir Socialism and the Dawn of Individualism*. London: Adam a Charles Black, 1908.

Killian, Lewis, and Charles Grigg. *Racial Crisis in America*. Englewood Cliffs, N. Prentice-Hall, 1964.

Kippis, Andrew. *Narrative of the Voyages Round the World Performed by Capt James Cook*. London: Bickers and Son, 1878.

Kiser, Clyde. *From Sea Island to City*. New York: Columbia University Press, 19

Kitson, Arthur. *Captain James Cook, the Circumnavigator*. New York: E. P. Dutt and Co., 1907.

Klineberg, Otto (Ed.) *Characteristics of the American Negro*. New York: Harp & Row, 1944.

Klineberg, Otto. *Race Differences*. New York: Harper & Row, 1935.

Korngold, Ralph. *Citizen Toussaint*. Boston: Little, Brown and Co., 1945.

Korwitz, Milton R. *The Alien and the Asiatic in American Law*. Ithaca: Corn University Press, 1946.

Kosa, John. *Land of Choice: The Hungarians in Canada*. Toronto: Toronto Univ sity Press, 1957.

Krader, Lawrence. *Peoples of Central Asia*. Bloomington: Uralic and Altaic Seri Indiana University, 1963.

Kramer, Judith R., and Seymour Leventman. *Children of the Gilded Ghetto: Conf Resolution of Three Generations of American Jews*. New Haven: Yale Univers Press, 1961.

Krueger, Nancy M. *Assimilation of Post-War Immigrants in Columbus, Ohio*. U published doctoral dissertation, Ohio State University, 1955.

Kuper, Hilda. *Indian People in Natal*. Pietermaritzburg, South Africa: Natal at University Press, 1960.

Kuper, Leo, *et al*. *Durban: A Study in Racial Ecology*. New York: Columbia U versity Press, 1958.

Farge, John, S.J. *The Catholic Viewpoint on Race Relations.* Garden City, N.Y.: Hanover House, 1960.

Piere, Richard T. *Sociology.* New York: McGraw-Hill Book Co., 1946.

urenti, Luigi. *Property Values and Race.* Berkeley: University of California Press. 1960.

a, H. C. *The Moriscos of Spain: Their Conversion and Expulsion.* Philadelphia: Lea Brothers and Co., 1901.

e, A. M. *Fraternities without Brotherhood.* Boston: Beacon Press, 1955.

e, A. M., and N. D. Humphrey. *Race Riot.* New York: Dryden Press, 1943.

e, Frank F. *Negro and White in a Connecticut Town.* New York: Bookman Asso- ciates, 1961.

ghton, Alexander H. *The Governing of Men.* Princeton: Princeton University Press, 1945.

wis, Hylan. *Blackways of Kent.* Chapel Hill, N.C.: University of North Carolina Press, 1955.

berson, Stanley. *Ethnic Patterns in American Cities.* New York: Free Press of Glencoe, 1963.

coln, Eric. *The Black Muslims in America.* Boston: Beacon Press, 1961.

d, Andrew W. *An Island Community: Ecological Succession in Hawaii.* Chicago: University of Chicago Press, 1938.

d, Andrew W. (Ed.) *Race Relations in World Perspective.* Honolulu: University of Hawaii Press, 1955.

d, Andrew W., and Robert Schmitt. *Hawaii's People.* Honolulu: University of Hawaii Press, 1955.

ton, Ralph (Ed.) *Acculturation in Seven American Indian Tribes.* New York: D. Appleton-Century Co., 1940.

ton, Ralph, *et al. The Science of Man in the World Crisis.* New York: Columbia University Press, 1945.

ton, Ralph. *The Study of Man.* New York: D. Appleton-Century Co., 1936.

s, Julius. *The Savage Hits Back.* New Haven: Yale University Press, 1937.

le, Kenneth L. *Negroes in Britain.* London: Kegan Paul, Trench, Trübner and Company, 1947.

ke, Alain, and B. J. Stern. *When Peoples Meet.* New York: Progressive Educa- ion Association, 1942.

an, Rayford W. *The Negro in American Life and Thought: The Nadir, 1877– 901.* New York: Dial Press, 1954.

man, Joseph D. *The Police and Minority Groups: A Manual Prepared for Use n the Chicago Park District Police Training School.* Chicago: Chicago Park District, 1947.

imer, Frank. *The Population of the Soviet Union: History and Prospects.* Geneva: League of Nations, 1946.

t, Albert J., and Bernice E. Lott. *Negro and White Youth: A Psychological Study n a Border-State Community.* New York: Holt, Rinehart & Winston, 1963.

cCrone, I. D. *Race Attitudes in South Africa.* London: Oxford University Press, 1937.

cGregor, Gordon. *Warriors without Weapons.* Chicago: University of Chicago Press, 1946.

MacIver, R. M., and Charles H. Page. *Society: An Introductory Analysis.* N
York: Rinehart and Co., 1949.

Mack, Raymond W. (Ed.) *Race, Class and Power.* New York: American Book C
1963.

MacLeod, William C. *The American Indian Frontier.* New York: Alfred A. Kno
1928.

Macmillan, W. M. *Bantu, Boer and Briton: The Making of the South African Nat
Problem.* London: Faber and Gwyer, Ltd., 1929.

Madigan, La Verne. *The American Indian Relocation Program.* New York: '1
Association on American Indian Affairs, 1956.

Mahajani, Urha. *The Role of Indian Minorities in Burma and Malaya.* Bombè
Vora and Co., 1960.

Malelu, Sharad J. *The Anglo-Indians: A Problem in Marginality.* Unpublisl
doctoral dissertation, Ohio State University, 1964.

Mandelbaum, D. G. *Soldier Groups and Negro Soldiers.* Berkeley and Los Angel
University of California Press, 1952.

Mangum, Charles S. *The Legal Status of the Negro.* Chapel Hill, N.C.: Univers
of North Carolina Press, 1940.

Manley, Douglas, *et al. The West Indian Comes to England.* London: Routlec
and Kegan Paul, Ltd., 1960.

Marais, J. S. *The Cape Coloured People, 1652–1937.* London: Longmans, Gre
and Co., 1939.

Marden, Charles F., and Gladys Meyer. *Minorities in American Society.* New Yo»
American Book Co., 1962.

Marrow, Alfred J. *Changing Patterns of Prejudice.* Philadelphia: Chilton Co., 19(

Masuoka, Jitsuichi, and Preston Valien. *Race Relations: Problems and Theo*
Chapel Hill, N.C.: University of North Carolina Press, 1961.

Mathews, Shailer. *A History of New Testament Times in Palestine.* New Yo»
Macmillan Co., 1921.

McCloy, Shelby T. *The Negro in France.* Lexington, Ky: University of Kentu(
Press, 1961.

McDonagh, E. C., and E. S. Richards. *Ethnic Relations in the United States.* N
York: Appleton-Century-Crofts, 1953.

McEntire, Davis. *Residence and Race.* Berkeley and Los Angeles: University
California Press, 1960.

McKay, Claude. *Harlem: Negro Metropolis.* New York: E. P. Dutton and Co., 19

McKay, Claude. *Harlem Shadows.* New York: Harcourt, Brace and Co., 1922.

McNickle, D'Arcy. *The Indian Tribes of the United States.* New York: Oxfe
University Press, 1962.

McNickle, D'Arcy. *They Came Here First.* Philadelphia: J. B. Lippincott Co., 19

McWilliams, Carey. *A Mask for Privilege: Anti-Semitism in America.* Boston: Lit»
Brown and Co., 1943.

McWilliams, Carey. *North from Mexico: The Spanish-Speaking People of the Uni*
States. Philadelphia: J. B. Lippincott Co., 1948.

Mead, Margaret. *The Changing Culture of an Indian Tribe.* New York: Colum»
University Press, 1932.

Mendelson, Wallace. *Discrimination: Based on the Report of the United Sta*
Commission on Civil Rights. Englewood Cliffs, N.J.: Prentice-Hall, 1962.

eriam, Lewis, and Associates. *The Problem of Indian Administration.* Baltimore: Johns Hopkins Press, 1928.

eyer, Peter, *et al. The Jews in the Soviet Satellites.* Syracuse: Syracuse University Press, 1963.

ill, John Stuart. *Principles of Political Economy.* 2 vols. New York: Colonial Press, 1899.

iller, Arthur S. *Racial Discrimination and Private Education: A Legal Analysis.* Chapel Hill, N.C.: University of North Carolina Press, 1957.

ller, H. A. *Races, Nations and Classes.* Philadelphia: J. B. Lippincott Co., 1924.

llin, Sarah Gertrude. *The South Africans.* New York: Boni and Liveright, 1927.

lls, C. Wright, Rose K. Goldsen, and Clarence Senior. *The Puerto Rican Journey.* New York: Harper & Row, 1950.

tchell, Glenford, and William Peace. *The Angry Black South.* New York: Corinth Books, 1962.

oney, James. *The Ghost Dance Religion.* 14th Annual Report, Part 2, Bureau of American Ethnology, Washington, 1896.

rdock, G. P. *Our Primitive Contemporaries.* New York: Macmillan Co., 1934.

rphy, H. B. M. *Flight and Resettlement.* Paris: UNESCO, 1955.

se, Benjamin. *Ten Years of Prelude: The Story of Integration Since the Supreme Court's 1954 Decision.* New York: Viking Press, 1964.

ers, Gustavus. *History of Bigotry in the United States.* New York: Random House, 1943.

rdal, Gunnar, with the assistance of Richard Sterner and Arnold Rose. *An American Dilemma: The Negro Problem and Modern Democracy.* New York: Harper & Row, 1944.

lson, A. M. *Awareness of In-group Attitudes.* Unpublished doctoral dissertation, Ohio State University, 1955.

rris, Hoke (Ed.) *We Dissent.* New York: St. Martin's Press, 1962.

vier, Sydney. *White Capital and Coloured Labour.* London: L. and V. Woolf, 929.

ison, John M. *Tecumseh and His Times.* New York: G. P. Putnam's Sons, 1938.

ley, Roi. *Black Odyssey: The Story of the Negro in America.* New York: Charles Scribner's Sons, 1948.

ley, Roi. *New World A-Coming.* Boston: Houghton Mifflin Co., 1943.

ngton, Mary White. *The Walls Came Tumbling Down.* New York: Harcourt, Brace and Co., 1947.

illa, Elena. *Up from Puerto Rico.* New York: Columbia University Press, 1958.

k, Robert E. *Race and Culture.* New York: Free Press of Glencoe, 1949.

k, R. E., and E. W. Burgess. *Introduction to the Science of Sociology.* Chicago: University of Chicago Press, 1924.

k, R. E., and H. A. Miller. *Old World Traits Transplanted.* New York: Harper Row, 1921.

ii, Raphael. *Between East and West.* Philadelphia: Jewish Publication Society, 953.

erson, Sheila. *Colour and Culture in South Africa.* London: Routledge and egan Paul, Ltd., 1953.

Patterson, Sheila. *Dark Strangers: A Sociological Study of the Absorption of Recent West Indian Migrant Group in Brixton, South London.* London: Tavistoc Publications, 1963.

Pettigrew, Thomas F. *A Profile of the Negro American.* Princeton, N.J.: D. V. Nostrand Co., 1964.

Pierson, Donald. *Negroes in Brazil.* Chicago: University of Chicago Press, 1942.

Pipes, Richard. *The Formation of the Soviet Union.* Cambridge: Harvard Universi Press, 1954.

Pitt-Rivers, G. H. L. *The Clash of Cultures and the Contact of Races.* Londo George Routledge and Sons, Ltd., 1927.

Poll, Solomon. *The Hasidic Community of Williamsburg.* New York: Free Press Glencoe, 1962.

Porteus, Stanley D. *Calabashes and Kings: An Introduction to Hawaii.* Palo Al Calif.: Pacific Books, 1945.

Powdermaker, Hortense. *After Freedom.* New York: Viking Press, 1939.

Powdermaker, Hortense. *Probing Our Prejudices.* New York: Harper & Row, 194

Powell, A. C., Jr. *Marching Blacks.* New York: Dial Press, 1945.

Price, Charles A. *Southern Europeans in Australia.* New York: Oxford Universi Press, 1964.

Price, Hugh D. *The Negro and Southern Politics.* New York: New York Universi Press, 1957.

Price, Willard. *Japan's Islands of Mystery.* New York: John Day Co., 1944.

Priestly, H. I. *The Coming of the White Man, 1492–1848.* New York: Macmillan C 1930.

Proudfoot, Merrill. *Diary of a Sit-in.* Chapel Hill, N.C.: University of North Car lina Press, 1962.

Putnam, Carleton. *Race and Reason.* Washington: Public Affairs Press, 1961.

Raab, Earl (Ed.) *American Race Relations Today.* Garden City, N.J.: Doubled & Co., 1962.

Rapkin, Chester, and William G. Grigsby. *The Demand for Housing in Racial Mixed Areas.* Berkeley: University of California Press, 1960.

Rappard, William E. *The Government of Switzerland.* Princeton, N.J.: D. V Nostrand Co., 1936.

Ravage, M. E. *An American in the Making: The Life Story of an Immigrant.* Ne York: Harper & Row, 1917.

Record, Wilson. *The Negro and the Communist Party.* Chapel Hill, N.C.: Universi of North Carolina Press, 1951.

Record, Wilson. *Race and Radicalism.* Ithaca: Cornell University Press, 1964.

Redding, J. Saunders. *They Came in Chains.* Philadelphia: J. B. Lippincott C 1950.

Redfield, Robert, and Alfonso Villa R. *Chan Kom: A Maya Village.* Washingt D.C.: Carnegie Institution, 1934.

Reid, Ira De A. *In A Minor Key: Negro Youth in Story and Fact.* Washington, D.C American Council on Education, 1949.

Reid, Ira De A. *The Negro Immigrant.* New York: Columbia University Press, 19

Reuter, E. B. (Ed.) *Race and Culture Contacts.* New York: McGraw-Hill Book C 1934.

Richmond, Anthony H. *Colour Prejudice in Britain.* London: Routledge and Kegan Paul, 1954.

Richmond, Anthony H. *The Colour Problem: A Study of Racial Relations.* Baltimore: Penguin Books, 1955.

Rihbany, A. M. *A Far Journey.* Boston: Houghton Mifflin Co., 1914.

Rischin, Moses. *The Promised City: New York's Jews, 1870–1914.* Cambridge: Harvard University Press, 1962.

Rister, Carl C. *Border Captives: The Traffic in Prisoners by Southern Plains Indians.* Norman, Okla.: Oklahoma University Press, 1940.

Roback, A. A. *A Dictionary of International Slurs.* Cambridge, Mass.: Sci-Art Publishers, 1944.

Roberts, E. F. *Ireland in America.* New York: G. P. Putnam's Sons, 1931.

Rohrer, John H., and Munro S. Edmonson. *The Eighth Generation: Cultures and Personalities of New Orleans Negroes.* New York: Harper & Row, 1960.

Rolland, Romain. *Mahatma Gandhi.* New York: Century Co., 1924.

Rose, Arnold, and Caroline Rose. *America Divided.* New York: Alfred A. Knopf, 1948.

Rose, Arnold. *The Negro's Morale: Group Identification and Protest.* Minneapolis: University of Minnesota Press, 1949.

Rose, Arnold. *Studies in the Reduction of Prejudice.* Chicago: American Council on Race Relations, 1947.

Rose, Peter I. *They and We.* New York: Random House, 1964.

Ruck, S. K. (Ed.) *The West Indian Comes to England.* London: Routledge and Kegan Paul, 1960.

Saenger, Gerhart. *The Social Psychology of Prejudice.* New York: Harper & Row, 1953.

Samuel, Maurice. *The Great Hatred.* New York: Alfred A. Knopf, 1941.

Sansom, G. B. *The Western World and Japan.* New York: Alfred A. Knopf, 1949.

Saron, Gustav, and Louis Hotz. *The Jews in South Africa.* New York: Oxford University Press, 1956.

Saveth, E. N. *American Historians and European Immigration, 1875–1925.* New York: Columbia University Press, 1948.

Schermerhorn, R. A. *These Our People.* Boston: D. C. Heath and Co., 1949.

Schmid, Calvin F. *Social Trends in Seattle.* Seattle: University of Washington Press, 1944.

Schmid, Calvin F., and Wayne W. McVey, Jr. *Growth and Distribution of Minority Races in Seattle, Washington.* Published by the Seattle Public Schools, 1964.

Schwarz, Solomon M. *The Jews in the Soviet Union.* Syracuse: Syracuse University Press, 1951.

Shapiro, Harry L. *The Heritage of the Bounty.* New York: Simon and Schuster, 1936.

Shay, Frank. *Judge Lynch: His First Hundred Years.* New York: Ives Washburn, Inc., 1938.

Sherman, Mandel, and T. R. Henry. *Hollow Folk.* New York: Thomas Y. Crowell Co., 1933.

Sherman, Charles B. *The Jews Within American Society: A Study in Ethnic Individuality.* Detroit: Wayne State University Press, 1961.

Shrieke, B. *Alien Americans.* New York: Viking Press, 1936.

Shuey, Audrey M. *The Testing of Negro Intelligence.* Lynchburg, Va.: J. P. Be Co., 1958.

Simmons, L. W. (Ed.) *Sun Chief: The Autobiography of a Hopi Indian.* New Have Yale University Press, 1942.

Simpson, George E., and J. Milton Yinger. *Racial and Cultural Minorities: A Analysis of Prejudice and Discrimination.* New York: Harper & Row, 1953.

Skinner, G. William. *Chinese Society in Thailand.* Ithaca: Cornell University Pres 1957.

Sklare, Marshall (Ed.) *The Jews: Social Patterns of an American Group.* New Yorl Free Press of Glencoe, 1958.

Smith, Bradford. *Americans from Japan.* Philadelphia: J. B. Lippincott Co., 1948.

Smith, W. C. *Americans in the Making.* New York: D. Appleton-Century Co., 193

Sorokin, P. A. *Contemporary Sociological Theories.* New York: Harper & Row, 192

Spellman, C. L. *Elm City: A Negro Community in Action.* Tallahassee: Flori A. and M. College, 1947.

Stanton, William. *The Leopard's Spots: Scientific Attitudes toward Race in Americ 1815–59.* Chicago: Chicago University Press, 1960.

Starkey, Marion L. *The Cherokee Nation.* New York: Alfred A. Knopf, 1946.

Stefansson, Vilhjalmur. *My Life with the Eskimo.* New York: Macmillan Co., 192

Stern, Curt. *Principles of Human Genetics.* San Francisco: W. H. Freeman and C 1949.

Steward, Julian H. (Ed.) *Handbook of South American Indians.* Smithsonian I stitution, Bureau of American Ethnology Bulletin 143. 5 vols. Washington, D.C Government Printing Office, 1946–1949.

Stibbe, E. P. *An Introduction to Physical Anthropology.* New York: Longman Green and Co., 1930.

Stonequist, E. V. *The Marginal Man.* New York: Charles Scribner's Sons, 1937.

Strandenraus, J. *The African Colonization Movement.* New York, Columbia Ur versity Press, 1961.

Strong, E. K. *The Second-Generation Japanese Problem.* Palo Alto, Calif.: Stanfor University Press, 1934.

Sutherland, Robert L. *Color, Class and Personality.* Washington: American Counc on Education, 1942.

Taft, Donald R., and Richard Robbins. *International Migrations.* New York: Ronal Press, 1955.

Tannenbaum, Frank. *Slave and Citizen: The Negro in the Americas.* New Yorl Alfred A. Knopf, 1947.

Taper, Bernard. *Gomillion versus Lightfoot.* New York: McGraw-Hill Book Cc 1962.

Thomas, Dorothy, and Richard Nishimoto. *The Spoilage.* Berkeley: University c California Press, 1946.

Thomas, Dorothy S. *The Salvage: Japanese American Evacuation and Resettlemen* Berkeley and Los Angeles: University of California Press, 1952.

Thomas, W. I., and Florian Znaniecki. *The Polish Peasant in Europe and Americ* 5 vols. Boston: R. G. Badger, 1918–1920.

Thompson, Daniel C. *The Negro Leadership Class.* Englewood Cliffs, N.J.: Prentic Hall, 1963.

hompson, Edgar T. (Ed.) *Race Relations and the Race Problem.* Durham. N.C.: Duke University Press, 1939.

hompson, Virginia, and Richard Adloff. *Minority Problems in Southeast Asia.* Palo Alto, Calif.: Stanford University Press, 1955.

indall, George B. *South Carolina Negroes, 1877–1900.* Columbia, S.C.: University of South Carolina Press, 1952.

oynbee, A. J. *A Study of History.* 6 vols. London: Oxford University Press, 1934.

ruesdell, L. F. *The Canadian Born in the United States.* New Haven: Yale University Press, 1943.

uck, R. D. *Not with the Fist.* New York: Harcourt Brace and Co., 1946.

umin, Melvin M. *Desegregation: Resistance and Readiness.* Princeton: Princeton University Press, 1958.

urney-High, H. H. *The Flathead Indians of Montana.* Memoirs of the American Anthropological Association, No. 48, 1937.

ander Zanden, James W. *American Minority Relations.* New York: Ronald Press, 1963.

ernant, Jacques. *The Refugee in the Post-War World.* New Haven: Yale University Press, 1953.

ickery, William E., and S. C. Cole. *Intercultural Education in American Education.* New York: Harper & Row, 1944.

allace, D. D. *History of South Carolina.* 4 vols. New York: American Historical Society, 1934.

alters, Leon K. *A Study of the Social and Marital Adjustment of Thirty-five American-Japanese Couples.* Unpublished master's thesis, Ohio State University, 1953.

are, Caroline. *Greenwich Village, 1920–1930.* Boston: Houghton Mifflin Co., 1935.

arner, Robert A. *New Haven Negroes.* New Haven: Yale University Press, 1940.

arner, W. L., et al. *Color and Human Nature.* Washington: American Council on Education, 1941.

arner, W. L., and Paul S. Lunt. *The Social Life of a Modern Community.* New Haven: Yale University Press, 1941.

arner, W. L., and Leo Srole. *The Social Systems of American Ethnic Groups.* New Haven: Yale University Press, 1945.

arner, W. L., and Paul S. Lunt. *The Status System of a Modern Community.* New Haven: Yale University Press, 1942.

atson, Goodwin. *Action for Unity.* New York: Harper & Row, 1947.

eatherford, W. D., and Charles S. Johnson. *Race Relations.* Boston: D. C. Heath and Co., 1934.

eaver, Robert C. *The Negro Ghetto.* New York: Harcourt, Brace and Co., 1948.

eld, Ralph F. *Brooklyn Is America.* New York: Columbia University Press, 1950.

eslager, C. A. *Delaware's Forgotten Folk.* Philadelphia: University of Pennsylvania Press, 1943.

essel, B. B. *An Ethnic Survey of Woonsocket, Rhode Island.* Chicago: University of Chicago Press, 1931.

eyl, Nathaniel. *The Negro in American Civilization.* Washington, D.C.: Public Affairs Press, 1961.

Wheeler, Geoffrey. *Racial Problems in Soviet Muslim Asia.* New York: Oxfor University Press, 1962.

White, L. C. *300,000 New Americans.* New York: Harper & Row, 1957.

Williams, Eric. *The Negro in the Caribbean.* Washington: Associates in Negro Fol Education, 1942.

Williams, G. D. *Maya-Speaking Crosses in Yucatan.* Harvard University, Peabod Museum Papers, Vol. 13, No. 1, 1931.

Williams, P. H. *South Italian Folkways in Europe and America.* New Haven: Yal University Press, 1938.

Williams, Robin M., Jr. *The Reduction of Intergroup Tensions.* Washington, D.C Social Science Research Council, 1947.

Williams, Robin M., Jr., *et al. Strangers Next Door: Ethnic Relations in America Communities.* Englewood Cliffs, N.J.: Prentice-Hall, 1964.

Willmott, D. E. *The Chinese of Semarang: A Changing Minority Community Indonesia.* Ithaca: Cornell University Press, 1960.

Wilner, D. M., Rosabelle P. Walkley, and S. W. Cook. *Human Relations in Inte racial Housing: A Study of the Contact Hypothesis.* Minneapolis: University Minnesota Press, 1955.

Wirth, Louis. *The Ghetto.* Chicago: University of Chicago Press, 1928.

Wissler, Clark. *Indians of the United States.* New York: Doubleday, Doran and C 1940.

Woods, Sister Frances Jerome. *Cultural Values of American Ethnic Groups.* Ne York: Harper & Row, 1956.

Woodward, C. Vann. *The Strange Career of Jim Crow.* New York: Oxford Universi Press, 1955.

Woofter, T. J., Jr. *Races and Ethnic Groups in American Life.* New York: McGra Hill Book Co., 1933.

Wright, Richard. *Black Boy.* New York: Harper & Row, 1945.

Wright, Richard. *Uncle Tom's Children.* Cleveland: World Publishing Co., 1943.

Wynes, Charles E. *Race Relations in Virginia, 1870–1902.* Charlottesville, Va University of Virginia Press, 1961.

Wynn, Daniel W. *The NAACP versus Negro Revolutionary Protest.* New Yor Exposition Press, 1955.

Young, Charles H., and Helen R. Reid. *The Japanese Canadians.* Toronto: Unive sity of Toronto Press, 1938.

Young, Donald. *American Minority Peoples.* New York: Harper & Row, 1932.

Young, Pauline V. *The Pilgrims of Russian Town.* Chicago: University of Chica Press, 1932.

Young, Whitney M., Jr. *To Be Equal.* New York: McGraw-Hill Book Co., 1964.

Zangwill, Israel. *The Melting Pot: Drama in Four Acts.* New York: Macmillan C 1921.

Zorbaugh, H. W. *The Gold Coast and the Slum.* Chicago: University of Chica Press, 1929.

Beveridge, A. J., 334 n, 405
Bierce, Ambrose, 321
Biesanz, John, 299, 405
Bilbo, Theodore G., 6, 197
Black Codes, 187, 347
Black Legion, 320
Black Muslims, 197, 386
Blau, Rabbi Joel, 385
Bloom, Leonard, 405
Blue, John T., 279
Blumenbach, 37
Boas, Franz, 281
Bodin, 55
Boehm, Max, 231
Bogardus, Emory S., his cycle of race relations, 98, 130–131, 134, 405
Bogardus social distance test, 288, 292 (table), 302
Bohemia, emigration from, 83
Bohn, Dorothy, 238 n
Bossard, James H. S., 295
Boycotts, as a weapon, 113–116
Boyd, William C., 40, 405
Brailsford, H. N., 157 n
Brameld, Theodore, 323, 405
Brand, D. D., 25
Brazil, assimilation in, 12, 135–138; social definition of Negro in, 27; two isolated tribes in, 67; attractiveness of, to emigrants, 89; insurrection of slaves in, 112; race relations in, 135–138; (compared with Hawaii, 142); amalgamation in, 136; slave trade in, 136; southern U.S. white immigration to, 267, 386; resistance to assimilation in, 268; opposition to Japanese immigration to, 340
British, in Malaya and Caribbean, 76; initial encouragement of amalgamation in India, 275
Britt, Albert, 394, 405
Britt, S. H., 213, 405, 408
Brooks, Maxwell R., 111, 187, 405
Broom, Leonard, 171, 172 (table), 405
Brother Daniel, 29
Brotz, Howard, 405
Brown, Demetra V., 258, 405
Brown, Earl, 110 n
Brown, F. J., 224 n, 405
Brown, G. G., 371 n
Brown, Sterling A., 119 n
Brown, W. O., 98; his cycle of race relations, 131–132; 134

Browne, Lewis, 307, 405
Brunner, E. deS., 360, 405
Bryan, William Jennings, 248
Buell, R. L., 183 n
Bureau of Indian Affairs, 25, 237
Burgess, Ernest W., 248 n, 305 n, 413
Burgess, M. Elaine, 405
Burlington, Vt., ethnic stratification in, 173–175
Burma, John H., 120, 280, 293, 391, 405
Burns, W. Haywood, 405
Bushmen, 206
Burrows, E. G., 386, 405

C

Cabot, John, 73
Cahnman, Werner J., 200, 290, 306, 405
Canada, control of immigration, 329
Cape Coloured, 3, 28, 47, 192, 201, 381
Capp, Al, 49
Caribbean Islands, British in, 76; insurrections in, 112–113; color distinctions in, 277
Carnegie Corporation Study of Negro in U.S.A., 55
Carroll, J. C., 113, 405
Carter, W. A., 405
Cash, W. J., 348, 405
Caste, definition of, 181
Caste system, in India, 182–183, 188–189
Category vs. group, 43
Catlin, George, 153, 405
Cayton, H. R., 354, 356, 358, 362, 366, 406
Chamberlain, H. S., 52
Cherokee Indians, expulsion from homes, 163–164. See also Indian in U.S.A.
Chicago, police training in, 15; Persian colony in, 199
Chickasaw Indians, successful in litigation, 123
Child, Irvin L., 405
China, Communist, flight from, 79
Chinatown, 206–209
Chinese, in Southeast Asia, 245–246; generally not assimilated, 245; immigration of, into Hawaii, 331
Chinese in U.S.A., good record of, in crime rates, 50; prejudice against, 207; increasing immigration of, 206–

Davis, A., 187 n, 358, 364 n, 366 n, 406
Davis, Ethelyn, 259 n, 406
Davis, S., 406
Dawes Act, 235
Day, Caroline Bond, 391, 406
Dean, John P., 406
Deasi, Rashmi, 406
De Groot, D. E., 95 n, 406
Delaware Indians. *See* Indians in U.S.A.
De Silva, H. R., 53
Deutsch, M., 406
DeWitt, General J. L., 166
Diaz, Bartholomew, 73
Dickson, Lenore, 304 n
Direct Action, as a form of conflict, 126–127; beginnings of, 10; effects of, 127
Discrimination, in favor of, in U.S.A., 7; in college fraternities, 8; against Jews, 210–213; against Negroes, 344–349; *vs.* prejudice, 300–304; definitions of, 300; attack upon, 325; Lincoln's protest against, 334; as method of domination, 341–349 (by system of etiquette, 341; by forbidding firearms, 343; by withholding education, 343–346; by denying the vote, 346–349; in Caribbean, 347)
Disease, extermination by, 152
Disorganization, as reaction to domination, 369–373
Dispersion, a type of migration, 74
"Displaced persons." *See* Migrations, forced
Displaced Persons Act, 93
Diversity of culture, desirability, 14
Dollard, John, 187 n, 310 n, 406
Dominance, reactions to, by subordinate group, disorganization, 369–373 (in Solomon Islands, 369; among Indians in U.S.A., 369–371; among Africans, 371; among immigrants to U.S.A., 371–373; among Negroes in U.S.A., 373; among Jews in ancient Palestine, 375; among Japanese-Americans, 376–377); reactions to, by dominant group, 378; techniques of gaining, 327–349 (by physical force, 328, by control of number, 329, by assimilation, 339, by discrimination, 341, by encouragement of cleavages), in subordinate group, 160, 351. *See also* Acceptance; Avoid-

ance; Assimilation; Aggression; Domination
Domination, of Huguenots, by English, 327; resolution of, through assimilation, 327; by whites in South Africa, 328; by *haoles* in Hawaii, 328. *See also* Dominance
Doyle, B. W., 203 n, 341 n, 406
Drachsler, Julius, 289 n, 406
Drake, St. Clair, 354, 356, 358, 362, 366, 406
Dreyfus case, 72
Driver, Harold E., 255, 406
Du Bois, W. E. B., 110, 402, 407
Dukhobors, 163
Duncan, H. G., 264 n, 266 n, 407
Dutch, in Java, 76; in Sumatra, 76; extermination, a policy of, 159
Dyer Anti-Lynching Bill, 108
Dynamic quality of race relations, 20–21

E

East Indians, migration of, to South Africa, 117. *See also* Republic of South Africa
Eaton, J. W., 261
Eckard, E. W., 391
Economic factors in migration, importance of, 81–84
Economic sanctions, as weapon, 115–116
Edict of Toleration (1782), 71
Edlefsen, John B., 103, 104
Edmonson, Munro S., 414
Edwards, G. Franklin, 407
Eisenstadt, S. N., 260 n, 407
Eisenhower, President, 238, 239, 338
Elkins, Stanley, 407
"Elmtown," stratification in, 175–178
Embree, E. R., 382 n, 407
Emigrants, to U.S.A., 88–90
Emigration, causes of, 81–84; policy against, in Japan, 165; of Southern whites, to Brazil, 267. *See also* Migrations
Encomienda, defined, 87, 183
Epstein, Benjamin R., 407
Eskelund, Karl, 293 n, 407
Eskimos, 67; effect of white man's diseases upon, 153
Estel, Leo, 41
Essien-Udoni, E. U., 407

Hughes, Henry, 16, 409
Hughes, Langston, 119, 287
Huguenots, religious persecution as motive for emigration of, 83; expulsion from France, 76; religion, a factor in assimilation of, 268; domination of English over, in South Carolina, 327
Humor, as a weapon, 120–121
Humphrey, N. D., 189 n, 411
Hungary, flight from, 78, 91; emigration from, 83
Hunt, Chester L., 17 n
Hunter, John, memoirs of, 297–298, 409
Hurst, Fannie, 390 n
Hutterites, 261–262
Hutton, J. H., 183 n, 189 n, 409
Huxley, Julian S., 32, 409
Hybrids, in Hawaii, 141; in England, 273; in India, 192, 274; in Yucatan, 281; in Pitcairn Island, 281; Boer-Hottentot, 281; Lapp-Norwegian, 282; distinction between cultural and racial, 285; in U.S.A., 193–195; in Jamaica, 171–173; in the Caribbean, 172; in Africa, 192; in Haiti, 193; the American *mestizo*, 193–195. *See also* Amalgamation; Intermarriage; Miscegenation

I

Idaho, Basques in, 103–104
Immigrants in U.S.A., 88–90. *See also* Immigration into U.S.A.
Immigration, defined, 79; correlation with business conditions, 82–83, 89; of Japanese, encouraged in Hawaii, 165. *See also* Immigration into U.S.A.; Immigration policies
Immigration Act of 1917, 335
Immigration Act of 1924, 336. *See also* Quota Act of 1921
Immigration into U.S.A., from Europe, 83, 88–90; from Canada, 89; ethnic composition of "old" and "new," 89–90; of Mennonites, 198; changing policies on, 331–339; first opposition to, 332–334; increase, after Civil War, 334; first federal law on, 334; later acts controlling, 334; change to restriction of, 335; varying arguments for restriction of, 335; discriminating

legislation on, 335. *See also* Immigrants in U.S.A.; Migrants from Europe to U.S.A.; Immigration policies
Immigration policies, of Canada, 329–330; of Australia, 330, of Hawaii, 331; of U.S.A., 331–339. *See also* Quota Act of 1921; Quota System in U.S.A.; McCarran-Walter Act
Impact of Western civilization on others, 4, 151, 369–371
Incas, 69, 73
Indenture, American colonial, 87, 185
India, flight of Moslems from, 79; early encouragement of intermarriage in, by British, 275; invasion into, 182; caste system in, 182–183. *See also* East Indians
Indian Council Fire, 403
Indian population, in U.S.A., distribution of, by states, (table) 239
Indian Removal Act, 164
Indian Reorganization Act of 1934, 237
Indian Rights Association, 403
Indians, assimilation of, a dominant policy in Brazil, 12; definition of, cultural rather than biological, in South and Central America, 25; attempts to enslave in West Indies, 87; friendship of Las Casas for, 88; amity toward, by ladinos, 101–102; dominance over, by ladinos, 125; amalgamation of, a dominant policy in Brazil, 136; in Canada, 153; evil effects of white man's culture on, 153–156; slow assimilation of, in Guatemala, 251–252
Indians in the U.S.A., impact of European culture on, 153–156, 232–240; assimilation of, advocated, 12; situations of, vary, 17; definition of, 24–26; numbers of, uncertain, 25; influence of, on our history and culture, 85–86; attempts to enslave, 87; use of litigation by, to gain rights, 123–124; resistance by Fox, to assimilation, 145–146; differences of various tribes of, in relation to whites, 147–149; Navajos, 151; Cherokees, 163–164; decimation of, by disease and vice, 153–156; plea of Delaware, 154; varied policies of whites toward, 232–240; citizenship, right to vote, con-

ferred upon, 235; Indian Reorganization Act of 1934, 237; population distribution of, (table) 239; resistance of, under Tecumseh, 393–395; organizations for improving conditions of, 403

Institute of Race Relations, 409

Insurrection, definition of, 112–113; slaves in Brazil, 112; Sepoy Mutiny, 112; slaves in U.S.A., 113

Integration, alternative to *apartheid*, 7

Integrationists, 353

I.Q. tests, cultural differences have influence on, 62–64

Intergroup cleavages. *See* Cleavages

Intergroup contact, antiquity of, 68

Intergroup relations, alternative term for race relations, 43

Intermarriage, approved of, by early British settlers in India, 275; in Hawaii, 289; of Jews, in Bible, 290; of Jews in modern times, 290; relation of, to assimilation, 288; Japanese-American, 294; Negro-white, 293; legal barriers to, 278. *See also* Miscegenation; Hybrids

Internal migration, 79–80, 189

International Refugee Organization, 91

Interracial contact, promotion of, 321

Intragroup cleavages, 357–366 (bases for, color, 358, age, 359, length of residence, 261, social class distinction, 364)

Ireland, immigration from, 83

Isolated societies today, 67–68

Israel, State of, assimilation in, 12–14; flight of Arabs from, 79

"I Was a Jew," anonymous account of "passing," 389–390

J

Jackson, Andrew, appeal of Cherokees to, 164

Jahoda, Marie, 406

Jamaica, status of hybrids in, 171–172; racial composition of population of, 172

Jamaica whites, 47, 285

Janowitz, Morris, 405

Japanese, in Hawaii, 165; in Brazil, 340. *See also* Japanese-Americans

Japanese-Americans, 165–168; expulsion from Pacific Coast area, 122, 165; reactions to discrimination by, 376–377; organizations of, 506

Japanese-American Citizens League, 506

Jefferson, Thomas, 233; on immigration, 332

Jennings, H. S., 281, 409

Jerome, Harry, 83, 409

Jett, S. C., 82 n

Jews, and Arabs, 3; attitudes of, vary, 17; definitions of, 28–29; population of, by countries, 30; religious persecution of, as motive for emigration, 83; migrations of, 70–72; expulsion of, from Palestine, 71; tolerance toward, in Austria (1782 edict), France, Holland, Prussia (1791), 71; refugees from Hitler, 77; as scapegoats, 111; refugees from Russia, 111; victims of pogroms in Russia, 111; Nazi policy to exterminate, 156; mass expulsion of, from Spain, 162; intermarriage of, 290; in ghettos, in privilege, 210, as persecution, 210–211; gradual emancipation of, in different countries, 212–213; in Burlington, Vt., 174; divergent views as to goal of, 221; cultural pluralism advocated for, 222; relationship with Negroes, 355; four periods of immigration of, to U.S.A., 362; cleavages among, 363; in ancient Palestine, 375; organizations of, 403. *See also* Anti-Semitism, Ghetto, Pogroms, Zionism

Jim Crow, 216

Johnson, Charles S., 186, 204, 219, 359, 364 n, 379, 380, 381, 400, 409

Johnson, Guy B., 107 n, 195, 314 n

Johnson, James Weldon, 10, 118, 409

Johnson, Robert, 373 n, 410

Jonassen, C. T., 263, 410

Jones, Maldwyn Allen, 410

Junek, O. W., 67, 410

K

Kalibala, E., 192

Kardiner, Abram, 410

Kaufman, H. F., 181, 410

Keller, A. G., 76, 308 n, 410

Kennedy, Raymond, 124, 249 n, 278 n

Kent, D. P., 95 n, 410

Non-violence, 116–118. *See also* Gandhi; Rev. Martin Luther King
Norris, Hoke, 413
North Viet Nam, flight from, 79

O

Oberg, Dr. K., visit to primitive tribe in Brazil, 67
O'Brien, R. W., 208
Olcott, Mason, 183 n
"Old Immigration," 89
Oliver, Lord, Governor of Jamaica, 173
Olivier, Sydney, 413
Organizations, for betterment of minority groups, 319–20, 402–403; diversity of goals, 320
Organizations, for promotion of discrimination, 320
Oskison, John M., 394 n, 413
Ots y Capdequi, Jose, 249 n
Ottley, Roi, 216, 356, 391, 413
Ovesey, Lionel, 410
Ovington, Mary W., 403 n, 413

P

Padilla, Elena, 354 n, 413
Page, Charles H., 315 n
Page, Patricia, 209 n
Pakistan, flight of Hindus from, 79
Palestine, expulsion of Jews from, 71. *See also* Zionism
Palgi, Phyllis, 260
Palmer, E. N., 151
Panunzio, C., 263
Park, R. E., 66, 98; cycle of race relations, 129–130, 135; 248 n, 263 n, 275 n, 276 n, 285, 305; nature of the race problem, 327–328; 371 n, 413
Parkes, James, 112
"Passing," 192, 389–392
Patai, Raphael, 260, 413
Patterson, Sheila, 413, 414
Peace, William, 413
Peace Movement of Ethiopia, 197
Pearson, Karl, 58 n
Penn, William, 83, 198
Peonage, 183
Petersen, W., 74 n
Pettigrew, Thomas F., 414
Pierson, Donald, 27, 112, 137, 138, 160, 257, 277, 340, 414

Pihlblad, C. T., 257, 289
Pilgrims, 91, 155–156
Pipes, Richard, 414
Pitcairn Island, 41, 281, 284
Pitt-Rivers, G. H. L., 414
Pluralism, 221; policy of, in Switzerland, 226–228, in Russia, 229–232, in U.S.A., in regard to Indians, 237–238; value and difficulties of, 241
Pogroms, 111–112
Pohlman, E. W., 189 n
Poland, expulsion from under Germans, 77; flight from, 91
Poles, emigration of, 83
Polish immigrants to U.S.A., demoralization of, 372
Poll, Solomon, 414
Poll tax, as a weapon, in Southern U.S.A., 126; constitutional amendment against, 126
Polynesians, decimated by disease, 153
Population, Jewish, 30; growth of, as result of contact, 151, 163
Porteus, S. D., 63, 98 n, 414
Portuguese, early explorations by, 72–73; in Brazil, 76
Powdermaker, Hortense, 55, 298, 358, 381, 383, 414
Powell, A. C., 7, 414
Prehistoric migrations, evidence for, 68–70; to America, 86
Prejudice, 297–325; nature, 298–300; definitions, 298–300; not innate, 305; rationalization, 315–319; means of reducing, 319–324; organizations for reduction of, 320; distinguished from discrimination, 300; dimensions of, 302–304; theories of, 304–315; against Chinese in California, 207, 306
Price, Charles A., 414
Price, Hugh D., 414
Price, Willard, 267, 414
Priestly, H. J., 343, 414
Proudfoot, Merrill, 414
Prussia, civil liberties to Jews, 71
Puerto Rico, social definition of Negro in, 28
Puerto Ricans, immigration of, into U.S.A., 3, 14, 23
Putnam, Carleton, 63, 414
Puyallup Indians, 143–145. *See also* Indians in U.S.A.
Pygmies, 206

Roberts, E. F., 357, 415
Roberts, S. H., 249 n
Robinson, Jacob, 232
Rogler, C. C., 28
Rohrer, John H., 415
Rolland, Romain, 118 n, 415
Roosevelt, F. D., 165, 190, 237
Roosevelt, Kermit, 114
Roosevelt, Theodore, 165
Rorschach tests, 102
Rose, Arnold, 307, 320, 324 n, 355, 356, 415
Rose, Arnold and Caroline, 65, 308 n, 380 n, 415
Rose, Peter I., 22, 415
Rosen, Alex, 406
Rosenwald, Julius, 355
Ross, E. A., 51
Ross, John (Cherokee chief), 362
Rostow, Eugene V., 168
Rothschild, Lionel de, 212
Roucek, J. S., 224, 405
Ruck, S. K., 415
Rufeisen, Oswald. See Brother Daniel
Russia, mass emigration from, 77; emigration from, 83; utilization of group conflicts by czars, 111. See also Soviet Union
Russian Molokans, 267, 287, 291

S

Saenger, Gerhart, 415
St. Vincent, Bory de, 37
Samuel, Maurice, 307, 415
Sanford, R. N., 311 n
Sansom, G. B., 415
Saron, Gustav, 415
Saveth, E. N., 415
Scandinavia, refugees welcomed in, 91
"Scapegoat" theory of prejudice, 308–309
Schermerhorn, R. A., 268, 356, 415
Schmid, Calvin, 200, 214–215, 415
Schmitt, Robert, 411
Schumann, F. L., 112 n
Schwarz, S. M., 231, 415
Scott, Winfield, 164
Segregation, voluntary, 198, 200, of Mennonites, 198, of other groups, 200, of some Negroes in U.S.A., 216–219; involuntary, 199–200, of Negroes in U.S.A., 199, in South Africa, 201, definition of, 198; nature of,

198; universality of, 200–202; spatial and social, 202–205; ruling of U.S. courts against, 205; patterns of, 206–219 (Chinatown, 206–209; the ghetto, 209–213; racial islands, 213–219); of Indians, in U.S.A., 234; alleged justification for, 316–318. See also Ghetto; Negro segregation
Senior, Clarence, 413
Senturia, J., 77 n, 163 n
"Separate but equal" principle in U.S.A., 190, 225, 345–346; sustained by Supreme Court in 1896, 345; decision against, by Supreme Court, in 1950, 346, in 1954, 346
Sepoy Mutiny, 112
Sequoya, 164
Shafter, Toby, 213 n
Shapiro, Harry L., 281, 282, 284, 415
Sharrett, Moshe, 29
Shay, Frank, 105, 107, 415
Shelby, G. M., 390 n
Sheppard, H. L., 356
Sherman, Charles B., 415
Sherman, Mandel, 68, 415
Shrieke, B., 160, 207 n, 416
Shuey, Audrey M., 64, 416
Silver Shirts, 320
Simmons, Leo W., 304, 416
Simpson, G. E., 300, 313, 379–380, 416
Sioux Indians. See Indians in U.S.A.
Sit-in. See Direct Action
Sitton, C., 346 n
Skinner, G. William, 416
Sklare, Marshall, 416
Slavery, justification of, 16. See also Negro slavery
Slave trade. See Negro slave trade
Smith, Bradford, 168 n, 416
Smith, W. C., 84, 138, 142, 199 n, 255 n, 257, 329, 372–373, 416
Smythe, H. H., 216 n
Snowden, F. M., 87 n
SNICK. See Student Nonviolent Coordinating Committee
Society of Forward Men, 320
Sorokin, P. A., 52 n, 56, 416
South Africa. See Republic of South Africa
Southern Christian Leadership Conference, 10
Southern Regional Council, 349
Soviet Union, discontent of minorities in, 4, 231–232; ethnic groups in, 5,

46–47; policy of cultural pluralism in, 229–232; expulsion of Germans from, 77; flight from, 91; Declaration of the Rights of Peoples of Russia, 230; Jews in, 231–232. *See also* Russia

Spain, expulsion of Moors from, 76; flight from Franco, out of, 77

"Specialties" of culture, defined, 33

Spellman, C. L., 219 n, 416

Srole, Leo, 178 n, 417

Stanton, William, 416

Starkey, Marion L., 163 n, 416

Statue of Liberty, inscription on, 331

Stefansson, V., 153, 416

Steggerda, M. S., 280 n, 406

Steinberg, Rabbi Milton, 222

Stephenson, C. M., 324 n

Stern, B. J., 160 n, 185 n, 230 n, 411

Stern, Curt, 274, 283, 416

Steward, Julian H., 25 n, 416

Stibbe, E. P., 40, 416

Stimson, Secretary of War, 166

Stoddard, Lothrop, 52

Stoney, S. G., 390 n

Stonequist, E. V., 47, 173, 276 n, 280, 286, 379, 380, 416

Strandenraus, J., 416

Stratification, definition of, 178; in Jamaica, 171–173; in South Africa, 173; in Burlington, Vt., 173–175; in Elmtown, 175–178; in rural New York community, 181–182; in India, 182–183; forms of, 178–195. *See also* Cleavages

Strauss, A. L., 294

Strikes, as weapon, 113–114

Strong, E. K., 360, 416

Strong, S. M., 373–374

Stuckert, Robert, 392

Student Nonviolent Coordinating Committee, 10, 191

Stuntz, Hugh, 371 n

Subordinate groups. *See* Minority and other subordinate groups

Sumner, Cid Ricketts, 390 n

Sumner, William Graham, 49, 308 n

Sun Chief (Hopi Indian), 304

Superiority, sense of, in all groups, 49

Supreme Court, decisions of, 122, 123, 190, 346

Supreme Order of the Star Spangled Banner, 320, 333

Sutherland, Robert L., 416

Sutton, H. E., 53

Sweatt, Herman, law case of, 122

Sweden, emigration from, 83

Swedes, uneven assimilation of, in Kansas, 257–258

Switzerland, refugees welcomed in, 91; policy of cultural pluralism in, 226–228; composition of population of, 227

T

Taft, D. R., 79 n, 416

Taft, President, 335

Tannenbaum, Frank, 416

Taper, Bernard, 349 n, 416

Tasmania, extermination of natives on, 158–159

Tax, Sol, 251–252

Tecumseh, 393–394

Thomas, Dorothy S., 416

Thomas, W. I., 187, 372, 416

Thompson, Daniel C., 369, 416

Thompson, Edgar, 187 n, 417

Thompson, Virginia, 417

Tindall, George B., 417

Tippecanoe, 395

Toland, John, 212

Tolstoy, 117

Toussaint L'Ouverture, 395–398

Toynbee, A. J., 4, 158, 277, 317, 417

"Trail of Tears," 163

Trinidad. *See* Caribbean Islands

Tristan da Cunha, 41, 49, 284

Truesdell, L. F., 417

Truman, President, 338

Tuck, Ruth D., 417

Tulto, Taos Indians, 382–384

Tumin, Melvin M., 417

Tungus, 99–101

Turner, Nat, 113

Turney-High, H. H., 369–370, 417

U

Ulotrichi, defined, 37

Uniformity in race relations, some features universal, 149

UN, Convention on Genocide, 161

UNRRA, 91

United Sons of America, 320